Accommodation

BB A   Price per person per night under £20

BB B   Price per person per night £20 – £25

BB C   Price per person per night £25 – £30

BB D   Price per person per night over £30

These prices are based on occupancy of a single room, per night including breakfast. However, if no single room is available two prices may be shown to indicate single and shared occupancy.

🏷   Ramblers Discount Vouchers accepted

☆   Box display advert

BB   Bed & Breakfast accommodation

DBB   Dinner, bed and breakfast

FB   Full board (breakfast, lunch and dinner)

SC   Self-catering accommodation

✗   Evening meal normally available (unless "book first") with average price/time served

✗ nearby   Evening meal available within a 10 minute walk

S, D, T, F   Number of single, double, twin or family rooms

Ⓓ   Clothes/boots drying facilities available

Ⓥ   Vegetarian evening meals always available

⊗   No smoking throughout the establishment

Ⓑ   At least one room has private bath/shower and/or toilet

⚄ (Stroud)   National railway station within 3km/2 miles (the station)

🍴   Packed lunch provided on request

☕   Tea/coffee making facilities in the bedrooms

★

◆   \ ...... diamond rating

Ⓢ Ⓖ   VisitBritain Silver or Gold award

Ⓦ   Walkers or Cyclists Welcome award

Ⓜ   The proprietor is a member of the Ramblers' Association

OFFA'S DYKE   Long distance path

CAIRNGORMS   National park

SOUTH DOWNS*   Proposed national park

KEY TO THE MAPS

National trail or long distance route (Scotland)   CWD

Other long distance path   SOL

County boundary

National park boundary

Indicates location of B&B in this guide   ● Tiverton

For path abbreviations see regional introductions

Editor: Dan French
Deputy Editor: Dominic Bates
Information Editor: Des de Moor

Design and production by Think Publishing
Project Editor: Emma Jones
Sub Editor: Rica Dearman
Art Director: Lou Millward
Designer: James Collins
www.thinkpublishing.co.uk
Cover photograph: Western Isles. David Robertson/Alamy
Front cover/back cover photographs: Perth & Kinross
Countryside Trust. Countryside Agency

Printed and bound by St Ives, Cornwall
walk BRITAIN 2006 is printed on Grapho Lux which is
manufactured using wood products certified by the Forestry
Stewardship Council

Trade distribution by Cordee Ltd
3a de Montfort Street, Leicester LE1 7HD
☎ 0116 254 3579 Email: sales@cordee.co.uk

Accommodation Advertising
☎ 020 7339 8527 Email: yearbook@london.ramblers.org.uk

Commercial Advertising
Think Publishing
The Pall Mall Deposit, 124-128 Barlby Road, London W10 6BL
☎ 020 8962 3020 Email: advertising@thinkpublishing.co.uk

Published by
The Ramblers' Association
2nd Floor, Camelford House
87-90 Albert Embankment, London SE1 7TW
☎ 020 7339 8500
Fax 020 7339 8501
Email: ramblers@london.ramblers.org.uk
www.ramblers.org.uk
Registered charity no. 1093577 and a company limited by
guarantee in England and Wales (no. 4458492)

Ramblers' Association Scotland
Kingfisher House, Auld Mart Business Park
Milnathort, Kinross KY13 9DA
☎ 01577 861222
Fax 01577 861333
Email: enquiries@scotland.ramblers.org.uk
www.ramblers.org.uk/scotland

Ramblers' Association Wales
3 Coopers Yard, Curran Road, Cardiff CF10 5NB
☎ 029 2064 4308
Fax 029 2064 5187
Email: cerddwyr@ramblers.org.uk
www.ramblers.org.uk/wales
www.ramblers.org.uk/cymru

Ramblers Holidays
Box 43, Welwyn Garden City AL8 6PQ
☎ 01707 331133
Fax 01707 333276
Email: info@ramblersholidays.co.uk
www.ramblersholidays.co.uk

ISBN 1 901184 68 4

CONTENTS

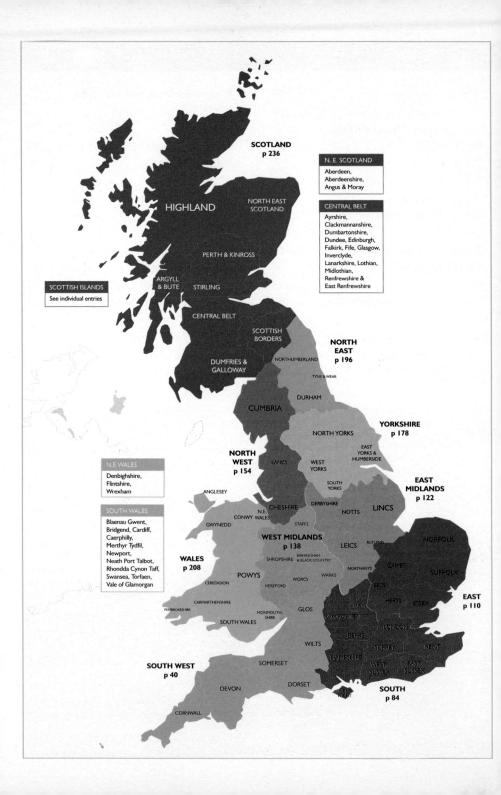

SCOTLAND
p 236

N. E. SCOTLAND
Aberdeen,
Aberdeenshire,
Angus & Moray

CENTRAL BELT
Ayrshire,
Clackmannanshire,
Dumbartonshire,
Dundee, Edinburgh,
Falkirk, Fife, Glasgow,
Inverclyde,
Lanarkshire, Lothian,
Midlothian,
Renfrewshire &
East Renfrewshire

HIGHLAND

NORTH EAST
SCOTLAND

PERTH & KINROSS

SCOTTISH ISLANDS
See individual entries

ARGYLL
& BUTE   STIRLING

CENTRAL BELT

SCOTTISH
BORDERS

DUMFRIES &
GALLOWAY   NORTHUMBERLAND

NORTH
EAST
p 196

TYNE & WEAR

DURHAM

CUMBRIA

NORTH YORKS

YORKSHIRE
p 178

EAST
YORKS &
HUMBERSIDE

N.E WALES
Denbighshire,
Flintshire,
Wrexham

NORTH
WEST
p 154   LANCS   WEST
YORKS

SOUTH
YORKS

EAST
MIDLANDS
p 122

SOUTH WALES
Blaenau Gwent,
Bridgend, Cardiff,
Caerphilly,
Merthyr Tydfil,
Newport,
Neath Port Talbot,
Rhondda Cynon Taff,
Swansea, Torfaen,
Vale of Glamorgan

ANGLESEY

CHESHIRE   DERBYSHIRE
N.E.
CONWY WALES
GWYNEDD   NOTTS   LINCS

STAFFS

WEST MIDLANDS
p 138   LEICS   RUTLAND   NORFOLK

WALES
p 208   SHROPSHIRE   BIRMINGHAM
& BLACK COUNTRY   WARKS   NORTHANTS   CAMBS   SUFFOLK

POWYS   WORCS   BEDS

CEREDIGION   HEREFORD   HERTS   EAST
p 110

CARMARTHENSHIRE   GLOS   BUCKS   ESSEX

PEMBROKESHIRE   MONMOUTH-
SHIRE   OXFORDSHIRE

SOUTH WALES   LONDON

BERKS   SURREY   KENT

WILTS

SOUTH WEST
p 40   SOMERSET   HAMPSHIRE   WEST
SUSSEX   EAST
SUSSEX

DORSET

DEVON   ISLE OF
WIGHT   SOUTH
p 84

CORNWALL

HOW TO USE THIS GUIDE

The guide is divided into eight English regions, Scotland and Wales. Each section contains a full colour map, a short introduction, contact details for local Ramblers Groups, a list of local walks guides, followed by the accommodation.

Local Ramblers Groups and Publications
Our Groups carry out conservation work in their localities and walk and socialise together. Each Group listed organises its own programme of led walks. Most walks are now on the Group Walks Finder on our website; otherwise you can request a programme by sending a SAE to the Group secretary. Many work from home and all are volunteers so if you telephone, please do so at reasonable times. Many Groups also publish details of upcoming walks and activities on their own websites, which are all linked from www.ramblers.org.uk/info/localgroups/

Most Groups have a mixed programme of walks but some specialise; for example some offer shorter walks or walks for families. There are also a number of Groups for people in their 20s-30s – we've highlighted these in blue. All details were correct in November 2005 but changes may take place during the year.

The books and guides listed cover a huge range of walks, from short circular strolls to long-distance paths, and are prepared by local walkers with local knowledge. They're available by mail order directly from the addresses shown. Where no p&p charge is shown this is included in the price. Publications specifically about long-distance paths can be found in the section beginning on p23. In addition, there is a selection available from the Ramblers Bookshop (see p306).

The Walker's Toolkit
This new section contains information that all walkers will find useful at some time or another. You can find out how to report an illegally blocked footpath; which kind of maps to use, and where to find out about public transport services – even a handy selection of equipment shops. We answer the most frequently asked questions about walkers' rights in the countryside, and explain how to find more detailed information about all aspects of walking and other outdoor activities.

ACCOMMODATION

The listings in the guide are organised by country/region then county or unitary authority order. Sometimes we have banded together authorities that are small in size or where there are fewer listings – see the key map opposite. Many of the entries in this guide come from members' recommendations. As we are not able to independently assess the establishments, this is a most valuable resource. Please keep your recommendations coming in (see Recommendation Form on p311).

BED & BREAKFAST
These entries are all listed under a 'place'. The place might be a village or town or even a hamlet and the choice is determined by a number of elements, such as the proximity to a long-distance path or national park; or occasionally at the request of an advertiser. If the place is situated in a national park, or within two miles of one of the long-distance paths listed on p23, the name of that national park or path is given after the place name.

SELF-CATERING
Prices for self-catering accommodation vary considerably by season; we give the lowest and highest cost per week. Where a proprietor lets more than one property, the price of the cheapest in low season and the most expensive in high season is given. You are advised to make full enquiries before booking.

Tourist board awards (see next page) may be different for each property let – in these cases we give the range of classifications awarded.

GROUP ACCOMMODATION
The group accommodation entries include many places tried and tested by Ramblers Groups and recommended to us. There is a variety of types, standards, prices and sizes. Some are self-catering (SC), others provide meals (BB, DBB, FB). There are hotels, hostels, university halls of residence, cabins in the woods, farmhouses – hopefully something for everyone.

HOSTELS, BUNKHOUSES & CAMPSITES

Some centres listed here are primarily for groups, but they should all be open to individuals as well. Any centres catering solely for groups are in Group Accommodation. In each case we state prices per night, and whether meals and/or self-catering facilities are available. Many hostels accept children at a reduced rate.

Categories of establishments are:

BHB = Bunkhouse Barn

A converted farm building, better equipped than the camping barn. Stoves and cooking facilities provided. Toilets may be chemical. Separate sleeping areas for males and females but little privacy. Bunk beds are provided.

B = Bunkhouse

Other kinds of converted buildings, simply but comfortably furnished. They can be run by hotels, sporting estates or individuals. Cooking facilities and utensils provided. Separate sleeping areas for males and females with beds or bunks. Showers and drying facilities provided.

C = Campsite

May be for tents only, plus tourers, or have hook-up facilities for caravans. In some sites static caravans are available. Some provide meals on-site.

CB = Camping Barn

A redundant farm building converted to provide basic shelter. Little or no privacy. Limited facilities. Toilets may be chemical. Sleeping areas are usually not divided between the sexes and there are wooden sleeping platforms. Camping barns are often described as 'stone tents'.

IH = Independent Hostel

A privately run hostel. The standards and conditions will vary from hostel to hostel. Some provide meals but the majority are self-catering. You will usually need to bring your own sheet sleeping bag liners.

OC = Outdoor Centre

Often available to groups only. See also Group accommodation.

YHA = Youth Hostel

A hostel which is a member of the Youth Hostels Association (see advertisement on p121 & p290 of the Walker's Toolkit).

TOURIST BOARD CLASSIFICATIONS

The AA, RAC, VisitBritain, VisitScotland and the Wales Tourist Board have reached an agreement to rate accommodation using a common set of standards: ★-★★★★★ for hotels and ◆-◆◆◆◆◆ (in England and Wales) for smaller guest accommodation. Self-catering establishments are rated ★-★★★★★. In addition, each organisation has its own special award scheme: RAC's sparkling diamond or warm welcome award; AA's red diamond award; VisitBritain's Silver and Gold awards. We only display VisitBritain's Silver ⑤ and Gold ⑥ awards in this guide.

In 2004 VisitBritain consulted with the Countryside Agency, the Ramblers' Association and the CTC among others to produce a national rating to meet the specific needs of walkers and cyclists. ⑩ indicates a Walkers Welcome or Cyclists Welcome award. While the Ramblers' Association is generally in favour of the new award, all the accommodation listed in this guide should welcome walkers, whether they have been inspected.

RAMBLERS DISCOUNT VOUCHER

All establishments marked with a ▀▄ in the 2006 edition of **walk BRITAIN** accept the vouchers. The amount of the discount is a maximum of £1 per night. Use a £1 voucher for a single night's stay, a £2 voucher for a two-night stay, and so on. Vouchers may be combined for a longer stay. Higher value vouchers can also be used for shorter stays, for example, a £4 voucher can be used for one, two or three nights at a discount of £1 per night.

Each voucher can only be used once. Photocopies will not be accepted. The voucher cannot be exchanged for services other than bed & breakfast.

Proprietors have the right to withhold the reduction in price if the visitor is already in receipt of another discount or if the customer booked through means other than **walk BRITAIN** 2006.

FURTHER INFORMATION

Six-figure grid references are given for each entry and the maps referred to are the Ordnance Survey Landranger series, scale 1:50 000. These are sometimes generated from the postcode and can be imprecise in some sparsely populated areas.

We have been asked to point out that any deposit paid is non-refundable in all circumstances, and in particular that any amount paid by credit card may not be returnable.

Finally, a disclaimer. The information in the guide is based on details received from proprietors during 2005. The Ramblers' Association cannot be held responsible for errors or omissions.

The Ramblers walk BRITAIN 2006 DISCOUNT VOUCHER

VALID FOR ONE NIGHT...

£1

...AT ANY B&B MARKED WITH A ◄ in walk BRITAIN 2006
Please refer to the terms and conditions on p6

The Ramblers walk BRITAIN 2006 DISCOUNT VOUCHER

VALID FOR UP TO TWO NIGHTS...

£2

...AT ANY B&B MARKED WITH A ◄ in walk BRITAIN 2006
Please refer to the terms and conditions on p6

The Ramblers walk BRITAIN 2006 DISCOUNT VOUCHER

VALID FOR UP TO THREE NIGHTS...

£3

...AT ANY B&B MARKED WITH A ◄ in walk BRITAIN 2006
Please refer to the terms and conditions on p6

The Ramblers walk BRITAIN 2006 DISCOUNT VOUCHER

VALID FOR UP TO FOUR NIGHTS...

£4

...AT ANY B&B MARKED WITH A ◄ in walk BRITAIN 2006
Please refer to the terms and conditions on p6

The great outdoors:
take a refresher
course

REGATTA
GREAT OUTDOORS ™
fresh air clothing

SUPPORTING US

PHOTO: CATHERINE LECKENBY

THE RAMBLERS' ASSOCIATION

The Ramblers' Association is much more than a walking club. We are a registered charity – the only one dedicated to:

- **Promoting** walking for everyone as a healthy, fun, inexpensive activity
- **Safeguarding** the countryside from unsightly and polluting developments
- **Increasing** opportunities for responsible access for everyone – irrespective of background – to our beautiful open countryside

- **Protecting** Britain's unique network of public paths
- **Providing** walking information and educating walkers about their rights and responsibilities

Because we receive no money from central government, we are entirely dependent upon the generosity of our members and supporters. The simplest way to help is to add your name to those of our 140,000 current supporters by joining. There is a special discounted rate for readers on p21.

BENEFITS OF MEMBERSHIP INCLUDE...

- **walk BRITAIN**, our annual handbook and accommodation guide
- **walk**, our quarterly colour magazine
- 10% off at Millets and Blacks, and discretionary discounts at many outdoor stores
- An annual membership card
- Up to four local/regional Area newsletters a year, where published

- Members can join a local Group of their choice and take part in its programme of walks and social events. More than 50 walking Groups cater specifically for people in their 20s-30s.
- Access to the Ramblers Map Library. The Library stocks all OS Landranger and Explorer maps, and members can borrow up to ten maps at a time for a small fee plus p&p. Contact the Map Library Service at our central office for details.

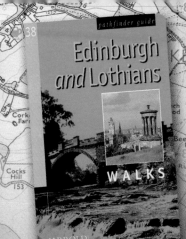

SUPPORTING OUR WORK WITH YOUR SKILLS AND TIME

Volunteering for the Ramblers is a brilliant way to share your passion for walking, while helping others to enjoy the benefits of walking at the same time. It's an opportunity to make new friends, it's fun and it keeps you fit.

You can volunteer for the Ramblers at a national, regional or local level, as an individual or as part of a group. You can get involved in practical outdoor activities or support our campaigns from home. Whatever you enjoy, we have opportunities to suit all lifestyles and interests.

WHAT WOULD YOU LIKE TO DO?

Get out and about – walking and practical work
- develop routes and lead walks
- report footpath problems
- carry out path surveys
- clear and maintain footpaths

Get passionate – support our campaigns
- lobby your MP and local authority
- respond to planning applications
- ensure paths are recorded on definitive maps
- promote walking through outreach and education
- inform others through media and publicity

Get involved – support your Area or Group
- organise a committee
- fundraise
- design a website
- compile a walks programme

Contact your local Area or Group to find out about volunteering opportunities where you live. Or look on our website for new one-off projects that are being added and updated regularly.

Many of our successes are down to the enormous contribution made by our volunteers. Without the support and dedication of so many people much of our work would not be possible. Volunteers are at the heart of what we do and we value the time given by everyone to help protect our outdoor environment and to promote walking as a healthy activity that can be enjoyed by all.

OTHER WAYS YOU CAN HELP

If you're already a member, here are some ways you can help us today, without putting your hand in your pocket.

Gift Aid – If you 'Gift Aid It', we can claim an extra 28p per pound donated, even on membership fees. This accounted for £300,000 last year, but this could double if all our supporters registered. So, if you pay income tax or capital gains tax, please Gift Aid today, or ☎ 020 7339 8511 for a form.

Direct Debit – Over 50% of members pay their subscriptions by direct debit, which saves them trouble and greatly reduces our administration costs and bank charges. Members can, of course, cancel this arrangement at any time.

Ramblers' Association credit card – If you switch to our card, run by the ethically guided Co-operative Bank, we receive £15 for every account opened, a further £2.50 when first used, plus a further 25p per £100 spent on the card. ☎ 0800 002 006 to apply, quoting reference 64309.

Ramblers' Insurance – We receive up to 10% of the premium for every home, travel or motor policy taken out with UIA Insurance – the insurer with principles. ☎ 0800 013 0064, quoting reference RAM2, visit www.ramblersinsurance.co.uk, or see the advert on p126.

Following in your footsteps – Once you have provided for your loved ones, why not leave the world a better place and include the Ramblers in your will? For a copy of our free guide to making and updating your will please ☎ 020 7339 8511 or see overleaf.

Ramblers Holidays was set up in 1946 to support the work of the Ramblers' Association, and still provides significant funds to the Ramblers' Association every year. For a brochure ☎ 01707 331133, or see inside back cover.

Our thanks go to Millets for their continuing support and sponsorship of this guide and we would like to draw your attention to their advertising on p262 and p293-296.

simple *pleasures*

The world is ever-changing, but the simplest pleasures remain the same.

At the Ramblers' Association, we want to make sure that these pleasures can be enjoyed forever.

Once you have provided for your loved ones, remembering the Ramblers in your will is a wonderful way to preserve for tomorrow the countryside that gives you such pleasure today.

www.ramblers.org.uk

The Ramblers' Association is a member of the Legacy Promotion Campaign

---

Please tell me how I can remember **The Ramblers** in my Will

☐ Please send me a free guide to making and updating my will

Registered charity number 1093577

Name _____

Address _____

_____

Postcode _____

I am a Ramblers member: Yes ☐   No ☐

Please return to:
John Wightman, The Ramblers' Association,
FREEPOST SW15, London SE1 7BR.

B

FREEDOM TO ROAM IN ENGLAND AND WALES

September 19th 2004 was a momentous day in the history of the Ramblers' Association, as the new right of access contained in Part I of the Countryside and Rights of Way Act 2000 – a statutory right to roam – was implemented in two English regions, the South East and the Lower North West. Other regions soon followed suit, and then on 28 May 2005 Wales opened up a staggering 22% of its land under the measures. The whole process was completed on 31 October 2005, when the East and West of England welcomed their new access rights: 8% of England's land is now available for walkers to enjoy.

A century of struggle

These events marked the culmination of a campaign for increased access to the countryside that has lasted for over a century, but reached a turning point with the Kinder Scout Mass Trespass in 1932, when six walkers were imprisoned following scuffles with gamekeepers. In 1935, the Ramblers' Association was formed, and the campaign for increased access to the countryside was integral to the organisation from the beginning.

In 1985 the Ramblers' Association launched its Forbidden Britain campaign, with a view to securing a new legal right of access. This brought the issue into the public eye once more and, after years of ceaseless campaigning, the Labour government elected in 1997 pledged to introduce a new statutory right of access to open countryside and registered common land across England and Wales. The resulting legislation – the Countryside and Rights of Way (CRoW) Act – finally received royal assent in November 2000.

The new right of access

The new right only provides a right of access on foot to mapped areas of open countryside, though any existing rights on the land will remain unaffected. Walkers are required to observe certain restrictions, while landowners who obstruct anyone seeking to exercise their new right will be committing a criminal offence. For more information and the latest news on commencement of access, please see www.ramblers.org.uk/freedom/

For more information on walkers' new rights and responsibilities (see p300).

Now that the new rights have come into force, the responsibility for managing access locally passes to the relevant access authority. It's important that access authorities (see Local Authorities on p276) use their new powers to ensure, for example, that misleading signs are removed and that walkers can get to the newly accessible areas. Walkers should contact the relevant access authority and the Ramblers' Association, using the form on p285, if they encounter any problems or misleading notices.

What now?

There is still much work to be done to maximise the public benefits of the CRoW Act. The Act has given us much new access, but in some areas, downland in particular, not as much as we'd hoped. The Ramblers' Association will be campaigning to increase the amount of land mapped as access land and in the coming year will be seeking an extension of the right of access to cover coastal land. Long-term aims include woodland areas.

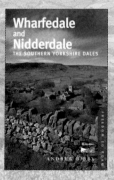
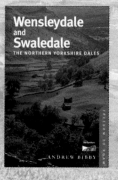
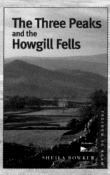
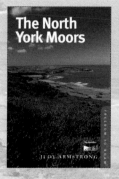

FOOTPATHS IN ENGLAND AND WALES

Britain's intricate network of rights of way in England and Wales provides intimate access to the furthest reaches of our countryside, but it is only as a result of 70 years' unstinting effort by the Ramblers' Association that many of these paths –140,000 miles (225,000km) of them in England and Wales – have survived for use today.

Changing the law

Since 1935, the Ramblers' Association has played a key role in the development of the legislation that seeks to protect those paths. In particular, the National Parks and Access to the Countryside Act 1949 required the production of definitive maps of rights of way, and the Countryside Act 1968 which introduced statutory signposting. During the passage of the Wildlife and Countryside Act through Parliament in 1981, we persuaded the House of Lords to defeat government proposals to abolish the right of appeal against path closures, and we played a key role in securing the Rights of Way Act 1990, which gives local authorities clear powers to enforce the law on keeping paths unobstructed where they cross cultivated fields. More recently, with the Countryside and Rights of Way Act 2000, we supported the government's introduction of provisions to enable any member of the public to serve notice on a highway authority to secure the removal of obstructions. This is proving highly effective and many paths are now being opened up as a result of its use by Ramblers footpath workers and others. The Parliamentary work continues with lobbying on the Natural Environment and Rural Communities Bill, which contains provisions that may help to resolve some of the problems surrounding the unsustainable use of recreational motor vehicles on rights of way.

Sadly, Acts of Parliament are not enough, and vigilance is still needed because much rights of way law is ignored or poorly enforced by local highway authorities. These councils have a duty to see that public rights of way are:
• properly maintained
• kept free from obstructions
• signposted where they meet surfaced roads
• waymarked where necessary along their route
• recorded on the official (definitive) map

Yet it is estimated there are over 200,000 obstacles and more than 110,000 missing signposts in England and Wales. That means a walker is likely to encounter an obstruction or problem every 2km/1 1/4 miles. So next time you are out walking and you encounter a problem please report it to the local authority with responsibility for that path. We try to make it as simple as possible for everybody to do this. We've produced a *Reporting Path Problems* (see p308) leaflet (available from our central office), or you can complete the form on p285, or on our website.

Grass roots successes

Ramblers footpath workers across the country are involved in casework to protect individual paths, and to extend and improve the path network. Examples abound. In July, Margaret Bowdery and her colleagues in the East Berkshire Group celebrated the opening of a safe route through a flood relief tunnel under the busy A404 – a motorway in all but name – which the public had been expected to cross on the level, dodging between cars. It took more than eight years to achieve this simple solution to the problem. And in Devon, Ron Bagshaw led the fight to prevent the deletion of a path at South Tawton on the edge of Dartmoor, from the definitive map. In both of these cases, the Association's Honorary Solicitor, Jerry Pearlman, brought his expertise to bear at public inquiries. Such legal work is crucial to the protection of the network, and the coming year will inevitably see action both in the magistrates' courts when we bring private prosecutions for obstruction, and possibly even in the House of the Lords as we challenge a court ruling which is preventing the addition of many paths to the definitive map.

Additionally we have many ongoing local footpath campaigns running up and down the country. Recent campaigns in Shropshire, Cornwall, Northamptonshire and Oxfordshire have led to increased funding for rights of way improvements in those counties. In Stoke-on-Trent an eight-year campaign culminated in the publication of the city's first ever definitive map of paths.

For more information about how you can help with footpath campaigns, please contact our central office.

WALKING HOLIDAYS THROUGHOUT THE UK

PHOTO: CATHERINE LECKENBY

COUNTRYSIDE PROTECTION

Back in the 1930s when the Ramblers' Association was in its youth, it was part of a movement not only to secure better access to the countryside but also to protect it. This is no less true today, and our charitable objective to defend the beauty of the countryside is just as relevant now as the pressures of development become ever greater.

Media attention on issues such as house building, renewable energy, road building, aviation and sustainable development have provided us with opportunities to get messages across that demonstrate the need for greater countryside protection for the health and well-being of the nation. Significant changes to the planning system, enshrined in the Planning and Compulsory Purchase Act 2004, have challenged us to change the way we campaign on these issues, in particular by focusing on regional and local decision-making, rather than what happens at county level. Nationally we continue to respond to consultations on planning guidance, work closely with

a range of like-minded organisations through Wildlife and Countryside Link (see p288) and provide newsletters, training and advice to volunteers on how they can make a difference locally.

In 2005 we continued to campaign for the creation of the South Downs National Park. The public inquiry ended in March and we hope to hear the announcement this year. We have stepped up our campaign for a change in the way renewable energy is funded and continued to oppose the most damaging schemes, such as Whinash wind farm on the borders of the Lake District National Park.

Countryside protection is dear to all walkers, and as such we intend to make it easier for everyone to be involved. If there is proposed development in your area that is causing you concern, or you'd like to know how you can influence the decisions made in your local area, please contact the countryside team at our central office for advice.

Today it's all a game for Rannoch, but for a walker or climber in trouble on Scotland's mountains he needs to be able to pla
it well. The dog's speed and superior sense of smell allow him to search many square miles a day in the sort of condition
that make human senses virtually useless.

Together with Kenny's knowledge of the mountains and handling skills, they make an expert team. The trust between them i
complete and built over many years. It certainly makes you think, in these days of avalanche transceivers and therma
imaging, that for many people when it's crunch time, a dog is still 'a man's best friend'.

TRUST IS EARNED berghaus

PROMOTING WALKING

The Ramblers' Association is working to inspire, encourage and support as many people as possible to walk for health, recreation and transport. We want everyone, of all ages, backgrounds and abilities, to feel able to walk close to home in safe and attractive environments, in towns and cities as well as in the countryside. We believe that making our environment more walker-friendly will help create a happier, healthier and more sustainable world for everyone.

New schemes nationwide

During 2005 we've been putting more resources than ever into this work. There are new promoting walking staff in our three offices, and a new strategy to help the Ramblers get more people on their feet.

In England, we're starting to work with councils and the health service to develop local healthy walking schemes, and trying innovative ways of getting people walking regularly even if a led walk isn't available. This work builds on our Walking Out projects in Stoke, Lincoln and Sheffield, where keen volunteers took out hundreds of new walkers on easy, local and accessible walks, including refugees who got special benefits from the walks.

With funds from the Scottish Executive through Paths to Health, a one-year Promoting Walking project in Scotland is helping to set up new groups across the country, aimed at new walkers or those returning to recreational walking. We're also encouraging existing Ramblers Groups to diversify their walks programmes with shorter walks appealing to a wider range of people, including families and those getting too fit for very short health walks. The work builds on our involvement in the Bums off Seats project in Fife over the last three years.

In Wales, the Cerrig Camu/Stepping Stones project is providing easy, friendly walks that fill the gap between health walks and more challenging rural walks. This nationwide project, funded by the Countryside Council for Wales, aims to offer a programme of walks in every Welsh local authority area. Cerrig Camu replaces our long established Lonc a Chlonc/Walk and Talk

programme and also features training courses for walk leaders: so far over 100 leaders have been trained.

Once again we've been involved in Britain on the Move, ITV's campaign to encourage everyone to improve their health and quality of life. Our ever-popular Welcome to Walking Week in September was a Britain on the Move event that also encompassed National Day of Walking and In Town Without My Car day.

Changing agendas

We're also helping to improve conditions for walkers by lobbying local authorities and government departments who, thanks to years of work by the Ramblers and other organisations, are now much more willing to promote walking as sustainable transport and healthy activity. In England the Department for Transport is supporting three sustainable travel towns: Darlington, Peterborough and Worcester, and Ramblers staff and volunteers have already worked with the council and Sustrans to help deliver walking information to the residents of Peterborough. In many other places Ramblers volunteers are contributing to an increasing number of local walking strategies.

Spreading the word

Getting information to the walking public in a useful and accessible form is another vital activity. This year we've launched a great new free colour leaflet for beginners, *Walking for You*, with many thousands of copies distributed through local health information points and doctors' surgeries. We've also reprinted our ever-popular *Take30* leaflet with its ten-week course of walking for health. Versions of these publications are also available from Ramblers Wales – these are bilingual and adapted for a Welsh audience.

Our acclaimed website has kept growing and now receives over 6million hits a month; the health and beginners' pages account for many of these hits and there's an increasing amount of local information on walking too.

THE RAMBLERS' ASSOCIATION IN SCOTLAND

There are almost endless opportunities to explore Scotland on foot; and new arrangements for outdoor access mean things are set to get even better in the coming years.

The Land Reform (Scotland) Act 2003 came into effect in February 2005 and introduced access arrangements that are among the best in Europe.

Ramblers' Association volunteers and staff played a key role in securing better protection for footpath networks, clearer rights of access to the wider countryside, and conservation of some of our most beautiful landscapes.

During 2006 we will continue to work to ensure the effective implementation of this access legislation. Local access forums are being set up in each local authority and national park authority area, and many Ramblers members are involved with these forums.

Ramblers Scotland is a founding partner in the Paths for All Partnership (see p290), launched in 1996 to promote paths in Scotland for people of all ages and ability, for walking, cycling and horse riding. The key objectives of the partnership are to achieve a significant increase in well-managed paths close to where people live, and to promote their use.

New national parks

The Ramblers has welcomed the creation of Scotland's first national park in Loch Lomond and the Trossachs and urged the park authority to ensure that the special recreational qualities of the area are maintained and enhanced in the future. The park was established on 8 July 2002 and covers 720 square miles.

A second park – the Cairngorms National Park – was officially opened on 1 September 2003. Although this is the biggest

national park in the UK there are serious concerns because Highland Perthshire was excluded from the park boundary for political reasons.

We have joined forces with other organisations to form PARC (Perthshire Alliance for the Real Cairngorms) to campaign for the inclusion of this area of Perthshire. If the Cairngorms are to achieve World Heritage Site status there needs to be integrated planning and management, and the widest possible boundary is needed to achieve this.

In June 2005 the Scottish Executive announced its intention to create Scotland's first coastal and marine national park. Scottish Natural Heritage is now setting up the consultation process for this third national park, and Ramblers Scotland is a member of the stakeholder group chaired by Scottish Natural Heritage to inform this process.

SPECIAL DISCOUNT MEMBERSHIP OFFER

If you are not yet a Ramblers member, use this coupon to get 20% off your first year's subscription, plus one month extra free for joining by Direct Debit. And if you are already a member why not introduce a friend to this special offer and give them this form? For your support you'll get a terrific range of benefits to help you to get the most out of walking:

■ walk BRITAIN, our annual handbook and accommodation guide

■ A lively colour magazine, walk

■ Membership of your local Ramblers Group

■ Access to our Ordnance Survey map library

■ 10% off at Millets and Blacks, and discretionary discounts at many outdoor shops

Your support will ensure we can keep working for walkers:

■ Protecting Britain's unique network of public paths

■ Increasing access for walkers

■ Safeguarding the countryside

■ Providing information, advice and support

IT IS A CONDITION OF THIS OFFER THAT YOU PAY BY DIRECT DEBIT

The Ramblers

Registered charity number 1093577

Yes, I/We would like to join the Ramblers

Title_____ Name(s)_____

Address_____

_____ Postcode _____

Date(s) of Birth _____ _____ RA Group (if you have a preference)_____

If you have no preference you will be placed in a group according to your postcode

B

Tick the box that suits you best: ☐ Individual £19.20 (normally £24) ☐ Joint* £25.60 (normally £32)

☐ Reduced Individual+ £14 ☐ Reduced Joint*+ £18

*Joint membership is available for two adults living at the same address,

+Reduced rates are available and are intended for people who, through whatever circumstances, cannot afford the standard rates. The offer is vaild until December 2005. The offer is not open to existing members.

We occasionally exchange member's names and addresses with other like-minded organisations, which may be of interest to you. These are for use once only, and will not lead to further mailings. However, if you would prefer to be excluded from any such exchanges, please tick this box. ☐

Instruction to your Bank or Building Society to pay by Direct Debit

DIRECT Debit

Please fill in the whole form and send it to: The Ramblers' Association, FREEPOST SW15, London SE1 7BR

Details of the Bank/Building Society

To: The Manager   Bank/Building Society

Address

Postcode

Name(s) of Account Holder(s)

Bank/Building Society account number

Originator's Identification Number 9 2 2 6 7 0

Branch Sort Code

Reference Number (for office use)

Instruction to your Bank/Building Society — Please pay The Rambler' Association Direct Debits from the account detailed in this Instruction subject to the safeguards assured by the Direct Debit Guarantee.

Signature(s)

Date

Banks/Building Societies may not accept Direct Debit Instructions for some types of account.

Walk on the Light side.

Nikon's new High Grade Light binoculars.
You'll keep walking...

... and you'll love it. Because Nikon's new HGL binoculars are so light you'll hardly notice them until you look through them. Multilayer coating makes for the brightest, sharpest images, even where there's little light. Waterproof, fog-free construction ensures you see your way through, wherever your walk takes you. The new HGL binoculars from Nikon. Time to enjoy the wild side.

10x42 HG L DCF

LONG DISTANCE PATHS

PERTH & KINROSS COUNTRYSIDE TRUST

These pages give information on a selection of long-distance paths and routes in Britain, offering many thousands of miles of excellent walking through a dramatic variety of landscapes. Nearly all of them can be used as the basis of shorter walks, or walked in short sections as well as in one longer trip.

Walking advice

If you are planning your first extended walking trip on a long-distance route we recommend you practise on day-walks before setting out to make sure you can comfortably walk the distance you intend to cover each day. Don't forget that unless you have arranged luggage transfer you will probably be carrying a heavier pack than you would on a day-walk.

EASY routes offer generally level walking through areas where transport and assistance are usually close at hand, and while attractive to all, they are especially recommended for the less experienced or energetic.

CHALLENGING routes have sections across difficult or remote terrain, which should only be attempted by those who have a little experience and navigational

skill and are properly equipped, especially in bad weather. The majority fall somewhere in between.

All routes are signed in their own right unless otherwise stated, though standards vary. We recommend you always take a path guide and map even when following a well-signed trail.

We only have room for a selection of routes in this guide. The Ramblers website lists many more and in much more detail – see www.ramblers.org.uk/info/ paths. The *Long Distance Walkers' Handbook* and its accompanying *Long Distance Path Chart*, compiled by the Long Distance Walkers Association, provide a comprehensive overview of routes over 32km/20 miles: both are available from the Ramblers Bookshop (see p306).

Accommodation

All routes listed are cross-referenced from the B&B section: accommodation within 3.2km/2 miles of paths listed here is indicated as such under its location. You can also use the path listings on the Ramblers website to search for accommodation.

Luggage carriers and hostel providers are listed in the Walker's Toolkit (p265). Many accommodation providers are also willing to transfer your luggage: look for the ! symbol in the accommodation section.

Maps

Sheet numbers refer to Ordnance Survey Explorer 1:25 000 maps: the latest editions of these show the exact line of route for almost all the trails listed. You can buy the full range of OS Explorer maps in both weatherproof and paper versions from Aqua3 through our website at a special discount, and we'll also receive a donation for every map sold: see www.ramblers.org.uk/ discountmaps. Strip maps and digital maps are available for some routes: these cover the route itself and some of the countryside on either side. For more on maps see p266.

Publications

Where indicated, these can be obtained from the Ramblers Bookshop: see p306 for details. Publications with ISBN numbers can be ordered from bookshops and internet retailers, or direct from the publisher, see Walker's Toolkit (p299). Some publications are less widely available, in which case we've given ordering details in the listing itself, with TIC indicating a Tourist Information Centre. Guides include at least sketch maps unless otherwise stated and those marked (OS) have extracts from Ordnance Survey mapping.

Comprehensive accommodation lists are available for some paths and are shown in the listings. Where a path website or printed publication has accommodation listings, we indicate this with the abbreviation (AC).

Symbols and abbreviations
✳ new listing
🛡 National Trail (England and Wales).
🛡 Long Distance Route (Scotland)
(AC) includes accommodation listings
(OS) includes Ordnance Survey map extracts
TIC Tourist/Visitor Information Centre
All photographs copyright Countryside Agency unless otherwise stated.

Angles Way
See Peddars Way and Norfolk Coast Path

Bembridge Trail
See Isle of Wight Coastal Path

Bournemouth Coast Path (E9)
See Solent Way

Cambrian Way
Cardiff to Conwy 440km/274 miles
CHALLENGING
A spectacular but very mountainous unsigned coast to coast route across Wales from north to south via the Brecon Beacons, Cader Idris and Snowdonia, devised by Ramblers volunteers.
MAPS OL12, OL13, OL17, OL18, OL23, 151, 152, 187, 213, 215
PUBLICATIONS GUIDEBOOK £5.50 + P&P FROM THE RAMBLERS BOOKSHOP (AC)
CONTACT CAMBRIAN WAY, 2 BEECH LODGE, 67 THE PARK, CHELTENHAM GL50 2RX, TONY.DRAKE@LINEONE.NET

Capital Ring
See London Loop

✳ Cateran Trail
Blairgowrie, Bridge of Cally and Spittal of Glenshee 101km/63 miles
A lengthy heart-shaped circular trail with a spur from Blairgowrie, over varied terrain from rolling pastures to the foothills of the Cairngorms with excellent views and stunning scenery throughout. Mostly moderate walking with a more challenging section from Enochdu to Spittal of Glenshee.
MAPS 381, 387
PUBLICATIONS THE CATERAN TRAIL
ISBN 1 898481 21 0, RUCKSACK READERS £10.99

CLEVELAND WAY

CONTACT PERTH AND KINROSS COUNTRYSIDE TRUST, ☎ 01738 475340
WWW.PKCT.ORG/CATERANTRAIL

Ceredigion Coast Path
See Pembrokeshire Coast Path

Chiltern Way
Circular via Hemel Hempstead with alternative routes 275km/172 miles total
Meandering, varied and largely rural trail offering a good cross-section of characteristic scenery in the Chilterns AONB. The original inner circuit runs between the Ridgeway and Dunstable Downs, with two more recent extensions linking with the Thames Path and Icknield Way.
MAPS 171, 172, 181, 182, 192, 193
PUBLICATIONS GUIDEBOOK £9.99 + P&P FROM THE RAMBLERS BOOKSHOP. TWO BOOKS OF LINKING CIRCULAR WALKS FROM THE CHILTERN SOCIETY.
CONTACT CHILTERN SOCIETY: SEE AONBS, P270

🛡 Cleveland Way
Helmsley to Filey Brigg 177km/110 miles
Horseshoe-shaped route that first follows the western and northern edges of the North York Moors National Park to Saltburn, then the beautiful coastline via Whitby and Scarborough: this last section is now part of the international North Sea Trail project. The whole route is accessible by public transport, and some sections are accessible for people with disabilities: contact the national trail officer for more information. The Link through the Tabular Hills connects Helmsley with the coast near Scalby via a more direct route (77km/48 miles), creating a complete circuit of the national park.
MAPS OL26, OL27, 301
PUBLICATIONS OFFICIAL GUIDEBOOK (OS) £12.99 + P&P. ACCOMMODATION AND INFORMATION GUIDE (AC) FREE + P&P FROM THE RAMBLERS BOOKSHOP. THE LINK THROUGH THE TABULAR HILLS GUIDEBOOK £3.95 + P&P FROM NORTH YORK MOORS NATIONAL PARK (P269). ALTERNATIVE GUIDEBOOK: THE CLEVELAND WAY AND THE YORKSHIRE WOLDS WAY WITH THE TABULAR HILLS WALK (OS) ISBN 1 85284 447 7, CICERONE £12.
LUGGAGE CARRIERS BRIGANTES, COAST TO COAST HOLIDAYS, SHERPA VAN
CONTACT NATIONAL TRAIL OFFICER ☎ 01439 770657
WWW.NATIONALTRAIL.CO.UK/CLEVELANDWAY (AC)

Clwydian Way
Circular from Prestatyn via Llangollen, Corwen and Denby 243km/152 miles total
A roughly bottle-shaped route through splendid but little-known walking country and historic towns in the Clwydian Range and the Vale of Clwyd. The main

CATERAN TRAIL

195km/122-mile circuit is complemented by an alternative 48km/30-mile moorland section linking Mynydd Hiraethog and Denbigh.
MAPS 255, 256, 264, 265
PUBLICATIONS GUIDEBOOK (OS) £6.95 + P&P FROM THE RAMBLERS BOOKSHOP
WWW.CLWYDIANWAY.CO.UK (AC)

Clyde Walkway
See West Highland Way

Coast to Coast Walk
St Bees to Robin Hoods Bay
304km/190 miles **CHALLENGING**
Unsigned route devised by Alfred Wainwright to link the Irish Sea and the North Sea via three national parks: the Lake District, Yorkshire Dales and the North York Moors. Popular and scenic, but notably remote and demanding, it was named the second best walk in the world in a recent experts' poll.
MAPS OL4, OL5, OL19, OL26, OL27, OL30, 302, 303, 304
HARVEY WEATHERPROOF STRIP MAPS, WEST AND EAST, £9.95 + P&P EACH FROM THE RAMBLERS BOOKSHOP
DIGITAL EXPLORER STRIP MAP £99.95 FROM MEMORY-MAP
PUBLICATIONS A COAST TO COAST WALK BY A WAINWRIGHT, ISBN 0 711222 36 3, FRANCES LINCOLN £11.99. CAMPING GUIDE £2.99 FROM ROCKUMENTARY PRESS, 11 CLIFF TOP, FILEY YO14 9HG, ROCKUMENTARYPRESS@YAHOO.CO.UK.
LUGGAGE CARRIERS BRIGANTES, COAST TO COAST HOLIDAYS, COAST TO COAST PACKHORSE, SHERPA VAN
HOSTEL BOOKING YHA

✳ Coleridge Way
Nether Stowey to Porlock
58km/36 miles
A walk linking the Quantock and Brendon hills, Exmoor National Park and the Somerset coast through a landscape that inspired the romantic poet Samuel Taylor Coleridge, including numerous delightful villages. Launched in 2005, the route has already proved popular despite being promoted only through the web, but signing and a printed guide are to follow.
MAPS OL9, 140
PUBLICATIONS FREE OVERVIEW LEAFLET FROM PORLOCK TIC ☎ 01643 863150; DETAILED DESCRIPTION AND MAPS ON WEBSITE BELOW.
WWW.QUANTOCKONLINE.CO.UK (AC)

🐚 Cotswold Way
Bath to Chipping Campden
163km/101 miles
Scenic, popular and undulating route along the Cotswold escarpment first proposed by Gloucestershire Ramblers in the 1950s. The route's relaunch as a national trail has been put back to 2007: for latest news about route improvements see National Trails website. Part of the Cotswold Round, a lengthy circular walk (see Macmillan Way).
MAPS OL45, 155, 167, 179
HARVEY WEATHERPROOF STRIP MAP £9.95 + P&P FROM THE RAMBLERS BOOKSHOP
PUBLICATIONS GUIDE £3.95 + P&P; HANDBOOK (AC, FACILITIES, TRANSPORT) £2.95 + P&P; BOTH FROM THE RAMBLERS BOOKSHOP. ALTERNATIVE GUIDE THE COTSWOLD WAY, ISBN 1 85284 449 3, CICERONE £12 (OS), INCLUDES MANY RECENT ROUTE IMPROVEMENTS.
LUGGAGE CARRIERS COMPASS, SHERPA VAN
CONTACT NATIONAL TRAIL OFFICE
☎ 01453 827004
WWW.NATIONALTRAIL.CO.UK/COTSWOLD

Cowal Way

Portavadie to Ardgartan near Arrochar 75km/47 miles
Across the Cowal peninsula from Loch Fyne to Loch Long, with grassy hills, heather moorland, forest plantations, prehistoric heritage and rich wildlife all within easy reach of Glasgow. Includes some more remote and strenuous sections.
MAPS 362, 363, 364
PUBLICATIONS GUIDE £4.99 + P&P FROM DUNOON VISITOR INFORMATION CENTRE
☎ 08707 200629, OR VIA WEBSITE BELOW.
CONTACT COLINTRAIVE AND GLENDARUEL COMMUNITY COUNCIL ☎ 01700 841311
WWW.COLGLEN.ORG.UK/COWALWAY (AC)

Cumbria Way
Ulverston to Carlisle 112km/70 miles
Through the heart of the Lake District National Park via Langdale and Borrowdale, Coniston, Derwent Water and Caldbeck. A good introduction to the area keeping mainly to the valleys, with some higher exposed ground.
MAPS OL4, OL5, OL6, OL7, 315
HARVEY WEATHERPROOF STRIP MAP £9.95 + P&P FROM THE RAMBLERS BOOKSHOP
PUBLICATIONS GUIDE £2.95 + P&P FROM THE RAMBLERS BOOKSHOP
LUGGAGE CARRIERS BRIGANTES, SHERPA VAN
HOSTEL BOOKING YHA

FIFE COASTAL PATH

Dales Way
Leeds, Shipley or Harrogate to Bowness-on-Windemere
205km/128 miles total **EASY**
Originally inspired by local Ramblers, this fairly easy-going, mainly waterside trail links the Yorkshire Dales and the Lake District. The original route runs from Ilkley to Bowness, and three links connect with big towns in the lower Dales.
MAPS OL2, OL7, OL19, OL30, 297 (MAIN ROUTE), 288 (SHIPLEY), 289 (LEEDS)
HARVEY WEATHERPROOF STRIP MAP INCLUDING ALL THREE LINKS £9.95 + P&P FROM THE RAMBLERS BOOKSHOP
PUBLICATIONS THE DALES WAY ISBN 1 85284 464 7, CICERONE £10 (OS): MOST RECENTLY UPDATED GUIDE, ONLY COVERS ROUTE FROM ILKLEY. HANDBOOK (AC, FACILITIES, TRANSPORT) £1.50 + P&P FROM THE RAMBLERS BOOKSHOP.
LUGGAGE CARRIERS BRIGANTES, SHERPA VAN
USER GROUP DALES WAY ASSOCIATION, 3 MOORFIELD ROAD, ILKLEY LS29 8BL
WWW.DALESWAY.ORG.UK (AC)

✳ Derwent Valley Heritage Way
Ladybower Reservoir, Bamford to Derwent Mouth, Shardlow
88km/55 miles **EASY**
Along the river Derwent from Ladybower Reservoir in the Peak District via the Derwent Valley Mills World Heritage Site and the city of Derby to its confluence with the river Trent near Shardlow. A fascinating combination of rich natural landscapes, industrial heritage and famous stately homes and estates such as Chatsworth and Haddon.
MAPS OL1, OL24, 259, 260
PUBLICATIONS THE DERWENT VALLEY HERITAGE WAY, ISBN 0 7117 2958 1, JARROLD £11.99 (OS). BASIC ROUTE DESCRIPTION AND OVERVIEW MAP ON WEBSITE BELOW.
WWW.NATIONALHERITAGECORRIDOR.ORG.UK

Epping Forest Centenary Walk

See Essex Way

Essex Way

Epping to Harwich
130km/81 miles EASY
Pioneered by Ramblers and CPRE members, this walk heads across quiet countryside via Dedham Vale and Constable country to finish at the Stour estuary. The unsigned 24km/15-mile Epping Forest Centenary Walk, created to celebrate the centenary of saving of the forest for public enjoyment, connects Manor Park in east London with Epping.
MAPS 174, 183, 184, 196, 197
PUBLICATIONS GUIDE BOOKLET £5 + P&P FROM THE RAMBLERS BOOKSHOP. CENTENARY WALK GUIDE £1 + 30P P&P FROM EPPING FOREST INFORMATION CENTRE ☎ 020 8508 0028, EPPING.FOREST@CORPOFLONDON.GOV.UK

Fife Coastal Path

North Queensferry to Newport on Tay 107km/67 miles

Around the firths of Forth and Tay, through historic towns and villages, excellent countryside and attractive beaches, combining surfaced seaside promenades and rougher coastal tracks. The route is now part of the international North Sea Trail.
MAPS 367, 370, 371
PUBLICATIONS GUIDE £12.99 + P&P FROM THE RAMBLERS BOOKSHOP. PATH MAPS AND OTHER USEFUL INFORMATION ON WEBSITE BELOW.
CONTACT FIFE COAST AND COUNTRYSIDE TRUST ☎ 01333 592591
WWW.FIFECOASTALPATH.COM (AC)

Glyndŵr's Way

Knighton to Welshpool
206km/128 miles
A beautiful route through mid Wales visiting many sites associated with the fifteenth century hero Owain Glyndŵr. Forms a rough triangle with Offa's Dyke Path as the third side and Machynlleth as its westernmost point.
MAPS 201, 214, 215, 216, 239
DIGITAL EXPLORER STRIP MAP £49.95 FROM MEMORY-MAP
PUBLICATIONS GUIDE (OS) £12.99 + P&P FROM THE RAMBLERS BOOKSHOP. FOR ACCOM GUIDE SEE OFFA'S DYKE PATH.
CONTACT NATIONAL TRAIL OFFICER ☎ 01654 703376
WWW.GLYNDWRSWAY.ORG.UK

GLYNDWR'S WAY

Great Glen Way

Fort William to Inverness
117km/73 miles
From the West Highland Way along the fault line of Glen Mor and the northwest shores of Loch Lochy and Loch Ness, following the course of the Caledonian Canal. Lower level and less demanding than some Scottish routes.
MAPS 392, 400, 416
HARVEY WEATHERPROOF STRIP MAP £9.95 + P&P FROM RUCKSACK READERS ☎ 01786 824 696
PUBLICATIONS GUIDEBOOK £10.99 + P&P, ACCOM & SERVICES GUIDE (AC) FREE + P&P FROM RUCKSACK READERS ☎ 01786 824696
LUGGAGE CARRIERS ABERCHALDER, GREAT GLEN BAGGAGE, GREAT GLEN TRAVEL, LOCH NESS INDEPENDENT HOSTELS IBHS
CONTACT GREAT GLEN WAY RANGER SERVICE ☎ 01320 366633
WWW.GREATGLENWAY.COM (AC)

Hadrian's Wall Path

Newcastle to Bowness-on-Solway
130km/81 miles
Along the line of the celebrated ancient monument and World Heritage Site, built in the year AD122 to mark the northern limit of the Roman empire, through contrasting surroundings from the bustling Newcastle quaysides to the remote North Pennines. Please help to look after the monument by following the conservation advice issued by the National Trail Office.
MAPS OL43, 314, 315, 316
HARVEY WEATHERPROOF STRIP MAP £9.95 + P&P FROM THE RAMBLERS BOOKSHOP
DIGITAL EXPLORER STRIP MAP £49.95 FROM MEMORY-MAP
PUBLICATIONS GUIDEBOOK (OS) £12.99 + P&P, ACCOM GUIDE (AC) FREE + P&P, ESSENTIAL GUIDE (FACILITIES, TRANSPORT, SUGGESTED ITINERARIES ETC) £3.95 + P&P FROM THE RAMBLERS BOOKSHOP. NUMEROUS SHORTER AND CIRCULAR WALKS GUIDES FROM NATIONAL TRAIL OFFICE (BELOW).
LUGGAGE CARRIERS BRIGANTES, SHERPA VAN, WALKERS BAGGAGE TRANSFER, WALKING SUPPORT
HOSTEL BOOKING YHA
CONTACTS NATIONAL TRAIL OFFICER ☎ 0191 269 1600
WWW.NATIONALTRAIL.CO.UK/HADRIANSWALL (AC)

HADRIAN'S WALL INFORMATION LINE
☎ 01434 322002
WWW.HADRIANS-WALL.ORG (AC)
USER GROUP HADRIAN'S WALL PATH TRUST C/O NATIONAL TRAIL OFFICER

Heart of England Way

Milford near Stafford to Bourton-on-the-Water
161km/100 miles
A green route across the West Midlands linking Cannock Chase with the Cotswolds, through mainly gentle low-lying country with woodlands, canals and agricultural land.
MAPS OL45, 205, 220, 221, 232, 244
PUBLICATIONS GUIDEBOOK £7.50 + P&P, ACCOM LIST (AC) FREE + P&P FROM THE RAMBLERS BOOKSHOP
USER GROUP HEART OF ENGLAND WAY ASSOCIATION, 50 GEORGE ROAD, WATER ORTON, BIRMINGHAM B46 1PE
WWW.HEARTOFENGLANDWAY.ORG

✳ Herefordshire Trail

Circular from Ledbury via Ross-on-Wye, Kington, Leominster and Bromyard 246.5km/154 miles

A circuit around the county visiting all the market towns, pretty villages and attractive countryside in between, including commons, woodlands, hills, farmlands, waterside and characteristic black and white architecture. Launched in 2005 by local Ramblers and soon to be signed.
MAPS OL13, OL14, 189, 190, 201, 202, 203
PUBLICATIONS THE HEREFORDSHIRE TRAIL, ISBN 1 901184 73 0. £5.95 + £2 P&P FROM THE BOOK SECRETARY, GAWSWORTH, NORTH ROAD, KINGSLAND HR6 9RU. CHEQUES TO HEREFORD GROUP OF THE RAMBLERS' ASSOCIATION.
WEBSITE WWW.HEREFORDSHIRETRAIL.COM (AC)

Icknield Way Path

Bledlow to Knettishall Heath near Thetford 206km/128 miles

Follows prehistoric trackways from the Chilterns into East Anglia, passing many sites of archaeological interest and connecting the Ridgeway and Peddars Way as part of a lengthy off-road route along ancient ways between the Dorset coast and the Wash (see Ridgeway). The original walking route runs from Ivinghoe Beacon; there are now alternative multi-user sections from Bledlow to Ivinghoe, running parallel to the Ridgeway, and from Aldbury to Pegsdon (Icknield Way Trail).
MAPS 181, 192, 195, 208, 209, 210, 226, 229
PUBLICATIONS GUIDEBOOK (FROM IVINGHOE)

£4.50 + P&P, ACCOM LIST (AC) £1 + P&P FROM THE RAMBLERS BOOKSHOP. GREATER RIDGEWAY GUIDE: SEE RIDGEWAY. BLEDLOW – IVINGHOE LEAFLET FROM BUCKINGHAMSHIRE COUNCIL, DOWNLOADABLE FROM THEIR WEBSITE UNDER WALKS AND RIDES (P276). ICKNIELD WAY TRAIL LEAFLET FROM NORTH CHILTERNS TRUST, ☎ 01582 412225, WWW.NORTHCHILTERNSTRUST.CO.UK. USER GROUP ICKNIELD WAY ASSOCIATION, 9 BOUNDARY ROAD, BISHOPS STORTFORD CM23 5LE WWW.ICKNIELDWAYPATH.CO.UK

Isle of Anglesey Coastal Path

Circular via Llanfaethlu, Amlwch, Beaumaris, Holyhead 200km/125 miles
Fairly easy walking through diverse coastal scenery almost entirely within an Area of Outstanding Natural Beauty, with many attractive villages. Easily accessed by bus (details in publications, below).
MAPS 262, 263
PUBLICATIONS ROUTE CARD PACK £1.99 FROM LLANFAIRPWLL TIC ☎ 01248 713177 OR VIEWABLE ON WEBSITE BELOW. FULL GUIDEBOOK SHOULD SOON BE AVAILABLE FROM SAME SOURCE. WEBSITE WWW.ANGLESEYCOASTALPATH.COM (AC)

Isle of Wight Coastal Path

Circular from Ryde 105km/65 miles
Attractive island circuit, via chines, saltmarshes, cliffs and holiday resorts, with plenty of accommodation and good public transport links. Connects with a number of other routes heading inland including the 22km/14-mile Tennyson Trail from Carisbrooke to Alum Bay and the 18km/11-mile Bembridge Trail from Shide to Bembridge.
MAPS OL29
PUBLICATIONS COASTAL PATH AND INLAND TRAILS GUIDE £3 + P&P FROM THE RAMBLERS BOOKSHOP, OR DOWNLOAD ROUTE GUIDES FROM TOURISM WEBSITE BELOW.
LUGGAGE CARRIER BAG TAG
CONTACT ISLE OF WIGHT TOURISM
☎ 01983 813800
WWW.ISLANDBREAKS.CO.UK/WALKING (AC)

Kelvin-Allander Walkway

See West Highland Way

Link through the Tabular Hills

See Cleveland Way

London Loop

Erith to Rainham via Kingston, circular route around Greater London 241km/150 miles EASY

A fascinating mix of waterside, parkland, nature reserves and countryside on the urban fringe, within easy reach of central London by public transport. The Loop and sister inner orbital path the Capital Ring (115km/72 miles via Woolwich, Crystal Palace, Richmond and Finsbury Park, fully opened in 2005) were pioneered by Ramblers volunteers and the London Walking Forum, and both are now Transport for London strategic walking routes.
MAPS 147, 160, 161, 162, 172, 173, 174
PUBLICATIONS LOOP AND RING GUIDEBOOKS (OS) £12.99 + P&P EACH FROM THE RAMBLERS BOOKSHOP. FREE LEAFLETS FOR MOST OF THE LOOP AND ALL OF THE RING ALSO AVAILABLE: ☎ 0870 240 6094 OR SEE WWW.TFL.GOV.UK/WALKING.

Macmillan Ways

Macmillan Way: Boston to Abbotsbury 464km/290 miles
Macmillan Way West: Castle Cary to Barnstaple 163km/102 miles
Abbotsbury-Langport Link: 38.5km/24 miles
Cross-Cotswold Pathway: Banbury to Bath 138km/86 miles
Cotswold Link: Chipping Campden to Banbury 33.5km/21 miles
A network of attractive routes linking the south coast, Bristol channel and North Sea coast of England, taking in the Cotswolds, the Quantocks and the Fens. The main route runs diagonally across England from south to east, while the western route links the north Devon coast to the east coast, or to the south coast via the Langport Link. The Cross-Cotswold option uses one of the most popular sections of the main route with additional town links providing public transport connections, while the Cotswold Link connects with the Cotswold Way to create the Cotswold Round, a 331km/207-mile circuit via Chipping Campden, Banbury, Cirencester and Bath.
MAPS MAIN ROUTE/ABBOTSBURY LINK: OL15, OL45, 117, 129, 142, 143, 156, 168, 191, 206, 207, 223, 233, 234, 235, 248, 249, 261
WEST: OL9, 128, 129, 140, 141, 142
CROSS-COTSWOLD PATHWAY/LINK: OL45, 155, 156, 168, 179, 191, 206
PUBLICATIONS MACMILLAN WAY GUIDEBOOK £9 + P&P, MACMILLAN WAY WEST GUIDEBOOK £6.25 + P&P FROM THE RAMBLERS BOOKSHOP. NORTH-SOUTH SUPPLEMENT FOR THE MAIN ROUTE, GUIDES TO OTHER LINKS AND SPURS, PLANNERS, UPDATE SHEETS, ACCOMMODATION LISTS AND NUMEROUS OTHER PUBLICATIONS AND

MERCHANDISE FROM USER GROUP BELOW.
USER GROUP MACMILLAN WAY ASSOCIATION
☎ 01789 740852
WWW.MACMILLANWAY.ORG

Mary Towneley Loop

See Pennine Bridleway

Midshires Way

Princes Risborough to Stockport 363km/230 miles
A walking link between southern and northern England, from the Ridgeway in the Chilterns to the Pennine Bridleway and Trans Pennine Trail via historic estates, farmland and the Peak District National Park. Generally gentle walking incorporating sections of numerous other trails including the North Bucks Way, Brampton Valley Way and High Peak Trail.
MAPS OL1, OL24, 181, 192, 207, 223, 233, 246, 259, 260
PUBLICATIONS WALKING THE MIDSHIRES WAY, ISBN 1 850058 778 7, SIGMA LEISURE £7.95.

Monarch's Way

Worcester to Shoreham 982km/610 miles
Britain's second longest signed route follows in the footsteps of Charles II on his flight from the Battle of Worcester, a meandering course from the West Midlands to the south coast taking in many historic sights. There are plans to extend it into France to cover the rest of the king's journey.
MAPS OL45, 116, 117, 119, 120, 121, 122, 129, 130, 131, 132, 141, 142, 143, 155, 167, 168. 204, 205, 218, 219, 220, 221, 242
PUBLICATIONS GUIDEBOOK IN THREE VOLS: 1 THE MIDLANDS £5.95 + P&P; 2 THE COTSWOLDS, THE MENDIPS AND THE SEA £6.95 + P&P; 3 THE SOUTH COAST, THE DOWNS AND ESCAPE £6.95 + P&P FROM THE RAMBLERS BOOKSHOP.
USER GROUP MONARCH'S WAY ASSOCIATION
☎ 0121 429 4397
WWW.MONARCHSWAY.50MEGS.COM

Nene Way

Badby to Sutton Bridge 177km/110 miles EASY
Along the valley of the river Nene as it first meanders through quiet Northamptonshire countryside then straightens out onto a canalised section towards Lincolnshire and the Wash.
MAPS 207, 223, 224, 227, 234, 235, 249
PUBLICATIONS LEAFLET PACK BADBY TO WANSFORD £3 + P&P FROM THE RAMBLERS BOOKSHOP. LEAFLET WANSFORD TO WHITTLESEA FREE FROM PETERBOROUGH COUNCIL PUBLIC RIGHTS OF WAY OFFICE (P279). LEAFLET WHITTLESEA TO

Avoid
at all
costs_

Frostbite occurs below
0°C when the skin
freezes and bloodflow
slows to your
extremities_

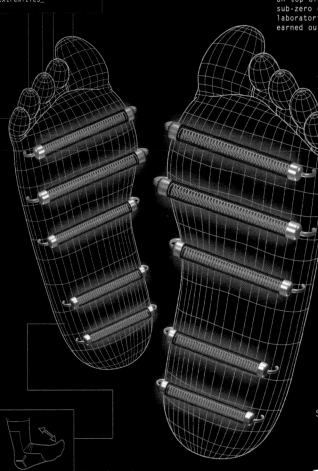

SUTTON BRIDGE FREE FROM CAMBRIDGESHIRE COUNCIL PUBLIC RIGHTS OF WAY OFFICE (P277).

Nidderdale Way

Circular from Pateley Bridge
85 km/53 miles

Around the valley of the river Nidd, an Area of Outstanding Natural Beauty on the edge of the Yorkshire Dales, including gritstone outcrops and rough, open moorland.
MAP 298 HARVEY WEATHERPROOF STRIP MAP £6.95 + P&P FROM THE RAMBLERS BOOKSHOP. PUBLICATIONS WALK CARD PACK £2.95 + P&P FROM THE RAMBLERS BOOKSHOP. CONTACT NIDDERDALE AONB (P270) WHO CAN ALSO GIVE INFORMATION ABOUT BUS SERVICES FOR WALKERS IN NIDDERDALE.

North Downs Way

Farnham to Dover 245km/153 miles
Along the chalk ridges and wooded downland of Surrey into Kent, with an optional loop via Canterbury, often running parallel to the ancient trackway of the Pilgrim's Way. The 55km/24-mile St Swithun's Way continues along the line of the trackway from Farnham to Winchester.
MAPS 137, 138, 145, 146, 147, 148, 150 (AND 132, 133, 144, 145 FOR ST SWITHUN'S WAY) HARVEY WEATHERPROOF STRIP MAPS: WEST (FARNHAM TO THE MEDWAY), EAST (MEDWAY TO DOVER), £9.95 EACH + P&P FROM THE RAMBLERS BOOKSHOP.
DIGITAL EXPLORER STRIP MAP £99.95 FROM MEMORY-MAP
PUBLICATIONS NORTH DOWNS WAY GUIDEBOOK (OS) £12.99, ST SWITHUN'S WAY CARD PACK £3.99 + P&P FROM THE RAMBLERS BOOKSHOP. ACCOMMODATION AND TRANSPORT DETAILS ON WEBSITE BELOW.
CONTACT NATIONAL TRAIL OFFICE
☎ 01622 221525
WWW.NATIONALTRAIL.CO.UK/NORTHDOWNS (AC)
ST SWITHUN'S WAY WEBSITE
WWW.HANTS.GOV.UK/WALKING/SWITHUNS/

Offa's Dyke Path

Chepstow to Prestatyn
283km/177 miles CHALLENGING

NORTH DOWNS WAY

A varied walk from the Severn estuary to the Irish Sea through the border country of England and Wales via Knighton, Welshpool and Llangollen, with around 100km/60 miles alongside the eighth century earthwork of Offa's Dyke itself. Although not as challenging as more mountainous routes, there are some remote sections with rough paths and many descents and climbs.
MAPS OL13, OL14, 201, 216, 240, 256, 265 HARVEY WEATHERPROOF STRIP MAPS: SOUTH (CHEPSTOW TO KNIGHTON) AND NORTH (KNIGHTON TO PRESTATYN), £9.95 EACH FROM OFFA'S DYKE ASSOCIATION OR HARVEY.
DIGITAL EXPLORER STRIP MAP £99.95 FROM MEMORY-MAP
PUBLICATIONS GUIDEBOOKS (OS) SOUTH CHEPSTOW TO KNIGHTON AND NORTH KNIGHTON TO PRESTATYN £12.99 + P&P EACH, OFFA'S DYKE & GLYNDŴR'S WAY ACCOM GUIDE (AC) £4 + P&P FROM THE RAMBLERS BOOKSHOP; ROUTE DESCRIPTIONS SOUTH TO NORTH AND NORTH TO SOUTH, A CAMPING AND BACKPACKING GUIDE, CIRCULAR WALKS BOOKS AND NUMEROUS OTHER ITEMS FROM OFFA'S DYKE ASSOCIATION.
LUGGAGE CARRIERS SHERPA VAN
USER GROUP/CONTACT OFFA'S DYKE ASSOCIATION ☎ 01547 528753
WWW.OFFASDYKE.DEMON.CO.UK

Peddars Way And Norfolk Coast Path

Knettishall Heath near Thetford to Cromer 146km/91 miles EASY
Effectively two routes: the Peddar's Way runs northwards through the Norfolk countryside to near Hunstanton, connecting with the Icknield Way path to form the last link in a continuous chain of ancient trackways from the south coast. The coast path then runs eastwards via Sheringham. Many sections are suitable for people with special access needs: more information from the National Trail Office. Two other easy routes connect to provide a lengthy circuit of Norfolk, the 90km/56-mile Weavers Way from Cromer to Great Yarmouth via the Broads, and the 123km/77-mile Angles Way eastwards along the Waveney and Little Ouse rivers back to Knettishall Heath.
MAPS 229, 236, 250, 251, 252, 252 (AND OL40 FOR WEAVERS WAY; OL40, 230, 231 FOR ANGLES WAY)
PUBLICATIONS PEDDARS WAY/COAST PATH/WEAVERS WAY GUIDE BOOKLET (AC) AND ANGLES WAY GUIDE BOOKLET (AC) £2.70 + P&P EACH FROM THE RAMBLERS BOOKSHOP. PEDDARS WAY AND NORFOLK COAST PATH OFFICIAL GUIDEBOOK (OS) ISBN 1 85410 852 2, AURUM

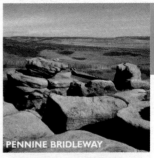

PENNINE BRIDLEWAY

£12.99. GREATER RIDGEWAY GUIDE: SEE RIDGEWAY.
CONTACT NATIONAL TRAIL OFFICE
☎ 01328 850530
WWW.NATIONALTRAIL.CO.UK/PEDDARSWAY (AC)

Pembrokeshire Coast Path

Amroth to Cardigan 299km/186 miles
Some of the most spectacular coastal walking in Britain, mainly along clifftops and almost all within the Pembrokeshire Coast National Park, including Wales' only marine nature reserve and 17 Sites of Special Scientific Interest (SSSIs). Some steep climbs but also sections suitable for people with special access needs. At Cardigan the path links with the 101km/63-mile Ceredigion Coastal Path, which is still under development but already walkable; both paths will eventually form part of a continuous walking route around the Welsh coast.
LUGGAGE CARRIERS PEMBROKESHIRE DISCOVERY, TONY'S TAXIS
MAPS OL35, OL36 (CEREDIGION COAST OL23, 198, 213)
PUBLICATIONS PEMBROKESHIRE COAST PATH GUIDEBOOK (OS) £12.99 + P&P, ACCOM GUIDE (AC) £2.50 + P&P FROM THE RAMBLERS BOOKSHOP. EASY ACCESS GUIDE £2.95 + P&P, WALK LEAFLETS FOR INDIVIDUAL SECTIONS AND CIRCULAR WALKS, VARIOUS OTHER PUBLICATIONS FROM PEMBROKESHIRE COAST NATIONAL PARK (P269). WALKING THE CEREDIGION COAST FREE + P&P FROM THE RAMBLERS BOOKSHOP OR DOWNLOADABLE FROM WWW.WALKCARDIGANBAY.COM (AC). WALKING THE CARDIGAN BAY COAST FROM CARDIGAN TO BORTH, ISBN 1 902302 09 5, KITTIWAKE £3.95.
CONTACT PEMBROKESHIRE COAST NATIONAL PARK ☎ 01437 720392
WWW.PEMBROKESHIRECOAST.ORG.UK (AC)

Pennine Bridleway

Hartington or Middleton Top to Byrness 560km/350 miles
Despite its name, this new national trail provides a great route for walkers as

A WALK THROUGH TIME

South of Galway and Limerick, the county of Clare is home to The Burren, one of Ireland's most spectacular regions. This is a territory of many surprises, and begins on an ancient grassy track, bordered by dry-stone walls. This is The Burren Way, a quiet 45km path, leading towards the Black Head Mountain, which is topped by an Iron Age fort.

The word 'Burren' comes from the Irish word for 'stony place', an apt description as it is surrounded by exposed limestone and rugged hills. Wild flowers such as eyebright, scarlet pimpernel and harebell thrive here, alongside orchids, mountain avens and maidenhair fern.

From Ballyvaughan, The Burren Way leads to the peak of Abbey Hill. Starting in a wildflower meadow, the walk then moves on to take in St Patrick's Holy Well, with engravings of Gothic and traditional Irish symbols in its walls.

At the top of the hill, amazing views show the Atlantic coast, then the pathway heads down the steep mountainside onto a gravel trail that was put into place during the Great Famine. The trail ends up back at Ballyvaughan.

For further information on attractions and accommodation in County Clare and the surrounding region please log on to www.shannonregiontourism.ie

well as horse-riders and cyclists, running roughly parallel to the Pennine Way but along easier paths to the west of the hilltops. The first substantial section, 188km/117 miles from the Peak District to the south Pennines, opened in 2004: this includes the Mary Towneley Loop, a 68km/42-mile circuit through the south Pennines around Todmorden and Bacup. A16km/10-mile loop via Settle and Malham in the Yorkshire Dales, not yet connected to the main trail, opened in 2005. The rest is mainly walkable already, though as yet unsigned: see website for the latest situation.
MAPS SOUTHERN SECTION OL1, OL21, OL24; NORTHERN SECTION OL2, OL19, OL41 HARVEY WEATHERPROOF STRIP MAP OF SOUTHERN SECTION £9.95 + P&P FROM THE RAMBLERS BOOKSHOP.
PUBLICATIONS GUIDEBOOK TO DERBYSHIRE/SOUTH PENNINES SECTION £12.99 + P&P, ACCOM AND SERVICES GUIDE (AC), FREE + P&P, FROM THE RAMBLERS BOOKSHOP.
CONTACT PENNINE BRIDLEWAY TEAM ☎ 0161 237 1061 WWW.NATIONALTRAIL.CO.UK/PENNINE BRIDLEWAY (AC)

Pennine Way
Edale to Kirk Yetholm 429km/268 miles CHALLENGING
A high and wild trail along the backbone of England from the Peak District to the Scottish borders. Pioneered by Ramblers activist Tom Stephenson, it is the oldest as well as one of the toughest of Britain's signed walking trails, and celebrated its 40th anniversary in 2005.
MAPS OL1, OL2, OL16, OL19, OL21, OL30, OL31, OL42, OL43
HARVEY WEATHERPROOF STRIP MAPS: SOUTH (EDALE TO HORTON), CENTRAL (HORTON TO GREENHEAD), NORTH (GREENHEAD TO KIRK YETHOLM), £9.95 EACH FROM BOOKSHOPS OR HARVEY.
DIGITAL EXPLORER STRIP MAP £99.95 FROM MEMORY-MAP
PUBLICATIONS GUIDEBOOKS SOUTH EDALE TO BOWES AND NORTH BOWES TO KIRK YETHOLM (OS) £12.99 + P&P EACH; TRANSPORT AND ACCOM LIST (OS) FREE + P&P FROM THE RAMBLERS BOOKSHOP.
LUGGAGE CARRIERS BRIGANTES, SHERPA VAN
HOSTEL BOOKING YHA (ASK ABOUT PENNINE HIGHLIGHTS AS A SHORTER ALTERNATIVE TO THE WHOLE WALK)
CONTACT NATIONAL TRAIL OFFICE ☎ 0113 246 9222 WWW.NATIONALTRAIL.CO.UK/PENNINEWAY (AC)

USER GROUP PENNINE WAY ASSOCIATION ☎ 01434 607088 WWW.PENNINEWAYASSOCIATION.CO.UK

Ridgeway
Overton Hill near Avebury to Ivinghoe Beacon 137km/85 miles
A route along 'Britain's oldest road' past the ancient hillforts of the North Wessex Downs, across the Thames and through the wooded countryside of the Chilterns. With the Wessex Ridgeway, Icknield Way and Peddars Way it forms a continuous 583km/363-mile walking route following ancient ways from the south coast to the Wash, the complete route of which is described in the Greater Ridgeway Guide, below.
MAPS 157, 170, 171, 181
HARVEY WEATHERPROOF STRIP MAP £9.95 + P&P FROM THE RAMBLERS BOOKSHOP
DIGITAL EXPLORER STRIP MAP £49.95 FROM MEMORY-MAP
PUBLICATIONS GUIDEBOOK (OS) £12.99 + P&P, COMPANION (AC) £3.95 + P&P, GREATER RIDGEWAY GUIDE (OS) £12.95 + P&P FROM CICERONE ☎ 01539 562069.
CONTACT NATIONAL TRAILS OFFICE ☎ 01865 810224 WWW.NATIONALTRAIL.CO.UK/RIDGEWAY (AC)
USER GROUP FRIENDS OF THE RIDGEWAY, 18 HAMPTON PARK, BRISTOL BS6 6LH WWW.RIDGEWAYFRIENDS.ORG.UK

Rob Roy Way
Drymen to Pitlochry 126km/79 miles
Connecting the West Highland Way with the Tay valley, this unsigned route includes rich woodlands, remote moors and heaths, dramatic mountain views, impressive built heritage and sites connected with Scotland's most famous outlaw, Rob Roy MacGregor (1671-1734).
LUGGAGE CARRIER BIKE AND HIKE, TROSSACHS TRANSFERS
MAPS 347, 365, 378, 386
PUBLICATIONS GUIDEBOOK £10.99 + P&P FROM THE RAMBLERS BOOKSHOP. WWW.ROBROYWAY.COM (AC)

Saints' Way
Padstow to Fowey 42km/26 miles
Attractive coast to coast trail across Cornwall, following a route possibly taken by the Celtic saints.
MAPS 106, 107
PUBLICATIONS GUIDE £3.99 + P&P FROM THE RAMBLERS BOOKSHOP.

Sandstone Trail
Frodsham to Whitchurch 51km/32 miles
An airy walk following the sandstone ridge that rises dramatically from the central Cheshire plain, including rock outcrops, woodlands, castles and historic churches. Can be walked easily in three sections of around 17km/10.5 miles each, with a seasonal weekend bus service.
LUGGAGE CARRIER BYWAYS BREAKS
MAPS 257, 267
PUBLICATIONS FREE LEAFLET + P&P FROM THE RAMBLERS BOOKSHOP, INFORMATION PACK (AC) FROM CHESHIRE COUNCIL COUNTRYSIDE SERVICES (P276) OR SEE WWW.CHESHIRE.GOV.UK/WALKING

Severn Way
Plylimon to Bristol 360km/225 miles
Britain's longest riverside walk follows the Severn from its source in the wild mid-Wales moorlands to its wide estuary on the Bristol channel via Welshpool, Shrewsbury, the World Heritage Site at Ironbridge, Worcester and Gloucester. The Way ends officially at Severn Beach (337km/210.5 miles) where a link path continues into central Bristol.
MAPS OL14, 154, 167, 190, 204, 214, 215, 216, 218, 240, 241, 242
PUBLICATIONS GUIDEBOOK £6.95 FROM RECREATION DEPARTMENT, ENVIRONMENT AGENCY MIDLANDS REGION, HAFREN HOUSE, WELSHPOOL ROAD, SHELTON, SHREWSBURY SY3 8BB. WEBSITE WWW.SEVERNWAY.COM (AC)

Shropshire Way
Shrewsbury, Wem, Grindley Brook, Long Mynd, Ludlow 264km/165 miles total
A tour devised by local Ramblers, combining bracing hill sections and celebrated sights including Wenlock Edge, the Long Mynd and the Wrekin with gentler, more pastoral walking in the valleys. A narrow, wiggling circuit from Shrewsbury with two alternative routes is combined with a spur to Grindley Brook and the Llangollen Canal. A good network of leisure buses operates in the area: see www.shropshirehillsshuttles.co.uk.
MAPS 203, 216, 217, 241, 242
PUBLICATIONS GUIDEBOOK £6.99 + P&P FROM THE RAMBLERS BOOKSHOP.

Wherever Swarovski is,
nature becomes
more fascinating.
Swarovski Pocket 8x20 B

Pocket 8x20

www.swarovskioptik.com

**Perfect for all outdoor activities,
ideal for the theatre,
or as a second binocular:**
Swarovski Pocket Binoculars fit into
pocket and provide a truly great view
experience. They have the world's m
complex optical system for compact
binoculars, as well as the patented
SWAROBRIGHT® prism coating for
optimum colour fidelity across the er
light spectrum. Individually adjustabl
removable, twist-up eyecups enable
an extremely large visual field - even
for spectacle wearers.

SWAROVSKI
OPTIK

Swarovski U.K. LTD. • Perrywood Business Park • Salfords, Surrey RH1 5JQ • Tel. 01737-856812 • Fax 01737-856

SOUTH DOWNS WAY

Solent Way
Christchurch to Emsworth
112km/70 miles

Across the south of Hampshire via beaches, clifftops, marshes, heaths, ancient woodlands, riverside villages and the historic waterfronts of Southampton and Portsmouth. The Way is signed from Milford but the Pub Walks title describes a route from Christchurch. The Bournemouth Coast Path, signed as European path E9, links Sandbanks (Poole) and the South West Coast Path to Milford: the new guide below includes sections with alternative clifftop and prom routes.
MAPS OL22, 119, 120 (AND OL15 FOR POOLE)
PUBLICATIONS PUB WALKS ALONG THE SOLENT WAY (INCLUDES COMPLETE LINEAR ROUTE) £7.95 + P&P; LEAFLET WITH ROUTE OVERVIEW, FREE + P&P FROM THE RAMBLERS BOOKSHOP. DETAILS ALSO AVAILABLE AT WWW.HANTS.GOV.UK/WALKING. EXPLORING THE BOURNEMOUTH COAST PATH, ISBN 1 85306 908 6, COUNTRYSIDE BOOKS £7.99.

South Downs Way
Eastbourne to Winchester
161km/101 miles

Exhilirating route along the rolling chalk downs of Sussex and Hampshire, through the heart of the future national park.
MAPS 119 (VERY SMALL PART), 120, 121, 122, 123, 132
HARVEY WEATHERPROOF STRIP MAP £9.95 + P&P FROM THE RAMBLERS BOOKSHOP.
PUBLICATIONS ALONG THE SOUTH DOWNS WAY GUIDE IN BOTH DIRECTIONS (AC) £6 + P&P FROM THE RAMBLERS BOOKSHOP. SOUTH DOWNS WAY OFFICIAL GUIDE (OS) ISBN 1 85410 966 9, AURUM £12.99.
CONTACT NATIONAL TRAIL OFFICER ☎ 023 9259 7618
WWW.NATIONALTRAIL.CO.UK/SOUTHDOWNS

✳ South Tyne Trail
Source of the South Tyne near Garrigill to Halwhistle 36.5km/23 miles EASY
Along the South Tyne and Tyne rivers through the remote and lesser-visited countryside of East Cumbria and the North Pennines to end near Hadrian's Wall. The route opened in 2004 with the help of local Ramblers. From Alston to Haltwhistle it follows an old railway line with easy access. More ambitious walkers can follow the full length of both the Tyne (Garrigill to Tynemouth 133km/83 miles) and North Tyne (Hexham to Alston and Deadwater 76km/47.5 miles) as both linear and linked circular walks using the additional publications below: note these longer routes include more challenging sections.
MAPS OL31, OL43
PUBLICATIONS SOUTH TYNE TRAIL LEAFLET £2 FROM EAST CUMBRIA COUNTRYSIDE PROJECT (BELOW). WALKING THE TYNE AND WALKING THE NORTH TYNE GUIDEBOOKS FROM NORTHUMBRIA RAMBLERS: SEE P199.
CONTACT EAST CUMBRIA COUNTRYSIDE PROJECT ☎ 01228 561601, ECCP@CARLISLE-CITY.GOV.UK

South West Coast Path
Minehead to Poole 1014km/630 miles

Britain's longest national walking route, a spectacular and massively popular continuous path around almost all of the southwest peninsula. Although never too remote, there are some arduous cliff top sections with steep climbs and descents. The national trail website below includes suggestions for short and easy walks as well as information about the whole trail.
MAPS OL9, OL15, OL20, 102, 103, 104, 105, 106, 107, 108, 109, 110, 111, 115, 116, 126, 139
DIGITAL EXPLORER STRIP MAPS, MINEHEAD TO FALMOUTH AND FALMOUTH TO POOLE, £99.95 EACH FROM MEMORY-MAP
PUBLICATIONS GUIDEBOOK, ROUTE DESCRIPTION ONLY, NO MAPS, (AC) £7 + P&P FROM THE RAMBLERS BOOKSHOP.
SOUTH WEST COAST PATH OFFICIAL GUIDES IN FOUR VOLUMES, AURUM £12.99 EACH (OS): MINEHEAD TO PADSTOW ISBN 1 85410 977 4, PADSTOW TO FALMOUTH ISBN 1 85410 850 6, FALMOUTH TO EXMOUTH ISBN 1 85410 768 2, EXMOUTH TO POOLE ISBN 1 85410 988 X.
SOUTH WEST COAST PATH THE OTHER WAY ROUND, ROUTE DESCRIPTION FROM POOLE TO MINEHEAD TO BE USED IN CONJUNCTION WITH OTHER GUIDES, £3.50 FROM SOUTH WEST COAST PATH ASSOCIATION WHO CAN ALSO SUPPLY OTHER LITERATURE AND MERCHANDISE.
CONTACT NATIONAL TRAIL OFFICER ☎ 01392 383560
WWW.SOUTHWESTCOASTPATH.COM (AC)
USER GROUP SOUTH WEST COAST PATH ASSOCIATION ☎ 01752 896237
WWW.SWCP.ORG.UK

✪ Southern Upland Way
Portpatrick to Cockburnspath
341km/212 miles CHALLENGING

Scenic coast to coast trail through southern Scotland via Sanquar, Moffatt and Melrose, combining some remote and demanding stretches with sections suitable for families. The route celebrated its 21st anniversary in 2005.
MAPS 309, 310, 318, 319, 320, 322, 328, 329, 330, 337, 338, 345, 346
PUBLICATIONS GUIDEBOOK (OS) £12.99 + P&P; ACCOM LEAFLET (AC) FREE + P&P FROM THE RAMBLERS BOOKSHOP. SHORTER WALKS LEAFLETS FROM RANGER SERVICES OR DOWNLOADABLE FROM WEBSITE.
LUGGAGE CARRIERS SOUTHERNUPLANDWAY.COM, WAY FORWARD
CONTACT RANGER SERVICE ☎ 01387 260184 (WEST) OR 01835 830281 (EAST)
WWW.DUMGAL.GOV.UK/SOUTHERNUPLANDWAY (AC)

✪ Speyside Way
Buckie to Craigelachie, Tomintoul or Aviemore 135km/84 miles (total)
Following the fast-flowing river Spey south from the Grampian coast through classic malt whisky country, along forest trails and an old railway track to the famous Highland resort of Aviemore.
MAPS 403, 419, 424
HARVEY WEATHERPROOF STRIP MAP £9.95 + P&P FROM THE RAMBLERS BOOKSHOP.
PUBLICATIONS GUIDEBOOK £9.99 +P&P; ACCOM GUIDE (AC) FREE + P&P FROM THE RAMBLERS BOOKSHOP.
CONTACT SPEYSIDE WAY RANGER'S OFFICE ☎ 01340 881266
WWW.SPEYSIDEWAY.ORG.UK (AC)

St Cuthbert's Way
Melrose to Lindisfarne 100km/62 miles
Pilgrimage path on the border between England and Scotland, following in the footsteps of a seventh-century saint and linking the Pennine and Southern Upland Ways. Easy except for a remote upland stretch between Kirk Yetholm and Wooler.
LUGGAGE CARRIERS CARRYLITE, SHERPA VAN
MAPS OL16, OL44, 339, 340
HARVEY ROUTE MAP (INCLUDED WITH GUIDE BELOW)
PUBLICATIONS GUIDE £9.99 + P&P FROM THE RAMBLERS BOOKSHOP.
CONTACT JEDBURGH TIC ☎ 01835 863435
WWW.STCUTHBERTSWAY.NET (AC)

St Swithun's Way
See North Downs Way

Staffordshire Way
Mow Cop Castle to Kinver
Edge 147km/92 miles
A north-south route across the
county, from gritstone hills on the
edge of the Peak District via the steep
wooded slopes of the Churnet Valley
('Staffordshire's Rhineland'), Cannock
Chase and more gentle pastoral
scenery and parkland to the sandstone
ridge of Kinver Edge. Sister path The
Way for the Millennium, designed for
easier walking, crosses at
Shugborough on its way from
Newport to Burton upon Trent
(65km/41 miles).
MAPS OL24, 218, 242, 244, 258, 259, 268
PUBLICATIONS GUIDEBOOK £5 + P&P, WAY
FOR THE MILLENNIUM GUIDEBOOK £3.50 + P&P,
ACCOM LEAFLET (AC) FOR BOTH PATHS FREE +
P&P FROM THE RAMBLERS BOOKSHOP.

Suffolk Coast and Heaths Path
Manningtree to Lowestoft
106km/92 miles EASY
Through the tranquil landscapes of an
Area of Outstanding Natural Beauty in
a less-visited part of England: beaches,
estuaries and wild heaths. The original
route starts at Felixstowe, while an
extension, the Stour and Orwell
Walk, negotiates the river estuaries via
Ipswich to Manningtree. The
96km/60-mile Sandlings Walk
provides an inland alternative through
the heathland between Ipswich and
Southwold.
MAPS OL40, 197, 212, 231
PUBLICATIONS SUFFOLK COAST AND STOUR
AND ORWELL PACKS INCLUDING PUBLIC
TRANSPORT (AC), £4 + P&P; SANDLINGS WALK
PACK, £4.75 + P&P FROM THE RAMBLERS
BOOKSHOP.
CONTACT SUFFOLK COAST AND HEATHS
PROJECT (P270)

Tees Link
See Teesdale Way

THAMES PATH

Teesdale Way
Dufton to Warrenby, Redcar
161km/100 miles
Along the Tees from its source in the
Cumbrian Pennines through wild and
remote moorland and gentler
countryside to the industrial cityscapes
of Teesside and on to the North Sea,
including ten circular walks. A shorter
path, the Tees Link, connects
Middlesbrough Dock to High Cliff
Nab, Guisborough (17km/10.5 miles)
via Guisborough Forest.
MAPS OL26, OL31, 304, 306
PUBLICATIONS THE TEESDALE WAY ISBN 1
85284 461 2, CICERONE £10 (OS, NEW 2005);
TEES LINK LEAFLET FROM TEES FOREST (P271)

Test Way
Inkpen Beacon to Totton
(Southampton) 70.5km/44 miles
A north-south route across
Hampshire from the
dramatic escarpment at
Inkpen along the course of the river
Test, one of southern England's finest
chalk streams, to its tidal marshes at
Southampton Water via Stockbridge,
Romsey and Totton. Divided into
eight sections, all but one of which
are linked by buses.
MAPS OL22, 131, 158
PUBLICATIONS LEAFLET TO BE USED IN
CONJUNCTION WITH OS MAPS, FREE + P&P FROM
THE RAMBLERS BOOKSHOP; DETAILED ROUTE
DESCRIPTION AT WWW.HANTS.GOV.UK/WALKING

Tennyson Trail
See Isle of Wight Coastal Path

Thames Path
Source of the Thames near Kemble
to London and Crayford Ness
311km/194 miles EASY
A splendid and very popular riverside
walk, pioneered by Ramblers
members, from the remote
Cotswolds to London, passing world-
famous sites such as Oxford, Windsor,
the central London riverfront and
Greenwich. The National Trail ends
officially at the Thames Barrier where
a well-signed 16km/10 mile extension
continues eastwards towards Erith
and the marshes. The whole route
through London is now one of
Transport for London's six strategic
walking routes.
MAPS 160, 161, 168, 169, 170, 171, 172, 173, 180
DIGITAL EXPLORER STRIP MAP £99.95 FROM
MEMORY-MAP
PUBLICATIONS GUIDEBOOK (OS) £12.99 +
P&P, COMPANION (AC ETC) £4.75 + P&P FROM
THE RAMBLERS BOOKSHOP; THE THAMES PATH

GUIDE FROM BARRIER TO SOURCE, ISBN 1 85284
436 1, CICERONE £12; DISCOVERING LONDON'S
WORKING RIVER FREE LEAFLET COVERING THAMES
PATH EXTENSION, ☎ 0870 240 6094 OR SEE
WWW.TFL.GOV.UK/WALKING.
CONTACT NATIONAL TRAIL OFFICE
☎ 01865 810224
WWW.NATIONALTRAIL.GOV.UK/THAMESPATH (AC)

Trans Pennine Trail
Southport to Chesterfield, Leeds,
York or Hornsea
560km/350 miles total EASY
Multi-user route from Merseyside to
Humberside via Stockport
(Manchester) and Doncaster, with
connecting spurs to Chesterfield via
Sheffield, Leeds via Wakefield, York
and Beverley linking all the major
cities of northern England,
interestingly mixing rural and urban
walking. Much of the route, which
was created with the help of local
Ramblers, is wheelchair and pushchair
accessible and easily reached by
public transport, and the section from
Liverpool to Hull is part of European
path E8. Walkers following the linear
coast-to-coast route from Southport
to Hornsea need only route maps 1
and 3 below, while map 2 covers the
central north-south spurs.
MAPS OL1, 268, 275, 276, 277, 278, 279, 285,
288, 289, 290, 291, 292, 293, 295
ROUTE MAPS: 1 IRISH SEA – YORKSHIRE; 2
DERBYSHIRE & YORKSHIRE; 3 YORKSHIRE –
NORTH SEA; £4.95 + P&P EACH FROM THE
RAMBLERS BOOKSHOP.
PUBLICATIONS VISITOR GUIDE (AC) £4.95 +
P&P FROM THE RAMBLERS BOOKSHOP, TO BE USED
IN CONJUNCTION WITH MAPS ABOVE.
CONTACT TRANS PENNINE TRAIL OFFICE
☎ 01226 772574
WWW.TRANSPENNINETRAIL.ORG.UK
USER GROUP FRIENDS OF THE TRANS
PENNINE TRAIL, 164 HIGH STREET, HOOK,
GOOLE DN14 5PL.

Two Moors Way
Ivybridge to Lynmouth
166km/103 miles
Appealing south-north route
through Devon, linking Dartmoor to
Exmoor and the north coast.
Unsigned across the moors.
MAPS OL9, OL20, OL28, 113, 114, 127
ILLUSTRATED ROUTE MAP £1.50 + 50P P&P FROM
TWO MOORS WAY ASSOCIATION
PUBLICATIONS GUIDEBOOK £4.95 + P&P;
ACCOM LIST (AC) 50P + P&P; BOTH FROM THE
RAMBLERS BOOKSHOP.
USER GROUP TWO MOORS WAY ASSOCIATION,
COPPINS, THE POPLARS, PINHOE, EXETER
EX4 9HH

Usk Valley Walk

Caerleon (Newport) to Brecon
77km/48 miles EASY
Along the broad and beautiful valley
of the river Usk between the Brecon
Beacons and the Black Mountains.
While there are a few short, sharp
climbs the route is generally on the
level, particularly along the canal
sections.
MAPS OL13, OL14, 152
PUBLICATIONS GUIDEBOOK £6.95 + 50P
P&P FROM MONMOUTHSHIRE COUNTY COUNCIL
COUNTRYSIDE SECTION (P282)

Valeways Millennium Heritage Trail

Circular from St Fagans
111km/69 miles
Meandering route through
the Vale of Glamorgan, a little-visited
but often beautiful area rich in history
in the southernmost part of Wales.
Circular via Peterston Super Ely,
Barry, Cowbridge, Llantwit Major, St
Bride's Major and Llanharry with
spurs to Ewenny Priory near Bridgend
and St Fagans. Numerous circular
walks using parts of the trail are
detailed on the website below.
MAP 151
PUBLICATIONS ROUTE CARD AND BOOKLET
PACK £6.99 + £1.50 P&P FROM VALEWAYS .
CONTACT VALEWAYS ☎ 01446 749000,
WWW.VALEWAYS.ORG.UK

Vanguard Way

See Wealdway

Viking Way

Barton-upon-Humber to Oakham
225km/140 miles EASY

A trail pioneered by
Ramblers volunteers from
the Humber Bridge south
along the Lincolnshire Wolds through
territory once occupied by Vikings to
Horncastle and Lincoln, finishing near
Rutland Water.
MAPS 234, 247, 272, 273, 281, 282, 284
PUBLICATIONS GUIDEBOOK £3.95 + P&P,
FACTSHEET (AC) FREE + P&P FROM
LINCOLNSHIRE COUNTY COUNCIL
☎ 01522 782070.

Way for the Millennium

See Staffordshire Way

Wealdway

Gravesend to Eastbourne
129km/80 miles
Attractive and surprisingly quiet walk
devised by local Ramblers from the

Thames estuary to the south coast
via the Kent and Sussex Weald and
Ashdown Forest. The southern
section runs parallel and sometimes
together with the Vanguard Way, an
107km/66-mile route from Croydon
to Newhaven. At Croydon you can
continue along the Wandle Trail for
19km/12 miles to join the Thames
Path at Wandsworth.
MAPS 123, 135, 147, 148, 163 (AND 146, 161
FOR VANGUARD WAY/WANDLE TRAIL)
PUBLICATIONS WEALDWAY GUIDEBOOK (OS)
£5 + P&P, VANGUARD WAY GUIDEBOOK £2.95
+ P&P FROM THE RAMBLERS BOOKSHOP.
WANDLE TRAIL FREE LEAFLET FROM SUTTON
LIBRARY ☎ 020 8770 4700 OR ONLINE AT
WWW.WANDLETRAIL.ORG.

Weavers Way

See Peddars Way

Wessex Ridgeway

Marlborough to Lyme
Regis 219km/136 miles
From deepest Wiltshire along ancient
paths via the edge of Salisbury Plain
and Cranbourne Chase to the
Dorset Coast. Connects with the
Ridgeway as part of a series of trails
linking Wessex and East Anglia.
MAPS 116, 117, 118, 130, 143, 157
PUBLICATIONS WILTSHIRE SECTION GUIDE
£4.50 + P&P FROM THE RAMBLERS BOOKSHOP.
COMPLETE GUIDE ISBN 1 85410 613 9, AURUM
£12.99 (OS). GREATER RIDGEWAY GUIDE: SEE
RIDGEWAY.

West Highland Way

Milngavie, Glasgow to Fort William
153km/95 miles CHALLENGING

A popular trail following
old drove, military and
coach roads from the
edge of Scotland's biggest city via its
largest freshwater loch, Loch
Lomond, and first national park to
the foot of its tallest mountain, Ben
Nevis, connecting with the Great
Glen Way. Two riverside walkways
effectively extend the walk in the
south through Glasgow city centre
and beyond: the Kelvin-Allander
Walkway from Milngavie to the
Clyde near the Tall Ship (14.5km/9
miles), and the Clyde Walkway from
Partick station to the Falls of Clyde at
New Lanark (64km/40 miles).
MAPS 347, 348, 364, 377, 384, 392 (AND 335,
342 AND 343 FOR THE WALKWAYS)
HARVEY ROUTE MAP £9.95 (INCLUDED WITH
GUIDE BELOW), DIGITAL EXPLORER STRIP MAP
£49.95 FROM MEMORY-MAP

YORKSHIRE WOLDS

PUBLICATIONS GUIDEBOOK £14.99 + P&P;
ACCOM LEAFLET (AC) FREE + P&P FROM THE
RAMBLERS BOOKSHOP. FIT FOR LIFE! MAP
INCLUDING ALL GLASGOW WALKWAYS AND THE
CLYDE WALKWAY LEAFLET PACK, BOTH FREE
FROM GLASGOW TIC, ☎ 0141 204 4400
LUGGAGE CARRIERS AMS, SHERPA VAN,
TRAVEL-LITE, TROSSACH TRANSFERS
INDEPENDENT HOSTELS IBHS
CONTACT WEST HIGHLAND WAY RANGER
☎ 01389 722199
WWW.WEST-HIGHLAND-WAY.CO.UK (AC)

Wye Valley Walk

Chepstow to Plylimon, Hafren
Forest 218km/136 miles
Along the the river Wye via
Monmouth, Hereford,
Builth Wells and Rhayader
to the source deep in rugged and
remote Hafren Forest, crisscrossing
the border of England and Wales
along dramatic limestone gorges and
through rolling countryside and
uplands.
MAPS OL13, OL14, 188, 189, 200, 214
PUBLICATIONS GUIDEBOOK £9 + P&P
FROM THE RAMBLERS BOOKSHOP. FREE ACCOM
LIST (AC) FROM WYE VALLEY AONB (P270).
WWW.WYEVALLEYWALK.ORG

Yorkshire Wolds Way

Hessle, Kingston upon Hull to Filey
127 km/79 miles
One of the least known national
trails, but well worth getting to know,
linking the North Sea coast and the
Cleveland Way with the Humber
through beautiful rolling chalk hills.
Ten new easy access sections are
described on the website below.
MAPS 293, 294, 300, 301
PUBLICATIONS GUIDEBOOK (OS) £12.99 +
P&P, ACCOM GUIDE (AC) FREE + P&P FROM THE
RAMBLERS BOOKSHOP. CIRCULAR WALKS GUIDES
AVAILABLE FROM NATIONAL TRAIL OFFICE.
CONTACT NATIONAL TRAIL OFFICER
☎ 01439 770657
WWW.NATIONALTRAIL.CO.UK/
YORKSHIREWOLDSWAY (AC)

Wear Páramo
and ramble on

...and on...and on...

Ramble on... in comfort

Páramo use Directional fabrics that move water away from you more effectively, and are more adaptable to changes in temperature than conventional systems. The benefit to you is a faster reaction to climate and activity changes than any other brand we know, and greater comfort as you stay drier regardless of the weather or how hard you are working.

Ramble on... without stopping

Forget awkward garment changes on the hill. Páramo combine intelligent ventilation with careful design to give you maximum performance with minimum weight.

Ramble on... for years and years

With Páramo waterproofs there's the guarantee of performance and comfort that will last. No laminates or coatings to break down, just strong (yet soft and quiet) fabrics that can be renewed with Nikwax care products, indefinitely.

Ramble on... to fellow walkers

If you buy one of our products, it will probably be because it was recommended to you. If you need convincing ask any of our customers if they'd give up their Páramo.

PÁRAMO – Leaders in comfort and performance

GOLD WINNER 2005 walk READER AWARDS

Find out more about Páramo's unique advantages – ring **01892 786444** for our latest activity catalogue or go online at **www.paramo.co.uk**

EUROPEAN LONG DISTANCE PATHS

E-paths, designated by the European Ramblers' Association (ERA), form an international network across the whole of Europe, linking the national and local path networks of member countries. The E-paths largely follow sections of existing trails and are not usually signed in their own right except at major junctions. For details of trails shown in green, see under the main entries in the previous section. For an overview of the E-paths, visit the ERA website (see p304). See also the E-paths section at www.ramblers.org.uk/info/paths.

ERA|EWU|FERP

E2 Atlantic – Mediterranean
Stranraer–Harwich or Dover 1400km/875 miles
An epic journey taking in the Southern Uplands, Pennines, Yorkshire coast, Wolds and Fens to connect with the ferry for Hoek van Holland. A western branch visits the Peak District, Cotswolds, Thames Valley and North Downs on its way to Dover (this branch continues from Oostende but there is currently no direct ferry: an alternative is the ferry to Calais and the E9 coastal path). The two routes rejoin in the Belgian Kempen and continue along the celebrated GR5 via the Ardennes, Lake Geneva and the French Alps to the Mediterranean coast at Nice. An Irish section to the Galway coast is planned, making a total length of 4850km/3030 miles.

FROM STRANRAER
SOUTHERN UPLAND WAY TO MELROSE 258KM/161 MILES
ST CUTHBERT'S WAY TO KIRK YETHOLM 51KM/32 MILES
PENNINE WAY TO MIDDLETON-IN-TEESDALE 180KM/113 MILES

EASTERN ROUTE VIA HARWICH
TEESDALE WAY AND TEES LINK TO GUISBOROUGH 125KM/77.5 MILES
CLEVELAND WAY TO FILEY 99KM/62 MILES
YORKSHIRE WOLDS WAY TO HESSLE THEN VIA HUMBER BRIDGE TO BARTON-UPON-HUMBER 131KM/82 MILES
VIKING WAY TO RUTLAND WATER 233KM/146 KM

HEREWARD WAY TO ELY 117KM/73 MILES
BETWEEN STAMFORD AND PETERBOROUGH THE HEREWARD WAY IS NOT THOROUGHLY SIGNED AND THE GUIDE IS CURRENTLY OUT OF PRINT: FOLLOW THE TORPEL WAY OVER ROUGHLY THE SAME ROUTE. INFORMATION FROM PETERBOROUGH COUNCIL (P279)
FEN RIVERS WAY TO CAMBRIDGE 27KM/17 MILES: GUIDE FROM CAMBRIDGESHIRE RAMBLERS (P111)
ROMAN ROAD LINK TO LINTON 18KM/11 MILES: NOT YET SIGNED AND NO GUIDE, BUT THE ROMAN ROAD IS OBVIOUS ON OS MAPS.
ICKNIELD WAY PATH TO STETCHWORTH 15KM/9.5 MILES
STOUR VALLEY PATH TO STRATFORD ST MARY 83KM/52 MILES: INFORMATION FROM DEDHAM VALE AND STOUR VALLEY AONB (P269)
ESSEX WAY TO RAMSEY THEN LINK PATH TO HARWICH INTERNATIONAL 28KM/17.5 MILES

WESTERN ROUTE VIA DOVER
PENNINE WAY TO STANDEDGE 200KM/125 MILES
OLDHAM WAY TO MOSSLEY 15KM/9.5 MILES: CONTACT OLDHAM COUNCIL (P279)
TAMESIDE TRAIL TO BROADBOTTOM 13KM/8 MILES: CONTACT TAMESIDE COUNCIL (P281)
ETHEROWGOYT VALLEY WAY TO COMPSTALL 8KM/5 MILES: CONTACT STOCKPORT COUNCIL (P280)
GOYT WAY TO MARPLE 4KM/2.5 MILES: CONTACT STOCKPORT COUNCIL
PEAK FOREST CANAL TO DISLEY 4KM/2.5 MILES: CONTACT BRITISH WATERWAYS (P288)
GRITSTONE TRAIL TO RUSHTON SPENCER 33KM/20.5 MILES: CONTACT CHESHIRE COUNCIL (P277)
STAFFORDSHIRE WAY TO CANNOCK CHASE 76KM/47.5 MILES
HEART OF ENGLAND WAY TO BOURTON-ON-THE-WATER 159KM/99.5 MILES
OXFORDSHIRE WAY TO KIRTLINGTON 41KM/25.5 MILES: CONTACT OXFORDSHIRE COUNCIL (P279)
OXFORD CANAL WALK TO OXFORD 16KM/10 MILES: CONTACT BRITISH WATERWAYS (P288)
THAMES PATH TO WEYBRIDGE 146KM/91 MILES
WEY NAVIGATION TO GUILDFORD 25KM/15.5 MILES: CONTACT NATIONAL TRUST ☎ 01483 561389
NORTH DOWNS WAY TO DOVER 193KM/120.5 MILES

E8 Atlantic – Istanbul
Liverpool–Hull 300km/188 miles
In Britain this path entirely follows the Trans Pennine Trail, connecting via the Dublin ferry with the Irish Waymarked Ways network. From Rotterdam it strikes out towards the Rhine Valley, the Romantische Straße, the Northern Carpathians

South West Coast Path via ferry
Poole Port

DES DE MOOR

and the Bulgarian Rodopi mountains to Svilengrad on the Turkish border, a total of 4390km/2750 miles, though some of the Eastern section of the route is incomplete.

E9 European Coastal Path

Plymouth – Dover 711km/444 miles, plus Isle of Wight loop 68 km/43 miles

Along or parallel to the south coast of England, including some of its most famous coastal sites and future national park. The path provides an alternative to the mainland route of the E9, with which it connects by ferry at Roscoff and Calais as well as several points in between. Additionally, it links the Saxon Shore Way and South West Coast Path to provide a continuous signed route of almost 1,000 miles around southern England from Gravesend to Minehead. The complete route will eventually stretch 5000km/3125 miles from Capo de São Vincente in the southwest corner of Portugal to Narva-Jõesuu on the Baltic coast at the Estonian-Russian border.

FROM PLYMOUTH

SOUTH WEST COAST PATH AND FERRY TO POOLE 343KM/214 MILES
BOURNEMOUTH COAST PATH (SEE SOLENT WAY) TO MILFORD ON SEA

30KM/19 MILES
SOLENT WAY TO LYMINGTON 11KM/7 MILES

ISLE OF WIGHT LOOP VIA FERRY TO YARMOUTH
ISLE OF WIGHT COASTAL PATH TO THE NEEDLES 11KM/7 MILES
TENNYSON TRAIL (SEE IOW COASTAL PATH) TO CARISBROOK 21KM/13 MILES
THEN LINK FROM THE NEEDLES TO NEWPORT 5KM/3.5 MILES
BEMBRIDGE TRAIL (SEE IOW COASTAL PATH) TO BEMBRIDGE 18KM/11 MILES
ISLE OF WIGHT COASTAL PATH TO RYDE 13KM/8 MILES THEN FERRY TO PORTSMOUTH

MAIN ROUTE
SOLENT WAY TO PORTSMOUTH, REJOINING ISLE OF WIGHT ALTERNATIVE 60KM/37.5 MILES.
SOLENT WAY TO LANGSTONE HARBOUR, HAVANT 16KM/10 MILES
STAUNTON WAY TO QUEEN ELIZABETH COUNTRY PARK 19KM/12 MILES: CONTACT HAMPSHIRE COUNCIL (P278)
SOUTH DOWNS WAY TO JEVINGTON 111KM/69.5 MILES
1066 COUNTRY WALK TO RYE 56KM/35 MILES: CONTACT BATTLE TIC
☎ 01424 773721
SAXON SHORE WAY TO DOVER 65KM/39 MILES: CURRENTLY NO GUIDEBOOK BUT SHOWN ON OS MAPS. CONTACT KENT COUNCIL (P278).

rtec.com

POLARTEC®
FORWARD FABRIC™

GLASTONBURY TOR AND SURROUNDING SOMERSET LEVELS

SOUTH WEST

J BEWLEY/SUSTRANS

CORNISH CLAY TRAILS

Last year the South West celebrated two special anniversaries. Exmoor National Park had its 50th birthday and the National Trust toasted 60 years since acquiring Sir Richard Acland's Holnicote Estate. The 12,500 acres of high moors, ancient forests, rivers and coastlines around Porlock Vale is still one of the largest gifts of land ever made to the Trust by a man who believed the land should rightfully belong to the people.

So Sir Richard would surely have been pleased to see the opening up of 96,000 hectares of access land in August when the right to roam came to Devon, Cornwall and western Somerset (Area 6). The new measures mean walkers can now explore the previously off-limits Gittisham Hill, near Honiton, and marvel at the panoramic views of Dartmoor and Exmoor from the summit of Codden Hill near Barnstaple.

> Walkers can now explore the previously off-limits Gittisham Hill, near Honiton, and marvel at the panoramic views of Dartmoor and Exmoor from the summit of Codden Hill near Barnstaple.

Three major new waymarked routes have also recently opened in the region. The Coleridge Way (see p24) trails 58km/36 miles from the Romantic poet's former home in Nether Stowey, over the Quantock and Brendon Hills into Exmoor. The Cornish Clay Trails bring together three walks among the historic mining pits and soaring spoil tips of mid-Cornwall's clay industry area. The three linear paths link Bugle, St Austell and Par with the Eden Project and Wheal Martyn China Clay Museum, and were specially designed to connect with local bus and train services. And July saw the launch of the Copper Trail: a 97km/60 mile circular route around Bodmin Moor that takes in Golitha Falls, Carburrow Tor and the Iron Age hillfort of Berry Castle.

But it's the genius of Sir Isambard Kingdom Brunel that organisers in Bristol hope will fascinate visitors to the South West in 2006. Brunel200 celebrates the bicentenary of the great Victorian engineer's birth with a range of events planned, including walks and trails around his greatest projects and the re-opening of steamliner SS Great Britain at Bristol's Great Western Dockyard after an extensive redevelopment.

Long Distance Paths

Coleridge Way	COL
Cotswold Way	CWD
Heart of England Way	HOE
Macmillan Way	MCM
Monarch's Way	MON
Offa's Dyke Path	OFD
Ridgeway	RDG
Saints' Way	STW
Severn Way	SVN
South West Coast Path	SWC
Thames Path	THM
Two Moors Way	2MS
Wessex Ridgeway	WXR
Wye Valley Walk	WVL

Public rights of way:

37,251km/23,133miles

Mapped access land:

399 sq km/154 sq miles
(Area 3, central southern)
961 sq km/371 sq miles
(Area 6, South West)

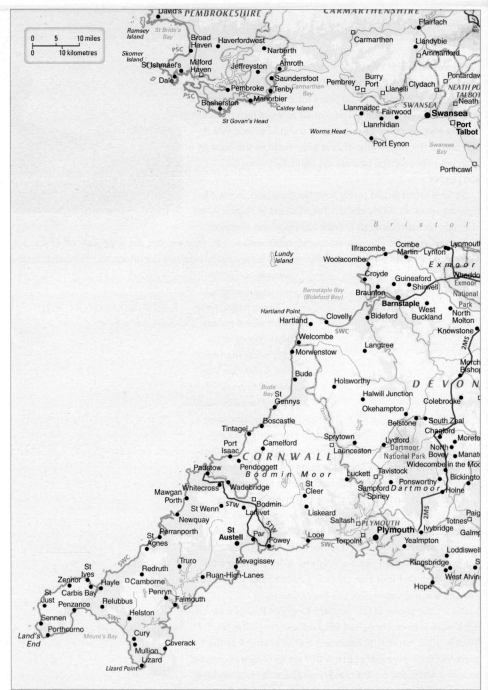

0   5   10 miles
0   10 kilometres

David's PEMBROKESHIRE   CARMARTHENSHIRE
Ramsey   St Bride's   Ffairfach
Island   Bay   Broad   Haverfordwest   Carmarthen   Llandybie
Skomer   Haven   Ammanford
Island   St Ishmael's Milford   Narberth   Pontardaw
          Dale   Haven   Jeffreyston   Amroth   NEATH PO
                                        Saundersfoot Pembrey Burry Llanelli Clydach   TALBOT
                  Pembroke Tenby Carmarthen   Port   Llanelli   Neath
              Bosherston   Manorbier Bay   SWANSEA
                        Caldey Island   Llanmadoc Fairwood   Swansea
              St Govan's Head   Port
                              Worms Head   Llanrhidian   Talbot
                                        Port Eynon   Swansea
                                                      Bay
                                                              Porthcawl

                                                      B r i s t o l
          Lundy   Ilfracombe Combe   Lynmoutl
          Island   Woolacombe   Martin Lynton
                                              E x m o o r
                            Croyde   Whaddo
                            Guineaford Shirwell Exmoor
                        Braunton   National
          Barnstaple Bay   Barnstaple   Park
          (Bideford Bay)   West   North
        Hartland Point   Clovelly Bideford Buckland Molton
              Hartland   SWC   Knowstone
          Welcombe   Langtree
          Morwenstow   Morch
                                                  Bishop
                Bude   D E V O N
          Bude   Holsworthy
          Bay St   Halwill Junction
              Gennys   Colebrooke
                        Okehampton
              Boscastle   Belstone South Zeal
          Tintagel   Chagford
          Port   Camelford Sprytown   Lydford Moreto
          Isaac   Launceston Dartmoor North
                  C O R N W A L L   National Park Bovey Manat
          Padstow Pendoggett   Luckett Widecombe in the Moo
          B o d m i n M o o r   Tavistock Bickingto
      Mawgan Whitecross Wadebridge St   Ponsworthy
      Porth   STW Cleer   Sampford Dartmoor Holne
          St Wenn   Bodmin   Spiney
      Newquay   STW Lanivet   Liskeard Saltash PLYMOUTH
          Perranporth   STN Par Fowey Looe Torpoint Ivybridge Galmp
      St Agnes St   SWC   Yealmpton
              Austell   Torpoint   Loddiswell
          Truro   Mevagissey   Kingsbridge S
      St   Redruth Ruan-High-Lanes   West Alvin
      Ives Hayle Camborne   Hope
  Zennor   Penryn
  St Carbis Bay Relubbus Falmouth
  Just Penzance   Helston
      Sennen   SWC
  Land's Porthcurno Cury
  End   Coverack
          Mullion
          Lizard
      Lizard Point

SOUTH WEST
LOCAL RAMBLERS GROUPS

AVON
AREA SECRETARY
See http://avon-area.members.beeb.net
or contact our central office for details.

GROUP SECRETARIES
Bath Mrs M Wright, 47 Dovers Park,
Bathford, Bath, BA1 7UD
☎ 01225 858047
www.tompson.demon.co.uk/
Bathramblers/Bathhome.htm
Bristol Mr John Wrigley,
14 Archfield Road, Cotham, Bristol,
BS6 6BE ☎ 0117 924 0125
www.bristolramblers.freeserve.co.uk/
Brunel Walking & Activity Penny
Richardson, 23 Rock Lane, Stoke
Gifford, Bristol, BS34 8PF
http://brunelwalking.org.uk
Kingswood Nicola Phelps,
10 Cloverlea Rd, Warmly,
Bristol, BS30 8LF
www.kingswoodramblers.pwp.
blueyonder.co.uk
Norton Radstock Mrs S Haddon,
4 Dymboro Close, Midsomer Norton,
Bath, BA3 2QS
Severnside Jill Fysh, 43a Springfields,
Ableton Lane, Severn Beach, Bristol,
BS35 4PP ☎ 01454 633001
www.severnside-ramblers.org.uk/
Southwold (Yate) Miss S S Naqui,
3 Brake Close, Sherbourne Park,
Bradley Stoke, Bristol, BS32 8BA
☎ 01179 697246
www.southwold-ramblers.co.uk/

CORNWALL
AREA SECRETARY
Mrs Christine James, Chy-Vean,
Tresillian, Truro, Cornwall, TR2 4BN
☎ 01872 520368
www.racornwall.org.uk

GROUP SECRETARIES
Bude/Stratton Mr P Judson,
Meadowcroft, Bagbury Road, Bude,
Cornwall, EX23 8QJ
☎ 01288 356597
Camel District (Wadebridge)
Mr R Sheppard, Bramleys, Marshall
Road, Nanstallon, Bodmin, Cornwall,
PL30 5LD ☎ 01208 832136
www.racamelgroup.org.uk
Caradon Mrs E M Honey, Penyoke
Lodge, Church Lane, Cargreen, Saltash,
Cornwall, PL12 6NS ☎ 01752 841361
Carrick Mr J B Jennings, 7 Moresk
Close, Truro, Cornwall, TR1 1DL
☎ 01872 278317
Cornwall 20s-30s New 20s-30s Group
(temporary name). Launches at AGM in

January 2006. Enquiries to Miss Sally
Berridge ☎ 07725 145857
sallyberridge@hotmail.com
Newquay Mrs D Hanks, 2 Brewers
Road, St Clement Vean, Truro,
Cornwall, TR1 1AJ ☎ 01872 222 367)
lawrence.hanks@homecall.co.uk
Restormel Mrs J C Sloan, Westering,
Old Hill, Grampound, Truro, TR2 4RY
☎ 01726 883214
West Cornwall (Penwith & Kerrier)
Mrs Sylvia Ronan, Trebant, Ludgvan,
Churchtown, Penzance, Cornwall,
TR20 8HH ☎ 01736 740542
sylv@west-cornwall-footpaths.com

DEVON
AREA SECRETARY
Mrs E M Linfoot, 14 Blaydon Cottages,
Blackborough, Cullompton, Devon,
EX15 2HJ ☎ 01884 266435
http://website.lineone.net/
~devon.ramblers

GROUP SECRETARIES
Bovey Tracey Mrs P Bray,
17 St Andrews Road, Paignton, Devon,
TQ4 6HA ☎ 01803 392182
Devon Bootlegs Dr M Sanderson,
51 Ribston Avenue, Exeter, EX1 3QE
www.geocities.com/devonbootlegs
East Devon Mr A Mack, 3 Cadbury
Gardens, East Budleigh, Budleigh
Salterton, EX9 7EU ☎ 01395 442748
Exeter & District Mrs J D Fly, Volant,
53 Bilbie Close, Cullompton, Devon,
EX15 1LG ☎ 01884 839 080
Moorland See www.ramblers.org.uk/
info/localgroups or contact our central
office for details
North Devon Mrs Pauline Newbound,
Mauretania, Town Bridge, Burrington,
Umberleigh, Devon, EX37 9LT
☎ 01769 520421
http://website.lineone.net/
~northdevon.ramblers/
Plymouth Ms Margaret Vatcher
(acting), 52 Glenholt Road, Glenholt,
Plymouth, Devon, PL6 7JD
☎ 01752 705868
www.plymouthramblers.org.uk/
South Devon Mr R A Woolcott,
The Lodge, 43 Seymour Drive,
Watcombe, Torquay, TQ2 8PY
☎ 01803 313430
South Hams Mr Peter Boult, Bridge
Cottage, Frogmore, Kingsbridge,
Devon, TQ7 2NU ☎ 01548 531701
Tavistock Mrs Rosemary Clarke,
39 Anderton Court, Whitchurch,
Tavistock, Devon, PL19 9EX
☎ 01822 615564

Teignmouth & Dawlish Mrs A
Mccallister , 21 Southdowns Road,
Dawlish, Devon, EX7 0LB ☎ 01626
864046 anne@mccallister.fsnet.co.uk
Tiverton Mrs M A Cox, 18 Anstey
Crescent, Tiverton, Devon, EX16 4JR
☎ 01884 256395
Totnes See www.ramblers.org.uk/info/
localgroups or contact our central office
for details

DORSET
AREA SECRETARY
See www.dorset-ramblers.co.uk or
contact our central office for details.

GROUP SECRETARIES
Dorset Young Walkers Miss Cheryl
Hadnutt, 112 Lions Lane, Ashley Heath,
Ringwood, BH24 2HW
☎ 07708 466236
www.dorsetyoungwalkers.org.uk/
East Dorset Mrs M H Kettlewell,
12 Limited Road, Bournemouth, BH9
1SS ☎ 01202 522467 (membership
enquiries J McDonald ☎ 01202 691709)
North Dorset Mr A T Combridge,
Green Bushes, North Rd, Sherborne,
Dorset, DT9 3JN ☎ 01935 812809
South Dorset Mr Stan Faris, 4 Long
Acre, New Street, Portland, Dorset,
DT5 1HH ☎ 01305 820957
West Dorset See
www.ramblers.org.uk/info/localgroups
or contact our central office for details

GLOUCESTERSHIRE
AREA SECRETARY
Mrs Karen Appleby, 46 Rendcomb
Drive, Cirencester, GL7 1YN
karen.appleby@openwork.uk.com

GROUP SECRETARIES
Cirencester Mrs Karen Appleby,
46 Rencomb Drive, Cirencester,
GL7 1YN ☎ 07854 816127
Cleeve Mrs Annie Clement,
22 Denham Close, Woodmancote,
Cheltenham, Glos, GL52 9TX
☎ 01242 674866
Forest of Dean Mr C Bolton,
Greenbank, Watery Lane,
Minsterworth, Gloucester, GL2 8JQ
☎ 01452 750471
http://website.lineone.net/~fredgray/
website.lineone.net/~fredgray
Gloucester See
www.ramblers.org.uk/info/localgroups
or contact our central office for details.
Gloucestershire Walking Group Miss
Sue Davis, 12 Kings Road, Cheltenham,
GL52 6BG ☎ 01242 234996
www.gwg.org.uk/

Mid-Gloucestershire Mrs Sheila Houston, 22 Leckhampton Road, Cheltenham, GL53 0AY
☎ 01242 210398
sheila210398@aol.com

North Cotswold Mr J D Clark, Stone Cottage, The Green, Lower Brailes, Banbury, Oxford, OX15 5HZ
☎ 01608 685 597

South Cotswold Mr B Smith & Mrs J Smith, 139 Thrupp Lane, Thrupp, Stroud, GL5 2DQ
☎ 01453 884 013
www.southcotswoldramblers.org.uk/

SOMERSET
AREA SECRETARY
Mrs M Henry, 22 Linden Grove, Taunton, Somerset, TA1 1EF
☎ 01823 333369
www.somersetramblers.org.uk/

GROUP SECRETARIES
Clevedon Mrs Sue Shewan, 25 Honeylands, Portishead, Bristol, BS20 6RB ☎ 01275 848075
www.somersetramblers.org.uk/

Family Countryside Walkers Mrs M Henry, 22 Linden Grove, Taunton, Somerset, TA1 1EF ☎ 01823 333369

Mendip Ms V Isbell, 2 Field Villas, Cannards Grave Road, Shepton Mallet, BA4 5RP ☎ 01749 347124

Sedgemoor See www.ramblers.org.uk/info/localgroups or contact our main office for details

Somerset Walking & Activity See www.ramblers.org.uk/info/localgroups or email swag@fsmail.net for details

South Somerset Mr I L Rendall, 3a Tintern, Abbey Manor Park, Yeovil, Somerset, BA21 3SJ ☎ 01935 421235
www.somersetramblers.co.uk/southsom.htm

Taunton Deane Mr A F Welsman, Stonegallows House, Stonegallowshill, Taunton, Somerset, TA1 5JS
☎ 01823 461811
www.tauntonramblers.org.uk/

West Somerset Geoff Taylor, 1 Culvercliffe Court, Minehead, TA24 5UP ☎ 01643 705288

Woodspring Ms D Smith, 50 Rowan Place, Weston-Super-Mare, BS24 7RQ ☎ 01934 518082

DID YOU KNOW?
Ramblers Group walks are now online at
www.ramblers.org.uk/walksfinder

WILTSHIRE & SWINDON
AREA SECRETARY
Mrs Joan Crosbee, 2 Kennet View, Fyfield, Marlborough, Wiltshire, SN8 1PU ☎ 01672 861359
www.ramblers-wilts.org.uk

GROUP SECRETARIES
Chippenham Mrs Kath Parkinson, 6 Silbury Road, Curzon Park, Calne, Wiltshire, SN11 0ES ☎ 01249 811445

Mid Wiltshire Mrs Linda Gilder, 1 Moggs Lane, Calstone, Calne, SN11 8QD ☎ 01249 822071

North East Wilts Mr Peter Gallagher, 10 Folkstone Road, Swindon, Wiltshire, SN1 3NH ☎ 01793 537472

South Wiltshire Mrs Barbara Wilmot, 9 Woodland Way, Laverstock, Salisbury, Wilts, SP1 1SB ☎ 01722 334329 (membership enquiries Brian Abel ☎ 01722 506561)

West Wiltshire Mrs Jill Elliott, 152 Bath Road, Bradford-On-Avon, Wilts, BA15 1SS ☎ 01225 862566

Wiltshire Wanderers Martin Lucas, 10 Foreman Street, Calne, SN11 8PE ☎ 01249 816467 http://homepage.ntlworld.com/ron-di/ypg.htm

SOUTH WEST

LOCAL RAMBLERS PUBLICATIONS

CORNWALL
NEW The Maritime Line: Trails from the Track
Walk card pack detailing nine walks, 3km/2 miles to 11km/7 miles, with most 8km/5 miles or under, generally easy-going, and all connecting with the Maritime Line, one of Cornwall's attractive branch lines running from Truro on the Great Western main line to Falmouth Docks. Includes linear walks linking all the stations between Truro and Penmere, and some circular options. Attractive and clear mapping, route descriptions and background information. A joint project of Carrick Ramblers and the Devon & Cornwall Rail Partnership. *Free from local stations and information centres, or send an SAE to Carrick Ramblers, 7 Moresk Close, Truro TR1 1DL.*

Rambles in the Roseland
(6 walks 4km/2.5 miles to 9km/5.5 miles)
Six Circular Coast and Country Walks on the Lizard
(6.5km/4 miles to 11km/7 miles)
Six Coastal Walks with Inland Returns in or on The Lizard
(5.5km/3.5 miles to 13km/8 miles)
Six Coastal Walks with Inland Returns in Penwith Book 1

(3km/2 miles to 11km/7 miles)
Six Coastal Walks with Inland Returns in Penwith Book 2
(3km/2 miles to 11km/7 miles)
Six Walks around Falmouth 1
(3km/2 miles to 11km/7 miles)
Six Walks around Falmouth 2
(3km/2 miles to 11km/7 miles)
Six North Cornwall Walks 1
(5km/3 miles to 9.5km/6 miles)
Six North Cornwall Walks 2
(5.5km/3.5 miles to 13km/8 miles)
Six Walks from Truro
(6.5km/4 miles to 11km/7 miles)
Wendron's Church and Chapels Walks
(6 walks 6.5km/4 miles to 8km/5 miles)
*All £1 + 25p p&p each from Publicity Officer, 2 Lanaton Road, Penryn TR10 8RB. Cheques to Cornwall Area, Ramblers' Association.
Penwith and Lizard booklets also available from Trebant, Ludgvan Churchtown, Penzance TR20 8HH. Cheques to Penwith/Kerrier Ramblers.*

Six North Cornwall Walks Book 1
Six North Cornwall Walks Book 2
Six short walks in each, all from car parks. Mainly around 6.5km/4 miles to 9.5km/6 miles. [2004]
Each £1.50 + 25p p&p from Pridham

House, Molesworth Street, Wadebridge PL27 7DS. Cheques to Ramblers' Association Camel District.

DEVON
Walks Around Dawlish
by Teignmouth and Dawlish Ramblers, published with Dawlish Town Council. Leaflet pack of seven illustrated walks around the town. *£2 from Dawlish Town Council, The Manor House, Old Town Street, Dawlish EX7 9AP, tel 01626 863388. Cheques to Dawlish Town Council.*

DORSET
A Rambler's Guide to the Dorset Jubilee Trail
A comprehensive guide with maps to this 145km/90-mile walk across Dorset from Forde Abbey to Bokerley Dyke. ISBN 1 901184 04 8. *£4.50 + 50p p&p from Jubilee Trail Contact, 19 Shaston Crescent, Dorchester DT1 2EB. Cheques to Ramblers Association - Dorset Area.*

GLOUCESTERSHIRE AND BRISTOL
Bristol Backs: Discovering Bristol on Foot
Compiled by Peter Gould, jointly published with Bristol City Council, ISBN 1 901184 52 8. 27 walks of between

3km/2 miles and 17.5km/11 miles in the city including street-based heritage walks, green trails, waterside strolls and a sculpture trail, with plentiful background descriptions. £6.99 + £1.50 p&p from 57 Somerset Road, Bristol BS4 2HT, bristolbacks@aol.com. Cheques to Bristol Group Ramblers' Association.

Bristol Triangular City Walk

A 28km/18-mile circuit of the city starting at Temple Meads station, easily walked as three sections of between 6 km/4 miles and 13km/8 miles connected by public transport. Includes the waterfront, Durdham Downs, Avon Gorge and Blaise Castle Estate as well as the heart and history of the city, developed by Bristol Ramblers in association with the City Council. Connects with South Bristol Circular Walk (see below). Colour leaflet £1.50 from 57 Somerset Road, Bristol BS4 2HT. Cheques to Bristol Group Ramblers' Association. Or free from local outlets.

Cirencester Circuit

A moderate 16km/10 mile walk around Cirencester, £1 + 40p p&p; and **Walks Around Cirencester** a moderate 9.5km/6 mile walk from Cirencester to Duntisbourne, 80p + 40p p&p from 80 Melmore Gardens, Cirencester GL7 1NS. Cheques to Cirencester Ramblers.

Cotswold Way Handbook & Accommodation Guide

ISBN 1 901184 62 5. £2.95 + 50p p&p from Mail Order Secretary, Tudor Cottage, Berrow, Malvern WR13 6JJ. Cheques to Ramblers' Association Gloucestershire Area.

NEW Favourite South Cotswold Walks Book One

by South Cotswold Ramblers (Spring 2006). 18 attractive half-day walks, several of which can be combined into day walks, in the Cotswolds Area of Outstanding Natural Beauty. A fully revised and extended issue of a best selling book first published in 1995. £3 + 95p p&p (reduced to 50p p&p for Ramblers members if you include your membership number). See also www.southcotswoldramblers.org.uk/books for further information and updates.

Forest of Dean East

40p + 30p p&p from Mail Order Secretary, Tudor Cottage, Berrow, Malvern WR13 6JJ. Cheques to Ramblers' Association Gloucestershire Area.

The Glevum Way

42km/26 mile circular walk around the outskirts of the city of Gloucester. 50p + 30p p&p from 12 Eardisland Road, Tuffley, Gloucester GL4 0BZ. Cheques to Ramblers' Association.

More Favourite Walks in the South Cotswolds

15 fully graded and illustrated walks of between 3km/2 miles and 22.5km/14 miles in the Cotswolds Area of Outstanding Natural Beauty. Special offer price £3 + 50p from Southcot, The Headlands, Stroud GL5 5PS. Cheques to South Cotswold Ramblers. See also www.southcotswoldramblers.org.uk/book s for further information and updates.

North Cotswold Diamond Way: 30 sparkling short walks

by Elizabeth Bell (North Cotswold Ramblers). Recently revised edition presenting this 96km/60-mile circular route via Moreton-on-Marsh, devised to celebrate the Ramblers' diamond jubilee in 1975, as 30 linked shorter (around 8km/5 mile) circular walks. £6.95 + £2 p&p from Holly Tree House, Evenlode GL56 0NT. Cheques to Ramblers' Association North Cotswold Group.

Samaritans Way South West: A Walk from Bristol to Lynton

by Graham Hoyle. Linking Bristol with the Cotswold Way National Trail at Bath, the Mendips, Cheddar, the Quantocks, Exmoor National Park and the South West Coast Path at Lynton, 160km/100 miles. Pocket guide with overprinted old OS map extracts. £5.45 from Samaritans Way SW Associationi, 6 Mervyn Road, Bristol BS7 9EL or email samaritansway@aol.com. Cheques to Samaritans Way SW.

Six Walks in Chipping Sodbury

by South Gloucestershire Council and Southwold Ramblers. Leaflets are Work and Play, Golf Course and Common, The Sodbury Round, Old Sodbury and Kingrove Common, Kingrove Common and Codrington, Paddocks and Ponds. Free from Chipping Sodbury Tourist Information Centre, The Clock Tower, Chipping Sodbury BS37 6AH, tel 01454 888686.

NEW South Bristol Circular Walk devised by Neil Buriton

A 37km/23-mile route following quiet streets and paths around the south of the city, from Temple Meads station via Troopers Hill, Whitchurch, Dundry and

Clifton Bridge. Lots of opportunities to split the walk into smaller sections via public transport, and a connection with the Bristol Triangular City Walk (see above). Developed by Bristol Ramblers and Bristol council. Excellent colour booklet with maps, route description, photos. Free from Bristol TIC.

Walk West

by Geoff Mullett (Avon Ramblers): 30 country walks of between 6.5km/4 miles and 22.5km/14 miles within easy reach of Bristol and Bath, including some in south Wales.

Walk West Again

by Geoff Mullett, ISBN 1 901184 61 7. A second volume of walks from 6.5km/4 miles to 19km/12 miles, within easy reach of Bristol and Bath. £7.99 each from 12 Gadshill Drive, Stoke Gifford, Bristol BS34 8UX. Cheques to Geoff Mullett. For information and updates visit walk-west.members.beeb.net

Waymarked Trails in the Forest of Dean and Highmeadow Woods.

Attractive leaflet describing two circular walks, the Beechenhurst Trail and the Highmeadow Trail. 60p + 30p p&p as North Cotswold Diamond Way above.

Yate Walks Leaflets

by Yate Town Council and Southwold Ramblers. Three leaflets: Brimshaw Manor Walk, Stanshawes Walk and Upstream & Downstream Walk. Free from Yate Town Council, Poole Court, Poole Court Drive, Yate BS37 5PP.

SOMERSET
Channel to Channel Seaton-Watchet

by Ken Young. 80km/50-mile rural walk across the southwest peninsula at its narrowest point, via the Blackdown Hills. £2 + 50p p&p from K Young, 14 Wilton Orchard, Taunton TA1 3SA. Cheques to Somerset Area Ramblers' Association.

Somerset Walks

by Taunton Deane Ramblers, illustrated by Ann Sharp, ISBN 1 901184 69 2. 16 circular walks 6.5km/4 miles to 22.5km/14 miles, including the Quantocks, Blackdown Hills, Brendon Hills, Somerset Levels and Exmoor, with notes on things to look out for, tea shops and pubs, but all from car parks. £2.95 + 50p p&p from Greenway Thatch, North Curry, Taunton TA3 6NH. Cheques to Taunton Deane Ramblers.

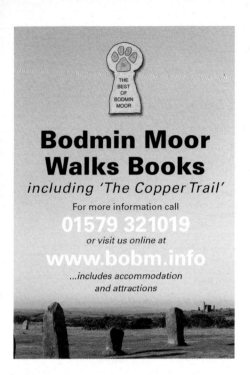

LOCAL RAMBLERS PUBLICATIONS continued

NEW **Walking for Pleasure**
edited by Mike Emmett (Taunton Deane
Ramblers). 14 circular walks exploring
the hidden countryside in and around
Taunton Deane, 6.5km/4 miles to
10.5km/6.5 miles. £2 + 50p p&p from
Fairacre, West Hatch, Taunton TA3 5RJ.
Cheques to Mike Emmett.

WILTSHIRE
**Northeast Wiltshire Ramblers
Publications**
**Nine Downland Walks between
Swindon and Marlborough**
between 5km/3 miles and 12km/7.5
miles on the Downs. £2
**Ten walks from village pubs near
Swindon**
by Pat Crabb. Short circular walks of
2km/1.5 miles to 8km/5 miles with bus
routes given where appropriate. £2
Twelve Walks around Marlborough:
between 5.5km/3.5 miles and 14.5km/9
miles. £1.80
20 Walks around Swindon
Between 3km/2 miles and 12km/7.5
miles, within a 30km/20-mile radius of
Swindon. £2.30
All from 21 Brynards Hill, Wootton
Bassett, Swindon SN4 7ER. Cheques to
Ramblers' Association NE Wilts Group.

**South Wiltshire Ramblers
Publications**
8 easy walks in the Salisbury Area
Route card pack
**10 shorter walks in the Salisbury
Area** Booklet
**10 longer walks in the Salisbury
Area** Route card pack
£3.50 each from 27 Richard Way,
Salisbury SP2 8NT. Cheques to Ramblers'
Association W3.

**West Wiltshire Ramblers
Publications**
Ten Walks in West Wiltshire
10 circular walks between 6.5km/4 miles
and 17.5km/11 miles, including some
near railway stations, with OS maps.
£2.50.

Walking in West Wiltshire Book 2
10 circular walks between 6.5km/4 miles
and 11km/7 miles, including some near
railway stations, with sketch maps. £1.25

Walking in West Wiltshire Book 3
10 circular walks between 8km/5 miles
and 16km/10 miles, including some near
railway stations, with sketch maps. £1.25
All from 68 Savernake Avenue, Melksham
SN12 7HE. Cheques to West Wilts
Ramblers' Association.

**The Kennet & Avon Wiggly Walks
Guide**
Three walks 3km/2 miles to 19km/12
miles, along the beautiful Vale of Pewsey
and the Kennet and Avon Canal,
connecting with Wigglybus services from
Devizes. Produced by the Kennt and
Avon Canal Rural Transport Partnership
with assistance from the Ramblers.
Free from 01249 460600.

Sarum Way
A circular walk around Salisbury and
Wilton. Booklet £3.50 from 27 Richard
Way, Salisbury SP2 8NT. Cheques to South
Wilts Ramblers Group.

Ten Walks Around Devizes
Varied walks of between 6.5km/4 miles
and 11km/7 miles starting at Devizes
market place, with maps, illustrations and
historical notes. £1.50 + 40p p&p from 1
Copings Close, Devizes SN10 5BW.
Cheques to Ramblers' Association Mid
Wilts Group.

12 Walks Around Chippenham
by Chippenham Ramblers, ISBN 1 000
3388 6. Varied selection of 4km/2.5-mile
to 11km/8-mile walks in excellent walking
country, all using public transport. £2 from
11A High Street, Sutton Benger SN15 4RE.
Cheques to RA Chippenham Group.

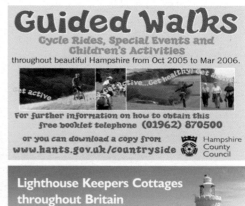

SOUTH WEST

BED & BREAKFAST

CORNWALL

● Boscastle
SOUTH WEST COAST PATH

The Old Coach House, Tintagel Road, PL35 0AS ☎ 01840 250398
www.old-coach.co.uk Map 190/098906
BB **B/C** ✗ nearby D4 T1 F3 Closed Xmas
🅑 🅓 ⊗ 🐾 👟 🚗 ! 🍴 ◆◆◆◆

🛏◀ Trerosewill Farm, Paradise , PL35 0BL ☎ 01840 250545
(Mrs Cheryl Nicholls) www.trerosewill.co.uk Map 190/098904
BB **C** ✗ nearby D3 T1 F2 Closed Xmas
🅑 🅓 ⊗ 🐾 👟 🚗 ! 🍴 Ⓜ ◆◆◆◆◆ⓢ

Lower Meadows, Penally Hill, PL35 0HF ☎ 01840 250570
(Anne & Adrian Prescott) www.lowermeadows.co.uk Map 190,200/101913
BB **D** ✗ nearby D4 T1 Closed Xmas
🅑 🅓 ⊗ 🐾 👟 🚗 ! ◆◆◆◆

● Bude
SOUTH WEST COAST PATH

🛏◀ Pencarrol Guest House, 21 Downs View, EX23 8RF ☎ 01288 352478
(M & E Payne) pencarrolbude@aol.com Map 190/207071
BB **C** ✗ nearby S2 D3 T1 F1 Closed Dec
🅑 🅓 ⊗ 🐾 👟 🚗 ! ◆◆◆◆

☆ 🛏◀ **Harefield Cottage**
Upton, EX23 0LY ☎ 01288 352350 (Sally-Ann Trewin)
www.coast-countryside.co.uk Map 190/202048
BB **B** ✗ book first £15, 6.30pm D1 T1 F1 Closed Xmas
🆅 🅑 🅓 ⊗ 🐾 👟 🚗 ! 🍴 ◆◆◆◆ⓢ

Harefield Cottage is only 250 yards from
the South West Coast Footpath.
Luxurious bedrooms. A hot tub in the
garden to relax those weary muscles.
Excellent homecooked meals on request.
We offer a pick-up and drop service with
luggage carried forward.

🛏◀ Tee-side Guest House, 2 Burn View, EX23 8BY ☎ 01288 352351
(Mrs June Downes) www.tee-side.co.uk Map 190/208066
BB **B** ✗ book first £12, 6:30pm S1 D2 T3 Closed Xmas
🆅 🅑 🅓 ⊗ 🐾 👟 🚗 ◆◆◆◆

The Greenhouse, 16 Burn View, EX23 8BZ ☎ 01288 355587
(Kevin & Yvette Queen) www.greenhousebude.co.uk Map 190/210066
BB **B** ✗ nearby D1 T1 F1
🅑 🅓 ⊗ 🐾 👟 ! 🍴 ◆◆◆◆ⓢ

🛏◀ Thornbury Cottage, 16 The Crescent, EX23 8LE ☎ 01288 352161
(Candida Brouwer) candidabbrouwer@hotmail.com Map 190/208061
BB **C** ✗ book first £15, 7-9pm S1 D1 T1 F1
🆅 🅑 🅓 ⊗ 🐾 👟 🚗 ! 🍴

● Camelford
🛏◀ The Countryman Hotel, Victoria Road, PL32 9XA
☎ 01840 212250 (Mrs Deborah Reeve)
www.cornwall-online.co.uk/countryman Map 200/108839
BB **C** ✗ book first £10, 7-8:30pm S2 D3 T2 F3 Closed Xmas
🆅 🅑 🅓 ⊗ 🐾 👟 🚗 ! 🍴 ◆◆◆ Guided walks.

● Carbis Bay (St Ives)
SOUTH WEST COAST PATH

🛏◀ Coast Vegetarian B&B, St Ives Rd, TR26 2RT ☎ 01736 795918
www.coastcornwall.co.uk Map 203/524385
BB **C** ✗ book first £7.45-£15, 6-8pm D5 T1 F2 Closed Xmas
🚌(Carbis Bay) 🆅 🅑 ⊗ 🐾 👟 👟

● Coverack (Helston)
SOUTH WEST COAST PATH

Mellan House, TR12 6TH ☎ 01326 280482 (Mrs Muriel Fairhurst)
hmfmelcov@aol.com Map 204/780186
BB **B** ✗ nearby S1 D1 T1 Closed Xmas 🅑 🅓 ⊗ 🐾 👟 🚗 ! 🍴

● Cury (Mullion)
SOUTH WEST COAST PATH

☆ **Cobblers Cottage**
Nantithet, TR12 7RB ☎ 01326 241342 (Mrs Hilary Lugg)
Map 203/681223
BB **C** ✗ book first £14, 6:30pm D2 T1 Closed Xmas
🅑 🅓 ⊗ 🐾 👟 ◆◆◆◆◆ⓢ

This picturesque 17th-century
riverside cottage, set in an acre
of beautiful gardens is situated
just 2½ miles from the SW Coast
Path. All bedrooms en-suite.
Evening dinner optional.
Colour brochure available.

● Falmouth
SOUTH WEST COAST PATH

Wickham, 21 Gyllyngvase Terrace, TR11 4DL ☎ 01326 311140
(Steve & Jenny Lake) www.wickham-hotel.co.uk Map 204/810318
BB **B/C** ✗ nearby S2 D2 T/F2 Closed Nov-Feb 🚌(Falmouth Town)
🅑 ⊗ 🐾 👟 ◆◆◆

● Fowey
SOUTH WEST COAST PATH & SAINTS' WAY

4 Daglands Road, PL23 1JL ☎ 01726 833164 (John & Carol Eardley)
www.jabedesign.co.uk/keverne Map 200/123518
BB **C** ✗ nearby D2 Closed Xmas 🅑 🅓 ⊗ 🐾 👟 ! 🍴 Ⓜ

Wringford, Golant, PL23 1LA
☎ 01726 832205 (Liz Barclay) Map 200/114548
BB **C** ✗ book first £12, 7-8pm S1 T1 Closed Dec-Jan
🆅 🅑 🅓 ⊗ 🐾 🚗 ! 🍴

🛏◀ Fowey Marine Guest House, 21 Station Road, PL23 1DF ☎ 01726 833920
(Evonne Jones) www.foweymarine.com Map 200/126521
BB **C/D** ✗ nearby S1 D2 T2 🆅 🅑 ⊗ 🐾 👟 ! 🍴 ◆◆◆

● Hayle
SOUTH WEST COAST PATH

54 Penpol Terrace, TR27 4BQ ☎ 01736 752855 (Mrs Anne Cooper)
annejohn@cooper827.fsnet.co.uk Map 203/558374
BB **C** ✗ nearby S1 D1 T1 Closed Xmas-Jan 🚌(Hayle) 🐾 👟 🚗 ! Ⓜ

● Helston
SOUTH WEST COAST PATH

🛏◀ Carmelin, Pentreath Lane, The Lizard, TR12 7NY ☎ 01326 290677 (Mrs
Jane Grierson) www.bedandbreakfastcornwall.co.uk Map 203/699126 BB **B**
✗ £11, 7-8pm S1 D1 Closed Xmas 🆅 🅑 🅓 ⊗ 🐾 👟 🚗 ! 🍴

SOUTH WEST

☆ **Tregaddra Farm**
Cury Cross Lanes, TR12 7BB ☎ 01326 240235 (Mrs June Lugg)
www.tregaddra.freeserve.co.uk Map 203/697216
BB **C** ✕ book first £15, 6:30pm D4 T1 Closed Xmas
Ⓥ Ⓑ Ⓓ ⊗ 🐾🛁🚗 ◆◆◆◆Ⓢ

Central Lizard Peninsula location in an area of outstanding natural beauty. Ideal base for walking the South West Coast Path (2 miles away). Luxurious en-suite bedrooms with magnificent views.
Heated indoor pool (May-Sept) and tennis court. Aga-cooked breakfasts.

● **Lanivet (Bodmin)**
SAINTS' WAY
Willowbrook, Old Coach Road, Lamorick, PL30 5HB ☎ 01208 831670
(Tony & Elaine Barnaby) willowbrookbandb@aol.com Map 200/037646
BB **C** ✕ book first £13 S1 D2 T1 Ⓥ Ⓓ ⊗ 🐾🛁🚗 ◆◆◆◆

● **Liskeard**
Elnor Guest House, 1 Russell Street, PL14 4BP ☎ 01579 342472
(Mr & Mrs B J Slocombe) elnor@btopenworld.com Map 201/250642
BB **B/C** ✕ nearby S4 D1 T1 F3 Closed Xmas ⋘(Liskeard)
Ⓑ Ⓓ 🐾🛁 ◆◆◆

Hopsland, Commonmoor, PL14 6EJ ☎ 01579 344480 (Linda Hosken)
www.hopslandholidays.co.uk Map 201/242694
BB **B** ✕ £7.50, 6.30pm D1 T1
Ⓥ Ⓑ Ⓓ ⊗ 🐾🛁🚗 See SC & Groups also.

● **Looe**
SOUTH WEST COAST PATH
Marwinthy Guest House, East Cliff, PL13 1DE ☎ 01503 264382 (Eddie Mawby)
www.marwinthy.co.uk Map 201/256533 BB **B** ✕ nearby D2 T1 F1 Closed Dec-Feb ⋘(Looe) Ⓑ Ⓓ 🛁🏊

☆ 🕊 **Schooner Point**
1 Trelawney Terrace, PL13 2AG ☎ 01503 262670 (Paul & Helen Barlow)
www.schoonerpoint.co.uk Map 201/252536
BB **B** ✕ nearby S2 D3 T1 F0 Closed Xmas ⋘(Looe)
Ⓥ Ⓑ Ⓓ ⊗ 🐾🛁 ◆◆◆

Relaxed B&B offering clean, fresh rooms in a happy family house with splendid river views. Set only 150m from South West Coast Path and Looe bridge
Non-smoking throughout. Widely appreciated breakfasts, including vegetarian.
One night stays accepted. Limited parking.

🕊 The Old Bridge House Hotel, The Quay, PL13 2BU ☎ 01503 263159
(Colin & Liz Clements) www.theoldbridgehouse.com Map 201/253534
BB **D** ✕ nearby S2 D5 T2 F2 ⋘(Looe)
Ⓥ Ⓑ Ⓓ ⊗ 🐾🛁 ◆◆◆

● **Luckett (Callington)**
🕊 Higher Trowes, PL17 8LH ☎ 01579 370890 (Jan & Phil Roper)
jan-roper@tiscali.co.uk Map 201/383737
BB **B** ✕ book first £5-£12, 6-9pm S1 T/F1 Closed Xmas
Ⓑ Ⓓ ⊗ 🐾🛁🚗 ! 🏊

● **Mawgan Porth (Newquay)**
SOUTH WEST COAST PATH
🕊 Trevarrian Lodge, Trevarrian, TR8 4AQ ☎ 01637 860156
www.trevarrianlodge.co.uk Map 200/851661
BB **C** ✕ book first £10, 6-7pm S2 D3 T1 F2
Ⓥ Ⓑ Ⓓ 🐾🛁🚗 ! ◆◆◆

🕊 Blue Bay Hotel, Trenance, TR8 4BA ☎ 01637 860324
(Pippa & James McLuskie) www.bluebaycornwall.co.uk Map 200/849671
BB **C/D** ✕ £16, 7-8:45pm D9 T1 F1 Closed Xmas
Ⓥ Ⓑ Ⓓ 🐾🛁🚗 ! 🏊

● **Mevagissey (St Austell)**
🕊 Honeycombe House, 61 Polkirt Hill, PL26 6UR ☎ 01726 843750
(Ian & Val Soper) www.honeycombehouse.com Map 204/015446
BB **C** ✕ nearby S1 D3 T1 Closed Xmas-Jan Ⓥ Ⓑ Ⓓ ⊗ 🐾🛁🚗 !

● **Morwenstow (Bude)**
SOUTH WEST COAST PATH
Cornakey Farm, EX23 9SS ☎ 01288 331260 (Monica Heywood)
Map 190/208157
BB **B** ✕ book first £12, 6:30pm D1 T1 F1 Closed Dec
Ⓥ Ⓑ Ⓓ ⊗ 🐾🛁🚗 ! ◆◆◆

● **Mullion (Helston)**
SOUTH WEST COAST PATH
Campden House, The Commons, TR12 7HZ ☎ 01326 240365 (Joan Hyde)
campdenhouse@aol.com Map 203/677194
BB **B** ✕ £8, 6:30pm onwards S2 D2 T1 F2 Closed Xmas
Ⓥ Ⓑ Ⓓ 🐾🛁🚗

Criggan Mill, Mullion Cove, TR12 7EU ☎ 01326 240496 (Mike & Jackie Bolton)
www.crigganmill.co.uk Map 203/667180
BB **B** ✕ book first £9 S4 D4 T4 F4 Closed Nov-Mar
Ⓥ Ⓑ Ⓓ 🐾🛁🚗 ! 🏊 ★★★★★ See SC also.

🕊 Trenance Farmhouse, TR12 7HB ☎ 01326 240639
www.trenancefarmholidays.co.uk Map 203/673185
BB **C/D** ✕ nearby D4 T1 Closed Nov-Feb
Ⓑ Ⓓ ⊗ 🐾🛁 ! 🏊 ◆◆◆◆

● **Newquay**
SOUTH WEST COAST PATH
Chichester, 14 Bay View Terrace, TR7 2LR ☎ 01637 874216 (S R Harper)
http://freespace.virgin.net/sheila.harper Map 200/813614
BB **B** ✕ book first £8, 6:30pm S1 D3 T2 F1 Closed Dec-Feb ⋘(Newquay)
Ⓥ Ⓑ Ⓓ 🐾🛁Ⓜ ◆

Roma Guest House, 1 Atlantic Road, TR7 1QJ ☎ 01637 875085
(Mrs P Williams) www.romaguesthouse.co.uk Map 200/803616
BB **B** ✕ book first £9, 6pm S1 D2 T1 F2 Closed Xmas ⋘(Newquay)
Ⓥ Ⓑ Ⓓ 🐾🛁 !

🕊 The Three Tees Hotel, 21 Carminow Way, TR7 3AY ☎ 01637 872055
(Greg & Fiona Dolan) www.3tees.co.uk Map 200/823622
BB **C** ✕ nearby D4 T1 F4 Closed Xmas ⋘(Newquay)
Ⓥ Ⓑ Ⓓ ⊗ 🐾🛁🚗 ◆◆◆

🕊 Dewolf Guest House, 100 Henver Rd, TR7 3BL ☎ 01637 874746
www.dewolfguesthouse.com Map 200/828620
BB **D** ✕ nearby S1 D3 T1 F1 ⋘(Newquay)
Ⓑ ⊗ 🐾🛁🚗 🏊 ◆◆◆

● Padstow
SOUTH WEST COAST PATH & SAINTS' WAY

☆ ◄■ Trevorrick Farm
St Issey, PL27 7QH ☎ 01841 540574 (Mr & Mrs M Benwell)
www.trevorrick.co.uk Map 200/921732
BB C ✗ nearby D2 T1 Closed Xmas
Ⓑ Ⓓ ⊗ ♨ ➴ ! ◆◆◆

Magnificent location near Padstow. Warm welcome — tea and homemade cake. Pub/restaurant half a mile. Ideal walking/touring base; visiting Eden. Easy footpath access to Camel Trail, Padstow and coast path. Heated swimming pool (seasonal).

● Par
SOUTH WEST COAST PATH & SAINTS' WAY

◄■ Palm Garden House, 3 Tywardreath Highway, PL24 2RW
☎ 01726 816112 (Pat Taylor)
http://website.lineone.net/%7Eroy10/New%20index.htm Map 200/077556
BB B ✗ book first £5.50-£14.50, 6:30pm onwards S1 D1 F1 ₩(Par)
Ⓥ Ⓓ ⊗ ♨ ♨ ➴ ! ♨

● Pendoggett (Port Isaac)
SOUTH WEST COAST PATH

◄■ Lane End Farm, PL30 3HH ☎ 01208 880013 (Mrs Linda Monk)
nabmonk@tiscali.co.uk Map 200/026793
BB B ✗ nearby S1 D1 T1 Closed Xmas
Ⓥ Ⓑ Ⓓ ⊗ ♨♨ ♨ ➴ ! Ⓜ ◆◆◆ See SC also.

● Penryn (Falmouth)
SOUTH WEST COAST PATH

◄■ 62 St Thomas Street, TR10 8JP ☎ 01326 374473 (Brian & Penny Ward)
Map 204/786341
BB A ✗ nearby S1 D2 T1 F1 Closed Nov-Feb ₩(Penryn) Ⓓ ♨ ♨ Ⓜ

● Penzance
SOUTH WEST COAST PATH

☆ ◄■ Torre Vene
Lescudjack Terrace, TR18 3AE ☎ 01736 364103 (Mrs G Ash)
Map 203/475308
BB B ✗ nearby S2 D4 T4 F4 Closed Xmas ₩(Penzance)
Ⓓ ♨ ♨

Well-appointed guesthouse, delightful views of harbour, Mount's Bay.
Friendly "home from home" atmosphere.
Ideal overnight stop for Isles of Scilly.
Close to railway, coach stations and coastal paths.
Good home cooking.
A warm welcome awaits you.

◄■ Woodstock Guest House, 29 Morrab Road, TR18 4EZ ☎ 01736 369049
(Anne & David Peach) www.woodstockguesthouse.co.uk Map 203/472300
BB C ✗ nearby S4 D2 T1 F1 Closed Xmas-Jan ₩(Penzance)
Ⓑ Ⓓ ⊗ ♨♨ ♨ ➴ ! ♨ Ⓜ ◆◆◆

◄■ The Dunedin, Alexandra Rd, TR18 4LZ ☎ 01736 362652 (John Bolton)
www.dunedinhotel.co.uk Map 203/466299
BB C ✗ nearby S1 D5 T1 F2 Closed Xmas ₩(Penzance)
Ⓑ Ⓓ ⊗ ♨ ◆◆◆◆

☆ Trewella Guest House
18 Mennaye Road, TR18 4NG ☎ 01736 363818 (Shan & Dave Glenn)
www.trewella.co.uk Map 203/469298
BB B ✗ nearby S2 D4 F2 Closed Nov-Feb ₩(Penzance)
Ⓑ ⊗ ♨ ◆◆◆

A warm welcome awaits you at Trewella.
Fully non-smoking, single to triple en-suite rooms.
One mile from main bus/train station, town centre 10 mins walk. Ideal centre for west Cornwall and South West Coast Path.
Discount for 3 or more days.
Email: shan.dave@lineone.net

☆ ◄■ Beechwood B&B
Alexandra Place, TR18 4NE ☎ 01736 360380 (Martin Miller)
www.beechwoodpenzance.co.uk Map 203/468298
BB C ✗ nearby D2 T2 F1 ₩(Penzance)
Ⓥ Ⓑ Ⓓ ♨♨ ♨ ➴ !

Beechwood is ideally situated as a base or stopover when walking the South West Coast Path, and just 100m from the promenade.

The town centre is five minutes' walk away with the mainline railway station, harbour and heliport for the Isles of Scilly.

Penrose Guest House, 8 Penrose Terrace, TR18 2HQ
☎ 01736 362782 (Marc White)
www.penrosegsthse.co.uk Map 203/475307
BB C ✗ nearby S1 D1 T1 F1 ₩(Penzance)
Ⓥ Ⓑ Ⓓ ⊗ ♨♨ ♨ ◆◆◆

Kimberley Guest House, 10 Morrab Road, TR18 4EZ ☎ 01736 362727
(Richard & Francesca Peterson) www.kimberleyhousepenzance.co.uk
Map 203/471299
BB B ✗ nearby S1 D2 T2 F1 ₩(Penzance)
Ⓥ Ⓑ Ⓓ ⊗ ♨ ♨

◄■ Glencree House, 2 Mennaye Road, TR18 4NG ☎ 01736 362026
(Helen Cahalane) www.glencreehouse.co.uk Map 203/469297
BB B/C ✗ nearby S3 D4 T2 F2 Closed Xmas ₩(Penzance)
Ⓥ Ⓑ Ⓓ ⊗ ♨♨ ♨ ➴ ! ♨ ◆◆◆

● Perranporth
SOUTH WEST COAST PATH

Chy An Kerensa, Cliff Road, TR6 0DR ☎ 01872 572470 (W Woodcock)
Map 200,203/754543
BB B/C ✗ nearby S2 D2 T2 F3 Closed Xmas
Ⓑ Ⓓ ♨♨ ♨ ! ♨ ◆◆◆

◄■ Cliffside Hotel, Cliff Rd, TR6 0DR ☎ 01872 573297 (Maureen Burch)
www.cliffsideperranporth.co.uk Map 200/754544
BB B ✗ book first £10, 6:30-7pm S3 D5 T1 F2 Closed Xmas
Ⓥ Ⓑ Ⓓ ♨ ♨

◄■ Penarth Guest House, 26 St Pirans Road, TR6 0BH
☎ 01872 573186 (Peter & Diana Freckleton)
www.penarthperranporth.co.uk Map 200/758542
BB C ✗ nearby S3 D2 T1 F1 Closed Dec-Jan
Ⓥ Ⓑ ♨♨ ♨ ♨

SOUTH WEST

● Port Isaac
SOUTH WEST COAST PATH

☆ **Anchorage**
The Terrace, PL29 3SG ☎ 01208 880629 (Colin & Maxine Durston)
www.anchorageportisaac.co.uk Map 200/999807
BB **C** ✕ book first £12, 7pm S2 D3 T1 F1 Closed Xmas-Jan
Ⓥ Ⓑ Ⓓ ⊗ 🐾🐕🖐️! ◆◆◆◆

Stunning sea views.

Perfectly situated on the North Cornwall Coast Path.

Contact Colin and Maxine Durston.

● Porthcurno (Penzance)
SOUTH WEST COAST PATH

🚐🚆 Sea View House, The Valley, TR19 6JX ☎ 01736 810638 (Susan Davis)
www.seaviewhouseporthcurno.com Map 203/383227
BB **C/D** ✕ book first £13, 7:30pm S1 D3 T/D2 Closed Nov-Feb
Ⓥ Ⓑ Ⓓ ⊗ 🐾🐕🖐️!🏕️Ⓜ

● Redruth
SOUTH WEST COAST PATH

🚐🚆 Tre Vab Yowann, 6 Trevingey Rd, TR15 3DG ☎ 01209 211352
(Margaret Johnson) http://members.fortunecity.com/yowann/index.htm
Map 203/694425
BB **B** ✕ book first £12.50, 7:30pm S1 D1 Closed Xmas 🚌(Redruth)
Ⓥ Ⓑ Ⓓ ⊗ 🐾🐕🖐️!🏕️ On Great Flat Lode Trail.

● Relubbus (Penzance)
SOUTH WEST COAST PATH

🚐🚆 Relubbus House, TR20 9EP ☎ 01736 762796 (Chris & Ann Hatton)
www.relubbushouse.co.uk Map 203/567319
BB **C** ✕ book first £10, 6-7pm D2 T2 Closed Xmas-Feb
Ⓥ Ⓑ Ⓓ ⊗ 🐾🐕🖐️!Ⓜ

● Ruan-High-Lanes (Truro)
SOUTH WEST COAST PATH

☆ **New Gonitor Farm**
TR2 5LE ☎ 01872 501345
newgonitorfarm@wanadoo.co.uk Map 204/905416
BB **C** ✕ nearby D1 T1 Closed Xmas
Ⓑ Ⓓ ⊗ 🐾🐕🖐️

Stay at our comfortable farmhouse in the beautiful Roseland. Wonderful coastal walks and NT gardens within the local area. Also, Lost Gardens of Heligan and Eden Project. En-suite rooms, traditional farmhouse fare.

● Sennen (Penzance)
SOUTH WEST COAST PATH

Treeve Moor House, TR19 7AE ☎ 01736 871284 (Liz Trenary)
www.firstandlastcottages.co.uk Map 203/353251
BB **D** ✕ nearby D2 T1 Closed Xmas
Ⓑ Ⓓ🖐️! ◆◆◆◆

● St Agnes
SOUTH WEST COAST PATH

Penkerris, Penwinnick Road, TR5 0PA ☎ 01872 552262 (Mrs Gill-Carey)
www.penkerris.co.uk Map 204/720501
DD **C** ✕ book first £12.50, 6:30pm S1 D2 T1
Ⓥ Ⓑ Ⓓ 🐾🐕🖐️ ◆◆

Kimberley B&B, West Polberro, TR5 0SS ☎ 01872 552044 (Neil Heathcote)
kimberley_sta@hotmail.com Map 200/716511
BB **B/C** ✕ nearby D2 T1
Ⓥ Ⓑ Ⓓ ⊗ 🐾🐕🚗! Wheelchair access.

● St Austell
SOUTH WEST COAST PATH

🚐🚆 Spindrift, London Apprentice, PL26 7AR ☎ 01726 69316 (Mrs Mcguffie)
www.spindrift-guesthouse.co.uk Map 204/007501
BB **C** ✕ nearby D1 F2 Closed Xmas
Ⓑ ⊗ 🖐️🏕️ ◆◆◆ See SC also.

● St Cleer (Liskeard)
SOUTH WEST COAST PATH

☆ 🚆 **Redgate Smithy**
Redgate, PL14 6RU ☎ 01579 321578 (Clive & Julie Ffitch)
www.redgatesmithy.co.uk Map 201/227685
BB **D** D2 T1 Closed Xmas
Ⓥ Ⓑ Ⓓ ⊗ 🖐️!🏕️ ◆◆◆◆

Welcoming B&B situated above beautiful Golitha Falls on southern edge of Bodmin Moor. Excellent walking, on moor or coast. On the Copper Trail. Area abounds with Cornish mining heritage and birds and wildlife on the moor. Lovely woodland garden. Brochure available.

☆ 🚆 **Trecarne House**
Penhale Grange, PL14 5EB ☎ 01579 343543 (Trish & Tom)
www.trecarnehouse.co.uk Map 201/247688
BB **D** ✕ nearby D2 F1 🚌(Liskeard)
Ⓥ Ⓑ Ⓓ ⊗ 🐾🐕🖐️🚗🏕️ ◆◆◆◆

Tranquility on the edge of historic Bodmin Moor in St Cleer. Easy access to moorland walking, close coastal footpaths. Informal, friendly atmosphere. Stunning views from tastefully-decorated bedrooms. Italian-style courtyard with BBQ facilities. Outdoor trampoline, tabletennis & table football. Close to Eden Project.

● St Gennys (Bude)
SOUTH WEST COAST PATH

Bears & Boxes Country Guest House, Penrose, Dizzard, EX23 0NX
☎ 01840 230318 (Robert & Francoise Holmes)
www.bearsandboxes.com Map 190/170986
BB **C** ✕ £13, 6:30-8pm D2 T1 F1
Ⓥ Ⓑ Ⓓ ⊗ 🐾🐕🚗!🏕️ ◆◆◆◆

● St Ives
SOUTH WEST COAST PATH

🚐🚆 Ren-roy Guest House, 2 Ventnor Terrace, TR26 1DY
☎ 01736 796971 (Mrs M E McPherson) Map 203/515405
BB **B** ✕ nearby S2 D2 T1 F1 Closed Xmas 🚌(St Ives)
Ⓑ Ⓓ 🐾🐕🚗!Ⓜ

✎◀ Ten Steps, Fish St, TR26 ILT ☎ 01736 798222 (Lydia Dean-Barrows)
www.tenstepsbandb.co.uk Map 203/519408
BB **C** ✖ nearby SI DI TI FI ⚌(St Ives)
Ⓥ Ⓑ Ⓓ ⊗🍴🛁🚗!🛏Ⓜ ◆◆◆◆

The Great Escape, 16 Park Avenue, TR26 2DN ☎ 01736 794617
www.g-escape.freeuk.com Map 203/516402
BB **D** ✖ nearby D3 Closed Jan ⚌(St Ives)
Ⓥ Ⓑ Ⓓ ⊗🛁🛏 Vegetarian food only.

● St Just (Penzance)
SOUTH WEST COAST PATH

☆ ✎◀ **Bosavern House**
TRI9 7RD ☎ 01736 788301 (Mrs C Collinson)
www.bosavern.com Map 203/371305
BB **D** ✖ nearby SI D3 T2 F2 Closed Xmas
Ⓑ Ⓓ ⊗🍴🛁🚗! ◆◆◆◆

17th-century country house offering centrally heated, comfortable accommodation. Most bedrooms have sea or moorland views; en-suite or private facilities. Lounge with log fire, TV & bar. Drying facilities. Home cooking using local produce. Half mile from the SW Coast Path.

The Farmhouse, Bollowal, TRI9 7NP ☎ 01736 788458 (Mrs Jo Hill)
johanna.hill@btinternet.com Map 203/359314
BB **B** ✖ nearby SI DI Closed Dec-Mar
⊗🛁🚗! See SC also.

✎◀ The Old Fire Station, 2 Nancherrow Terrace, TRI9 7LA ☎ 01736 786463
(Angus & Liz Baxter) www.oldfirestationstjust.com Map 203/369315
BB **C** ✖ nearby D2 TI
Ⓥ Ⓑ Ⓓ ⊗🍴🛁🚗!

● St Wenn (Bodmin)
SAINTS' WAY

☆ **Tregolls Farm**
PL30 5PG ☎ 01208 812154 (Mrs Marilyn Hawkey)
www.tregollsfarm.co.uk Map 200/983661
BB **B/C** ✖ book first £13, 7pm D2 TI Closed Xmas
Ⓥ Ⓑ Ⓓ🍴🛁🚗! ◆◆◆◆ See SC also.

Grade II listed farmhouse with beautiful countryside views from all windows. 2 guest bedrooms. Farm trail links up to Saints' Way footpath. Pets corner. Eden, Helligan, Fowey and Padstow all within 25 minutes drive.

Treliver Farm, PL30 5PQ ☎ 01726 890286 (Jenny Tucker)
jenny@tucker600.freeserve.co.uk Map 200/980655
BB **C** ✖ £15, until 8:30pm DI TI FI
Ⓥ Ⓑ Ⓓ ⊗🍴🛁🚗 ◆◆◆◆

● The Lizard (Helston)
SOUTH WEST COAST PATH

Trethvas Farm, TRI2 7AR ☎ 01326 290720 (Mrs G Rowe)
trethvasfarm@amserve.com Map 203/709136
BB **C** ✖ nearby DI TI F/DI Closed Nov-Feb
Ⓑ Ⓓ ⊗🍴🛁! ◆◆◆◆

Parc Brawse House, Penmenner Road, TRI2 7NR ☎ 01326 290466 (Jo Charity)
www.cornwall-online.co.uk/parcbrawsehouse Map 203/701120
BB **D** ✖ nearby S3 D2 T2 FI Ⓥ Ⓑ ⊗🍴🛁🚗!🛏 ◆◆◆

● Tintagel
SOUTH WEST COAST PATH

Bossiney House Hotel, PL34 0AX ☎ 01840 770240 (John & Pauline Gibbs)
www.bossineyhouse.co.uk Map 200/066887
BB **D** ✖ book first £18, 7-9pm D9 T9 FI Closed Xmas-Jan
Ⓥ Ⓑ Ⓓ ⊗🍴🛁!🛏Ⓜ ★★

Bosayne Guest House, Atlantic Road, PL34 0DE ☎ 01840 770514
(Julie & Keith Walker) www.bosayne.co.uk Map 200/050890
BB **B/C** ✖ nearby S3 D2 TI F2 Closed Xmas
Ⓑ Ⓓ ⊗🍴🛁! ◆◆◆

● Truro
The Bay Tree, 28 Ferris Town, TRI 3JH ☎ 01872 240274 (Ann Talbot)
Map 204/821448
BB **B** ✖ nearby SI DI T2 FI ⚌(Truro) Ⓥ Ⓓ ⊗🛁🛏

● Wadebridge
SAINTS' WAY

✎◀ The Paddock, Edmonton, PL27 7JA ☎ 01208 812832 (Sue Russell)
www.paddock-bedandbreakfast.co.uk Map 200/964727
BB **B** ✖ book first £7.50, 6-8pm SI DI TI FI Closed Xmas
Ⓥ Ⓑ Ⓓ🍴🛁!🛏 ◆◆◆

● Whitecross (Wadebridge)
SOUTH WEST COAST PATH

✎◀ The Old Post Office, Atlantic Highway, PL27 7JD ☎ 01208 812620
www.bywaysactivityholidays.co.uk Map 200/966722
BB **B** ✖ book first £7 DI T2
Ⓑ Ⓓ🍴🛁🚗!🛏 ◆◆◆

● Zennor (St Ives)
SOUTH WEST COAST PATH

Trewey Farm, TR26 3DA ☎ 01736 796936 (Mrs N I Mann)
Map 203/454384
BB **B** ✖ nearby SI D2 TI F2 Closed Dec Ⓥ Ⓓ ⊗🛁🛏

✎◀ Boswednack Manor, TR26 3DD ☎ 01736 794183 (Dr E Gynn)
boswednack-manor@cornwall-county.com Map 203/442378
BB **B** ✖ nearby SI D2 TI FI Closed Nov-Mar
Ⓥ Ⓑ Ⓓ ⊗🍴🛁! See SC also.

DEVON

● Bampton (Tiverton)
Rows Farmhouse, EX16 9LD ☎ 01398 331579 (Mr & Mrs H Brooks)
suzannah@dircon.co.uk Map 181/946227
BB **C** ✖ book first £10 DI TI FI Closed Xmas
Ⓥ Ⓑ Ⓓ🍴🛁🚗!🛏

● Barnstaple
SOUTH WEST COAST PATH & MACMILLAN WAY WEST

✎◀ The Yeo Dale Hotel, Pilton Bridge, EX31 IPG ☎ 01271 342954
www.yeodalehotel.co.uk Map 180/556338
BB **D** ✖ nearby S3 D3 T2 F3 ⚌(Barnstaple)
Ⓑ Ⓓ🛁🚗! ◆◆◆◆

SOUTH WEST

Beer
SOUTH WEST COAST PATH

🚶🍳◀ Bay View Guest House, Fore Street, EX12 3EE ☎ 01297 20489
(Mr & Mrs R Oswald) Map 192/230891
BB **B/C** ✖ nearby SI D5 TI FI 🅱 🄳 🐕♿ 🛏 ◆◆◆

🚶🍳◀ Colebrooke House, Fore Street, EX12 3JL ☎ 01297 20308
(Wendy & Dave) Map 192/230891
BB **B** ✖ nearby D2 TI F3 🆅 🅱 🄳 ⊗ 🐕♿🚗! 🛏 Ⓜ

Belstone (Okehampton)
DARTMOOR

🚶🍳◀ Moorlands House, EX20 1QZ ☎ 01837 840549
www.moorlands-house.co.uk Map 191/620935
BB **C** ✖ nearby D2 TI Closed Xmas
🅱 🄳 🐕♿🚗🛏

Bickington (Newton Abbot)
DARTMOOR

🚶🍳◀ Rentor, TQ12 6JW ☎ 01626 821213 (Mr & Mrs P Warren)
rentorbnb@aol.com Map 191/801721
BB **B/C** ✖ nearby SI DI TI Closed Dec-Jan 🅱 🄳 ⊗ 🐕♿🚗

Bideford
SOUTH WEST COAST PATH & TARKA TRAIL

The Mount, Northdown Road, EX39 3LP ☎ 01237 473748
(Heather & Andrew Laugharne) www.themount1.cjb.net Map 190/449269
BB **D** ✖ nearby S2 D3 TI FI Closed Xmas
🅱 🄳 🐕♿🚗! ◆◆◆◆

Corner House, The Strand, EX39 2ND ☎ 01237 473722 (Chris & Sally Stone)
www.cornerhouseguesthouse.co.uk Map 190,180/452268
BB **C** ✖ nearby SI D2 TI F2 Closed Xmas 🆅 🄳 ⊗ 🐕♿🛏

☆ 🚶🍳◀I **Southdown Cottage**
Higher Clovelly, EX39 5SA ☎ 01237 431504 (Mrs Mary McColl)
maryfmcoll@hotmail.com Map 190/297236
BB **B** ✖ book first £10 SI DI TI FI
🆅 🅱 🄳 🐕♿🚗! 🛏

Lovely cosy cottage. Bright en-suite & standard rooms with TV, tea/coffee and wonderful views. Lifts to/from South West Coast Path anywhere between Barnstaple and Bude, so make us your base for a while. Breakfast a speciality.

Braunton
SOUTH WEST COAST PATH

North Cottage, 14 North Street, EX33 1AJ ☎ 01271 812703 (Mrs Jean Watkins)
north_cottage@hotmail.com Map 180/485367
BB **B** ✖ nearby S2 DI TI FI Closed Xmas
🅱 🄳 🐕♿! 🛏 Ⓜ

🚶🍳◀ St Merryn B&B, HIgher Park Rd, EX33 2LG ☎ 01271 813805
(Ros Bradford) www.st-merryn.co.uk Map 180/496364
BB **D** ✖ book first £12, 7-7:30pm SI DI TI FI Closed Xmas
🆅 🅱 🄳 ⊗ 🐕♿🚗! 🛏

The Firs, Higher Park Road, EX33 2LG ☎ 01271 814358 (Alison Benning)
bennings@sosi.net Map 180/498364
BB **C** ✖ nearby DI TI 🆅 🅱 🄳 ⊗ 🐕♿🚗!

Brixham
SOUTH WEST COAST PATH

Homeleigh B&B, 49 New Road, TQ5 8NL ☎ 01803 850781 (Carol Hemus)
www.homeleigh-brixham.co.uk Map 202/920559
BB **A** ✖ nearby SI D2
🆅 🄳 ⊗ 🐕♿

🚶🍳◀ Nods Fold B&B, Mudstone Lane, TQ5 9EQ ☎ 01803 856138
www.nodsfold.co.uk Map 202/930555
BB **D** ✖ nearby DI
🆅 🅱 🄳 ⊗ 🐕♿🚗!

Budleigh Salterton
SOUTH WEST COAST PATH

Ropers Cottage, Ropers Lane, Otterton, EX9 7JF ☎ 01395 568826 (Mrs Earl)
Map 192/081851
BB **B** ✖ nearby SI TI Closed Xmas
🅱 🄳 ♿🛏

Burrowshot (Axminster)
MONARCH'S WAY, WESSEX RIDGEWAY & SOUTH WEST COAST PATH

☆ 🚶🍳◀ **Hedgehog Corner**
Lyme Road, EX13 5SU ☎ 01297 32036 (Joy Raymond)
www.smoothhound.co.uk/hotels/hedgehog.html Map 193/316959
BB **C** ✖ nearby D2 TI 🚌(Axminster)
🆅 🅱 🄳 ⊗ 🐕♿🛏 Ⓜ

A warm welcome at this tranquil haven set back from the road in three acres of award-winning grounds.

A cosy home from home where nothing is too much trouble to ensure your comfortable stay. Two miles from Lyme Regis.

Chagford (Newton Abbot)
DARTMOOR
TWO MOORS WAY

Cyprian's Cot, 47 New Street, TQ13 8BB ☎ 01647 432256 (Shelagh Weeden)
www.cyprianscot.co.uk Map 191/701874
BB **B** ✖ nearby SI DI TI Closed Xmas
🅱 🄳 ♿! 🛏
Luggage transfer off-season only.

Clovelly (Bideford)
SOUTH WEST COAST PATH

The New House, EX39 5TQ ☎ 01237 431303
www.clovelly.co.uk Map 190/317248
BB **D** ✖ book first £20, 7-8:30pm D2 T3 F2 Closed Xmas
🆅 🐕♿ Ⓜ ★★

Colebrooke (Crediton)
TWO MOORS WAY

The Oyster, EX17 5JQ ☎ 01363 84576 (Pearl Hockridge)
Map 191/770008
BB **B** ✖ nearby D2 TI 🚌(Yeoford)
🅱 🄳 🐕♿! 🛏

● Colyford (Colyton)
SOUTH WEST COAST PATH

☆ Horriford Farm
EX24 6HW ☎ 01297 552316 (Colin and Valerie Pady)
www.datacottage.com/horriford.htm Map 192/237922
BB **C** ✕ book first £12.50, 7pm S2 D2 T1 F1 Closed Xmas
Ⓥ Ⓑ Ⓓ ⊛ 🍴🛏🚗🚪!

16th C. character farmhouse set in quiet valley near ford. En-suite double & twin bedrooms & single bedrooms. Log fires in winter. Close to SW Coast Path & East Devon Way.
horriford@datacottage.com

● Colyton
🐾◀ Sunnyacre, Rockerhayne Farm, Northleigh, EX24 6DA ☎ 01404 871422
(Mrs Norma Rich) sunnyacre@tesco.net Map 192,193/213963
BB **B** ✕ book first £7, 6:30pm D1 T1 F1 Ⓥ Ⓓ 🍴🛏🚪!🧺 ◆◆◆

● Combe Martin
EXMOOR
SOUTH WEST COAST PATH

☆ 🐾◀ The Royal Marine Public House Hotel
Seaside, EX34 0AW ☎ 01271 882470 (M J Lethaby)
www.theroyalmarine.co.uk Map 180/576472
BB **C** ✕ book first £5-£10, 6-10pm D4 T1 F1
Ⓥ Ⓑ Ⓓ🍴🛏🚪!

A warm welcome by the sea awaits you from resident proprietors Pat and Merv.
Five beautiful en-suite rooms with beach views.
Award winning licensee for food and service.
We specialise in home cooked food.
Mini breaks 1, 2, 3, 4 days, mid-week/weekends.

🐾◀ Mellstock House, Woodlands, EX34 0AR ☎ 01271 882592
(Mary Burbidge) www.mellstockhouse.co.uk Map 180/575473
BB **B** ✕ book first £12, 7pm S1 D4 T1 F1 Closed Xmas
Ⓥ Ⓑ Ⓓ⊛🍴🛏! ◆◆◆◆

● Croyde (Braunton)
SOUTH WEST COAST PATH
Combas Farm, Putsborough, EX33 1PH ☎ 01271 890398 (Mrs Gwen Adams)
Map 180/449396
BB **C** ✕ nearby S1 D2 T1 F/T2 Closed Xmas-Jan
Ⓑ Ⓓ⊛🍴 ◆◆◆

● Dartmouth
DARTMOOR
SOUTH WEST COAST PATH
🐾◀ Hill View House, 76 Victoria Road, TQ6 9DZ ☎ 01803 839372
(Suzanne White) www.hillviewdartmouth.co.uk Map 202/872512
BB **D** D3 T2 Closed Jan 🚌(Kingswear) Ⓑ Ⓓ⊛🛏! ◆◆◆◆Ⓖ

● Exeter
Park View Hotel, 8 Howell Road, EX4 4LG ☎ 01392 271772
www.parkviewexeter.co.uk Map 192/917933
BB **C** ✕ nearby S1 D7 T3 F2 Closed Xmas 🚌(Exeter Central)
Ⓑ Ⓓ⊛🍴🛏 ◆◆◆

The Old Mill, Mill Lane, EX2 8SG ☎ 01392 259977
Map 192/915903
BB **A** ✕ nearby S1 D1 T2 F1 🚌(Exeter St Davids)
Ⓥ Ⓓ⊛⊙ Wheelchair access.

● Exmouth
SOUTH WEST COAST PATH
Sholton Guest House, 29 Morton Road, EX8 1BA ☎ 01395 277318 (Ann Jones)
Map 192/999807
BB **B** ✕ nearby S1 D3 T2 F1 Closed Xmas 🚌(Exmouth) Ⓑ Ⓓ🛏
🐾◀ Clinton House, 41 Morton Road, EX8 1BA ☎ 01395 271969
(John Thorogood) www.clinton-house.com Map 192/999807
BB **B** ✕ nearby S1 D2 T1 F2 🚌(Exmouth) Ⓥ Ⓑ Ⓓ⊛🛏

● Galmpton (Kingsbridge)
SOUTH WEST COAST PATH

☆ 🐾◀ Burton Farmhouse & Garden Room Restaurant
TQ7 3EY ☎ 01548 561210 www.burtonfarm.co.uk Map 202/693403
BB **D** ✕ £18, 7-9pm S1 D4 T3 F6
Ⓥ Ⓑ Ⓓ⊛🍴🛏!🧺 ◆◆◆◆Ⓢ
Wheelchair access and facilities for disabled visitors.

A warm welcome and comfortable en-suite farmhouse accommodation with excellent home cooking. Direct access from the South West Coast Path through our own farmland. An abundance of other nature walks, green lanes and beautiful countryside to explore. Ideal base for walking holidays.

● Guineaford (Marwood)
SOUTH WEST COAST PATH
🐾◀ Highfield, EX31 4EA ☎ 01271 373779 (Mrs Carol Edwards)
www.guineaford.co.uk Map 180/551375
BB **C** ✕ nearby D1 Closed Dec-Jan
Ⓥ Ⓑ Ⓓ⊛🍴🛏🚗! See SC also.

● Halwill Junction (Holsworthy)
🐾◀ Market House, EX21 5TN ☎ 01409 221339 (Mrs Caroline Halliwell)
ctandf@aol.com Map 190/447990
BB **B** ✕ £12, 7pm D1 T1 Closed Xmas Ⓥ Ⓑ Ⓓ🍴🛏🧺

● Hartland (Bideford)
SOUTH WEST COAST PATH
🐾◀ West Titchberry Farm, Hartland Point, EX39 6AU ☎ 01237 441287
(Mrs Y Heard) Map 190/242272
BB **B** ✕ book first £12, 6:30pm D1 T1 F1 Ⓥ Ⓑ Ⓓ⊛🍴🛏🚗!

☆ Elmscott Farm
EX39 6ES ☎ 01237 441276 (Mrs Thirza Goaman)
Map 190/231215
BB **C** ✕ book first £12, 6pm D1 T1 F1 Closed Xmas
Ⓥ Ⓑ Ⓓ⊛🍴🛏🚗! ◆◆◆◆

Comfortable farmhouse, ideally situated on the South West Coast Path.
All rooms en-suite or with private facilities.
Beautiful coastal scenery.

☆ Gawlish Farm
EX39 6AT ☎ 01237 441320 (Mrs Jill George)
Map 190/256263
BB **B** ✕ book first £10, 6.30pm D1 T2 Closed Xmas
Ⓥ Ⓑ Ⓓ 🍳🛏🚗!🛁 ◆◆◆

You will be warmly
welcomed to this tastefully
furnished farmhouse.
Beautifully quiet
countryside on route to the
South West Way.

● Holne (Ashburton)
DARTMOOR
TWO MOORS WAY

Chase Gate Farm, TQ13 7RX ☎ 01364 631261 (Anne & David Higman)
www.chasegatefarm.com Map 202/716703
BB **B** D2 T1 Closed Xmas
Ⓑ Ⓓ 🍳🛏!🛁

● Holsworthy

☆ Leworthy Farmhouse
Pyworthy, EX22 6SJ ☎ 01409 259469 (Mrs Pat Jennings)
www.leworthyfarmhouse.co.uk Map 190/322012
BB **D** ✕ nearby D3 T2 F1
Ⓑ Ⓓ⊗ 🍳🛏🚗! ◆◆◆◆Ⓢ

Charming Georgian farmhouse in quiet backwater.
Beautifully prepared en-suite rooms. Ample fresh milk, teas, biscuits, pretty
bone china, fresh flowers, soft carpets and crisp bed linen.
A welcoming home with antiques, objets d'art and extensive collection of books,
poetry and glossy magazines. A peaceful guests' lounge with ticking clocks,
sparkling china, comfy sofas, old prints and Chinese carpets.
Have a scrumptious full English breakfast with buttery fried potatoes and
mushrooms, kippers, delicious local bacon and free-range eggs. Or choose
creamy organic porridge, yogurt, dried fruits and nuts, muesli, prunes and fresh
fruit salad.
Lovely coastal walks and quiet country lanes nearby.

● Honiton
The Crest, Moorcox Lane, EX14 9JU ☎ 01404 831419 (Mrs Suzanne Kidwell)
Map 192,193/220999
BB **C** ✕ £10.50, 6-7pm D1 T1 F1
Ⓥ Ⓑ Ⓓ⊗ 🍳🛏🛁 Wheelchair access.

● Hope Cove (Kingsbridge)
SOUTH WEST COAST PATH

☆ The Cottage Hotel
TQ7 3HJ ☎ 01548 561555
www.hopecove.com Map 202/676401
BB **D** ✕ book first £16.95, 7:30-8:30pm S10 D/T20 F5 Closed Jan
Ⓥ Ⓑ Ⓓ 🍳🛏🛁 ★★Ⓢ Price includes dinner!

The hotel enjoys a magnificent position
in this pretty and secluded fishing
village. By heritage coastline and
National Trust land. Ideally situated for
walks. Log fire in winter. Drying
facilities. Group rates available. Friendly
& efficient service. Good food & wine.

● Ilfracombe
SOUTH WEST COAST PATH

The Woodlands, Torrs Park, EX34 8AZ ☎ 01271 863098 (Mark O'Brien)
www.thewoodlands-hotel.co.uk Map 180/511472
BB **B** ✕ nearby S2 D6 T1 F1 Closed Xmas
Ⓑ Ⓓ⊗ 🍳🛏! ◆◆◆◆Ⓢ

Norbury House Hotel, Torrs Park, EX34 8AZ ☎ 01271 863888
(Andy Walters) www.norburyhousehotel.co.uk Map 180/511473
BB **C** ✕ book first £13, 6:30pm D2 F4
Ⓥ Ⓑ Ⓓ⊗ 🍳🛏🚗!🛁 ◆◆◆

Greyven House, 4 St James Place, EX34 9BH ☎ 01271 862505 (Trevor Jacobs)
www.ilfracombe-tourism.co.uk/greyvenhouse Map 180/521478
BB **B** ✕ nearby S1 D4 T3 F1 Closed Dec
Ⓥ Ⓑ Ⓓ⊗ 🍳🛏! ◆◆◆

● Ivybridge
DARTMOOR
TWO MOORS WAY

Hillhead Farm, Ugborough, PL21 0HQ ☎ 01752 892674
(Mrs Jane Johns) www.hillhead-farm.co.uk Map 202/674564
BB **C** ✕ nearby D2 T1 Closed Oct-Dec
Ⓑ Ⓓ⊗ 🍳🛏🚗!🛁 ◆◆◆◆Ⓢ

☆ Kevela
4 Clare Street, PL21 9DL ☎ 01752 893111 (Ray & May Dunn)
ray@kevela.co.uk Map 202/632559
BB **C** ✕ nearby D2 T1 〰(Ivybridge)
Ⓑ Ⓓ⊗ 🍳🛏!🛁

Ray and May offer you a warm welcome at Kevela, centrally situated in Ivybridge
close to all amenities and with easy access to Dartmoor, the coast and the
historical towns and villages of South Hams.
All rooms en-suite with TV and tea & coffee making facilities.
Full English breakfast.
Pubs and restaurants nearby. Parking.
B&B from £30 per person

● Kingsbridge
SOUTH WEST COAST PATH

Ashleigh House, Ashleigh Road, TQ7 1HB ☎ 01548 852893
(Nick & Jan Alen) www.ashleigh-house.co.uk Map 202/731439
BB **D** ✕ nearby D5 T1 F2 Closed Dec
Ⓥ Ⓑ Ⓓ⊗ 🛏🛁Ⓜ ◆◆◆

● Knowstone (South Molton)
TWO MOORS WAY
West Bowden Farm, EX36 4RP ☎ 01398 341224 (Mrs J Bray)
Map 181/833224
BB **C** ✕ book first £11, 6:30pm S1 D3 T2 F2 Closed Xmas
V B D 🐴🛁🚗!🏠 ◆◆◆

● Langtree (Great Torrington)
Tor View, 28 Fore Street, EX38 8NG ☎ 01805 601140 (Mrs Sheila Mears)
www.tarka-country.co.uk/torview Map 190/447156
BB **B** ✕ book first £11.50, 7-8pm S1 D1 T1
V B D ⊗ 🐴🛁🚗!🏠 Ⓜ

● Loddiswell (Kingsbridge)
SOUTH WEST COAST PATH
Blackwell Park, TQ7 4EA ☎ 01548 821230 (Mrs A Kelly)
anne.kelly@tiscali.co.uk Map 202/714517
BB **C** ✕ £10, 6:30pm S1 D1 T2 F2 Closed Nov-Mar
V B D 🐴🛁🏠

● Lydford (Okehampton)
DARTMOOR

☆ 🍴 **Lydford House**
EX20 4AU ☎ 01822 820347
www.lydfordhouse.com Map 201,191/517852
BB **C** ✕ nearby S2 D3 T2 F2
V B D 🐴🛁🏠 ◆◆◆◆

Set amidst the spectacular scenery of Dartmoor National Park near to Lydford Gorge, an ideal location for walking or cycling.
A warm relaxed atmosphere. Beautifully appointed, spacious rooms, licensed teamrooms, cycle hire and walks in every direction. Excellent local restaurants.

● Lynmouth
EXMOOR
SOUTH WEST COAST PATH & TWO MOORS WAY

☆ **Tregonwell & The Olde Sea-Captain's House**
1 Tors Road, EX35 6ET ☎ 01598 753369 (Mr & Mrs C & J Parker)
www.smoothhound.co.uk/hotels/tregonwl.html Map 180/727494
BB **C** ✕ nearby S1 D5 T1 F2 Closed Xmas & Jan
B D ⊗ 🐴🛁🚗!🏠 ◆◆◆

Awarded 'England's B&B of the Year'. Warm welcome guaranteed at the best place for you Exmoor ramblers. Our elegant Victorian riverside guesthouse is snuggled in wooded valleys, waterfalls, England's highest clifftops & most enchanting harbour. Pretty en-suite bedrooms with dramatic views. Log fires. Garaged parking. Group discounts.

☆ **Glenville House**
2 Tors Road, EX35 6ET ☎ 01598 752202 (Tricia & Alan Francis)
www.glenvillelynmouth.co.uk Map 180/727494
BB **B/C** ✕ nearby S1 D4 T1 Closed Dec-Feb
B D ⊗ 🐴🛁🚗!Ⓜ ◆◆◆◆

Elegant Victorian house in idyllic riverside setting. Lovely licensed B&B. Tastefully decorated bedrooms. Picturesque harbour and village. Dramatic Exmoor scenery & spectacular valley/coastal walks. Peaceful, tranquil, romantic - a very special place.

☆ **The Bath Hotel**
EX35 6EL ☎ 01598 752238 (Mrs S L Hobbs)
www.torslynmouth.co.uk Map 180/723496
BB **D** ✕ book first £18, 7-8:30pm S1 D10 T7 F4 Closed Dec-Jan
V B D ⊗ 🐴🛁🏠 ★★

Friendly, family-run two-star establishment with good facilities and excellent food. 22 bedrooms, all ensuite with TV, tea & coffee. Situated on edge of Exmoor, an ideal location for a walking holiday. Special group rates available.

☆ **River Lyn View**
26 Watersmeet Road, EX35 6EP ☎ 01598 753501 (Carol Sheppard)
www.riverlynview.com Map 180/725508
BB **B** ✕ nearby D4 T1
B D 🐴🛁🚗!🏠

River Lyn View offers comfortable B&B. Rooms are en-suite & overlook the East Lyn River situated on the edge of Exmoor near the picturesque harbour in Lynmouth with its spectacular coastal views. Ideal for walking holidays. Major credit cards accepted. Email: riverlynview@aol.com

● Lynton
EXMOOR
SOUTH WEST COAST PATH & TWO MOORS WAY
🍴 Lee House, 27 Lee Road, EX35 6BP ☎ 01598 752364
(Mike & Lesley Tucker) www.leehouselynton.co.uk Map 180/717495
BB **C** ✕ nearby D6 T2 F1 Closed Xmas
B D ⊗ 🐴🛁! ◆◆◆◆

☆ **The Denes**
15 Longmead, EX35 6DQ ☎ 01598 753573 (John McGowan)
www.thedenes.com Map 180/715495
BB **B/C** ✕ book first £13, 6:30-8pm D3 T2 FT/3 Closed Xmas
V B D ⊗ 🐴🛁🚗!🏠 ◆◆◆◆

Glorious place, Good food, Great value. An ideal base for exploring Exmoor or stop-over for SW Coast Path trekkers. Drying facilities. Car parking. Licensed. Evening meals. En-suites rooms available. From £20-26 pppn. Open all year. Major credit cards accepted.

☆ ▪ ◀ **Meadpool House**
Brendon, EX35 6PS ☎ 01598 741215 (Nigel & Vivienne Wood)
www.whatsonexmoor.co.uk/meadpool Map 180/771482
BB **B** ✗ nearby D2 TI Closed Xmas
Ⓑ Ⓓ ☺ 🍴🛏🚗 !

Luxury, smoke-free B&B on East Lyn river. ¼ mile walk to Lynmouth via wooded gorge. Upstream to open moor through 'Doone Valley'. Coast Path 2 miles, pub ¼ mile. Bedrooms (with TVs) are en-suite or with private bathroom. Lounge. From £20pppn.

▪ ◀ Sandrock Hotel, Longmead, EX35 6DH ☎ 01598 753307
(Len & Liz Gunn) www.thesandrockhotel.co.uk Map 180/715493
BB **D** ✗ £12, 6-9pm S2 D4 T3 F3
Ⓥ Ⓑ Ⓓ 🍴🛏🚗 !🅿 ★★

☆ **North Cliff Hotel**
North Walk, EX35 6HJ ☎ 01598 752357
www.northcliffhotel.co.uk Map 180/718497
BB **D** ✗ £14-£18, 6-10pm SI D7 T2 F4 Closed Jan
Ⓥ Ⓑ Ⓓ ☺ 🍴🛏🚗 !🅿 ★

Family run hotel on South West Coast Path, near Watersmeet, Lorna Doone Valley.
All rooms have a view across Lynmouth Bay and are en-suite.
Drying room. Restaurant/bar. Car Park. Open all year.

Croft House, Lydiate Lane, EX35 6HE ☎ 01598 752391
www.smoothhound.co.uk/hotels/crofthou.html Map 180/714494
BB **C** ✗ nearby S2 D5 T2 FI Ⓥ Ⓑ Ⓓ ☺ 🛏!

● Manaton (Newton Abbot)
    DARTMOOR
    TWO MOORS WAY

▪ ◀ Hazelcott B&B, TQ13 9UY ☎ 01647 221405 (Nigel Fisher)
www.dartmoordays.com Map 191/751822
BB **D** ✗ book first £17.50, 7:30pm D2 TI FI
Ⓥ Ⓑ Ⓓ ☺ 🍴🛏🚗 !🅿 ◆◆◆◆

● Morchard Bishop (Crediton)
    TWO MOORS WAY

Beech Hill Community, EX17 6RF ☎ 01363 877228
http://mysite.wanadoo-members.co.uk/beechhill Map 191/782086
BB **A** ✗ book first £5, 7pm TI F3 Closed Xmas
Ⓥ Ⓓ ☺ 🍴🛏!🅿

▪ ◀ Beggar's Roost, Fore Street, EX17 6NX ☎ 01363 877398
(Annie Hargreaves) www.stephenhargreaves.com Map 191/768076
BB **C** ✗ book first £13, 6-8pm DI Closed Dec ⋙(Morchard Road)
Ⓥ Ⓓ ☺ 🛏🚗 !🅿

● Moretonhampstead (Newton Abbot)
    DARTMOOR
    TWO MOORS WAY

Great Slon Combe Farm, TQ13 8QF ☎ 01647 440595 (Mrs Trudie Merchant)
www.greatsloncombefarm.co.uk Map 191/736862
BB **C** D2 TI Ⓥ Ⓑ Ⓓ 🍴🛏🚗 !🅿 ◆◆◆◆ Ⓢ

Little Wooston Farm, TQ13 8QA ☎ 01647 440551 (Jeanne Cuming)
jeannecuming@tesco.net Map 191/760887
BB **A** ✗ book first £6-8, 6:30-7pm SI DI FI Closed Xmas
Ⓥ Ⓓ 🍴🛏🚗 🅿 ◆◆◆

☆ **Cookshayes Country Guest House**
33 Court Street, TQ13 8LG ☎ 01647 440374 (Julie Saunders)
www.cookshayes.co.uk Map 191/751860
BB **B** ✗ book first £14, 6:30pm SI D5 TI FI
Ⓥ Ⓑ Ⓓ 🍴🛏!🅿 ◆◆◆

Beautiful mid-Victorian house set in large gardens on the edge of Dartmoor. Minutes away from village centre. Most rooms en-suite.
Email:cooksayes@aol.com

● Newton Abbot (Torquay)
▪ ◀ Branscombe House B&B, 48 Highweek Village, TQ12 1QQ
☎ 01626 356752 (Miles Opie)
www.branscombe-house.co.uk Map 191/845721
BB **D** ✗ nearby D2 TI ⋙(Newton Abbot)
Ⓑ Ⓓ ☺ 🍴🛏🚗 !

● Newton Popplford (Sidmouth)
    SOUTH WEST COAST PATH

Milestone, High ST., EX10 0DU ☎ 01395 568267
Map 192/081896
BB **C** ✗ nearby S2 DI T/DI
Ⓑ Ⓓ ☺ 🍴🛏🚗

● North Bovey
    DARTMOOR
    TWO MOORS WAY

▪ ◀ Lower Hookner Barn, TQ13 8RS ☎ 01647 221282 (Jenny Pryce-Davies)
lowerhookner@hotmail.com Map 191/714825
BB **B** ✗ book first £11, 7:30pm onwards DI TI FI Closed Xmas
Ⓥ Ⓑ Ⓓ ☺ 🍴🛏🚗 !🅿

● North Molton
Zeales, East Street, EX36 3JQ ☎ 01598 740356 (Martin & Stella Hickman)
www.zeales.co.uk Map 180/742297
BB **B** ✗ book first £10 D/F2 TI
Ⓥ Ⓑ Ⓓ ☺ 🍴🛏🚗

● Okehampton
    DARTMOOR

Northlake, Stockley, EX20 1QH ☎ 01837 53100 (Pam Jeffrey)
www.northlakedevon.co.uk Map 191/610953
BB **B** ✗ book first £8 SI DI TI Closed Xmas
Ⓥ Ⓑ Ⓓ ☺ 🍴🛏🚗 !🅿

● Ottery St Mary
▪ ◀ Fluxton Farm, EX11 1RJ ☎ 01404 812818 (Mrs E A Forth)
Map 192/086934
BB **C** ✗ nearby S2 D2 T3 Closed Xmas
Ⓑ Ⓓ 🛏🅿 ◆◆ Oct-May weekend stays only. Must be cat lovers!

● **Paignton**

SOUTH WEST COAST PATH

Culverden Hotel, 4 Colin Road, TQ3 2NR ☎ 01803 559786
www.culverdenhotel.co.uk Map 202/893614
BB **B** ✗ nearby S2 D2 T2 F2 ∿(Paignton)
Ⓥ Ⓑ ⊗ 🐾👤🏠 ◆◆◆

● **Plymouth**

SOUTH WEST COAST PATH

✖🍽️ Mount Batten Centre, 70 Lawrence Rd, Mount Batten, PL9 9SJ
☎ 01752 404567 www.mount-batten-centre.com Map 201/487532
BB **A-D** ✗ book first £up to £13, 5-9pm Closed Xmas ∿(Plymouth)
Ⓥ Ⓑ Ⓓ 🐾👤Ⓜ

George Guest House, 161 Citadel Road, The Hoe, PL1 2HU ☎ 01752 661517
www.accommodationplymouth.co.uk Map 201/478540
BB **B** ✗ nearby S1 D3 T1 F1 ∿(Plymouth)
Ⓥ Ⓑ Ⓓ 🐾👤🏠👤!🏠 ◆◆◆

☆ ✖🍽️ **Mariners Guest House**
11 Pier Street, West Hoe, PL1 3BS ☎ 01752 261778 (Jim Steven)
www.marinersguesthouse.co.uk Map 201/472538
BB **B** ✗ nearby S2 D4 T1 F1 ∿(Plymouth)
Ⓥ Ⓑ Ⓓ ⊗ 🐾👤! ◆◆◆

Attractive Victorian guesthouse situated 100 yards from the
seafront.
Central for local attractions.
Stroll through woods and grounds of Saltram House
overlooking the Plym Estuary.
Ideal base for exploring wild and picturesque Dartmoor.
Breathtaking scenery along coastal walks.

✖🍽️ The Rusty Anchor Guesthouse, 30 Grand Parade, West Hoe, PL1 3DJ
☎ 01752 663924 (Jan Taylor) Map 201/472536
BB **C** ✗ nearby D4 T1 F2 ∿(Plymouth)
Ⓥ Ⓑ Ⓓ ⊗ 🐾👤🏠

● **Ponsworthy (Newton Abbot)**

DARTMOOR
TWO MOORS WAY

Old Walls Farm, TQ13 7PN ☎ 01364 631222 (Mrs E Fursdon)
Map 191/701747
BB **B** S1 D1 T1 Closed Xmas
Ⓑ Ⓓ 🐾👤!🏠

● **Rackenford (Tiverton)**

EXMOOR
TWO MOORS WAY

✖🍽️ Creacombe Parsonage Farm, Creacombe, EX16 8EL ☎ 01884 881260
(Mrs C Poole) www.creacombe.com Map 181/820185
BB **B** ✗ book first £12.50, 6-8pm T2 F1 Closed Xmas
Ⓥ Ⓑ Ⓓ ⊗ 🐾👤🏠!🏠

● **Sampford Spiney (Yelverton)**

DARTMOOR

✖🍽️ Withill Farm, PL20 6LN ☎ 01822 853992 (Pam Kitchin)
withillfarm1@aol.com Map 201/548726
BB **B** ✗ nearby D2 T1 Closed Xmas
Ⓑ Ⓓ 🐾👤🏠 ! 🏠 See SC also.

● **Seaton**

SOUTH WEST COAST PATH

✖🍽️ Beach End, 8 Trevelyan Road, EX12 2NL ☎ 01297 23388 (Hilary Bevis)
Map 192/251899
BB **C** ✗ nearby D2 T1 Ⓥ Ⓑ Ⓓ ⊗ 👤!Ⓜ ◆◆◆◆Ⓢ

● **Shirwell (Barnstaple)**

The Spinney Guest House, EX31 4JR ☎ 01271 850282 (Mrs Janet Pelling)
www.thespinneyshirwell.co.uk Map 180/590370
BB **B/C** ✗ book first £15, 7pm S1 D2 T1 F1 Closed Xmas
Ⓥ Ⓑ Ⓓ ⊗ 👤🏠 ◆◆◆◆Ⓢ

● **Sidmouth**

SOUTH WEST COAST PATH

Canterbury House, Salcombe Road, EX10 8PR ☎ 01395 513373
(Mrs A Garton-Penaluna) cgh@eclipse.co.uk Map 192/127878
BB **B/C** ✗ book first £12, 6pm S1 D4 T2 F3 Closed Xmas
Ⓥ Ⓑ Ⓓ ⊗ 👤🏠 ◆◆◆

✖🍽️ Newland Guest House, Temple Street, EX10 9BA ☎ 01395 514155
Map 192/126881
BB **B** ✗ nearby S1 D3 T2 F2 Ⓥ Ⓑ Ⓓ ⊗ 🐾👤🏠!🏠

✖🍽️ Ryton Guest House, 52-54 Winslade Road, EX10 9EX ☎ 01395 513981
(Mrs G Bradnam) www.ryton-guest-house.co.uk Map 192/126885
BB **B** ✗ nearby S3 D1 T2 F4 Closed Dec-Jan
Ⓥ Ⓑ Ⓓ ⊗ 🐾👤🏠!🏠 ◆◆◆

☆ ✖🍽️ **Rose Cottage**
Coburg Road, EX10 8NF ☎ 01395 577179 (Jackie Cole)
www.rosecottage-sidmouth.co.uk Map 192/123874
BB **D** ✗ nearby D3 T1
Ⓥ Ⓑ ⊗ 🐾👤🏠 !

Cosy, characterful Grade II-listed cottage
with pretty garden available to guests. 200
yards from seafront, shops, bistros, theatre
and cinema.
Family home - children welcome. Each room
has TV and en-suite or private
bathroom. Non-smoking, parking available at request. Organic food used.

● **Slapton (Kingsbridge)**

SOUTH WEST COAST PATH

Old Walls, TQ7 2QN ☎ 01548 580516 (V J Mercer)
Map 202/823449 BB
B/C ✗ nearby S1 D2/F2 T1 Closed Xmas
Ⓥ Ⓑ Ⓓ ⊗ 🐾👤🏠!🏠Ⓜ

● **South Zeal (Okehampton)**

DARTMOOR

☆ **Poltimore Guest House**
EX20 2PD ☎ 01837 840209 (Ben & Diane Radford)
www.poltimore-southzeal.co.uk Map 191/652932
BB **D** ✗ nearby S1 D3 T2 Closed Xmas
Ⓑ Ⓓ 🐾👤🏠

Luxurious thatched guest house.
Log fire in own lounge. Set on the
northern edge of Dartmoor National
Park. Real ale pubs within easy
walking distance. Abundant wildlife
and fantastic walking. Painting and
navigation courses available.

Cawsandside, Throwleigh Road, EX20 2QD ☎ 01837 840353
(John Draper) draperjt@tinyworld.co.uk Map 191/657914
BB **C** ✗ book first £15, approx 7:30pm DI T2
Ⓥ Ⓑ Ⓓ ⊗ 🚗🛏 🚗 ! 🏛

● Sprytown (Lifton)

☆ **The Old Coach House at the Thatched Cottage**
PL16 0AY ☎ 01566 784224 (Paul & Cathy Fullegar)
www.theoldcoach-house.co.uk Map 201/412855
BB **D** ✗ nearby S4 DI T2 F3
Ⓥ Ⓑ Ⓓ ⊗ 🚗🛏 🚗 ! ◆◆◆ Wheelchair access.

Attractively converted 16th-century coach house offering spacious en-suite accommodation with TV & CD players, tea/coffee making facilities and individual access.

Situated in a quiet hamlet in the Tamar Valley on the Devon/Cornwall border.

Ideal base to explore the beauty of Dartmoor, Bodmin Moor and Lydford Gorge, or stop-over for coastal path trekking.

Full English, continental or vegetarian breakfast. Large private car park. Warm welcome from Cathy and Paul.

● Teignmouth
SOUTH WEST COAST PATH

Brunswick House, 5 Brunswick Street, TQ14 8AE ☎ 01626 774102
(Margrethe & Pete Hockings) margrethehockings@hotmail.com
Map 192/941727
BB **B/C** ✗ nearby SI D4 T/F3 FI 🚶(Teignmouth)
Ⓑ Ⓓ ⊗ 🚗🛏 🏛

● Tiverton

Bridge Guest House, 23 Angel Hill, EX16 6PE ☎ 01884 252804
www.smoothhound.co.uk/hotels/bridgegh.html Map 181/953125
BB **C** ✗ book first £16, 6:30-7pm S5 D2 TI F2 Closed Xmas
Ⓥ Ⓑ Ⓓ 🚗🛏 ◆◆◆

Angel Guest House, 13 St Peter Street, EX16 6NU ☎ 01884 253392
(Tony Evans) cerimar@eurobell.co.uk Map 181/954126
BB **B** ✗ nearby SI D3 TI F2 Ⓑ Ⓓ ⊗ 🚗🛏 ◆◆◆

● Torquay
SOUTH WEST COAST PATH

Westbourne Hotel, 106 Avenue Road, TQ2 5LQ ☎ 01803 292927
(Marjorie Riley) www.westbournehoteltorquay.co.uk Map 202/904646
BB **D** ✗ book first £13.50, 6-7pm SI D3 T2 F2 Closed Xmas-Jan 🚶(Torre)
Ⓥ Ⓑ Ⓓ ⊗ 🚗🛏 ! ◆◆◆◆

Headland View, 37 Babbacombe Downs, Babbacombe, TQ1 3LN
☎ 01803 312612 www.headlandview.com Map 202/926654
BB **C** ✗ nearby D6 Closed Dec-Jan 🚶(Torquay)
Ⓥ Ⓑ Ⓓ ⊗ 🚗🛏 🚗 ◆◆◆◆

Aries House, I Morgan Avenue, TQ2 5RP ☎ 01803 404926
arieshousetorquay@yahoo.co.uk Map 202/912643
BB **B** ✗ nearby S2 D2 T2 F2 🚶(Torquay) Ⓥ Ⓑ Ⓓ ⊗ 🚗🛏

☆ **Meadfoot Bay Hotel**
Meadfoot Sea Road, TQI 2LQ ☎ 01803 294722 (Tracey Tyerman)
www.meadfoot.com Map 202/926632
BB **D** ✗ book first £15, 7-7:30pm S3 D12 T5 FI Closed Dec-Feb
🚶(Torquay) Ⓥ Ⓑ 🚗🛏 ◆◆◆◆

This comfortable, quiet and friendly hotel is close to the harbour, beaches and local amenities. We are in an ideal location for exploring the South West Coast Path which is just 200 yards from the hotel as well as other local walks in Torbay and the surrounding area.
All bedrooms are en-suite with colour television and beverage making facilities. Towels and complimentary toiletries are provided.
Email: stay@meadfoot.com

● Upottery (Honiton)

Lower Luxton Farm, EX14 9PB ☎ 01823 601269 (Mrs Elizabeth Tucker)
www.lowerluxtonfarm.co.uk Map 192,193/217110
BB **B** ✗ book first £9, 7pm DI FI
Ⓥ Ⓑ Ⓓ ⊗ 🚗🛏 🚗 🏛

● Welcombe (Bideford)
SOUTH WEST COAST PATH

Cranham House, EX39 6ET ☎ 01288 331351 (Jennifer Jones)
www.cranhamhouse.co.uk Map 190/224192
BB **C** ✗ £15-£18.50, 6-8pm D2 Closed Xmas
Ⓥ Ⓑ Ⓓ ⊗ 🚗🚗 !

● West Alvington (Kingsbridge)

☆ **Youngcombe Farmhouse**
TQ7 3BE ☎ 01548 560147 (Sally & Michael Webb)
www.youngcombefarm.co.uk Map 202/720422
BB **C** SI DI TI FI Closed Xmas
Ⓥ Ⓑ Ⓓ ⊗ 🚗🛏 🚗 🏛

Charming traditional Devon farmhouse set in beautiful countryside, I mile from main road.
Tastefully decorated bedrooms. Lovely peaceful garden.
On 4 mile walk Salcombe/Kingsbridge, 5 miles from coastal path, 10 miles Dartmoor.

● West Buckland (Barnstaple)
MACMILLAN WAY WEST

Huxtable Farm, EX32 0SR ☎ 01598 760254 (Jackie & Antony Payne)
www.huxtablefarm.co.uk Map 180/665308
BB **D** ✗ book first £22, 7:30pm D3 TI F2 Closed Dec-Jan
Ⓥ Ⓑ Ⓓ ⊗ 🚗🛏 🚗 ! ◆◆◆Ⓢ

● Widecombe-in-the-Moor (Newton Abbot)
DARTMOOR
TWO MOORS WAY

Lower Blackaton, TQ13 7UB ☎ 01364 621369 (Judy Lomax)
www.lowerblackaton.co.uk Map 191/694780
BB **B** ✕ book first £10, 7:30pm S1 T2 F2 Closed June-Aug
Ⓥ Ⓑ Ⓓ ⊗ 🐾 🛏 ! 🛁 See SC also.

● Woolacombe
SOUTH WEST COAST PATH

Clyst House, Rockfield Road, EX34 7DH ☎ 01271 870220 (Ann Braund)
Map 180/455441
BB **C** ✕ nearby S1 D1 T1 F1 Closed Nov-Feb Ⓓ ⊗ 🐾 🛁

● Yealmpton
SOUTH WEST COAST PATH

☆ **Kitley House Hotel**
Kitley Estate, PL8 2NW ☎ 01752 881555
www.kitleyhousehotel.com Map 202/559514
BB **D** ✕ £30, 7-9pm S1 D9 T2 F7
Ⓥ Ⓑ Ⓓ 🐾 🛏 ! 🛁 ★★★

Historic country house set in 600 acres of private estate. Overlooks lake and private woodland. Very quiet with own walks. Dartmoor 15 mins—close to SW Coast Path. Range of bedrooms including suites, full restaurant and lounge service available. Extensive gardens and wildlife around house. Satellite TV and CD. All rooms en-suite with shower. Private car parking.

DORSET

● Abbotsbury (Weymouth)
SOUTH WEST COAST PATH & MACMILLAN WAY

Swan Lodge, DT3 4JL ☎ 01305 871249
Map 194/578852
BB **C** ✕ £7, 6-9:30pm D3 T2 Closed Xmas
Ⓥ Ⓑ Ⓓ 🐾 🛁 🛁 ◆◆◆

● Blandford Forum

▨🍽 Portman Lodge, Whitecliff Mill Street, DT11 7BP ☎ 01258 453727
www.portmanlodge.co.uk Map 194/884067
BB **C** ✕ book first £15, 7-9pm D2 T1 Closed Jan
Ⓥ Ⓑ ⊗ 🐾 🛁 🛏 ! Ⓜ ◆◆◆◆◆

● Bournemouth
NEW FOREST
SOUTH WEST COAST PATH

St Michaels Guest House, 42 St Michaels Road, Westcliff, BH2 5DY
☎ 01202 557386 (Mrs E Davies) www.stmichaelsfriendlyguesthouse.co.uk
Map 195/082910
BB **B** ✕ £6, 6pm S1 D2 T2 F1 Closed Xmas 🚍(Bournemouth)
Ⓥ Ⓓ 🐾 🛁 🛁

Devenshire Guest House, 40 St Michaels Road, BH2 5DY ☎ 01202 291610
(Mrs K Ferns) Map 195/082910
BB **B** ✕ nearby S1 D3 T2 F1 🚍(Bournemouth)
Ⓥ Ⓓ 🐾 🛁 🛁

● Bridport
SOUTH WEST COAST PATH & MONARCH'S WAY

☆ **Britmead House**
154 West Bay Road, DT6 4EG ☎ 01308 422941
www.britmeadhouse.co.uk Map 193/465912
BB **C** ✕ nearby D4 T2 F2 Closed Xmas
Ⓑ Ⓓ ⊗ 🐾 🛁 🛏 ! 🛁 ◆◆◆◆

An elegant Edwardian house, situated within walking distance of West Bay harbour and the SW Coast Path, part of the World Heritage Site. We offer comfortable en-suite accommodation with many thoughtful extras. Parking, non-smoking. Dogs welcome by arrangement.

☆ 🍽 **Eypes Mouth Country Hotel**
Eype, DT6 6AL ☎ 01308 423300 (Kevin & Glenis French)
www.eypesmouthhotel.co.uk Map 193/448914
BB **D** ✕ £23, 7-9pm S2 D12 T3 F1
Ⓥ Ⓑ Ⓓ 🐾 🛁 🛏 ! 🛁 ★★

The hotel nestles between the clifftops and downland that form the Heritage Coastline. Close to SW Coast Path, the hotel enjoys stunning seaviews, peace and tranquility, superb food using the best of local produce and offers a high standard of hospitality.

Fleet Cottage, 152 West Bay Road, DT6 4AZ ☎ 01308 458698
(Janice Warburton) janicewarburton@supanet.com Map 193/465915
BB **B** ✕ book first £7, 6:30pm D/S2 T1 F1 Closed Xmas
Ⓥ Ⓑ Ⓓ 🐾 🛁 🛏 🛁

Green Lane House, Dorchester Road, DT6 4LH ☎ 01308 422619
(Christine Prideaux) greenlanehouse@aol.com Map 193/483932
BB **B** ✕ book first £12 S1 D1 T1 F1 Closed Xmas
Ⓥ Ⓑ Ⓓ ⊗ 🐾 🛁 🛏

Saxlingham House, West Road, Symondsbury, DT6 6AA ☎ 01308 423629
(Valerie Nicholls)
http://members.freezone.co.uk/saxlingham/Saxlingham.htm Map 193/448930
BB **C** ✕ nearby D2 T1 Closed Dec-Feb
Ⓑ Ⓓ ⊗ 🛁 See SC also.

▨🍽 Eypeleaze Bed & Breakfast, 117 West Bay Road, DT6 4EQ
☎ 01308 423363 (Ann Walker) www.eypeleaze.co.uk Map 193/467912
BB **B** ✕ nearby T1
Ⓑ Ⓓ ⊗ 🐾 🛁 ! ◆◆◆◆Ⓢ

☆ ►═◄ **At Home**
134 West Bay Road, DT6 4AZ ☎ 01308 458880 (Linda Bane)
www.dorset-coast.co.uk Map 193/465914
BB **B/C** ✕ nearby D2 T1
Ⓥ Ⓑ Ⓓ ⊗ 🍴🛏🚗 ! 🏠 ◆◆◆Ⓦ

Family-run superior bed & breakfast,
en-suite with bath/shower.
Within walking distance of Bridport
market town, Jurassic Coast, SW Coast
Path and Monarch's Way. Excellent
English breakfast using local produce.
Check website for special offers.

►═◄ Highway Farm, West Road, DT6 6AE ☎ 01308 424321 (Pauline Bale)
www.highwayfarm.co.uk Map 116/443928
BB **D** ✕ book first £12, 7pm D1 T1 F1
Ⓥ Ⓑ Ⓓ ⊗ 🍴🛏🚗 ! ◆◆◆◆Ⓦ

● **Cerne Abbas (Dorchester)**
WESSEX RIDGEWAY
►═◄ Badger Hill, 11 Springfield, DT2 7JZ ☎ 01300 341698
(Patricia Hammett) Map 194/663014
BB **C** ✕ nearby D1 T1
Ⓑ Ⓓ ⊗ 🍴🛏🏠Ⓜ ◆◆◆◆

Abbots, 7 Long St, DT2 7JF ☎ 01300 341349 (Robert Lamb)
www.3lambs.com/abbots Map 194/665011
BB **D** ✕ nearby D2 T2 Closed Xmas
Ⓑ ⊗ 🍴🛏🚗 🏠

● **Charmouth (Bridport)**
SOUTH WEST COAST PATH
►═◄ Cliffend B&B, Higher Sea Lane, DT6 6BD ☎ 01297 561047
www.cliffend.org.uk Map 116/364931
BB **D** ✕ nearby D2 Closed Dec-Feb
Ⓑ Ⓓ ⊗ 🍴🛏🚗 ! ◆◆◆◆

● **Chideock (Bridport)**
SOUTH WEST COAST PATH & MONARCH'S WAY
►═◄ Frogmore Farm, DT6 6HT ☎ 01308 456159 (Mrs S Norman)
Map 193/434925
BB **C** ✕ book first £14, 7pm D1 T1 F1
Ⓥ Ⓑ Ⓓ ⊗ 🍴🛏🚗 ! 🏠

►═◄ Rose Cottage, Main Street, DT6 6JQ ☎ 01297 489994
(Sue & Mick Kelson) www.rosecottage-chideock.co.uk Map 193/423927
BB **C** ✕ nearby D1 T1 Closed Xmas
Ⓑ Ⓓ ⊗ 🍴🛏 ◆◆◆◆ Closed Sun-Tues.

►═◄ The Cabin, Duck Street, DT6 6JR ☎ 01297 489573 (Cathy Roberts)
www.chideock.co.uk Map 193/421927
BB **D** ✕ book first £7 D1
Ⓥ Ⓑ ⊗ 🍴🛏🚗 !

● **Donhead St Mary (Shaftesbury)**
WESSEX RIDGEWAY
►═◄ Cedar Lodge, 5 Dewey's Place, SP7 9LW ☎ 01747 829240
(Lorraine Dewey) www.cedarlodge.org.uk Map 183/902227
BB **C** ✕ nearby D2 T1 Closed Nov-Feb
Ⓥ Ⓑ Ⓓ ⊗ 🍴🛏🚗 ! ◆◆◆Ⓦ

● **Dorchester**

☆ ►═◄ **Churchview Guest House**
Winterbourne Abbas, DT2 9LS ☎ 01305 889296
www.churchview.co.uk Map 194/618905
BB **D** ✕ £15, 7pm S1 D4 T3 F1 Closed Xmas
Ⓥ Ⓑ Ⓓ 🍴🛏🚗 ! 🏠 ◆◆◆Ⓢ See Groups also.

Our beautiful 17th-century guest house
set in picturesque countryside makes an
ideal rambling base. Period dining room,
two lounges, licensed bar. Delicious
evening meals. Non-smoking. Groups are
our speciality. Call Michael & Jane Deller.
Email: stay@churchview.co.uk

►═◄ Cowden House, Fry's Lane, Godmanstone, DT2 7AG ☎ 01300 341377
(Tim Mills) www.cowdenhouse.co.uk Map 194/666970
BB **C** ✕ book first £15, 7:30pm D1 T2 F1 Closed Xmas
Ⓥ Ⓑ Ⓓ ⊗ 🍴🛏🚗 ! 🏠

►═◄ Aquila Heights, 44 Maiden Castle Road, DT1 2ES ☎ 01305 267145
(Joan Cox) www.aquilaheights.co.uk Map 194/683896
BB **C** ✕ nearby S2 D2 T2 F1 Closed Xmas ♨(Dorchester South)
Ⓥ Ⓑ Ⓓ ⊗ 🍴🛏 ◆◆◆ Wheelchair access.

● **Ibberton (Blandford Forum)**
WESSEX RIDGEWAY
Manor House Farm, DT11 0EN ☎ 01258 817349 (Mrs C Old)
Map 194/788077
BB **B** ✕ nearby D2 T1 Closed Xmas Ⓑ ⊗ 🍴🛏🏠

● **Langton Matravers (Swanage)**
SOUTH WEST COAST PATH
Kamloops, Haycrafts Lane, BH19 3EE ☎ 01929 439193 (Mr D V Joseph)
info@kamloops.co.uk Map 195/983792
BB **C/D** ✕ nearby D/T3 Closed Xmas
Ⓑ Ⓓ ⊗ 🍴🛏🚗 !

● **Lyme Regis**
SOUTH WEST COAST PATH, WESSEX RIDGEWAY & MONARCH'S WAY
Lucerne, View Road, DT7 3AA ☎ 01297 443752 (Owen Keith Lovell)
http://lymeregis.com/lucerne Map 193/338923
BB **C** S1 D3 T1 Closed Xmas Ⓑ ⊗ 🛏🚗 ★★★

The Orchard Country Hotel, Rousdon, DT7 3XW ☎ 01297 442972
(Mr P Wightman) www.orchardcountryhotel.com Map 193/296916
BB **D** ✕ book first £17.50, 7:15pm S1 D6 T4 Closed Dec-Feb
Ⓥ Ⓑ Ⓓ ⊗ 🍴🛏 ◆◆◆◆

Charnwood Guest House, 21 Woodmead Road, DT7 3AD ☎ 01297 445281
(Wayne & Ann Bradbury) www.lymeregisaccommodation.com
Map 193/339924
BB **C** ✕ nearby S1 D4 T2 F1 Closed Xmas Ⓑ Ⓓ ⊗ 🛏Ⓜ ◆◆◆◆

►═◄ Thatch, Uplyme Rd, DT7 3LP ☎ 01297 442212 (Frank & Wendy Rogers)
thatchbb@aol.com Map 193/335924
BB **C** ✕ nearby S1 D1 T1 Ⓑ Ⓓ ⊗ 🍴🛏🚗 ! 🏠 ◆◆◆◆

● **Norden (Wareham)**
Three Barrows Farm, BH20 5DU ☎ 01929 480797 (Mrs Valerie Bull)
Map 195/938841
BB **C** ✕ nearby D1 T1 F1 Closed Xmas Ⓑ Ⓓ ⊗ 🍴🛏🚗 ! 🏠

● Pimperne (Blandford Forum)
🚶🍴 The Old Bakery, Church Road, DT11 8UB ☎ 01258 455173
(John & Joyce Tanner) jjtanners@hotmail.com Map 195/905092
BB **B** ✕ book first £8, 7:30-8pm S1 D/T1 T1
Ⓥ Ⓑ Ⓓ ⊗ 🐾🛏️🚗!🏕️ ◆◆◆

● Poole
SOUTH WEST COAST PATH
The Laurels, 60 Britannia Road, BH14 8BB ☎ 01202 265861 (Mrs North)
www.thelaurelsbandb.freeservers.com Map 195/033913
BB **C** ✕ nearby S1 D1 T1 F1 🚶(Parkstone) Ⓑ Ⓓ🛏️

● Portesham (Weymouth)
SOUTH WEST COAST PATH
Lavender Cottage, 9 Malthouse Meadow, DT3 4NS ☎ 01305 871924
(Mrs Joan Haine) joanhaine@sagainternet.co.uk Map 194/599856
BB **B** ✕ nearby D1 T1 Closed Nov-Feb Ⓓ ⊗ 🛏️🚗!

🚶🍴 Bridge House, 13 Frys Close, DT3 4LQ ☎ 01305 871685 (Thea Alexander)
www.bridgehousebandb.co.uk Map 194/602858
BB **C** ✕ nearby D2 Closed Xmas
Ⓑ Ⓓ ⊗ 🛏️🚗 ◆◆◆◆

● Preston (Weymouth)
SOUTH WEST COAST PATH & MACMILLAN WAY
🚶🍴 Pebble Villa, 13 Enkworth Road, DT3 6JT ☎ 01305 837469 (Karina Hill)
www.pebblevilla.co.uk Map 194/693821
BB **D** ✕ nearby D1 Closed Dec-Jan 🚶(Weymouth)
Ⓥ Ⓑ Ⓓ ⊗ 🛏️🚗!

● Puddletown (Dorchester)
🚶🍴 Zoar House, DT2 8SR ☎ 01305 848498 (Mrs J Stephens)
Map 194/762942
BB **B** ✕ nearby S1 D1 T1 F1 Ⓑ Ⓓ ⊗ 🐾🛏️🏕️

● Seaborough (Beaminster)
MONARCH'S WAY & WESSEX RIDGEWAY
Seaborough Manor Farm, DT8 3QY ☎ 01308 868272 (Mrs V Barber)
www.seaboroughmanor.co.uk Map 193/431060
BB **C** ✕ book first £12, 6-8pm S1 D2 Closed Xmas
Ⓥ Ⓑ Ⓓ 🐾🛏️🚗!

● Sherborne
MACMILLAN WAY
🚶🍴 Honeycombe View, Lower Clatcombe, DT9 4RH ☎ 01935 814644
(Mrs D Bower) Map 183/637179
BB **B** ✕ nearby T1 Closed Xmas 🚶(Sherborne)
Ⓑ Ⓓ ⊗ 🛏️

● Shillingstone (Blandford Forum)
WESSEX RIDGEWAY
Pennhills Farm, Sandy Lane, Off Lanchards Lane, DT11 0TF ☎ 01258 860491
(Mrs Rosemary Watts) Map 194/819102
BB **B** D/F1 T/S1 Closed Xmas
Ⓑ Ⓓ ⊗ 🐾🛏️🚗!🏕️ ◆◆◆

● Sturminster Newton
Newton House, DT10 2DQ ☎ 01258 472783 (Margie Fraser)
carolinepass@lineone.net Map 194/783135
BB **C** ✕ nearby S2 D2 T1 Closed Xmas
Ⓑ Ⓓ ⊗ 🐾!

Northwood Cottages, 2 Northwood Cottages, Manston, DT10 1HD
☎ 01258 472666 (Jonathan & Poppy Sewell)
www.northwoodcottages.co.uk Map 183/812170
BB **D** ✕ book first £16.50, 7pm S2 D2 Closed Xmas
Ⓥ Ⓑ Ⓓ ⊗ 🐾🛏️ ◆◆◆◆

● Swanage
SOUTH WEST COAST PATH
Hermitage Guesthouse, 1 Manor Road, BH19 2BH ☎ 01929 423014
(Susan Pickering) www.hermitage-online.co.uk Map 195/031785
BB **B** ✕ nearby D2 T1 F4 Closed Jan Ⓓ ⊗ 🛏️🏕️ Ⓜ

☆ **The Limes Hotel**
48 Park Road, BH19 2AE ☎ 01929 422664
www.limeshotel.net Map 195/033783
BB **D** ✕ nearby S3 D2 T4 F3
Ⓑ Ⓓ ⊗ 🐾🛏️🚗!🏕️ ◆◆◆

Swanage-Just off Coast Path.
Close to town and the beach.
Wonderful for walking.
Car park, bar, laundry.
Open all year for B&B.
Families, groups and pets are welcome.
Website: www.limeshotel.net

Sandhaven, 5 Ulwell Rd, BH19 1LE ☎ 01929 422322 (Janet Foran)
Map 195/030798
BB **C** ✕ nearby S1 D4 T2 F2 Closed Xmas
Ⓥ Ⓑ Ⓓ 🐾🛏️🏕️ ◆◆◆

Perfick Piece, Springfield Road, BH19 1HD ☎ 01929 423178 (Mrs Elaine Hine)
www.perfick-piece.co.uk Map 195/028788
BB **B** ✕ book first £8.50, 6pm S1 D1 T1 F1
Ⓥ Ⓑ Ⓓ 🐾🛏️ ◆◆◆ Evening meals in winter only.

🚶🍴 Sandringham Hotel, 20 Durlston Rd, BH19 2HX ☎ 01929 423076
(Mr & Mrs T Silk) www.smoothhound.co.uk/hotels/sandringham.html
Map 195/033782
BB **D** ✕ book first £15 (groups only), 6:30-7pm S2 D3 T2 F4 Closed Xmas
Ⓥ Ⓑ 🐾🛏️🚗!🏕️ ◆◆◆ See Groups also.

Beachway Private Hotel, 19 Ulwell Road, BH19 1LF ☎ 01929 423077
(Mrs Helen Holt) beachway.19ulwellroad@fsmail.net Map 195/030799
BB **B** ✕ nearby S2 D2 T2 F2 Ⓥ Ⓑ Ⓓ 🐾🛏️🛏️

Bella Vista Hotel, 14 Burlington Road, BH19 1LS ☎ 01929 422873
(Deirdre McAlpin) www.bellavista-hotel.co.uk Map 195/032800
BB **D** ✕ nearby D4 T2 F3 Closed Nov-Feb
Ⓥ Ⓑ Ⓓ ⊗ 🐾🛏️🏕️ ◆◆◆◆ Wheelchair access.

Danesfort Hotel, 3 Highcliffe Road, BH19 1LW ☎ 01929 424224
(Mrs Hilary Anderson) www.danesforthotel.co.uk Map 195/031798
BB **D** ✕ book first £15, 7pm S1 D2 T2 F3
Ⓥ Ⓑ Ⓓ 🐾🛏️🚗!

The Oxford, 3-5 Park Road, BH19 2AA ☎ 01929 422247 (Robin Creed)
www.oxfordhotelswanage.co.uk Map 195/032784
BB **C** ✕ nearby S2 D6 T1 F3 Ⓥ Ⓑ ⊗ 🐾🛏️ ◆◆◆

● Sydling St Nicholas (Dorchester)
WESSEX RIDGEWAY
City Cottage, DT2 9NX ☎ 01300 341300 (Mrs J Wareham)
Map 194/632994
BB **B** ✕ nearby S1 D1 Closed Xmas Ⓓ 🐾

Magiston Farm, DT2 9NR ☎ 01300 320295 (Mrs Barraclough)
Map 194/637967
BB **B** ✕ book first £12, 7pm S1/2 D1 T3 Closed Xmas
Ⓥ Ⓑ 🛏️🍴🛁♨️ ◆◆◆

🍴🛏️ Hazel Cottage, 1 Waterside Walk, DT2 9PJ ☎ 01300 341618
(Penny & Charles Cordy) www.hazelcottagedorset.co.uk Map 194/633995
BB **D** ✕ nearby D/T1
Ⓥ Ⓑ Ⓓ 🍴🛏️🛁 ◆◆◆◆Ⓢ

● Tarrant Launceston (Blandford)
🍴🛏️ Ramblers Cottage, DT11 8BY ☎ 01258 830528
www.ramblerscottage.co.uk Map 195/943094
BB **D** ✕ nearby D3
Ⓥ Ⓑ Ⓓ 🍴🛏️🛁♨️!🍴 ◆◆◆◆

● Wareham
Ashcroft, 64 Furzebrook Road, Stoborough, BH20 5AX ☎ 01929 552392
(Mr & Mrs Cake) www.ashcroft-bb.co.uk Map 195/929850
BB **C** ✕ nearby S1 D1 T1 F1 Closed Xmas ♨️(Wareham)
Ⓑ Ⓓ 🍴🛏️🛁♨️ ◆◆◆◆

🍴🛏️ Hyde Cottage, Furzebrooke Rd, Stoborough, BH20 5AX ☎ 01929 553344
(D & J Bryer) hydecottbb@yahoo.co.uk Map 195/927853
BB **B** ✕ book first £10, 6:30-7:30pm S1 D1 T1 F2 Closed Xmas
♨️(Wareham) Ⓥ Ⓑ Ⓓ 🍴🛏️🛁♨️!🍴

🍴🛏️ Birchfield, 2 Drax Ave, BH20 4DJ ☎ 01929 552462 (Diana Hutton)
www.birchfieldbedandbreakfast.co.uk Map 195/922885
BB **B** ✕ nearby S1 D1 T1 Closed Dec-Jan ♨️(Wareham)
Ⓑ Ⓓ 🍴🛏️🛁♨️!

● Weymouth
SOUTH WEST COAST PATH
🍴🛏️ Hotel Rembrandt, 12-18 Dorchester Rd, DT4 7JU ☎ 01305 764000
www.hotelrembrandt.co.uk Map 194/679805
BB **D** ✕ £12.50-£14.50, 6:30-9:15pm S14 D29 T24 F8 Closed Xmas
♨️(Weymouth) Ⓥ Ⓑ Ⓓ 🍴🛏️🛁Ⓜ ★★★

Kimberley Guest House, 16 Kirtleton Avenue, DT4 7PT ☎ 01305 783333
(Ken & Ann Jones) Kenneth.Jones@btconnect.com Map 194/679802
BB **B** ✕ book first £7.50, 6pm S2 D6 T1 F2 Closed Xmas ♨️(Weymouth)
Ⓥ Ⓑ Ⓓ 🍴🛏️🛁! ◆◆◆

🍴🛏️ Cunard Guest House, 45/46 Lennox Street, DT4 7HB ☎ 01305 771546
(Mr & Mrs Harris) www.cunardguesthouse.co.uk Map 194/681798
BB **B/C** ✕ nearby S2 D5 T2 F1 ♨️(Weymouth)
Ⓑ Ⓓ 🍴🛏️🛁♨️!🍴Ⓜ ◆◆◆

🍴🛏️ Harbour Lights Guesthouse, 20 Buxton Rd, DT4 9PJ ☎ 01305 783273
(Mrs Diane Quick) http://harbourlights-weymouth.co.uk Map 194/672779
BB **C** ✕ nearby S2 D5 T1 F2 Closed Nov-Feb ♨️(Weymouth)
Ⓥ Ⓑ Ⓓ 🍴🛏️🛁 ◆◆◆◆

🍴🛏️ Channel View Guest House, 10 Brunswick Terrace, DT4 7RW
☎ 01305 782527 (Martin & Alison Weller) www.channelviewweymouth.co.uk
Map 194/682799
BB **C** ✕ nearby S2 D3 T1 F1 Closed Xmas ♨️(Weymouth)
Ⓑ Ⓓ 🍴🛁! ◆◆◆◆

🍴🛏️ Greenwood Guest House, 1 Holland Rd, DT4 0AL ☎ 01305 775626
(Sharon Arnold) www.greenwoodguesthouse.co.uk Map 194/674793
BB **C** ✕ nearby D3 T2 F1 Closed Xmas ♨️(Weymouth)
Ⓑ Ⓓ 🍴🛏️🛁♨️!🍴

🍴🛏️ Galway Guest House, 7 Abbotsbury Road, DT4 0AD ☎ 01305 783319
(Mrs E Wilcox) lynwlc@aol.com Map 194/674792
BB **B** ✕ nearby S1 D2 T1 F3 Closed Dec ♨️(Weymouth)
Ⓥ Ⓓ 🍴🛏️🛁♨️!

St John's Guesthouse, 7 Dorchester Road, DT4 7JR ☎ 01305 775523
(Mrs Jan Massey) www.stjohnsguesthouse.co.uk Map 194/681800
BB **C** ✕ nearby D7 T2 F2 Closed Xmas ♨️(Weymouth)
Ⓥ Ⓑ 🍴🛏️ ◆◆◆ Wheelchair access.

Weymouth Sands, 5 The Esplanade, DT4 8EA ☎ 01305 839022
www.weymouthsands.co.uk Map 194/682788
BB **C** S3 D4 T2 ♨️(Weymouth) Ⓥ Ⓑ 🍴🛁🛏️

☆ 🍴🛏️ **Old Harbour View**
12 Trinity Road, DT4 8TJ ☎ 01305 774633 (Peter & Anna Vincent)
Map 194/678786
BB **D** ✕ nearby D2 Closed Xmas ♨️(Weymouth)
Ⓥ Ⓑ Ⓓ 🍴🛏️🛁

Idyllic Georgian harbourside townhouse, offering two charming double bedrooms, with harbourside restaurants & pubs on its doorstep. Ferries to Jersey & Guernsey. This B&B sits on the Jurassic Coastal Pathway, an ideal base to explore the amazing prehistoric coastline.

● Winterborne Kingston
🍴🛏️ West Acres, West Street, DT11 9AT ☎ 01929 471293 (Mr & Mrs Jenkins)
www.westacres-bedandbreakfast.co.uk Map 194/854976
BB **B** ✕ book first £10, 7:30pm D1 T1 F1 Closed Xmas
Ⓥ Ⓓ 🍴🛏️🛁♨️!🍴

GLOUCESTERSHIRE

● Blockley (Moreton-in-Marsh)
MONARCH'S WAY & HEART OF ENGLAND WAY
The Malins, 21 Station Road, GL56 9ED ☎ 01386 700402
www.chippingcampden.co.uk/themalins.htm Map 151/169354
BB **B** ✕ nearby D2 T2 Ⓑ Ⓓ 🍴🛏️🛁♨️! ◆◆◆◆

🍴🛏️ Grange Cottage B&B, Mill Lane, GL56 9HT ☎ 01386 700251
(Guy Heitmann) ramblers@garden-designer.biz Map 151/163347
BB **C** ✕ book first £12 D1 T1
Ⓥ Ⓑ Ⓓ 🍴🛏️🛁♨️!🍴

● Brookthorpe (Gloucester)
COTSWOLD WAY

☆ 🍴🛏️ **Brookthorpe Lodge**
Stroud Road, GL4 0UQ ☎ 01452 812645 (Robert & Diana Bailey)
www.brookthorpelodge.demon.co.uk Map 162/835128
BB **C** ✕ book first £13.95, until 7pm S3 D2 T3 F2 Closed Xmas
Ⓥ Ⓑ Ⓓ 🍴🛏️🛁♨️!🍴 ◆◆◆

Elegant Georgian house set in lovely countryside at the foot of the Cotswold escarpment between Gloucester & Stroud. Family run, traditional service and delicious breakfasts. Excellent walking country & ideal base for Cotswolds, Cheltenham and Bath. Good access to M5.

● Cam (Dursley)
COTSWOLD WAY

☆ **Foresters**
31 Chapel Street, GL11 5NX ☎ 01453 549996 (Mrs Victoria Jennings)
www.foresters-inn.co.uk Map 162/750002
BB **C** ✗ book first £10-14, 6-8:30pm D2 T2 F1 ⋙(Cam & Dursley)
Ⓥ Ⓑ Ⓓ ⊗ ♨ ♿ ♨ ♨ ◆◆◆◆

18th-century cosy former village inn with pretty walled garden. Spacious en-suite beamed bedrooms and visitor lounge with open fire and central heating. Drying facilities available.

Excellent walking on our doorstep and a wealth of attractions/villages and cities to visit: Westonbirt, Slimbridge, Bath, Cotswold Way, Berkeley Castle, Gloucester, Bristol, Cheltenham, Tetbury.
Close to Jct 13/14 M5. Dogs welcome by arrangement.
10% reduction for 7 nights stay. Discounts for 2 nights or more.
Colour TVs/tea/coffee facilities. 4 poster-beds/2 twins.

● Charlton Kings (Cheltenham)
COTSWOLD WAY

☆ ⋘ **Charlton Kings Hotel**
London Road, GL52 6UU ☎ 01242 231061
www.charltonkingshotel.co.uk Map 163/977201
BB **D** ✗ £18-£20, 7-9pm S2 D5 T5 F1
Ⓥ Ⓑ Ⓓ ♨ ♿ ♨ ★★★

Ideally situated on edge of town, ½ mile from Cotswold Way. All rooms beautifully refurbished with bath/shower, most have views of the Cotswold Hills. Set in an acre of gardens, ample parking. Restaurant open every night. Conde Nast Johansens Recommended.
enquiries@charltonkingshotel.co.uk.

22 Ledmore Road, GL53 8RA ☎ 01242 526957 (Geraldine White)
www.cotswoldstudio.co.uk Map 163/967207
BB **B** ✗ nearby S1 D1 T1 Closed Xmas ⋙(Cheltenham)
Ⓑ Ⓓ ⊗ ♨ ♿ ♨ ! Ⓜ

California Farm, Capel Lane, GL54 4HQ ☎ 01242 244746
Map 163/023196
BB **C** ✗ book first £12-£15, 7pm S1 D2 T1 Closed Xmas
Ⓥ Ⓑ Ⓓ ⊗ ♨ ♿ ♨ !

● Chedworth (Cheltenham)
MONARCH'S WAY & MACMILLAN WAY

⋘ The Vicarage, GL54 4AA ☎ 01285 720392 (George & Pattie Mitchell)
canongeorgemitchell@btinternet.com Map 163/052118
BB **B** ✗ nearby S1 T1 Ⓑ Ⓓ ⊗ ♨ ♿ ♨ ◆◆◆

● Chipping Campden
COTSWOLD WAY & HEART OF ENGLAND WAY

Weston Park Farm, Dovers Hill, GL55 6UW ☎ 01386 840835
(Mrs J Whitehouse) www.cotswoldcottages.uk.com Map 151/130390
BB **C** ✗ nearby D1 F1 Closed Xmas
Ⓑ Ⓓ ♨ ♿ ♨ ! ◆◆◆ See SC also.

⋘ Lygon Arms Hotel, High Street, GL55 6HB ☎ 01386 840318
www.lygonarms.co.uk Map 151/153394
BB **D** ✗ book first £6-£20, 6-10pm S2 D/T5 T2 F2 Closed Xmas
Ⓥ Ⓑ Ⓓ ♨ ♿ ♨ ! ♨ ◆◆◆◆

The Old Bakehouse, Lower High Street, GL55 6DZ ☎ 01386 840979
(Sarah Drinkwater) oldbakehouse@chippingcampden-cotswolds.co.uk
Map 151/150392
BB **C/D** ✗ nearby D3 T1 F1 Closed Xmas
Ⓑ Ⓓ ♨ ♿ !

Frances Cottage, Lower High St, GL55 6DY ☎ 01386 840894 (Jill Slade)
www.visitcotswolds.co.uk/francescottage.htm Map 151/147390
BB **C/D** ✗ nearby D1 T1 Closed Dec-Feb
Ⓑ Ⓓ ⊗ ♨ ♿ !

● Chipping Sodbury
MONARCH'S WAY & COTSWOLD WAY

The Moda Hotel, 1 High St, BS37 6BA ☎ 01454 312135 (Jo Macarthur)
www.modahotel.com Map 172/726822
BB **D** ✗ nearby S4 D4 T1 F1 Closed Xmas ⋙(Yate)
Ⓑ Ⓓ ♨ ♿ ♨ ♨ ◆◆◆◆

● Cirencester
MONARCH'S WAY

Royal Agricultural College, GL7 6JS ☎ 01285 652531 (Conference Department)
www.rac.ac.uk/ Map 163/004011
BB **B** ✗ book first £19, 7pm S12 T7 Closed Xmas
Ⓥ Ⓑ Ⓓ ♨ ♿ ★★★

● Clearwell (Coleford)
WYE VALLEY WALK

☆ ⋘ **Tudor Farmhouse Hotel**
High Street, GL16 8JS ☎ 01594 833046
www.tudorfarmhousehotel.co.uk Map 162/573080
BB **D** ✗ £20, 7-9pm S6 D12 T2 F2 Closed Xmas
Ⓥ Ⓑ Ⓓ ♨ ♿ ♨ ! ♨ ★★★

A cosy 13th-century stone built hotel with 2 AA Rosettes restaurant in the historic & pretty village of Clearwell in the Forest of Dean is the ideal setting for a relaxed or active holiday. Near the Wye Valley Walk & Offa's Dyke with walking also available from the hotel.
All rooms en-suite with some having jacuzzi baths and four-poster beds.
Drying room & cycle storage available. Pets welcome.

● Cleeve Hill (Cheltenham)
COTSWOLD WAY
Heron Haye, Petty Lane, GL52 3PW ☎ 01242 672516
(Edward Saunders) dick.whittamore@virgin.net Map 163/987273
BB **B** ✕ nearby S1 D2 Closed 1-12 Ⓓ ⊛ 🐾 ! 🐾

● Cold Ashton (Bristol)
COTSWOLD WAY
Toghill House Farm, BS30 5RT ☎ 01225 891261 (D Bishop)
www.toghillhousefarm.co.uk Map 172/731724
BB **D** ✕ nearby D/S5 T/S3 F/S3 Ⓑ Ⓓ ⊛ 🐾 👶 🐾 ◆◆◆◆

● Dursley
COTSWOLD WAY
☛◀ 7 Prospect Place, off May Lane, GL11 4JL ☎ 01453 543445
(Mrs Cecilia Boyle) ceciliaboyle@hotmail.com Map 162/755980
BB **B** ✕ book first £10.50-£12.50, 8pm S1 D1 T1 Closed Xmas
▲▲(Cam, Dursley) Ⓥ Ⓓ 🐾 👶 🚗 ! 🐾

● English Bicknor (Coleford)
WYE VALLEY WALK
☛◀ Dryslade Farm, GL16 7PA ☎ 01594 860259 (Mrs Daphne Gwilliam)
www.drysladefarm.co.uk Map 162/579149
BB **D** ✕ nearby D1 T1 F1 Closed Xmas
Ⓑ Ⓓ ⊛ 🐾 👶 🚗 ! 🐾 ◆◆◆◆

● Fairford
THAMES PATH
☛◀ Kempsford Manor, GL7 4EQ ☎ 01285 810131
www.kempsfordmanor.co.uk Map 163/158969
BB **D** ✕ book first £12.50, 7:30-8:30pm S2 D2 F1
Ⓥ Ⓑ Ⓓ ⊛ 🐾 👶 🚗 🐾 ◆◆◆

● Guiting Power
Guiting Guest House, GL54 5TZ ☎ 01451 850470 (Barbara Millar)
www.guitingguesthouse.com Map 163/099245
BB **D** ✕ book first £25, 7pm S1 D6 T1 F1 Closed Xmas
Ⓥ Ⓑ Ⓓ ⊛ 🐾 👶 🚗 ! 🐾 ◆◆◆◆◆Ⓢ

● Hailes (Cheltenham)
COTSWOLD WAY & HEART OF ENGLAND WAY
☛◀ Home Orchard Cottage, Salters Lane, GL54 5PB ☎ 01242 604894
(Louisa & John Davison) www.homeorchardcottage.co.uk Map 150/048301
BB **C** ✕ book first £10, 7pm D1 T1 Ⓥ Ⓓ ⊛ 🐾 👶 🐾

● Hasfield (Gloucester)
SEVERN WAY
☛◀ Rural Cottage B&B, Rust's Meadow, Hasfield Road, GL19 4LL
☎ 01452 700814 (Liz Dawson) Map 162/809279
BB **B** ✕ book first £7.50 D1 T1 Ⓥ Ⓑ Ⓓ ⊛ 🐾 🚗 ! 🐾

● King's Stanley (Stonehouse)
COTSWOLD WAY
Old Chapel House, Broad Street, GL10 3PN ☎ 01453 826289 (Jean Hanna)
www.geocities.com/bandbinuk Map 162/813033
BB **B** ✕ book first £6 upwards, 6:30-7:30pm S2 D1 T1 F1 Closed Xmas
▲▲(Stonehouse) Ⓥ Ⓑ Ⓓ 🐾 👶 !

☛◀ Vally Views, 12 Orchard Close, Middleyard, GL10 3QA ☎ 01453 827458
(Mrs Pam White) Map 162/819032
BB **C** ✕ book first £5+, 7pm D1 T1 Closed Xmas ▲▲(Stonehouse)
Ⓥ Ⓑ Ⓓ ⊛ 🐾 👶

● Lechlade
THAMES PATH
Cambrai Lodge, Oak Street, GL7 3AY ☎ 01367 253173 (Mr John Titchener)
Map 163/214998
BB **C** ✕ nearby S2 D3 T2 Ⓑ Ⓓ ⊛ 🐾 👶 🐾 ◆◆◆◆Ⓢ

☛◀ Leventen House, High St, GL7 3AD ☎ 01367 252592 (Ms Elizabeth Reay)
emreay@aol.com Map 163/212995
BB **D** ✕ nearby S1 D1 Closed Xmas Ⓑ Ⓓ ⊛ 👶

● Little Sodbury (Chipping Sodbury)
COTSWOLD WAY
New Crosshands Farm, BS37 6RJ ☎ 01454 316366 (Mrs Deborah Snell)
debsnell@tiscali.co.uk Map 172/761826
BB **C** ✕ book first £10-£15, 7:30pm S3 D3 T3 F1 Closed Xmas
Ⓥ Ⓑ ⊛ 🐾 🚗 !

● Long Newnton (Tetbury)
MONARCH'S WAY
☛◀ Church Farm, GL8 8RS ☎ 01666 502352 (Mrs Angela Tucker)
meg.tucker@virgin.net Map 173,163/910927
BB **C** ✕ book first £12.50, 7-9pm D2 T1
Ⓥ Ⓑ Ⓓ ⊛ 🐾 👶 🚗 ! 🐾

● Mitcheldean
☛◀ Gunn Mill House, Lower Spout Lane, GL17 0EA ☎ 01594 827577
(David Lucas) www.gunnmillhouse.co.uk Map 162/674159
BB **C/D** ✕ book first £15.50, 7pm D4 T2 F1
Ⓥ Ⓑ Ⓓ ⊛ 🐾 👶 🚗 ! 🐾 ◆◆◆◆Ⓢ

● Naunton (Cheltenham)
☛◀ Foxhill B&B, Old Stow Road, GL54 5RL ☎ 01451 850496 (Sue Guyatt)
www.smoothhound.co.uk/hotels/foxhillnaunton Map 163/099232
BB **D** D2 T1 F1 Ⓥ Ⓑ Ⓓ ⊛ 🐾 👶 🚗 ! 🐾 ◆◆◆◆

● Newland (Coleford)
WYE VALLEY WALK
☛◀ Tan House Farm, GL16 8NQ ☎ 01594 832222 (Peter Chamberlain)
christie.arno3@virgin.net Map 162/552091
BB **C** ✕ nearby S1 D3 T1 Closed Xmas
Ⓑ Ⓓ ⊛ 🐾 👶 🚗 ! 🐾 ◆◆◆

● North Nibley (Dursley)
COTSWOLD WAY

☆ **Nibley House**
GL11 6DL ☎ 01453 543108 (Diana A Eley)
john@eley7143.freeserve.co.uk Map 162/737958
BB **C** ✕ nearby D2 T2 F1 Closed Xmas
Ⓥ Ⓑ Ⓓ ⊛ 🐾 👶 ! 🐾

Relax... Splendid views.
Relax... 2½ acres of garden.
Relax... 400 years of history.
Relax... Hospitality.
Relax... Where to stay on the
Cotswold Way?
Relax... You've found it.

Burrows Court, Nibley Green, GL11 6AZ ☎ 01453 546230 (Peter Rackley)
www.burrowscourt.co.uk Map 162/732967
BB **D** D3 T2 F1 Closed Jan-Feb Ⓥ Ⓑ Ⓓ ⊛ 🐾 👶 🚗 🐾

SOUTH WEST

● **Old Sodbury (Bristol)**
MONARCH'S WAY & COTSWOLD WAY

Denison Cottage, Combs End, BS37 6SQ ☎ 01454 311510
(Mrs Susan Holbrook) Map 172/754806
BB **B** ✕ nearby TI Closed Xmas D ⊗ 🐾🛁🚗❗

● **Painswick (Stroud)**
COTSWOLD WAY

🔹🛏 Skyrack, The Highlands, GL6 6SL ☎ 01452 812029 (Wendy Hodgson)
www.painswick.co.uk/skyrack Map 162/868105
BB **C** ✕ nearby S2 D/FI T/FI Closed Xmas
B D ⊗ 🐾🛁🚗❗🏕 ◆◆◆

Orchard House, 4 Court Orchard, GL6 6UU ☎ 01452 813150
(Mrs Barbara Harley) www.painswick.co.uk Map 162/866095
BB **B/C** ✕ nearby DI TI Closed Xmas
B ⊗ 🐾🛁🚗❗Ⓜ

The Falcon Inn, New Street, GL6 6UN ☎ 01452 814222 (Fiona Layfield)
www.falconinn.com Map 162/866097
BB **D** ✕ book first £9, 7-9:30pm D4 T4 F4
V B D 🐾🛁🚗❗ ★★

🔹🛏 Meadowcote, Stroud Road, GL6 6UT ☎ 01452 813565 (Mr & Mrs A Lock)
Map 162/865095
BB **C** ✕ nearby S2 D2 Closed Dec-Feb B D ⊗ 🐾🛁🚗 ◆◆◆◆

Cardynham House, The Cross, GL6 6TX ☎ 01452 814006 (John Paterson)
www.cardynham.co.uk Map 162/868098
BB **D** ✕ book first £24.50, 7pm onwards D6 F3
V B 🛁 ◆◆◆◆

🔹🛏 Wren's Nest, 3 Painswick Heights, Yokehouse Lane, GL6 7QS
☎ 01452 812347 (Patricia Moroney) bsimplybetter@tiscali.co.uk
Map 162/873086
BB **C** ✕ book first £12, 7-9pm DI TI V B D ⊗ 🐾🛁🚗

● **Slimbridge**
SEVERN WAY

May Cottage, Shepherd's Patch, GL2 7BP ☎ 01453 890820
(Peter & Sue Gibson) www.smoothhound.co.uk/hotels/maycottage1
Map 162/721044
BB **C** ✕ nearby TI Closed Xmas B D ⊗ 🐾🛁

● **Southam (Cheltenham)**
COTSWOLD WAY

Pigeon House Cottage, next Tithe Barn, Southam Lane, GL52 3NY
☎ 01242 584255 (B J Holden) www.pigeonhousecottage.co.uk
Map 163/973255
BB **C** ✕ nearby D2 T2 Closed Xmas V B D ⊗ 🐾🛁🚗❗

● **Stanton (Broadway)**
COTSWOLD WAY

Shenberrow Hill, WR12 7NE ☎ 01386 584468 (Mrs Angela Neilan)
michael.neilan1@btopenworld.com Map 150/071342
BB **C** ✕ nearby D2 T2 F2 Closed Xmas
B D ⊗ 🐾🛁🚗❗🏕 ◆◆◆

● **Stow-On-The-Wold (Cheltenham)**
HEART OF ENGLAND WAY, MONARCH'S WAY & MACMILLAN WAY

The Limes, Evesham Road, GL54 1EJ ☎ 01451 830034
(Helen & Graham Keyte) thelimes@zoom.co.uk Map 163/181264
BB **B** ✕ nearby D3 TI FI Closed Xmas B D 🛁🏕

Corsham Field Farm House, Bledington Road, GL54 1JH ☎ 01451 831750
(Robert Smith) www.corshamfield.co.uk Map 163/217250
BB **B/C** ✕ nearby D2 T2 F3 Closed Xmas B D ⊗ 🛁🏕 ◆◆◆

Fifield Cottage, Fosse Lane, GL54 1EH ☎ 01451 831056 (Valerie Keyte)
Map 163/189258
BB **B** ✕ nearby DI TI FI Closed Xmas V B D 🛁🏕

● **Stroud**
COTSWOLD WAY

The Downfield Hotel, 134 Cainscross Road, GL5 4HN ☎ 01453 764496
(Maura & Nigel) www.downfieldhotel.co.uk Map 162/841051
BB **C** ✕ book first £12, 6:30-8:15pm S4 D8 T7 F2 Closed Xmas 🚶(Stroud)
V B D 🐾🛁🚗❗🏕 ◆◆◆

Pretoria Villa, Wells Road, Eastcombe, GL6 7EE ☎ 01452 770435
(Mrs Glynis Solomon) www.bedandbreakfast-cotswold.co.uk Map 163/891064
BB **C** ✕ book first £20, 7-8:30pm SI DI TI Closed Xmas
V B D ⊗ 🐾🛁🚗❗ ◆◆◆◆Ⓢ

Rusland, Bourne Lane, Brimscombe, GL5 2RQ ☎ 01453 882165
(Freda Watson) www.charles.freda.freeuk.com Map 162/869025
BB **B** ✕ nearby DI TI Closed Xmas 🚶(Stroud)
B D ⊗ 🐾🛁🚗

Braemar, Selsley West, GL5 5LG ☎ 01453 826102 (Mrs D Wear)
www.cotswoldsbraemarbb.co.uk Map 162/828035
BB **B** ✕ book first £10, 7pm SI D2 F2 Closed Xmas 🚶(Stroud)
V B D ⊗ 🐾🛁🚗❗

🔹🛏 Journeys End, Chapel Lane, Ebley, GL5 4TD ☎ 01453 752099
(Jane Fletcher) www.cotswold-way.co.uk/journeysend Map 162/827048
BB **C** ✕ book first £11.50, 7-9pm DI TI Closed Xmas 🚶(Stroud)
V B D ⊗ 🐾🛁🚗❗

🔹🛏 Hillenvale Guest House, The Plain, Whiteshill, GL6 6AB ☎ 01453 753441
(Bob & Sue Baker) www.hillenvale.co.uk Map 162/840068
BB **C** ✕ nearby DI T2 Closed Xmas 🚶(Stroud)
B D ⊗ 🐾🛁🚗❗ ◆◆◆

● **Tormarton (Badminton)**
COTSWOLD WAY & MONARCH'S WAY

Chestnut Farm, GL9 1HS ☎ 01454 218563 www.chestnut-farm.co.uk
Map 172/768790
BB **B/D** ✕ £10, 8pm D5 T2 Closed Xmas V B D ⊗ 🐾🛁🚗🏕

● **Uley (Dursley)**
COTSWOLD WAY

Hodgecombe Farm, GL11 5AN ☎ 01453 860365 (Mrs Catherine Bevan)
www.hodgecombefarm.co.uk Map 162/790985
BB **C** ✕ book first £16, 7pm D2 FO Closed Nov-Mar
V B D ⊗ 🐾🛁🚗❗ ◆◆◆

● **Winchcombe (Cheltenham)**
COTSWOLD WAY

Gower House, 16 North Street, GL54 5LH ☎ 01242 602616 (Mrs S Simmonds)
gowerhouse16@aol.com Map 150,163/025284
BB **C** ✕ nearby DI T2 Closed Xmas B D ⊗ 🐾🛁❗Ⓜ ◆◆◆◆

🔹🛏 Cleevely Cottage, Wadfield Farm, Corndean Lane, GL54 5AL
☎ 01242 602059 (Mrs C M Rand) cleevelybxb@hotmail.com
Map 150/025263
BB **B** ✕ book first £10, 6:30pm DI TI FI Closed Xmas
V B D ⊗ 🐾🛁🚗❗🏕 ◆◆◆◆

Blair House, 41 Gretton Road, GL54 5EG ☎ 01242 603626 (Mrs S Chisholm) chissurv@aol.com Map 150,163/023287
BB **C** ✘ nearby S2 D1 T1 Closed Dec-Jan
Ⓑ Ⓓ ⊗ ⛤ ◆◆◆◆

━━ Glebe Farm, Wood Stanway, GL54 5PG ☎ 01386 584791
(Ann Flavell-Wood) www.woodstanway.co.uk Map 150/065313
BB **C** ✘ book first £17, 6.30pm D1 T2 Closed Xmas
Ⓥ Ⓑ Ⓓ ⛤🐾🚗🐴

━━ Wood Stanway Farmhouse, Wood Stanway, GL54 5PG ☎ 01386 584318
(Maggie Green) www.woodstanwayfarmhouse.co.uk Map 150/062311
BB **C** ✘ book first £12, 6-7pm D1 T1 F1 Closed Xmas
Ⓥ Ⓑ Ⓓ ⛤🐾🚗❗🐴

☆ ━━ **The Old White Lion**
37 North St, GL54 5PS ☎ 01242 603300 (John & Jason Hobbs)
www.theoldwhitelion.com Map 150,163/024284
BB **D** ✘ £6-£14, 6-9pm S2 D4 T2
Ⓥ Ⓑ Ⓓ ⛤🐾👤🐴

The Old White Lion is a 15th-century inn and restaurant situated in the centre of Winchcombe, an ancient and pretty little Cotswold town about 8 miles east of Cheltenham.
All rooms are en-suite with TV, phone, hair dryer, tea/coffee and internet access.

━━ One Silk Mill Lane, GL54 5HZ ☎ 01242 603952 (Jenny Cheshire)
jenny.cheshire@virgin.net Map 150,163/026284
BB **B** ✘ nearby T2 Closed Xmas
Ⓑ Ⓓ ⊗ ⛤🐾🚗❗ ◆◆◆◆

Gaia Cottage, 50 Gloucester St, GL54 5LX ☎ 01242 603495
(Brian & Sally Simmonds) briansimmonds@onetel.com
Map 150,163/022282
BB **D** ✘ nearby D1 T1 Ⓑ Ⓓ ⊗ ⛤🐾👤Ⓜ ◆◆◆◆

● Wyck Rissington (Cheltenham)
HEART OF ENGLAND WAY
━━ Hope Lodge, GL54 2PN ☎ 01451 822466 (Mr & Mrs R Pye)
www.hopelodge.com Map 163/189217
BB **D** D1 T1 Closed Dec-Feb
Ⓥ Ⓑ Ⓓ ⊗ ⛤🐾🚗❗ ◆◆◆◆ See SC also.

SOMERSET

● Axbridge
Waterside, Cheddar Road, BS26 2DP ☎ 01934 743182 (Gillian Aldridge)
www.watersidecheddar.co.uk Map 182/438545
BB **B** ✘ book first £10, 7pm S1 D2 T1
Ⓥ Ⓑ Ⓓ ⊗ ⛤🐾🐴 ◆◆◆

● Bath
COTSWOLD WAY
Cranleigh, 159 Newbridge Hill, BA1 3PX ☎ 01225 310197
www.cranleighguesthouse.com Map 172/724656
BB **D** ✘ nearby D4 T2 F2 Closed Xmas ⚒(Bath Spa)
Ⓑ Ⓓ ⊗ 👤🚗❗ ◆◆◆◆

Brocks, 32 Brock Street, BA1 2LN ☎ 01225 338374 (Marion Dodd)
www.brocksguesthouse.co.uk Map 172/746652
BB **D** ✘ nearby D3 T1 F2 Closed Xmas ⚒(Bath Spa)
Ⓑ Ⓓ ⊗ 👤 ◆◆◆◆

☆ ━━ **Marlborough House**
1 Marlborough Lane, BA1 2NQ ☎ 01225 318175
www.marlborough-house.net Map 172/742651
BB **D** S7 D7 T1 F2 ⚒(Bath Spa)
Ⓥ Ⓑ ⊗ ⛤🐾🚗🐴Ⓜ ◆◆◆◆ Vegetarian food only.

Elegant vegetarian B&B in Bath. Rambler friendly with knowledgable hosts who are walkers themselves. Happily enlighten our guests on Bath's many fabulous walks as well as heritage sites. Beautiful en-suite rooms furnished with antiques. Children and pets welcome.

☆ ━━ **Number 30 Crescent Gardens**
BA1 2NB ☎ 01225 337393 (David Greenwood)
www.numberthirty.com Map 172/744650
BB **D** ✘ nearby S1 D5 T1 Closed Xmas ⚒(Bath Spa)
Ⓑ Ⓓ ⊗ ⛤🐾👤Ⓜ ◆◆◆◆Ⓢ

4 diamond standards of comfort and housekeeping in our Victorian house in Bath city centre. Non-smoking. Vegetarian options. All rooms en-suite, light and airy. No pets.

☆ ━━ **Crescent Guest House**
21 Crescent Gardens, Upper Bristol Rd, BA1 2NA ☎ 01225 425945
(John & Gilly Deacon) www.crescentbath.co.uk Map 172/744650
BB **D** ✘ nearby S1 D4 T1 Closed Xmas ⚒(Bath Spa)
Ⓑ Ⓓ ⊗ 👤 ◆◆◆◆Ⓢ Veggie breakfasts.

Enjoy a warm welcome at our city centre Victorian home. Comfort, award-winning standards of service & cleanliness, & generous breakfasts (for omnivores & herbivores) prepared from fresh local ingredients. 5 mins stroll to the shopping centre and Bath's many attractions.

━━ Athole Guest House, 33 Upper Oldfield Park, BA2 3JX ☎ 01225 334307
www.atholehouse.co.uk Map 172/742641
BB **D** ✘ nearby S2 D3 T1 F1 ⚒(Bath Spa)
Ⓥ Ⓑ Ⓓ ⊗ ⛤🐾❗ ◆◆◆◆◆ⒼⓌ

Astor House, 14 Oldfield Road, BA2 3ND ☎ 01225 429134
astorhouse.visitus@virgin.net Map 172/742640
BB **D** ✘ nearby D5 T1 F2 ⚒(Bath Spa)
Ⓥ Ⓑ Ⓓ ⊗ ⛤👤 ◆◆◆◆

━━ Lindisfarne Guest House, 41a Warminster Road, BA2 6XJ
☎ 01225 466342 (Ian & Carolyn Tiley) www.bath.org/hotel/lindisfarne.html
Map 172/776658 BB **D** ✘ nearby D2 T1 F1 Closed Jan ⚒(Bath Spa)
Ⓥ Ⓑ ⊗ ⛤🐾🚗❗ ◆◆◆◆

Flaxley Villa, 9 Newbridge Hill, Lower Weston, BA1 3PW ☎ 01225 313237
(Mary Cooper) www.stilwell.co.uk Map 172/730652
BB **C** ✘ nearby S1 D2 T2 F2 ⚒(Bath Spa) Ⓥ Ⓑ ⊗ 👤 ◆◆◆

● Bridgwater (Wembdon)
MACMILLAN WAY WEST

Cokerhurst Farm, 87 Wembdon Hill, TA6 7QA ☎ 01278 422330
(Mrs D Chappell) www.cokerhurst.clara.net Map 182/280378
BB **C/D** ✗ nearby D1 T1 F1 Closed Xmas ⩓(Bridgewater)
🄱 🄳 ⊗ 🐾🛦 ⇨ ! ◆◆◆◆

● Bristol
MONARCH'S WAY

Mayfair Lodge, 5 Henleaze Road, Westbury-on-Trym, BS9 4EX
☎ 0117 962 2008 (Mrs A Kitching)
www.smoothhound.co.uk/hotels/mayfairlodge.html Map 172/573761
BB **C** ✗ nearby S5 D2 T2 Closed Xmas 🄱 ⊗ 🛦 ◆◆◆

● Chard
🚩⊲ Ammonite Lodge, 43 High Street, TA20 1QL ☎ 01460 63839
www.ammonitelodge.co.uk Map 193/319085
BB **C** ✗ nearby S2 D3 T2 🆅 🄱 🄳 ⊗ 🐾🛦 ◆◆◆◆

● Charlton Horethorne (Sherborne)
MONARCH'S WAY & MACMILLAN WAY

Beech Farm, Sigwells, DT9 4LN ☎ 01963 220524 (Susan Stretton)
stretton@beechfarmsigwells.freeserve.co.uk Map 183/642231
BB **A** ✗ nearby S1 D1 T1 F1 Closed Xmas 🄱 🄳 ⊗ 🐾🛦 ⇨ ! 🐎

● Cheddar
Constantine, Lower New Road, BS27 3DY ☎ 01934 741339
(Sue & Barry Mitchell) Map 182/450531
BB **B** ✗ book first £10, 6:30pm S1 D2 T/D1 F1 Closed Dec
🆅 🄱 🄳 🐾🛦 ◆◆◆

🚩⊲ Bay Rose House, The Bays, BS27 3QN ☎ 01934 741377
(Andrea & Martin Kay) www.bayrose.co.uk Map 182/463538
BB **D** ✗ book first £12, 7-9pm D1 T1 F1 Closed Xmas
🆅 🄱 🄳 ⊗ 🐾🛦 ⇨ ! ◆◆◆

☆ **Tor Farm Guesthouse**
Nyland, BS27 3UD ☎ 01934 743710 (Mr & Mrs Ladd)
www.torfarm.co.uk Map 182/462507
BB **D** ✗ book first £20, 7pm D4 T2 F2
🆅 🄱 🐾🛦 ⇨ ! 🐎 ◆◆◆◆Ⓦ

Tucked away down a quiet country lane, this guesthouse offers eight en-suite rooms - five of which are on the ground floor with private terraces.
Ideal base for Mendip walks and Somerset Levels.
Heated outdoor pool. Large car park.

● Chew Stoke (Bristol)
MONARCH'S WAY

Orchard House, Bristol Road, BS40 8UB ☎ 01275 333143 (Mrs Ann Hollomon)
www.orchardhse.ukgateway.net Map 182, 172/561618
BB **C** ✗ nearby S1 D1 T2 F1
🄱 🄳 🐾🛦 ⇨ ! ◆◆◆

● Chipping Sodbury (Bristol)
MONARCH'S WAY & COTSWOLD WAY

🚩⊲ Kingrove Farm, BS37 6DY ☎ 01454 312314 (Mrs Mary Watson)
Map 172/731813
BB **C** ✗ nearby S2 D2 T1 🆅 🄱 🄳 ⊗ 🐾🛦 🐎

● Coxley (Wells)
MONARCH'S WAY

🚩⊲ Tynings House, Harters Hill Lane, BA5 1RF ☎ 01749 675368
(Tish Hopkins) www.tynings.co.uk Map 182,183/530430
BB **C** ✗ book first £20, 6-7:30pm S1 D2 T1
🆅 🄱 🄳 ⊗ 🐾🛦 ⇨ ◆◆◆◆

● Crewkerne
MONARCH'S WAY

🚩⊲ George Hotel and Courtyard Restaurant, Market Square, TA18 7LP
☎ 01460 73650 (Frank E Joyce MHCIMA)
www.thegeorgehotelcrewkerne.co.uk Map 193/441098
BB **C/D** ✗ £5-£15, 7-9pm S3 D5 T2 F3 ⩓(Crewkerne)
🆅 🄱 🄳 🐾🛦 ◆◆◆

Honeydown Farm, Seaborough Hill, TA18 8PL ☎ 01460 72665
(Catherine Bacon) www.honeydown.co.uk Map 193/430072
BB **C** ✗ book first £16, 7pm D2 T1 Closed Xmas ⩓(Crewkerne)
🆅 🄱 🄳 ⊗ 🐾🛦 ⇨ ! ◆◆◆◆

● Dulverton
EXMOOR
COLERIDGE WAY

Town Mills, TA22 9HB ☎ 01398 323124 (Mrs Jane Buckingham)
www.townmillsdulverton.co.uk Map 181/914279
BB **C** ✗ nearby D4 T1 Closed Xmas 🄱 🄳 🛦 ◆◆◆◆Ⓢ

🚩⊲ Marsh Bridge Cottage, TA22 9QG ☎ 01398 323197 (Mrs C Nurcombe)
Map 181/904288 BB **B/C** ✗ book first £15.50, 7pm D1 T1 F1
🆅 🄱 🄳 ⊗ 🐾🛦 ⇨ 🐎

● Dunster (Minehead)
EXMOOR
SOUTH WEST COAST PATH & MACMILLAN WAY WEST

☆ 🚩⊲ **The Yarn Market Hotel**
High Street, TA24 6SF ☎ 01643 821425 (Penny Bale)
www.yarnmarkethotel.co.uk Map 181/992437
BB **D** ✗ £20, 5:30-8:30pm S6 D12 T3 F3 ⩓(Dunster)
🆅 🄱 🄳 ⊗ 🐾🛦 ⇨ ! 🐎 Ⓜ ★★★ See Groups also.

Our small hotel provides a friendly atmosphere, home cooking, en-suite single, double, four-poster and family rooms all with colour TV & tea/coffee. Residents' lounge, packed lunches and drying facilities available. Open all year.
B&B from £40 (£60 with evening meal). 3 nights £105 (£165). Special offer for walking parties (10-50 people) - 3 nights B&B from £90 (£135).
An ideal centre for exploring Exmoor.
Email Penny Bale: yarnmarket.hotel@virgin.net

● Exebridge
EXMOOR

2 Staghound Cottages, TA22 9AZ ☎ 01398 324453 (Penny Richards)
www.staghound.co.uk Map 181/930243
BB **B** ✗ nearby S1 D1 T1 Closed Xmas 🄱 🄳 ⊗ 🐾🛦 ⇨ !

SOUTH WEST

● Holford (Bridgwater)
MACMILLAN WAY WEST & COLERIDGE WAY

Forge Cottage, TA5 IRY ☎ 01278 741215 (Mrs Susan Ayshford)
Map 181/158413
BB **A** ✗ book first £8, 6-7pm D2 TI Closed Xmas
Ⅴ Ⅾ 🐾🛏🚗🍴🏠

● Minehead
EXMOOR
SOUTH WEST COAST PATH & MACMILLAN WAY WEST

Fernside, The Holloway, TA24 5PB ☎ 01643 707594 (Colin & Maureen Smith)
catman.do@btopenworld.com Map 181/966464
BB **B** ✗ book first £10, 6-6:30pm D2 FI Closed Xmas
Ⅴ Ⅾ ⊛🐾🛏 ◆◆◆

☆ **Lyn Valley Guest House**
3 Tregonwell Road, TA24 5DT ☎ 01643 703748 (Margaret & Julian Hills)
www.lynvalleyminehead.co.uk Map 181/973463
BB **C** ✗ nearby SI D3 T3 FI Closed Xmas
Ⅴ Ⅾ ⊛🛏🏠 ◆◆◆

Comfortable spacious family guest house on quiet residential road. 2 minutes walk from town centre, seafront, restaurants and steam railway. Close to start of South West Coast Path.

🚋🍴 The Parks Guesthouse, 26 The Parks, TA24 8BT ☎ 01643 703547
(Jackie & Richard Trott) www.parksguesthouse.co.uk Map 181/964462
BB **C** ✗ nearby D3 T2 F2 Closed Xmas
Ⅾ ⊛🐾🛏🚗🍴 ◆◆◆◆Ⓦ

🚋🍴 Kenella House, 7 Tregonwell Rd, TA24 5DT ☎ 01643 703128
(Steve and Sandy Poingdestre) www.kenellahouse.co.uk Map 181/972461
BB **D** ✗ book first £15, 7:30pm D4 T2 Closed Xmas
Ⅴ Ⅾ ⊛🐾🛏🚗🍴🏠 ◆◆◆

Higher Rodhuish Farm, TA24 6QL ☎ 01984 640253 (Jennifer & Alan Thomas)
jennifer@higherrod.wanadoo.co.uk Map 181/011397
BB **B** ✗ book first £10 D2 TI Ⅾ 🐾🛏🚗🍴🏠 ◆◆◆

● Nether Stowey (Bridgwater)
MACMILLAN WAY WEST & COLERIDGE WAY

🚋🍴 The Old Cider House, 25 Castle Street, TA5 ILN ☎ 01278 732228
www.theoldciderhouse.co.uk Map 181/191397
BB **D** ✗ book first £12.50, approx 7:30pm D2 T3
Ⅴ Ⅾ ⊛🐾🛏🏠 ◆◆◆◆

🚋🍴 Castle of Comfort Hotel, Dodington, TA5 ILE ☎ 01278 741264
(Carol & Nigel Venner) www.castle-of-comfort.co.uk Map 181/173399
BB **D** ✗ book first £28.50, 7:30-8:30pm SI D3 TI FI Closed Xmas
Ⅴ Ⅾ Ⅾ ⊛🐾🛏🚗🍴🏠 ◆◆◆◆◆Ⓢ

● North Cadbury
MACMILLAN WAY & MONARCH'S WAY

🚋🍴 Ashlea House, High Street, BA22 7DP ☎ 01963 440891
(Mr & Mrs J Wade) www.ashleahouse.co.uk Map 183/635274
BB **C/D** ✗ book first £12-£14, 7pm DI TI Closed Xmas-Apr
Ⅴ Ⅾ Ⅾ ⊛🐾🛏🚗🍴 ◆◆◆◆Ⓢ

● North Petherton (Bridgwater)
Quantock View Guest House, Bridgwater Road, TA6 6PR ☎ 01278 663309
www.quantockview.com Map 182/300341
BB **C** ✗ book first £10, 6:30-7pm SI DI TI FI Closed Xmas
🚋(Bridgwater) Ⅴ Ⅾ Ⅾ ⊛🐾🛏🚗🍴🏠 ◆◆◆

● Porlock (Minehead)
EXMOOR
SOUTH WEST COAST PATH & COLERIDGE WAY

Leys - The Ridge, Off Bossington Lane, TA24 8HA ☎ 01643 862477
(Mrs J Stiles-Cox) Map 181/892469
BB **B** ✗ nearby S2 D/TI Closed Xmas
Ⅾ ⊛🐾🛏 ◆◆◆◆

🚋🍴 The Lorna Doone Hotel, High Street, TA24 8PS ☎ 01643 862404
(R G Thornton) porlockld@yahoo.com Map 181/887469
BB **C** ✗ book first £14, 6.15-8.30pm S4 D4 T4 F2 Closed Xmas
Ⅴ Ⅾ Ⅾ ⊛🐾🛏🏠 ◆◆◆

Silcombe Farm, Culbone, TA24 8JN ☎ 01643 862248 (Mrs E J Richards)
Map 181/833482
BB **B** ✗ book first £11, 7.30pm SI DI T2 Closed Xmas
Ⅴ Ⅾ Ⅾ ⊛🐾🛏🚗🍴🏠

● Shipham
Herongates, Horseleaze Lane, BS25 IUQ ☎ 01934 843280
(Mrs Helen Stickland) herongates@hotmail.com Map 182/437579
BB **B** ✗ nearby DI TI FI Closed Xmas
Ⅾ Ⅾ ⊛🐾🛏 ◆◆◆◆

● South Cadbury (Yeovil)
MACMILLAN WAY & MONARCH'S WAY

Lower Camelot B&B, Lower Camelot, BA22 7HA ☎ 01963 440581
(Mrs Julie Verney) www.southcadbury.co.uk Map 183/633256
BB **C** ✗ nearby D/T3 Closed Jan-Feb Ⅴ Ⅾ Ⅾ ⊛🐾🛏🚗🍴

● Taunton
🚋🍴 Blorenge House, 57 Staplegrove Road, TA1 IDG ☎ 01823 283005
(Mr & Mrs Painter) www.blorengehouse.co.uk Map 193/223250
BB **D** ✗ nearby S5 D8 T8 F3 Closed Xmas 🚋(Taunton)
Ⅾ Ⅾ 🐾🛏🏠 ◆◆◆◆

● Washford (Watchet)
MACMILLAN WAY WEST & COLERIDGE WAY

🚋🍴 Green Bay B&B, TA23 0NN ☎ 01984 640303 (Mrs Ann Morgan)
www.greenbaybedandbreakfast.co.uk Map 181/049410
BB **B** ✗ book first £8, 6-7:30pm DI T/S2
Ⅴ Ⅾ Ⅾ 🐾🛏🍴🏠 ◆◆◆

☆ 🚋🍴 **Monkscider House**
TA23 0NS ☎ 01984 641055
www.monksciderhouse.com Map 181/050410
BB **C** ✗ book first £10 SI DI TI
Ⅴ Ⅾ Ⅾ ⊛🐾🛏🚗 ◆◆◆◆Ⓢ

Monkscider House is the perfect HQ for hikers, situated between Exmoor & the Quantocks and offering luxurious & spacious accommodation in a converted farmhouse. Fortify yourself with a fabulous breakfast using all local produce. Close to the Coleridge Trail.

● Wells
MONARCH'S WAY

Cadgwith House, Hawkers Lane, BA5 3JH ☎ 01749 677799
(Elspeth Fletcher) www.cadgwithhouse.co.uk Map 182/559462
BB **C** SI DI TI FI Closed Xmas Ⓑ Ⓓ ⊗ 🏠♿🐾! 🛏 ◆◆◆◆

☆ ◄ The Crown At Wells
Market Place, BA5 2RP ☎ 01749 673457
www.crownatwells.co.uk Map 182,183/550457
BB **D** ✕ book first £15, 6pm onwards S2 D7 T4 F2
Ⓥ Ⓑ Ⓓ 🏠♿🛏 ★★

Superbly located 15th-century coaching inn, overlooked by Wells Cathedral and Bishop's Palace. The Crown provides comfortable and affordable accommodation. Fabulous food served in popular restaurant, bar and courtyard. Warm welcome and friendly service, in a relaxed atmosphere.

● Westonzoyland (Bridgwater)
MACMILLAN WAY WEST

Staddlestones, 3 Standards Road, TA7 0EL ☎ 01278 691179
(Liz & John Knight) www.staddlestonesguesthouse.co.uk Map 182/352348
BB **D** ✕ nearby D2 TI Ⓥ Ⓑ Ⓓ ⊗ 🏠♿🐾! ◆◆◆◆◆Ⓢ

● Wheddon Cross (Minehead)
EXMOOR
COLERIDGE WAY & MACMILLAN WAY WEST

Exmoor House, TA24 7DU ☎ 01643 841432
www.exmoorhouse.com Map 181/924388
BB **D** ✕ book first £18, 7:30pm D3 TI FI Closed Dec-Jan
Ⓥ Ⓑ Ⓓ ⊗ 🏠♿🐾! 🛏 ◆◆◆◆◆Ⓢ

☆ ◄ The Rest And Be Thankful Inn
TA24 7DR ☎ 01643 841222 (Ronald Kingston)
www.restandbethankful.co.uk Map 181/922388
BB **D** ✕ £10, 7-9pm SI D2 TI FI
Ⓥ Ⓑ Ⓓ 🏠♿! ◆◆◆◆Ⓢ

Located near the centre of Exmoor National Park, the inn is ideally situated for exploring the moor with its red deer and ponies.

The bar, with its real log fires in winter, provides snacks and offers homecooked main meals at lunch and dinner. Good quality en-suite accommodation offering twin, double and single rooms.

An ideal stopover for those walking the Coleridge Way. Full English or vegetarian breakfasts included.

● Williton (Taunton)
MACMILLAN WAY WEST & COLERIDGE WAY

Hartnells, 28 Long Street, TA4 4QU ☎ 01984 634777 (Myra King)
m.king_hartnells@tiscali.co.uk Map 181/080412
BB **C** ✕ nearby SI T2 Closed Xmas Ⓑ Ⓓ ⊗ 🏠♿🐾! 🛏 ◆◆◆

● Winsham (Chard)
MONARCH'S WAY & WESSEX RIDGEWAY

☆ ◄ Gabriels
Fore Street, TA20 4DX ☎ 01460 30275
www.staygabriels.co.uk Map 193/375064
BB **C/D** ✕ £14, 4-9pm D2 TI Closed Xmas
Ⓥ Ⓑ Ⓓ ⊗ 🏠♿! 🛏 ◆◆◆◆Ⓢ

Winsham is a good base for exploring Dorset's World Heritage coastline and is on the Liberty Trail, with Jubilee Trail, Monarch's Way and Wessex Ridgeway close by.
Lifts offered to and from pubs, walks or stations. All rooms en-suite with TV.

Fulwood House, Ebben Lane, TA20 4EE ☎ 01460 30163 (Elizabeth & Carl Earl)
carleton.earl@virgin.net Map 193/377066
BB **D** ✕ nearby D2
Ⓥ Ⓑ Ⓓ ⊗ 🏠♿🐾 Ⓜ ◆◆◆◆

● Withypool (Minehead)
EXMOOR
TWO MOORS WAY & MACMILLAN WAY WEST

Hamiltons, TA24 7QP ☎ 01643 831431 (Mrs Ina Gage)
Map 181/846355
BB **B/C** ✕ nearby SI D3 TI
Ⓑ Ⓓ ⊗ 🏠♿🐾! 🛏

● Woolminstone (Crewkerne)
MONARCH'S WAY & WESSEX RIDGEWAY

Barn Cottage B&B, Lyminster Farm, TA18 8QP ☎ 01460 75313
(Adrienne Pyke) barncottagebandb@aol.com Map 193/414790
BB **C** ✕ book first £15, 6-8pm DI TI Closed Dec-Jan ᨓ(Crewkerne)
Ⓥ Ⓑ Ⓓ ⊗ 🏠♿! Ⓜ

WILTSHIRE

● Ashton Keynes (Swindon)
THAMES PATH

The Firs, High Rd, SN6 6NX ☎ 01285 860169 (Karen Shaw)
www.thefirsbandb.co.uk Map 173,163/045941
BB **C** ✕ nearby SI D2 TI
Ⓑ Ⓓ 🏠♿🐾! 🛏 Ⓜ

● Bradford-on-Avon
MACMILLAN WAY

Bradford Old Windmill, 4 Masons Lane, BA15 1QN ☎ 01225 866842
(Priscilla & Peter Roberts) www.bradfordoldwindmill.co.uk Map 173/826611
BB **D** ✕ book first £21, 8pm SI D3 FI Closed Nov-Feb
ᨓ(Bradford-on-Avon) Ⓥ Ⓑ Ⓓ ⊗ 🏠♿ Ⓜ ◆◆◆◆◆

● Bremhill (Calne)
Lowbridge Farm, SN11 9HE ☎ 01249 815889 (Elizabeth Sinden)
Map 173/987737
BB **C** ✕ £10.50, 7-9pm TI FI
Ⓥ Ⓓ ♿🐾! 🛏 Jacuzzi available.

● Cricklade (Swindon)
THAMES PATH

☆ 🚄 **Leighfield Lodge**
Lodge Farm, Malmesbury Road, Leighfield, SN6 6RH ☎ 01666 860241
(Mrs Claire Read)   www.leighfieldlodge.com   Map 173,163/063916
BB **D** ✕ book first £18 D1 T1
Ⓥ Ⓑ Ⓓ ⊛ 🐾 🛏 🖐 ! ◆◆◆◆

Peaceful location on working farm. Collection from Cricklade for Thames Path available.

All rooms en-suite bath and shower, colour TV and tea & coffee making facilities. Clothes and boots dried over the Aga.

Evening meals by prior arrangement - bring your own wine.

● Devizes
WESSEX RIDGEWAY

Rockley, London Road, SN10 2DS ☎ 01380 723209 (Jean & Richard Bull)
www.rockley.org.uk Map 173/003618
BB **B** ✕ nearby S2 D1 T3 F1 Closed Xmas
Ⓑ Ⓓ ⊛ 🐾 🛏 🖐

🚄 The Gatehouse, Wick Lane, SN10 5DW ☎ 01380 725283
(Mrs L Stratton) www.visitdevizes.co.uk Map 173/006605
BB **B** ✕ nearby S1 D1 T1 Closed Xmas
Ⓑ Ⓓ ⊛ 🐾 🛏 🚗 ! ◆◆◆

☆ 🚄 **Rosemundy Cottage**
London Road, SN10 2DS ☎ 01380 727122
www.rosemundycottage.co.uk Map 173/014621
BB **D** ✕ nearby D4
Ⓥ Ⓑ Ⓓ ⊛ 🐾 🛏 🚗 ! ◆◆◆◆

Alongside the Kennet & Avon Canal, just off Wessex Ridgeway, and a short walk to the town centre. Facilities include guest office, sitting room and garden with swimming pool and seasonal BBQ. All rooms double en-suite. Four-poster and ground floor rooms available. Good base for varied walks. Double/3-night offers.

● Inglesham (Swindon)
THAMES PATH

Evergreen, 3 College Farm Cottages, SN6 7QU ☎ 01367 253407
(Mr & Mrs G Blowen) www.evergreen-cotswolds.co.uk Map 163/204959
BB **C** ✕ nearby S2 D1 Closed Xmas
Ⓑ Ⓓ ⊛ 🐾 🛏 🖐 !

● Ludwell (Shaftesbury)
WESSEX RIDGEWAY

Birdbush Farm, SP7 9HH ☎ 01747 828252 (Mrs Ann Rossiter)
annrossiter@fsmail.net Map 184/913229
BB **B** ✕ nearby S1 D1 Closed Nov-Feb
Ⓓ ⊛ 🐾 🛏 🖐 !

● Malmesbury

🚄 Mayfield House Hotel, Crudwell, SN16 9EW ☎ 01666 577409
(Chris Marston) www.mayfieldhousehotel.co.uk Map 173,163/954928
BB **D** ✕ £18, 6:30-8:45pm S3 D12 T9 F2
Ⓥ Ⓑ Ⓓ 🐾 🛏 🚲 ★★ See Groups also.

● Marlborough
WESSEX RIDGEWAY

☆ **Browns Farm**
SN8 4ND ☎ 01672 515129 (Hazel J Crockford)
www.smoothhound.co.uk/hotels/brownsfarmbb.html Map 173/198678
BB **B** ✕ nearby D2 T1 F1
Ⓑ Ⓓ ⊛ 🐾 🛏 🚗 🚲

Attractive farmhouse set on the edge of the Savernake Forest. Large comfortable rooms offering views over open farmland. Ideal base for walkers & cyclists. Close to The Ridgeway, Avebury and Wansdyke.

● Marshfield (Chippenham)
COTSWOLD WAY & MACMILLAN WAY

Knowle Hill Farm, Beeks Lane, SN14 8BB ☎ 01225 891503 (Cynthia Bond)
Map 173/825729
BB **C** ✕ book first £8, 7pm D1 T1 F1
Ⓥ Ⓑ Ⓓ 🐾 🛏 🚗 ! 🚲

● Mere
MONARCH'S WAY

Castleton House, Castle St, BA12 6JE ☎ 01747 860446 (Gail Garbutt)
www.castletonhouse.com Map 183/811323
BB **C** ✕ book first £15, 7:30-8:30pm D1 T1 F1 Closed Xmas
Ⓥ Ⓑ Ⓓ 🐾 🛏 🚗 ! ◆◆◆◆

● Ogbourne St George (Marlborough)
RIDGEWAY

Foxlynch, Bytham Road, SN8 1TD ☎ 01672 841307 (Mr G H Edwins)
Map 173/190740
BB **A** ✕ nearby S1 F1 Ⓑ Ⓓ 🐾 🛏 🚗 ! 🚲 Bunkroom only.

☆ 🚄 **Parklands Hotel & Restaurant**
High Street, SN8 1SL ☎ 01672 841555 (Mark Bentley)
www.parklandshoteluk.co.uk Map 174/200744
BB **D** ✕ book first £8.95, 7-9pm S2 D3 T6 Closed Xmas
Ⓥ Ⓑ Ⓓ 🐾 🛏 🚗 ! 🚲 ◆◆◆◆

Set in the tiny Wiltshire village of Ogbourne St George, Parklands Hotel offers comfortable, peaceful accommodation and an excellent restaurant in a family run hotel. Conveniently located for the Ridgeway path.

To see more details, please visit our website.

● Salisbury

🚄 Hayburn Wyke Guest House, 72 Castle Road, SP1 3RL ☎ 01722 412627
www.hayburnwykeguesthouse.co.uk Map 184/142309
BB **C/D** ✕ nearby D3 T2 F2 🚌(Salisbury) Ⓑ Ⓓ 🛏 ◆◆◆

🚄 Byways House, 31 Fowler's Rd, SP1 2QP ☎ 01722 328364
(Barbara Bouffard) www.bed-breakfast-stonehenge.co.uk Map 184/149299
BB **D** ✕ nearby S4 D7 T7 F5 Closed Xmas 🚌(Salisbury)
Ⓑ 🐾 🛏 🚲 ◆◆◆

SOUTH WEST

● Warminster

WESSEX RIDGEWAY

Farmers' Hotel, 1 Silver Street, BA12 8PS ☎ 01985 213815
www.farmershotel.yahoo.uk Map 183/871451
BB **B** ✗ £9, 6-10pm S9 D4 T7 F3 Closed Xmas ▲▲(Warminster)
Ⓥ Ⓑ Ⓓ 🍴🛁🛏 ◆

● West Overton (Marlborough)

RIDGEWAY & WESSEX RIDGEWAY

Cairncot, SN8 4ER ☎ 01672 861617 (Mrs Rachel Leigh)
www.cairncot.co.uk Map 173/131680
BB **C** ✗ nearby S1 D1 Ⓓ 🐕🍴🛁🚗🛏🏵 ◆◆◆

● Wroughton (Swindon)

RIDGEWAY

2 Greens Lane, SN4 0RJ ☎ 01793 813982 (Christine Spooncer)
Map 173/150182
BB **B** ✗ nearby T2 Ⓑ Ⓓ🏵 🍴🐕🛏🏵

SELF-CATERING

CORNWALL

● Ashton

Chycarne Farm Cottages ☎ 01736 762473 (Pauline & Graham Ross)
www.chycarne-farm-cottages.co.uk
£100-£405 Sleeps 1-4. 9 cottages. Closed Nov, Feb, Mar Beautiful rural
location, overlooks Mounts Bay. 🏵 🏵 ★★★

● Bodmin

☆ **Ruthern Valley Holidays**
☎ 01208 831395 (Tim & Eileen Zair)
www.self-catering-ruthern.co.uk
£220-£630 Sleeps 4-6. 8 lodges, 4 bungalows, 6 static caravans.
Closed Nov-Feb David Bellamy Gold Award for conservation. 🏵 ★★★★

Mid Cornwall.
A small holiday retreat in 7.5 acres of park
and woodland. Lodges/caravans. 10 miles to
the north or south coasts – Eden Project.
Close to Camel Trail and Saints' Way.
No bar, no disco, no bingo!
Email: ruthern.valley@btconnect.com

● Boscastle

Bremor Holidays ☎ 01840 230340 (Mrs P A Rogers)
www.bremorholidays.co.uk
£125-£320 Sleeps 2. 1 cottage. Easy access to coastal footpath. 🏵 ★★★

☆ **Venn Down Farmhouse**
☎ 01840 250599 (Diane Bentall)
www.venndownfarmhouse.co.uk
£200-£525 Sleeps 2-4 + cot. 2 apartments.
Kennel only for dogs, max 2. 🏵 🏵 ★★★★

Two luxurious apartments adjacent to 18th
century farmhouse standing in 12 acres of
grounds, finished to a high standard. Tranquil
location. Distant sea views. Near Boscastle
harbour, Tintagel, Polzeath, Port Isaac. Stunning
coastal walks, sandy beaches, Cornish villages,
restaurants, pubs and cream teas.

Tony & Enid Pryer ☎ 01242 238865
£150-£320 Sleeps 4. 1 house. Designated parking for two cars. 🏵

● Bude

☆ **Flexbury House**
☎ 01600 772918 (Sarah Watkins)
www.flexburyhouse.com
£350-£950 Sleeps 2-10 + 2 cots. 1 detached house.
5 minutes from coast, town, pub. 🏵 ★★★★

Large 4 bedroomed
Victorian House.

Excellent location NT
coastal path/beach
4 minutes walk.

Bude town centre
10 minutes.

Nearest pub, corner shop 5 minutes. Walkers' paradise.

Stunning walks from the door. Come home to the smell of your aga-cooked
casserole, and soak away your weary legs in our extra deep bath.

Drying and laundry facilities. Very well equipped house. Discount for smaller
parties out of season.

Honeysuckle Cottage ☎ 01288 355496 (Dennis Mobbs)
www.honeysucklecottage.co.uk
£180-£400 Sleeps 2. 1 cottage. Indoor pool. Laundry. 🏵 ★★★★

Rockhaven ☎ 01288 359175 (Mrs Anderson)
£170-£330 Sleeps 4. 1 chalet. Coastal path access at back gate. 🏵

● Camelford

Roughtor House ☎ 01840 211242 (Mrs Ashton) ashtonda1@aol.com
£150-£295 Sleeps 2-4. 1 cottage.
Near Bodmin Moor, South West Coast Path. 🏵

● Fowey

Fowey Harbour Cottages ☎ 01726 832211 (David Hill)
wwww.foweyharbourcottages.co.uk
£150-£1,000 Sleeps 2-6. 10 cottages & flats.
On Cornish Coast Path & Saints' Way. 🏵 ★★-★★★★

Izzy Minx Cottage ☎ 07813 890768 (Julie Yardley)
www.izzyminx.co.uk
£160-£430 Sleeps 5. 1 cottage.
Fabulous cottage on South West Coast Path. 🏵 🏵

● Helford

Helford Cottages ☎ 01326 231666 (Pam Royall)
www.helfordcottages.co.uk
£165-£895 Sleeps 2-9. 12 cottages. Enchanting creekside cottages on
coastal footpath. 🏵 🏵 ★★★-★★★★

● Helston

Glebe Hall Cottages ☎ 01326 221155 (Julian & Ali Rand)
www.glebehallcottages.co.uk
£200-£610 Sleeps 4-6. 4 cottages.
Swimming pool, pub serving food opposite. 🏵

● Launceston

East Gate Barn ☎ 01566 782573 (Jill Goodman) www.eastgatebarn.co.uk
£250-£460 Sleeps 2-4. 1 barn conversion.
Footpath walk-guides to Bodmin Moor. ⊗ ★★★★ RA member

● Liskeard

Brian & Terri Shears ☎ 01579 321019 www.trengale.co.uk
£210-£890 Sleeps 1-6. 3 cottages, 1 annexe.
Stunning rural location, suitable all year. 🐾 ★★★★

Cutkive Wood Holiday Lodges ☎ 01579 362216 (Andy Lowman)
www.cutkivewood.co.uk
£120-£410 Sleeps 1-6. 6 lodges.
Idyllic rural location, moors, coasts, countryside. 🐾 See Groups also.

Hopsland Holidays ☎ 01579 344480 (Linda Hosken)
www.hopslandholidays.co.uk
£185-£550 Sleeps 4-6. 3 cottages.
150yrds to Bodmin Moor. ⊗ ★★★★ See B&B and Groups also.

Agnes Ambrose ☎ 01503 240629 www.jopesmill.co.uk
£250-£450 Sleeps 4. 1 mill cottage.
Water mill, river, lake, large garden. ⊗

● Mevagissey

☆ **Craftsmen Cottage**
☎ 01726 843037 (Mrs S Franklin)
www.craftsmencottage.co.uk
£195-£470 Sleeps 4-6. 1 cottage.
Almost 200 years old. ⊗

A spacious two-bedroomed three storey cottage.
Traditional Cornish fishing village, bright and fully
equipped to a high standard.
Excellent base for coastal and inland walks, 100yds from
the harbour.
Ten miles to Eden Project and extremely close to
Heligan Gardens.

● Mullion

Criggan Mill ☎ 01326 240496 (Mike & Jackie Bolton) www.crigganmill.co.uk
£170-£715 Sleeps 2-6. 25 timber lodges.
Coastal path 200yds, village 1 mile. 🐾 ★★★★★ See B&B also.

Gweltek ☎ 01326 290443 (Barbara Downing) www.wetoes.com
£195-£450 Sleeps 6. 1 cottage.
SW Coast Path & sea. Golf, gardens. 🐾

Trenance Farm Cottages ☎ 01326 240639 (Tamara)
www.trenancefarmholidays.co.uk
£180-£675 Sleeps 2-6. 9 cottages.
Within 5 mins walk of SW Coast Path. 🐾 ★★★

● Newquay

Betty Barry ☎ 01637 876104 betty.barry@btinternet.com
£115-£350 Sleeps 2-6. 1 apartment.
Facilities for walkers, cyclists, surfers, fisherfolk. ⚓(Newquay) ★★

● Padstow

Yellow Sands Cottages ☎ 01637 881548 (Sharon Keast)
www.yellowsands.co.uk
£200-£750 Sleeps 1-6. 6 cottages.
Coastal footpath 200 metres, idyllic location. 🐾 ★★★★

☆ **Bosca Brea**
☎ 01208 814472 (Mrs Alison Mitchell)
alisonm.trevalsa@btinternet.com
£145-£340 Sleeps 1-4. 1 bungalow.
Saints' Way and coastal path nearby. 🐾

Detached bungalow in peaceful hamlet of
Tregonce. Views across Little Petherick Creek
and towards Padstow from ½ acre private
grounds. Close access to Saints' Way, Camel
Trail and SW Coast Path. Wadebridge, Padstow,
surfing and sandy beaches approx. 5 miles by
road.

● Polperro

Graham Wright ☎ 01579 344080
£175-£495 Sleeps 2-8. 2 cottages.
Miles of unspoilt National Trust cliff walks. 🐾

● Polzeath

☆ **Westpoint Holiday Cottage**
☎ 01395 567304 (Claire Mills)
claire@blagdon-house.fsnet.co.uk
£650-£1,200 Sleeps 8. 1 house.
Stunning seaviews. 5 mins to coast path. ⊗

Westpoint is a perfectly situated
house with stunning seaviews, close to
the coastal walk.
Four bedrooms.
Short breaks available.
Brochure on request.

● Port Isaac

Lane End Farm ☎ 01208 880013 (Mrs Linda Monk) nabmonk@tiscali.co.uk
£165-£460 Sleeps 4. 1 bungalow.
Beautiful views. Convenient coast path, moors. ⊗ 🐾 ★★★ RA member.
See B&B also.

● Rock

☆ **Mariners Lettings**
☎ 020 7384 9105 (Claire Tordoff)
www.marinersrock.com
£475-£1,045 Sleeps 4-6. 5 houses.
Beautiful views over Camel estuary. 🐾 ★★★-★★★★

Luxury fully equipped and beautifully
furnished houses; private terraces; wonderful
views over Camel estuary; 2 mins from beach;
200yds to Mariners Pub/restaurants; on
South West Coast Path. All houses fully
equipped including washing machine, bed
linen and towels.

● St Austell

Spindrift ☎ 01726 69316 (Mrs McGuffie) www.spindrift-guesthouse.co.uk
£200-£500 Sleeps 2-4. 3 varying types.
Between Heligan Gardens and Eden Project. ⊗ 🐾 ★★★
See B&B also.

● St Dennis

Ginny ☎ 01726 821715   barrieandginny@providencechapel.freeserve.co.uk
£100-£500 Sleeps 2-6. 1 studio flat, 1 cabin.
Closed Jan-Feb (cabin)   ⊗

● St Ives

St Ives Cottage ☎ 020 8870 3228 (Sue Kibby)
www.btinternet.com/~stives.cottage
£200-£500 Sleeps 4. 1 cottage.
Near Hepworth Museum. Walker friendly owners.   ⊗ ⋙(St Ives) ★★★

☆ Dolphins Holiday Cottage
☎ 07963 338531 (Steve & Jill Lane)
www.dolphins.uk.com
£239-£595 Sleeps 4-6 +child. 1 cottage.
Sea views, near Tate. Adjoins South West Coast Path.   ⊗ ⋙(St Ives)

- Overlooks The Beach
- Comfortable Family Home
- Garden & Sheltered Courtyard
- Peaceful Relaxing Location
- Available Year Round
- Short Walk To Beaches Harbour, Restaurants,Galleries, & Tate St Ives.
- Perfect For Walking The South West Coast Path

Email: dolphins.hols@ntlworld.com

● St Just

Scilly Sun Cottages ☎ 01736 788458 (Mrs Jo Hill)   www.scillysuncottages.com
£135-£475 Sleeps 5. 2 cottages.
200 yds SW Coast Path   ⊗ 🛁 See B&B also.

● St Keverne

☆ Cobb Cottage
☎ 01798 344169 (Mrs S Harding)
sharding@lineone.net
£160-£495 Sleeps 6. 1 cottage. 🛁

Traditional Cornish cottage situated on The Lizard in the village of St Keverne. Three bedrooms, sleeping 6. Fully equipped. Ideal for walking the coastal path. Lovely local beaches. Dogs allowed.

● St Teath

Tredarrup ☎ 01208 850994 (Mrs Bailey) www.tredarrup.com
£370-£998 Sleeps 4-6. 1 barn, 1 cottage.
Stunning views, near good local walks.   ⊗ ★★★★

● St Wenn

☆ Tregolls Farm
☎ 01208 812154 (Mrs Marilyn Hawkey)
www.tregollsfarm.co.uk
£200-£850 Sleeps 2-8. 4 converted barns.
Clothes drying facilities. Saints Way. ★★★★ See B&B also.

Quality barn conversion in a picturesque valley overlooking fields of cows and sheep. Farm trail links up with Saints' Way footpath. Pets corner. Games room. BBQs. Central heating and log burners. Only 20 minutes drive from Eden or Padstow.

● The Lizard

Most Southerly House ☎ 01326 290300 (Mr G Sowden)
george@sowden7000fsworld.co.uk
£180-£250 Sleeps 2-3. 1 clifftop chalet.   Closed Nov-Mar
On coastal path, magnificent sea views.   ⊗

● Zennor

Boswednack Manor ☎ 01736 794183 (Dr E Gynn)
boswednack-manor@cornwall-county.com £195-£370 Sleeps 4. 1 cottage.
Walks leaflets, organic garden, sea sunsets.   ⊗ See B&B also.

DEVON

● Aveton Gifford

Marsh Mills ☎ 01548 550549 (Mrs M Newsham) www.marshmills.co.uk
£275-£300 Sleeps 2-3. 1 cottage annexe.
Own sun terrace, gardens, orchard & parking.   ⊗ 🛁

● Barnstaple

☆ Highfield
☎ 01271 373779 (Carol Edwards)
www.guineaford.co.uk
£249-£583 Sleeps 2-6 +cot. 1 cottage.   Closed Nov-May
Quiet village, near Exmoor, town and beaches.   ⊗ See B&B also.

Fully equipped cottage, level accommodation, sleeps 2-6 plus cot, views over pretty village and countryside. Conservatory entrance on garden level. Steps or slope to parking area. Church, chapel, pub, Marwood Hill Gardens. Ideal for Exmoor, coastal walks and market town.

☆ Mrs Marcia White
☎ 01271 850501
www.plaistowbarton.co.uk
£199-£880 Sleeps 2-5. 1 cottage.
Luxury cottage, beautiful location. Garden, dishwasher.   ⊗

Luxury, tranquil, three-bedroom 17th century cottage. Beautiful rural location. Completely refurbished to a very high standard. Luxury bathroom, 4-poster bed, Inglenook fireplace, large garden, dishwasher, washer/dryer. Excellent for magnificent coastal walks and stunning Exmoor. Visit our website now!

● Belstone
DARTMOOR

Coombe Head Farm ☎ 01837 840108 (Jackie Day)
www.coombeheadfarm.co.uk
£200-£350 Sleeps 4 + cot. 1 cottage.
Superb barn conversion, weekend breaks available.   🚭 ★★★

● Bishops Nympton

☆ **North Hayne Farm Cottages**
☎ 01769 550807 (Mr & Mrs Dixon)
www.northhaynefarmcottages.co.uk
£262-£867 Sleeps 2-6 + cot. 7 cottages.
Hot tubs, children's farm, games room.   🚭

Seven character stone cottages in idyllic peaceful courtyard setting, sleeping 2-34 plus cots. Ten acres, many animals, free donkey rides, games room, play barn, private hot tubs, free laundry/drying facilities. Excellent base for Exmoor National Park (5 miles).

● Brayford

☆ **The Old Stables**
☎ 01271 830238 (Mr & Mrs Summers)
www.the-old-stables.net
£250-£420 Sleeps 2. 1 cottage.
🚭 ★★★★

Luxurious and spacious one bedroomed cottage with private garden, situated close to Exmoor, coastal walks, beaches and beautiful north Devon countryside. Fully centrally heated, the cottage is open all year and provides an excellent base for exploring the area.

● Bucks Mills

☆ **Marks Cottage**
☎ 01481 266906 (Jenny & Steve Oliver)
www.markscottage.co.uk
£295-£745 Sleeps 2-6. Fisherman's cottage.
Central heating, aga, laundry.   🚭

Picturesque 4 bedroom semi-detached fisherman's cottage furnished to high standard. Located in Bucks Mills, a traditional rural fishing village on South West Coast Path in North Devon Coast Area Of Outstanding Natural Beauty. Surrounded by National Trust woodland. A walker's paradise, only steps to magnificent coastal cliff-top walks as well as sheltered cove with rock pools and partly sandy beach. Excellent base to explore Tarka Trail, Clovelly and Hartland.

● Chulmleigh
Rodney & Margaret Davies ☎ 01769 581250   http://eggesford-barton.co.uk
£506-£1,803 Sleeps 6-10. 3 cottages.
On Tarka Trail. Beautiful forest walks.   🚭 ᴍᴍ(Eggesford) 🐾

● Combe Martin
EXMOOR

Northcote Manor Farm ☎ 01271 882376 (Pat Bunch)
www.northcotemanorfarm.co.uk
£200-£895 Sleeps 4-6. 5 cottages.   Closed Nov
Tranquil location near coast and Exmoor.   🚭 🐾 ★★★★

Kentisbury Grange ☎ 01271 883454 (Roy Shindler)
www.kentisburygrange.co.uk
£145-£445 Sleeps 2-6. 4 cabins, 19 caravans..   Closed Oct-Mar
Quiet countryside retreat on fringe of Exmoor. 🐾 ★★★★

● Dunsford
DARTMOOR

Mrs Jean May ☎ 01647 252784 lesjmay@aol.com
£160-£310 Sleeps 2-4. 2 cottages.
Peaceful farmland, lovely views, woodland walks.   🚭

● East Prawle

☆ **Kittiwake Cottage**
☎ 01548 511471 (Lou & Bill Bonham)
www.kittiwakecottage.com
£275-£600 Sleeps 4-6. 1 cottage.
Sea views. Log burner. Sunny garden.   🚭

Restored fisherman's cottage. Well equipped and comfortably furnished. South West Coast Path - 5 minutes' walk. Dartmoor - 40 minutes' drive. Stunning coastal scenery. Great beaches. Numerous walks from the door. Rare birds. Village pubs, shop and café. Brochure available.

● Hartland

☆ **Yapham Cottages**
☎ 01237 441916 (Jane Young)
www.yaphamcottages.com
£260-£630 Sleeps 2-4. 3 cottages.
Stunning, tranquil coastal location. Central heating.   🚭 ★★★★

3 beautiful 4 star cottages sleeping 2-4.

Stunning coastal location. Set in landscaped gardens within seven acres of lovely grounds, including woodland walk and wild flower meadow. 1 mile from South West Coast Path. On the breathtaking and unspoilt Hartland Peninsula, Yapham enjoys complete tranquillity yet is perfect for visiting nearby tourist attractions; Exmoor, Dartmoor, The Eden Project.

Our cottages are beautifully furnished including central heating. Excellent home cooked meals and dishes can be provided. Delicious cream tea on arrival, plus chocolates and flowers. Short breaks available.

Country Cottage Plus ☎ 01237 441476 (Clive Edwards)
www.countrycottageplus.co.uk
£395-£1,995 Sleeps 4-10. 3 cottages.
Three cottages, three pools. Farm. Coastal. 🛏 ★★★★

Devon Chalet ☎ 07860 450162 (Mrs McArdell) www.devonchalet.com
£120-£520 Sleeps 4. 2 chalets.   Closed Mid Jan-mid Mar
Picturesque Clovelly, Tarka Trail, Hartland Point. ⊗ 🛏

● Honiton
Twistgates Farm ☎ 01404 861173 (Mrs Gray) www.twistgatesfarm.co.uk
£180-£535 Sleeps 2-5. 3 cottages.
Woodburner, laundry area, meals available. Rural.
⊗ 🛏 ★★★-★★★★

● Lynton
EXMOOR
South Dean Cottage ☎ 01598 763732 (Trevor & Vicki)
www.southdeancottage.co.uk
£300-£450 Sleeps 6. 1 cottage.   Half a mile from cliff walk. ⊗ 🛏

Devon Holidays 4U ☎ 01865 875356 (Emma & Andrew Firth)
www.devonholidays4u.co.uk
£405-£900 Sleeps 4 +cot. 4 cottages/apts.
On the coast. Exceptionally well equipped. ⊗ 🛏 ★★★-★★★★

● Moretonhampstead
DARTMOOR

☆ **Budleigh Farm**
☎ 01647 440835 (Judith Harvey)
www.budleighfarm.co.uk
£140-£495 Sleeps 2-6. 7 varying types.
Heated outdoor swimming pool (summer only). 🛏 ★★-★★★★

Climb our hill and admire Dartmoor from the site of an Iron Age fort. There's not much left of the fort, but the view is stunning.
Visit historic cities, secret villages, tumbling streams, superb beaches; admire bluebell woods and wildflowers; roam Dartmoor, and sleep soundly after walking the Tors. Short breaks.

FOUND SOMEWHERE
THAT'S NOT IN THIS GUIDE?
Fill in the Recommendation Form on
p311 and send it to the editor at our
central office or email:
yearbook@london.ramblers.org.uk

● Oare
EXMOOR

☆ **Cloud Farm**
☎ 01598 741234 (Jill Harman)
www.doonevalleyholidays.co.uk
£235-£770 Sleeps 2-8. 3 cottages.
Idyllic riverside setting. Perfect walking base. 🛏 ★★★ See Hostels also.

Cloud Farm's idyllic riverside setting in the tranquility of the Exmoor National Park's Doone Valley provides perfect 'away-from-it-all' holidays and short breaks all year round. Three farmhouse cottage accommodations, all newly refurbished, set in an unspoilt paradise for walking, relaxing, exploring, watching wildlife, or riding from our stables (all ages and levels).

Excellent base for touring nearby villages and walking the South West Coast Path. Shop, off-licence, tearoom, gardens, laundry facilities on-site.

● Okehampton
DARTMOOR

☆ **East Hook Holiday Cottages**
☎ 01837 52305 (Mrs M E Stevens)
www.easthook-holiday-cottages.co.uk
£175-£480 Sleeps 2-6. 3 cottages.
Outstanding location, on Tarka Trail/Cycleway 27. 🛏 ★★-★★★★

Heart of glorious Devon with beautiful panoramic view of Dartmoor. Set in own grounds, three idyllic country cottages with oak beams and log fire. Wonderful charm and ambience. Comfortable, peaceful and relaxing.

● Sidmouth
Ann Bowden ☎ 01392 841984 philann@bowthom.fsnet.co.uk
£145-£460 Sleeps 4. 1 bungalow.   Closed Jan
Rural location on Jurassic Heritage Coast. ⊗ 🛏

● Tavistock
DARTMOOR
Langstone Manor ☎ 01822 613371 (Jane Kellett)
http://langstone-manor.co.uk
£160-£564 Sleeps 2-7. 2 cottages, 2 apts, 7 static caravans.   Closed Dec-Feb
Direct access onto Dartmoor. Bar meals. ⊗ 🛏 ★★★★ See Hostels also.

● Teignmouth
Bowden Close House ☎ 01803 328029 (Sarah Farquharson)
www.bowdenclose.co.uk
£209-£630 Sleeps 3-4. 6 cottages/apts.
South West Coast Path on doorstep. ⊗ ★★★

● Walkhampton
DARTMOOR

Withill Farm ☎ 01822 853992 (Mrs P Kitchin) withillfarm@aol.com
£172-£360 Sleeps 2-4. 1 cottage.
Small farm close to open moor. 🛏 See B&B also.

● Whimple
Lower Southbrook Farm ☎ 01404 822989 (Angela Lang)
www.lowersouthbrookfarm.co.uk
£185-£420 Sleeps 4-6. 3 cottages.
Comfortable accommodation in delightful rural situation. 🛏 ★★★

● Widecombe-in-the-Moor
DARTMOOR

☆ **Wooder Manor**
☎ 01364 621391 (Mrs Angela Bell) www.woodermanor.com
£160-£1,000 Sleeps 2-12. 5 varying types.
Beautiful quiet location, with central heating.
🛏 ★★★-★★★★ Access category 2.

Cottages in picturesque valley, surrounded by moors and granite tors. Peaceful location with lovely walks from the doorstep. Clean and well equipped. Central heating. Gardens. Off-road easy parking. Open all year. Good food at two local inns. Colour brochure. Groups welcome.

Lower Blackaton Farm ☎ 01364 621369 (Judy Lomax)
www.lowerblackaton.co.uk
£500-£1,400 Sleeps 6-11. 1 farmhouse/cottage.
Renovated farmhouse, superb moorland/farmland scenery.
Ⓧ 🛏 See B&B also.

● Witherage

☆ **Newhouse Farm Cottages**
☎ 01884 860266 (Mr Keith Jenkins)
www.newhousecottages.com
£236-£1,519 Sleeps 1-40. 8 cottages.
Peaceful location, stunning views. Swimming pool. 🛏

Eight beautifully converted well-equipped cosy Grade II listed stone barns, some with wood burning stoves. Choice of accommodation from one bedroom with four-poster bed to our five bedroom barn sleeping ten. Set in 23 acres of peaceful meadows with many enjoyable local walks.

DORSET

● Abbotsbury

☆ **Gorwell Farm**
☎ 01305 871401 (Mrs J M Pengelly) www.gorwellfarm.co.uk
£200-£925 Sleeps 2-8. 6 cottages.
Coastal path, Macmillan Way. Wheelchair access.
Ⓧ 🛏 ★★★★-★★★★★ Access category 2.

Relax, unwind and leave the car keys behind, in a comfortable well equipped cottage whilst you enjoy the unsurpassed network of footpaths in this beautiful area of west Dorset. Cottages to suit all ages with log fires and fenced gardens.

● Bridport
Saxlingham House ☎ 01308 423629 (Valerie Nicholls)
http://members.freezone.co.uk/saxlingham/Saxlingham.htm
£225-£300 Sleeps 4. 1 cottage.   Closed Oct-Feb
Set in beautiful Dorset countryside.   Ⓧ 🛏 See B&B also.

● Dorchester
The Barn ☎ 01305 849344 (Mrs E J Peckover)
www.stables-pallington.co.uk
£240-£390 Sleeps 2. 1 stable conversion.   Closed Nov-Feb
Central location, Dorset World Heritage Coast. 🛏 ★★★★

● Stoke Abbott
Jon and Sue Evans ☎ 01308 867100
http://mysite.wanadoo-members.co.uk/dorsethideaway
£120-£250 Sleeps 2. 1 log cabin.
Short breaks available on a nightly basis.   Ⓧ

● Sturminster Newton
The Homestead ☎ 01258 471390 (Terry & Carol Townsend)
www.townsend.dircon.co.uk
£210-£260 Sleeps 4. 1 apartment, 1 lodge.
Picturesque peaceful location. Ideal walking country.   Ⓧ ★★★

● Sutton Poyntz
☆ **Ebenezer Cottage**
☎ 07778 524199 (Cathy Varley)
www.ebenezercottage.co.uk
£305-£700 Sleeps 4 +cot. 1 cottage.
SW Coast Path. World Heritage site.   Ⓧ ★★★★

Ebenezer Cottage. Charming 4-star three bed terraced cottage on picturesque millstream lane in Sutton Poyntz. Explore the SW Coast Path and savour spectacular views towards the Jurassic coastline in the heart of the World Heritage Site.

● Swanage
Alrose Villa Apartments ☎ 01929 426318 (Jacqui Wilson)
www.alrosevilla.co.uk £180-£460 Sleeps 2-6. 4 apartments.   Closed Nov-Feb
100m to beach. Some baconies. Sea views. 🛏 ★★★

☆ **California Barn**

☎ 01929 425049 (Karen Delahay)
www.californiacottage.co.uk
£475-£1,000 Sleeps 11 +cots. 1 house.
Wheelchair accessible, large studio/meetings room. 🚭 🐾 ★★★★

California Barn. luxury stone barn on stunning Jurassic Heritage Coast. Wheelchair accessible. Pets. Garden and south facing patio with seaviews to Isle of Wight. Access to large studio/meeting room. Arts tuition, archaeological and wildlife tours/talks available. Excellent walking and wildlife.

● Uploders
Springside Cottages ☎ 01305 871585 (Mr Alan Spargo)
www.springsidecottages.com
£180-£600 Sleeps 2-5. 1 cottage annexe, 1 cottage.
Superb coast and country walking area.   🚭 ★★★

● Weymouth

☆ **Dream Cottages**

☎ 01305 789000   http://dream-cottages.co.uk
£335-£1,330 Sleeps 2-12. 25 cottages, apts and barns.
Cottages perfect for coast and country.
🚭 🚣(Weymouth) 🐾 ★★-★★★★

With over 150 cottages we can accommodate those wanting a small cosy retreat to those wanting a large family home, in a countryside or coastal setting. Many cottages are perfectly appointed for beautiful walks along the Dorset Coast World Heritage Site

GLOUCESTERSHIRE

● Blockley
Skylark Cottage ☎ 01451 832575 (Ruth Lucas)   www.skylarkcottage.co.uk
£295-£475 Sleeps 2-4. 1 cottage.
Cotswold cottage. Stunning views. Extensive walking.   🚭 ★★★★

● Chipping Campden
Weston Park Farm ☎ 01386 840835 (Mrs J Whitehouse)
http://cotswoldcottages.uk.com
£150-£500 Sleeps 2-5. 1 coach house flat, 2 cottages.
Magnificently situated on Cotswold Way. 🐾 See B&B also.

● Dursley
Two Springbank ☎ 01453 543047 (Mrs F A Jones)
lhandfaj32lg@surefish.co.uk
£141-£225 Sleeps 4. 1 cottage.
Tranquil village setting near Cotswold Way.   🚭 🚣(Cam & Dursley) ★★★

● Elkstone
The Grannery ☎ 01242 870375 (Mrs Lois Eyre)
www.cottageguide.co.uk/grannery
£180-£300 Sleeps 1-2. Wing of country house.   Closed Jan
Comfortable, walker-friendly, map-loan, optional extras.   🚭 🐾

● Mitcheldean

☆ **Church Farm**

☎ 01594 541211 (Lucy & John Verity)
www.churchfarm.uk.net
£200-£350 Sleeps 2-3. 2 apartments.   Closed Feb
Situated on farm in Forest of Dean.   🚭 🐾 ★★★

The apartments are situated in a high-standard converted granary on our farm, offering direct walking in 20,000 acres of the Forest of Dean. Trails lasting from 30mins to three hours take you through oak woodland, tranquil ponds, with magnificent views over the Wye and Severn rivers. Pets welcome.

● Stanton

☆ **Charity Farm**

☎ 01386 584339 (Mrs V Ryland)
www.myrtle-cottage.co.uk/ryland.htm
£215-£550 Sleeps 2-6. 2 cottages.
Idyllic situation near Cotswold Way. 🐾 ★★★

Charming cotswold stone cottages in picturesque village on the Cotswold Way. Pretty gardens offer 'al fresco' dining. Village pub serves food and Broadway has a selection of pubs and restaurants. Walk the hills or visit National Trust houses and gardens.

● Stow-on-the-Wold
Mr & Mrs Richard Rye ☎ 01451 822466
www.hopelodge.com £450-£550 Sleeps 4-5. 1 cottage.   🚭 🐾

☆ **Flagstone Farm Cottages**

☎ 01451 832215 (Ann Whitney)
www.cotswoldfarmhouse.com
£290-£2,240 Sleeps 2-16. 6 cottages.
Spacious. Most bedrooms have ensuite. 🐾

Six spacious barn conversions, sleeping 14, 12, 8, 6, 4 and 2.
Easily accessible from all areas of the UK. Situated two miles west of Stow-on-the-Wold.
Many facilities – tennis, table tennis, snooker. 14 acres of grounds situated in the heart of the Cotswolds.

Email: awhitney@btconnect.com

● Winchcombe
The Cotswold Retreat ☎ 01242 603124 (Mark Grassick)
www.thecotswoldretreat.co.uk
£150-£400 Sleeps 2-6. 2 cottages.
Great location on Cotswold Way. 🐾 ★★★★

SOMERSET

● Axbridge
Waterfront Farm Cottage ☎ 01934 733202 (Mrs Marina Parrett)
badgworthfarm@aol.com
£250-£350 Sleeps 2. 1 cottage.
River frontage, and private fishing.   🚭 🐾

● Burrowbridge

Hillview ☎ 01823 698308 (Mrs Ros Griffiths)
£150-£185 Sleeps 2. Bungalow annexe.
Fully equipped, central heating. Rural location. ⊗ 🛁 ★★★

● Cheddar

☆ **Home Farm**
☎ 01934 842078 (Chris & Sue Sanders)
www.homefarmcottages.com
£240-£685 Sleeps 1-8. 4 cottages.
⊗ ★★★★

Four beautifully converted stone barns
with original beams. Set in two acres of
an Area of Outstanding Natural Beauty,
and surrounded by farm and National
Trust land. Many local walks.
All cottages are comfortable warm
and fully equipped.

Sungate Holiday Apartments ☎ 01934 842273 (Mrs M M Fieldhouse)
http://sungateholidayapartments.co.uk
£120-£175 Sleeps 1-5. 4 apartments.
Fully equipped with laundry facilities available. ⊗ 🛁 ★★★

☆ **Bradley Cross Farm**
☎ 01934 741771 (Judy Credland)
www.bradleycrossfarm.org.uk
£150-£210 Sleeps 2. 1 cottage.   Closed Oct-Mar
Panoramic views over the Somerset Levels. 🛁

Single room stone built cottage with bunk
beds and bathroom, on
working farm. Situated high on the Mendip
Hills, one mile from Cheddar Gorge, with
spectacular views over the Somerset Levels.

Close to the West Mendip Way walk.

Venns Views ☎ 01934 741920 (Lawrence Leigh-Coop)
leigh-coop@ukonline.co.uk
£150-£300 Sleeps 2. 4 studio flats.   Closed Dec-Jan
Small apartments, big views, private parking. 🛁

● Crewkerne

Mrs Z Morgan ☎ 01460 77259
£100-£150 Sleeps 2-4. 1 property.
Listed building in rural setting. ⚓(Crewkerne) 🛁 RA member

● Exford
EXMOOR

Court Farm ☎ 0845 226 7154 (Mr & Mrs Horstmann)
www.courtfarm.co.uk
£180-£325 Sleeps 2-5. 3 cottages.
Adjacent to river with private gardens. 🛁 ★★★★

● Ilminster

Mrs Barbara Garfield ☎ 01481 253145
garfieldgsy@cwgsy.net
£200-£350 Sleeps 4. 1 cottage.
Set in heart of Blackdown hills. ⊗ 🛁 ★★★

● Porlock
EXMOOR

☆ **The Pack Horse**
☎ 01643 862475 (Linda & Brian Garner)
www.thepackhorse.net
£220-£480 Sleeps 2-6. 4 apartments, 1 cottage.
Located in idyllic National Trust village. 🛁 ★★★-★★★★

Our self-catering apartments and cottage are
situated in this unique location alongside the
shallow river Aller overlooking the famous Pack
Horse Bridge. Enjoy immediate access from our
doorstep to the beautiful surrounding countryside, pretty villages, spectacular coast & Exmoor.
Open all year. Short breaks. Private parking.

● Porlock Weir
EXMOOR

☆ **Woodlands**
☎ 01793 731449 (Peter & Anita Gantlett)
gantlettp@aol.com
£460-£990 Sleeps 8-10. 1 house.
Ideal for exploring Exmoor/SW Coast Path. ⊗ 🛁

Comfortable spacious house in idyllic
situation overlooking quaint harbour of
Porlock Weir. Superb sea views from almost
all rooms. 4 bedrooms, 2 sitting rooms,
kitchen, utility, shower room, bathroom,
log fire. Full CH and electricity included.
Good food nearby. Brochure.

● Simonsbath
EXMOOR

Wintershead Farm ☎ 01643 831222 (Jane Styles)
www.wintershead.co.uk
£195-£650 Sleeps 2-6. 5 cottages.   Closed Jan-Feb
Ideal base for a walking holiday. 🛁 ★★★★

● Withypool
EXMOOR

Newland House ☎ 01643 831693 (Alex Stokes) flying.flo@virgin.net
£150-£210 Sleeps 2. 1 flat.
2 minutes from Two Moors Way. ⊗

WILTSHIRE

● Castle Combe

Well Cottage ☎ 07919 357363 (Steve Boyle)
www.wellcottagecastlecombe.co.uk
£350-£770 Sleeps 4-6. 1 cottage.
Secluded period cottage, near Cotswold Way. 🛁

● Devizes

The Old Stables ☎ 01380 862971 (Jon & Judy Nash)
www.tichbornes.co.uk £252-£448
Sleeps 4. 3 cottages.
Converted stables in rural Wiltshire. ⊗ 🛁 ★★★★

● Marlborough

☆ **Dairy Cottage**
☎ 01672 515129 (Hazel & Mark Crockford)
crockford@farming.co.uk
£300-£650 Sleeps 6-8. 1 cottage.
Peaceful bungalow on edge of Savernake Forest. ⊗ 🐾 ★★★

Dairy Cottage is situated on Brown's Farm, which is a working dairy/arable farm. Set on the edge of Savernake Forest overlooking open farmland, Dairy Cottage offers peace and tranquility for a true north Wiltshire holiday. A modern spacious, well-equipped bungalow with open fire awaits your arrival.

DORSET

☆ **Churchview Guesthouse** (BB)
Winterbourne Abbas, Dorchester DT2 9LS ☎ 01305 889296
(Michael & Jane Deller) www.churchview.co.uk Map 194/618905
BB £33-£37 Max 17.
✗ 🐾 Ⓑ Ⓓ ⊗ ! 🚗 ◆◆◆◆ See B&B also.

Our beautiful 17th-century guest house is ideal for groups wishing to explore west Dorset. We cater for up to 17 (more by arrangement with local B&Bs). Delicious evening meals. Two lounges and bar. Group rates. Call Michael & Jane Deller.
Email: stay@churchview.co.uk

GROUPS

CORNWALL

Cutkive Wood Holiday Lodges (SC) St Ives ☎ 01579 362216
(Andy & Jackie Lowman) www.cutkivewood.co.uk Grid ref: SX 292676
SC £120-£410 Min 1, max 30. 6 lodges. Ⓓ ⊗ See SC also.

The Field of Dreams (BB/SC) Sancreed, Penzance ☎ 01736 788304
(John Hawken) www.thefieldofdreams.co.uk Grid ref: 298405
BB £25, FB £40, SC £800-£1,500 Min 8, max 20. 1 residential centre.
✗ 🐾 Ⓓ ⊗ 🚗 !

Hopsland (BB/SC) Commonmoor, Liskeard PL14 6EJ ☎ 01579 344480
(Linda Hosken) www.hopslandholidays.co.uk Grid ref: SX257696
BB £20, SC £185-£550 Min 1, max 16. Cottages.
✗ 🐾 Ⓑ Ⓓ ⊗ 🚗 ★★★★ See B&B and SC also.

DEVON

☆ **Royal York & Faulkner Hotel** (BB)
Sidmouth ☎ Freephone 0800 220714
www.royalyorkhotel.net
DBB £33.90-£50.60 Min 30, max 90. Closed Jan
✗ 🐾 Ⓑ Ⓓ ★★Ⓢ

Beautifully appointed Regency hotel in a superb position on the centre of Sidmouth's elegant esplanade and adjacent to the picturesque town centre.

Family run with a long-standing reputation for hospitality and service, offering all amenities and excellent facilities.

Located on the Jurassic Coast, a World Heritage site, the area is ideally situated for walking the superb coastal paths and inland walks offering stunning flora, fauna and views. Regular host to Ramblers Groups.

Email: stay@royalyorkhoyel.net

Sandringham Hotel (BB) 20 Durlston Rd, Swanage BH19 2HX ☎ 01929 423076 (Mr & Mrs Silk) www.smoothhound.co.uk/hotels/sandringham.html
Map 195/033782 BB £27-£37 Max 25. Closed mid-July-Aug
✗ 🐾 Ⓑ Ⓓ ! 🚗 See B&B also.

SOMERSET

☆ **Yarn Market Hotel** (BB)
25-31 High Street, Dunster TA24 6SF ☎ 01643 821425 (Penny Bale)
www.yarnmarkethotel.co.uk
BB £30 ✗ Min 10, max 50. 1 hotel.
🐾 Ⓑ Ⓓ ⊗ 🚶(Dunster) ★★★ ! 🚗 See B&B also.

Our small hotel provides a friendly atmosphere, home cooking, en-suite single, double, four-poster and family rooms all with colour TV and tea/coffee. Residents' lounge, packed lunches and drying facilities available. Open all year. B&B from £40 (£60 with evening meal). 3 nights £105 (£160). Special offer for walking parties (10-50 people) - 3 nights B&B from £90 (£135). An ideal centre for exploring Exmoor.
Email Penny Bale: yarnmarket.hotel@virgin.net

FOUND SOMEWHERE THAT'S NOT IN THIS GUIDE?
Fill in the Recommendation Form on p311 and send it to the editor at our central office or email:
yearbook@london.ramblers.org.uk

WILTSHIRE

COTSWOLD WAY

☆ Mayfield House Hotel (BB)
Crudwell, Malmesbury SN16 9EW ☎ 01666 577409 (Max or Chris)
www.mayfieldhousehotel.co.uk Map 173/954928
DBB £36 Min 2, max 46.

✕ 🐾 Ⓑ Ⓓ See B&B also.

Explore the Cotswolds.
Friendly country house hotel in the heart of the Cotswolds. Excellent restaurant.
Fresh food and plenty of it! Proprietor run, 26 lovely bedrooms, regularly used
by walking groups. Group rates from £36pppn DBB.
reception@mayfieldhousehotel.co.uk
AA 2 stars, AA Rosette Award-winning food.

HOSTELS, BUNKHOUSES & CAMPSITES

CORNWALL

SOUTH WEST COAST PATH

The Old Chapel Zennor Backpackers/Cafe (IH) Zennor, St Ives TR26 3BY
☎ 01736 798307 www.backpackers.co.uk/zennor
Bednight £12 ✕ 🐾 Ⓓ ⊗

DEVON

☆ Cloud Farm (C)
Oare, Lynton ☎ 01598 741234
www.doonevalleyholidays.co.uk Grid ref: 794468
Bednight £5-7.50
✕ nearby Ⓓ ★★★ See SC also.

Cloud Farm's idyllic riverside setting in
the tranquility of the Exmoor National
Park's Doone Valley, provides perfect
'away-from-it-all' camping all year. Three
spacious riverside camping/caravan fields,
set in an unspoilt paradise for walking,
relaxing, watching wildlife, or riding from
our stables (all ages and levels).

Excellent base for touring nearby villages
and walking the South West Coast Path.

Shop, selling food and camping supplies. Laundry facilities and new shower
block on-site.

DARTMOOR
TWO MOORS WAY

Langstone Manor (C) Moortown, Tavistock, PL19 9JZ ☎ 01822 613371
(Jane Kellett) www.langstone-manor.co.uk Map 201/528734
Camping £8 Closed Nov-mid-Mar ✕ Ⓑ Ⓓ ★★★★ See SC also.

SOMERSET

MACMILLAN WAY WEST

Bowdens Crest Caravan & Camping Park (C) Bowdens, Langport TA10 0DD
☎ 01458 250553 www.bowdenscrest.co.uk
Camping £4 Caravans for hire. ✕ 🐾 Ⓑ ★★★

PUBS

CORNWALL

● Morwenstow
SOUTH WEST COAST PATH

☆ The Bush Inn
Crosstown, Morwenstow, Bude EX23 9ST
☎ 01288 331242 (Rob or Ed) www.bushinn-morwenstow.co.uk
✕ Ⓥ Large groups bookings. Please leave muddy boots at the door.
B&B accommodation available.

A 13th-century
freehouse in a
stunning
location just
off the South
West Coast
Path.

Once a haunt
for smugglers
and wreckers,
this historic pub has provided sustenance for weary travellers for hundreds of
years and is situated halfway between Bude and Hartland on one of the most
dramatic stretches of the north Cornish coast.

Open all day serving home-cooked food and Cornish real ales. Children and dogs
welcome. A quarter of a mile from the coast.

SOMERSET

● Stogumber

☆ The White Horse Inn
High Street TA4 3TA
☎ 01984 656277 (John Trebilcock) www.whitehorsestogumber.co.uk
✕ Ⓥ Large groups bookings. Leave muddy boots at the door.
Accommodation available.

The White Horse is a Grade II-listed
freehouse in the picturesque village
of Stogumber in glorious countryside
on the slopes of the Quantock Hills.
The extensive menu uses fresh local
produce and award-winning locally-
brewed real ales are a speciality.

SOUTH WEST

SOUTH DOWNS WAY

SOUTH

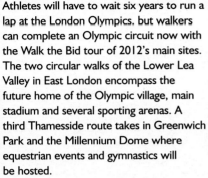

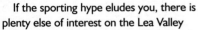
LEA VALLEY

Athletes will have to wait six years to run a lap at the London Olympics, but walkers can complete an Olympic circuit now with the Walk the Bid tour of 2012's main sites. The two circular walks of the Lower Lea Valley in East London encompass the future home of the Olympic village, main stadium and several sporting arenas. A third Thameside route takes in Greenwich Park and the Millennium Dome where equestrian events and gymnastics will be hosted.

If the sporting hype eludes you, there is plenty else of interest on the Lea Valley trails both natural and man-made. Kestrels, kingfishers and herons can be spotted around the old canal basins and ford locks, while eels, perch and carp inhabit the River Lea. Several historic buildings also lie en-route, including the Grade I-listed House Mill, Britain's largest surviving eighteenth-century tidal mill, and the ornate Italian and Gothic styled Abbey Mills Pumping Station known as the 'cathedral of sewage'.

> Kestrels, kingfishers and heron can be spotted around the old canal basins and ford locks, while eels, perch and carp inhabit the River Lea.

Last September, the Capital Ring formally launched. The 115km/72-mile path makes a fascinating journey through London's parks, riversides, streets and woodland, crossing the Thames at Woolwich and Richmond (see London Loop, p27). Or try the culture-driven Discover London Trails – also unveiled last year – offering eleven half and full-day walks to over 100 museums and galleries.

Beyond the M25, the Serpent Trail opened its stiles to the public in April: a 103km/64-mile route that snakes its way between Haslemere, Petworth, Midhurst and Petersfield over 1,000 acres of fragile West Sussex heathland. The region also boasts the country's first new national parks for 50 years: the New Forest, and later this year, the South Downs. And after running five years over-schedule, the 170m-tall Spinnaker Tower opens at Portsmouth Harbour, so walkers of the Solent Way can enjoy spectacular views of the footpath from the glass-floored viewing deck and 110m crow's nest.

Long Distance Paths

Chiltern Way	CHI
Icknield Way	ICK
Isle of Wight Coastal Path	IWC
London Loop	LNL
Macmillan Way	MCM
Midshires Way	MDS
Monarch's Way	MON
North Downs Way	NDN
Ridgeway	RDG
Solent Way	SOL
South Downs Way	SDN
Test Way	TST
Thames Path	THM
Wealdway	WLD

Public rights of way:
34,376km/21,348 miles

Mapped access land:

590 sq km/228 sq miles
(Areas 1, 3, 7, 8)

0   5   10 miles

0   10 kilometres

Explore Lee Valley Regional Park

If you enjoy walking, wildlife, countryside, heritage, fantastic open spaces with great places to stay, then the Lee Valley Regional Park is the place for you. The park stretches for 10,000 acres between Ware in Hertfordshire to the River Thames at East India Dock Basin and provides leisure activities which suit all ages, tastes and abilities.

☎ 0845 677 0615*

www.leevalleypark.org.uk

*Calls charged at local call rate from a BT land line

Lee Valley Park

Open spaces and sporting places

SOUTH
LOCAL RAMBLERS GROUPS

BERKSHIRE
AREA SECRETARY
Mr Cliff Lambert, Marandella, 1
Lawrence Mead, Kintbury, Hungerford,
RG17 9XT ☎ 01488 608108

GROUP SECRETARIES
Berkshire Walkers Caroline
Mcdonagh, 49 Sharnwood Drive,
Calcot, Reading, Berkshire, RG31 7YD
www.berkshirewalkers.org.uk
East Berkshire Mr Gerald Barnett,
9 Fremantle Road, High Wycombe,
Bucks, HP13 7PQ ☎ 01494 522404
(Membership enquiries Mrs Welch
☎ 01753 662139)
www.eastberksramblers.org/
Loddon Valley Mrs J Eves, 4 Carlton
Close, Woodley, Reading, Berks,
RG5 4JS ☎ 0118 9690318 (Membership
enquiries Mrs Curtis ☎ 0118 9403158)
www.lvra.org.uk/
Mid Berkshire Ms E Cuff, Donkey
Pound Cottage, Beech Hill, Reading,
Berkshire, RG7 2AX ☎ 0118 988 2674
www.mbra.org.uk/
Pang Valley Dr C Howlett, Reading,
RG30 2AL ☎ 0118 9590436
South East Berks Mr John Moules,
50 Qualitas, Roman Hill, Bracknell,
Berks, RG12 7QG ☎ 01344 421002
http://members.aol.com/seberksra
West Berkshire Mrs J Bowman,
4 Cansfield End, Northcroft Park,
Newbury, Berks, RG14 1XH
☎ 01635 35902
www.wberksramblers.org.uk/
Windsor & District Miss J M Clark,
7 Dyson Close, Windsor, Berkshire,
SL4 3LZ ☎ 01753 866 545

BUCKINGHAMSHIRE & WEST MIDDLESEX
AREA SECRETARY
Mr D Bradnack, 47 Thame Road,
Haddenham, Aylesbury, Bucks, HP17
8EP ☎ 01844 291069 (before 9pm)
www.bucks-wmiddx-ramblers.org.uk/

GROUP SECRETARIES
Amersham & District Mrs M Moody,
White Cottage, 93 St Leonard's Road,
Chesham Bois, Amersham, HP6 6DR
☎ 01494 727504
Aylesbury & District Mr G Seymour,
108 Northern Road, Aylesbury,
HP19 9QY ☎ 01296 583562
www.aylesbury-ramblers.me.uk
Chiltern 20s-30s Walking Group
John Wainwright, 21 Milton Way,
Houghton Regis, Dunstable, Beds,
LU5 5UF

☎ 01582 864972
www.chilterns2030s.co.uk
Hillingdon & District See
www.hillingdonramblers.org.uk or
contact our central office for details
MK & North Bucks 20s-30s John
Frankland (contact), 2 Yeats Close,
Newport Pagnell, Bucks, MK16 8RD
☎ 01908 612938
www.mk-northbucks2030s.org.uk/
Milton Keynes & District Mr John
West, 45 Blackdown, Fullers Slade,
Milton Keynes, MK11 2AA
☎ 01908 564055
www.mkramblers.freeserve.co.uk
North West London Miss H O Lee,
12b Wellesley Road, Harrow,
Middlesex, HA1 1QN ☎ 020 8863 7628
heatherlee@onetel.com
West London Mr T Berry, 128 Park
Lane, South Harrow, Middlesex,
HA2 8NL ☎ 020 8422 3284
www.btinternet.com/
~westlondongroupra/
Wycombe District Mr John
Esslemont, 4 Park Farm Way, Lane End,
High Wycombe, Buckinghamshire,
HP14 3EG ☎ 01494 881597
(membership enquiries Mrs A Shipley
☎ 01494 862699)
www.geocities.com/perrir_uk/walking/
frames.html

HAMPSHIRE
AREA SECRETARY
Mr D Nixon, 27 Brading Avenue,
Southsea, Hants, PO4 9QJ
☎ 023 9273 2649
www.hants.gov.uk/hampshireramblers

GROUP SECRETARIES
Alton See www.ramblers.org.uk/info/
localgroups or contact our central office
for details.
Andover Mr P Wood, 9 Kingsmead,
Anna Valley, Andover, Hampshire,
SP11 7PN ☎ 01264 710 844
www.hants.gov.uk/ raag
Eastleigh Mrs P D Beazley,
16 Windover Close, Bitterne,
Southampton, SO19 5JS
☎ 02380 437443) www.hants.org.uk/
eastleighramblers
**Hampshire 20s & 30s Walking
Group** Miss R V Lee & Mr P Lewis, 9
Thistle Road, Hedge End, Southampton,
SO30 4TS ☎ 023 8033 2069
(membership enquiries ☎ 0798 6655660)
www.hants.gov.uk/hantswalk2030
Meon Mrs C Coxwell, 19 New Road,
Fareham, Hants, PO16 7SR
☎ 01329 827790

New Forest Mrs Audrey Wilson,
16 West Road, Dibden Purlieu,
Southampton, SO45 4RJ
☎ 023 8084 6353
www.newforestramblers.org.uk
North East Hants See
www.ramblers.org.uk/info/localgroups
or contact our central office for details.
North Hampshire Downs
Mr Mike Taylor, 19 Inkpen Gardens,
Lychpit, Basingstoke, Hants, RG24 8YQ
☎ 01256 842468
www.hants.org.uk/ramblersnhd
Portsmouth Mrs M G Haly,
95 Winstanley Road, Stamshaw,
Portsmouth, Hants, PO2 8JS
☎ 023 92693874
Romsey Mr T W Radford,
67 Rownhams Lane,
North Baddesley,
Southampton, SO52 9HR
☎ 02380 731279
www.romseynet.org.uk/ramblers/
ramblers.htm
South East Hants Mr D Nixon,
27 Brading Avenue, Southsea, Hants,
PO4 9QJ ☎ 023 9273 2649
www.hants.org.uk/sehantsramblers
Southampton John Catchlove,
4 Sandringham Court, 18 Winn Rd,
Southampton, SO17 1EN
☎ 023 8055 3883
www.hants.gov.uk/sotonram
Waltham Mrs W E Bassom,
3 Mayfair Court, Botley,
Southampton, SO30 2GT
☎ 01489 784946
Wessex Weekend Walkers
Ms H E Stacey, 18 Langham Close,
North Baddesley, Southampton,
SO52 9NT ☎ 07884 486676
www.wessexweekendwalkers.org.uk
Winchester Mrs P Farncombe,
7 Fairfax Close, Winchester, SO22 4LP
☎ 01962 620126
www.hants.gov.uk/wramblers

HERTFORDSHIRE & NORTH MIDDLESEX
See East

INNER LONDON
AREA SECRETARY
Mr D Purcell, 8 Dryburgh Mansions,
London, SW15 1AJ ☎ 020 8788 1373
www.innerlondonramblers.org.uk

GROUP SECRETARIES
Blackheath Ms D O'Toole,
67 Flintmill Crescent, London, SE3 8LU
☎ 020 8319 8593
www.blackheathramblers.org.uk

SOUTH

LOCAL RAMBLERS GROUPS continued

Hammersmith & Wandsworth Mrs M Jones, 27 Rannoch Road, London, W6 9SS ☎ 07796 684522 (membership enquiries Mr Esbester ☎ 020 8646 5545)

Hampstead & District Mr K D Jones, Flat 4, 144 Agar Grove, Camden, London, NW1 9TY ☎ 020 7485 2348 (evenings only)

Kensington, Chelsea & Westminster Ms J M Mack, 8n Grove End House, Grove End Road, London, NW8 9HN ☎ 020 7289 0305 (membership enquiries Susan Gunning ☎ 020 7589 6600) http://users.whsmithnet.co.uk/ kcw.ramblers

Metropolitan Walkers Miss K White, Ground Floor Flat, 32 Leigh Road, London, N5 1AH ☎ 020 7226 3583 or 07799 667022 www.metropolitan-walkers.org.uk

North East London Ms S Milsome, 6 Belgrave Lodge, 36 Wellesley Road, London, W4 4BN ☎ 020 8994 0171 http://nelr.co.uk

South Bank Mrs Vivien Scorer, 11 Rope Street, London, SE16 7TE ☎ 020 7252 2506

ISLE OF WIGHT

AREA SECRETARY
Mr Mike Marchant, Merry Meeting, Ryde House Drive, Binstead Road, Ryde, Isle Of Wight, PO33 3NF ☎ 01983 564909

GROUP SECRETARIES
Isle of Wight Mr David Skelsey, Madeira, Hunts Road, St Lawrence, Ventnor, Isle Of Wight, PO38 1XT ☎ 01983 854540

Wight Sole Mr Gary Clarke, 70 Newport Road, Cowes, Isle Of Wight, PO31 7PN ☎ 01983 299511

KENT

AREA SECRETARY
Mr Arthur Russ, 7 Barnfield Road, Riverhead, Sevenoaks, Kent, TN13 2AY ☎ 01732 453863) www.kentramblers.org.uk/

GROUP SECRETARIES
Ashford (Kent) Mr P B Whitestone, Summer Hill, Fosten Green, Biddenden Ashford, Kent, TN27 8ER ☎ 01580 291596 www.Ashford-Ramblers.co.uk

Bromley Miss Barbara Phelps, 60 St Georges Road West, Bromley, Kent, BR1 2NW barbara.phelps@btopenworld.com

Canterbury Mr R Cordell, 162 Broadway, Herne Bay, Kent, CT6 8HY ☎ 01227 361 902

raycordell162@hotmail.com

Dartford Mr N E Turvey, 84 Park Avenue, Northfleet, Kent, DA11 8DL ☎ 01474 323790

Maidstone Mr P D Royall, 18 Firs Close, Aylesford, Maidstone, Kent, ME20 7LH ☎ 01622 710782 (membership enquiries W Williams ☎ 01634 371906) www.maidstoneramblers.org.uk

Medway Mrs D M Ashdown, 94a Hollywood Lane, Wainscott, Rochester, Kent, ME3 8AR

North West Kent Mr Ken Conie, 63 Crofton Avenue, Orpington, Kent, BR6 8DY ☎ 01689 851358

Sevenoaks Mrs S E Penzer, 62 Oakhill Road, Sevenoaks, Kent, TN13 1NT ☎ 01732 461536

Tonbridge & Malling Miss B Stead, 43 Copse Hill, Leybourne, West Malling, Kent, ME19 5QR

Trailfinders (East Kent) 20s-40s Claire Spencer, 29 Primrose Drive, Kingsnorth, Ashford, Kent, TN23 3NP ☎ 01233 503266

Tunbridge Wells Miss M I Coulstock, 29 St Peters Street, Tunbridge Wells, Kent, TN2 4UX ☎ 01892 536715

West Kent Walking Mr N Houghton, 4 Swangleys Lane, Knebworth, Hertfordshire, SG3 6AA http://home.freeuk.net/wkwo/

White Cliffs Mrs R Hodges, 25 William Avenue, Folkestone, Kent, CT19 5TL ☎ 01303 258022) rhonahodges@hotmail.com

OXFORDSHIRE

AREA SECRETARY
Mr P Lonergan, 35 Cherwell Close, Abingdon, Oxon, OX14 3TD ☎ 01235 202784) http://ramblers-oxon.org.uk

GROUP SECRETARIES
Bicester & Kidlington Mr Colin Morgan, 11 Spruce Drive, Bicester, OX26 3YE ☎ 01869 369603

Cherwell Hazel Lister, 3 Bowling Green, Farthinghoe, Brackley, NN13 5PQ ☎ 01295 710227 hazel@lister8280.fsbusiness.co.uk

Didcot & Wallingford Mrs V Tilling, The Cedars, Brookfield Close, Wallingford, OX10 9EQ ☎ 01491 839221 janicetilling@aol.com

Henley & Goring Eileen Burroughs, 43 Elizabeth Road, Henley-On-Thames, RG9 1RA ☎ 01491 572490 (membership enquiries Tony Brown ☎ 01491 575500)

Oxford Mrs E M Steane & Mr J Steane, 36 Harpes Road, Summertown, Oxford, OX2 7QL ☎ 01865 552531

Oxon 20s & 30s Walking Group Miss J A Cockram, 76 Cornwallis Road, Oxford, OX4 3NL ☎ 01865 772327/07930 645901 www.34 brinkster.com/ oxon2030walkers

Thame & Wheatley Mrs J E Noyce, 27 Worminghall Road, Ickford, Aylesbury, Bucks, HP18 9JB ☎ 01844 339969

Vale of White Horse Mr P Lonergan, 35 Cherwell Close, Abingdon, Oxon, OX14 3TD ☎ 01235 202784) patlon@ntlworld.com

West Oxfordshire Mr Clive Jones, 49 Harefields, Oxford, OX2 8HG ☎ 01865 514663

SURREY

AREA SECRETARY
Mr G Butler, 1 Leaside Court, Lower Luton Road, Harpenden, Herts, AL5 5BX ☎ 01582 767062 Butlergc1@aol.com

GROUP SECRETARIES
Croydon Mr W Haug, 22 Danvers Way, Caterham, Surrey, CR3 5FJ ☎ 01883 344 011 www.croydonramblers.org.uk

East Surrey Mrs C Isham, 25 Wheeler Avenue, Oxted, Surrey, RH8 9LF ☎ 01883 717966 www.eastsurreyramblers.org.uk/

Epsom & Ewell Mr D J Newman, 56a Acacia Grove, New Malden, Surrey, KT3 3BU ☎ 0208 949 3471 www.epsomandewellramblers.co.uk

Farnham & District Ms G Ross, 10 Ridgway Hill Road, Farnham, Surrey, GU9 8LS ☎ 01252 722930 www.farnhamramblers.org.uk/

Godalming & Haslemere Mrs C Chard, 1 Hill House, Ockford Road, Godalming, GU7 1QX ☎ 01483 416907 www.godalmingandhaslemereramblers. org.uk

Guildford Mr P & Mrs C Hackman, 2 Downside Road, Guildford, GU4 8PH ☎ 01483 573633

http://guildfordramblers.mysite. freeserve.com

Kingston Mr M Lake, 87 Porchester Road, Kingston Upon Thames, Surrey, KT1 3PW ☎ 020 8541 3437 (membership enquiries Mrs R O'Keeffe ☎ 020 8946 8380) www.geocities.com/kingstonramblers

Mole Valley Mrs J Kucera, 120 Carlton Road, Reigate, Surrey, RH2 0JF ☎ 01737 765158 (membership enquiries Mrs Marles ☎ 01372 454012) http://myweb.tiscali.co.uk/ molevalleyramblers

SOUTH

LOCAL RAMBLERS GROUPS continued

Reigate Mr Glyn Jones, 12 Briars Wood, Horley, Surrey, RH6 9UE
☎ 01293 773198
www.reigateramblers.org.uk

Richmond Mr W Westcott, 47 Capel Gardens, Pinner, Middx, HA5 5RF
☎ 020 8429 0886 (membership enquiries Mrs Sharp ☎ 020 8748 0049)
www.richmondramblers.co.uk/

Staines Pat Pratley, 76 Hetherington Rd, Charlton Village, Shepperton, Middlesex, TW17 0SW
☎ 01932 711355
www.stainesramblers.co.uk/

Surrey Area Weekend Walkers See www.saww.org.uk. or contact our central office for details.

Surrey Heath Mrs C Norris, 11 Warwick Close, Camberley, Surrey, GU15 1ES ☎ 01276 26821

Surrey Under 40s Mr D E Ebdon, Leafdale Cottage, London Road, Addington, West Malling, Kent, ME19 5PL ☎ 01732 843351
www.surreyyoungwalkers.org.uk

Sutton/Wandle Valley Peter Rogers, 8 Claygate Court, All Saints Road, Sutton, Surrey, SM1 3DB
☎ 020 8641 4339 (membership enquiries ☎ 020 8643 2605)
ww.suttonandwandlevalleyramblers.org.uk

Woking & District Miss S Woodcock, Skerries, 6 Connaught Crescent, Brookwood, Woking, GU24 0AN
☎ 01483 489 053)
http://web.ukonline.co.uk/ wokingramblers/

SUSSEX
AREA SECRETARY
Mr Nigel Sloan, Kervesridge, Kerves Lane, Horsham, West Sussex, RH13 6ES ☎ 01403 258055
(membership enquiries P Brannigan
☎ 01243 824135)
www.sussex-ramblers.org.uk

GROUP SECRETARIES
Arun-Adur Miss G M Agate, 136 Abbey Road, Sompting, Lancing, Sussex, BN15 0AD
☎ 01903 761352

Beachy Head Miss M O'Brien, Southease, Folkington Lane, Folkington, Polegate, BN26 5SA ☎ 01323 482068

Brighton & Hove Mrs F M Leenders, 14 Middle Road, Brighton, BN1 6SR
☎ 01273 501233
www.brightonandhoveramblers.org.uk/

Crawley & North Sussex
Mrs V Sherrington, 37 Cook Road, Crawley, RH10 5DJ
☎ 01293 535852

Heathfield & District Mrs R Brown, Chant House, Eridge Lane, Rotherfield, Nr Crowborough, Sussex, TN6 3JU
☎ 0189 285 2153

High Weald Walkers Mr N Singer, Croft Lodge, Bayhall Road, Tunbridge Wells, Kent, TN2 4TP
☎ 01892 523821
www.highwealdwalkers.org.uk/

Horsham & Billingshurst See www.sussex-ramblers.org.uk/ horsham/horsham.htm or contact our central office for details.

Mid Sussex Mrs Celia Parrott, 27 Dale Avenue, Hassocks, West Sussex, BN6 8LP
☎ 01273 843715

Rother Mr L E Pringle, Merrymead, 57 Westfield Lane, St Leonards-On-Sea, TN37 7NE ☎ 01424 752452
www.rotherramblers.org.uk

South West Sussex Mrs Anne Parker, 11 Palmers Field Avenue, Chichester, West Sussex, PO19 6YE
☎ 01243 536080
http://southwestsxramblers.mysite.wan adoo-members.co.uk

Sussex Young Walkers Ms B Bruzon, 30 Northiam Road, Eastbourne, BN20 8LP ☎ 01323 639172
www.sussexyoungwalkers.fsnet.co.uk/

LOCAL RAMBLERS PUBLICATIONS

BERKSHIRE
The Chairman's Walk around the perimeter of West Berkshire
edited by Geoff Vince, ISBN 1 901184 59 5. A series of 25 linear walks, each of about 7km/4 miles, grouped in 10 sections and completing a 158km/98-mile circuit. Guide contains maps, route guides, public transport and local interest information and photographs. £7 + £1 p&p from West Berks Ramblers, 38 Kipling Close, Thatcham RG18 3AY. Cheques to West Berks Ramblers.

Rambling for Pleasure Footpath maps for East Berkshire
Cookham & District a superb area of walking country in the Thames Valley easily accessible by rail. 50p
Hurley & District highlights the dense network of footpaths linking the Thames Path with the quiet meadows and wooded slopes surrounding Warren Row and Knowl Hill. 50p
Windsor & The Great Park ISBN 1 874258 10 4. The only guide to show all the paths and areas open to the public on foot in the Park, plus footpaths in surrounding areas and other features of

interest. 50p + 30p p&p per map from East Berks RA Publications, PO Box 1357, Maidenhead SL6 7FP. Cheques to East Berks RA Publications.
Rambling for Pleasure Guides
Along the Thames 5th edition, ISBN 1 874258 09 0. 24 walks of 3km/2 miles to 9.5km/6 miles between Runnymede and Sonning, £2.95
Around Reading 1st Series, ISBN 1 874258 12 0 and 2nd Series, ISBN 1 974258 16 3. Two books each of 24 easy country walks of 5km/3 miles to 16km/10 miles through Berkshire, Oxfordshire and north Hampshire, within an 11km/7-mile radius of Reading. £2.95 each.
In East Berkshire ISBN 1 874258 15 5. 24 mainly flat walks of 5km/3 miles to 12km/7.5 miles around Maidenhead, Wokingham, Bracknell and Ascot, including 6 from stations, £2.95
Kennet Valley & Watership Down ISBN 1 874258 13 9. 24 walks of 4km/2.5 miles and 11km/7 miles exploring the hidden countryside between Reading, Newbury and Basingstoke. Some modest hills. £2.95 + 50p p&p per guide from East Berks RA

Publications, PO Box 1357, Maidenhead SL6 7FP. Cheques to East Berks RA Publications.

Three Castles Path
ISBN 1 874258 08 2. A 96km/60-mile route from Windsor to Winchester with six circular walks, £2.95 + 50p p&p from East Berks RA Publications, PO Box 1357, Maidenhead SL6 7FP. Cheques to East Berks RA Publications.

21 Walks for the 21st Century
Walks on the Berkshire/Wiltshire border of between 8km/5 miles and 14.5km/9 miles, on a set of colour laminated cards with maps, directions, points of interest and transport details . £6 + £1 p&p from West Berks Ramblers, 38 Kipling Close, Thatcham RG18 3AY. Cheques to West Berks Ramblers.

BUCKINGHAMSHIRE
Best Walks in Bucks by Bus and Train.
Although the printed edition is no longer available, up-to-date detailed route descriptions are now available online at www.bucks-wmiddx-ramblers.org.uk.

Walks in South Bucks
by West London Ramblers. 17 short
walks. £1.50 from 128 Park Lane, Harrow
HA2 8NL. Cheques to West London Group
Ramblers' Association.

HAMPSHIRE
Avon Valley Path
55km/34-mile route from Salisbury to
Christchurch. £2.99 including p&p.
More Than the New Forest
by New Forest Ramblers, ISBN 1
901184 75 7. 12 cartoons, forest lore
and walking anecdotes, from prehistory
to the national park. Now only £1 post
free.
**More Walks Around the New
Forest**
17 walks between 5km/3 miles and
13km/8 miles covering the whole of the
National Park, with detailed maps, route
descriptions, points of special interest and
colour photos. £2.50 including p&p.
Walking the Wessex Heights
Detailed maps and route descriptions for
a 123km/ 77-mile route and 14 circular
walks. £1.99 including p&p.
**NEW Walks Around the New
Forest National Park**
17 newly surveyed and updated short
and medium length routes into the heart
of the new national park and along its
borders, plus carefully researched route
maps, times and walk directions. £3.50 +
50p p&p.
All from 9 Pine Close, Dibden Purlieu,
Southampton SO45 4AT. Cheques payable
to the New Forest Group, Ramblers'
Association.

King's Way
by Pat Miles, ISBN 0 86146 093 X
(Meon Group). A 72km/45-mile walk
from Portchester to Winchester, divided
into easy stages. £3.25 + £1 p&p from
19 New Road, Fareham PO16 7SR.
Cheques to Ramblers Association
Meon Group.

**12 Walks in and Around
Winchester**
Moderate-level walks in town and
countryside varying from 3km/2 miles to
14.5km/9 miles. £1.50 + 50p p&p from
Underhill House, Beech Copse, Winchester
SO22 5NR. Cheques to Winchester
Ramblers.

**Rural Rambles from the villages
around Alton**
by Alton and District RA. 10 circular walks

from 9.5km/6 miles to 16km/10 miles
starting from villages, including details of
places of interest, pubs and public
transport. Ideal for visitors to east
Hampshire and Jane Austen's house
at Chawton
Walks From Alton.
10 walks from 6km/3.75 miles to
14km/8.75 miles through typical Hampshire
landscapes, all starting in the town.
£3.50 for both books from Green Bank,
Wilsons Road, Headley Down, Bordon
GU35 8JG. Cheques to Alton and District
Ramblers.

ISLE OF WIGHT
**12 Favourite Walks on the Isle of
Wight**
**12 More Favourite Walks on the
Isle of Wight**
**12 Walks from Country Towns on
the Isle of Wight**
Walks of between 5km/3 miles and
14.5km/9 miles, with simple maps and
route descriptions, all suitable for the
infrequent walker.
All £2 + 40p p&p each from Dibs, Main
Road, Rookley, Ventnor PO38 3NQ.
Cheques payable to Mrs Joan Deacon.

KENT
**NEW Ashford Ring Walk and 7
Loop Walks**
by Fred Wright (Ashford Ramblers). A
35km/22-mile loop circling Ashford,
linking outer villages, and connected by
seven loops of around 13km/8 miles to
the town centre. £2.50 from 93 Rylands
Road, Kennington, Ashford TN24 9LR.
Cheques to Ashford Ramblers.

**Maidstone Circular Walk Part 1
and Part 2:**
Two sets of six walk cards describing a
circular route around Maidstone. Each
£1.80 + 50p p&p from Little Preston
Lodge, Coldharbour Lane, Aylesford
ME20 7NS. Cheques to Ramblers'
Association — Maidstone Group.

Walks to Interesting Places
in Sussex & Kent and **Walks in the
Weald** (Heathfield & District Group): see
under Sussex.

LONDON
Rural Walks around Richmond
by Ramblers' Association Richmond
Group. 21 walks of between 3km/2
miles and 24km/15 miles, many with
various short options, in a London

borough rich in green space, including
Richmond Park, Bushy Park, Barnes and
the Thames. Eight walks have details of
wheelchair-accessible sections, including
one route that is accessible throughout.
£1.80 + 45p p&p from 59 Gerard Road,
London SW13 9QH. Cheques to
Margaret Sharp.

SURREY
Four Stations Way
18.5km/11 mile route via stations from
Godalming to Haslemere. Illustrated in
both directions on two laminated A4
cards. £1.50 + 50p p&p from Kate Colley,
6 Hill Court, Haslemere GU27 2BD.
Cheques to Godalming and Haslemere
Ramblers Group.

The Highlights of Surrey
A series of 48 online walks originally
devised by members of Surrey Ramblers
to mark the Millennium in 2004. Lengths
from 3km/2 miles to 13.5km/8.5 miles
with some linking walks, and 30 of the
walks starting from train stations. The
walk descriptions are in simple route card
style and you will need to be able to use
an OS map.
http://surreyhilitewalks.mysite.wanadoo-
members.co.uk/

**Twenty-five Favourite Walks in
West Surrey & Sussex**
by Godalming and Haslemere Ramblers,
revised edition, ISBN 1 901184 63 3.
Variety of circular walks offering both
short and long options between
5.5km/3.5 miles and 25.5km/16 miles.
£4.95 + 50p p&p from Elstead Maps.
Cheques to Elstead Maps.

SUSSEX
Sussex Diamond Way
Midhurst — Heathfield: 96km/60 mile
walk across the county. Free + £1 p&p.

**Walks to Interesting Places in
Sussex & Kent**
(Heathfield Ramblers), ISBN 0 900613
99 8.
21 walks from 4km/2.5 miles across easy
terrain, including some linear walks
returning on preserved railways. £3.50.
Walks in the Weald
Revised 2nd edition. 36 walks from
5km/3 miles to 16km/10 miles (average
10km) across varied terrain. £3.50.
All from Cobbetts, Burnt Oak Road, High
Hurstwood, Uckfield TN22 4AE. Cheques
to Heathfield and District Ramblers Group.

SOUTH

BED & BREAKFAST

BERKSHIRE

● Ascot
Englemere Lodge, London Road, SL5 8DE ☎ 01344 627700 (Martin Langford)
www.englemerelodge.co.uk Map 175/911687
BB **D** ✕ nearby D/T3 ⋙(Ascot) Ⓥ Ⓑ Ⓓ ⊗ 🐾 ♿

● Hungerford
TEST WAY
Alderborne, 33 Bourne Vale, RG17 0LL ☎ 01488 683228
www.honeybone.co.uk Map 174/333682
BB **B** ✕ nearby S2 T2 Closed Xmas ⋙(Hungerford)
Ⓑ Ⓓ ⊗ 🐾♿🚗!Ⓜ ♦♦♦♦

Whitegates, Hungerford Park, RG17 0UR ☎ 01488 681806 (Carol Shanahan)
carol@negu.co.uk Map 174/359689
BB **D** ✕ nearby S1 D1 T1 ⋙(Hungerford) Ⓥ Ⓓ ⊗ 🐾♿🚗!Ⓜ

● Maidenhead
THAMES PATH
🍴◀ Sheephouse Manor Guest House, Sheephouse Road, SL6 8HJ
☎ 01628 776902 (Mrs C J Street)
www.sheephousemanor.co.uk Map 175/898831
BB **D** S2 D1 Closed Xmas ⋙(Maidenhead)
Ⓑ Ⓓ ⊗ 🐾♿!♿ ♦♦♦

● Newbury
Goodwin's Bed and Breakfast, 19 Kimbers Drive, Speen, RG14 1RQ
☎ 01635 521571 (Mrs Sandra Goodwin)
www.the-process.com/sandra Map 174/456681
BB **B** ✕ nearby S1 D1 T1 ⋙(Newbury)
Ⓥ Ⓑ Ⓓ ⊗ 🐾♿🚗!Ⓜ ♦♦

● Windsor
THAMES PATH
🍴◀ The Laurells, 22 Dedworth Road, SL4 5AY ☎ 01753 855821 (Mrs Joyce)
Map 175,176/952765
BB **B** ✕ nearby S1 T2 Closed Xmas ⋙(Central & Riverside)
Ⓑ Ⓓ ⊗ 🐾♿

Clivore, 12 Parsonage Lane, SL4 5EN ☎ 01753 868052
clivorest@tiscali.co.uk Map 175,176/953766
BB **C** ✕ nearby S2 D2 ⋙(Windsor Central) Ⓥ Ⓓ ⊗ ♿!

BUCKINGHAMSHIRE

● Edlesborough (Dunstable)
RIDGEWAY, ICKNIELD WAY & CHILTERN WAY
Ridgeway End, 5 Ivinghoe Way, LU6 2EL ☎ 01525 220405 (Mr & Mrs Lloyd)
www.ridgewayend.co.uk Map 165/974183
BB **C** ✕ nearby S1 D1 T1 F1 Closed Xmas Ⓑ Ⓓ ⊗ 🐾🚗!

● Marlow
THAMES PATH & CHILTERN WAY
Merrie Hollow, Seymour Court Hill, Marlow Road, SL7 3DE ☎ 01628 485663
(Mr & Mrs B Wells) Map 175/837889
BB **B** ✕ book first £12, 7-8pm D1 T1 Closed Xmas ⋙(Marlow)
Ⓥ Ⓓ ⊗ 🐾♿🚗♿ ♦♦♦

Acha Pani, Bovingdon Green, SL7 2JL ☎ 01628 483435 (Mrs Mary Cowling)
mary@achapani.freeserve.co.uk Map 175/834869
BB **B** S1 D1 T1 ⋙(Marlow) Ⓑ Ⓓ 🐾♿🚗♿ ♦♦♦

🍴◀ 18 Rookery Court, SL7 3HR ☎ 01628 486451 (Gill Bullen)
www.bandbmarlow.co.uk Map 175/849869
BB **D** ✕ nearby S1 D1 ⋙(Marlow)
Ⓑ Ⓓ ⊗ 🐾♿🚗!♿ ♦♦♦♦Ⓢ

🍴◀ Compleat Cottage, SL7 1RL ☎ 01628 478704 (Sheila Gaunt)
sheilagaunt@aol.com Map 175/851858
BB **C** ✕ £5, 6-9pm S1 ⋙(Marlow) Ⓥ Ⓑ Ⓓ ⊗ 🐾♿🚗!♿Ⓜ

● Saunderton (High Wycombe)
RIDGEWAY, CHILTERN WAY & MIDSHIRES WAY
Hunters Gate, Deanfield, HP14 4JR ☎ 01494 481718 (Mrs Anne Dykes)
www.huntersgatebandb.co.uk Map 165/809975
BB **B** ✕ nearby D2 T1 ⋙(Saunderton)
Ⓑ Ⓓ 🐾♿🚗!♿Ⓜ ♦♦♦

● Wendover (Aylesbury)
RIDGEWAY & CHILTERN WAY
26 Chiltern Road, HP22 6DB ☎ 01296 622351 (Mrs E C Condie)
Map 165/865082
BB **A** ✕ nearby S1 T/F1 Closed Xmas ⋙(Wendover)
Ⓓ ⊗ ♿♿Ⓜ ♦

● West Wycombe (High Wycombe)
CHILTERN WAY
The Swan Inn, HP14 3AE ☎ 01494 527031
Map 175/829945
BB **C** ✕ nearby S1 D2 T1 F1 Closed Xmas ⋙(Saunderton)

HAMPSHIRE

● Alton
🍴◀ The Manor House, Holybourne, GU34 4HD ☎ 01420 541321
(Clare Whately) clare@whately.net Map 186/734411
BB **D** ✕ nearby D1 T1 ⋙(Alton)
Ⓑ Ⓓ ⊗ 🐾♿🚗!♿ ♦♦♦♦Ⓢ

● Ashurst (Southampton)
NEW FOREST
TEST WAY
🍴◀ The Barn Vegetarian Guest House, 112 Lyndhurst Rd, SO40 7AY
☎ 023 8029 2531 (Richard & Sandra Barnett) www.veggiebarn.net
Map 196/338105
BB **D** ✕ book first £14, 6:30pm D1 T1 Closed Xmas ⋙(Ashurst)
Ⓥ Ⓑ Ⓓ ⊗ ♿♿

● Blashford (Ringwood)
Fraser House, Salisbury Road, BH24 3PB ☎ 01425 473958 (Mr & Mrs Burt)
www.fraserhouse.net Map 195/151066
BB **C** D4 T2 Ⓥ Ⓑ ⊗ 🐾♿♿ ♦♦♦♦

● Boldre (Brockenhurst)
NEW FOREST
SOLENT WAY
🍴◀ Hilden B&B, Southampton Road, SO41 8PT ☎ 01590 623682
(Mrs A Arnold-Brown) www.newforestbandb-hilden.co.uk Map 196/307989
BB **C** ✕ nearby D/F3 ⋙(Brockenhurst)
Ⓑ Ⓓ ♿🚗!♿

● Broughton (Stockbridge)
MONARCH'S WAY & TEST WAY

Kings, Salisbury Road, SO20 8BY ☎ 01794 301458 (Ann Heather)
Map 185/300336
BB **B** ✗ book first £7.50-£10 D1 T1 Closed Xmas
Ⓥ Ⓑ Ⓓ 🐾♿🚗❗

● Buriton (Petersfield)
SOUTH DOWNS*
SOUTH DOWNS WAY

Nursted Farm, GU31 5RW ☎ 01730 264278 (Mrs M Bray)
Map 197/754214
BB **B** ✗ nearby D1 T2 F1 Closed Xmas/Mar-Apr ⋙(Petersfield)
Ⓓ⊗🐾🚗

● Burley (Ringwood)
NEW FOREST

Holmans, Bisterne Close, BH24 4AZ ☎ 01425 402307 (Robin & Mary Ford)
Map 195/229025
BB **D** ✗ nearby D2 T1 Closed Xmas
Ⓑ Ⓓ⊗♿🚗❗🍴 ◆◆◆◆Ⓖ Stables available for guests' horses.

● Cadnam
NEW FOREST

Kingsbridge House, Southampton Road, SO40 2NH ☎ 023 8081 1161
(Linda Goodrich) www.kingsbridgehousebandb.co.uk Map 196/296135
BB **C** ✗ nearby D2 F1
Ⓥ Ⓑ Ⓓ⊗🐾♿🚗❗ ◆◆◆◆ See SC also.

● Chineham (Basingstoke)
☆ 🍽◀ **The Hampshire Centre Court**
Centre Drive, Great Binfields Road, RG24 8FY ☎ 01256 319700
www.marstonhotels.com Map 185,186/658542
BB **D** ✗ £27.50, 7-9.45pm S27 D55 F1
Ⓥ Ⓑ 🐾♿ ★★★★ Wheelchair access.

Conveniently located close to the Basingstoke Canal and surrounding countryside, the hotel is the ideal place to relax, with extensive swimming, tennis, gym, sauna and spa facilities. Comfortable and stylish bedrooms. Please ask about our exclusive rates for walking parties.

● Dummer (Basingstoke)
☆ 🍽◀ **Oakdown Farm**
RG23 7LR ☎ 01256 397218 (Mrs E Hutton)
Map 185/587472
BB **B/C** ✗ nearby D1 T2
Ⓓ⊗🐾🚗❗Ⓜ ◆◆◆

Wayfarers Walk 200 metres. North of Junction 7 M3. Secluded position. Evening meal locally. Lifts available. Car parking.

● East Meon (Petersfield)
SOUTH DOWNS*
SOUTH DOWNS WAY

Dunvegan Cottage, Frogmore Lane, GU32 1QJ ☎ 01730 823213
(Jenny d'Amato) www.dunvegan.btinternet.co.uk Map 185/688217
BB **C** ✗ nearby D2 T3 F1 Closed Xmas
Ⓑ Ⓣ⊗🐾♿🏠❗🍴 ◆◆◆◆

● Fordingbridge (Alderholt)
NEW FOREST

Alderholt Mill, Sandleheath Road, SP6 1PU ☎ 01425 653130
(Mr & Mrs R Harte) www.alderholtmill.co.uk Map 195/119143
BB **C** ✗ book first £15, 7-8:30pm S1 D3 T1 Closed Xmas
Ⓥ Ⓑ Ⓓ⊗🐾🚗❗🍴 ◆◆◆◆ See SC also.

● Freefolk (Whitchurch)
🍽◀ The Old Rectory, RG28 7NW ☎ 01256 895408 (Sue Etridge)
Map 185/487487
BB **C/D** ✗ nearby D1 T1 F1 Closed Xmas ⋙(Whitchurch)
Ⓑ Ⓓ🐾🚗❗🍴 ◆◆◆Ⓦ

● Hambledon (Waterlooville)
MONARCH'S WAY
🍽◀ Mornington House, Speltham Hill, PO7 4RU ☎ 023 9263 2704
(Mr & Mrs Lutyens) Map 196/644149
BB **B** ✗ nearby T2 Closed Xmas Ⓓ 🐾♿🚗🍴

● Headley (Bordon)
☆ 🍽◀ **The Holly Bush Inn**
High Street, GU35 8PP ☎ 01428 712211 (Joan, John or Colin)
www.headley-village.com/hollybush Map 186/822362
BB **D** ✗ £9, 6-9pm D1 T1
Ⓥ Ⓓ🐾♿🚗❗🍴

Situated on the edge of the North Downs, a warm welcome is waiting for you. Food is served until 9pm (4pm on Sundays) in the bar, dining area or outside if the weather is fine. The choice is yours from the snack menu to main meals. To go with the good food is an excellent selection of wines and ales, including Courage Best and the occasional guest ale.

● Highclere (Newbury)
Westridge (Open Centre), Star Lane - off A343, RG20 9PJ ☎ 01635 253322
Map 174/436604
BB **A** ✗ nearby T2 Closed Xmas Ⓓ♿ Booking ahead essential.

● Ibthorpe (Andover)
TEST WAY

Staggs Cottage, Windmill Hill, Hurstbourne Tarrant, SP11 0BP ☎ 01264
736235 (Mr & Mrs Norton) www.staggscottage.co.uk Map 185/374536
BB **C** ✗ book first £10, 6-9pm D1 T2
Ⓥ Ⓓ🐾🚗🍴Ⓜ ◆◆◆◆

● Lymington
NEW FOREST & SOLENT WAY

◆━◢ The Anchorage, Kings Farm Lane, Hordle, SO41 0HD ☎ 01425 622375 (Jean & Ken Aitken) http://theanchorage.mysite.wanadoo-members.co.uk Map 195/277950   BB **B** ✕ nearby S1 T1 Closed Xmas ⋙(Sway)
🅑 🄳 ⊗ 🍳🛏🚗❗Ⓜ

● Lyndhurst
NEW FOREST

◆━◢ Stable End, Emery Down, SO43 7FJ ☎ 023 8028 2504 (William & Mary Dibben)   dibbenfam@aol.com Map 196/290089
BB **D** ✕ nearby D1 T1 ⋙(Ashurst) 🅑 🄳 ⊗🛏🚗❗ ◆◆◆

☆ ━◢ **Ormonde House Hotel**
Southampton Road, SO43 7BT ☎ 02380 282806 (Paul Ames)
www.ormondehouse.co.uk Map 196/305083
BB **D** ✕ book first £15-£19, 6:30-8pm S1 D17 T4 F1 Closed Xmas
⋙(Ashurst) Ⓥ 🅑 🄳 🍳🛏❗🌢 ★★

Perfect base for walking; Ormonde House Hotel & Pinewood Cottage lie opposite the open forest, within walking distance of Lyndhurst village. Furnished to a high standard the hotel has 19 pretty en-suite bedrooms with colour TV & hairdryers. Pinewood Cottage Suites are self-contained, fully serviced and have full kitchens with washing machines, dryers & dishwashers.
Pets are welcome. Privately owned & renowned for its excellent home cuisine.
Discounts for midweek 4 day breaks & for parties of min. 6 out of season.
Email: enquiries@ormondehouse.co.uk

☆ ━◢ **Rufus House Hotel**
Southampton Rd, SO43 7BQ ☎ 02380 282930 (Paul & Alma Carter)
www.rufushousehotel.co.uk Map 196/304082
BB **C/D** ✕ nearby S1 D9 T1 F2 Closed Xmas
Ⓥ 🅑 🄳 ⊗🍳🛏🚗❗ ◆◆◆◆

Delightful Victorian house set in beautiful gardens. Superb location, close to village & opposite open forest. Relaxed, friendly atmosphere offering outstanding accommodation at affordable prices. Extensive knowledge of local walks and attractions. Complementary flasks of tea/coffee. Extended stay discounts.

☆ **Burwood Lodge**
27 Romsey Road, SO43 7AA ☎ 023 8028 2445
www.burwoodlodge.co.uk Map 196/299083
BB **D** ✕ nearby S1 D3 T1 F2
Ⓥ 🅑 🄳 ⊗🍳🛏🚗

Burwood Lodge Guest House is a beautiful Edwardian property which offers bed & breakfast accommodation to a high standard and is set in half an acre of grounds with ample private parking to the front.

The Penny Farthing Hotel & Cottages, Romsey Road, SO43 7AA
☎ 023 8028 4422 www.pennyfarthinghotel.co.uk Map 196/298082
BB **D** ✕ nearby S3 D12 T3 F2 Closed Xmas
🅑 🄳🛁 ◆◆◆◆ See SC also.

● New Milton
NEW FOREST

St Ursula, 30 Hobart Road, BH25 6EG ☎ 01425 613515 (Mr & Mrs M Pearce) Map 195/239947
BB **C** ✕ nearby S2 D1 T2 F1 ⋙(New Milton)
🅑 🄳 ⊗🍳🛏🚗❗🌢 ◆◆◆◆ Access Category 3.

● Petersfield
SOUTH DOWNS®
SOUTH DOWNS WAY

◆━◢ Heath Farmhouse, GU31 4HU ☎ 01730 264709 (Mrs P Scurfield) www.heathfarmhouse.co.uk Map 197/757224
BB **C** D1 T1 F1 Closed Xmas ⋙(Petersfield)
🅑 🄳 ⊗🍳🛏❗🌢 ◆◆◆ Veggie breakfasts.

◆━◢ 1 The Spain, Sheep St, GU32 3JZ ☎ 01730 263261 (Jennifer Tarver) allantarver@ntlworld.com Map 197/748232
BB **D** ✕ nearby D2 T1 Closed Xmas ⋙(Petersfield)
🅑 🄳 🍳🛏🌢 ◆◆◆◆

● Ringwood

Fraser House, Salisbury Road, Blashford, BH24 3PB ☎ 01425 473958 (Mr & Mrs M Burt) www.fraserhouse.net Map 195/149068
BB **C/D** D4 T2 Closed Xmas ⊗🍳🛏🌢 ◆◆◆◆

● Romsey
MONARCH'S WAY & TEST WAY

Roselea, Hamdown Crescent, East Wellow, SO51 6BJ ☎ 01794 323262 (Penny Cossburn) www.roselea.info Map 185/306189
BB **B** ✕ book first £15.50, 7pm S1 D1 T1 Closed Xmas
Ⓥ 🅑 🄳 ⊗🍳🛏🚗🌢 ◆◆◆◆

● Stockbridge
MONARCH'S WAY & TEST WAY

Carbery Guest House, Salisbury Hill, SO20 6EZ ☎ 01264 810771 Map 185/350351
BB **D** ✕ book first £15, 7pm S4 D4 T2 F1 Closed Xmas
Ⓥ 🅑 🄳🍳🛏 ◆◆◆

● Winchester
MONARCH'S WAY & SOUTH DOWNS WAY

◆━◢ St Margaret's, 3 St Michael's Road, SO23 9JE ☎ 01962 861450 (Mrs Brigid Brett) www.winchesterbandb.com Map 185/479290
BB **C** ✕ nearby S2 D1 T1 Closed Xmas ⋙(Winchester)
🄳 ⊗🛁 ◆◆◆

◆━◢ 5 Compton Road, SO23 9SL ☎ 01962 869199 (Gillian Davies) vicb@csma-netlink.co.uk Map 185/476291
BB **B** ✕ nearby T2 F1 Closed Xmas ⋙(Winchester)
🄳 ⊗🍳🛏🚗❗Ⓜ ◆◆◆

◆━◢ Brookside, Back St, St Cross, SO23 9SB ☎ 01962 854820 (Jane Harding) www.brookside-stcross.co.uk Map 185/477279
BB **D** ✕ nearby D1 T1 Closed Xmas ⋙(Winchester)
🅑 🄳 ⊗🍳🛏🚗❗ ◆◆◆◆Ⓦ

ISLE OF WIGHT

● Bembridge
ISLE OF WIGHT COASTAL PATH

Sea Change, 22 Deachfield Road, PO35 5TN ☎ 01983 875558
(Vi & Richard Beet) www.seachangewight.co.uk Map 196/654875
BB **C/D** ✕ nearby D2 TI Closed Nov-Feb
B ⊛ 🍴 ♨ ! ◆◆◆◆⑤

● Bonchurch (Ventnor)
ISLE OF WIGHT COASTAL PATH

☆ **The Lake Hotel**
Shore Road, PO38 IRF ☎ 01983 852613
www.lakehotel.co.uk Map 196/572778
BB **D** ✕ £10, 6:30-7pm S2 D8 T6 F4 Closed Xmas 🚌(Shanklin)
V B D 🍴♨ ◆◆◆◆

Visiting beautiful Bonchurch? We offer comfortable en-suite accommodation in a country house hotel set in beautiful 2-acre garden. Same family run for last 40 years with assured first-class food and comfort. Special 4-night break including car-ferry, dinner/breakfast £175.

☆ ▪🚗◀ **Bonchurch Manor**
Bonchurch Shute, PO38 INU ☎ 01983 852868
www.bonchurchmanor.com Map 196/577782
BB **D** ✕ book first £10, 7pm S2 D4 T2 F4 V B D ⊛ 🍴♨🚗!
♨ ◆◆◆ Rail link coach to Shanklin station.

An outstanding 1830's Victorian country house, set in gardens providing spectacular views over the sea. Located in literary Bonchurch, close to the Downs, coastal paths and beaches of Bonchurch and Ventnor.
Known for our warmth and good food.
WiFi internet access everywhere.

● Brighstone
ISLE OF WIGHT COASTAL PATH

Buddlebrook Guest House, Moortown Lane, PO30 4AN ☎ 01983 740381
www.buddlebrookguesthouse.co.uk Map 196/426832
BB **C** ✕ nearby D2 TI Closed Xmas
B D ⊛ ♨ 🚗 !♨

● Chale
ISLE OF WIGHT COASTAL PATH

Cortina, Gotten Lane, PO38 2HQ ☎ 01983 551292 (Mrs E L Whittington)
Map 196/487791
BB **B** ✕ nearby DI TI
D ⊛ 🍴 🚗 ! Veggie breakfasts.

▪🚗◀ Butterfly Paragliding, Sunacre, The Terrace, PO38 2HL ☎ 01983 731611
(Miranda Botha) www.paraglide.uk.com Map 196/484774
BB **B** ✕ nearby T2 FI Closed Dec-Mar
D ⊛ 🍴 🚗 ! Organic & vegetarian food.

● Freshwater
ISLE OF WIGHT COASTAL PATH

The Traidcraft Shop, 119 School Green Road, PO40 9AZ ☎ 01983 752451
(Mr & Mrs C Murphy) Map 196/340870
BB **B** ✕ nearby DI TI Closed Xmas D ♨! Ⓜ ◆◆

☆ ▪🚗◀ **Rockstone Cottage**
Colwell Chine Road, PO40 9NR ☎ 01983 753723 (Bob Hurle & Nicky Drew)
www.rockstonecottage.co.uk Map 196/329876
BB **C** ✕ nearby D2 T2 FI
B D ⊛ 🍴♨🚗! ◆◆◆◆⑤

Family run guesthouse built in 1790. 400 yards to the beach, surrounded by lovely hill and coastal walks. Guest lounge and dining room. All rooms en-suite, TV, tea/coffee. Relaxing garden. No children under 12 or pets except guide dogs. Open Christmas.

● Rookley
Sundowner B&B, Niton Rd, PO38 3NX ☎ 01983 721350
(Pauline & Peter Wade) www.sundowner.iowight.com Map 196/508835
BB **B** ✕ nearby D2 T/FI Closed Xmas B D ⊛ 🍴♨🚗♨

● Ryde
ISLE OF WIGHT COASTAL PATH

Rowantrees, 63 Spencer Road, PO33 3AF ☎ 01983 568081 Map 196/585926
BB **B** ✕ nearby S2 DI Closed Xmas 🚌(Ryde Esplanade)
D ⊛ ♨ 🚗 !♨ Ⓜ

▪🚗◀ Sea View, 8 Dover Street, PO33 2AQ ☎ 01983 810976 (Diana Davies)
seaviewbandbinryde@hotmail.com Map 196/595926 BB **B** ✕ nearby
DI TI Closed Xmas 🚌(Ryde Esplanade) ⊛ 🍴♨ ◆◆◆

● Sandown
ISLE OF WIGHT COASTAL PATH

▪🚗◀ Heathfield House, 52 Melville St, PO36 8LF ☎ 01983 400002
www.heathfieldhousehotel.com Map 196/595841
BB **C** ✕ nearby S3 D2 TI F2 Closed Xmas 🚌(Sandown)
B D ⊛ 🍴♨ ◆◆◆

● Shanklin
ISLE OF WIGHT COASTAL PATH

▪🚗◀ Atholl Court, I Atherley Road, PO37 7AT ☎ 01983 862414 (Louise Bond)
www.atholl-court.co.uk Map 196/582818
BB **B** ✕ nearby, Xmas S3 D2 T3 🚌(Shanklin) B 🍴♨ ◆◆◆

The Edgecliffe Hotel, Clarence Gardens, PO37 6HA ☎ 01983 866199
(Mick & Dru Webster) www.wightonline.co.uk/edgecliffehotel
Map 196/585820
BB **C** ✕ book first £10.95, 6:30pm S2 D3 T2 F3 🚌(Shanklin)
V B D ⊛ 🍴♨ ◆◆◆◆

● Ventnor
ISLE OF WIGHT COASTAL PATH

▪🚗◀ St Andrew's Hotel, Belgrave Rd, PO38 IJH ☎ 01983 852680
www.standrewsventnor.com Map 196/559774
BB **C** ✕ book first £14, 6:30pm (Mon-Thurs) D5 T3 F2
V B D ⊛ 🍴♨🚗

▪🚗◀ Hill House, 22 Spring Hill, PO38 IPF ☎ 01983 854581 (Barbara Roscoe)
www.hillhouse-ventnor.co.uk Map 196/565777
BB **C** ✕ nearby SI DI TI FI B D ⊛ 🍴♨🚗! ◆◆◆

SOUTH

☆ **Hillside Hotel**
151 Mitchell Avenue, PO38 IDR ☎ 01983 852271
hillside-hotel@btconnect.com Map 196/565779
BB **C** ✕ book first £16, 7:30pm onwards S2 D7 T2 FI Closed Xmas
Ⓥ Ⓑ Ⓓ 🐕🛏🚗! 🎱 ★★

Simply delightful in summer & a comfortable retreat in winter. Built circa 1789, Hillside is Ventnor's oldest & only thatched hotel. Set in 2 acres of grounds, at the foot of St Boniface Downs, with sea views. All bedrooms en-suite with TV. Licensed bar. Extensive choice of breakfast & evening menu. Dogs welcome.

☆ 🖢◀ **Cornerways**
39 Madeira Road, PO38 IQS ☎ 01983 852323 (Steve & Carol)
www.cornerwaysventnor.co.uk Map 196/570777
BB **C** ✕ book first £10, 6:30pm D3 T2 F3
Ⓥ Ⓑ 🐕🛏🎱 ◆◆◆◆

Cornerways is a Victorian country house in a quiet location with magnificent views of both the sea and St Boniface Down. It is within easy reach of Ventnor and the beautiful village of Bonchurch.

Tower House, Zig Zag Road, PO38 IDD ☎ 01983 857507 (Rita Wills)
www.wightonline.co.uk/towerhouse Map 196/558776
BB **B** ✕ nearby D3 TI F3 Ⓑ Ⓓ 🐕🛏🎱

● **Yarmouth**
  ISLE OF WIGHT COASTAL PATH
🖢◀ Wavells B&B & Bike Hire, The Square, PO41 0NP ☎ 01983 760738
www.yarmouthiw.fsworld.co.uk Map 196/355896
BB **C** ✕ nearby SI D3 TI FI Ⓑ Ⓓ 🐕🛏🚗 Ⓜ No children under 8.

Alvina Cottage, Station Road, PO41 0QX ☎ 01983 761528 (Karen Clements)
doughnut.1@virgin.net Map 196/356894
BB **C** ✕ nearby SI DI Closed Dec-Feb Ⓥ Ⓑ Ⓓ 🐕🛏🚗!

KENT

● **Bilsington (Ashford)**
Willow Farm, Stone Cross, TN25 7JJ ☎ 01233 721700 (Mrs Hopper)
www.willowfarmenterprises.co.uk Map 189/028366
BB **D** ✕ nearby SI DI TI FI Ⓓ 🐕🚗! ◆◆◆

● **Brenchley (Tonbridge)**

☆ 🖢◀ **Hononton Cottage**
Palmers Green Lane, TN12 7BJ ☎ 01892 722483 (Simon Marston)
www.smoothhound.co.uk/hotels/hononton.html Map 188/687417
BB **D** ✕ nearby DI TI Closed Xmas 🚶(Paddock Wood)
Ⓑ Ⓓ 🐕🛏🚗! 🎱 ◆◆◆◆ Ⓢ

Picturesque 16th C. listed farmhouse sympathetically modernised with wealth of exposed beams on a quiet lane in Kent orchards. Ideal base for walkers with High Weald Landscape Trail passing the door. Full English breakfast with local produce where possible.

● **Charing (Ashford)**
23 The Moat, TN27 0JH ☎ 01233 713141 (Mrs Margaret Micklewright)
m.micklewright@btinternet.com Map 189/955492
BB **C** ✕ nearby TI Closed Nov-Mar 🚶(Charing) Ⓑ Ⓓ 🐕🛏Ⓜ

● **Chartham (Canterbury)**
The Barn Oast, Nickle Farm, CT4 7PF ☎ 01227 731255 (Mrs Mary Arnold)
www.thebarnoast.co.uk Map 179/092561
BB **C** ✕ nearby DI TI FI Closed Xmas 🚶(Chartham) Ⓑ Ⓓ 🐕🛏

● **Chilham (Canterbury)**
🖢◀ The Old Alma, Canterbury Road, CT4 8DX ☎ 01227 731913
(Mrs Jo Niven) oldalma@aol.com Map 189,179/079538
BB **D** ✕ nearby DI T2 🚶(Chilham)
Ⓥ Ⓑ Ⓓ 🐕🛏🚗! ◆◆◆

● **Cranbrook**
The Hollies, Old Angley Road, TN17 2PN ☎ 01580 713106 (Mrs D M Waddoup)
digs@waddoup.freeserve.co.uk Map 188/775367
BB **C** ✕ book first £10, 7pm SI TI FI Closed Xmas 🚶(Staplehurst)
Ⓑ Ⓓ 🐕🛏🚗🎱

● **Deal**
Ilex Cottage, Temple Way, Worth, CT14 0DA ☎ 01304 617026 (Mrs Stobie)
www.ilexcottage.com Map 179/335560
BB **D** ✕ nearby DI TI FI Closed Xmas 🚶(Sandwich)
Ⓑ Ⓓ 🐕🛏🚗! 🎱 ◆◆◆◆

🖢◀ Sparrow Court, Chalk Hill Road, Kingsdown, CT14 8DP ☎ 01304 389253
(Hon Mrs E G Maude) www.farm-stay-kent.co.uk/popups/sparrowcourt.html
Map 179/374481 BB **D** ✕ nearby DI TI Closed Xmas 🚶(Walmer)
Ⓑ Ⓓ 🐕🛏🚗! 🎱 ◆◆◆◆

● **Dover**
Bleriot's, 47 Park Avenue, CT16 IHE ☎ 01304 211394 (M J Casey)
www.bleriots.net Map 179/316422
BB **B/C** ✕ nearby SI D3 T2 F2 Closed Xmas 🚶(Dover Priory)
Ⓑ 🛏 ◆◆◆

🖢◀ Maison Dieu B&B Guesthouse, 89 Maison Dieu Road, CT16 IRU
☎ 01304 204033 (Diane French) www.maisondieu.com Map 179/319418
BB **C** ✕ nearby S3 D2 TI FI 🚶(Dover Priory)
Ⓥ Ⓑ Ⓓ 🐕🛏 ◆◆◆

● **Dymchurch (Romney Marsh)**
Waterside Guest House, 15 Hythe Road, TN29 0LN ☎ 01303 872253
www.watersideguesthouse.co.uk Map 189/105298
BB **D** ✕ £6.50, 5:30-7:30pm D2 T2 FI Closed Xmas
Ⓥ Ⓓ 🐕🛏 ◆◆◆◆

● **Etchinghill (Folkestone)**
One Step Beyond, Westfield Lane, CT18 8BT ☎ 01303 862637 (John & Jenny Holden) johnosb@rdplus.net Map 189,179/166394
BB **B** ✕ book first £10 SI DI Closed Xmas
Ⓥ Ⓑ Ⓓ 🐕🛏🚗!

● **Folkestone**
🖢◀ Wycliffe Hotel, 63 Bouverie Road West, CT20 2RN ☎ 01303 252186
(Mike & Kate Sapsford) www.wycliffehotel.com Map 189,179/219357
BB **C** ✕ book first £14, 6:30pm S3 D5 T4 F2 🚶(Folkestone Central)
Ⓥ Ⓑ Ⓓ 🛏🚗! 🎱

Pigeonwood House, Grove Farm, Arpinge, CT18 8AQ ☎ 01303 891111
www.pigeonwood.com Map 189,179/193387
BB **C** ✕ nearby D1 T1 F1 Closed Nov-Jan ♨(Folkestone West)
B ⊗ 🍵🛏🚗! ◆◆◆◆

● Gillingham
✉ Mayfield Guest House, 34 Kingswood Road, ME7 1D7 ☎ 01634 852606
(A Z Sumner) Map 178/776685
BB **B** ✕ nearby S4 D2 T2 F2 ♨(Gillingham)   B 👜 ◆◆

● Grafty Green

☆ ✉ **Foxes Earth Bed & Breakfast**
ME17 2AP ☎ 01622 858350 (Pat & Keith Anderson)
www.foxesearthbedandbreakfast.co.uk Map 189/871486
BB **C** ✕ nearby S1 D2 ♨(Headcorn/lenham)
V B ⊗ 🍵🛏🚗!

Foxes Earth Grafty Green is ideally situated in the beautiful Weald of Kent countryside - a walkers' paradise! The Pilgrim's Way, Green Sandway and North Downs Way, plus many other public footpaths are in easy reach for the discerning walker/rambler.

● Harrietsham (Maidstone)
✉ Homestay, 14 Chippendayle Drive, ME17 1AD ☎ 01622 858698
(Mrs Barbara Beveridge) www.kent-homestay.info Map 189/870527
BB **B/C** ✕ nearby T2 Closed Xmas ♨(Harrietsham)
B ⊗ 🍵🛏🚗👜 ◆◆◆◆

● Herne Bay
✉ Hobbit Hole, 41a Pigeon Lane, CT6 7ES ☎ 01227 368155 (Jean Herwin)
hobhole@aol.com Map 179/185669
BB **C** ✕ nearby S1 D1 T1 F1 Closed Xmas ♨(Herne Bay)
B ⊗ 🚗! Ⓜ ◆◆◆

● Hythe

☆ ✉ **The Hythe Imperial**
Prince's Parade, CT21 6AE ☎ 01303 267441
www.marstonhotels.com Map 189,179/169344
BB **D** ✕ £32.50, 7-9.30pm S17 D55 T23 F5
V B 🍵🛏 ★★★★ Wheelchair access.

Victorian splendour on Hythe seafront, convenient for North Downs and Romney Marsh. Fantastic modern leisure facilities and spa. Set in 50 acres with own golf course. Restaurant and two bars. Please ask about our exclusive rates for walking parties.

● Otford (Sevenoaks)
9 Warham Road, TN14 5PF ☎ 01959 523596 (Mrs Patricia Smith)
Map 188/526590
BB **B** ✕ nearby S1 D1 T1 Closed Xmas ♨(Otford)
D ⊗ 🍵🛏🚗👜 ◆◆

● Rochester
255 High Street, ME1 1HQ ☎ 01634 842737 (Mrs E Thomas)
thomasbandb@btinternet.com Map 178/748681
BB **A** ✕ nearby D1 T1 F1 Closed Xmas ♨(Rochester) B D 🍵🚗

✉ St Martin, 104 Borstal Road, ME1 3BD ☎ 01634 848192 (Mrs H Colvin)
icolvin@stmartin.freeserve.co.uk Map 178/736673
BB **B** ✕ book first £8, To suit. D1 T2 Closed Xmas ♨(Rochester)
V D 🍵🛏🚗!👜 Ⓜ ◆◆◆

● Sandwich
Le Trayas, Poulders Road, CT13 0BB ☎ 01304 611056 (Mrs R A Pettican)
www.letrayas.co.uk Map 179/322576
BB **B** ✕ nearby D1 T2 Closed Xmas ♨(Sandwich)
B D ⊗ 🍵🛏🚗!

● Shepherdswell (Dover)
✉ Sunshine Cottage, The Green, Mill Lane, CT15 7LQ ☎ 01304 831359
(B & L Popple) www.sunshine-cottage.co.uk Map 179/261478
BB **C/D** ✕ nearby D/S4 T/S1 F1 ♨(Shepherdswell)
B D ⊗ 🍵🛏🚗 ◆◆◆◆Ⓢ

● Stelling Minnis (Canterbury)
✉ Great Field Farm, Misling Lane, CT4 6DE ☎ 01227 709223 (Mrs L Castle)
www.great-field-farm.co.uk Map 189,179/134452
BB **D** ✕ nearby D2 T1 F1 Closed Xmas
B D ⊗ 🍵🛏🚗! ◆◆◆◆Ⓢ

● Tenterden
Old Burren, 25 Ashford Rd, TN30 6LL ☎ 01580 764442 (Gill Pooley)
www.oldburren.co.uk Map 189/886337
BB **C** ✕ nearby D2 Closed Xmas
B D ⊗ 🍵🛏👜 ◆◆◆◆

● Walderslade Woods (Chatham)

☆ ✉ **Bridgewood Manor**
Bridgewood Roundabout, ME5 9AX ☎ 01634 201333
www.marstonhotels.com Map 188,178/747634
BB **D** ✕ £32.50, 7-10pm D74 T26
V B 🍵🛏 ★★★★ Wheelchair access.

Relax at the comfortable Bridgewood Manor. Convenient for North Downs Way and Saxon Shore Way, the hotel offers a restaurant, bar and modern Leisure Club. Well-equipped bedrooms around beautiful courtyard. Please ask about our exclusive rates for walking parties.

● Wye (Ashford)
Selsfield, Oxtenturn Road, TN25 5AZ ☎ 01233 812133 (Joan & John Morris)
morij@tesco.net Map 189,179/052457
BB **C** ✕ nearby S1 D1 T1 Closed Xmas ♨(Wye) D ⊗ 🍵🛏

LONDON

● Brentford
THAMES PATH
✉ Primrose House, 56 Boston Gardens, TW8 9LP ☎ 020 8568 5573
(Garrie & Constance Williams) www.primrosehouse.com Map 176/164786
BB **D** ✕ nearby D2 T1 Closed Xmas ♨(Brentford)
B ⊗ 🛏🚗!👜 ◆◆◆◆

SOUTH

● Central London
THAMES PATH

St Athan's Hotel, 20 Tavistock Place, WC1H 9RE ☎ 020 7837 9140
www.stathanshotel.com Map 176,177/300823
BB **D** ✕ nearby S16 D20 T10 F8 Closed Xmas ♨(Euston/King's Cross)
Ⓑ Ⓓ 🛁 ◆

☆ ♥ Cardiff Hotel
5-9 Norfolk Square, W2 1RU ☎ 020 7723 3513 (Debbie & Andrew Davies)
www.cardiff-hotel.com Map 176/268812
BB **D** ✕ nearby S25 D22 T9 F5 Closed Xmas ♨(Paddington)
Ⓑ 🛁 ◆◆◆

15 minutes from Heathrow Airport by express train, the Cardiff Hotel overlooks a quiet garden square just 2 minutes walk form Paddington station. Rooms have a TV, phone, hairdryer and tea making facilities. Hearty English breakfast included.

☆ ♥ Lincoln House Hotel
33 Gloucester Place, W1U 8HY ☎ 020 7486 7630
www.lincoln-house-hotel.co.uk Map 176/279814
BB **D** ✕ nearby S6 D6 T4 F7 ♨(Paddington)
Ⓑ 🛁 !

A delightfully hospitable B&B hotel. In Central London's West End, offering Georgian charm and modern comforts. En-suite rooms with fast internet connection. Close to Oxford Street shopping, Theatreland and nightlife. On airports' bus route. Ideal for business and leisure.

● Hammersmith
THAMES PATH

91 Langthorne St, SW6 6JU ☎ 020 7381 0198 (Brigid Richardson)
www.londonthameswalk.co.uk Map 176/236770
BB **C/D** ✕ nearby S1 D2 T1 Closed Xmas ♨(Hammersmith)
Ⓑ Ⓓ ⊗ 🛁 ◆◆◆

● Islington (London)
THAMES PATH

☆ ♥ Kandara Guest House
68 Ockendon Road, N1 3NW ☎ 020 7226 5721 (Mrs Avril Harmon)
www.kandara.co.uk Map 176,177/327845
BB **D** ✕ nearby S4 D3 T1 F4 ♨(King's Cross)
Ⓥ Ⓓ ⊗ 🛁 ◆◆◆

Family run guest house in quiet residential road, close to the Angel Islington. Nine bus routes and two tube stations provide good public transport to all parts of London. Free overnight street parking and free secure cycle storage.

● Putney
THAMES PATH

One Fanthorpe Street, SW15 1DZ ☎ 020 8785 7609 (Pip & Robert Taylor)
www.bbputney.com Map 176/233758
BB **D** ✕ book first £20, 8pm D1 T1 Closed Xmas ♨(Putney)
Ⓥ Ⓑ Ⓓ ⊗ 🐾 Ⓜ

● Richmond-upon-Thames
LONDON LOOP & THAMES PATH

♥ Ivy Cottage, Upper Ham Road, Ham Common, TW10 5LA
☎ 020 8940 8601 (David Taylor) www.dbta.freeserve.co.uk Map 176/178717
BB **C** ✕ nearby S1 D1 T2 F1 Closed Xmas
Ⓑ Ⓓ 🍵🛁🚗!🐾 ◆◆◆

● Twickenham
LONDON LOOP & THAMES PATH

♥ 33 Arlington Road, St Margarets, TW1 2AZ ☎ 020 8287 7492
(David & Silvia Kogan) www.33arlingtonroad.co.uk Map 176/170744
BB **D** ✕ nearby S1 D1 Closed Xmas ♨(St Margarets)
Ⓓ ⊗ 🛁 Ⓜ ◆◆◆◆

● Wimbledon
LONDON LOOP & THAMES PATH

Beggars Roost, 6 Augustus Road, SW19 6LN ☎ 020 8788 9438
(Mrs Pamela O'Neill) Map 176/246732
BB **B** ✕ book first £10, 6:30pm S1 T4 Closed Xmas ♨(Southfields)
Ⓥ Ⓓ ⊗ 🛁

OXFORDSHIRE

● Binfield Heath (Henley-on-Thames)
THAMES PATH & CHILTERN WAY

♥ Teapot Cottage, Shiplake Row, RG9 4DR ☎ 01189 470263 (Clare Jevons)
www.teapot-cottage.co.uk Map 175/752784
BB **C** ✕ nearby D2 T1 ♨(Shiplake) Ⓑ Ⓓ ⊗ 🍵🛁🚗

● Burford

☆ ♥ The Inn For All Seasons
The Barringtons, OX18 4TN ☎ 01451 844324 (Matthew R Sharp)
www.innforallseasons.com Map 163/204120
BB **D** ✕ £16, 6:30-9:30pm S5 D5 T5 F2 Closed Xmas
Ⓥ Ⓑ Ⓓ 🍵🛁🚗!🐾 ★★★

16th C. family run Cotswold Inn in The Windrush Valley with many local historic walks. 10 en-suite rooms, a well stocked cellar & a kitchen famous for its use of local produce. An ideal place for small groups. Drying rooms & ample secure parking. Small enough to care, large enough to be professional.

● Chipping Norton
♥ 1 Lower Barns, Salford, OX7 5YP ☎ 01608 643276 (Mrs Barnard)
Map 163/287279 BB **A** T1 Closed Xmas Ⓑ Ⓓ ⊗ 🛁🚗!🐾

● Faringdon
THAMES PATH

♥ Sudbury House Hotel, London Street, SN7 8AA ☎ 01367 241272
(Andrew Ibbotson) www.sudburyhouse.co.uk Map 164/294954
BB **D** ✕ £23.50, 7-9:30pm D39 T10 F2 Closed Xmas
Ⓥ Ⓑ Ⓓ 🍵🛁🚗!🐾 Ⓜ ★★★

● Frieth (Henley-on-Thames)
CHILTERN WAY

♥ St Katharine's, Parmoor, RG9 6NN ☎ 01494 881037
(Mrs Bethan Macleod) www.srpf.webspace.fish.co.uk Map 175/794893
BB **B** ✕ book first £5, 6-8pm S8 D3 T12 F2 Closed Xmas
Ⓥ Ⓑ Ⓓ ⊗ 🍵🛁🚗!🐾

● Goring-on-Thames (Reading)
RIDGEWAY, THAMES PATH & CHILTERN WAY

Northview House, Farm Rd, RG8 0AA ☎ 01491 872184 (I. Sheppard)
hi@goring-on-thames.freeserve.co.uk Map 175/603808
BB B ✕ nearby D2 T1 Closed Xmas ▬(Goring & Streatley)
⊡ ⊛ 🛏🛁 🏡 Ⓜ

● Henley-on-Thames
THAMES PATH & CHILTERN WAY

Lenwade, 3 Western Road, RG9 1JL ☎ 01491 573468 (Mrs J Williams)
www.w3b-ink.com/lenwade Map 175/760817
BB D ✕ nearby D2 T1 Closed Xmas ▬(Henley-on-Thames)
⒝ ⊡ ⊛ 🛏🛁🏡 🔔 Ⓜ ◆◆◆◆◆

Mrs Margery Meek B&B, RG9 2ER ☎ 01491 574300 (Margery Meek)
margery@meek1661.fsnet.co.uk Map 175/756831
BB D ✕ nearby S1 D1 ▬(Henley-on-Thames)
Ⓥ ⊡ 🛏🛁🏡 🔔

● Letcombe Regis (Wantage)
RIDGEWAY

Quince Cottage B&B, OX12 9JP ☎ 01235 763652 (Louise Boden)
www.rboden.supanet.com Map 174/380865
BB C ✕ nearby D2
Ⓥ ⊡ ⊛ 🛏🛁🏡 🔔

● Long Hanborough (Witney)
Wynford House, 79 Main Rd, OX29 8JX ☎ 01993 881402 (Carol Ellis)
www.accommodation.uk.net/wynford.htm Map 164/424142
BB D ✕ nearby D1 T1 F1 Closed Xmas ▬(Hanborough)
⒝ ⊡ ⊛ 🛏🛁🔔

● Long Wittenham (Abingdon)
THAMES PATH

Witta's Ham Cottage, High Street, OX14 4QH ☎ 01865 407686
(Mrs Jill Mellor) martin.mellor@sjpp.co.uk Map 174,164/546937
BB D ✕ nearby S1 D1 T1 Closed Xmas ▬(Culham)
⊡ ⊛ 🛏🛁🏡 🔔 ◆◆◆◆⑤

● Milton Common (Thame)

☆ The Oxford Belfry
OX9 2JW ☎ 01844 279381
www.marstonhotels.com Map 164,165/651035
BB D ✕ £32.50, 7-9.30pm S3 D84 T43
Ⓥ ⒝ 🛏🛁 ★★★★ Wheelchair access.

Explore Oxford whilst enjoying the countryside. Set in 17 acres with excellent leisure facilities. Popular bar, restaurants and picturesque courtyard. Close to many attractions including Blenheim Palace and the Oxford Way. Please ask about our exclusive rates for walking parties.

● Moulsford-on-Thames (Wallingford)
THAMES PATH, RIDGEWAY & CHILTERN WAY

White House, OX10 9JD ☎ 01491 651397 (Mrs Maria Watsham)
www.stayatwhitehouse.co.uk Map 174/591837
BB D ✕ nearby S1 D1 T1 Closed Xmas
⒝ ⊡ ⊛ 🛏🛁🏡 🔔 ◆◆◆◆⑤

● Nettlebed (Henley-on-Thames)
RIDGEWAY

Park Corner Farm House, RG9 6DX ☎ 01491 641450 (Mrs S Rutter)
parkcorner_farmhouse@hotmail.com Map 175/688891
BB C S1 T2 Closed Xmas ⊡ ⊛ 🛏🛁🏡 🔔🏠 ◆◆◆

● North Stoke (Wallingford)
RIDGEWAY & CHILTERN WAY

Footpath Cottage, The Street, OX10 6BJ ☎ 01491 839763 (Mrs Tanner)
Map 175/610863 BB B ✕ book first £12 S1 D2 Ⓥ ⒝ 🛏🛁🏡

● Nuffield (Henley-on-Thames)
RIDGEWAY & CHILTERN WAY

14 Bradley Road, RG9 5SG ☎ 01491 641359 (Diana Chambers)
diana.chambers@rwethameswater.com Map 175/681882
BB C ✕ nearby D2 T1 Closed Xmas ⒝ ⊡ ⊛ 🛏🛁🏡 🔔🏠

● Pishill (Henley-on-Thames)
CHILTERN WAY

Bank Farm, RG9 6HS ☎ 01491 638601 (Mrs E Lakey)
e.f.lakey@btinternet.com Map 175/713898
BB B ✕ nearby D2 T1 Closed Xmas ⊡ ⊛ 🛏🛁🏡 🔔 ◆◆

● Shillingford (Wallingford)
THAMES PATH

The Kingfisher Inn, 27 Henley Road, OX10 7EL ☎ 01865 858595
(Alexis or Mayumi) www.kingfisher-inn.co.uk Map 174,164/595928
BB D ✕ £10, 7:30-9:30pm D5 T1 Closed Xmas
Ⓥ ⒝ ⊡ 🛏🛁🏡 🔔 ◆◆◆◆

● Shipton-under-Wychwood (Chipping Norton)

Court Farm, Mawles Lane, OX7 6DA ☎ 01993 831515 (Belinda Willson)
enquiries@courtfarmbb.com Map 163/279177
BB D ✕ nearby D2 T1 ▬(Shipton-under-Wychwood)
Ⓥ ⒝ ⊡ ⊛ 🛏🛁🏡 🏠 ◆◆◆◆⑤

● Stoke Row (Henley-on-Thames)
CHILTERN WAY & RIDGEWAY

Stag Hall, Stoke Row Road, RG9 5NX ☎ 01491 680338
stag_hall@hotmail.com Map 175/686835
BB C ✕ nearby D1 F1 Ⓥ ⒝ ⊡ 🛏🛁🏡 🔔🏠 ★★★

● Swyncombe (Henley-on-Thames)
RIDGEWAY & CHILTERN WAY

Pathways, Cookley Green, RG9 6EN ☎ 01491 641631
(Mrs Ismayne Peters) ismayne.peters@tesco.net Map 175/695901
BB C ✕ book first £9, 7-8pm D1 T2 Closed Xmas
Ⓥ ⒝ ⊡ ⊛ 🛏🛁🔔

● Tackley (Kidlington)

55 Nethercote Road, OX5 3AT ☎ 01869 331255 (June Collier)
www.colliersbnb.com Map 164/482206
BB C ✕ nearby D1 T1/F1 ▬(Tackley) ⊡ ⊛ 🛏🛁🏡 🔔🏠 ◆◆◆

● Wallingford
THAMES PATH, RIDGEWAY & CHILTERN WAY

Little Gables, 166 Crowmarsh Hill, OX10 8BG ☎ 01491 837834
(Jill & Tony Reeves) www.stayingaway.com Map 175/627887
BB D ✕ nearby S1 D/S2 T/S3 F/S2 ▬(Cholsey)
⒝ ⊡ ⊛ 🛏🛁🔔 ◆◆◆◆ Veggie breakfasts.

SOUTH

● **Wantage**

RIDGEWAY

Lockinge Kiln Farm, The Ridgeway, Chain Hill, OX12 8PA ☎ 01235 763308 (Mrs Stella Cowan) www.lockingekiln.co.uk Map 174/423833
BB **B** ✕ book first £10, 7pm D1 T2 Closed Xmas-Feb Ⓥ Ⓓ ⊗ 🐾👢!

● **Witney**

▪☜ Hawthorn House, 79 Burford Road, OX28 6DR ☎ 01993 772768 (Joanne & Paul Donohoe) www.hawthornhouse.netfirms.com
Map 164/346102 BB **D** ✕ nearby D2 T3 Ⓥ Ⓑ ⊗ 🐾👢🛋

● **Woodstock (Witney)**

☆ **Gorselands Hall**
Boddington Lane, OX29 6PU ☎ 01993 882292 (Mr & Mrs N Hamilton)
www.gorselandshall.com Map 164/399135
BB **D** ✕ nearby D4 T1 F1 Closed Xmas ⋙(Hanborough)
Ⓑ Ⓓ ⊗ 👢🛋 ◆◆◆◆Ⓢ

Lovely old Cotswold stone country house with oak beams and flagstone floors in delightful rural setting. Large secluded garden. Good walking country. Ideal for Blenheim Palace, the Cotswolds and Oxford. All rooms en-suite. Lounge with snooker table. Winter discounts. Fax: 01993 883629.

● **Wootton (Woodstock)**
8 Manor Court, OX20 1EU ☎ 01993 811186 (Mrs Nancy Fletcher)
Map 164/438199
BB **C** ✕ nearby S1 D1 Closed Dec Ⓑ Ⓓ ⊗ 🐾👢🚗

SURREY

● **Bowlhead Green (Godalming)**
Heath Hall Farm, GU8 6NW ☎ 01428 682808 (Mrs Susanna Langdale)
www.heathhallfarm.co.uk Map 186/918388
BB **C** ✕ book first £12 S1 D1 T1 F1 Closed Xmas
Ⓥ Ⓑ Ⓓ ⊗ 🐾👢🚗🛋 ◆◆◆

● **Charlwood**
▪☜ Trumbles, Stan Hill, RH6 0EP ☎ 01293 863418 (Julia Roberts)
www.trumbles.co.uk Map 187/236418
BB **D** ✕ nearby D3 T1 F2 Ⓑ Ⓓ ⊗ 🐾👢🚗! ◆◆◆◆

● **Cranleigh**
The White Hart, Ewhurst Road, GU6 7AE ☎ 01483 268647
pasilver@netcomuk.co.uk Map 187/060390
BB **C** ✕ £5-£10, 6-9pm S2 D7 T3 F2 Ⓥ Ⓑ Ⓓ 🐾👢🛋

● **Dorking**
▪☜ 5 Rose Hill, RH4 2EG ☎ 01306 883127 (Margaret Walton)
www.altourism.com/uk/walt.html Map 187/166491
BB **C** ✕ book first £16, 7:30pm onwards D2 T1 F1 ⋙(Dorking North)
Ⓥ Ⓑ Ⓓ ⊗ 🐾👢!🛋

Fairdene Guest House, Moores Road, RH4 2BG ☎ 01306 888337
(Clive Richardson) zoe.richardson@ntlworld.com Map 187/169496
BB **D** ✕ nearby D2 T2 F2 Closed Xmas ⋙(Dorking)
Ⓑ Ⓓ ⊗ 🐾👢🚗!🛋 ◆◆◆

☆ **Hindover**
21 St Pauls Rd West, RH4 2HT ☎ 01306 742306 (Susan Aitchison)
www.hindover.co.uk Map 187/164488
BB **D** ✕ nearby S1 D1 T1 F1 ⋙(Dorking)
Ⓥ Ⓓ ⊗ 🐾👢🚗! ◆◆◆◆

Large Edwardian house with comfortable, spacious rooms. All rooms have armchairs, TVs & hairdryers. Ironing facilities available. Conveniently situated for the North Downs Way, Polsden Lacy and numerous walks in the Surrey Hills. Close to good pubs and restaurants. hindover@aol.com

☆ **Claremont Cottage**
Rose Hill, RH4 2ED ☎ 01306 885487 (Mrs Jan Stammers)
www.claremontcott.co.uk Map 187/164489
BB **D** ✕ nearby S3 D2 T1 ⋙(Dorking)
Ⓥ Ⓑ Ⓓ ⊗ 🐾👢🚗 ◆◆◆◆ Internet access available.

Olde worlde cottage, formerly coach house and stables, with modern amenities. Very close to town centre yet peaceful location down own lane. Picturesque garden setting. All rooms individually styled and en-suite. Easy access to London, M25 and beauty spots.

● **Forest Green (Dorking)**
Bridgham Cottage, Horsham Rd, RH5 5PP ☎ 01306 621044 (Max Taylor)
http://mysite.freeserve.com/bridcott Map 187/123400
BB **D** ✕ nearby S1 D1 T1 Closed Xmas
Ⓑ Ⓓ ⊗ 🐾👢🚗🛋 ◆◆◆◆

● **Guildford**
25 Scholars Walk, Ridgemount, GU2 7TR ☎ 01483 531351
Map 186/988498 BB **D** ✕ nearby S2 ⋙(Guildford) Ⓑ ⊗ 👢

Highfield House, 18 Harvey Rd, GU1 3SG ☎ 01483 534946 (Mike & Jo Anning)
Map 186/001494 BB **C** ✕ nearby D1 T1 Closed Xmas ⋙(Guildford)
Ⓑ Ⓓ ⊗ 👢🚗 Ⓜ

● **Horley**
The Turret Guest House, 48 Massetts Road, RH6 7DS ☎ 01293 782490
www.theturret.com Map 187/286426
BB **D** ✕ nearby S2 D3 T2 F3 ⋙(Horley/Gatwick)
Ⓑ ⊗ 🐾👢Ⓜ ◆◆◆ Veggie breakfasts.

The Lawn Guest House, 30 Massetts Rd, RH6 7DF ☎ 01293 775751
(Adrian Grinsted) www.lawnguesthouse.co.uk Map 187/283428
BB **D** ✕ nearby D3 T3 F6 Closed Xmas ⋙(Horley/Gatwick)
Ⓑ Ⓓ ⊗ 👢🚗🛋 ◆◆◆◆Ⓢ

Whitehatch Guest House, Oldfield Road, RH6 7EP ☎ 01293 785391
(Lorna & Marino Giammarini) www.findaukbusiness.co.uk/whitehatch
Map 187/278424 BB **D** ✕ nearby D5 ⋙(Horley/Gatwick)
Ⓑ Ⓓ ⊗ 👢🚗!

● **Oxted**
▪☜ Pinehurst Grange Guesthouse, East Hill (A25), RH8 9AE
☎ 01883 716413 (Laurie Rodgers)
laurie.rodgers@ntlworld.com Map 187/392525
BB **D** ✕ nearby S1 D1 T1 Closed Xmas ⋙(Oxted) Ⓓ ⊗ 🐾👢

Meads, 23 Granville Road, RH8 0BX ☎ 01883 730115 (Helen Holgate)
holgate@meads9.fsnet.co.uk Map 187/399530
BB **D** ✕ nearby S0 D2 T1 Closed Xmas ₩₩(Oxted)
Ⓑ Ⓓ ⊛ 🐴🖐🚗 ! ◆◆◆◆

● Shalford (Guildford)
▪━◀ The Laurels, 23 Dagden Road, GU4 8DD ☎ 01483 565733
(Mrs M J Deeks) Map 186/000475
BB **B** ✕ book first £8, 7-8pm D1 T1 ₩₩(Shalford)
Ⓥ Ⓑ Ⓓ ⊛ 🐴🖐🚗 ! 🏠 Ⓜ ◆◆◆

EAST SUSSEX

● Alfriston
SOUTH DOWNS WAY & WEALDWAY
Dacres, BN26 5TP ☎ 01323 870447 (Mrs Patsy Embry) Map 199/518028
BB **C** ✕ nearby T1 Closed Xmas ₩₩(Berwick)
Ⓑ Ⓓ ⊛ 🖐!

▪━◀ 5 The Broadway, BN26 5XL ☎ 01323 870145 (Mrs Janet Dingley)
janetandbrian@dingley5635.freeserve.co.uk Map 199/516030
BB **C** ✕ nearby S1 D1 T1 Closed Xmas Ⓑ Ⓓ ⊛ 🐴🖐🚗 !

Pleasant Rise Farm, BN26 5TN ☎ 01323 870545 (Mrs Savage)
Map 199/517028
BB **C** ✕ nearby D1 Closed Oct-Dec ₩₩(Berwick)
Ⓥ Ⓑ Ⓓ ⊛ 🐴🖐🏠

● Blackboys (Uckfield)
WEALDWAY
Rangers Cottage, Terminus Rd, TN22 5LX ☎ 01825 890463
(David & Elizabeth Brown) rangerscottage@evemail.net Map 199/518207
BB **C/D** ✕ nearby D1 T1 Closed Xmas Ⓑ Ⓓ 🐴🖐🚗 ! ◆◆◆◆

● Chiddingly (Lewes)
WEALDWAY
▪━◀ Hale Farm House, BN8 6HQ ☎ 01825 872619 (David & Sue Burrough)
www.halefarmhouse.co.uk Map 199/555145
BB **C** ✕ book first £7.50, 6-8pm T2 F1 Closed Xmas
Ⓥ Ⓑ Ⓓ ⊛ 🐴🖐🚗🏠 ◆◆◆◆

● Colemans Hatch (Hartfield)
WEALDWAY
Gospel Oak, TN7 4ER ☎ 01342 823840 (Mrs L Hawker)
lindah@thehatch.freeserve.co.uk Map 187/447327
BB **D** ✕ book first £14, 7-8pm D1 T1
Ⓥ Ⓑ Ⓓ ⊛ 🐴🖐🏠 Ⓜ ◆◆◆

● Danehill (Haywards Heath)
Green Acres, Horsted Lane, RH17 7HP ☎ 01825 790863 (Mrs J M Jennings)
Map 187,198/397278
BB **A** ✕ book first £7, 6-8:30pm S1 D1 T1
Ⓥ Ⓑ Ⓓ ⊛ 🐴🖐 Ⓜ

● Denton (Newhaven)
SOUTH DOWNS WAY
▪━◀ Lupin Cottage, 46 Denton Road, BN9 0QB ☎ 01273 517419
(Mrs Kathryn Coevoet) chris@coevoet.fsnet.co.uk Map 198/454024
BB **C** ✕ £8.95, 6:30-9:30pm D2 ₩₩(Newhaven)
Ⓥ Ⓑ Ⓓ ⊛ 🐴🚗

● East Dean (Eastbourne)
SOUTH DOWNS*
SOUTH DOWNS WAY & WEALDWAY
▪━◀ The Welkin, 2 The Link, BN20 0LB ☎ 01323 423384
(Mrs Phyll Workman) phyll.workman@tesco.net Map 199/560989
BB **B** ✕ book first £10 S1 T1 Closed Xmas Ⓥ Ⓑ Ⓓ ⊛ 🐴🖐🚗

● East Hoathly (Lewes)
WEALDWAY
▪━◀ Aberdeen House B&B, 5 High Street, BN8 6DR ☎ 01825 840219
(Jo Gardiner) jo@aberdeenhouse.freeserve.co.uk Map 199/522162
BB **D** ✕ nearby D3 T1 F1 Ⓥ Ⓑ Ⓓ ⊛ 🐴🖐🚗 ! ◆◆◆◆

● Eastbourne
SOUTH DOWNS WAY & WEALDWAY
Ambleside Hotel, 24 Elms Avenue, BN21 3DN ☎ 01323 724991 (J Pattenden)
www.smoothhound.co.uk/hotels/ambleside.html Map 199/616989
BB **B** S2 D6 T6 ₩₩(Eastbourne) Ⓑ Ⓓ 🖐🏠

Brayscroft Hotel, 13 South Cliff Avenue, BN20 7AH ☎ 01323 647005
www.brayscrofthotel.co.uk Map 199/609980
BB **D** ✕ book first £14, 6pm S1 D3 T2 Closed Xmas ₩₩(Eastbourne)
Ⓥ Ⓑ Ⓓ ⊛ 🐴🖐🚗 ◆◆◆◆Ⓖ

▪━◀ The Atlanta Hotel, 10 Royal Parade, BN22 7AR ☎ 01323 730486
(Jason Osbourne) www.hotelatlanta.co.uk Map 199/619993
BB **C** ✕ book first £10, 6pm S6 D4 T3 F2 Closed Xmas-Jan
₩₩(Eastbourne) Ⓥ Ⓑ ⊛ 🐴🖐! ◆◆◆

Southcroft, 15 South Cliff Ave, BN20 7AH ☎ 01323 729071 (Andrew Johnson)
www.southcrofthotel.co.uk Map 199/609980
BB **D** ✕ £12, 6pm D3 T2 Closed Xmas ₩₩(Eastbourne)
Ⓥ Ⓑ Ⓓ ⊛ 🐴🖐! ◆◆◆◆

▪━◀ The Cherry Tree Hotel, 15 Silverdale Road, Lower Meads, BN20 7AJ
☎ 01323 722406 (Lynda Couch-Smith) www.cherrytree-eastbourne.co.uk
Map 199/609980 BB **C** ✕ nearby S2 D4 T2 F1 ₩₩(Eastbourne)
Ⓥ Ⓑ ⊛ 🐴🖐🏠! Ⓢ

Camberley Hotel, 27-29 Elms Avenue, BN21 3DN ☎ 01323 723789
(Pat Estevez) Map 199/616989
BB **B** ✕ book first £8, 6pm S2 D3 T3 F4 Closed Nov-Feb ₩₩(Eastbourne)
Ⓥ Ⓑ Ⓓ ⊛ 🖐🚗

● Fairwarp (Uckfield)
WEALDWAY
Broom Cottage, Browns Brook, TN22 3BY ☎ 01825 712942 (Jane Rattray)
Map 198/472272
BB **C** ✕ nearby S1 D1 T1 Ⓑ Ⓓ ⊛ 🐴🖐🏠 ◆◆◆◆

● Groombridge (Tunbridge Wells)
WEALDWAY
▪━◀ Ventura, The Ridge, Withyam Road, TN3 9QU ☎ 01892 864711
(Brenda Horner) Map 188/521369
BB **B** ✕ book first £10, 6:30-7pm S1 D/F1 T1 Closed Xmas
Ⓥ Ⓑ Ⓓ 🐴🖐🚗!🏠

● Hailsham
WEALDWAY
▪━◀ Longleys Farm Cottage, Harebeating Lane, BN27 1ER ☎ 01323 841227
(David & Jill Hook) Map 199/598105
BB **B** ✕ nearby D1 T1 F1
Ⓑ Ⓓ ⊛ 🐴🖐🚗🏠 ◆◆◆

SOUTH

● Hastings

☆ **White Cottage**
Battery Hill, Fairlight, TN35 4AP ☎ 01424 812528 (John & June Dyer)
juneandjohn@whitecottagebb.fsnet.co.uk Map 199/873123
BB **D** ✕ nearby D3 TI Closed Nov-Jan
🅱 🅳 ⊛ ♨ 🚗 ◆◆◆◆

 We are a peaceful, friendly run B&B with beautiful gardens for our guests to enjoy. We have three doubles and one twin room, all en-suite (two with sea views). Tea/coffee making facilities and TV in all rooms. Extensive breakfast menu.

⌐► Grand Hotel, Grand Parade, St Leonards, TN38 0DD ☎ 01424 428510
(Peter Mann) www.grandhotelhastings.co.uk Map 199/802089
BB **B** ✕ book first £15, 5-7pm S3 D9 T7 F4 ⋙(Warrior Square)
📺 🅱 🅳 ⊛ 🎣♨ 🚗 ❗ ◆◆◆

● Heathfield
Spicers Bed and Breakfast, 21 Spicers Cottages, Cade Street, TN21 9BS
☎ 01435 866363 (Graham & Valerie Gumbrell)
www.spicersbb.co.uk Map 199/605212 BB **D** ✕ book first £12-£15, 6-8pm
SI DI TI 📺 🅱 🅳 ⊛ 🎣♨ 🚗 ❗🐾 ◆◆◆◆

● Horam (Heathfield)
WEALDWAY
⌐► Oak Mead Nursery, Cowden Hall Lane, TN21 9ED ☎ 01435 812962
(Mrs Barbara Curtis) Map 199/592171
BB **B/C** ✕ nearby SI DI TI Closed Dec-Feb 🅱 🅳 ⊛ 🎣♨ 🚗

● Lewes
SOUTH DOWNS*
SOUTH DOWNS WAY
Settlands, Wellgreen Lane, Kingston, BN7 3NP ☎ 01273 472295
(Mrs Diana Artlett) diana-a@solutions-inc.co.uk Map 198/398082
BB **D** ✕ nearby DI TI Closed Xmas ⋙(Lewes)
🅳 ⊛ 🎣♨ 🚗 ❗ ◆◆◆◆⑤

⌐► Bethel, Kingston Ridge, Kingston, BN7 3JX ☎ 01273 478658
(Tim & Nancy Lear) www.lewes-area-bed-and-breakfast.com/bethel
Map 198/387085 BB **C/D** ✕ nearby DI T2 Closed Xmas ⋙(Lewes)
🅱 🅳 ⊛ 🎣♨ 🚗 ❗

B&B Number 6, Gundreda Rd, BN7 1PX ☎ 01273 472106 (Jackie Lucas)
www.stayinlewes.co.uk Map 198/406105
BB **C** ✕ nearby D2 TI Closed Xmas ⋙(Lewes)
🅱 🅳 ⊛ 🎣♨ 🚗 ❗ ◆◆◆⑤

● Mayfield
April Cottage Guest House and Tearoom, West Street, TN20 6BA
☎ 01435 872160 (Miss B Powner) Map 188,199/585269
BB **C** ✕ nearby SI D/SI T/SI Closed Xmas 🅱 🅳 🎣🐾

● Newhaven
SOUTH DOWNS*
SOUTH DOWNS WAY
⌐► Newhaven Lodge, 12 Brighton Rd, BN9 9NB ☎ 01273 513736
(Jan Cameron) NewhavenLodge@aol.com Map 198/442013
BB **C** ✕ nearby S2 DI TI F3 Closed Xmas ⋙(Newhaven)
🅱 🎣♨ ❗ ◆◆◆

● Nutley (Uckfield)
WEALDWAY
⌐► West Meadows B&B, Bell Lane, TN22 3PD ☎ 01825 712434
(Alex Everett) www.westmeadows.co.uk Map 187,198/437276
BB **C** ✕ nearby D2 TI Closed Xmas
🅱 🅳 ⊛ 🎣♨ 🚗 ❗🐾 ◆◆◆◆⑤

● Rye

☆ ⌐► **Jeake's House**
Mermaid Street, TN31 7ET ☎ 01797 222828 (Mrs J Hadfield)
www.jeakeshouse.com Map 189/919203
BB **D** ✕ nearby SI D7 TI F2 ⋙(Rye)
🅱 🅳 ♨🐾 ◆◆◆◆◆⑤

 Dating from 1534, this listed building stands in Rye's medieval town centre.
Breakfast is served in the elegant galleried hall and features traditional, vegetarian, devilled kidneys and fish dishes.
Stylishly restored bedrooms combine luxury and modern amenities.
After rambling the Romney Marshes you can relax in the book-lined bar with a drink.
Bike hire nearby.
Private car park.

Flackley Ash Hotel, Peasmarsh, TN31 6YH ☎ 01797 230651
www.flackleyashhotel.co.uk Map 199,189/881233
BB **D** ✕ £24.50, 7-9:30pm D23 T18 F4 Closed Xmas
📺 🅱 🅳 🎣♨ ❗🐾 ★★★

⌐► Little Saltcote, 22 Military Rd, TN31 7NY ☎ 01797 223210
(Barbara & Denys Martin) littlesaltcote.rye@virgin.net Map 189/923212
BB **D** ✕ nearby D2 F3 Closed Xmas ⋙(Rye)
🅱 🅳 ⊛ 🎣♨ 🚗 ❗🐾 ◆◆◆◆

⌐► Culpeppers, 15 Love Lane, TN31 7NE ☎ 01797 224411
www.culpeppers-rye.co.uk Map 189/918209
BB **C** ✕ book first £, 6-6:30pm S2 TI ⋙(Rye)
📺 🅱 🅳 ⊛ 🎣♨ 🚗 🐾 ◆◆◆⑤

⌐► The Windmill Guest House, Ferry Road, TN31 7DW ☎ 01797 224027
(Brian Elliott) www.ryewindmill.co.uk Map 189/916203
BB **D** ✕ nearby SI T/D4 ⋙(Rye)
📺 🅱 🅳 ⊛ 🎣♨ ◆◆◆◆

● Streat
SOUTH DOWNS*
SOUTH DOWNS WAY
North Acres, BN6 8RX ☎ 01273 890278 (Mrs Valerie Eastwood)
www.northacres-streat.co.uk Map 198/353154
BB **C** ✕ nearby S2 DI TI Closed Xmas ⋙(Plumpton)
🅳 ⊛ 🎣♨ 🚗 ❗

● Wilmington (Polegate)

SOUTH DOWNS WAY & WEALDWAY

📷◀ Crossways Hotel, BN26 5SG ☎ 01323 482455 (David Stott)
www.crosswayshotel.co.uk Map 199/547048
BB **D** ✕ book first £33.95, 7:30-8:30pm S2 D3 T2 Closed Xmas-Jan
📶(Polegate) Ⓥ Ⓑ Ⓓ 🐾♿! ◆◆◆◆◆

● Withyham

WEALDWAY

☆ **Dorset House**
TN7 4BD ☎ 01892 770035 (Meg Stafford)
www.dorset-house.co.uk Map 188/496356
BB **C** ✕ nearby T2
Ⓓ ⊛ 🐾♿🚗!

A family-run B&B with two twin rooms in separate annexe in Withyham, near Hartfield.
The Wealdway and High Weald Landscape Trail pass close by.
The Dorset Arms pub is opposite for excellent evening meals.

WEST SUSSEX

● Amberley (Arundel)

SOUTH DOWNS*

SOUTH DOWNS WAY & MONARCH'S WAY

📷◀ Woodybanks Cottage, Crossgates, BN18 9NR ☎ 01798 831295
(Mr & Mrs G Hardy) www.woodybanks.co.uk Map 197/041136
BB **C** ✕ nearby D1 T1 Closed Xmas 📶(Amberley)
Ⓓ ⊛ 🐾♿🚗! ◆◆◆◆ Some facilities for disabled guests.

● Arundel

SOUTH DOWNS WAY & MONARCH'S WAY

Arden Guest House, 4 Queen's Lane, BN18 9JN ☎ 01903 882544
Map 197/019068 BB **C** ✕ nearby D5 T3 Closed Xmas 📶(Arundel)
Ⓑ ⊛ ♿ ◆◆◆

📷◀ Dellfield, 9 Dalloway Road, BN18 9HJ ☎ 01903 882253 (Mrs J M Carter)
jane@heron-electric.com Map 197/006064
BB **B** ✕ nearby S1 T1 Closed Dec 📶(Arundel) Ⓑ Ⓓ ⊛ 🐾♿Ⓜ

● Burgess Hill

📷◀ The Homestead, Homestead Lane, Valebridge Road, RH15 0RQ
☎ 01444 246899 (Sue & Mike Mundy) www.burgess-hill.co.uk
Map 198/323208 BB **C** ✕ nearby S1 D1 T2 F1 Closed Xmas
📶(Wivelsfield) Ⓑ Ⓓ ⊛ 🐾♿🚗 ◆◆◆◆

● Bury (Pulborough)

SOUTH DOWNS*

SOUTH DOWNS WAY & MONARCH'S WAY

📷◀ Harkaway, 8 Houghton Lane, RH20 1PD ☎ 01798 831843
(Mrs Carol Clarke) www.harkaway.org.uk Map 197/012130
BB **B** ✕ nearby S2 D1 T1 Closed Xmas 📶(Amberley)
Ⓑ Ⓓ ⊛ 🐾♿🚗! ◆◆◆

📷◀ Arun House, RH20 1NT ☎ 01798 831736 (Jan & Chris Briggs)
www.arunhousesussex.co.uk Map 197/010137
BB **B/C** ✕ book first £10, 6:30-8:30pm S1 D1 T1 F1 Closed Xmas
📶(Amberley) Ⓥ Ⓓ ⊛ 🐾♿🚗!🏵 ◆◆◆

● Charlton (Chichester)

SOUTH DOWNS*

MONARCH'S WAY & SOUTH DOWNS WAY

☆ **Woodstock House Hotel**
PO18 0HU ☎ 01243 811666 (Aidan F Nugent)
www.woodstockhousehotel.co.uk Map 197/889129
DD **D** ✕ nearby S2 D6 T4 F1 Closed Xmas
Ⓑ Ⓓ ⊛ 🚗!🏵 ◆◆◆◆

Situated in magnificent South Downs just 1 mile from South Downs Way. Converted from an old farmhouse our licensed B&B hotel has 13 en-suite bedrooms with all modern amenities. Our local inn for dinner is just 1 minute's walk.

● Chichester
5 Willowbed Avenue, PO19 8JD ☎ 01243 786366 (Mrs D A Pring) Map
197/870038 BB **A** ✕ nearby S2 D1 T1 📶(Chichester)
Ⓑ Ⓓ ⊛ ♿🏵

● Clayton (Hassocks)

SOUTH DOWNS*

SOUTH DOWNS WAY

Dower Cottage, Underhill Lane, BN6 9PL ☎ 01273 843363 (Mrs C Bailey)
www.dowercottage.co.uk Map 198/309136
BB **D** ✕ nearby S1 D2 T1 F2 Closed Xmas 📶(Hassocks)
Ⓑ Ⓓ ⊛ 🐾♿

● Cocking (Midhurst)

SOUTH DOWNS*

SOUTH DOWNS WAY

Downsfold, Bell Lane, GU29 0HU ☎ 01730 814376 (Malcolm & Janet Hunt)
www.downsfold.co.uk Map 197/876176
BB **C** ✕ nearby D1 T1 Closed Xmas Ⓓ ⊛ 🐾🚗!

The Blue Bell, Bell Lane, GU29 0HN ☎ 01730 813449 (Kate & Mark Walford)
www.thebluebell.org.uk Map 197/877175
BB **D** ✕ £8.95, 6:30-9:30pm D2 T1 Ⓥ Ⓑ 🐾♿🚗

● Ditchling (Hassocks)

SOUTH DOWNS*

SOUTH DOWNS WAY

South Cottage, 2 The Drove, BN6 8TR ☎ 01273 846636 Map 198/326153
BB **C** ✕ nearby D2 T1 Closed Xmas 📶(Hassocks) Ⓓ ⊛ 🐾🚗🏵

● East Grinstead

VANGUARD WAY

📷◀ Cranston House, Cranston Road, RH19 3HW ☎ 01342 323609
www.cranstonhouse.co.uk Map 187/397385
BB **D** ✕ book first £6 (snacks), 7-8pm S2 D2 T5 F1 Closed Xmas
📶(East Grinstead) Ⓥ Ⓑ Ⓓ ⊛ 🐾♿ ◆◆◆◆

● Fulking (Henfield)

SOUTH DOWNS*

SOUTH DOWNS WAY & MONARCH'S WAY

Knole House, Clappers Lane, BN5 9NH ☎ 01273 857387 (Jill Bremer)
www.knolehouse.co.uk Map 198/249124
BB **D** ✕ book first £15, 7-8pm S2 D1 T1 F1
Ⓥ Ⓑ Ⓓ ⊛ 🐾♿🚗!

SOUTH

● **Graffham (Petworth)**
SOUTH DOWNS WAY

Brook Barn, GU28 0PU ☎ 01798 867356 (Mr & Mrs S A Jollands)
brookbarn@hotmail.com Map 197/929180
BB **D** ✕ nearby D1 Closed Xmas 🅱 🅳 🐾 👜 🏠 ◆◆◆◆◆Ⓢ

● **Heyshott (Midhurst)**
SOUTH DOWNS*
SOUTH DOWNS WAY

Little Hoyle, Hoyle Lane, GU29 0DX ☎ 01798 867359 (Robert & Judith Ralph)
www.smoothound.com/littlehoyle Map 197/906187
BB **D** ✕ nearby D1 Closed Xmas 🅱 🅳 ⊗ 🐾 👜 🚗 ◆◆◆◆

● **Ifield Green (Crawley)**
April Cottage, 10 Langley Lane, RH11 0NA ☎ 01293 546222
(Brian & Liz Pedlow) www.aprilcottageguesthouse.co.uk Map 187/253379
BB **B/C** ✕ nearby D1 T2 F1 ⋙(Ifield)
🅱 ⊗ 🐾 👜 🚗 ! ◆◆◆◆ Guide dogs welcome.

● **Lindfield (Haywards Heath)**

☆ **Copyhold Hollow**
Copyhold Lane, Borde Hill, RH16 1XU ☎ 01444 413265 (Frances B G Druce)
www.copyholdhollow.co.uk Map 187,198/330267
BB **D** ✕ book first £20, 7pm S1 D2 T1 F2 ⋙(Haywards Heath)
🆅 🅱 🅳 ⊗ 👜 ! 🏠 ◆◆◆◆ⒼⓌ

A warm welcome in a 16th-century home.
Oak beams, inglenook fireplace in guests'
sitting room, cotton bedcovers, down duvets.
Home-baked bread and local produce for
breakfast. The surrounding countryside
complements the large garden enhancing the
tranquility. Details of local walks available.

● **Poynings (Brighton)**
SOUTH DOWNS WAY

☆ 🍴 **Cobby Sands Bed & Breakfast**
The Street, BN45 7AQ ☎ 01273 857821 (Mrs Angie Gill)
www.cobbysands.com Map 198/262119
BB **D** ✕ nearby
D1 T1 🆅 🅳 ⊗ 🐾 👜 🚗

Luxury detached country house with direct
access to the South Downs Way. Excellent pub
(Royal Oak) under two minutes' walk away.
Luxury bathroom with jacuzzi and separate
shower room.
All bedrooms have views across the South
Downs (see picture and website).

● **Pulborough**
SOUTH DOWNS WAY

Barn House Lodge, Barn House Lane, RH20 2BS ☎ 01798 872682
suehj@aol.com Map 197/052185
BB **C** ✕ nearby D1 T1 ⋙(Pulborough) 🆅 🅱 ⊗ 👜 ◆◆◆◆

● **Shoreham-by-Sea**
MONARCH'S WAY & SOUTH DOWNS WAY

🍴 Rutland House, 418 Upper Shoreham Road, BN43 5NE ☎ 01273 461681
(Elaine & Andrew Gill) elainegill@hotmail.co.uk Map 198/210059
BB **C** ✕ book first £12, 7:30pm S1 D3 T2 F1 ⋙(Shoreham-by-Sea)
🆅 🅱 🅳 ⊗ 🐾 👜 ! Wheelchair access.

● **South Harting (Petersfield)**
SOUTH DOWNS*
SOUTH DOWNS WAY

Torberry Cottage, Torberry Farm, GU31 5RG ☎ 01730 826883
(Mrs Maggie Barker) www.visitsussex.org/torberrycottage Map 197/767200
BB **C** ✕ nearby D1 T1 Closed Xmas 🅱 🅳 ⊗ 🐾 👜 🚗 ! ◆◆◆◆

● **Steyning**
SOUTH DOWNS*
MONARCH'S WAY & SOUTH DOWNS WAY

5 Coxham Lane, BN44 3LG ☎ 01903 812286 (Mrs J Morrow) Map 198/176116
BB **A** ✕ nearby S1 T2 Closed Nov-Feb 🅱 🅳 👜 🚗 !

🍴 Springwells Hotel, 9 High Street, BN44 3GG ☎ 01903 812446
www.springwells.co.uk Map 198/177112
BB **D** ✕ nearby S2 D3 T4 F1 Closed Xmas
🅱 🅳 🐾 👜 ! 🏠 ◆◆◆◆

Buncton Manor Farm, Steyning Rd, Wiston, BN44 3DD ☎ 01903 812736
(Nancy Rowland) www.bunctonmanor.supanet.com Map 198/148138
BB **B** D1 T1 Closed Nov 🆅 🅳 ⊗ 🐾 👜 !

Northfield Cottage, Kings Barn Lane, BN44 3YR ☎ 01903 815862
(Jennifer Shanahan) mob.club@virgin.net Map 198/188123
BB **D** ✕ book first £5, 6-8pm D1 T1 Closed Xmas
🅱 🅳 ⊗ 🐾 👜 🚗 ! 🏠

🍴 Uppingham, Kings Barn Villas, BN44 3FH ☎ 01903 812099
(Mrs Diana Couling) www.uppingham-steyning.co.uk Map 198/182111
BB **C** ✕ nearby S2 D2 🅱 🅳 ⊗ 🐾 👜 🚗 ! 🏠 Ⓜ

● **Worthing**
🍴 Manor Guest House, 100 Broadwater Rd, BN14 8AN ☎ 01903 236028
(Sandy Colbourne) www.manorworthing.com Map 198/147040
BB **D** ✕ £7, 6-8pm S1 D2 T1 F2 ⋙(Worthing)
🆅 🅱 🅳 ⊗ 🐾 👜 🚗 ! 🏠 ◆◆◆

Tudor Guesthouse, 5 Windsor Road, BN11 2LU ☎ 01903 210265
(Claire Bellezza) www.tudor-worthing.co.uk Map 198/159028
BB **D** ✕ book first £10, 6pm S2 D3 T4 Closed Dec ⋙(Worthing)
🆅 🅱 🅳 ⊗ 🐾 👜 🚗 ! ◆◆◆◆

SELF-CATERING

HAMPSHIRE

● **East Meon**
SOUTH DOWNS*

Church Farm House ☎ 01730 823256 (Christopher Moor)
www.gardenchalet.co.uk
£100-£180 Sleeps 2. 1 chalet.
Beautiful village, near South Downs Way. ⊗ 🏠

● **Fordingbridge**
NEW FOREST

Alderholt Mill ☎ 01425 653130 (Sandra Harte) www.alderholtmill.co.uk
£220-£480 Sleeps 2-6. 3 flats.
Working water mill conversion. Rural setting. ⊗ 🏠 ★★★
See B&B also.

☆ Sandy Balls Holiday Centre
☎ 01425 653042 (Tracey Farmer)
www.sandy-balls.co.uk
£148-£1,113 Sleeps 2-6. 136 lodges/homes. 230 touring/camping pitches.
Closed Jan   Set in 120 acres of woodland. 🏠 ★★★★★

Nestled in 120 acres of glorious woods and parkland, Sandy Balls is the ideal
retreat from the hustle and bustle of every day living for weekend, midweek and
holiday breaks — at any time of year — with the New Forest on
its doorstep.
With its own nature reserve, wildlife and bordering the river Avon, it's a
Rambler's delight!
Other facilities include horse riding, cycle hire, fishing, swimming and gym and
leisure centre — as well as a shop, Woodside Inn and Italian restaurant.
Nearby places to visit:
Hampshire/Dorset coastline
Beaulieu Motor Museum
Paultons Park
Marwell Zoo
WestQuay
Gunwharf & the Historic Naval Dockyard Portsmouth

● Lymington
NEW FOREST

The Old Exchange ☎ 01590 679228 (Sarah Alborino)
www.newforestretreats.co.uk £300-£600 Sleeps 2-7. 1 apartment.
Short breaks available all year.   ⊗ ♨(Sway) ★★★

● Lyndhurst
NEW FOREST

Penny Farthing Hotel & Cottages ☎ 023 802 84422 (Mike)
www.pennyfarthinghotel.co.uk
£525-£950 Sleeps 4-8. 5 varying types.
Quality inspected properties in village centre.   ⊗ ★★★★ See B&B also.

Kingsbridge House ☎ 023 8081 1161 (Linda Goodrich)
www.kingsbridgehousebandb.co.uk
£190-£300 Sleeps 2 + cot. 1 annexe of house.
Comfortable accommodation. Ideal location for the forest.   ⊗ See B&B also.

● Petersfield
The Privett Centre ☎ 01730 828238 (Centre Manager)
www.privettcentre.org.uk
£150-£200 (per night) Sleeps 20. 1 Victorian schoolhouse.
In Area of Outstanding Natural Beauty.   ⊗ See Groups also.

● Ringwood
NEW FOREST

Crofton ☎ 01425 471829 (Mrs J Hordle) www.croftonewforest.co.uk
£300-£650 Sleeps 4-5. 2 bungalows.
Ideal location to explore forest and coast.   ⊗ 🏠 ★★★★★

● Romsey
1 Thatched Cottage ☎ 01794 340460 (Mrs R J Crane)
£197-£325 Sleeps 5. 1 cottage.
Thatched country cottage. Bed linen provided.   ♨(Dunbridge) 🏠

☆ Brook Farm Cottages
☎ 01794 389334 (Sarah de Sigley)
www.quidity.com/brookfarmcottages
£525-£665 Sleeps 2. 4 cottages.
Adjoining the Test Way.   ⊗ 🏠 ★★★★

This beautifully converted timber-framed
barn has four luxurious cottages catering
principally for adults looking for a
country retreat. Set in a secluded
courtyard with the grounds of a 16th-
century Grade II listed farmhouse just
north of Romsey, adjoining the Test Way.

● Sway
NEW FOREST

Mrs Helen Beale ☎ 01590 682049 £160-
£380 Sleeps 2-6. 1 cottage, 2 flats.
Comfortable accommodation in excellent walking area.   ♨(Sway) 🏠 ★★★

● Winchester
SOUTH DOWNS*

Mrs Barbara Crabbe ☎ 01962 777887 crabbesleg@dsl.pipex.com
£200 Sleeps 2 adults 2 children. 1 apartment.
On Pilgrims Way. Pub half mile.   ⊗ 🏠

ISLE OF WIGHT

● Bonchurch

☆ Westfield Lodges
☎ 01983 852268 (Toby Brading)
www.westfieldlodges.co.uk
£205-£570 Sleeps 2-6. Lodges and apartments.
Indoor heated pool. Tennis court.   ⊗ ♨(Shanklin) 🏠

In the sunniest, prettiest part of the island in
an AONB with 500 miles of well maintained
sign-posted paths and 60 miles of coastland.
Westfield Lodges apartments offer superb
accommodation all year round, with a heated
swimming pool.
Email: info@westfield01983.fsnet.co.uk

● Newport

☆ Brockley Barns
☎ 01983 537276 (Sally Mitchell)
www.brockleybarns.co.uk
£269-£890 Sleeps 4-10. 3 cottages.
Beautiful country location with abundant wildlife.   ⊗

An 18th century barn, situated in the
courtyard garden of a five-acre
smallholding on the outskirts of Newport,
has been converted to create three cottages. Wonderful views of nearby Parkhurst
Forest. Very close to the Tennyson and
Shepherds' Trails, and Carisbrooke Castle.

SOUTH

● Niton

Ramblers' Retreat ☎ 0781 292 3897 (Patrick Fraher)
www.netguides.co.uk/wight/ramblersretreat.html
£175-£285 Sleeps 4. 1 chalet.   Closed Nov-Mar
Recently refurbished. Perfect base for walkers. ⊗

☆ Wight Heaven
☎ 01983 551501 (John & Barbara Sheppard)
www.now.dial.pipex.com/wightheaven.htm
£160-£325 Sleeps 2-3. 1 chalet.   Closed Jan-Feb
Peaceful setting, gardens. Adjoins coastal path. ⊗ ★★

 Comfortably furnished chalet on the southern tip of the island. Small securely gated site with tree-lined garden. Adjoins outstanding countryside. Delightful village pub and shops only a short walk away. Double bedroom, bedsettee in lounge area. Kitchen. Shower. Short drive/bus-ride from many villages, events and attractions.

● Sandown

Brackla Apartments ☎ 01983 403648 (Lindsay Heinrich)
www.brackla-apartments.co.uk
£250-£680 Sleeps 2-6. 3 apartments.   Well-equipped. Close station.
Ferry bookings arranged. ⊗ ⋙(Sandown) ★★★★

● Shanklin

☆ Lyon Court
☎ 07766 368719 (Paul Humphreys)
www.lyoncourtshanklin.co.uk
£190-£650 Sleeps 2-6. 8 apartments.
Overlooks Shanklin Down. Bus and rail links. ⊗ ⋙(Shanklin) ★★★

 Elegant Country House in an idyllic setting, yet close to Shanklin Old Village with pubs and restaurants. Nearby access to Shanklin Down, Worsley Trail and Coast Path. Laundry. Sauna, heated outdoor pool. Apartments have central heating and fully equipped kitchen.

☆ YMCA Isle of Wight
☎ 01983 862441 www.ymca-fg.org
£271-£1,904 Sleeps 4-24. 2 properties.
Linen included. Short breaks off season.
⊗ ⋙(Lake Station, Shanklin) ★★★ See Groups also.

 In the grounds of a beautiful Victorian building used as a group holiday centre. The Lodge, for 10-24 SC (or meals in main buiding). Mostly twin/group rooms. Close to cliff path and sandy beach. Great base for Island walking. Also, apartment for four.

● Capel-le-Ferne

☆ Eagles Nest House
☎ 07774 161280 (Celia Allen)
www.eaglesnesthouse.co.uk
£650-£1,200 Sleeps 6-8. 1 house.   Closed Oct-May
Heated pool, spa bath, water bed. ⊗ 🛏

 Stunning, mediterranean style house on Saxon Shore Way overlooking Warren Nature Reserve and Weir Bay. Sleeps 6/8, south and west facing terraces, indoor pool and conservatory.

State of the art kitchen, comfortable TV lounge. Two en-suite double bedrooms, one double and one single, plus luxury bathroom.
Superb walks from the house with access to the North Downs Way. Many local hostelries catering for every palate are within walking distance.

Email: nodandcelia@btinternet.com

● Holmbury St Mary

Gill Hill ☎ 01306 730210
£240-£400 Sleeps 2-4. 2 units.
Converted farm buildings on Greensand Way 🛏 ★★★ Access Category 1.

● Rye

☆ Cadborough Farm
☎ 01797 225426 (Jane Apperly)
www.cadborough.co.uk
£185-£395 Sleeps 2. 5 cottages.
Newly converted. Full GCH. Linen included. ⊗ ⋙(Rye) 🛏 ★★★★

 5 newly converted individual farm cottages providing luxurious and spacious accommodation for two people. Located 1 mile from Rye with direct access to 1066 Country Walk. Full gas c/h. Linen and towels included. No smoking. One small well behaved dog welcome.

Email: info@cadborough.co.uk Fax: 01797 224097

● Wadhurst

☆ **Bardown Farm**
☎ 01580 200452 (Alison Wortley)
www.bardownfarm.co.uk
£385-£750 Sleeps 4. 3 cottages.
Working farm. Luxury accommodation. Outdoor pool. ⊛ ∿(Stonegate)

Beautiful Sussex barn on working sheep-farm in area of outstanding natural beauty. Newly converted into three luxury cottages with oak beams and bespoke kitchens. Stunning panoramic views from private gardens and outdoor heated pool. Excellent footpath network from farm.

WEST SUSSEX

● Compton
SOUTH DOWNS*

Yew Tree House ☎ 023 9263 1248 (Mr J Buchanan)
d.buchanan@btinternet.com
£180-£295 Sleeps 2. 1 flat. Ideal for walking the South Downs. ⊛ 🏠 ★★★

● Henfield
SOUTH DOWNS*

☆ **New Hall**
☎ 01273 492546 (Mrs M W Carreck)
£240-£400 Sleeps 4-5. 1 cottage, 1 flat.
On footpath close to South Downs.
🏠 ★★★

Self-contained flat and 17th century cottage in two wings of manor house, set in three and a half acres of mature gardens, surrounded by farmland and footpaths. Half a mile from river Adur and Downslink long distance footpath. Two and a half miles from the South Downs Way.

GROUPS

HAMPSHIRE

The Privett Centre (SC) Church Lane, Privett ☎ 01730 828238
www.privettcentre.org.uk SC £150 + pn Max 20. Converted School.
Ⓓ ⊛   See SC also.

☆ **The Wessex Centre** (BB)
Sparsholt College, Sparsholt, Winchester SO21 2NF ☎ 01962 797259
(Sue Reeves) www.thewessexcentre.co.uk Map 185/423319
Min 6, max 250.
✕ 🐾 Ⓑ Ⓓ ∿(Winchester) ★★Ⓢ

Stunning venue offering comfortable en-suite bedrooms, good food, sports facilities and friendly atmosphere, within 400 acre working farm. Ideal base for exploring the South Downs Way, Clarendon Way and Test Way. Please book in advance. Groups of 6 or more. Open all year round.

ISLE OF WIGHT

☆ **YMCA Isle of Wight** (BB/SC)
Winchester House, Sandown Rd, Shanklin PO37 6HU ☎ 01983 862441
www.ymca-fg.ork
FB £26 +, SC £00 1 pw Min 10, max 150. Closed Xmas
✕ 🐾 ⊛ ∿(Lake Station, Shanklin) See SC also.

Beautiful Victorian building sleeps 135. Mostly bunk-bedded twin/group rooms. Great food - welcoming staff. Cliff-top position. Gloriously sandy beach. Great base for Island walking. Also, The Lodge, for 10-24 SC or meals in main building. Short breaks off season.

HOSTELS, BUNKHOUSES & CAMPSITES

HAMPSHIRE

SOUTH DOWNS*

Wetherdown Hostel (C/IH), The Sustainability Centre, Droxford Rd, GU32 1HR
☎ 01730 823549 www.earthworks-trust.com Map 197/676190
B&B £20 ✕(book first) 🐾(book first) Ⓓ ⊛

KENT

☆ **Palace Farm Hostel** (IH)
Down Court Rd, Doddington ☎ 01795 886200
www.palacefarm.com Grid ref: 935577
Bednight £16
✕ nearby 🐾 Ⓑ Ⓓ ⊛ ★★★

Luxury 30 bed hostel accommodation in the Kent Downs AONB on a family farm in village with pub. Enjoy this beautiful area with many self-guided walks. Ensuite rooms, comfortable beds and bunks, kitchen, garden, BBQ, continental breakfast and linen included.

SURREY

Puttenham Camping Barn (CB), Home Farm Barn, Puttenham GU3 1AR
☎ 01306 877978 (Sarah Hart)
www.puttenhamcampingbarn.co.uk Map 186/933479
Bednight £8 Closed Nov-March ✕ nearby ⊛ ∿(Wanborough)

WEST SUSSEX

SOUTH DOWNS*
SOUTH DOWNS WAY

Washington Caravan & Camping Park (C) London Rd, Washington, RH20 4AJ
☎ 01903 892869 (Max F Edlin) www.washcamp.com
Camping £6 ✕ nearby
🐾 Ⓓ ∿ (Worthing) ★★★★ Wheelchair access and toilet.

SOUTH

PEDDARS WAY

EAST

ST ALBANS MUSEUMS

VERULAMIUM PARK WITH ST ALBANS ABBEY

For many people, going for a walk means leaving life's stresses behind and getting away from it all – which usually involves turning off the mobile phone. But walkers in St Albans are being encouraged to stay on their phones to experience the town as it was in Roman times.

This spring, the Museum of St Albans is launching a self-guided walking tour of Verulamium – the ancient Roman settlement that lies beneath Verulamium Park – using any WAP-enabled mobile phone. Colour pictures, diagrams, audio tracks and text information will be sent to your phone showing for example, where the basilica and forum once stood or describing of the Roman graveyard buried beneath the lake that exists today. If the toga era doesn't appeal, there are plans to extend the guides on offer to include Victorian and Tudor St Albans and even a poetry-themed tour of the city.

> Walkers in St Albans are being encouraged to stay on their phones to experience the town as it was in Roman times.

The BBC is offering similar mobile-guided tours of Great Yarmouth and has teamed up with the tourist information centre to loan out WAP-enabled handsets. The 4km/2.5-mile circular tour begins on the beach and journeys into the town's streets, explaining how it was once England's fifth richest town and detailing its links with Nelson, herrings and bodysnatchers.

In Essex, the Roach Valley Way celebrates its 10th anniversary this year after recent restoration and the introduction of a distinctive new blue-and-white waymark. Staff and pupils of Deanes School in Thundersley, near Byfleet, who helped establish the way with the local council, also worked to renew the route as part of a student community action programme. The 37km/23-mile circuit tracks along the banks of both the Roach and Crouch estuaries, crossing creeks, marshland, pretty villages, open country and the ancient Hockley Woods. Each year Rochford & Castle Point Ramblers' Group walk the entire path in each direction on successive days.

Long Distance Paths

Chiltern Way	CHI
Essex Way	ESX
Icknield Way	ICK
London Loop	LNL
Nene Way	NEN
Peddars Way & Norfolk Coast Path	PNC
Suffolk Coast & Heaths Path	SCH

Public rights of way:
25,240km/15,674 miles

Mapped access land:

181 sq km/70 sq miles
(Area 8, East)

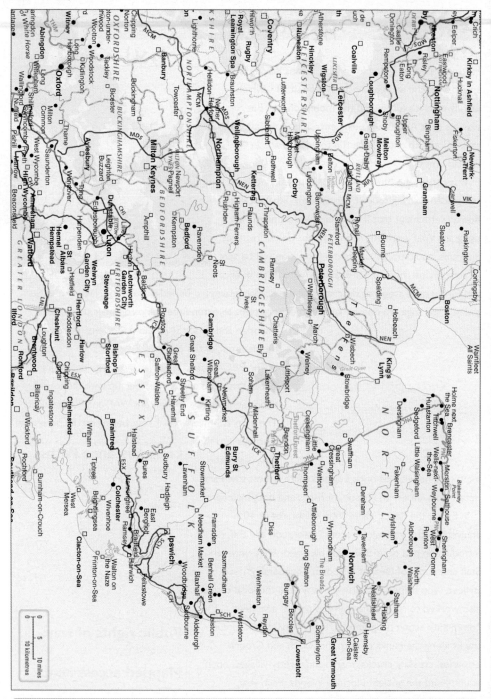

EAST
LOCAL RAMBLERS GROUPS

BEDFORDSHIRE
AREA SECRETARY
See www.ramblers.org.uk/info/localgroups
or contact our central office for details

GROUP SECRETARIES
Ivel Valley Mrs R Bryce, 7 Wood
Close, Biddenham, Bedford,
MK40 4QG
☎ 01234 272898
www.ivelvalleywalkers.org.uk
Lea & Icknield Miss S H Lewis,
21 Simpson Close, Leagrave, Luton,
LU4 9TP ☎ 01582 847273
Leighton Buzzard Mr John Hartley,
57 The Paddocks, Leighton Buzzard,
Beds, LU7 2SX ☎ 01525 372525
http://leightonramblers2.mysite.
wanadoo-members.co.uk/
North Bedfordshire Mrs Linda
Tongue, 25 Field Cottage Road, Eaton
Socon, St Neots, Cambs, PE19 8HA
☎ 01480 350345
Ouse Valley Mrs B M Leaf,
117 High Street, Blunham,
Bedfordshire, MK44 3NW
www.ousevalleyramblers.co.uk

CAMBRIDGESHIRE & PETERBOROUGH
AREA SECRETARY
Miss J Cartwright, 8 Willoughby
Avenue, Market Deeping,
Peterborough, PE6 8JE
☎ 01778 344831
http://web.ukonline.co.uk/
cambs.ramblers

GROUP SECRETARIES
Cambridge Ms J Tuffnell, 62 Beche
Road, Cambridge, CB5 8HU
☎ 01223 362881
**Cambridge 20s & 30s Walking
Group** Mr M Bingam & Miss A Ahmed,
8 Coachmans Lane, Baldock, SG7 5BN
☎ 01480 352733
www.walkcambridge.org
East Cambridgeshire Mrs Sue
Summerside, Mow Fen Hall, 4a Silt
Road, Littleport, Ely, Cambs, CB6 1QD
☎ 01353 861435
Fenland Mrs S L Ledger, 18 Alexandra
Road, Wisbech, Cambs, PE13 1HS
☎ 01945 587135
Huntingdonshire Mr William
Thompson, 2 Bankers Walk, Ramsey,
Huntingdon, Cambs, PE26 1EG
☎ 01487 812022
Peterborough Mr P Bennett,
93 Woodhurst Road, Stanground,
Peterborough, Cambs, PE2 8PQ
☎ 01733 553828

Peterborough Younger Walkers
Miss K L Hornsby, 11 Albany Walk,
Peterborough, PE2 9JN
☎ 01733 557381
http://web.ukonline.co.uk/
cambs.ramblers/ pbg_20-30_info.htm

ESSEX
AREA SECRETARY
Mr L Banister, 41 Gordon Avenue,
Highams Park, London, E4 9QT
☎ 020 8527 8158

GROUP SECRETARIES
Basildon Greenway Mr D J Tucker,
5 Mount Close, Wickford, Essex, SS11
8HF ☎ 01268 734932 (membership
enquiries ☎ 01375 670464)
Brentwood Mr R V Carpenter,
43 Arnolds Avenue, Shenfield,
Brentwood, Essex, CM13 1ET
☎ 01277 220781
www.brentwoodramblers.org.uk/
Chelmer & Blackwater Mrs Pauline
Ellis, 85 Hoynors, Danbury,
Chelmsford, CM3 4RL ☎ 01245 227727
Colchester Kevin Clark, Vine Cottage,
366 London Road, Stanway, Colchester,
CO3 8LU ☎ 01206 210510
www.colchester-ramblers.ccom.co.uk
East Essex Friends Mrs Nancy Hunt
(acting), 'Peatlands', 27 Runsell View,
Danbury, Chelmsford, CM3 4PE
☎ 01245 227988
Essex Friends Mrs Jeanie Lamb,
96 Waverley Crescent, Wickford,
Essex, SS1 7LS ☎ 01268 768546
www.eastessexfriends.plus.com
Essex Young Ramblers A Vincent-
Jones, Flat 14, Nelmes Court,
Hornchurch, Essex, RM11 2QL
☎ 01708 473253
Havering & East London Mr Ken
Richards, 26 Arundel Road, Harold
Wood, Romford, Essex, RM3 0RT
☎ 01708 375559
http://uk.geocities.com/helramblers
Lea Valley Friends Mrs Margaret
Brown, 11 Harford Road, London,
E4 7NQ ☎ 020 8529 1602
Maldon & Dengie Hundred
Ms J Mcgregor, 29 Doubleday Drive,
Heybridge, Maldon, CM9 4TL
☎ 01621 842595
www.maldondengieramblers.org.uk
North West Essex Mr David Harvey,
18 Clydesdale Road, Braintree, Essex,
CM7 2NX ☎ 01376 342090
Redbridge Mrs Wendy Rogers,
4 Kershaw Close, Hornchurch, Essex,
RM11 1SW ☎ 01708 456771
www.redbridgeramblers.org.uk

Rochford & Castle Point Mrs Janet
Paton, 11 Arundel Gardens, Rayleigh,
Essex, SS6 9GS ☎ 01268 786620
www.btinternet.com/~bta.wga/
rochford-ramblers
South East Essex Mrs Carol Clark,
146 Kenneth Road, Benfleet, SS7 3AN
☎ 01268 758855
www.e-cox.fsnet.co.uk
Stort Valley Mr Chris Abbott,
68 Glebelands, Harlow, Essex,
CM20 2PB ☎ 01279 305 725
www.geocities.com/stortvalleywalkers
Tendring District Mrs Ann Jones,
Wayside, Hall Road, Great Bromley,
Colchester, Essex, CO7 7TS
☎ 01206 230563
www.tendringramblers.co.uk
Thurrock Mr S G Dyball, 29 Bishops
Road, Corringham, Stanford Le Hope,
Essex, SS17 7HB ☎ 01375 676442
Uttlesford Mrs A Corke, Roston
House, Dunmow Road, Thaxted,
Dunmow, CM6 2LU ☎ 01371 830 654
West Essex Mr P B Spence,
6 Oak Glen, Hornchurch, Essex,
RM11 2NS ☎ 01708 702095

HERTFORDSHIRE & NORTH MIDDLESEX
AREA SECRETARY
Mr D S Allard, 8 Chilcourt, Royston,
Herts, SG8 9DD ☎ 01763 242677
www.herts-northmiddlesex
ramblers.org.uk

GROUP SECRETARIES
Dacorum Mr N T Jones,
47 Cedar Walk, Hemel Hempstead,
Herts, HP3 9ED
☎ 01442 211794
East Hertfordshire Miss P A
Hemmings, 16 Smiths Green, Debden,
Saffron Walden, CB11 3LP
☎ 01799 541308
Finchley & Hornsey Mrs J Haynes,
33 Links Road, Cricklewood, London,
NW2 7LE ☎ (membership enquiries
Mrs V Mallindine ☎ 020 8883 8190)
www.herts-northmiddlesex-
ramblers.org.uk
North Hertfordshire Mr R T Jarvis,
17 Moormead Close, Hitchin, Herts,
SG5 2BA ☎ 01462 422837
www.herts-northmiddlesex-
ramblers.org.uk
North London & South Herts
Mr M Noon, 100 Wynchgate, London,
N14 6RN ☎ 020 8886 0348
(membership enquiries 020 8441 0920)
www.herts-northmiddlesex-
ramblers.org.uk

LOCAL RAMBLERS GROUPS continued

Royston & District Mrs K L Heale, 4 The Brambles, Royston, SG8 9NQ ☎ 01763 246988

Watford & Three Rivers Mrs V M Buckley, 4 Firbank Drive, Watford, Herts, WD19 4EL ☎ 01923 222591

NORFOLK
AREA SECRETARY
Miss E Martin, 111 Belvoir Street, Norwich, Norfolk, NR2 3AZ ☎ 01603 612644 http://homepage. ntlworld.com/bcmoore/NorfolkRA

GROUP SECRETARIES
Fakenham Mrs A Easton, Pear Tree Cottage, The Street, Little Snoring, Fakenham, Norfolk, NR21 0AJ ☎ 01328 878872

Great Yarmouth Mrs P A Sharrock, Aldebaran, The Street, West Somerton, Norfolk, NR29 4EA ☎ 01493 393671

King's Lynn Mrs L Jones, 8 Lancaster Drive, Long Sutton, Spalding, PE12 9BD

Mid-Norfolk Mrs Carol Jackson, Mandola, Mill Street, Elsing, Dereham, Norfolk, NR20 3EJ ☎ 01362 637752

Norwich Mr D J Goddard, 49 Lindford Drive, Eaton, Norwich, Norfolk, NR4 6LR http://homepage.ntlworld.com /bcmoore/NorwichRA

Sheringham & District Mr Don Davenport, 'Malbank', 20 Newhaven Close, Cromer, Norfolk, NR27 0BD ☎ 01263 514955

Southern Norfolk Mrs J Aldridge, Wacton Common, Long Stratton, Norwich, NR15 2UP ☎ 01508 530289

Wensum Mr Tony Smith, 3 Priors Drive, Old Catton, Norwich, NR6 7LJ ☎ 01603 423085

SUFFOLK
AREA SECRETARY
Mr P Snelling, 12 Market Place, Lavenham, Suffolk, CO10 9QZ ☎ 01787 248079

GROUP SECRETARIES
Alde Valley Miss M B Perry, 16 Chapel Road, Saxmundham, Suffolk, IP17 1BG ☎ 01728 604712

Bury St Edmunds Mrs J M Bolwell, 42 Cloverfields, Sandpit Lane, Thurston,

Bury St. Edmunds, Suffolk, IP31 3TJ ☎ 01359 231301 www.burystedmundsramblers.org.uk

Ipswich & District Mr John Laycock, 8 Church Lane, Henley, Ipswich, Suffolk, IP6 0RQ ☎ 01473 831236 www.ipswichramblers.co.uk

Newmarket & District Mrs C C Lee, Corner Cottage, Sharps Lane, Horringer, Bury St Edmunds, IP29 5PW ☎ 01284 735971 www.newmarketramblers.co.uk

Stour Walking Group Miss L Ward, Two Rose Cottage, 46 Head Street, Halstead, CO9 2BX ☎ 01787 479761 www.stourwalkinggroup.co.uk

Stowmarket Mrs B Peart, 8 Elmsett Close, Stowmarket, Suffolk, IP14 2NU ☎ 01449 675315 www.stowmarketramblers.org.uk

Sudbury Mrs I Kay, 6 Chaplin Walk, Great Cornard, Sudbury, Suffolk, CO10 0YT ☎ 01787 370019 www.sudburyra.freeserve.co.uk

Waveney Lionel Hardy, 24 Meadow Gardens, Beccles, Suffolk, NR34 9PA ☎ 01502 716253

LOCAL RAMBLERS PUBLICATIONS

BEDFORDSHIRE
Leighton Buzzard Millenium Walks
(Leighton Buzzard Group). Ten tried and tested walks from gentle strolls to day treks, illustrated in full colour with OS map extracts. *Free + first class stamp from 8 Carlton Grove, Leighton Buzzard LU7 3BR.*

CAMBRIDGESHIRE
Guide to the Fen Rivers Way
Describes this 80km/50-mile route, part of E2, from Cambridge to Ongar Hill, on the Wash north of King's Lynn, with some circular walks of 6.5km/4 miles to 13km/8 miles linked to the main route. *£4.50 from 52 Maids Causeway, Cambridge CB5 8DD. Cheques to Cambridge Group of the Ramblers' Association.*

NEW **Twenty Rambles in Huntingdonshire Revisited**
by Huntingdonshire Ramblers, ISBN 1 901184 77 3. Walks in lowland countryside in the former county, 8km/5 miles to 21km/13 miles, spiral bound in handy pocket size, sketch maps, no public transport details. Revised and updated second edition of a book first published in 1998. *£4 + 50p p&p from 8 Park View, Needingworth, St Ives PE27 4TJ. Cheques to Huntingdonshire Group Ramblers.*

Walks in East Cambridgeshire
ISBN 0 9522518 0 9.
Circular lowland walks from 9.5km/6 miles to 19km/12 miles.
Walks in South Cambridgeshire
ISBN 0 9522518 3 3.
Circular lowland walks from 8km/5 miles to 19km/12 miles.
Walks on the South Cambridgeshire Borders
ISBN 0 9522518 2 5.
20 easy to moderate walks of from 8km/5 miles to 19km/12 miles along the boundaries with Essex, Hertfordshire and Bedfordshire.
All £4.50 each from 52 Maids Causeway, Cambridge CB5 8DD. Cheques to Cambridge Group of the Ramblers' Association.

ESSEX
Camuplodunum
by Colchester Ramblers. 40km/25 miles around Colchester via Great Horkesley and Mersea Road. No printed guide, but a full route description, updated in 2004, is available on Colchester Ramblers website (p113).

The Ramblers Millennium Walk
37km/23 mile walk around Southend-on-Sea and district. *£1 + A5 SAE from Southend Borough Council Leisure Services*

Department, Civic Centre, Victoria Avenue, Southend-on-Sea SS2 6ER. Cheques to Southend Borough Council.

15 Walks in South East Essex for all the Family
ISBN 901184 17 X.
17 More Walks in and around South East Essex
ISBN 1 901184 50 1.
Short Walks in the area of Southend-on-Sea
Walks of 6.5km/4 miles to 14.5km/9 miles. *£2.25 each including postage from 146 Kenneth Road, Thundersley SS7 3AN. Cheques to S E Essex Ramblers Group.*

HERTFORDSHIRE
Ten Walks in North Herts
by North Hertfordshire Ramblers, ISBN 0 900613 90 4. Ten mainly easy walks of 9.5km/6 miles for enjoyment in all seasons, most accessible by public transport and each a personal favourite of one of the Group. *£2.50 + 21p p&p from 55 Derby Way, Stevenage SG1 5TR. Cheques to North Herts Ramblers Group.*

NORFOLK
NEW **Angles Way**
(new edition 2005) edited by Sheila Smith, ISBN 1 901184 84 6. 125km/78mile route following the

Waveney Valley along the Norfolk/
Suffolk border from Great Yarmouth in
the Norfolk Broads to Knettishall Heath
in the Suffolk Brecks, and completing the
circuit of the Peddars Way National Trail
and Weavers Way. Includes maps,
accommodation and public transport
information. £2.70 + 30p p&p.

Iceni Way
edited by Sheila Smith, ISBN 1 901184
64 1. 134.5km/84-mile route from
Knettishall Heath in Breckland to the
coast at Hunstanton along the Little and
Great Ouse Valleys. First 24km/15miles
from Knettishall to Thetford is a useful
footpath link for Peddars Way or Angles
Way with transport and other facilities in
Thetford. Guide includes maps,
accommodation details and transport
information. £2.70 + 30p p&p.
NEW **Walking the Peddars Way
& Norfolk Coast Path with
Weavers Way**
(new edition 2005), edited by Ian
Mitchell, ISBN 1 901184 83 8. Concise
guide covering a total distance of
239km/149miles, the National Trail from
Knettishall Heath to Holme-next-the Sea
then along the coast to Cromer, and an
inland route from Cromer to Great
Yarmouth. Combined with the Angles
Way they provide a circular route of
364km/227miles. Guide includes maps,
accommodation and public transport
information. £2.70 + 30p p&p.
*All from Caldcleugh, Cake Street, Old
Buckenham, Attleborough NR17 1RU;
post free if three or more guides are
ordered together. Cheques to Ramblers'
Association Norfolk Area.*

Nelson's Heritage Walks
by Allan Jones (King's Lynn Ramblers).
16 circular walks with maps and
illustrations based on people, places or
events associated with Lord Nelson to
mark his bicentenary. Walks range from
5km/3 miles to 16km/10 miles, a few
using sections of the Peddars Way and
Norfolk Coast Path National Trail. No
public transport details, though town
walks in Great Yarmouth, Downham
Market, Norwich and King's Lynn are
included. £2.70 + 40p p&p.
West Norfolk Walkaway - 2
by Ian Smith (King's Lynn Ramblers),
ISBN 1 901184 55 2. 16 easy circular
walks between 7km/4.5 miles and
19.5km/12 miles, in the area of the
Peddar's Way between King's Lynn and
Fakenham. Sketch maps, route
descriptions and details of local
features. £2.10 + 40p p&p. Both from
42 Elvington, Springwood, King's Lynn
PE30 4TA. Cheques to Ramblers'
Association.

SUFFOLK
Cornard and Beyond
by Laurie Burroughs, ISBN 1 901194 65
X (Sudbury Ramblers). 4 short easy walks
of 6.5km/4 miles or less through the
countryside around Cornard.
Glemsford and Beyond by Lesley Pilbrow
(Sudbury Ramblers). A4 route cards with
three walks of 6.5km/4 miles to 9.5km/6
miles, all starting at Glemsford's fifteenth
century church. Both £1.20 + 50p p&p
each from 6 Chaplin Walk, Great Cornard,
Sudbury CO10 0YT. Cheques to Sudbury
and District Ramblers.

**East Suffolk Line Walks: Station
to Station Ipswich to Lowestoft**
by Roger Wolfe, ISBN 0 9547865 0 5.
11 varied and attractive walks linking
the stations along the East Suffolk Line
through both remote rural areas and
parkland on the urban fringe, ranging
from a short stroll beside a tidal estuary
(2.5km/1.5 miles) to a lengthy field
path and woodland walk (16km/10
miles). All the walks link together so
you can join together sections to taste
or even treat the route as a single long
distance path of over 112km/70 miles.
Jointly published by the East Suffolk
Travellers Association, Suffolk Ramblers
and Railfuture. £2 from East Suffolk
Travellers Association, 15 Clapham
Road South, Lowestoft NR32 1RQ,
or downloadable at
www.eastsuffolklinewalks.co.uk.

Rural Rambles Round Beccles
(Waveney Ramblers) 12 walks,
5.5km/3.5 miles to 13km/8 miles
Rural Rambles Round Lowestoft
(Waveney Ramblers) 11 walks, 6.5km
/4 miles to 16km/10 miles
Rural Rambles Round Southwold
(Waveney Ramblers) 12 walks, 8km/5
miles to 13km/8 miles
*All £1.80 + 35p p&p each, as Waveney
Way below.*

Waveney Way
(Waveney Ramblers). 115km/72 mile
circular walk from Lowestoft. £2.10 +
35p p&p from 1 Church Close,
Redenhall, Harleston IP20 9QS. Cheques
to Ramblers' Association.

EAST

BED & BREAKFAST

BEDFORDSHIRE

● Luton
ICKNIELD WAY
🚋🍴 4 Friars Way, Farley Hill, LU1 5PR ☎ 01582 724086 (T & J Wilson)
jeanandtom70@hotmail.com Map 166/077203
BB **B** ✗ book first £8 S1 D3 T1 F1 Closed Xmas ⋙(Luton Midland Road)
Ⓥ Ⓑ Ⓓ 🐾🛁🏠

● Ravensden (Bedford)
Tree-Garth, Church End, MK44 2RP ☎ 01234 771745 (Sue & Bruce Edwards)
treegarth@ukonline.co.uk Map 153/079547
BB **C** ✗ nearby S1 D1 T1 Closed Xmas
Ⓓ☺🐾🛁🚗 ◆◆◆◆

CAMBRIDGESHIRE

● Cambourne (Cambridge)

☆🚋🍴 **The Cambridge Belfry**
Cambourne, CB3 6BW ☎ 01954 714600
www.marstonhotels.com Map 153/TL 319601
BB **D** ✗ £32.50, 7-9:30pm D96 T24
Ⓥ Ⓑ🐾🛁 ★★★★ Wheelchair access.

A comfortable, modern four-star hotel with excellent facilities, The Cambridge Belfry is located in Cambourne, just 8 miles from Cambridge, a city itself offering enjoyable walks amongst the colleges and beside the River Cam.

With choice of dining in the main Bridge restaurant or the separate brasserie and bar area, this hotel is the place to stay when exploring the Cambridgeshire countryside with its woods and ridges.

Relax in the Reflections Leisure Club, with its heated indoor swimming pool, body treatments and massages in the spa, gym, sauna and steam room.

Please ask about our exclusive rates for walking parties.

● Cambridge
145 Gwydir Street, CB1 2LJ ☎ 01223 356615 (Mrs M Sanders)
www.thegwydirhouse.co.uk/index.php Map 154/462579
BB **B** ✗ nearby T1 Closed Xmas ⋙(Cambridge)
Ⓓ☺🐾🛁🚗!

Dykelands Guest House, 157 Mowbray Road, CB1 7SP ☎ 01223 244300
(Alison Tweddell) www.dykelands.com Map 154/471561
BB **C** ✗ nearby S1 D3 T2 F3 Closed Xmas ⋙(Cambridge)
Ⓑ Ⓓ☺🛁🏠 ◆◆◆

● Great Shelford (Cambridge)
Norfolk House, 2 Tunwells Lane, CB2 5LJ ☎ 01223 840287 (Mrs Janet Diver)
Map 154/463521 BB **C** ✗ nearby D1 T2 Closed Xmas
⋙(Great Shelford) Ⓑ Ⓓ☺🛁

● Great Wilbraham (Cambridge)
The Sycamore House, 56 High Street, CB1 5JD ☎ 01223 880751
(B W & E A Canning) www.thesycamorehouse.co.uk Map 154/549572
BB **C** ✗ nearby S1 D2 Closed Xmas
Ⓑ Ⓓ☺🐾🛁🚗🏠Ⓜ ◆◆◆◆

● Kirtling (Newmarket)

☆ **Hill Farm**
Newmarket Road, CB8 9HQ ☎ 01638 730253 (Mrs Ann Bailey)
Map 154/682583
BB **C** ✗ nearby S1 D1 T1 Closed Xmas
Ⓑ Ⓓ🐾🛁🚗🏠 ◆◆◆

Picturesque 400-year-old farmhouse with superb views of rural Studland. Tea/coffee facilities, CH, en-suites available. Log fires, TV lounge, games room. Excellent home-cooking with menu choice. Special diets by arrangement. Licensed. Fire certificate. Access at all times. £30 single room, £55 double.

● Streetly End (West Wickham)
ICKNIELD WAY
🚋🍴 Chequer Cottage, CB1 6RP ☎ 01223 891522 (Debbie Stills)
www.chequercottage.com Map 154/615482
BB **D** ✗ book first £12, 7pm D2 T1 F1
Ⓥ Ⓑ Ⓓ☺🐾🛁🚗! ◆◆◆◆

● Welney (Wisbech)
Stockyard Farm B&B, Wisbech Rd, PE14 9RQ ☎ 01354 610433
(Mrs C Bennett) Map 143/528944
BB **C** ✗ nearby D1 T1 Closed Xmas
Ⓓ☺🐾🛁🏠 Veggie breakfasts.

ESSEX

● Bradfield (Manningtree)
ESSEX WAY
Emsworth House, Ship Hill, CO11 2UP ☎ 01255 870860 (Penny Linton)
www.emsworthhouse.co.uk Map 168,169/142310
BB **D** ✗ nearby S3 D2 T1 F1 Closed Xmas
Ⓑ Ⓓ☺🐾🛁🚗! ◆◆◆◆

● Colchester
ESSEX WAY
Scheregate Hotel, 36 Osborne Street, CO2 7DB ☎ 01206 573034 (J Powell)
Map 168/996250 BB **D** ✗ nearby S15 D6 T8 F1 Closed Xmas
⋙(Colchester) Ⓑ Ⓓ🛁 ◆◆

● Great Chesterford (Saffron Walden)
ICKNIELD WAY

Mill House, CB10 1NS ☎ 01799 530493 (Mrs Christine King)
Map 154/504431
BB **A** ✕ nearby S1 D4 T1 Closed Xmas
⚑(Great Chesterford) ▢ ☺ ⚑♿☕♨ 🏠

● Ramsey (Harwich)
ESSEX WAY

Woodview Cottage, Wrabness Road, CO12 5ND ☎ 01255 886413 (Anne Cohen)
www.woodview-cottage.co.uk Map 168,169/191310
BB **D** ✕ book first £4 (light supper) S1 D1 F1 Closed Xmas ⚑(Wrabness)
Ⓥ Ⓑ ▢ ☺ ⚑♿☕♨ 🏠 ◆◆◆◆Ⓢ

HERTFORDSHIRE

● Hemel Hempstead
CHILTERN WAY

Alexandra Guest House, 40-42 Alexandra Road, HP2 5BP ☎ 01442 242897
www.alexandraguesthouse.co.uk Map 166/057074
BB **C** ✕ nearby S6 D5 T4 F3 Closed Xmas ⚑(Hemel Hempstead)
Ⓥ Ⓑ⚑♿☕ ◆◆◆

● Lilley (Luton)

🚩⊷ Putteridge Bury B&B, Dog Kennel Farm, LU2 8LQ ☎ 01462 769888
(Alison Balfour-Lynn) www.putteridgebury.com Map 166/121258
BB **C** ✕ nearby D1 T2 F2 ⚑(Luton Parkway)
Ⓥ Ⓑ ▢ ⚑♿☕♨!🏠

● Tring
RIDGEWAY & CHILTERN WAY

Rangers Cottage, Tring Park, Wigginton, HP23 6EB ☎ 01442 890155
(Sally Dawson) www.rangerscottage.com Map 165/936102
BB **D** ✕ nearby D2 T1 Closed Xmas ⚑(Tring)
Ⓑ ▢ ☺ ⚑♿♨ ◆◆◆◆

NORFOLK

● Aldborough

Butterfly Cottage, The Green, NR11 7AA ☎ 01263 768198 (Mrs Janet Davison)
www.butterflycottage.com Map 133/184343
BB **C** ✕ nearby S1 D1 T1 F1 Ⓑ ▢⚑♿☕♨!🏠 ◆◆◆

● Aylsham (Norwich)

☆ 🚩⊷ **The Old Pump House**
2 Holman Road, NR11 6BY ☎ 01263 733789
www.smoothhound.co.uk/hotels/oldpumphouse.html Map 133,134/190269
BB **C** ✕ book first £20, 6.30pm S1 D3 T1 F1 Closed Xmas
Ⓥ Ⓑ ▢ ☺ ⚑♿☕♨ ◆◆◆◆Ⓢ

18th C family home by thatched pump near marketplace, convenient for Weavers Way. Centrally located heated rooms (4 en-suite) with TV and hot drinks. Hearty breakfasts in pine-shuttered sitting room overlooking peaceful garden. Evening meals Oct-April by arrangement. Non-smoking.

● Brancaster (King's Lynn)
PEDDARS WAY & NORFOLK COAST PATH

The Ship, Main Rd, PE31 8AP ☎ 01485 210333
www.shipinnbrancaster.co.uk Map 132/774438
BB **C** ✕ £7.75, 7-9pm D3 T1 F1 Closed Xmas
Ⓥ Ⓑ ☺ ⚑♨! ★★★

● Cromer
PEDDARS WAY & NORFOLK COAST PATH

The White Cottage, 9 Cliff Drive, NR27 0AW ☎ 01263 512728 (Mrs J. Boocock)
www.whitecottagecromer.co.uk Map 133/224419
BB **D** ✕ nearby D2 T1 ⚑(Cromer)
Ⓑ ▢ ☺ ⚑♿♨ ◆◆◆◆

Birch House, 34 Cabbell Road, NR27 9HX ☎ 01263 512521 (Mrs W Lawrence)
www.birchhousenorfolk.co.uk Map 133/216421
BB **C** ✕ book first £12.50 S1 D3 T2 ⚑(Cromer)
Ⓥ Ⓑ ☺ ⚑♿☕♨! ◆◆◆

● Dersingham (King's Lynn)
PEDDARS WAY & NORFOLK COAST PATH

☆ **Holkham Cottage**
34 Hunstanton Road, PE31 6HQ ☎ 01485 544562 (Jane Curtis)
www.holkhamcottage.co.uk Map 132/685305
BB **C** ✕ book first £10, 6:30pm S1 D2 T1   Ⓥ Ⓑ ▢ ☺ ⚑♿☕♨!
🏠 ◆◆◆◆ Accommodation suitable for disabled guests.

Holkham Cottage is a large, detached Edwardian house with a beautiful garden. A perfect, tranquil base for exploring the countryside. Situated near Royal Sandringham and set in wonderful walking country. Peddars Way & Norfolk Coast Path close by.

● Great Cressingham (Swaffham)
PEDDARS WAY & NORFOLK COAST PATH

The Vines, IP25 6NL ☎ 01760 756303 (Mike & Vanessa Woolnough)
www.thevines.fsbusiness.co.uk Map 144/850016
BB **B** ✕ nearby D2 T1 F1
Ⓑ ▢ ☺ ⚑♿☕♨!🏠 ◆◆◆◆

● Hickling (Norwich)

Black Horse Cottage, The Green, NR12 0YA ☎ 01692 598691 (Yvonne Pugh)
www.blackhorsecottage.com Map 134/410234
BB **C** ✕ nearby S1 D2 Closed Xmas
▢ ☺ ⚑♿☕♨! ◆◆◆◆

● Holme-next-the-Sea (Hunstanton)
PEDDARS WAY & NORFOLK COAST PATH

Seagate House, 60 Beach Rd, PE36 6LG ☎ 01485 525510 (Mrs Norma Hasler)
dshinholme@aol.com Map 132/698435
BB **D** ✕ nearby D2 T1 Closed Xmas
Ⓑ ▢ ☺ ♿♨! ◆◆◆◆

● Hunstanton
PEDDARS WAY & NORFOLK COAST PATH

🚩⊷ The Gables, 28 Austin Street, PE36 6AW ☎ 01485 532514
(Mrs Barbara Bamfield) www.thegableshunstanton.co.uk Map 132/674411
BB **C/D** ✕ book first £14.99, 6:30pm D2 T2 F3 Closed Xmas
Ⓥ Ⓑ ▢ ☺ ⚑♿☕♨!Ⓜ ◆◆◆◆ Discounts for groups.

● Little Cressingham (Thetford)
PEDDARS WAY & NORFOLK COAST PATH

☆ **Sycamore House B&B**
IP25 6NE ☎ 01953 881887 (Mr J Wittridge)
Map 144/872001
BB **B** ✕ nearby S2 D2 T1 Closed Xmas
🅱 🅳 🐾 👵 🛏 !

Sycamore House is a large country home in a tranquil village. Close to Thetford Forest, which is host to many activities to suit people of all ages. It is situated on the Peddars Way and near the historical market towns of Watton, Swaffham and Thetford.

● Little Walsingham
◼ The Black Lion Hotel, Friday Market Place, NR22 6DB ☎ 01328 820235
(Christabel Napiper) www.blacklionwalsingham.com Map 132/933366
BB **D** ✕ £10, 7-9:30pm D5 T2
🆅 🅱 🅳 🐾 👵 🛏 ! ◆◆◆◆

● Morston (Holt)
PEDDARS WAY & NORFOLK COAST PATH
Scaldbeck Cottage, Stiffkey Rd, NR25 7BJ ☎ 01263 740188 (E Hamond)
eandnhamond@dialstart.net Map 133/004440
BB **C** ✕ nearby D1 T1 Closed Dec-Jan 🅳 ⊗ 👵 🛏

● Neatishead (Norwich)
◼ Regency Guest House, The Street, NR12 8AD ☎ 01692 630233
(Sue Wrigley) www.norfolkbroads.com/regency Map 133,134/340210
BB **C** ✕ book first £ D1 T1 F1
🅱 🅳 🐾 👵 ! ◆◆◆◆

● North Walsham

☆ ◼ **Green Ridges**
104 Cromer Road, NR28 0HE ☎ 01692 402448 (Yvonne Mitchell)
www.greenridges.com Map 133/272307
BB **D** ✕ book first £14.99, 5:30-8:30pm D1 T1 F1 ⋀⋀(North Walsham)
🆅 🅱 🅳 ⊗ 🐾 👵 🛏 ! ◆◆◆◆

Offering superior en-suite accommodation for the discerning traveller & delicious home-cooked home-grown produce. Conveniently situated within walking distance of town centre. Comfort and quality at a price you'll like.

● Norwich
◼ Foxhole Farm, Windy Lane, Foxhole, Saxlingham Thorpe, NR15 1UG
☎ 01508 499226 (John & Pauline Spear) foxholefarm@hotmail.com
Map 134/218971 BB **B** ✕ book first £15 D1 T1
🆅 🅱 🅳 ⊗ 🐾 👵 ◆◆◆◆

For an explanation of the symbols used in this guide see the Key to Abbreviations & Symbols on p1

● Old Hunstanton (Hunstanton)
PEDDARS WAY & NORFOLK COAST PATH

☆ ◼ **The Neptune Inn & Restaurant**
85 Old Hunstanton Road, PE36 6HZ ☎ 01485 532122
www.theneptune.co.uk Map 132/686422
BB **D** ✕ book first £30, 6-9pm S1 D5 T1
🆅 🅱 ⊗ 🐾 👵 🛏 ! 🐾 ◆◆◆◆⊛

Award-winning accommodation and restaurant, near to the Peddars Way and Norfolk Coast Path and bird reserves. All bedrooms en-suite, TV, DVD, coffee and tea making facilities. Only fresh local produce served in our AA rosette restaurant.

● Salthouse (Holt)
PEDDARS WAY & NORFOLK COAST PATH
Cumfus Bottom, Purdy Street, NR25 7XA ☎ 01263 741118
Map 133/073437
BB **C** ✕ nearby D2 T1 Closed Xmas 🅱 🅳 🐾 👵 ! 🛏

● Sedgeford (Hunstanton)
PEDDARS WAY & NORFOLK COAST PATH
Park View, PE36 5LU ☎ 01485 571352 (Mrs J Frost)
Map 132/711366 BB **B** ✕ book first £10 S1 D1 T1 Closed Xmas-Jan
🆅 🅱 🅳 ⊗ 🐾 👵 🛏 ! 🛏

● Sheringham
PEDDARS WAY & NORFOLK COAST PATH
Oakleigh, 31 Morris Street, NR26 8JY ☎ 01263 824993 (Mrs Diana North)
dnorthoak@hotmail.com Map 133/157434
BB **B/C** ✕ nearby S1 D1 Closed Nov-Mar ⋀⋀(Sheringham)
🅱 🅳 ⊗ 🐾 👵 ! 🛏

◼ Elmwood, 6 The Rise, NR26 8QA ☎ 01263 825454
Map 133/160426 BB **B** ✕ nearby D1 T1 Closed Xmas ⋀⋀(Sheringham)
🅱 🅳 ⊗ 👵 🛏 ! 🛏 🅜

◼ Bay Leaf Guest House, 10 St Peters Rd, NR26 8QY ☎ 01263 823779
(Graham & Ros) bayleafgh@aol.com Map 133/156431
BB **C/D** ✕ £3-£6 (bar snacks), 5-9pm D3 T2 F2 Closed Xmas
⋀⋀(Sheringham) 🆅 🅱 ⊗ 🐾 👵 ◆◆◆◆

● Stalham (Norwich)
Landell, Brick Kiln Lane, Ingham, NR12 9SX ☎ 01692 582349
(Mrs Barbara Mixer) www.landell.co.uk Map 133,134/385255
BB **C** ✕ book first £12 D1 T1 F1 Closed Xmas
🅱 🅳 ⊗ 🐾 👵 🛏 ! 🛏 🅜

● Stowbridge (King's Lynn)
◼ Narwiss Lodge, 22 The Causeway, PE34 3PP ☎ 01366 384734
narwisslodge@btinternet.com Map 143/608070
BB **B/C** ✕ nearby S1 D/T/F1 Closed April-May
🆅 🅱 🅳 ⊗ 🐾 👵 🛏 🅜

● Taverham (Norwich)
◼ Foxwood Guest House, Fakenham Road, NR8 6HR ☎ 01603 868474
www.foxwoodhouse.co.uk Map 133/154152
BB **C** ✕ book first £10, 6:30pm D1 T2 Closed Xmas
🆅 🅱 🅳 ⊗ 🐾 👵 🛏 !

● Thompson (Thetford)
PEDDARS WAY & NORFOLK COAST PATH

College Farm, IP24 1QG ☎ 01953 483318 (Lavender Garnier)
collegefarm@amserve.net Map 144/933966
BB **C** ✗ nearby D2 T1   B   D 🐾♨🚗🛏

Thatched House, Mill Rd, IP24 1PH ☎ 01953 483577 (Brenda Mills)
thatchedhouse@amserve.com Map 144/919967
BB **C** ✗ nearby D1 T2 Closed Xmas
V B D 🐾🐾♨🚗!🛏 Ⓜ

● Titchwell (King's Lynn)
PEDDARS WAY & NORFOLK COAST PATH

┌──┐
☆ **Briarfields**
Main Street, PE31 8BB ☎ 01485 210742
www.norfolkhotels.co.uk Map 132/757438
BB **C** ✗ £12.50, 6:30-9pm D11 T7 F4
V B D 🐾🐾♨🚗🛏 ★★

Briarfields is a renovated barn complex with sea views situated next to the RSPB
reserve and marshes at Titchwell. We are the perfect getaway to explore the
north Norfolk coast with Sandringham, Norfolk Lavender, Peddars Way and
Holkham Hall nearby.
Old beams and oak floors, log fire, excellent bar & restaurant dishes, afternoon
teas, real ales, four-poster beds and exceptional views of the RSPB marshes.
All bedrooms are en-suite including family rooms.
We offer bed & breakfast packages and discounted rates over the winter period.
└──┘

● Wells-next-the-Sea
PEDDARS WAY & NORFOLK COAST PATH

Meadowside, Two Furlong Hill, NR23 1HQ ☎ 01328 710470 (C & L Shayes)
Map 132/913433
BB **C** ✗ nearby D1 T1 Closed Xmas   B   D 🐾♨ Ⓜ

Fern Cottage B&B, Standard Road, NR23 1JU ☎ 01328 710306 (Linda Pearce)
www.ferncottage.co.uk Map 132/918435
BB **D** ✗ nearby D2 Closed Xmas   B   D 🐾♨

● West Runton
PEDDARS WAY & NORFOLK COAST PATH

┌──┐
☆ **Homefield Guest House**
48 Cromer Road, NR27 9AD ☎ 01263 837337 (Lisa Sargeant)
www.homefieldguesthouse.co.uk Map 133/182427
BB **C** ✗ nearby D4 T2 ⚶(West Runton)
V B D 🐾🐾♨🚗! ◆◆◆

Quality, period guesthouse located in
pretty coastal village of West Runton.
Clean, comfortable rooms, packed lunches
available on request and walking
reference books for guests to borrow.
Village serviced by train, coach and bus
routes. Private car park.
└──┘

● Weybourne
PEDDARS WAY & NORFOLK COAST PATH

Sedgemoor, Sheringham Road, NR25 7EY ☎ 01263 588533 Map 133/113429
BB **B** ✗ nearby D2 Closed Xmas ⚶(Weybourne)   D 🐾🚗🛏

SUFFOLK

● Aldeburgh
SUFFOLK COAST & HEATHS PATH

▪⚶◀ The Toll House, 50 Victoria Road, IP15 5EJ ☎ 01728 453239
Map 156/458570
BB **C** ✗ nearby D5 T2
V B D 🐾🐾♨! ◆◆◆◆

● Beccles
Catherine House, 2 Ringsfield Road, NR34 9PQ ☎ 01502 716428
(Mr & Mrs W T Renilson) Map 156/418897
BB **B** ✗ nearby D3 Closed Xmas ⚶(Beccles)
V B D 🐾♨ ◆◆◆

▪⚶◀ Pinetrees, Park Drive, NR34 7DQ ☎ 01502 470796 (Sue Bergin)
www.pinetrees.net Map 156/435900
BB **C** ✗ nearby D3 ⚶(Beccles)
V B D 🐾🐾🚗! Wheelchair access.

● Benhall Green (Saxmundham)
SUFFOLK COAST & HEATHS PATH

┌──┐
☆ ▪⚶◀ **Honeypot Lodge**
Aldecar Lane, IP17 1HN ☎ 01728 602449
www.saxmundham.info Map 156/383609
BB **C** ✗ book first £7.50 D1 T1 ⚶(Saxmundham)
V B D 🐾🐾♨🚗! ◆◆◆◆

Set in a quiet acre of Suffolk
countryside, 2 miles from
Saxmundham and 7 miles
from Aldeburgh.
Easy access to Suffolk Coastal
Walk, RSPB Minsmere and NT
Dunwich heath.
└──┘

● Blaxhall (Woodbridge)
SUFFOLK COAST & HEATHS PATH

▪⚶◀ The Ship Guesthouse, School Road, IP12 2DY ☎ 01728 688316
shipblaxhall@aol.com Map 156/367570
BB **C** ✗ nearby T4   B   D 🐾🐾♨🚗!🛏 ◆◆

● Bungay
▪⚶◀ 22 Quaves Lane, NR35 1DF ☎ 01986 892907 (Mrs M Sheppard)
bigoolholidays@tiscali.net Map 156/336895
BB **B** ✗ nearby S1 D1 T1 Closed Xmas   B   D 🐾🐾♨🚗!

● Bures (Sudbury)
▪⚶◀ Queens House, Church Square, CO8 5AB ☎ 01787 227760
(Roger Arnold) www.queens-house.com Map 155/908341
BB **D** ✗ book first £14 D3 T2 F1 Closed Xmas ⚶(Bures)
V B D 🐾🐾🚗!🛏 ◆◆◆◆

EAST

● Bury St Edmunds

Rose Cottage & Laurels Stables, Horringer-cum-Ickworth, IP29 5SN
☎ 01284 735281   Map 155/825613
BB **C** ✕ nearby DI T2 Closed Xmas ✸(Bury St Edmunds)
Ⓓ ⊛ 🐾♿🛏 Access Category I.

⊶ Oak Cottage, 54 Guildhall Street, IP33 IQF ☎ 01284 762745
(Sheila Keeley) sheekee@talk21.com Map 155/852638
BB **B/C** ✕ book first £15, 6:30-7pm SI DI TI FI ✸(Bury St Edmunds)
Ⓥ Ⓑ Ⓓ ⊛ 🐾♿🚗!🛏Ⓜ

● East Bergholt (Colchester)

ESSEX WAY & SUFFOLK COAST & HEATHS PATH
Rosemary, Rectory Hill, CO7 6TH
☎ 01206 298241 (Mrs Natalie Finch) Map 155,169/073344
BB **B** ✕ nearby SI T3 Closed Xmas ✸(Manningtree)
Ⓓ ⊛ 🐾🚗🛏 ◆◆◆

● Framsden (Stowmarket)

Greggle Cottage, Ashfield Rd, IP14 6LP ☎ 01728 860226 (Jim & Phil Welland)
wellands@ukgateway.net Map 156/194609
BB **C** SI DI T/DI Closed Xmas Ⓑ ⊛ 🐾♿🚗!🛏

● Lavenham (Sudbury)

Brett Farm, The Common, CO10 9PG ☎ 01787 248533 (Mrs M Hussey)
www.brettfarm.com Map 155/923491
BB **D** D2 TI Closed Xmas ✸(Sudbury)
Ⓑ Ⓓ ⊛ 🐾♿🚗! ◆◆◆◆

● Reydon (Southwold)

SUFFOLK COAST & HEATHS PATH
49 Halesworth Road, IP18 6NR ☎ 01502 725075 (Miss E A Webb)
www.southwold.info Map 156/498770
BB **C** ✕ nearby D2 TI Closed Xmas
Ⓑ Ⓓ ⊛ 🐾♿!🛏

● Saxmundham

⊶ Georgian Guest House, 6 North Entrance, IP17 IAY ☎ 01728 603337
www.thegeorgian-house.com Map 156/385634
BB **D** ✕ nearby D4 TI F2 Closed Xmas ✸(Saxmundham)
Ⓑ Ⓓ ⊛ 🐾♿🚗!🛏 ◆◆◆◆◆Ⓢ

● Somerleyton (Lowestoft)

Laurel House, The Street, NR32 5QB ☎ 01502 732714 (Christine Nichols)
arnoldalfrednichols@yahoo.co.uk Map 134/483972
BB **C** ✕ nearby S2 D2 ✸(Somerleyton)
Ⓥ Ⓓ ⊛ 🐾♿🚗!

● Sudbourne (Woodbridge)

Long Meadows, Gorse Lane, IP12 2BD
☎ 01394 450269 (Mrs A Wood) Map 156/412532
BB **B** ✕ book first £10, 7:30pm SI DI TI Closed Xmas
Ⓥ Ⓑ Ⓓ ⊛ 🐾♿🚗!🛏 ◆◆◆

● Wenhaston (Halesworth)

⊶ Rowan House, Hall Road, IP19 9HF ☎ 01502 478407
(Mrs Patricia Kemsley) rowanhouse@freeuk.com Map 156/427749
BB **B** ✕ book first £12, 7:30pm DI TI Closed Xmas
Ⓥ Ⓑ Ⓓ 🐾♿🚗!🛏 ◆◆◆◆

● Woodbridge

☆ **French's Farm**
Debach, IP13 6BZ ☎ 01473 277126 (Maggie Jennings)
www.treadsuffolk.co.uk/ffbbmain.htm Map 156/243552
BB **B/C** ✕ book first £9.50 SI D2 TI FI Closed Xmas
Ⓥ Ⓑ Ⓓ ⊛ 🐾♿🚗!Ⓜ See Walking Holidays also.

Beautiful 16th-century former farmhouse,
Grade II-listed. Guest lounge, log fires,
homemade breads & preserves. Grounds
with large ponds. Access: Woodbridge,
Dunwich Framlingham, Heritage Coast.
Friendly, welcoming hosts.
Email: maggie@treadsuffolk.co.uk

Deben Lodge, Melton Road, IP12 INH ☎ 01394 382740 (Rosemary Schlee)
Map 169/278498 BB **B** ✕ nearby S2 DI TI ✸(Woodbridge)
Ⓥ Ⓓ ⊛ ♿🛏 ◆◆Ⓦ Oxfam B&B Scheme.

SELF-CATERING

NORFOLK

● Castle Acre

Mrs A C C Swindell ☎ 01534 727480 www.castleacre.org
£175-£350 Sleeps 6. I cottage.
Delightful village on the Peddars Way. 🛏 ★★★

● Cley-next-the-Sea

☆ **Archway Cottage**
☎ 01992 511303 (Mrs V Jackson)
£200-£480 Sleeps 2-7. I cottage.
Character cottage, comfortable and well-equipped
⊛ 🛏 ★★★

Archway Cottage, Cley-next-the-Sea.
Comfortable and well-equipped
character cottage – sleeps 7.
Another cottage in Wells-next-the-Sea.
Also telephone: 01992 503196

● Wells-next-the-Sea

Ms Lesley Whitby ☎ 020 7485 0573 l.whitby@ucl.ac.uk
£265-£340 Sleeps 2. I cottage.
Traditional flint cottage by saltmarshes. ⊛ ★★★

● West Runton

Mrs J Marquart ☎ 01603 454801 jackie.marquart@tiscali.co.uk
£180-£300 Sleeps 3. I flint cottage.
Near coastal path and National Trust woods.
⊛ ✸(West Runton) 🛏

SUFFOLK

● **Aldeburgh**
Lesley Valentine ☎ 01986 798609 www.aldeburgh-cragside.co.uk
£200-£410 Sleeps 3. 1 flat.
Ground floor flat, comfortable and warm. Ⓖ ▲▲▲▲

Beach Cottage ☎ 01728 746475 (Fiona Kerr) www.eastonfarmpark.co.uk
£421-£824 Sleeps 7. 1 cottage.
Seaside location. Ample parking. Ⓖ 🏠 ★★★★

● **Bures**
Coppins Farm ☎ 01787 269297 (John McGlashan) http://coppinsfarm.co.uk
£250-£350 Sleeps 4. 1 showman's living van.
Little lanes, woodland, wildflowers. Ⓖ ᴘᴘ(Bures)

● **Darsham**

> ☆ **Priory Farm Country Holidays**
> ☎ 01728 668459 (Mrs Bloomfield)
> www.holidaysatprioryfarm.co.uk
> £225-£425 Sleeps 2-4. 2 properties.   Weekly lets and short breaks.
> Ⓖ ᴘᴘ(Darsham) ★★★ Access category 2.
>
>
>
> The Granary and the Mallards are superb barn conversions. Well equipped for your comfort and convenience. Centrally heated. Weekly or short breaks. Close to good woodland and heathland walking areas that are rich in beauty, history and culture.

● **Southwold**
The Old Orchard ☎ 01502 575880 (Adrienne & Michael Wolfers)
www.oldorchard.netfirms.com
£213-£586 Sleeps 4. 4 cottages.
Indoor swimming pool. Farm walks, owls! Ⓖ ᴘᴘ(Brampton) 🏠

GROUPS

NORFOLK

PEDDARS WAY & NORFOLK COAST PATH

Deepdale Granary Group Hostel (SC) Burnham Deepdale ☎ 01485 210256
www.deepdalefarm.co.uk Map 132/804441
Max 18. ✕nearby 🐾 Ⓑ Ⓓ Ⓖ ★★★Ⓦ See Hostels also.

HOSTELS, BUNKHOUSES & CAMPSITES

NORFOLK

PEDDARS WAY & NORFOLK COAST PATH

Deepdale Backpackers and Camping (C/IH) Burnham Deepdale
☎ 01485 210256 www.deepdalefarm.co.uk Map 132/803443
Bednight £10.50 ✕nearby Ⓑ Ⓓ Ⓖ 🏠 🐾 ★★★★Ⓦ See Groups also.

EAST

VIEW FROM BLACK ROCKS IN CROMFORD TOWARDS MATLOCK

EAST MIDLANDS

With the constant pressure on Britain's woodlands from planners and developers, a major project aiming to actively expand forested areas may seem surprising. But such is the ambition of the National Forest which hopes to cover a third of the 518 sq km/200 square miles across Leicestershire, Derbyshire and Staffordshire, and is already half way towards its target.

THE 'DRAGON'S BACK', SOUTH OF BUXTON

Linking the ancient forests of Needwood and Charnwood, the new planting is transforming the stripped industrial landscape that surrounds the ex-mining towns of Coalville and Swadlincote, and enhancing existing local tourist spots, such as historic Ashby de la Zouch. But most importantly for walkers, the National Forest has created 16 waymarked trails within its boundaries, all circular routes ranging from three to 22 miles. The Birthday Walk celebrates the forest's tenth birthday and is a ten-mile tour of the project's past successes, taking in ten new woodland areas including the Sence Valley Forest Park – a former open-cast mine turned wildlife sanctuary where otters and abundant birdlife can be spotted.

The arrival of the right to roam opened up several new areas of the Peak District to walkers. The startling contours of the Dragon's Back hills, south of Buxton, are now accessible via a series of fellsides from Hollins Hill to High Wheeldon. And more moorland and spectacular sandstone escarpments on Combs and Black Edge, near Chapel-en-le-Frith, are no longer out-of-bounds.

Having impressed Hollywood's Tom Hanks and Ron Howard during filming of the Da Vinci Code, Lincolnshire continues to capitalise on its Warhol-moment of fame.

Having impressed Hollywood's Tom Hanks and Ron Howard during filming of the Da Vinci Code, Lincolnshire continues to capitalise on its Warhol-moment of fame with a second Discover Greater Lincoln Weekend in March. As well as guided tours of Lincoln's starring cathedral, there are organised walks of Posterngate's Roman wall and the 375-acre Natural World Centre in Whisby. And Lincolnshire Ramblers will offer even more walking options during the second Lincolnshire Wolds Walking Festival in May and June with over 50 led-walks planned.

Long Distance Paths

Derwent Valley Heritage Way	DER
Macmillan Way	MCM
Midshires Way	MDS
Nene Way	NEN
Pennine Bridleway	PNB
Pennine Way	PNN
Staffordshire Way	SFS
Trans Pennine Trail	TPT
Viking Way	VIK

Public rights of way:

19,780km/12,283 miles

Mapped Access land:

 323 sq km/125 sq miles (Area 7, West)

15 sq km/6 sq miles (Area 8, East)

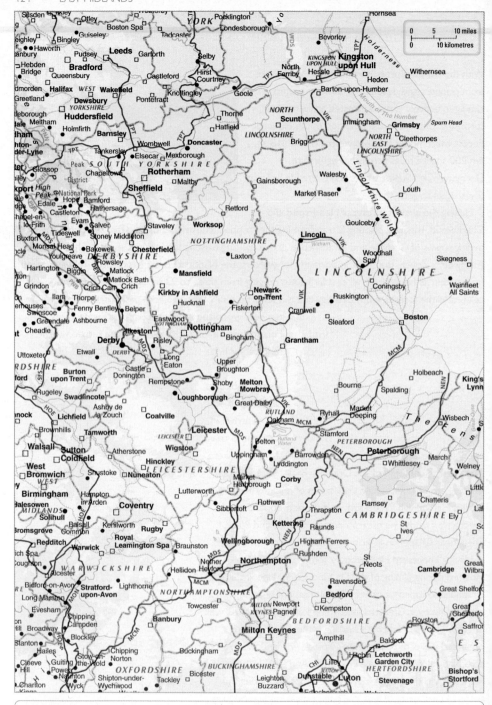

DERBYSHIRE

AREA SECRETARY
Mr John Hayes, The Old Rectory, Old Brampton, Chesterfield, Derbyshire, S42 7JG ☎ 01246 569260

GROUP SECRETARIES
Amber Valley Mrs M A Siddons, Overdene, Ridgeway Lane, Nether Heage, Nr Belper, Derbyshire, DE56 2JT
www.ambervalleyramblers.org.uk
Derby & South Derbyshire Mrs P Vaughan, 'Greenways', 13 Evans Avenue, Allestree, Derbys, DE22 2EL
☎ 01332 558552
www.derbyramblers.org.uk
Derbyshire Dales Mrs Mandy Higton, 231 Chesterfield Road, Matlock DE4
☎ 01629 582681
www.derbyshiredalesramblers.org.uk
Derbyshire Family Rambling Group
☎ 01332 841975 or 01332 554756
www.derbyshirefamilyrambling.org.uk
Erewash District Tony Beardsley, 14 York Avenue, Sandiacre, Nottingham, NG10 5HB ☎ 0115 917 0082
www.erewashramblers.org.uk

LEICESTERSHIRE & RUTLAND

AREA SECRETARY
Mrs E Sandeman, 39 Maple Way, Earl Shilton, Leicestershire, LE9 7HW
☎ 01455 848166
http://uk.geocities.com/ramblingjohn/Leics.html

GROUP SECRETARIES
Coalville Mr Malvern Irons (acting), 14 Coverdale, Whitwick, LE67 5BP
www.trig222.f9.co.uk/coalvilleramblers
Hinckley Mrs B Elliston, 20 Surrey Close, Burbage, Hinckley, Leics, LE10 2NY ☎ 01455 238881
www.hinckleyramblers.cjb.net
Leicester Mr T G Bates, 9 Main Street, Scraptoft, Leicester, LE7 9TD
☎ 0116 241 8887
http://leicesterramblers.co.uk
Leicestershire & Rutland Walking Group Andrew Hann, 119 Beatrice Road, Leicester, LE3 9FJ
☎ 0116 224 6171
www.lrwg.org.uk
Loughborough & District Mrs Joyce Noon, 8 Ribble Drive, Barrow-Upon-Soar, Loughborough, Leics, LE12 8LJ
☎ 01509 414519
http://uk.geocities.com/ramblingjohn/Loughborough.html

Lutterworth Mrs Y Coulson, 12 Elmhirst Road, Lutterworth, Leicestershire, LE17 4QB
☎ 01455 552265
Melton Mowbray Gill Lant, 94 Scalford Road, Melton Mowbray, LE13 1JZ
☎ 01664 500516
www.meltonra.org.uk
Rutland Joy Coleman, 6 Shannon Way, Oakham, Rutland, Leics, LE15 6SY
☎ 01572 755813
www.rutland-ramblers.co.uk

LINCOLNSHIRE

AREA SECRETARY
Mr S W Parker, 129 Broughton Gardens, Brant Road, Lincoln, LN5 8SR
☎ 01522 534655 (includes answerphone)
www.lincscountyramblers.co.uk

GROUP SECRETARIES
Boston Mrs Sheila Pratt, Capri, Whitehouse Lane, Fishtoft, Boston, PE21 0BH ☎ 01205 369835
www.lincscountyramblers.co.uk
Gainsborough Mr M A Clapham, 69 Beckett Avenue, Gainsborough, Lincolnshire, DN21 1EJ
☎ 01427 615871
www.lincscountyramblers.co.uk
Grantham See www.ramblers.org.uk/info/localgroups for the latest details or visit www.lincscountyramblers.co.uk
Grimsby & Louth Mr A E Johnson, 50 Gayton Rd, Cleethorpes, DN35 0HN
☎ 01472 509396
http://uk.geocities.com/tjrambler
Horncastle Mr G Vessey, 51 Elm Crescent, Burgh Le Marsh, Skegness, PE24 5EG ☎ 01754 810049
www.lincscountyramblers.co.uk
Lincoln Mrs M Glen, 130 Fulmar Road, Harts Holme Fields, Lincoln, LN6 0LA
www.lincscountyramblers.co.uk
Lincolnshire Walking Group
Mrs H Bridgen, 45 Mareham Lane, Sleaford, NG34 7LA
www.lincswalkinggroup.org.uk
Scunthorpe Mrs V Bowser, 4 Orchid Rise, Church Lane, Scunthorpe, DN15 7AB ☎ 01724 336757
www.lincscountyramblers.co.uk
Skegness Mr A Malcolm, 9 Winston Drive, Skegness, Lincs, PE25 2RE
☎ 01754 899 878
www.skegnessramblers.gothere.uk.com
Sleaford Mr Dave Houghton, 19 Eastgate, Heckington, Sleaford, Lincs, NG34 9RB ☎ 01529 461220
www.lincscountyramblers.co.uk/

Spalding Mrs W A Hicks, 2 Jubilee Close, Spalding, Lincolnshire, PE11 1YD
☎ 01775 725531
www.spaldingramblers.org.uk
Stamford Mrs F Jacklin, 15 Perth Road, Stamford, Lincs, PE9 2TX
☎ 01780 752736
www.lincscountyramblers.co.uk

NORTHAMPTONSHIRE

AREA SECRETARY
Mrs Pamela Barrett, 132 Wellingborough Road, Earls Barton, Northampton, NN6 0JS ☎ 01604 812556
www.northants-area-ra.info

GROUP SECRETARIES
Daventry Mrs P Alexander, 14 Coronation Road, Newnham, Daventry, NN11 3EY ☎ 01327 310945
Kettering Miss E M Wildman, 36 Skeffington Close, Geddington, Northants, NN14 1BA
☎ 01536 741222
mary@wildman7292.fsnet.co.uk
Northampton Miss J Hammond, 37 Knights Court, Little Billing, Northampton, NN3 9AT
☎ 01604 518517
www.northamptonra.org.uk
Northants 20s & 30s Walking Group See www.letsgetreadytoramble.org.uk for the latest details or visit www.ramblers.org.uk/info/localgroups
Wellingborough & District Mrs Pamela Barrett, 132 Wellingborough Road, Earls Barton, Northampton, NN6 0JS ☎ 01604 812556
www.wellingboroughramblers.org.uk

NOTTINGHAMSHIRE

AREA SECRETARY
Mr Rod Fillingham, 1 Albany Close, Arnold, Nottingham, NG5 6JP
☎ 0115 9204066
www.nottsarearamblers.co.uk

GROUP SECRETARIES
Broxtowe Dr A H Brittain, 23 Banks Road, Toton, Nottingham, NG9 6HE
☎ 0115 9720 258
www.broxtoweramblers.co.uk
Collingham Mrs L J Piper, 92 High Street, Collingham, Newark, NG23 7NG ☎ 01636 892795
Dukeries Mr A Gamble, 35 Greenwood Crescent, Boughton, Newark, Notts, NG22 9HX
☎ 01623 861376 See Area website
Gedling Mrs J M Fillingham, 1 Albany Close, Arnold, Nottingham, NG5 6JP
☎ 0115 9204066
www.innotts.co.uk/ramblers

LOCAL RAMBLERS GROUPS continued

Hucknall See Area website or contact our central office for details

Mansfield & Sherwood Walking Group Mr M Lawson, 2 Northfield Drive, Mansfield, Nottingham, NG18 3DD ☎ 01623 460941 www.mansfield-ramblers.co.uk

Newark Mrs C Grant, 16 Elizabeth Road, Newark, Notts, NG24 4NP ☎ 01636 681994 www.newarkramblers.co.uk

Nottingham Mrs E M Collison, 13 Overdale Road, Basford, Nottingham, NG6 0LR ☎ 0115 970 8796 See Area website

Notts Derby Walking Group Ms C Anderson, 8 Berridge Road, Nottingham, NG7 6LZ ☎ 07904 381911 www.ndwg.co.uk

Notts Weekend Walkers Kevin Matthews, 44 The Downs, Silverdale, Nottingham, NG11 7DY ☎ 0115 914 5653 notts.walkers@ntlworld.com See Area website

Ravenshead Allan Rogers, 63 Quarry Road, Ravenshead, Nottingham, NG15 9AP ☎ 01623 797321

Retford Mrs J Anson, Townrows Farm, High Street, Elkesley, Notts, DN22 8AJ ☎ 01777 838 763 See Area website

Rushcliffe Mr R Parrey, 61 West Leake Road, Kingston On Soar, Notts, NG11 0DN ☎ 0115 9830730 www.theburks.org/ramblers

Southwell Mr M Macdonald, 61 Bullpit Road, Balderton, Newark, Nottingham, NG24 3LY ☎ 01636 677395 See Area website

Vale of Belvoir Mrs L Pitt, 4 Rockingham Grove, Bingham, Nottingham, NG13 8RY ☎ 01949 876146 See Area website

Worksop Ms S J Mcguire, 44 Sandy Lane, Worksop, Notts, S80 1SW ☎ 01909 500278 See Area website

LOCAL RAMBLERS PUBLICATIONS

NEW **Walk East Midlands** edited by Chris Thompson of Nottinghamshire Ramblers. This book brings together the expertise of six Ramblers Areas to create the definitive volume of circular walks in an English region that, as the preface admits, 'has a recognition problem'. A substantial book offering 50 walks, most with short and long options, all with public transport links, avoiding the obvious honeypots of the Peak District and exploring instead the surprisingly varied landscapes of Derbyshire, Leicestershire, Lincolnshire, Northamptonshire, Nottinghamshire and Rutland, from flat fens to limestone uplands, river valleys and lush woodlands. Even the shorter options can be on the long side (up to 16km/10 miles) but otherwise this is a laudable enterprise, published jointly with Sigma Leisure (ISBN 1 85058 824 4. *£8.95, order from bookshops or publisher, see p299).*

DERBYSHIRE

NEW **Chesterfield Round Walk** devised by Chesterfield and Northeast Derbyshire Ramblers and written by Rob Haslam. A colour leaflet, including maps, of this new 55km/34-mile walk around Chesterfield, launched in June 2005. *£1.50 + 50p p&p from Membership Secretary, 195 Old Road, Chesterfield S40 3QH. Cheques to Chesterfield and North East Derbyshire Ramblers' Group.*

Walks Through Derbyshire's Gateway Favourite walks of the Bolsover Ramblers in their own backyard. Five leaflets with clear maps and route descriptions, each describing a single circular walk of between 6.5km/4 miles and 13km/8 miles, *free from local outlets or send an*

SAE to 34 Lime Tree Avenue, Glapwell, Chesterfield S44 5LE.

LINCOLNSHIRE

NEW **Danelaw Way** by Brett Collier. A 100km/60-mile walk in five stages between Lincoln and Stamford, the 'burghs' of the ancient Danelaw. The spiral bound guide includes sketch maps and extracts from poetry. The author, a well-known local veteran Ramblers campaigner, had just completed work on the book before his death in 2005. The book has been published in his memory. *£5.95 + 80p p&p from 39 Fiskerton Rd, Reepham, Lincoln LN3 4EF. Cheques to Lincoln Group Ramblers' Association.*

Gingerbread Way A Grantham Perimeter Country Walk (Grantham Group). 40km/25 mile challenging circuit developed to celebrate the RA's Golden Jubilee in 1985. Booklet with route description and OS 1:50 000 map, *£1.20 post free from Tweedsdale, Aviary Close, Grantham NG31 9LF. Cheques to Grantham Ramblers.*

Lindsey Loop by Brett Collier, ISBN 1 901184 13 7 (2nd edition). 154km/96 miles through the Lincolnshire Wolds Area of Outstanding Natural Beauty between Market Rasen and Louth, in eight stages. *£5.95 + 70p p&p.*

Plogsland Round by Brett Collier, ISBN 1 901184 41 2. A 75km/47 mile circular walk around Lincoln. *£5.50 + 60p p&p. All from 2 Belgravia Close Lincoln LN6 0QJ. Cheques to Lincoln Group Ramblers' Association.*

The Silver Lincs Way Linking Grimsby & Louth A 40km/25-mile walk through the Lincolnshire Wolds via Ludborough using footpaths, bridleways and quiet lanes. A parallel bus service offers good public transport connections. Established by Grimsby/Louth Ramblers to mark their 25th anniversary, in conjunction with the Lincolnshire Wolds countryside service and with funding from Awards for All.

Circular Walks from the Silver Lincs Way Linking paths and circular options from the Silver Lincs Way, giving a choice of walks from 3km/2 miles up to 21.5km/13.5 miles. *Both colour leaflets with maps, points of interest and route descriptions, free from local information outlets or by sending an SAE to 50 Gayton Road, Cleethorpes DN35 0HN.*

Towers Way by Alan Nash, Janet Nash, Tony Broad. A meandering 160km/100-mile route linking 40 churches between Barton Upon Humber and Lincoln Cathedral, as an alternative to the Viking Way. *Route description available from 39 Fiskerton Road, Reepham, Lincoln LN3 4EF; publication to follow.*

Country Walks in Kesteven by N S P Mitchell. 30 circular walks, many with shorter options, from 2.5km/1.5 miles to 14.5km/9 miles, within a 24km/15-mile radius of Grantham. Walk descriptions and sketch maps. This book has been revised and expanded many times since its original appearance in 1975. *£3.50 post free from Tweedsdale, Aviary Close, Grantham NG31 9LF. Cheques to Grantham Ramblers.*

EAST MIDLANDS

BED & BREAKFAST

DERBYSHIRE

● Alsop en le Dale (Ashbourne)
PEAK DISTRICT
PENNINE BRIDLEWAY

Dove Top Farm, Coldeaton, DE6 1QR ☎ 01335 310472 (Mrs Ann Wainwright)
www.dovetopfarm.co.uk Map 119/147566
BB **B** ✗ book first £10 D1 F1 Closed Dec-Feb
Ⓥ Ⓑ Ⓓ ⊗ 🐾 👐 🚗 🏠

● Ashbourne
●⊂■ Mercaston Hall, Mercaston, DE6 3BL ☎ 01335 360263
(Angus & Vicki Haddon) www.mercastonhall.com Map 119, 128/279419
BB **D** ✗ nearby D1 T2 Closed Xmas
Ⓑ Ⓓ ⊗ 🐾 👐 🚗 🏠 ◆◆◆◆

●⊂■ Compton House, 27-31 Compton, DE6 1BX ☎ 01335 343100
(Jane Maher) www.comptonhouse.co.uk Map 128,119/180464
BB **C** ✗ book first £15, 7pm D3 T1 F1
Ⓥ Ⓑ ⊗ 🐾 👐 🚗 ! 🏠 ◆◆◆◆ Tissington Trail on doorstep.

Mona Villas B&B, Church Lane, Middle Mayfield, DE6 2JS ☎ 01335 343773
www.mona-villas.fsnet.co.uk Map 128,119/149448
BB **B** ✗ nearby D2 T1 Closed Xmas
Ⓑ Ⓓ ⊗ 🐾 👐 🚗 ◆◆◆◆

● Bakewell
PEAK DISTRICT
DERWENT VALLEY HERITAGE WAY

Mandale House, Haddon Grove, nr Over Haddon, DE45 1JF ☎ 01629 812416
(Mrs J Finney) www.mandalehouse.co.uk Map 119/184664
BB **C/D** ✗ nearby D2 T1 Closed Dec-Jan
Ⓑ Ⓓ ⊗ 🐾 👐 🚗 ! ◆◆◆◆

●⊂■ 1 Glebe Croft, Monyash Rd, DE45 1FG ☎ 01629 810013 (Mrs P Green)
www.glebecroft-bakewell.co.uk Map 119/215684
BB **D** ✗ nearby D2 T1 Closed Xmas
Ⓑ Ⓓ ⊗ 🐾 👐 🚗 ! Ⓜ ◆◆◆◆Ⓢ

●⊂■ Holly Cottage, By Pilsley Post Office, Bun Alley, Pilsley, DE45 1UH
☎ 01246 582245 (Julie & Phil Rodgers) www.hollycottagebandb.co.uk
Map 119/241709 BB **D** ✗ nearby D1 T1 Closed Xmas
Ⓑ Ⓓ ⊗ 🐾 👐 🚗 ! ◆◆◆◆

● Bamford (Hope Valley)
PEAK DISTRICT

☆ **Pioneer House**
Station Road, S33 0BN ☎ 01433 650638 (Janet Treacher)
www.pioneerhouse.co.uk Map 110/207825
BB **B** ✗ nearby D2 T1 Closed Xmas ⋘(Bamford)
Ⓑ Ⓓ ⊗ 🐾 👐 🚗 Ⓜ ◆◆◆◆Ⓢ

Begin your day with a hearty breakfast, and return and relax in the traditional style and comfort of your spacious en-suite room. Our delightfully furnished period home is the ideal base for exploring the Peak District and the Derbyshire Dales. For more information, call Janet Treacher or visit our website.

The White House, S33 0BG ☎ 01433 651487 (Fiona Middleton)
Map 110/200818
BB **B** ✗ nearby S2 D2 T1 Closed Xmas ⋘(Bamford)
Ⓓ 🐾 👐 🚗 🏠 ◆◆◆

● Belper
MIDSHIRES WAY

Woodlands B&B, Sawmills, DE56 2JQ
☎ 01773 856178 (Gill & David Hirst)
dhirst316@aol.com Map 119/364522
BB **C** ✗ book first £5, 7-8pm D1 T1 F1 Closed Xmas ⋘(Ambergate)
Ⓥ Ⓑ Ⓓ ⊗ 🐾 👐 🏠

● Biggin-by-Hartington (Buxton)
PEAK DISTRICT

☆ ●⊂■ **Biggin Hall Hotel**
SK17 0DH ☎ 01298 84451
www.bigginhall.co.uk Map 119/153594
BB **D** ✗ book first £17.50, 7pm S1 D8 T8 F3
Ⓥ Ⓑ Ⓓ ⊗ 🐾 👐 🏠 ★★

Small 17th century Old Hall, 1,000ft up in the Peak District National Park, close to Dovedale, in peaceful open countryside with beautiful uncrowded footpaths and bridleways.

Baths en-suite, log fires, warmth, comfort, quiet, and fresh home cooked dinner. Licensed. Telephone for a free brochure
or
Fax: 01298 84681
Email: enquiries@bigginhall.co.uk

● Birch Vale (Hayfield)
MIDSHIRES WAY & PENNINE BRIDLEWAY

Sycamore Inn, Sycamore Rd, SK22 1AB ☎ 01663 747568
www.sycamoreinn.co.uk Map 110/013869
BB **C** ✗ £7-£12, until 9pm S6 D6 T3 F2 Closed Xmas
⋘(New Mills Central) Ⓥ Ⓑ Ⓓ 🐾 👐 🏠 ◆◆◆◆

● Buxton
PEAK DISTRICT
MIDSHIRES WAY

The Old Manse, 6 Clifton Road, Silverlands, SK17 6QL
☎ 01298 25638 (T W & P A Cotton)
www.oldmanse.co.uk Map 119/063734
BB **B** ✗ book first £11, 6:30pm S1 D4 T2 F2 Closed Xmas ⋘(Buxton)
Ⓥ Ⓑ Ⓓ ⊗ 🐾 👐 ◆◆◆

Linden Lodge, 31 Temple Rd, SK17 9BA ☎ 01298 27591 (Mrs Eileen Blane)
www.lindentreelodge.co.uk Map 119/052727
BB **B** ✗ nearby D1 T1 Closed Xmas ⋘(Buxton)
Ⓑ Ⓓ ⊗ 🐾 👐 ◆◆◆◆

☆ Devonshire Lodge Guest House

2 Manchester Road, SK17 6SB ☎ 01298 71487 (Mrs S Pritchard)
www.devonshirelodgeguesthouse.co.uk Map 119/055738
BB **C** D2 T1 Closed Dec-Feb ⋙(Buxton)
🅱 🅳 ⊛ 🕭 ♦♦♦♦⑤

Set in the elegant town of Buxton, in the heart of the English Peak District,
Devonshire Lodge is a friendly, family-run guest house offering quality
accommodation. This fine Victorian house is just three minutes walk from the
Opera House, Pavilion Gardens and the town centre.

☆ ⋙◀ Portland Hotel

32 St Johns Road, SK17 6XQ ☎ 01298 22462
www.portlandhotelbuxton.net Map 119/054734
BB **C** ✕ £10, 7-9pm S5 D8 T9 ⋙(Buxton)
Ⓥ 🅱 🅳 🐾🕭🦮

Rambler friendly, Peak District National Park hotel.

- 22 ensuite rooms with singles available (no single supplement)
- Real ale bar
- Traditional, fresh local food
- B&B and DBB rates available
- Competitive rates for groups
- Packed lunches available if required
- Drying facilities
- Open socialising area available
- Modern but homely atmosphere with friendly and efficient service
- Car and coach parking and bike storage available
- Across the road from the famous Buxton Opera House

Please contact us to ascertain availability. portland.hotel@btinternet.com

☆ Kingscroft Guest House

10 Green Lane, SK17 9DP
☎ 01298 22757 (David Sedgwick) Map 119/056727
BB **D** ✕ nearby S2 D5 T2 ⋙(Buxton)
Ⓥ 🅱 🅳 🐾🕭🚗!🦮 ♦♦♦♦⑤Ⓦ

We welcome you to stay in our late Victorian luxury
guest house, situated in a central yet quiet position
in Buxton, in the heart of the Peak District. Here
you will find everything you need for a relaxing
break in comfortable surroundings with period
decor and furnishings. Enjoy our hearty, delicious
home cooked and veggie breakfasts.

● Calver (Hope Valley)
PEAK DISTRICT

Pear Tree Cottage, Main Street, S32 3XR ☎ 01433 631243 (Dianne Payne)
diannepayne1@aol.com Map 119/238745
BB **B** ✕ nearby S2 D1 Closed Xmas ⋙(Grindleford)
Ⓥ 🅱 🅳 ⊛ 🐾🕭🚗!

⋙◀ Bridge End, Dukes Drive, Curbar, S32 3YP ☎ 01433 630226
(Catherine Hunt) hunt@g3fwb.wanadoo.co.uk Map 119/247744
BB **C** ✕ nearby T1 ⋙(Grindleford)
🅱 🅳 ⊛ 🐾🕭🚗!🦮

● Castleton (Hope Valley)
PEAK DISTRICT
PENNINE WAY & PENNINE BRIDLEWAY

☆ Rambler's Rest

Mill Bridge, S33 8WR ☎ 01433 620125 (Mary Gillott)
www.ramblersrest-castleton.co.uk Map 110/150831
BB **B/C** ✕ nearby S2 D5 T2 F1 Closed Xmas ⋙(Hope)
🅱 🅳 🐾🕭🦮 ♦♦♦

A 17th C. guesthouse in the picturesque village
of Castleton. The house is pleasant and olde
worlde with 5 bedrooms, 3 en-suite.
All have central heating, colour TV and tea
making facilities.
Own car park.

Cryer House, S33 8WG ☎ 01433 620244 (Mr & Mrs T Skelton)
fleeskel@aol.com Map 110/149829
BB **B** ✕ nearby D2 Closed Xmas ⋙(Hope)
🅱 🅳 🐾🕭 ♦♦♦

⋙◀ Dunscar Farm, S33 8WA ☎ 01433 620483 (Janet Glennerster)
www.dunscarfarm.co.uk Map 110/143835
BB **D** ✕ nearby D3 T2 Closed Xmas ⋙(Hope)
🅱 🅳 ⊛ 🕭🚗! ♦♦♦

⋙◀ Bargate Cottage, Market Place, S33 8WQ ☎ 01433 620201
(Fiona Saxon) www.bargatecottage.co.uk Map 110/150827
BB **D** ✕ nearby D2 T1 Closed Xmas ⋙(Hope)
🅱 🅳 ⊛ 🐾🕭🚗! ♦♦♦♦ Guide dogs welcome.

⋙◀ Four Seasons B&B, Spital House, How Lane, S33 8WJ ☎ 01433 620655
(Jenny Humphreys) www.4seasonsbb.co.uk Map 110/152830
BB **D** ✕ nearby S4 D4 T3 F3 ⋙(Hope)
Ⓥ 🅱 🅳 ⊛ 🐾🕭🚗!🦮 Stair lift available.

EAST MIDLANDS

☆ ▧◀ Losehill Hall
Peak District National Park Centre, S33 8WB ☎ 01433 620373
www.losehill.org.uk Map 110/153838
BB **C** ✗ book first £16.50, 6pm S23 D1 T16 F1 Closed Xmas ⋙(Hope)
Ⓥ Ⓑ Ⓓ ⊗ 🐾 ◆◆◆

Set in 27 acres of beautiful parkland in the heart of the Peak District, Losehill Hall offers stunning scenery, a relaxed environment and friendly staff. Close to the Pennine Way and Limestone Way. We also offer Walking and Navigation Skills holidays.

● Chapel-en-le-Frith (High Peak)
PEAK DISTRICT

☆ ▧◀ High Croft Guesthouse
High Croft, Manchester Road, SK23 9UH ☎ 01298 814843 (Elaine Clarke)
www.highcroft-guesthouse.co.uk Map 119/041799
BB **C** ✗ nearby D4 ⋙(Chapel-en-le-Frith)
Ⓥ Ⓑ Ⓓ ⊗ 🐾 🐾 🚗 ! 🛏 ◆◆◆◆◆Ⓦ

An Edwardian country house within 1.5 acres of established gardens, with outstanding views of the Peak District countryside from all rooms!

Enjoy walking directly from the house or explore further afield knowing you always return to a relaxing and peaceful environment.

● Crich
MIDSHIRES WAY & DERWENT VALLEY HERITAGE WAY

Clovelly Guest House, Roe's Lane, DE4 5DH ☎ 01773 852295 (Janice Lester)
Map 119/352545
BB **B** ✗ book first £6, 6pm S1 D2 Closed Xmas ⋙(Whatstandwell)
Ⓥ Ⓓ ⊗ 🐾 🛏 🚗 ! ◆◆

● Crich Carr (Whatstandwell)
PEAK DISTRICT
MIDSHIRES WAY & DERWENT VALLEY HERITAGE WAY

▧◀ Riverdale, Middle Lane, DE4 5EG ☎ 01773 853905 (Mrs V A Durbridge)
www.riverdaleguesthouse.co.uk Map 119/336542
BB **B/C** ✗ book first £12, 7pm D2 T1 Closed Xmas ⋙(Whatstandwell)
Ⓥ Ⓑ Ⓓ ⊗ 🐾 🛏 🚗 🛏 Ⓜ ◆◆◆◆

● Derby
DERWENT VALLEY HERITAGE WAY

▧◀ A38woodlands.com B&B, 300 Burton Road, DE23 6AD ☎ 01332 293658
(Mr E Wilamowski) www.a38woodlands.com Map 128/345351
BB **B** ✗ nearby S2 D2 T2 F2 ⋙(Derby Midland) Ⓥ Ⓑ ⊗ 🐾

● Edale (Hope Valley)
PEAK DISTRICT
PENNINE WAY & DERWENT VALLEY HERITAGE WAY

Brookfield, S33 7ZL ☎ 01433 670227 (J E Chapman) Map 110/113847
BB **B** ✗ nearby D1 T1 Closed Nov-Mar ⋙(Edale)
Ⓓ ⊗ 🐾 🛏 ◆◆◆

▧◀ Mam Tor House, S33 7ZA ☎ 01433 670253 (Caroline Jackson)
www.mamtorhouse.co.uk Map 110/123858
BB **B** T2 F1 Closed Xmas ⋙(Edale)
Ⓓ ⊗ 🐾 🛏 🛏 ◆◆◆

☆ ▧◀ Rambler Country House Hotel
Lane Head Green, S33 7ZA ☎ 01433 670268 (David Cairney)
www.theramblerinn.co.uk Map 110/123855
BB **D** ✗ £10, 12-9:30pm S1 D3 T1 F4 ⋙(Edale)
Ⓥ Ⓑ 🐾 🛏 ◆◆◆

An attractive country house situated in Edale Valley, which lies in a beautiful setting below Kinder Scout and at the start of the Pennine Way - England's first and most famous long-distance footpath.

All our rooms are en-suite with colour TV, coffee & tea making facilities, hair dryer and phone.
You can see our hotel and rooms in the Virtual Tour on our website.

● Etwall (Derby)
▧◀ The Barn Retreat, Tara Buddhist Centre, Ashe Hall, Ash Lane, DE65 6HT
☎ 07875 250716 (Judy Chau) www.thebarnretreat.co.uk Map 128/257332
BB **C** ✗ nearby S5 T1 Ⓥ Ⓑ Ⓓ ⊗ 🐾 🛏 ◆◆◆ On-site cafe.

● Eyam (Hope Valley)
PEAK DISTRICT

Crown Cottage, Main Road, S32 5QW ☎ 01433 630858 (Angela Driver)
www.crown-cottage.co.uk Map 119/215766
BB **C** ✗ nearby D3 T1 Closed Xmas ⋙(Grindleford)
Ⓑ Ⓓ ⊗ 🐾 🛏 🚗 ! 🛏 ◆◆◆◆

● Fenny Bentley (Ashbourne)
PEAK DISTRICT

▧◀ Cairn Grove, Ashes Lane, DE6 1LD ☎ 01335 350538 (Mrs Thelma Wheeldon) www.cairngrove.co.uk Map 119/173501 BB **C** ✗ nearby D2 T1
Closed Xmas Ⓑ Ⓓ ⊗ 🐾 🚗 ! 🛏 ◆◆◆◆

● Foolow
PEAK DISTRICT, DERWENT VALLEY HERITAGE WAY & PENNINE BRIDLEWAY

☆ ▧◀ Housley Cottage
Housley S32 5QB ☎ 01433 631505 (Kevin Tighe)
http://housley.mysite.wanadoo-members.co.uk Map 119/194759
BB **B** ✗ nearby D3 T3 F1 Closed Dec-Jan
Ⓑ Ⓓ ⊗ 🐾 🚗 ! ◆◆◆◆

A 16th C. farm cottage set in open countryside with views from all rooms over rolling fields. Within 10 minutes walk of the pretty village of Foolow and the Bull's Head Inn. Public footpaths pass by our garden gate leading to Millers Dale, Monsal Head, Chatsworth House and the plague village of Eyam.

● Glossop

PEAK DISTRICT

PENNINE WAY, TRANS PENNINE TRAIL & PENNINE BRIDLEWAY

▪☞◀ Birds Nest Cottage, 40 Primrose Lane, SK13 8EW ☎ 01457 853478 (Sandra Newman) birds@nest49.freeserve.co.uk Map 110/025939 BB **B** ✕ nearby S2 T2 F2 ▲▲▲(Glossop)
🅱 🅳 ⊗ 🍵 ⛏ 🚗 🏵 Mini kitchen for guests. Veggie breakfasts.

● Grangemill (Matlock)

PEAK DISTRICT

MIDSHIRES WAY & PENNINE BRIDLEWAY

Avondale Farm, DE4 4HT ☎ 01629 650820 (Louise Wragg) www.avondalefarm.co.uk Map 119/244577
BB **C** ✕ nearby T1 Closed Xmas 🅱 🅳 ⊗ ⛏ 🚗 ! 🏵 ◆◆◆◆Ⓢ

● Hartington (Buxton)

PEAK DISTRICT

MIDSHIRES WAY & PENNINE BRIDLEWAY

Bank House, Market Place, SK17 0AL ☎ 01298 84465 (Mrs H Harrison) Map 119/128604 BB **C** ✕ book first £10-£13.50, 6:30pm S1 D1 T1 F2 Closed Xmas 🅥 🅱 🅳 ⊗ 🍵 ⛏ 🚗 ! ◆◆◆

● Hathersage (Hope Valley)

PEAK DISTRICT

DERWENT VALLEY HERITAGE WAY

☆ **Cannon Croft**
Cannonfields, S32 1AG ☎ 01433 650005 (Mrs Sandra Oates) www.cannoncroft.fsbusiness.co.uk Map 110/226815
BB **D** ✕ nearby D3 T2 F2 ▲▲▲(Hathersage)
🅱 🅳 ⊗ 🍵 ⛏ ◆◆◆◆Ⓖ Veggie breakfasts.

Stunning panoramic views.

Famous for our hospitatlity and breakfast: try Sundancer eggs or porridge with whiskey for example!

The standard of cleanliness is exceptional, as is the friendliness and caring attention provided throughout your stay, in keeping with our gold award status. Off road and private parking. All rooms en-suite.

Recommended by Holiday Which? Country Walking and Food and Travel Magazines. AA 4 RED dimanonds and Egg Cup Award also.

Sladen Cottage, Castleton Road, S32 1EH ☎ 01433 650104 (Mrs Julie Colley) www.sladencottage.co.uk Map 110/227814
BB **D** ✕ book first £15 (groups only), 7.30pm D3 T3 F1 Closed Xmas ▲▲▲(Hathersage) 🅥 🅱 🅳 ⊗ 🍵 ⛏ 🚗 ! ◆◆◆◆

Polly's B&B, Moorview Cottage, Cannonfields, S32 1AG ☎ 01433 650110 (Polly Fisher) Map 110/225815 BB **B** ✕ nearby D2 T1 Closed Xmas ▲▲▲(Hathersage) 🅱 🅳 ⊗ 🍵 ⛏ 🚗 !

● Hope (Hope Valley)

PEAK DISTRICT & DERWENT VALLEY HERITAGE WAY

▪☞◀ Old Hall Cottage, Edale Road, S33 6ZF ☎ 01433 621601 (Mrs Glen) www.visitpeakdistrict.co.uk Map 119/173813 BB **D** ✕ nearby D1 ▲▲▲(Hope) 🅥 🅱 🅳 ⊗ 🍵 ⛏ 🚗 ! ◆◆◆ Guide dogs by arrangement.

☆ ▪☞◀ **Underleigh House**
Off Edale Road, S33 6RF ☎ 01433 621372 (Vivienne Taylor) www.underleighhouse.co.uk Map 110/164849
BB **D** ✕ nearby S/D5 T1 ▲▲▲(Hope)
🅥 🅱 🅳 ⊗ 🍵 ⛏ 🚗 ! 🏵 ◆◆◆◆◆Ⓢ

Charming cottage and barn conversion in a stunning location. Ideal for exploring the Peak District with superb walks from the door. Delicious breakfasts feature local and homemade specialities. Winner of Derbyshire Food Awards 'Best Breakfast' 2004. Welcoming and relaxing atmosphere.

● Ilam (Ashbourne)

PEAK DISTRICT

▪☞◀ Throwley Hall Farm, DE6 2BB ☎ 01538 308202 (Mrs M A Richardson) www.throwleyhallfarm.co.uk Map 119/110526
BB **C** D2 T1 F1 🅱 🅳 ⊗ 🍵 ⛏ 🚗 ! 🏵 ◆◆◆◆

● Matlock

PEAK DISTRICT

DERWENT VALLEY HERITAGE WAY

☆ **Glendon**
Knowleston Place, DE4 3BU ☎ 01629 584732 (Mrs S Elliott) Map 119/301598
BB **B/C** ✕ nearby D2 T2 F1 Closed Xmas ▲▲▲(Matlock)
🅱 🅳 ⊗ 🍵 ⛏ ◆◆◆◆

This Grade II listed building by the river and park is on the Heritage Way. It is conveniently situated near the town centre and bus/rail stations. Comfortable, well equipped accommodation in a relaxed atmosphere. Large private car park.

☆ **Woodside**
Stanton Lees, DE4 2LQ ☎ 01629 734320 (Mrs K M Potter) www.stantonlees.freeserve.co.uk Map 119/254633
BB **C** ✕ nearby D2 T1 Closed Xmas
🅱 🅳 ⊗ 🍵 ⛏ ◆◆◆◆

When visiting the Peak District enjoy a friendly welcoming B&B in a rural Peakland village with panoramic views. Ideal for walking, sightseeing, birdwatching. En-suite bedroom, TV, hospitality tray. Non-smoking. Chatsworth, Bakewell, Matlock 4½ miles. derwentkk@potter8378.freeserve.co.uk

Riverbank House, Derwent Avenue, DE4 3LX ☎ 01629 582593 bookings@riverbankhouse.co.uk Map 119/299599
BB **D** ✕ nearby D3 T1 F2 Closed Xmas ▲▲▲(Matlock)
🅱 🅳 ⊗ 🍵 ⛏ Ⓜ ◆◆◆◆

● Matlock Bath (Matlock)

PEAK DISTRICT

DERWENT VALLEY HERITAGE WAY

▪☞◀ The Firs, 180 Dale Road, DE4 3PS ☎ 01629 582426 (Bernhard Trotman) bernhard@thefirs180.demon.co.uk Map 119/295594
BB **C** ✕ nearby D1 T/D2 Closed Xmas ▲▲▲(Matlock Bath)
🅱 🅳 🍵 ⛏ 🚗 ! 🏵 ◆◆◆

● Monsal Head (Bakewell)
PEAK DISTRICT

☆ **Castle Cliffe**
DE45 1NL ☎ 01629 640258 (Mrs J Mantell)
www.castle-cliffe.com Map 119/185716
BB **C** ✕ nearby D3 T2 F2
B D ⊗ 🐾 ♿ 🅿 ! 🏛 ◆◆◆◆

Stunning position overlooking the beautiful Monsal Dale.
Noted for its friendly atmosphere, hearty breakfasts and exceptional views.
Drinks in the garden or around an open log fire in winter.
Choice of dinner venues within an easy stroll.
Walks in all directions. Groups of all sizes welcome.
Guest lounge available and licensed to sell drinks.
Plenty of car parking space.

● Risley
MIDSHIRES WAY

Braeside Guest House, 113 Derby Rd, DE72 3SS ☎ 01159 395885
www.braesideguesthouse.co.uk Map 129/457357
BB **D** ✕ nearby D4 T2
B D ⊗ 🐾 ♿ ◆◆◆

● Rowsley (Matlock)
PEAK DISTRICT
DERWENT VALLEY HERITAGE WAY

🍴 Eastfield, Chatsworth Road, DE4 2EH ☎ 01629 734427
www.east-field.co.uk Map 119/260662
BB **B** ✕ nearby D1 T2 Closed Xmas
D 🐾 ♿ 🅿 ! Ⓜ

● Stoney Middleton (Hope Valley)
PEAK DISTRICT
DERWENT VALLEY HERITAGE WAY

🍴 Lovers Leap, The Dale, S32 4TF ☎ 01433 630300
www.loversleap.biz Map 119/227756
BB **C** ✕ £15-£18, 7pm-12am D3 Ⓥ B ⊗ 🐾 ♿ ! 🏛

● Swinscoe (Ashbourne)
🍴 Dog and Partridge Country Inn, DE6 2HS ☎ 01335 343183
(Jenny Stelfox) www.dogandpartridge.co.uk Map 119/133481
BB **D** ✕ £7.95, 5:30-10pm S4 D10 T6 F10
Ⓥ B D 🐾 ♿ ! 🏛 ★★

● Thorpe (Ashbourne)
PEAK DISTRICT
PENNINE BRIDLEWAY

The Old Orchard, Stoney Lane, DE6 2AW ☎ 01335 350410 (Mrs B Challinor)
www.theoldorchardguesthouse.co.uk Map 119/157503
BB **C** ✕ nearby D2 Closed Nov-Feb
B D ⊗ 🐾 ♿ 🅿 ! 🏛 ◆◆◆

☆ 🍴 **Hillcrest House**
Dovedale, DE6 2AW ☎ 01335 350436 (Margaret Sutton)
hillcresthouse@freenet.co.uk Map 119/152505
BB **C** ✕ book first £14 S1 D4 T1 F1 Closed Xmas
Ⓥ B D ⊗ 🐾 ♿ 🅿 ! ◆◆◆◆

Start your day with a full English
breakfast and finish off with a
nightcap in our lounge. Plenty of
off road car parking. All king-size
beds and four-posters. En-suite,
TV, tea/coffee making facilities,
radio alarm and hairdryer.

Jasmine Cottage, DE6 2AW ☎ 01335 350465 (Liz Round) Map 119/155502
BB **C** ✕ nearby D1 T1 Closed Xmas B D ⊗ 🐾 ♿ ♿

● Tideswell (Buxton)
PEAK DISTRICT
PENNINE BRIDLEWAY

Rockingham Lodge, Market Square, SK17 8LQ ☎ 01298 871684
(Nick Brelsford) www.peaksaccommodation.co.uk Map 119/151758
BB **C** ✕ nearby D1 T2 Closed Xmas
B D ⊗ 🐾 ♿ ! Ⓜ See SC also.

● Whaley Bridge (High Peak)
MIDSHIRES WAY & PENNINE BRIDLEWAY

Springbank Guest House, 3 Reservoir Rd, SK23 7BL ☎ 01663 732819
(Margot Graham) www.whaleyspringbank.co.uk Map 110/011813
BB **C** ✕ book first £8, 7pm D2 T2 F1 🚌(Whaley Bridge)
Ⓥ B D ⊗ 🐾 ♿ 🅿 ! ◆◆◆

🍴 Jordell Arms, 39 Market Street, SK23 7AA ☎ 01663 719265
(Pete Cruickshank) pcruickshank@btinternet.com Map 110/009814
BB **B** ✕ book first £6, 9pm S2 D5 T2 🚌(Whaley Bridge)
Ⓥ B D 🐾 ♿ 🏛

● Youlgreave (Bakewell)
PEAK DISTRICT
PENNINE BRIDLEWAY & MIDSHIRES WAY

The Old Bakery, Church Street, DE45 1UR ☎ 01629 636887 (Anne Croasdell)
www.cressbrook.co.uk/youlgve/oldbakery Map 119/210643
BB **B** ✕ nearby D2 T2 Closed Xmas B D ⊗ 🐾 ♿ ! ◆◆◆

The Farmyard Inn, Main St, DE45 1UW ☎ 01629 636221 (Joanne Healey)
sjghealey@aol.com Map 119/208641
BB **C** ✕ £7, 7-9pm D2 T1 F1 Ⓥ B D 🐾 ♿ ! ◆◆◆

LEICESTERSHIRE

● Great Dalby (Melton Mowbray)
MIDSHIRES WAY

Dairy Farm, 8 Burrough End, LE14 2EW ☎ 01664 562783 (Mrs L Parker)
dairyfarm@tesco.net Map 129/744141
BB **B** ✕ nearby D2 T1 Closed Xmas B D 🐾 ♿ 🅿 ! 🏛 ◆◆◆

● Loughborough
Peachnook Guest House, 154 Ashby Road, LE11 3AG ☎ 01509 264390
(Valerie Wood) www.smoothhound.co.uk/hotels/peachno-html Map 129/529196
BB **A/B** ✕ nearby S1 D1 T1 F2 Closed Xmas 🚌(East Midlands)
B 🐾 ♿ ◆◆ Special diets catered for.

● Rempstone (Loughborough)
MIDSHIRES WAY
▪◢ Guesthouse At Rempstone, LE12 6RH ☎ 01509 881886 (Mark Cosgrove)
www.guesthouse-rempstone.co.uk Map 129/577243
BB **B** ✕ £6, 7pm S4 D3 T4 F2 Ⓥ Ⓑ Ⓓ ⛄♨!🏠

● Shoby (Melton Mowbray)
Shoby Lodge Farmhouse Bed & Breakfast, Shoby Lodge Farm, LE14 3PF
☎ 01664 812156 (Linda Lomas) Map 129/669214
BB **C** D2 TI Closed Xmas Ⓥ Ⓑ Ⓓ ⊗ ⛄♨ ◆◆◆◆Ⓢ

● Upper Broughton (Melton Mowbray)
MIDSHIRES WAY

☆ **Sulney Fields**
Colonel's Lane, LE14 3BD ☎ 01664 822204 (Hilary Collinson)
hillyc@hotmail.com Map 129/683262
BB **C** ✕ nearby SI D2 T2
Ⓥ Ⓑ Ⓓ ⊗ ⛄♨🚗🏠 Stair lift available.

Spacious accommodation in this large family house, set in a quiet position, with stunning views across the Vale of Belvoir.
Convenient for the Leicestershire Round Walk and the Grantham Canal.
Choice of pubs within one mile.

LINCOLNSHIRE

● Cranwell (Sleaford)
VIKING WAY
▪◢ Byards Leap Cottage, NG34 8EY ☎ 01400 261537 (Anne Wood)
Map 130/011498
BB **B** ✕ book first £12, 6:30pm onwards DI TI Closed Xmas
Ⓥ Ⓓ ⊗ ⛄🚗 ! ◆◆◆ Special diets. Guide dogs welcome.

● Goulceby (Louth)
▪◢ Goulceby Post, Ford Way, LN11 9WD ☎ 01507 343230
www.goulcebypost.co.uk Map 122/256791
BB **C** ✕ book first £10, 7pm TI
Ⓥ Ⓑ Ⓓ ⊗ ⛄♨🚗 ! ◆◆◆ Wheelchair access. See SC also.

● Lincoln
VIKING WAY
Old Rectory Guest House, 19 Newport, LN1 3DQ ☎ 01522 514774
(Tony Downes) Map 121/975722 BB **B** ✕ nearby SI D3 TI FI Closed Xmas
🚌(Lincoln) Ⓑ ⊗ ⛄♨ ◆◆◆

● Market Rasen
VIKING WAY
▪◢ Waveney Cottage, Willingham Road, LN8 3DN ☎ 01673 843236
(Mrs J Bridger) www.waveneycottage.co.uk Map 121,113/111890
BB **C** ✕ book first £10.50, 6pm D/FI T2 Closed Xmas 🚌(Market Rasen)
Ⓥ Ⓑ Ⓓ ⊗ ⛄♨🚗 ◆◆◆◆

● Ruskington (Sleaford)
Sunnyside Farm, Leasingham Lane, NG34 9AH ☎ 01526 833010
(Daphne Luke) www.sunnysidefarm.co.uk Map 121/074502
BB **B** ✕ nearby DI TI 🚌(Ruskington) Ⓑ Ⓓ ⛄🚗!🏠 ◆◆◆

● Wainfleet (Skegness)
▪◢ Willow Farm, Thorpe Fendykes, PE24 4QH ☎ 01754 830316
www.willowfarmholidays.co.uk Map 122/452611
BB **B** ✕ £5, 6-9pm DI TI Closed Xmas 🚌(Thorpe Culvert)
Ⓥ Ⓑ Ⓓ ⛄♨🚗!🏠

● Walesby (Market Rasen)
VIKING WAY
▪◢ Blaven, Walesby Hill, LN8 3UW ☎ 01673 838352 (Jacqy Braithwaite)
www.blavenhouse.co.uk Map 113/135924 BB **D** D2 TI Closed Xmas
Ⓑ Ⓓ ⊗ ⛄🚗🏠 ◆◆◆◆◆

● Woodhall Spa
VIKING WAY
Claremont Guest House, 9/11 Witham Road, LN10 6RW ☎ 01526 352000
(Claire Brennan) www.woodhall-spa-guesthouse-bedandbreakfast.co.uk
Map 122/191630 BB **A/B** ✕ nearby S3 D2 TI F5 Closed Xmas
Ⓑ Ⓓ ⊗ ⛄♨!🏠 ◆◆

NORTHAMPTONSHIRE

● Braunston (Daventry)
The Old Castle, London Road, NN11 7HB ☎ 01788 890887
Map 152/533660
BB **B** ✕ nearby S3 D2 TI FI Closed Dec-Jan Ⓑ Ⓓ ♨🏠

● Hellidon (Daventry)

☆ ▪◢ **Hellidon Lakes**
NN11 6GG ☎ 01327 262550
www.marstonhotels.com Map 151/512578
BB **D** ✕ £29.95, 7-9:45pm S7 D75 T28
Ⓥ Ⓑ ⛄♨ ★★★★ Wheelchair access.

Hellidon Lakes offers splendid views overlooking lakes and rural countryside, with many wonderful walks through conservation villages, delightful hamlets, meadows and pastures nearby.

Our golf course and comfortable bedrooms allow Hellidon Lakes to offer you a rejuvenating break.

The hotel is situated in 220 acres of walkable rolling countryside on the borders of Warwickshire and Northamptonshire.

Please ask about our exclusive rates for walking parties.

EAST MIDLANDS

● Nether Heyford (Northampton)
NENE WAY & MIDSHIRES WAY
◄ Heyford B&B, 27 Church Street, NN7 3LH ☎ 01327 340872
(Pam Clements) http://heyfordguesthouse.co.uk Map 152/659586
BB **C** ✗ nearby S1 T3 Closed Xmas Ⓑ Ⓓ 🍵☕🍴🐾❗🛏 ◆◆

● Sibbertoft (Market Harborough)
The Wrongs, LE16 9UJ ☎ 01858 880886 (Mrs M J Hart)
www.brookmeadow.co.uk Map 141/666829
BB **B** ✗ nearby S1 D1 Closed Xmas Ⓓ ⊗ 🍵☕🍴🛏 See SC also.

NOTTINGHAMSHIRE

● Fiskerton (Southwell)
◄ The Three Firs B&B, 21 Marlock Close, NG25 0UB ☎ 01636 830060
(Christine & Peter Jakeman) www.threefirs.co.uk Map 120/734512
BB **C** ✗ nearby S2 D1 Closed Xmas 🚐(Fiskerton)
Ⓑ Ⓓ ⊗ 🍵☕🍴

● Laxton (Newark)
Manor Farm, Moorhouse Road, NG22 0NU ☎ 01777 870417 (Mrs Pat Haigh)
Map 120/724666
BB **B** ✗ nearby D1 F2 Closed Xmas Ⓓ 🍵☕🍴🛏 ◆◆◆

● Mansfield
◄ Bridleways Holiday Homes & Guest House, Newlands Rd, Forest Town,
NG19 0HU ☎ 01623 635725 (Gillian & Michael Rand)
www.stayatbridleways.co.uk Map 120/579624
BB **C** ✗ nearby S5 D4 T1 F1 Ⓑ ⊗☕ ◆◆◆

RUTLAND

● Barrowden (Oakham)
High House, Wakerley Rd, LE15 8EP ☎ 01572 747354 (Mrs P Dawson)
www.highhouse.net Map 141/949002
BB **D** ✗ book first £15, 6-7:30pm D2 T2 Closed Xmas
Ⓥ Ⓑ Ⓓ 🍵☕🍴❗

● Belton-in-Rutland (Oakham)
MACMILLAN WAY

☆ ◄ **The Old Rectory**
LE15 9LE ☎ 01572 717279
www.theoldrectorybelton.co.uk Map 141/814010
BB **C** ✗ nearby S1 D2 T3 F1 Closed Xmas
Ⓑ Ⓓ ⊗🍵☕🍴❗🛏 ◆◆◆ See SC also.

Macmillan Way, Leicestershire Round,
Rutland Water, Barnsdale gardens.
Comfortable B&B accommodation in
conservation village.
Pub 200 yards, serving meals by
arrangement. Packed lunch available
with 24hrs notice.

● Lyddington (Oakham)
◄ Lydbrooke, 2 Colley Rise, LE15 9LL ☎ 01572 821471 (Pauline Brown)
lydbrookebb@hotmail.com Map 141/872973
BB **C** ✗ nearby S1 D1 T1 Closed Xmas Ⓑ Ⓓ ⊗ 🍵☕🚐

● Oakham
MACMILLAN WAY & VIKING WAY
◄ The Old Wisteria Hotel, 4 Catmose Street, LE15 6HW ☎ 01572 722844
(Emad Saleeb) www.wisteriahotel.co.uk Map 141/862086
BB **D** ✗ book first £from £12.50, 7-9pm S7 TD/18 🚐(Oakham)
Ⓥ Ⓑ Ⓓ 🍵☕🛏 ★★★ See Groups also.

● Ryhall
MACMILLAN WAY
◄ Manorcroft, Essendine Road, PE9 4HE ☎ 01780 754876
(Mrs Julie Headland) birchhouse@hotmail.com Map 130/036114
BB **C** ✗ nearby D1 T2 Closed Xmas
Ⓑ Ⓓ ⊗ ☕🚐

● Uppingham
◄ Meadow Sweet Lodge, South View, LE15 9TU ☎ 01572 822504
Map 141/867995
BB **C** ✗ nearby T1 Closed Xmas Ⓑ Ⓓ ⊗ 🍵☕🚐❗🛏

SELF-CATERING

DERBYSHIRE

● Ashbourne
Windlehill Farm ☎ 01283 732377 (Keith & Joan Lennard)
www.windlehill.btinternet.co.uk
£140-£450 Sleeps 2-6. 1 apt, 1 cottage.
Beamed barns on small organic farm. ⊗ 🛏 ★★★★

Ann Brown ☎ 01335 344799
ann@canalside00.freeserve.co.uk
£280 Sleeps 3. 1 cottage.
Available for short breaks. Good walking countryside. ⊗ 🛏 RA member

☆ **Sandybrook Country Park**
☎ 01335 300000 (Pinelodge Holidays Ltd)
www.pinelodgeholidays.co.uk/sandybrook.ihtml
£260-£950 Sleeps 2-8. 41 pine lodges. Pinelodges sleep 2-8.
Indoor swimming pool. 🛏 ★★★-★★★★ See Matlock also.

Luxurious pinelodges
with glorious views,
excellent base for
Peak District.

Children's adventure
playground, soft play
and indoor pool.
Woodland walk.

The Coach House bar and restaurant serves an extensive menu and takeaways.

The luxurious pinelodges have satellite television and video recorders.
Fully fitted kitchens and a range of appliances. Each has a verandah with garden
furniture. All linen is included. Weeks and short breaks available year round.
Email: enquiries@pinelodgeholidays.co.uk

☆ **Offcote Grange Cottage Holidays**
☎ 01335 344795 (Pat Walker)
www.offcotegrange.com
£900-£1,900 Sleeps 10-14 + 2 cots. 2 cottages. Oak beams, log fires, beautiful gardens. ⊗ ★★★★★ Car collection from station

Hillside Croft and Billy's Bothy

Two large, luxurious 5-star five-bedroom detached country cottages in peaceful rural locations, own landscaped gardens within beautiful scenery. Patio and BBQs. Private parking.

Each with separate lounge and dining rooms, exceptional farmhouse kitchens, quality bath/shower rooms. Billy's Bothy is all en-suite.

An excellent walking area, central Derbyshire, ideal base for all attractions. Close to Chatsworth House and Carsington Water. Soon — gymnasium, sauna and conference facility.

☆ **Granary Court**
☎ 01283 820917 (Lynne Statham)
www.granarycourt.demon.co.uk
£300-£1,800 Sleeps 1-26. 4 barn conversions, 1 cottage. Spa, great dining room, games room. ⊗ ★★★★ RA member. See Groups also.

Situated on the Staffordshire and Derbyshire borders, this venue offers plenty of scope for different grades of walking and outdoor activities. After a day's exertion, relax in our spa or book an on-site treatment with our therapists. Very relaxing.

● Ashford-in-the-Water
PEAK DISTRICT

1, Sunny Lea ☎ 01629 815285 (Mrs D Furness)
£220-£395 Sleeps 4 + cot. 1 cottage.
Beamed cottage, high standard, owner maintained. ⊗ ★★★★

● Bakewell
PEAK DISTRICT

Mr Chris Swaap ☎ 01629 812359
www.bolehillfarm.co.uk
£220-£590 Sleeps 2-6. 8 cottages.
Walks from the door. Groups accepted. ★★★-★★★★

● Buxton
PEAK DISTRICT

Northfield Farm ☎ 01298 22543 (Liz Andrews)
www.northfieldfarm.co.uk
£90-£485 Sleeps 2-9. 4 barn conversions.
Excellent walking. Stunning views, great 'local'. ★★★

● Chapel-en-le-Frith
PEAK DISTRICT

Saffi House ☎ 01298 812441 (Carole Coe) www.saffihouse.co.uk
£375-£800 Sleeps 9 + cot. 1 cottage.
Spacious 3 storey, all modern amenities. ⊗ ∿∿(Chapel-en-le-Frith)

● Chinley
PEAK DISTRICT

Pam Broadhurst ☎ 01663 750566
www.cotebank.co.uk
£230-£600 Sleeps 2-6. 2 cottages.
Footpaths from the door. ∿∿(Chinley) ★★★★

● Curbar
PEAK DISTRICT

Curbar Cottages ☎ 01433 631885 (Mr & Mrs Pierce)
http://curbarcottages.com
£165-£275 Sleeps 2-6. 2 cottages.
Newly renovated. Can let as one.  ★★★

● Eyam
PEAK DISTRICT

☆ **Dalehead Court Country Cottages**
☎ 01433 620214 (Mrs Dorothy Neary)
www.peakdistrictholidaycottages.com
£185-£485 Sleeps 2-6. 3 cottages. Unique village square setting, private parking. ⊗ ★★★★-★★★★★ See Hope also.

Historic Eyam. A fine house, a delightful 17th century barn and cosy cottage overlooking Derbyshire's most historic village square.
Exceptional decor and furnishings; walled courtyard garden and private parking. Village inn, shops 2 mins.
Breaks from £115. Phone for a brochure or email laneside@lineone.net

● Hartington
PEAK DISTRICT

Patrick Skemp ☎ 01298 84447
www.cotterillfarm.co.uk
£220-£950 Sleeps 2-6. 6 cottages. Superb location and views, near River Dove. ⊗ ★★★★-★★★★★ RA member.

☆ **Sheen Cottage**
☎ 01270 874979 (Janice Mills)
www.sheencottage.co.uk
£190-£360 Sleeps 1-4. 1 cottage.
Open fire, beams, warm and cosy. ⊗

Lovely Grade II listed cottage. Modernised to high standards while maintaining character & charm. Clean, warm and welcoming. Excellent base for exploring White Peak. Adjoins quiet pub serving good food. Includes heating, electricity, coal, logs and bed linen. Email: janice@sheencottage.co.uk

Mr & Mrs Lawrenson ☎ 01538 300487
www.cottageguide.co.uk/peakdistrictcottage
£165-£260 Sleeps 2-3. 1 cottage.
Dovedale/Manifold valleys. The Roaches nearby. ★★★

● Hope
PEAK DISTRICT

Mrs Gill Elliott ☎ 01433 620640
www.farfield.gemsoft.co.uk
£225-£550 Sleeps 2-7. 3 cottages. Spacious, well-equipped accommodation in scenic location. ⊗ ∿∿(Hope) ★★★★

EAST MIDLANDS

☆ **Laneside Farm Holiday Cottages**
☎ 01433 620214 (Mrs Dorothy Neary) ·
www.peakdistrictholidaycottages.com ·
£170-£380 · Sleeps 2-4. · 3 cottages. · Delightful riverside setting bordering
Hope village. · ⊗ ⋙(Hope) ⌂ · ★★★★ · See Eyam also.

Hope — riverside setting. Award-winning
conversion of 3 beamed farm barns into
delightful self-catering cottages. River &
hill walks abound. Train/buses nearby for
walk and ride-back options. Conveniently
located near village amenities.
Breaks from £110. Phone for a brochure or email laneside@lineone.net

● **Hope Valley**
PEAK DISTRICT

Peak Farm Holidays ☎ 01433 620635 (Mrs Angela Kellie)
www.peakfarmholidays.co.uk £275-£450 Sleeps 4-6. 3 cottages.
Tennis court, gardens, farm walks, fishing. ⊗ ⋙(Bamford) ⌂ ★★★★

● **Matlock**
PEAK DISTRICT

☆ **Darwin Forest Country Park**
☎ 01629 732428 (Pinelodge Holidays LTD)
www.pinelodgeholidays.co.uk/darwin_forest.ihtml
£260-£950 Sleeps 2-8. 85 pine lodges. Pinelodges sleep 2-8, indoor
swimming pool. ⌂ ★★★-★★★★ See Ashbourne also.

Set in 44 acres of
stunning woodland,
excellent base for
exploring Peak
District.
Tennis courts,
children's play areas,
indoor pool, sauna,
steam, gym and
beauty therapy.
The Forester's Inn serves an extensive menu and takeaways.

The luxurious pinelodges have satellite television and DVD players.
Fully fitted kitchens and a range of appliances. Each has a verandah with garden
furniture. All linen is included. Weeks and short breaks available year round.

Email: enquiries@pinelodgeholidays.co.uk

● **Tideswell**
PEAK DISTRICT

Rockingham Lodge ☎ 01298 871684 (Nick Brelsford)
www.peaksaccommodation.co.uk
£175-£420 Sleeps 4-6. 1 cottage. RA member ⊗ See B&B also.

LEICESTERSHIRE

● **Market Harborough**
Brookmeadow ☎ 01858 880886 (Mary & Jasper Hart)
www.brookmeadow.co.uk £160-£450 Sleeps 3-6. 3 chalets. Peaceful
lakeside setting, camping. Jurassic Way. ⌂ ★★★-★★★★ See B&B also.

LINCOLNSHIRE

● **Louth**
Louth Holiday Home ☎ 0117 9315033 (Julia Mullet)
www.louth-holidayhome.co.uk £180-£250 Sleeps 3. 1 house.
Victorian townhouse with private parking. ⊗ ★★★ RA member.

☆ **Goulceby Post**
☎ 01507 343230 (Gordon and Louise Reid)
www.goulcebypost.co.uk
£175-£250 Sleeps 2. 1 cottage.
⊗ ★★★★ See B&B also.

Situated in the heart of the Lincolnshire Wolds
on the Viking Way, this delightful
cottage is an ideal base for a walking
holiday. Fully central heated, luxury bedroom
and lounge with wonderful views.
Own parking space and drying facilities.
Bay Tree Cottage

● **Spilsby**
Carlton Cottage ☎ 01790 754754 (Janet Toynton) janehake@cheerful.com
£145-£250 Sleeps 5-6. 1 cottage. Three bedrooms, south-facing courtyard. ⊗

NORTHAMPTONSHIRE

● **Byfield**
Manor Cottage ☎ 01327 260104 (Mrs H Cousins)
£224 Sleeps 2. 1 flat. Off road parking in four acres. ⊗

RUTLAND

● **Belton-in-Rutland**
The Old Rectory ☎ 01572 717279 (Richard & Vanessa Peach) bb@iepuk.com
£150-£295 Sleeps 2-5. 1 apartment.
On Macmillan Way and Leicestershire Round. ⊗ ⌂ See B&B also.

GROUPS

DERBYSHIRE
PEAK DISTRICT

The Glenorchy Centre (SC) United Reformed Church, Coldwell Street,
Wirksworth, DE4 4FB ☎ 01629 824323 (Mrs E M Butlin)
www.glenorchycentre.org.uk Grid Ref: SK287541
SC £990 Max 30. Closed Dec-Feb ✄ nearby Ⓓ ⋙(Cromford)

☆ **Granary Court** (BB/SC)
Draycourt-in-the-Clay, Ashbourne
☎ 01283 820917 (Lynne Statham)
SC £300+ 1 barn conversion. Min 10, max 26.
✄ 🐾 Ⓑ Ⓓ ⊗ ★★★★ See SC also.

Great for groups. Situated on the
Staffordshire/Derbyshire borders this
venue offers plenty of scope for
different grades of walking or outdoor
activities. Wonderful Garden Room to
dine or relax in with catering available.
Adult spa and treatments available.

RUTLAND

The Old Wisteria Hotel (BB) 4 Catmose St, Oakham, Rutland, LE15 6HW
☎ 01572 722844 www.wisteriahotel.co.uk Map 141/862086
DBB £47.50 Min 15, max 45.
✄ 🐾 Ⓑ Ⓓ ⊗ ⋙(Oakham) ★★★ See B&B also.

ELLESMERE, SHROPSHIRE

WEST MIDLANDS

MARTIN GOULDING,
WWW.BRITISHWILDBOAR.ORG.UK

WILD BOAR SOW

The right to roam may have arrived in the West Midlands only last October, but beasts thought extinct in Britain over 300 years ago have been enjoying such freedom of the region for considerably longer. The 400lb creatures were first spotted in Ross-on-Wye in the late 1990s when one reportedly chased a horse-rider across a field, and a local pig farmer claimed his sows were tampered with by their hairier betusked cousins after breaking into his enclosure.

The culprits? Wild boar, and a breeding population of over 30 animals now roams Herefordshire. Thought to have originated from a defunct wild boar farm in the area, they have now spread to the Forest of Dean and parts of Warwickshire, where police reported sightings in Coughton, Alcester, Ettington and Wootton Wawen.

The naturally shy and retiring animals are in fact difficult to sight – active mainly at night, they sleep for much of the day. But they are certainly an added attraction for keen-eyed walkers embarking on the Herefordshire Trail, which launched in June. The 248km/154-mile circular route from Ledbury tracks straight through the wild boar hotspot of Ross-on-Wye to Kington, Leominster and Bromyard, flanked by the spectacular Malvern Hills to the east and the brooding westerly Black Mountains.

> The 400lb creatures were first spotted in Ross-on-Wye when one reportedly chased a woman horse-rider across a field, and a local pig farmer claimed his sows were tampered with by their hairier betusked cousins.

Last May, 150 hectares of Shropshire woodland were dedicated for public access by owner and Ramblers member Ann Dyer. The three areas of bluebell woods at Westhope, near Craven Arms, further extend access along the 24km/15-mile limestone ridge of Wenlock Edge and offer some attractive new links with existing routes, such as the Marches Way and waymarked walks from the Secret Hills Discovery Centre. The visitor attraction has also recently opened a 37km/23-mile all-weather track around its Onny Meadows site especially for families and wheelchair-users, and introduced GEOcaching – a series of outdoor treasure hunts using GPS navigation.

Long Distance Paths

Heart of England Way	HOE
Herefordshire Trail	HRT
Macmillan Way	MCM
Monarch's Way	MON
Offa's Dyke Path	OFD
Sandstone Trail	SAN
Severn Way	SVN
Shropshire Way	SHS
Staffordshire Way	SFS
Wye Valley Walk	WVL

Public rights of way:

21,308km/13,232 miles

Mapped access land:

 190 sq km/73 sq miles
(Area 7, West)

WEST MIDLANDS
LOCAL RAMBLERS GROUPS

HEREFORDSHIRE
AREA SECRETARY
Mr Phil Long, 5 Gillow Cottages, St. Owens Cross, Hereford, HR2 8LE
☎ 01989 730697

GROUP SECRETARIES
Hereford Mr A W Lee, 61 Bredon Grove, Malvern, Worcs, WR14 3JS
☎ 01684 575044

Leadon Vale Mrs I C Gibson, 41 Jubilee Close, Ledbury, Herefordshire, HR8 2XA ☎ 01531 635139

Mortimer Mrs P A Bickerton, 35 Mortimer Drive, Orleton, Ludlow, Shropshire, SY8 4JW ☎ 01568 780827

Ross-on-Wye Mr Sam Phillips, Thelsam, Chapel Road, Ross-On-Wye, Herefordshire, HR9 5PR
☎ 01989 563874

SHROPSHIRE
AREA SECRETARY
Mrs Marion Law, 3 Mead Way, Shifnal, Shropshire, TF11 9QB ☎ 01952 462855
www.shropshireramblers.org.uk

GROUP SECRETARIES
Broseley & Wenlock
See www.ramblers.org.uk/info/ localgroups or contact our central office for details

Market Drayton Mrs H J Morris, 10 Golf Links Lane, Wellington, Telford, TF1 2DS (Contact our central office for further details.)

Oswestry Mrs A Parker, 11 St Johns Hill, Ellesmere, Shropshire, SY12 0EY
☎ 01691 623026

Shrewsbury & Mid-Shropshire
Mrs Chris Cluley, Birches Farm, Clun, Craven Arms, Shropshire, SY7 8NL
☎ 01588 640243

Shropshire Young Ramblers Paul Tanner, 4 Bridge Way, Shawbury, Shrewsbury, SY4 4PG

South Shropshire Ms S Sharp, Brookside, Eagle Lane, Cleobury Mortimer, Kidderminster, DY14 8RA
☎ 01299 271099

Telford & East Shropshire
Mrs A R Sumner, 18 Shrewsbury Road, Edgmond, Newport, Shropshire, TF10 8HU ☎ 01952 810444

STAFFORDSHIRE
AREA SECRETARY
Geoff Budd, 28 Cricketers Close, Burton-On-Trent, DE15 9EH
☎ 01283 561535
http://homepages.tesco.net/~staffsra

GROUP SECRETARIES
Biddulph Mr N Oakden, Dukes Well, Cloudside, Congleton, Cheshire, CW12 3QG ☎ 01260 226617
www.biddulphra.freeuk.com

Bilston Mrs J Tyler, 50 Wellington Place, Wednesfield, Willenhall, West Midlands, WV13 3AB ☎ 01902 633849
www.bilstonramblers.org.uk

Chase & District Mr R Roobottom, Flat 19 Winchester Court, Wildwood Ringway, Stafford, ST17 4TB
☎ 01785 663131

East Staffordshire Mrs Jane King, 39 Faraday Avenue, Stretton, Burton on Trent, Staffs, DE13 0FX
☎ 01283 543483

Leek Mrs Shirley Lunt, 17 Rennie Crescent, Cheddleton, Leek, ST13 7HD ☎ 01538 360907
www.raleek.co.uk

Lichfield Mrs P Evans, 9 Gillespie Close, Fradley Chase, Fradley, Staffs, WS13 8SN ☎ 01543 444566

Mid Staffordshire Mrs S A Benn, 11 Porlock Avenue, Stafford, Staffs, ST17 0HS ☎ 01785 603646
http://homepage.ntlworld.com/brian.benn/ra

Sandwell Miss V Dubois, 47 Gladys Road, Smethwick, B67 5AW
☎ 0121 525 8955
www.sandwellramblers.org.uk

Staffordshire Walking Group
Mr Philip Patrick, 65 Stoney Lane, Cauldon, Stoke-On-Trent, ST10 3EP
☎ 07968 313014
www.staffs-walkers.org.uk

Stoke/Newcastle Mr Graham Evans, 65 Pacific Road, Trentham, Stoke On Trent, Staffs, ST4 8RS
☎ 01782 642872 (membership enquiries ☎ 01782 846838)
http://hyperhelp.co.uk/ra/index.htm

Stone Mr G Greensides, Ambleside, 111 Lichfield Road, Stone, Staffs, ST15 8QD ☎ 01785 813067
www.stoneramblers.com

Stourbridge Mrs D Pearce, 17 Ibstock Drive, Stourbridge, West Midlands, DY8 1NW
☎ 01384 359463

Walsall Mrs Alice Harrison, 30 Clarendon Place, Pelsall, Walsall, West Midlands, WS3 4NL ☎ 01922 683411

Wolverhampton See www.ramblers.org.uk/info/localgroups or contact our central office for details.

WARWICKSHIRE
AREA SECRETARY
Mr Michael Bird, 16 Melford Hall Road, Solihull, West Midlands, B91 2ES
☎ 0121 705 1118
www.warwickshire.freeserve.co.uk

GROUP SECRETARIES
Bear Group Steven Bick, 11 Normandy Close, Hampton Magna, Warwick, Warwickshire, CV35 8UB
☎ 01926 400842

Castle Bromwich Mr A R Moore, 436 Bromford Road, Birmingham, B36 8JH ☎ 07779 205183
www.iccastlebromwichramblers.co.uk

City of Birmingham Ms C D Dittrich, 10 Peel Walk, Harborne, Birmingham, B17 8SR
www.bhamramblers.btinternet.co.uk

Coventry Mr T C O'Sullivan, 94 Dunhill Avenue, Coventry, CV4 9PX ☎ 02476 471404
http://members.aol.com/coventryra

Mid Warwickshire Mrs B Shone, 23 Stephenson Close, Old Milverton Rd, Leamington Spa, Warks, CV32 6BS
☎ 01926 335999
www.midwarksramblers.org

Rugby Mr Tony Harris, 16 Fishers Close, Kilsby, Rugby, Warks, CV23 8XH ☎ 01788 822996
http://uk.geocities.com/rugbyramblers

Solihull Mrs S M Woolley, 36 Alderwood Place, Princes Way, Solihull, West Midlands, B91 3HX
☎ 0121 7055753
www.icsolihullramblers.co.uk

South Birmingham Mrs C Stefaniak, 12 Henlow Road, Birmingham, B14 5DT ☎ 0121 680 3853
www.icsbramblers.co.uk

Southam Mr C Haywood, 44 Pendicke Street, Southam, Warks, CV47 1PF
☎ 01926 812820
http://members.aol.com/southamra/southam.htm

Stratford upon Avon Mrs E M Leavesley, 16 Icknield Row, Alcester, Warwicks, B49 5EW ☎ 01789 764798
www.stratfordramblers.com

Sutton Coldfield Mr Geoff Jones, 3 Shenstone Close, Four Oaks, Sutton Coldfield, West Midlands, B74 4XB
☎ 0121 353 0405
www.suttoncoldfieldramblers.co.uk

West Midlands Walking Group
28 Seymour Close, Coventry, CV3 4ER
☎ 01299 878904 www.wmwg.co.uk

WEST MIDLANDS

HEREFORDSHIRE
WALKING FESTIVALS

27TH - 31ST DECEMBER 2005 & 17TH - 25TH JUNE 2006

Herefordshire & THE WYE VALLEY

Herefordshire is a wonderful place to walk. Whether your taste is for the occasional stroll, family walking days out or serious daily hikes, the varied landscapes and rich environment of the County can provide you with whatever you require.

There are more than 2,100 miles of public rights of way in Herefordshire, through some of the most beautiful countryside in Britain, including the Wye Valley and the Malvern Hills. There is a Cathedral city, fine market towns and picturesque villages, ancient castles and churches, hills and rivers, orchards and woodland, hop yards and meadows. We even have our own long distance trail all within the County. The Herefordshire Trail is a 154 mile circular route linking all the market towns in the County and taking in the wonderful and varied countryside along the way. Other long distance trails that pass through the County include the Wye Valley Walk, the Mortimer Trail and Offa's Dyke Path. In June and December of each year Herefordshire hosts its' very own Walking Festival. The Winter Festival is held between Christmas and New Year (27th - 31st December 2005) has 12 walks around the county. The Summer Festival held on 17th-25th June offers participants 60 walks during the 9 day Festival many of these walks linked to local food and drink.

To find out more about our

Walking Festivals

visit **www.walkingfestival.com**
or to receive information about Herefordshire visit
www.visitherefordshire.co.uk
e mail tourism@herefordshire.gov.uk
or telephone **01432 260621**

HEREFORDSHIRE Walking Festivals

LOCAL RAMBLERS GROUPS continued

WORCESTERSHIRE

AREA SECRETARY
Mr R A Hemmings, 25 Whinfield Road,
Worcester, WR3 7HF ☎ 01905 451142

GROUP SECRETARIES
Bromsgrove Mrs J Deakin,
106 Salwarpe Road, Charford,
Bromsgrove, Worcs, B60 3HS
☎ 01527 875385

Evesham Ms D K Harwood
(acting), 12 Queen's Rd, Evesham,
Worcs, WR11 4JN
www.communigate.co.uk/
worcs/ramblersevesham
Redditch Mrs A Hawkins,
58 Cherington Close,
Redditch, B98 0BB
(Contact our central office
for further details)

Worcester See
www.ramblers.org.uk/info/localgroups
or contact our central office for details.
Worcester 20s & 30s Mr James Baker,
19 St Peters Crescent, Droitwich,
Worcestershire, WR9 8QD
☎ 01905 799036
Wyre Forest Hugh Buttress, 132 Elan
Avenue, Stourport On Severn,
Worcester, DY13 8LR ☎ 01299 878 181

LOCAL RAMBLERS PUBLICATIONS

BIRMINGHAM AND THE BLACK COUNTRY
Birmingham Greenway
by Fred Willits, ISBN 1 869922 40 9.
From the southern to the northern
boundary of Birmingham using footpaths,
riversides and towpaths. *£4.95 + £1 p&p
from Meridian Books, 40 Hadzor Road,
Oldbury B68 9LA*

Waterside Walks in the Midlands
by Birmingham Ramblers, ISBN 1
869922 09 3 22. Walks by brooks,
streams, pools, rivers and canals in
Derbyshire, Shropshire, Staffordshire,
Warwickshire and Worcestershire.
£4.95 + £1 p&p.
More Waterside Walks in the Midlands
by Birmingham Ramblers, ISBN 1
869922 31 X. A second collection of
Midlands walks. *£5.95 + £1 p&p.
Both from Meridian Books as Birmingham
Greenway above.*

Walks Around Stourbridge
a range of easy walks between 6km/4
miles and 12km/8 miles. *£4.50 inc p&p
from Mrs J Crowe (Secretary), 29 Stennels
Avenue, Halesowen B62 8QJ. Cheques
payable to Ramblers' Association –
Stourbridge Group.*

HEREFORDSHIRE
NEW **The Herefordshire Trail**
by Hereford Ramblers, ISBN 1 901184
73 0.
A 246km/154-mile circuit of

Herefordshire visiting all eight market
towns in the county, some delightful
villages and attractive countryside.
Ringbound colour guide dividing the
route into 15 manageable sections of
around 16km/10 miles each, most with
public transport connections, with
detailed route descriptions, tempting
photos and very clear maps. *£5.95 + £2
p&p from The Book Secretary, Gawsworth,
North Road, Kingsland HR6 9RU. Cheques
to Hereford Group of the Ramblers'
Association.*

Our Favourite Herefordshire Walks
by Hereford Ramblers, ISBN 0 9511995
9 5. 12 easy to moderate walks of
between 6.5 km/4 miles to 19 km/12
miles, scattered around the county. *£3.95
post free: ordering details as for
Herefordshire Trail above.*

SHROPSHIRE
Ramblers Guide to the Shropshire Way
by Shropshire Ramblers, ISBN 1 946679
44 4. MU Publishers *£6.99 + p&p.*

STAFFORDSHIRE
Our Favourite Walks
12 walks of between 11km/7 miles and
22.5km/14 miles, mainly in Staffordshire
but venturing into Derbyshire and
Shropshire. *£2.95 + 35p p&p or A5 SAE
from 46 Grange Crescent, Penkridge,
Stafford ST19 5LU
Cheques to Ramblers' Association, Mid
Staffs Group.*

Walks Around Stone
(Stone Ramblers). 12 walks each from
Westridge Port and from Downs Banks,
between 1.5km/1 mile and 11km/7 miles
with route descriptions, maps and
guidance on healthy walking in plastic
cover. *£3 + 50p p&p from 1 Vanity Close,
Oulton, Stone ST15 8TZ. Cheques to
Ramblers' Association Stone Group.*

WARWICKSHIRE
Warwick District Walks
*£2 post free from Mr P Heelis, 7 Almond
Grove, Warwick CV34 5TB. Cheques to
Mid-Warwickshire Ramblers' Association.*

WORCESTERSHIRE
**Bromsgrove Ramblers 30 mile
circular walk in the countryside
around Bromsgrove**
48km/30-mile circuit around Bromsgrove
from Wychbold via Chaddesley Corbett
and Alvechurch, devised to celebrate the
30th anniversary of the local Ramblers
Group. Leaflet has route description and
overview map and would need to be
used in conjunction with the local OS
map. *£1.50 from 13 Victoria Road,
Bromsgrove B61 0DW. Cheques to
Ramblers' Association Bromsgrove Group.*

Walks in the Vale of Evesham
2nd edition: 12 walks, all reasonably easy,
of between 2.5km/1.5 miles and
11.5km/7.25 miles, in and around
Evesham. *£3 + A5 SAE from 12 Queens
Road, Evesham WR11 4JN. Cheques to
RA Vale of Evesham Group.*

WEST MIDLANDS

YOUNG AT HEART?
The Ramblers' Association now has Groups for members in their 20s and 30s. To find the
nearest one to you see the Local Ramblers Groups highlighted in blue in the relevant region.
Alternatively, start your own!
Call Kevin Matthews for details ☎ 0115 9145653   kevin.matthews5@ntlworld.com.

BED & BREAKFAST

BIRMINGHAM & THE BLACK COUNTRY

● Hampton in Arden(Solihull)
HEART OF ENGLAND WAY

🖻◄◀ The Cottage, Kenilworth Road, B92 0LW ☎ 01675 442323 (Roger)
www.smoothhound.co.uk/hotels/cottage.html Map 139/224792
BB **D** ✕ nearby S4 D4 T2 F2 Closed Xmas ⋀⋀(Hampton in Arden)
🅱 🅳 ♿ ☎ 🏊 ♦♦♦♦

● Solihull
HEART OF ENGLAND WAY

🖻◄◀ Ivy House, Warwick Road, Heronfield Knowle, B93 0EB ☎ 01564 770247
(Mr & Mrs J Townsend) www.smoothhound.co.uk/hotels/ivyguest.html
Map 139/194750 BB **D** ✕ nearby S3 D2 T2 F1 Closed Xmas
⋀⋀(Dorridge) 🅱 ⊛ ♿ 🏊 ♦♦♦

HEREFORDSHIRE

● Brockhampton (Hereford)
WYE VALLEY WALK & HEREFORDSHIRE TRAIL

Ladyridge Farm Guest House, HR1 4SE ☎ 01989 740220 (Carol Grant)
carolgrant@ladyridgefarm.fsworld.co.uk Map 149/592320
BB **B** ✕ book first £11, 6:30-8pm S1 D2 T1
🆅 🅳 ⊛ ☎ ♿ 🍴 🏊 ♦♦♦♦

● Clyro (Hay-on-Wye)
HEREFORDSHIRE TRAIL

🖻◄◀ Baskerville Arms Hotel, HR3 5RZ ☎ 01497 820670 (Lyn & Phil Strahan)
www.baskervillearms.co.uk Map 161,148/214438
BB **D** ✕ £10, 6-9pm S1 D9 T2 F1
🆅 🅱 🅳 ☎ ♿ 🚗 🏊

● Collington (Bromyard)
HEREFORDSHIRE TRAIL

The Granary, Church House Farm, HR7 4NA ☎ 01885 410345
(Margaret Maiden) Map 149,138/655600
BB **B** ✕ £13+, 6-9pm D1 T4 Closed Xmas
🆅 🅱 🅳 ☎ ♿ 🏊 ♦♦♦

● Eaton Bishop (Hereford)
The Ancient Camp Inn, Ruckhall, HR2 9QX ☎ 01981 250449
(Kathryn Mackintosh) www.theancientcampinn.co.uk Map 161,149/449393
BB **D** ✕ book first £, 7-9pm D4 T1 Closed Xmas
🆅 🅱 🅳 ⊛ ☎ ♿ 🚗

● Fownhope (Hereford)
WYE VALLEY WALK & HEREFORDSHIRE TRAIL

Pippins, Capler Lane, HR1 4PJ
☎ 01432 860677 (Ann Corby) Map 149/581340
BB **B** ✕ nearby T2 Closed Xmas 🅱 🅳 ⊛ ☎ ♿ 🚗 !

● Goodrich (Ross-on-Wye)
WYE VALLEY WALK & HEREFORDSHIRE TRAIL

🖻◄◀ Jolly's Of Goodrich, HR9 6HX ☎ 01600 890352
www.jollysofgoodrich.co.uk Map 162/574194
BB **B** ✕ nearby D1 T1 F1 Closed Xmas 🅱 ⊛ ☎ ♿

☆ Granton House B&B
HR9 6JE ☎ 01600 890277 (John & Liz Bloxham)
www.grantonhouse.co.uk Map 162/571189
BB **D** ✕ nearby D2 T1 Closed Xmas
🆅 🅱 🅳 ⊛ ☎ ♿ 🚗 !

Attractive period house in peaceful location, once owned by Victorian artist Joshua Cristall. Footpaths from door to Coppet Hill, River Wye & Symonds Yat. Ideal base for exploring this AONB. Superb en-suite accommodation and delicious breakfasts served.

● Hereford
WYE VALLEY WALK

🖻◄◀ Hopbine Hotel, Roman Road, HR1 1LE ☎ 01432 268722
(Mrs Doreen Horne) info@hopbinehotel123.fsnet.co.uk Map 149/512420
BB **D** ✕ nearby S4 D6 T6 F4 ⋀⋀(Hereford)
🅳 ☎ ♿ 🚗 ! ♦♦

● How Caple
HEREFORDSHIRE TRAIL

The Falcon Guest House, HR1 4TF ☎ 01989 740223 (Barbara Cole)
www.falconguesthouse.co.uk Map 149/605323
BB **B** ✕ book first £8.50, 6:30-9pm D1 T2 F1
🆅 🅱 🅳 ⊛ ☎ ♿ 🚗 🏊

● Kington
OFFA'S DYKE & HEREFORDSHIRE TRAIL

☆ 🖻◄◀ Burton Hotel
Mill Street, HR5 3BQ ☎ 01544 230323
www.hotelherefordshire.co.uk Map 148/296565
BB **D** ✕ £8.50, 6:30pm onwards S2 D6 T5 F3
🆅 🅱 🅳 ☎ ♿ 🚗 🏊 ★★★

A family-run 3-star hotel with local reputation for good ales and food with relaxed ambience. Even after a cold, wet walk you can be refreshed in our new inviting pool, spa and fitness club - free to hotel guests.

Church House, Church Road, HR5 3AG ☎ 01544 230534 (Mr & Mrs Darwin)
www.churchhousekington.co.uk Map 148/291567
BB **D** ✕ nearby D1 T1 Closed Xmas
🅳 ⊛ ☎ ♿ ! 🏊

Southbourne, Newton Lane, HR5 3NF ☎ 01544 231706 (Geoff & Patsy Cooper)
southbourne@kayoss.co.uk Map 148/290570
BB **A** ✕ book first £10, 7pm S1 D2 T2 Closed Xmas
🆅 🅳 ⊛ ☎ ♿ ! Green Tourism Award.

● Ledbury
HEREFORDSHIRE TRAIL

☆ **Church Farm**
Coddington, HR8 1JJ ☎ 01531 640271 (Mrs Jane West)
www.dexta.co.uk Map 149/719426
BB **C** S1 D2 T1 Closed Xmas & Jan
Ⓑ Ⓓ 🍳 👤 🌿 ◆◆◆

Share our lovely 16th-century listed home. Working farm with quiet, happy relaxed atmosphere. Aga-cooked breakfasts. Good food available locally. Log fires. Excellent walking. Malvern Hills close by. Over 20 years' experience.

● Much Birch (Hereford)
HEREFORDSHIRE TRAIL

☆ 🛏◀ **Pilgrim Hotel**
Ross Road, HR2 8HJ ☎ 01981 540742
www.pilgrimhotel.co.uk Map 149/498310
BB **D** ✕ £20, 7-9pm S4 D12 T4 F2 Closed Xmas
Ⓥ Ⓑ Ⓓ 🍳 👤 🚗 ! 🌿 ★★★

Beautiful country house hotel set in 4 acres of parkland, in sleepy village of Much Birch. A wonderful base for a walking holiday, convenient for the Wye Valley Walk. Cosy beamed bar and award winning restaurant. Country breaks: DBB from £38 pp.

● Much Marcle (Ledbury)
WYE VALLEY WALK & HEREFORDSHIRE TRAIL

🛏◀ New House Farm, HR8 2PH ☎ 01531 660604 (Anne Jordan)
Map 149/640320 BB **A** ✕ book first £12.50 D1 T1 Closed Xmas
Ⓥ Ⓑ Ⓓ 🍳 👤 🚗 ! ◆◆◆

● Ross-on-Wye
WYE VALLEY WALK & HEREFORDSHIRE TRAIL

Sunnymount Hotel, Ryefield Road, HR9 5LU ☎ 01989 563880
(Denise & Bob Robertson) sunnymount@tinyworld.co.uk Map 162/606242
BB **C** ✕ nearby S1 D4 T2 Ⓑ Ⓓ 🍳 👤 🚗 ! 🌿 ◆◆◆◆

Radcliffe Guest House, HR9 7BS ☎ 01989 563895 (Mrs Sue Wall)
www.radcliffeguesthouse.co.uk Map 162/597242
BB **C** ✕ nearby S1 D2 T2 F1 Closed Xmas Ⓑ Ⓓ 🍳 👤 🚗 ! ◆◆◆

● Stoke Lacy
HEREFORDSHIRE TRAIL

☆ **Dovecote Barn**
HR7 4HJ ☎ 01432 820968 (Judy Young)
www.dovecotebarn.co.uk Map 149/619494
BB **C** ✕ book first £23 D1 T1 Closed Xmas
Ⓥ Ⓑ Ⓓ 🍳 👤 🚗 ! 🌿

A warm welcome awaits at this 17th C. barn, on the edge of the village in a beautiful conservation area. Locally sourced organic food, lavish breakfasts and dinners, or free lifts to excellent pubs nearby. Between Malvern Hills and Black Mountains/Beacons.

● Weobley
HEREFORDSHIRE TRAIL

🛏◀ Mellington House, Broad St, HR4 8SA ☎ 01544 318537
mellingtonhouse@weobley.freeserve.co.uk Map 148,149/402516
BB **C** ✕ nearby D1 T1 F1 Closed Xmas
Ⓑ Ⓓ 🍳 🍳 👤 🚗 ! 🌿 See SC also.

SHROPSHIRE

● Abdon (Craven Arms)
SHROPSHIRE WAY

Earnstrey Hill House, SY7 9HU ☎ 01746 712579 (Mrs Jill Scurfield)
Map 137/587873 BB **C/D** ✕ book first £18.50 D1 T2 Closed Xmas
Ⓥ Ⓑ Ⓓ 🍳 🍳 👤 🚗 ! ◆◆◆◆

● Bayston Hill (Shrewsbury)
SHROPSHIRE WAY

Lythwood Hall B&B, 2 Lythwood Hall, Lythwood, SY3 0AD ☎ 07074 874747
(Julia Bottomley) lythwoodhall@amserve.net Map 126/470085
BB **B** ✕ £12, 6-8pm S2 D1 T1 ᴡᴡᴡ(Shrewsbury)
Ⓥ Ⓓ 🍳 🍳 👤 🚗 ! 🌿 Ⓜ ◆◆◆

● Bishop's Castle
SHROPSHIRE WAY

🛏◀ The Old Brick Guesthouse, 7 Church Street, SY9 5AA ☎ 01588 638471
(Norm & Rosie Reid) www.oldbrick.co.uk Map 137/323885
BB **D** ✕ nearby D2 T1 F1 Ⓑ Ⓓ 🍳 🍳 👤 🚗 ! 🌿

🛏◀ Boars Head Hotel, Church Street, SY9 5AE ☎ 01588 638521
www.boarsheadhotel.co.uk Map 137/322884
BB **D** ✕ £8.50, Until 9pm D1 T2 F1
Ⓥ Ⓑ Ⓓ 🍳 🍳 👤 🚗 ! 🌿 ◆◆◆

Old Time, 29 High Street , SY9 5BE ☎ 01588 638467 (Jane Carroll)
www.oldtime.co.uk Map 137/323888
BB **C** ✕ nearby D2 T1 Ⓑ Ⓓ 🍳 🍳 👤 🚗 ! 🌿

Claremont, Bull Lane, SY9 5BW ☎ 01588 638170 (Mrs Audrey Price)
www.priceclaremont.co.uk Map 137/324889
BB **C** ✕ nearby D1 T2 F1 Closed Xmas Ⓑ Ⓓ 🍳 🍳 👤 🚗 ! 🌿

🛏◀ The Porch House, 33/35 High Street, SY9 5BE ☎ 01588 638854
(Gill Lucas) www.theporchhouse.com Map 137/323888
BB **D** ✕ nearby D/T2 Closed Xmas
Ⓑ Ⓓ 🍳 🍳 👤 🚗 ! See SC also

● Broseley
🛏◀ Orchard House, 40 King Street, TF12 5NA ☎ 01952 882684
(Diane Kaiser) mkbroseley@yahoo.co.uk Map 127/671022
BB **B** ✕ nearby D1 T1 F1 Closed Xmas Ⓑ Ⓓ 🍳 🍳 👤 🚗 ◆◆◆

● Burwarton (Bridgnorth)
SHROPSHIRE WAY

🛏◀ Peace Haven, The Old School, WV16 6QG ☎ 01746 787566
(Keith Wilkins) www.findpeacehaven.co.uk Map 138/619853
BB **D** ✕ book first £15, 7-9pm D1 T1 F1 Ⓥ Ⓑ Ⓓ 🍳 🍳 👤 🚗 !

● Church Stretton
SHROPSHIRE WAY

🛏◀ Belvedere Guest House, Burway Road, SY6 6DP ☎ 01694 722232
www.belvedereguesthouse.co.uk Map 137/451941
BB **C** ✕ nearby D4 T1 F2 Closed Xmas ᴡᴡᴡ(Church Stretton)
Ⓑ Ⓓ 🍳 🍳 👤 🚗 ! 🌿 ◆◆◆◆

☆ Brereton's Farm
Woolston, SY6 6QD ☎ 01694 781201 (Joanna Brereton)
www.breretonsfarm.co.uk   Map 137/424871
BB **C**   D1 T1   Closed Xmas-Jan
Ⓑ Ⓓ ⊗ 🐾♨🏠 ◆◆◆◆

Victorian farmhouse on working farm with spacious en-suite rooms offering specatacular views, peace and tranquility in abundance! Long Mynd and Stiperstones nearby, as are Ludlow, Ironbridge and Powis Castle. Perfect base for south Shropshire holiday.

☆ ⚑ Brookfields Guest House
Watling Street North, SY6 7AR ☎ 01694 722314 (Angie & Paul Bradley)
www.smoothhound.co.uk/hotels/brookfieldsgh.html   Map 137,138/459937
BB **C/D** ✗ book first £16 (groups only), 6:30-7:30pm   S1 D2 T1 F1 Closed Xmas ⚑(Church Stretton) Ⓥ Ⓑ Ⓓ ⊗ 🐾♨🚗! ◆◆◆◆Ⓢ

Large comfortable Edwardian house & grounds, ample parking. Stroll to town & train station. Luxury en-suite bedrooms. Ideal base for walkers & tourers. Great views of Long Mynd. Licensed. Non-smoking. Drying room. Special rates for weekly or party bookings.

☆ Malt House Farm
Lower Wood, SY6 6LF ☎ 01694 751379 (Lyn Bloor)
Map 137,138/466974
BB **B** ✗ book first £15, 7pm   D2 T1   Closed Dec
Ⓥ Ⓑ Ⓓ ⊗ 🐾♨ ◆◆◆

The Malthouse is a century-old working farm situated on the lower slopes of the Long Mynd Hills AONB. Peace, quiet and stunning scenery. Excellent walking from our door. Many places of interest to visit. Half an hour drive from Ludlow, Shrewsbury and Ironbridge Gorge.
All rooms en-suite, colour television, hairdryers and beverage tray.
Comfortable guest lounge.
Home cooked dinners available in the beamed dining room. Fully licensed.
Warm welcome.
Regret: no children or pets.

☆ The Longmynd Hotel
Cunnery Road, SY6 6AG ☎ 01694 722244
www.longmynd.co.uk   Map 137/449935
BB **D** ✗ £25, 6:45-9pm   S6 D23 T13 F8   ⚑(Church Stretton) Ⓥ Ⓑ Ⓓ 🐾♨🏠 ★★★ See Groups also.

Breathtaking views, fine restaurant and bar facilities. Ideal location for walking the Shropshire hills and touring the area. Special interest packages and many amenities (incl. sauna, outdoor heated pool, golf, croquet) available.
Email: info@longmynd.co.uk

Rheingold, 9 The Bridleways, SY6 7AN ☎ 01694 723969
(Mrs Margaret Knight)   Map 137,138/462934
BB **C** ✗ book first £15, 7.15pm   D2   Closed Xmas   ⚑(Church Stretton) Ⓑ ⊗ 🐾♨ ◆◆◆◆

⚑ Ragdon Manor, Ragdon, SY6 7EZ ☎ 01694 781389 (Wendy Clark)
www.ragdonmanorbandb.co.uk   Map 137,138/455915
BB **C**   D1 T1   Closed Xmas   ⚑(Church Stretton) Ⓑ Ⓓ ⊗ 🐾♨🚗🏠 ◆◆◆◆

Sayang House, Hope Bowdler, SY6 7DD ☎ 01694 723981
(Patrick & Madeline Egan)   www.sayanghouse.com   Map 137,138/476924
BB **D** ✗ book first £15, 6:30pm onwards   D3 T1 F/D2   Closed Xmas   ⚑(Church Stretton) Ⓥ Ⓑ Ⓓ 🐾♨🚗! 🏠 ◆◆◆◆

Old Rectory House, Burway Road, SY6 6DW ☎ 01694 724462 (Mike Smith)
info@oldrectoryhouse.co.uk   Map 137/452938
BB **C**   D2 T1   Closed Xmas   ⚑(Church Stretton) Ⓥ Ⓑ Ⓓ ⊗ 🐾♨🚗 ◆◆◆◆

● Cleobury (Kidderminster)
Cox's Barn, Bagginswood, DY14 8LS ☎ 01746 718415 (Dinah M Thompson)
www.southshropshire.org.uk/coxsbarn   Map 138/682805
BB **C** ✗ book first £8-£12, 6:30-8:30pm   D3
Ⓥ Ⓑ Ⓓ ⊗ 🐾♨🏠 ◆◆◆◆

● Clun
SHROPSHIRE WAY
Clun Farm House, High Street, SY7 8JB ☎ 01588 640432
(Anthony & Sue Whitfield)   www.clunfarmhouse.co.uk   Map 137/302808
BB **C** ✗ book first £18-£20   S2 D/F1 T/D1 F1   Closed Xmas
Ⓥ Ⓑ Ⓓ 🐾♨🚗! 🏠

⚑ Hurst Mill Farm, SY7 0JA ☎ 01588 640224 (Mrs J Williams)
Map 137/323811
BB **C** ✗ book first £10, 6-8pm   D1 T1 F1   Closed Xmas   ⚑(Craven Arms) Ⓥ Ⓑ Ⓓ 🐾♨🚗! 🏠 Ⓜ ◆◆◆

☆ ⚑ Crown House
Church Street, SY7 8JW ☎ 01588 640780 (Reg Maund & Judy Bailey)
Map 137/300805
BB **B/C** ✗ nearby   S1 D1 T1   Closed Xmas
Ⓑ Ⓓ ⊗ 🐾♨🚗! 🏠 Ⓜ ◆◆◆ Veggie breakfasts.

Walking the Shropshire Way or Offa's Dyke? If you visit Clun, visit us! We welcome muddy boots, wet anoraks and happy people. We have superb accommodation in self-contained annexe. Lifts and luggage transfers by arrangement.

▨🛏 Glebelands, 25 Knighton Road, SY7 8JH ☎ 01588 640442
(John & Judy Adamson) info@skietoile.co.uk Map 137/299805
BB **B** ✕ nearby T2 Closed Xmas-Mar
Ⓑ Ⓓ ⊗ 🍵🖐️🚗❗ ◆◆◆

▨🛏 The White Horse Inn, The Square, SY7 8JA ☎ 01588 640305
www.whi~.lun.co.uk Map 137/300808
BB **C** ✕ £10, 6:30-8:30pm D1 F3 Closed Xmas
Ⓥ Ⓑ Ⓓ 🍵🖐️🚗❗🅟 ★★★

● Ellesmere
Hordley Hall, Hordley, SY12 9BB ☎ 01691 622772 (Mrs Hazel Rodenhurst)
Map 126/381308 BB **C** ✕ book first £12-£14, 6-7pm S1 D2 T1
Ⓥ Ⓑ Ⓓ ⊗ 🍵🖐️🚗 ◆◆◆◆

● Gobowen (Oswestry)
Clevelands, Station Road, SY11 3JS ☎ 01691 661359 (Miss O Powell)
Map 126/302334 BB **A** ✕ nearby S2 D1 Closed Xmas 🚗(Gobowen) ⊗🅟

● High Ercall (Telford)
SHROPSHIRE WAY & SEVERN WAY
▨🛏 The Mill House, Shrewsbury Road, TF6 6BE ☎ 01952 770394
(Judy Yates) www.ercallmill.co.uk Map 126/584163
BB **D** ✕ nearby D1 T1 F1 Closed Xmas Ⓑ Ⓓ ⊗ 🍵🖐️🚗❗🅟 ◆◆◆◆

● Hope Bagot (Ludlow)
SHROPSHIRE WAY

☆ **The Croft Cottage**
Cumberley Lane, SY8 3LJ ☎ 01584 890664 (Elizabeth Hatchell)
www.croftcottagebedandbreakfast.co.uk Map 137/582741
BB **C** ✕ nearby D1 T1 Closed Xmas
Ⓑ Ⓓ ⊗ 🖐️🚗❗🅟 ◆◆◆◆ Minimum booking 2 people for 2 nights.

Enjoy our wildlife cottage garden with babbling brook and pool. Watch badgers, revel in the peace and quiet and eat our honey, eggs and jam for breakfast. Private ground-floor wing let to one party of 2-4 people only. Non-smoking throughout.

● Ironbridge
SHROPSHIRE WAY & MONARCH'S WAY
▨🛏 Post Office House, 6 The Square, TF8 7AQ ☎ 01952 433201
(Janet Hunter) www.pohouse-ironbridge.fsnet.co.uk Map 127/673034
BB **D** ✕ nearby D1 T1 F1 Ⓑ Ⓓ 🍵🖐️❗🅟 ◆◆◆

● Leintwardine (Craven Arms)
SHROPSHIRE WAY
Kinton Thatch, Kinton, SY7 0LT ☎ 01547 540611 (Anna Ecclestone)
www.tuckedup.com/stayat/795/Kinton_Thatch.php Map 148,137/409746
BB **D** ✕ book first £17.50, 7pm D/F1 T/F1
Ⓥ Ⓑ Ⓓ ⊗ 🍵🖐️🚗❗🅟

● Llansilin (Oswestry)
Heulfron, SY10 7QX ☎ 01691 791296 Map 125/174273 BB **C** ✕ book
first £12.50, 7pm D1 T1 Closed Nov-Jan Ⓑ Ⓓ ⊗ 🍵🖐️🚗❗🅟 ★★★

● Ludlow
SHROPSHIRE WAY
Bull Hotel, 14 The Bull Ring, SY8 1AD ☎ 01584 873611 (Philip Maile)
http://bull-ludlow.co.uk Map 137,138/512747 BB **D** ✕ nearby D2 T1 F1
Closed Xmas 🚗(Ludlow) Ⓑ 🍵🖐️🚗🅟 ◆◆◆

☆ **Cecil Guest House**
Sheet Road, SY8 1LR ☎ 01584 872442 (Ron Green)
Map 137,138/525742
BB **B** ✕ book first £18, 6:30pm S2 D2 T4 F1 Closed Xmas 🚗(Ludlow)
Ⓥ Ⓑ Ⓓ 🍵🖐️🚗❗🅟 ◆◆◆

Comfortable guesthouse offering relaxed atmosphere, freshly cooked food & spotlessly clean surroundings. 9 bedrooms (7 ensuite), with CH & TV. Residents bar & lounge. Smoking only in bar. Off-street parking. Double/ twin ensuite £28-£31pp (dual occupancy) £38-£41 (single) Standard single £22.   Fax/Tel: 01584 872442

▨🛏 The Mount Guest House, 61 Gravel Hill, SY8 1QS ☎ 01584 874084
(Mandy Callender) www.themountludlow.co.uk Map 137,138/515751
BB **D** ✕ nearby S1 D3 T1 Closed Xmas 🚗(Ludlow)
Ⓑ Ⓓ ⊗ 🍵🖐️🚗❗🅟 Ⓜ ◆◆◆

▨🛏 Wheatsheaf Inn, Lower Broad Street, SY8 1PQ ☎ 01584 872980
www.wheatsheaf-ludlow.co.uk Map 137,138/512743
BB **D** ✕ £8-£9, 6-9:30pm D4 T1 🚗(Ludlow)
Ⓥ Ⓑ 🍵🖐️🚗❗🅟 ◆◆◆◆

● Melverley (Oswestry)
SEVERN WAY
▨🛏 Church House, SY10 8PJ ☎ 01691 682754 (Jane Sprackling)
www.members.aol.com/melverley Map 126/332166
BB **C** ✕ nearby D1 T1 Closed Xmas
Ⓑ Ⓓ ⊗ 🍵🖐️🚗 🅟 ◆◆◆◆

● Myddle (Shrewsbury)
▨🛏 Oakfields, Baschurch Road, SY4 3RX ☎ 01939 290823 (Mrs Gwen Frost)
Map 126/465235 BB **B** ✕ nearby D1 T1 F1 🚗(Yorton)
Ⓓ ⊗ 🍵🖐️🅟 ◆◆◆

● Norbury (Bishops Castle)
SHROPSHIRE WAY
Shuttocks Wood, SY9 5EA ☎ 01588 650433 (Ann Williams)
www.smoothhound.co.uk/hotels/shuttock.html Map 137/367924
BB **B** ✕ book first £12.50, 6:30-7pm D2 T2 Closed Xmas
Ⓥ Ⓑ Ⓓ ⊗ 🍵🖐️🚗❗ ◆◆◆◆

● Oswestry
OFFA'S DYKE
B.J's, 87 Llwyn Rd, SY11 1EW ☎ 01691 650205 (Barbara Williams)
barbara@williams87.fsnet.co.uk Map 126/294303
BB **B** ✕ nearby D1 T1 Closed Xmas Ⓓ 🍵🖐️🚗 ◆◆◆

● Shrewsbury
SHROPSHIRE WAY
Lucroft Hotel, Castlegates, SY1 2AD ☎ 01743 362421
(Pia Widen & John Brookes) www.lucrofthotel.co.uk Map 126/492128
BB **B** ✕ nearby S4 D4 T3 F1 Closed Xmas 🚗(Shrewsbury) Ⓑ 🖐️

▨🛏 Abbey Court House, 134 Abbey Foregate, SY2 6AU ☎ 01743 364416
(Mrs V.A Macleod) www.abbeycourt.biz Map 126/503122
BB **D** ✕ nearby S2 D3 T4 F1 🚗(Shrewsbury) Ⓑ 🍵🖐️ ◆◆◆◆

● Trefonen (Oswestry)
The Pentre, SY10 9EE ☎ 01691 653952 (Helen & Stephen Gilbert)
www.thepentre.com Map 126/238260 BB **D** ✕ book first £16, 7:30pm
D1 T1 F1 Closed Xmas Ⓥ Ⓑ Ⓓ ⊗ 🍵🖐️🚗❗🅟 ◆◆◆◆

● Wem (Shrewsbury)
SHROPSHIRE WAY
Forncet, Soulton Road, SY4 5HR
☎ 01939 232996 (Mrs Anne James)   Map 126/521292
BB **C** ✗ nearby S1 D1 T1 Closed Xmas ᴍᴍ(Wem) Ⓓ ⊗ 🐾 ♿ 🚗

● Whixall (Whitchurch)
SHROPSHIRE WAY
Roden View, Dobson's Bridge, SY13 2QL ☎ 01948 710320 (Jean James)
www.roden-view.co.uk Map 126/493343
BB **B** ✗ £10, 6-8:30pm D1 T2 F1 Ⓥ Ⓑ Ⓓ ⊗ 🐾 ♿ 🏠 ◆◆◆◆

● Woodside (Clun)
SHROPSHIRE WAY
The Old Farmhouse, SY7 0JB ☎ 01588 640695 (Conor Digby)
www.theoldfarmhousebandb.co.uk Map 201/310800
BB **B** ✗ book first £12.50, 6-8pm D2 T2 Closed Xmas
Ⓥ Ⓑ Ⓓ ⊗ 🐾 ♿ 🚗 ! 🏠 ◆◆◆◆

STAFFORDSHIRE

● Cheadle (Stoke-on-Trent)
STAFFORDSHIRE WAY
The Old Convent, Bank Street, ST10 1NR ☎ 01538 756356
(David & Kate Scorey) Map 119/008432 BB **A** ✗ nearby D2 T1 Closed Xmas
Ⓓ ⊗ 🐾 ♿ 🏠

● Endon (Stoke-on-Trent)
STAFFORDSHIRE WAY
Hollinhurst Farm, Park Lane, ST9 9JB ☎ 01782 502633 (Mr J.Ball)
www.smoothhound.co.uk/hotels/hollinhurst.html Map 118/942531
BB **B** ✗ nearby D2 T1 F1 Closed Xmas
Ⓑ ⊗ 🐾 ♿ 🚗 ! 🏠 ◆◆◆

● Greendale (Oakamoor)
STAFFORDSHIRE WAY
🚌➤ The Old Furnace, ST10 3AP ☎ 01538 703331
www.oldfurnace.co.uk Map 128,119/041435
BB **B** ✗ book first £7.50 S2 D2 T1
Ⓥ Ⓓ ⊗ 🐾 🚗 ! See SC also.

● Grindon (Leek)
PEAK DISTRICT

☆ **Summerhill Farm**
ST13 7TT ☎ 01538 304264 (Mrs P Simpson)
www.summerhillfarm.co.uk Map 119/083534
BB **B** ✗ book first £12, 6:30-7pm D2 T/D1 F1 Closed Xmas
Ⓥ Ⓑ Ⓓ ⊗ 🐾 ♿ 🚗 🏠 ◆◆◆◆

Tastefully furnished, en-suite facilities, tea/coffee, colour TV. Amid rolling countryside overlooking the Dove and Manifold Valleys – wonderful for walkers. Ideally situated for Buxton, Chatsworth House, the Potteries and Alton Towers. Email: info@summerhillfarm.co.uk, or visit our website.

● Horton (Leek)
STAFFORDSHIRE WAY
Croft Meadows Farm, ST13 8QE
☎ 01782 513039 (Mrs Irene Harrison) Map 118/921577
BB **B** ✗ book first £10 S3 D1 T1 Ⓥ Ⓑ Ⓓ ⊗ 🐾 ♿ 🚗 ! Ⓜ

● Waterhouses (Stoke-on-Trent)
PEAK DISTRICT
Leehouse Farm, Leek Road, ST10 3HW ☎ 01538 308439 (Josie Little)
Map 119/081503 BB **B** D2 T1 · Closed Xmas
Ⓑ Ⓓ ⊗ 🐾 ♿ 🚗 ! · ◆◆◆◆ Ⓢ

WARWICKSHIRE

● Balsall Common (Coventry)
HEART OF ENGLAND WAY
🚌➤ Avonlea, 135 Kenilworth Road, CV7 7EU ☎ 01676 533003 (Frank Welsh)
avonlea135@btinternet.com Map 139/236778
BB **C** ✗ nearby S1 D1 T2 ᴍᴍ(Berkswell) Ⓥ Ⓓ ⊗ 🐾 ♿ !

● Bidford-on-Avon
HEART OF ENGLAND WAY
🚌➤ Fosbroke House, 4 High Street, B50 4BU ☎ 01789 772327 (M Swift)
www.smoothhound.co.uk/hotels/fosbroke.html Map 150/101519
BB **D** ✗ nearby D1 T1 F1 Closed Xmas Ⓑ Ⓓ ⊗ ♿ ◆◆◆◆

● Coughton (Alcester)
HEART OF ENGLAND WAY & MONARCH'S WAY

☆ 🚌➤ **Coughton Lodge**
B49 5HU ☎ 01789 764600 (Graham Cooke)
www.coughtonlodge.co.uk Map 150/079604
BB **C** ✗ nearby D9 T/F3
Ⓥ Ⓑ Ⓓ ⊗ 🐾 ♿ 🚗 ! ◆◆◆◆ Ⓦ

Attractive Grade II-listed half-timbered building tastefully developed from the original Coughton Court land agent's office. Ground floor rooms set around an internal courtyard/watergarden provide the perfect place to relax and explore rural Warwickshire. Ideal for walkers.

● Kenilworth
Banner Hill Farmhouse Accom., Rouncil Lane, CV8 1NN ☎ 01926 852850
(Mrs Patricia Snelson) Map 140/268708
BB **C** ✗ book first £8.50 S2 D2 T4 F2 Ⓥ Ⓑ Ⓓ 🐾 ♿ ! 🏠

● Lighthorne
Church Hill Farm, CV35 0AR ☎ 01926 651251 (Susan Sabin)
www.churchillfarm.co.uk Map 151/336558
BB **C** ✗ nearby D2 T1 Ⓥ Ⓑ Ⓓ ⊗ 🐾 ♿ ◆◆◆◆

● Long Marston (Stratford-upon-Avon)
HEART OF ENGLAND WAY
Church Farm, CV37 8RH ☎ 01789 720275 (Mrs Taylor)
www.churchfarmhouse.co.uk Map 151/153484 BB **B** ✗ nearby
D1 T/F1 F/D1 Closed Xmas Ⓑ Ⓓ ⊗ 🐾 ♿ 🚗 🏠 ◆◆◆◆

● Shustoke (Coleshill)
HEART OF ENGLAND WAY
Priory Farmhouse, B46 2AZ
☎ 01675 481550 (Mrs Margaret Manley) Map 139/220900
BB **C** ✗ nearby S2 D2 T1 F1 Closed Xmas Ⓑ Ⓓ 🐾 ♿ 🚗 🏠

● Stratford-upon-Avon
HEART OF ENGLAND WAY
🚌➤ The Hunter's Moon Guesthouse, 150 Alcester Road, CV37 9DR
☎ 01789 292888 (Rosemary & David Austin)
www.huntersmoonguesthouse.com Map 151/186552 BB **C** ✗ nearby
S2 D2 T2 F1 Closed Xmas ᴍᴍ(Stratford-upon-Avon) Ⓑ Ⓓ ⊗ ♿ ◆◆◆

☆ ▪☜◄ **Stratford Manor**
Warwick Road, CV37 0PY ☎ 01789 731173
www.marstonhotels.com Map 151/230587
BB **D** ✗ £32.50, 7-9.45pm D41 T63
Ⓥ Ⓑ 🐾♿ ★★★★ Wheelchair access

Perfectly located for the Welcombe Hills Nature Reserve, Stratford Manor is a
modern hotel with excellent leisure facilities situated in the pleasant
Warwickshire countryside, only 4 miles from historic Stratford-upon-Avon with
its picturesque canal walks, including Wilmcote - home to the well-kept house of
Shakespeare's mother.

The hotel offers a new bar and restaurant, and the Reflections Leisure Club offers
a sauna, swimming pool, gym and tennis courts.

Ideal for exploring the area, especially Warwick Castle, Leamington Spa and
Stratford-upon-Avon.

Please ask about our exclusive rates for walking parties.

☆ ▪☜◄ **Stratford Victoria**
Arden Street, CV37 6QQ ☎ 01789 271000
www.marstonhotels.com Map 151/197551
BB **D** ✗ £29.50, 6-9:30pm S10 D52 T32 F8 ♠(Stratford-upon-Avon)
Ⓥ Ⓑ 🐾♿ ★★★★ Wheelchair access

Stratford Victoria is a convenient base for exploring historic Stratford-upon-
Avon and its variety of walks, with many starting from the River Avon via field
paths, bridleways and a disused railway.

Located in the town centre, near to the train station, guests can walk to many of
the town's attractions, such as Shakespeare's theatre and house.

Enjoy great food and fine wines in our award-winning restaurant.
A comfortable modern hotel incorporating the style and character of Victorian
architecture.

Please ask about our exclusive rates for walking parties.

☆ ▪☜◄ **Parkfield Guest House**
3 Broad Walk, CV37 6HS ☎ 01789 293313 (Jo & Roger Pettitt)
www.parkfieldbandb.co.uk Map 151/197546
BB **C** ✗ nearby S1 D3 T2 F1 Closed Xmas ♠(Stratford-upon-Avon)
Ⓑ Ⓓ⊛ 🐾♿ ♦♦♦

Attractive Victorian house in quiet location, 5 mins
walk to town centre and Royal Shakespeare Theatre, 1
min from Greenway leading to Heart of England Way.
Most rooms en-suite, with colour TV.
Full English or vegetarian breakfast. Brochure on
request. Large private car park. Non-smoking.
Email: parkfield@btinternet.com

WORCESTERSHIRE

● Ashton under Hill (Evesham)
▪☜◄ Holloway Farm House, WR11 7SN ☎ 01386 881910 (M Sanger-Davies)
www.hollowayfarmhouse.btinternet.co.uk Map 150/998382
BB **B** ✗ nearby T2 F1 Closed Xmas Ⓑ Ⓓ 🐾♿ ➠ ! 🛏

● Bewdley
SEVERN WAY
Bank House, 14 Lower Park, DY12 2DP ☎ 01299 402652 (Fleur Nightingale)
http://bewdley-accommodation.co.uk Map 138/789754
BB **C** ✗ nearby S2 D1 T1 Closed Xmas Ⓓ ⊛ 🐾♿ ♦♦♦

Severn Valley Guest House, 240 Westbourne St, DY12 1BS ☎ 01299 402192
(Linda & Julian) www.severnvalleyguesthouse.co.uk Map 138/790754
BB **C** ✗ nearby S2 D2 T2 F2 Ⓑ 🐾♿ 🛏

● Broadway
COTSWOLD WAY
Old Station House, Station Drive, WR12 7DF ☎ 01386 852659
www.broadway-cotswolds.co.uk/oldstationhouse.html Map 150/090380
BB **D** ✗ nearby S1 D2 T2 F1 Closed Xmas
Ⓑ Ⓓ ⊛ 🐾♿ ! ♦♦♦♦Ⓢ

Brook House, Station Road, WR12 7DE
☎ 01386 852313 (Mrs Marianne Thomas)
enquiries@brookhousebroadway.wanadoo.co.uk Map 150/090379
BB **C/D** ✗ nearby S1 D2 T1 F1 Closed Xmas Ⓑ Ⓓ ♿ 🛏

● Evesham
▪☜◄ Anglers View B&B, 88-90 Albert Rd, WR11 4LA ☎ 01386 442141
(Sarah Tomkotowicz) Map 150/033441
BB **C** ✗ book first £5 S2 D1 T3 F2 ♠(Evesham)
Ⓥ Ⓓ ⊛ 🐾♿ ➠ ! 🛏 Veggie breakfasts.

● Great Malvern
SEVERN WAY
Croft Guest House, Bransford, WR6 5JD ☎ 01886 832227 (Mrs Ann Porter)
www.croftguesthouse.com Map 150/795524
BB **C** ✗ book first £10-£12.50, 7-7:30pm D4 T/F1
Ⓑ Ⓓ ⊛ 🐾♿ 🛏 ♦♦♦

Bredon House Hotel, 34 Worcester Road, WR14 4AA ☎ 01684 566990
(Sue Reeves) www.bredonhousehotel.co.uk Map 150/775463
BB **D** ✗ book first £15 S2 D4 T2 F1 Closed Xmas ♠(Great Malvern)
Ⓥ Ⓑ Ⓓ 🐾♿ ➠ ! 🛏 ♦♦♦♦

WEST MIDLANDS

☆ Abbey Hotel

Abbey Road, WR14 3ET ☎ 01684 892337
www.sarova.co.uk/sarova/hotelcollection/abbey/ Map 150/775458
BB **D** ✗ £23.50, 7-9:30pm S10 D47 T37 F9 Closed Xmas
⋘(Great Malvern) Ⓥ Ⓑ 🐾🛋🚲Ⓜ ★★★

The Abbey is an historic hotel situated at the foot of the Malvern Hills. The bedrooms are comfortable; many have breathtaking views. The Priory View restaurant is open for evening meals and the bar serves refreshments throughout the day.

Local walking attractions include:
Malvern Hills
Wye Valley
Severn Valley
Family rooms and group accommodation are available. For further information please see our website or contact us quoting Ramblers' Association.

● Malvern Wells

🏃‍♂️🍴Chestnut Hill, Oaklands, off Green Lane, WR14 4HU ☎ 01684 564648
pat@chestnut55.freeserve.co.uk Map 150/776422
BB **C** ✗ nearby S1 D3 T1 Closed Xmas-Jan ⋘(Great Malvern)
Ⓑ Ⓓ ⊗🐾🛋Ⓜ ◆◆◆

● Pershore

🏃‍♂️🍴Jofran House, 31 Cherry Orchard, WR10 1EL ☎ 01386 555653
www.jofranhouse.co.uk Map 150/948462
BB **B** ✗ nearby S1 D1 T1 Closed Xmas ⋘(Pershore)
Ⓑ Ⓓ ⊗🐾🛋 ◆◆◆◆

SELF-CATERING

HEREFORDSHIRE

● Kington

Crossing Cottage ☎ 01625 582550 (N Passey) www.crossingcottage.info
£216-£400 Sleeps 6. 1 cottage.
Rural riverside cottage. Offa's Dyke Path.   ⊗🛋

● Llangarron

Angela Farr ☎ 01600 750333 www.farrcottages.co.uk
£150-£650 Sleeps 2-25. 4 cottages.
Picturesque village, walks across open countryside. 🛋 ★★★

● Ross-on-Wye

Main Oaks ☎ 01531 650448 (Mrs P Unwin) www.mainoaks.co.uk
£220-£760 Sleeps 2-7. 6 farm cottages.
Beside River Wye, short breaks available. 🛋 ★★★-★★★★★

Fiddlers Rest Cottage ☎ 01989 750853 (Lisa Lown)
www.fiddlersrestcottage.co.uk
£180-£200 Sleeps 2. 1 cottage annexe.
Cosy, secluded rural accommodation. Country walks.   ⊗🛋

● Whitbourne

Dial House ☎ 01886 821534 (Mrs Anne Evans) www.whitbourne-estate.co.uk
£360-£630 Sleeps 11 +cot. 19th century farmhouse.
Spacious, personally maintained, 5 bedrooms. Fishing.   ⊗🛋 ★★★

SHROPSHIRE

● Bishop's Castle

☆ The Byre

☎ 01743 891412 (Yvonne and John Hart) yj.hart@virgin.net
£170-£240 Sleeps 2. 1 studio.
Garden. Glorious countryside. Warm welcome guaranteed.
⊗ Guide dogs accepted.

Luxurious, detached studio nestling in the heart of the tranquil Shropshire Hills on small farm. Oak beams and floor. No steps. Panoramic views of the Stiperstones Hills. Long Mynd, Offa's Dyke and Shropshire Way nearby. Walks from door. AONB.

☆ The Porch House

☎ 01588 638854 (Gill Lucas) www.theporchhouse.com
£172-£285 Sleeps 2-4. 2 apartments.
Historic Elizabethan town centre house. Short breaks.
⊗ See B&B also

Two recently converted apartments each with central heating, open fires and retaining many original features. Off road parking and cycle store. Real ale pubs and good choice of restaurants within a short walk. Close to Long Mynd, Stiperstones and Offa's Dyke.
Email: info@theporchhouse.com

Maureen Thuraisingham ☎ 01588 638560   www.thefirscolebatch.co.uk
£185-£280 Sleeps 2-4. I bungalow.
Open views, garden, log stove, spacious. 🐾 ★★★

Annette Bedford ☎ 01588 620770   www.bordercottages.co.uk
£248-£609 Sleeps 1-7. I cottage, I flat.
Relaxing and picturesque country house setting. ⊗ 🐾 ★★★★★

☆ Hope Park Farm Cottages
☎ 01743 891518 (Sue Ashwin)
£180-£400 Sleeps 2-4.
2 cottages.   Closed Feb

Quality barn conversion – spacious rooms. Lovely gardens, glorious views. Birdwatching and walking from the door to stone circles and hill forts. Stiperstones, Long Mynd, Kerry Ridgeway, Offa's Dyke, Shropshire Way close by. Sorry no children or pets.

● Church Stretton
Lower Barn ☎ 01694 781427 (Mrs Carol Morris)
£160-200 Sleeps 2. I cottage.
Pretty, comfortable. Logburner. Between Longmynd/Wenlock Edge. 🐾

☆ The Pottery
☎ 01694 723511 (Chris Cotter)
www.stmem.com/the-pottery
£225-£300 Sleeps 2-4. I cottage.   Wood-burning stove. Central heating, utility room. ⋒(Church Stretton) ⊗ ★★★ Guide dogs allowed.

Eco-friendly converted pottery on side of Long Mynd. Solar heated water in summer. Excellent base for walking/cycling the Shropshire Hills. Double bedroom (converts to twin). En-suite shower room. Double sofa bed in living room. Mob: 07793 196 100
Email: pottery1@mac.com

● Clun

☆ Pooh Hall Cottages
☎ 01588 640075 (Sue Murray)
www.pooh-hallcottages.co.uk
£275-£425 Sleeps 2. 3 cottages.
Woodland walks from the gate. ⊗ 🐾 ★★★★-★★★★★

Three individual stone cottages for two, each equipped to the highest standard. Stunning views over Clun (I mile) and beyond. Walks from the gate, Offa's Dyke, Long Mynd, Mortimer Trail nearby. Adults only.
Email: pooh-hall@realemail.co.uk

● Craven Arms
Hesterworth ☎ 01588 660487 (Roger & Sheila Davies)
www.hesterworth.co.uk
£123-£426 Sleeps 2-8. II cottages & flats.
Beautiful area, caring owners, short breaks. ⋒(Broome) 🐾 ★★-★★★

● Ludlow

☆ Suttton Court Farm
☎ 01584 861305 (Jane Cronin)
www.suttoncourtfarm.co.uk
£208-£500 Sleeps 2-6. 6 cottages.
Short breaks all year (minimum 2 nights) 🐾 ★★★★

Six special cottages set around a peaceful, rural, courtyard in the Corvedale. Walk from the door or explore further afield in the beautiful south Shropshire countryside. Enjoy a cream tea or evening meal on your return (by prior arrangement).

Goosefoot Barn ☎ 01584 861326 (Sally Loft)   www.goosefootbarn.co.uk
£190-£460 Sleeps 2-6. 4 cottages.
Tranquil setting. Games room. Short breaks.   ⊗ 🐾 ★★★★

☆ Mocktree Barns
☎ 01547 540441 (Clive & Cynthia Prior)
www.mocktreeholidays.co.uk
£195-£410 Sleeps 1-6 +cot. 5 cottages.   Country walking from door.
Transport available. ⊗ 🐾 ★★★ Access Category I.

Comfortable well-equipped, character cottages in lovely peaceful countryside. Gardens, wildlife, super views. Great walks from the door. Offa's Dyke, Mortimer Trail, Herefordshire Trail, Shropshire Hills all convenient. Guides and transport offered.
Groups welcome. Disabled friendly. Short breaks (3 night minimum).

Mrs Jean Mellings ☎ 01584 873315
www.mellings.freeserve.co.uk
£370-£750 Sleeps 6 +cot. I cottage.
Cottage, village location, garden. Near Ludlow.
⊗ 🐾 ★★★★★

● Marshbrook

☆ Lodge Cottage
☎ 020 8694 1823 (Tanya English & Mark Stopard)
www.lodgecottageshropshire.co.uk
£170-£275 Sleeps 4-6. I cottage.
Private wood, lovely views. ⊗ 🐾

A cosy, comfortable stone cottage on the edge of the Long Mynd – with 4.5 acres of private bluebell woods and garden. Great views and good food pub around the corner! Wood stove, exposed beams plus good road and rail access (near Church Stretton). Ideal base for walkers.

WEST MIDLANDS

STAFFORDSHIRE

● Calton
PEAK DISTRICT

☆ Field Head Farmhouse Holidays
☎ 01538 308352 (Janet Hudson)
www.field-head.co.uk
£565-£1,195   Sleeps 11-14. 1 farmhouse.
Groups welcome, Sky TV, spa bath.   ⊗ 🛁 ★★★★

Grade II listed farmhouse, 5 bedrooms, 2 bathrooms, spa bath/shower room. Well equipped, secluded location set in beautiful surroundings close to Dovedale and the Manifold Valley. Open all year, short breaks, bargain mid-week breaks. info@field-head.co.uk

● Oakamoor

☆ The Old Furnace
☎ 01538 703331 (Annette Baxter)
www.oldfurnace.co.uk
£27-£40 per day Sleeps 1-3. 1 annexe.   Transport available.
Adjoins Staffordshire Way ⊗ 🛁 ★★★ See B&B also.

Comprising three single beds in two rooms, The Annexe is situated beside a trickling stream in beautiful Dimmingsdale. Superb walking all around; Staffordshire Way and National Trust Nature Reserve both 400 yards. Adjoins Peak District National Park. Short breaks available all year.

WORCESTERSHIRE

● Great Malvern
Rosehill Cottage ☎ 01684 561074 (Mrs Gwyn Sloan)
sloaniain@hotmail.com   £190-£220 Sleeps 2. 1 detached studio.
Situated in Malvern Hills, stunning views.   ⊗ 🛁 ★★★

☆ Fly2Barn

☎ 01684 772263 (Peter Gilbert)

www.fly2barn.com

Secluded. Converted calf pens. All inclusive. King size bedroom, lounge with double sofa-bed, heating, kitchen diner, shower room (en-suite bathroom to bedroom if needed), patio. Ideal walks for the Cotswold and Malvern hills. Close to rivers Severn and Avon.

● West Malvern
Greenbank ☎ 01684 567328 (Mr D G Matthews)
matthews.greenbank@virgin.net
£150-£210 Sleeps 2-4. 1 flat.
Conservatory, drying room; near Worcestershire Way. ᴡᴡ(Colwall) 🛁 ★★★

GROUPS

☆ The Talbot Hotel (BB)
Leominster, HR6 8EP ☎ 01568 616347
www.smoothhound.co.uk/hotels/talbot2.html
Min 10, max 42 BB £31-£32 ᴡᴡ(Leominster)
✕ 🍴 B D ! ★★★

Originally a 15th century coaching house sympathetically updated with ensuite bedrooms. Ideal location for ramblers visiting Herefordshire. Designated Black and White Trail through picturesque villages and beautiful countryside. Group rates offered for Ramblers Group block-bookings. Email: talbot@bestwestern.co.uk

☆ Longmynd Hotel (BB)
Cunnery Rd, Church Stretton ☎01694 722244 (Rowena Jones)
www.longmynd.co.uk Map 137/449935
DBB £43+ Min 20, max 100 ᴡᴡ(Church Stretton)
✕ 🍴 B D See B&B also.

Breathtaking views, fine restaurant and bar facilities. Ideal location for walking the Shropshire hills and touring the area. Special interest packages and many amenities (incl. sauna, outdoor heated pool, golf, croquet) available. Email: info@longmynd.co.uk

HOSTELS, BUNKHOUSES & CAMPSITES

HEREFORDSHIRE

Berrow House Camping/Bunkhouse (C/B/1H/OC) Hollybush, Ledbury HR8 1ET
☎ 01531 635845
www.berrowhouse.co.uk Map 150/763368
Bednight £7 ⊗
Near Worcestershire Way and Three Choirs Way.

SHROPSHIRE

Sallow View (C) Park Lane, Craven Arms
☎ 01588 6732295 (Mr Steve Rudge)
www.sallowview.co.uk Map 137/422825
£50 per night (min 4 people)
ᴡᴡ(Craven Arms) ✕ nearby D

153

The Cardigan area is truly a walker's paradise. Whether you're looking for a taste of beautiful Cardigan Bay, Pembrokeshire Coastal Path, the mysterious Teifi Valley or the magical Preseli Hills – Cardigan Festival of Walking has it all!

©Janet Baxter 2004

CARDIGAN FESTIVAL OF WALKING
GŴYL CERDDED ABERTEIFI
6 – 8 OCTOBER / HYDREF 2006

For further details contact Menter Aberteifi   Tel: 01239 615554
Email: info@menter-aberteifi.co.uk   Website: www.visitcardigan.com

THE LAKE DISTRICT NEAR KESWICK

NORTH WEST

HEN HARRIER

It is rare for wildlife to warrant 24-hour protection and a special police operation. But the hen harrier is so rare that the RSPB believes it risks extinction without the help of a £40,000 scheme launched in the North West last year. The stakeout focused on a harrier nest in the King's Forest of Geltsdale in Cumbria where a pair of the birds had settled. Previous incidents of shooting and poisoning hen harriers and the theft of their eggs had prevented any nesting in the area for two years.

But it's the beautiful wooded valleys and heath-covered peat moorland of the Forest of Bowland in Lancashire that are the real base for the fight to conserve the hen harrier. A record 28 chicks fledged from ten nests in the forest last year. All Bowland harriers are wing-tagged and the RSPB is keen to know of any sightings during winter months when they leave the area. So far the magnificent birds of prey have been spotted as far away as East Anglia, Wales and the Isle of Wight.

In addition to the hen harrier, hawk-eyed walkers can spot merlin and peregrine falcons, snipe, curlews, redshanks and lapwings.

In May the right to roam extended to the Upper North West, increasing access land to more than half-a-million hectares across four national parks, and opening up much of the Forest of Bowland where access had been restricted by rigorous gamekeeping. Covering 80,000 hectares from Hornby and Bentham on the banks of the river Lune in the north, to the northern edge of the Ribble Valley in the south, the AONB is so appealing that even the Queen has professed wanting to retire there.

A 74km/46-mile circular walk called Journey through the Centre of the Kingdom takes in many of Bowland's highlights and passes through the pretty village of Dunsop Bridge – once declared by Ordnance Survey to be the centre of Britain. The Bowland festival each June also offers guided walks across the forest where, in addition to the hen harrier, hawk-eyed walkers can spot merlin and peregrine falcons, snipe, curlews, redshanks and lapwings.

Long Distance Paths

Coast to Coast Walk	C2C
Cumbria Way	CMB
Dales Way	DLS
Hadrian's Wall Path	HWP
Midshires Way	MDS
Pennine Bridleway	PNB
Pennine Way	PNN
Sandstone Trail	SAN
Staffordshire Way	SFS
Teesdale Way	TSD
Trans Pennine Trail	TPT

Public rights of way:

21,318km/13,239 miles

Mapped access land:

1,272 sq km/491 sq miles (Area 2, Lower North West)
3,929 sq km/1,517 sq miles (Area 4, Upper North West)

NORTH WEST
LOCAL RAMBLERS GROUPS

MANCHESTER & HIGH PEAK
AREA SECRETARY
See www.ramblers.org.uk/info/localgroups/ for current details or visit www.manchester-ramblers.org.uk

GROUP SECRETARIES
Bolton Mr D Smethurst, 15 Heaton Court Gardens, Chorley New Road, Bolton, Lancs, BL1 5DG
☎ 01204 849229
http://homepage.ntlworld.com/boltonramblers
Bury Mrs M Smith, 87 Bankhouse Road, Bury, Lancashire, BL8 1DY
☎ 0161 764 8598
Mad Walkers (Manchester & District) David Lacey, 18 Hyde Grove, Sale, M33 7TE www.madwalkers.org.uk
New Mills Mrs C L Thompson
☎ 01663 734850 (before 9pm)
www.nmramblers.freeserve.co.uk
Oldham Janet Hewitt, 2 Hillside Avenue, Carrbrook, Stalybridge, Cheshire, SK15 3NE ☎ 01457 834769
www.oldhamramblers.org.uk
Rochdale Mrs S Blatcher, 5 Enfield Close, Rochdale, Lancashire, OL11 5RT
☎ 01706 641041
Stockport Mrs L Sangster, 98 Mile End Lane, Great Moor, Stockport, SK2 6BP
☎ 0161 4838774
www.stockportramblers.org.uk
Wigan & District Mr K Rourke, 8 Hawthorn Avenue, Orrell, Wigan, WN5 8NQ ☎ 01942 203265
www.cms.livjm.ac.uk/wiganramblers

MERSEYSIDE AND WEST CHESHIRE
AREA SECRETARY
Miss G F Thayer, 53 Bramwell Avenue, Prenton, Wirral, CH43 0RQ
☎ 0151 608 9472

GROUP SECRETARIES
Cestrian (Chester) Ms F Parsons, 32 Wetherby Way, Little Sutton, South Wirral, CH66 4NY
☎ 0151 3391178
Liverpool Mrs M Hems, 19 Moorcroft Road, Liverpool, L18 9UG
☎ 07980 856101
www.liverpoolramblers.co.uk
Merseyside 20s-30s Walkers Ms B Roche, 212 Pilch Lane, Liverpool, L14 0JQ ☎ 07880 535 221
www.fillyaboots.org.uk
Southport Mr D Wall, 22 Dunbar Crescent, Southport, Merseyside, PR8 3AB ☎ 01704 579924

St Helens Mrs C Walsh, 13 Owen Street, Toll Bar, St Helens, WA10 2DW
☎ 01744 601608
Wirral Mr A Wall, 35 Mount Avenue, Bebington, Wirral, CH63 5QY
☎ 0151 608 0586

LAKE DISTRICT
AREA SECRETARY
Peter Jones, 44 High Fellside, Kendal, LA9 4JG ☎ 01539 723705
www.ralakedistrict.ukf.net

GROUP SECRETARIES
Carlisle Miss A M Cole, 101 Etterby Lea Crescent, Stanwix, Carlisle, Cumbria, CA3 9JR ☎ 01228-546544
See Area website
Furness Mrs P Leverton, 6 Churchill Drive, Millom, Cumbria, LA18 5DD
☎ 01229 772217 See Area website
Grange over Sands Mrs Wendy Bowen, Hollyhow, Hazelrigg Lane, Newby Bridge, Ulverston, Cumbria, LA12 8NY ☎ 015395 31785
See Area website
Kendal Mr Lester Mather, 5 Airethwaite, Kendal, Cumbria, LA9 4SP ☎ 01539 731788 See Area website
Lancaster Dr Brian Jones, 116 North Road, Carnforth, Lancs, LA5 9LX
☎ 01524 732305 See Area website
Penrith Dave Dixon, Oaklea, Beacon Edge, Penrith, CA11 8BN
☎ 01768 863155 See Area website
Summit Good Mr Paul Strzoda, 8 Highcroft Drive, Allithwaite, Grange-Over-Sands, LA11 7QL
☎ 015395 33523 See Area website
West Cumbria Mr David Woodhead, Cropple How, Birkby, Ravenglass, Cumbria, CA18 1RT
☎ 01229 717270 See Area website

MID LANCASHIRE
AREA SECRETARY
Mr D Kelly, 4 Buttermere Close, Bamber Bridge, Preston, Lancs, PR5 4RT ☎ 01772 312027
www.lancashire-ramblers.org.uk

GROUP SECRETARIES
Chorley Mrs J Tudor Williams, Oaklands, 5 The Bowers, Chorley, Lancs, PR7 3LA www.lancashire-ramblers.org.uk/chorley
Fylde Mr D J Stokes, 7 Cedar Close, Newton With Scales, Kirkham, Lancs, PR4 3TZ ☎ 01772 671134
www.ramblersassociation-fyldegroup.org.uk
Garstang & District Mrs C Stenning, 20 Meadowcroft Avenue, Catterall,

Garstang, Lancs, PR3 1ZH
☎ 01995 601170
Lancashire Walking Mrs R Kirk, 20 Cranleigh, Standish, Wigan, WN6 0EU www.lypwc.org.uk
Preston Mr A Manzie, 3 Ruthin Court, Dunbar Road, Ingol, Preston, Lancs, PR2 3YE ☎ 01772 736467
www.prestonra.co.uk
South Ribble Mr B A Kershaw, 2 Moss Way, New Longton, Preston, Lancs, PR4 4ZQ
West Lancashire Mr W G Wright, 49 Riverview, Tarleton, Preston, Lancs, PR4 6ED ☎ 01772 812034
www.westlancsramblers.org.uk

NORTH EAST LANCASHIRE
AREA SECRETARY
Mrs S Baxendale, 101 Blackburn Road, Clayton-Le Moors, Accrington, Lancs, BB5 5JT ☎ 01254 235049

GROUP SECRETARIES
Blackburn & Darwen Miss M G Brindle, 103 School Lane, Guide, Blackburn, BB1 2LW ☎ 01254 671269
Burnley & Pendle Mrs M Broadley, 18 Station Road, Padiham, Lancashire, BB12 8EB ☎ 01282 778 153
Clitheroe Mr B Brown, 2 Chorlton Terrace, Barrow, Whalley, Clitheroe, Lancs, BB7 9AR ☎ 01254 822851
Hyndburn Mr P J Bedson, 8 Mill Street, Church, Accrington, Lancs, BB5 4EJ
☎ 01254 399559
www.hyndburnramblers.co.uk
Rossendale Mr Peter Aizlewood, Lynwood, 265 Haslingden Old Road, Rossendale, BB4 8RR
☎ 01706 215085
www.waidew.btinternet.co.uk

SOUTH & EAST CHESHIRE
AREA SECRETARY
See www.ramblers.org.uk/info/localgroups/ for the latest details.

GROUP SECRETARIES
Congleton Mrs J Rishworth, 54 Bailey Crescent, Congleton, Cheshire, CW12 2EW ☎ 01260 271869
East Cheshire Mr Ian Mabon, 'Highwinds', 15 Churchfields, Bowdon, Altrincham, Cheshire, WA14 3PL
☎ 0161 928 3437 (fax also)
South Cheshire Mr P Callery, 45 Broughton Lane, Wistaston, Crewe, CW2 8JR ☎ 01270 568714
www.ramblerssouthcheshire.org.uk

Explore the biggest leisure centre in the British Isles

If your boots are made for walking, then the Isle of Man Walking Festival is for you. Next year's event will be bigger than ever and is on from the 19th to the 23rd of June 2006 with registration on the 18th of June. We'll also be launching our first mini-walking festival in mid-October 2006, so watch this space.

Six night festival packages include return travel, accommodation, walks, and social events including a quiz night, and The Blister Ball, all from only £279 pp.

To book, call 01624 66 11 77 or visit www.isleofmanwalking.com

Isle OF man

VisitIsleofMan.com

LOCAL RAMBLERS GROUPS continued

NORTH AND MID CHESHIRE

AREA SECRETARY
Mrs D Armitage, Birchtree Bungalow,
Red Lane, Appleton, Warrington,
WA4 5AB ☎ 01925 268540
http://nmc-ramblers.org.uk

GROUP SECRETARIES
Halton Mr Phil Williams, 21 Castner
Avenue, Weston Point, Runcorn,
WA7 4EG http://nmc-ramblers.org.uk

North & Mid Cheshire Under 40
Mr D Heys, 18 Rhuddlan Road, Rhyl,
LL18 2PR www.cheshirewalkers.org.uk

Vale Royal and Knutsford Mrs D
Armitage, Birchtree Bungalow, Red
Lane, Appleton, Warrington, WA4 5AB
http://nmc-ramblers.org.uk

Warrington Mr M & Mrs B Elebert,
Yellow Lodge, Park Lane, Higher
Walton, Warrington, WA4 5LW
http://nmc-ramblers.org.uk

LOCAL RAMBLERS PUBLICATIONS

CUMBRIA
The Cumbria Way
by John Trevelyan, ISBN 1 855681 97 8
(Lake District Ramblers/Dalesman).
Concise guide to this popular
112kmk/70-mile route from Ulverston to
Carlisle, with sketch maps, route
description and background information.
*£2.99 free postage from Lakeing,
Grasmere, Ambleside LA22 9RW.
Cheques to Lake District Ramblers.*

**Walks Around Carlisle & North
Cumbria**
ISBN 0 9521458 0 4 (Carlisle Ramblers).
17 fairly easy walks of between 8km/5
miles and 14.5km/9 miles in the lowland
countryside around Carlisle, including the
Eden Valley and Hadrian's Wall. *£3.50
post free to members, + 50p p&p to non-
members from 24 Currock Mount, Carlisle
CA2 4RF. Cheques to Carlisle Ramblers.*

NEW **More Walks Around Carlisle
and North Cumbria**
ISBN 1 904350 43 6 (Carlisle Ramblers).
Well-stuffed book of 37 circular and linear
walks including countryside, coast and
Hadrian's Wall. From 4km/2.5 miles to
23km/14 miles, with quite a few options
under 8km/5 miles. Some public
transport walks, several starting from
Carlisle itself and several of the walks
interconnect for more options. Sketch
maps, background details. *£4 from Little
Gables, Brampton CA8 2HZ. Cheques
to Ramblers' Association.*

Walks in the Kendal Area Book 1
3rd edition, ISBN 0 904350 40 1.
18 low level walks within 16km/10 miles
of Kendal.
Walks in the Kendal Area Book 3
2nd Edition, ISBN 0 904350 37 1.
Mostly lower level walks of between
6.5km/4 miles and 24km/15 miles within

16km/10 miles of Kendal.
*Each £2.95 post free from 6 Orchard
Close, Sedgwick, Kendal LA8 0LJ. Cheques
to RA Kendal Group.*

LANCASHIRE AND
MANCHESTER
Cown Edge Way (Manchester Area)
32km/20-mile walk in six sections from
Hazel Grove, Stockport to Gee Cross,
Woodley, with notes on history, fauna
and flora, maps and drawings. *£1 from 31
Wyverne Road, Manchester M21 0ZW.
Cheques to Ramblers' Association
Manchester Area.*

Rambles Around Oldham
by Oldham Ramblers. 20 easy walks of
between 6.5km/4 miles and 16km/10
miles, all connecting with bus services,
including sites of biological importance.
*£3.50 + 50p p&p from 682 Ripponden
Road, Oldham OL4 2LP. Cheques to
Oldham Ramblers Book Account.*

**25 Walks in the Ribble and Hodder
Valleys**
by Clitheroe Ramblers, ISBN 1 901184
72 2. 25 walks from 6.5km/4 miles to
9.5km/6 miles all selected by members of
the Group. *£5.99 from 1 Albany Drive,
Salesbury, Blackburn BB1 9EH. Cheques to
The Ramblers' Association Clitheroe Group
Social Account.*

Walks Around Heywood
by S Jackson and D M Williams (Rochdale
Ramblers). 20 easy to moderate walks of
5km/3 miles to 10km/6 miles in
Heywood and surrounding area, with
public transport details and local
information. A new edition of a booklet
originally published by Heywood Civic
Society. *£3 + 50p p&p from 152 Higher
Lomax Lane, Heywood OL10 4SJ. Cheques
to Ramblers' Association Rochdale Group.*

Walks from the Limestone Link
ISBN 0 904350 41 X.
17 easy walks of between 2km/1.5 miles
and 16km/10 miles in the beautiful
limestone area north of Lancaster, and
the 19km/12-mile Limestone Link path.
Includes maps and sketches.

Walks in the Lune Valley
ISBN 0 904350 39 8.
14 walks of between 4km/2.5 miles and
24km/15 miles, and the Lune Valley
Ramble, 37km up the north bank of the
river and 38.5km/24 miles down the
south bank. Includes maps and sketches.

Walks in North West Lancashire
15 easy walks of between 6.5km/4 miles
and 14.5km/9 miles in the areas
surrounding the rivers Lune, Keer and
Wyre and parts of Silverdale and
Arnside and Forest of Bowland AONBs,
including sketch maps and notes on
public transport.
*All £2.95 + 45p p&p each from 116
North Road, Carnforth LA5 9LX. Cheques
to Ramblers' Association Lancaster Group.*

NEW **Walks Round Lancaster City**
Five easy walks between 7km/4miles and
8km/5 miles from the city centre which
can be combined into one 24km/15mile
walk through the surrounding countryside.

NEW **More Walks in North West
Lancashire**
21 walks of between 5km/3 miles and
14.5km/9 miles in the areas surrounding
the rivers Lune, Keer and Wyre and parts
of Silverdale and Arnside and Forest of
Bowland AONBs, including sketch maps
and notes on public transport. Most are
easy but nine are in access areas and
include rough walking.
*Both available from Ramblers' Association
Lancaster Group (see p157).*

NORTH WEST

BED & BREAKFAST

CHESHIRE

● Altrincham
TRANS PENNINE TRAIL
◄ 46-48 Barrington Road, WA14 1HN ☎ 0161 928 4523 (Oasis Hotel)
www.oasishotel.co.uk Map 109/769885
BB **D** ✕ £10, 5:30-10:30pm S10 D11 T9 F3 ⋘(Altrincham)
Ⅴ Ⓑ Ⓓ 🛏️👤 ★★

● Church Minshull (Crewe)
Higher Elms Farm, Cross Lane, Minshull Vernon, CW1 4RG ☎ 01270 522252
(Mrs A M Charlesworth)
http://members.aol.com/tomsworld/higherelmsfarmhomepage.html
Map 118/669607
BB **C** ✕ nearby S1 D1 T1 F1 Ⓑ Ⓓ ⊗ 🛏️👤🚗🏕️ ◆◆◆

● Congleton
STAFFORDSHIRE WAY
◄ Yew Tree Farm, North Rode, CW12 2PF ☎ 01260 223569
(Mrs Sheila Kidd) www.yewtreebb.co.uk Map 118/890665
BB **C** ✕ book first £15, 6:30pm D1 F1 Closed Xmas
Ⅴ Ⓑ Ⓓ ⊗ 🛏️👤🚗 ◆◆◆◆

● Crewe

☆ ◄ **Crewe Hall**
Weston Road, CW1 6UZ ☎ 01270 253333
www.marstonhotels.com Map 118/732540
BB **D** ✕ £37.50, 7-9:30pm D63 T2 ⋘(Crewe)
Ⅴ Ⓑ 🛏️👤 ★★★★ Wheelchair access.

An ideal base for a multitude of walks in the attractive Cheshire countryside, including the Shropshire Union and Trent & Mersey Canals, Crewe Hall is a beautiful four-star stately home with a sympathetic modern wing.

Enjoy a break in the comfortable and stylish West Wing and dine in the Brasserie with its unique revolving bar while soaking in the atmosphere of history.

Convenient for the Little Moreton Walk and Crewe station.

Please ask about our exclusive rates for walking parties.

● Macclesfield
◄ Ryles Arms, Hollin Lane, Higher Sutton, SK11 0NN ☎ 01260 252244
(Ian Brown) www.rylesarms.com Map 118/939695
BB **C** ✕ £9, 5:30-9pm D3 T1 F1 Closed Xmas
Ⅴ Ⓑ Ⓓ ⊗ 🛏️👤 ◆◆◆◆

● Nantwich
◄ Downstream, 44 Marsh Lane, CW5 5LH ☎ 01270 625125 (Nancy Cleave)
www.downstream.me.uk Map 118/644519
BB **B** ✕ nearby F1 Closed Xmas ⋘(Nantwich) Ⓑ Ⓓ ⊗ 🛏️👤 Ⓜ

● Northwich
Ash House Farm, Chapel Lane, Acton Bridge, CW8 3QS ☎ 01606 852717
(Mrs S M Schofield) www.ashhousefarm.co.uk Map 117/587755
BB **C** S1 D1 T1 F1 ⋘(Acton Bridge) Ⓑ Ⓓ 🛏️👤🚗🏕️ ◆◆◆◆

● Rainow (Macclesfield)
PEAK DISTRICT
STAFFORDSHIRE WAY
Harrop Fold Farm, SK10 5UU ☎ 01625 560085
www.harropfoldfarm.co.uk Map 118/966781
BB **C/D** ✕ book first £15, 6-8pm D1 T1 F1
Ⅴ Ⓑ Ⓓ ⊗ 🛏️👤🚗! ◆◆◆◆

☆ ◄ **Common Barn Farm B&B**
Smith Lane, SK10 5XJ ☎ 01625 574878 (Rona Cooper)
www.cottages-with-a-view.co.uk Map 118/968764
BB **D** ✕ nearby S2 D1 T2 F1
Ⅴ Ⓑ Ⓓ ⊗ 🛏️👤🚗! See SC also.

A luxury barn conversion with en-suite facilities in all rooms, including power showers and under-floor central heating. Fully accessible room with en-suite wetroom and wheelchair-friendly bathroom. Situated in the Peak District National Park with unrivalled views across the Cheshire plain to the Welsh mountains.

● Romiley (Stockport)
Upper Watermeetings Barn, Watermeetings Lane, SK6 4HJ ☎ 01614 270220
www.watermeetingsbarn.com Map 109/954905
BB **C** ✕ nearby S1 D1 T1 F1 Closed Xmas ⋘(Romiley)
Ⓑ Ⓓ 👤🚗🏕️

● Siddington (Macclesfield)
◄ The Golden Cross Farm, SK11 9JP
☎ 01260 224358 (Hazel Rush) Map 118/848707
BB **B** ✕ nearby S2 D2 Closed Xmas Ⓑ Ⓓ ⊗ 🛏️👤 ◆◆◆

● Spurstow (Tarporley)
SANDSTONE TRAIL
Haycroft Farm, Peckforton Hall Lane, CW6 9TF ☎ 01829 260389
(Richard Spencer) www.haycroftfarm.co.uk Map 117/554573
BB **B** ✕ nearby S2 D2 T2 F1 Closed Xmas
Ⓓ ⊗ 🛏️👤!🏕️ ◆◆◆◆ See Groups also.

● Wincle (Macclesfield)
PEAK DISTRICT
Hill Top Farm, SK11 0QH ☎ 01260 227257 (Mrs Susan Brocklehurst)
c_brock_22@hotmail.com Map 118/965661
BB **C** ✕ book first £12, 6-6:30pm D1 T1
Ⅴ Ⓑ Ⓓ ⊗ 🛏️👤🚗 ◆◆◆◆

● Wybunbury (Nantwich)

☆ ◨◀ **Lea Farm**
Wrinehill Road, CW5 7NS ☎ 01270 841429 (Mrs Jean E Callwood)
www.smoothhound.co.uk/hotels/leafarm.html Map 118/716489
BB **C** ✕ nearby D1 T1 F1
🅱 🅳 ⟨symbols⟩ ◆◆◆

Charming farmhouse set in landscaped
gardens where peacocks roam. 150 acres of
peaceful family farm.
Delightful bedrooms. All amenities, some
en-suite rooms.
Snooker/pool table. Fishing available.
Email: contactus@leafarm.freeserve.co.uk

CUMBRIA

● Alston
PENNINE WAY

◨◀ Greycroft, Middle Park, The Raise, CA9 3AR ☎ 01434 381383
(Mrs P M Dent) www.greycroft.co.uk Map 86/706463
BB **C** ✕ nearby D1 T/F1 Closed Xmas
🅱 🅳 ⟨symbols⟩ ◆◆◆◆Ⓢ

High Field, Bruntley Meadows, CA9 3UX ☎ 01434 382182 (Mrs Celia Pattison)
cath@cybermoor.org.uk Map 87/720461
BB **A** ✕ £8, 7-9pm S1 D1 T1 F1 Closed Xmas Ⓥ 🅱 🅳 ⟨symbols⟩

◨◀ The Cumberland Hotel, Townfoot, CA9 3HX ☎ 01434 381875
(Helen & Guy Harmer) www.alstoncumberlandhotel.co.uk Map 86,87/717464
BB **C** ✕ £7.50+, 6-9pm D2 T2 F1 Closed Xmas
Ⓥ 🅱 🅳 ⟨symbols⟩

Lowbyer Manor Country House, Hexham Road, CA9 3JX ☎ 01434 381230
www.lowbyer.com Map 86,87/717469
BB **D** ✕ nearby S1 D5 T2 F1 Ⓥ 🅱 🅳 ⟨symbols⟩ ◆◆◆◆

● Ambleside
LAKE DISTRICT
COAST TO COAST WALK & CUMBRIA WAY

☆ ◨◀ **Broadview Guest House**
Low Fold, Lake Road, LA22 0DN ☎ 015394 32431 (Alan & Sue Clarke)
www.broadview-guesthouse.co.uk Map 90/377036
BB **D** ✕ nearby D3 T1 F2 Closed Xmas
🅱 🅳 ⟨symbols⟩ ◆◆◆

Comfortable non-smoking B&B in Ambleside, short
stroll from village and Lake Windermere at
Waterhead. Always a warm welcome and a hearty
breakfast. Packed lunches, morning weather
reports and drying facilities.
Walks start from our front door.
Special breaks available all year.

◨◀ Lyndale Guest House, Lake Road, LA22 0DN ☎ 015394 34244
(Alison Harwood) www.lyndale-guesthouse.co.uk Map 90/377036
BB **C** ✕ nearby S2 D2 T2 F2
🅱 🅳 ⟨symbols⟩ ◆◆◆

◨◀ Brantfell House, Rothay Road, LA22 0EE ☎ 015394 32239
(Chris & Jane Amos) www.brantfell.co.uk Map 90/374041
BB **C** ✕ nearby S1 D6 T2 Ⓥ 🅱 🅳 ⟨symbols⟩ ◆◆◆◆

☆ ◨◀ **The Old Vicarage**
Vicarage Road, LA22 9DH ☎ 015394 33364
www.oldvicarageambleside.co.uk Map 90/373044
BB **D** ✕ nearby D8 T2 F2
🅱 🅳 ⟨symbols⟩Ⓜ ◆◆◆◆

Quality Bed & Breakfast accommodation.
Quiet central location. Own car park. Pets
welcome. All bedrooms have TV, hairdryer,
alarm clock radio, video, mini fridge,
kettle, CH, private bath/shower and WC.
Indoor heated pool, sauna and hot-tub.
Email: the.old.vicarage@kencomp.net

☆ ◨◀ **Croyden House**
Church Street, LA22 0BU ☎ 015394 32209 (Sylvia & John Drinkall)
www.croydenhouseambleside.co.uk Map 90/376043
BB **C** ✕ nearby S3 D6 T4 F2 Closed Xmas
🅱 🅳 ⟨symbols⟩

A guest house centrally situated on a quiet
street 2 minutes walk from the main bus stop
and centre of Ambleside.
Offering a friendly welcome, generous home
cooked breakfasts, comfortable rooms with TV,
tea/coffee making facilities and private
car park.

☆ **Nab Cottage**
Rydal, LA22 9SD ☎ 015394 35311 (Liz & Tim Melling)
www.rydalwater.com Map 90/355064
BB **C** ✕ book first £15, 7pm S1 D2 T2 F2 Closed July-Aug
Ⓥ 🅱 🅳 ⟨symbols⟩ ◆◆◆

A Grade II listed 16th C. cottage
overlooking Rydal Water. Once
home of Thomas de Quincey and
Hartley Coleridge. Superb walks in
every direction. Delicious home
cooked food. Informal atmosphere.
Email: tim@nabcottage.com

☆ ◨◀ **Smallwood House Hotel**
Compston Road, LA22 9DJ ☎ 015394 32330
www.smallwoodhotel.co.uk Map 90/375044
BB **D** ✕ £20, 6:30-7pm S2 D4 T3 F3 Closed Xmas
Ⓥ 🅱 🅳 ⟨symbols⟩ ◆◆◆◆ See Groups also.

We pride ourselves on a
quality, friendly service in
the traditional way.

Dinners and packed lunches.
Drying facilities.
Group discounts.
Winter breaks.
Leave your cars in our car-
park and walk from here.

Please telephone Anthony or
Christine Harrison for a full
brochure and tariff.

enq@smallwoodhotel.co.uk

☆ Stepping Stones
Under Loughrigg, LA22 9LN ☎ 015394 33552 (Amanda Rowley)
www.steppingstonesambleside.com Map 90/366055
BB **D** ✕ nearby D3 T1 Closed Xmas
Ⓑ Ⓓ ⊗ ♨ ◆◆◆◆ See SC also.

Lakeland stone Victorian house, set in outstanding location with spectacular views over river, stepping stones and fells. Beautifully appointed, spacious bedrooms with period furnishings. Walks from door. Landscaped gardens with ample private parking.

● Appleby-in-Westmorland

☆ ▪◀ Limnerslease
Bongate, CA16 6UE ☎ 017683 51578 (Mrs Kathleen Coward)
http://mysite.freeserve.com/limnerslease Map 91/689200
BB **B** ✕ nearby D2 T1 Closed Xmas ⚏(Appleby)
Ⓓ ⊗ 🐾🐾

Limnerslease is a charming guest house situated in the historic picturesque market town of Appleby-in-Westmorland. You are assured a warm welcome and clean, comfortable accommodation. 5 mins walk from town centre and 10 mins walk from the famous Carlisle to Settle line.

☆ ▪◀ Bongate House
CA16 6UE ☎ 017683 51245 (Anne & Malcolm Dayson)
www.bongatehouse.co.uk Map 91/689200
BB **B/C** ✕ nearby S1 D3 T2 F2 Closed Nov-Feb ⚏(Appleby)
Ⓥ Ⓑ Ⓓ 🐾🐾🚗! 🐾 ◆◆◆◆

Attractive comfortable Georgian guesthouse in acre of garden. 8 bedrooms, 5 en-suite all with CH, TV and beverage facilities. Hearty breakfasts & lovely walks. Lakes, Pennines and Eden Valley. Groups welcome. Selection of eating places close at hand. information@bongatehouse.co.uk

● Arnside
Willowfield Hotel, The Promenade, LA5 0AD ☎ 01524 761354
(Janet & Ian Kerr) www.willowfield.uk.com Map 97/456788
BB **C** ✕ book first £15, 7pm S2 D3 T4 F2 ⚏(Arnside)
Ⓥ Ⓑ Ⓓ ⊗ 🐾🐾🚗! ◆◆◆◆ Evening meal weekends only.

● Bampton (Penrith)

☆ Mardale Inn
CA10 2RQ ☎ 01931 713244 (Neil & Katherine Stocks)
www.mardaleinn.co.uk Map 90/514181
BB **D** ✕ £8.95, 6-8pm D3 T3
Ⓥ Ⓑ ⊗ 🐾🐾🚗! 🐾 ◆◆◆

Cosy, non-smoking, 18th century inn with en-suite accommodation, near Haweswater. Wooden beams, log fire, real ales and over 30 malt whiskies. Home-made food featuring local produce. Tranquil location surrounded by beautiful countryside, by Coast to Coast Walk.

● Bampton Grange (Penrith)
Crown & Mitre Hotel, CA10 2QR ☎ 01931 713225
www.crownandmitrehotel.co.uk Map 90/520179
BB **C** ✕ £5.95-£8.50, 6-9:30pm S2 D2 T1 F2 Closed Xmas
Ⓥ Ⓑ Ⓓ 🐾🐾🐾

● Boot (Eskdale)
The Post Office, Dale View, CA19 1TG ☎ 019467 23236 (John & Leigh Gray)
www.booteskdale.co.uk Map 89,90/176010
BB **B** ✕ nearby S1 D2 T1 Closed Xmas ⚏(Dalegarth)
Ⓓ 🐾🐾

▪◀ Wha House, CA19 1TH ☎ 019467 23322
mariehodgkiss@aol.com Map 89,90/190009
BB **B** ✕ nearby S1 D1 T2
Ⓥ Ⓓ ⊗ 🐾🐾 Guest kitchen available. See SC also.

● Borrowdale (Keswick)

☆ ▪◀ Royal Oak Hotel
CA12 5XB ☎ 017687 77214
www.royaloakhotel.co.uk Map 90/259148
BB **D** ✕ £10, 7pm S2 D5 T2 F6 Closed Xmas
Ⓥ Ⓑ Ⓓ 🐾🐾🐾🚗! 🐾 ★

Traditional, family-run Lakeland hotel situated beside Stonethwaite Beck in the heart of Borrowdale. Good home cooking, cosy bar, open fire and friendly service. Brochure, tariffs and special mid-week and long weekend breaks available.

● Bowness-on-Solway
Kings Arms, CA7 5AF ☎ 016973 51426
www.kingsarmsbowness.wanadoo.co.uk Map 85/222627
BB **C** ✕ £5.50, 6-9pm T2 F2 Closed Xmas
Ⓥ Ⓓ 🐾🐾🐾! 🐾

● Bowness-on-Windermere (Windermere)

☆ Lingwood
Birkett Hill, LA23 3EZ ☎ 015394 44680 (Mrs J Fry)
www.lingwood-guesthouse.co.uk/ Map 96,97/402963
BB **C/D** ✕ nearby D3 T1 F2 Closed Xmas ⚏(Windermere)
Ⓑ Ⓓ ⊗ ♨ ◆◆◆◆

A modern, family-run guest house in a quiet location but within 400 yards of Lake Windermere. A 10-minute walk from the end of the Dales Way and free off-road parking whilst you walk it!

● Brampton
HADRIAN'S WALL

New Mills House, CA8 2QS ☎ 016977 3376 (Janet Boon)
www.newmillshouse.co.uk Map 86/549617
BB **C** ✗ book first £12.50+, 7:30-8pm D1 T1 Closed Xmas ⋙(Brampton)
Ⓥ Ⓑ Ⓓ ⊛ ⛟ 🕭 ◆◆◆

● Brough (Kirkby Stephen)
🚩◀ The Castle Hotel, Main St, CA17 4AX ☎ 01768 341252 (Tracey Letaief)
www.castlehotelbrough.co.uk Map 91/794146
BB **B** ✗ £6.95, 6-8:30pm S3 D6 T3 F2 Ⓥ Ⓑ Ⓓ ⛟🕭🚗!

● Broughton-in-Furness
LAKE DISTRICT

Middlesyke, Church Street, LA20 6ER ☎ 01229 716549
(David & Sarah Hartley) Map 96/208876
BB **C** ✗ nearby D2 Closed Xmas ⋙(Foxfield)
Ⓑ Ⓓ ⊛ ⛟🕭!🕭Ⓜ ◆◆◆◆Ⓢ

● Buttermere (Cockermouth)
COAST TO COAST WALK

☆🚩◀ **Dalegarth Guest House**
CA13 9XA ☎ 017687 70233 (Ramblers Holidays)
www.dalegarthguesthouse.co.uk Map 89,90/186160
BB **B** ✗ book first £, 7pm D4 T5 Closed Nov-Mar
Ⓑ Ⓓ ⊛ ⛟ Ⓜ

Our guesthouse is situated in the grounds of the Hassness Estate on the shore of Buttermere 1¼ miles south of Buttermere village. Bed and breakfast from £22 per person. Ask about midweek specials.

● Caldbeck (Wigton)
LAKE DISTRICT
CUMBRIA WAY

☆🚩◀ **The Briars**
Friar Row, CA7 8DS ☎ 016974 78633 (Dorothy H Coulthard)
Map 90/325399
BB **B** ✗ nearby S1 D1 T1 Closed Xmas
Ⓑ Ⓓ ⊛🕭! ◆◆◆

Situated in Caldbeck village, overlooking Caldbeck Fells. Ideal for touring Lake District, Scottish Borders and Roman Wall. We are right on the Cumbria Way. Near Reivers cycle route. Tea-making facilities. Rooms en-suite with TV. 2 mins walk to village inn.

☆ **Swaledale Watch**
Whelpo, CA7 8HQ ☎ 016974 78409 (Mr & Mrs Savage)
www.swaledale-watch.co.uk Map 90/309396
BB **D** ✗ nearby D2 T1 F1 Closed Xmas
Ⓑ Ⓓ ⊛ ⛟🕭🚗! ◆◆◆◆Ⓢ

Enjoy comfort, beautiful surroundings and peaceful countryside on our farm. Central for touring or walking the northern fells. Lifts to and from Caldbeck village available. A warm welcome awaits you. Ideal for the Cumbria Way. All rooms have private facilities.

● Carlisle
HADRIAN'S WALL, CUMBRIA WAY & PENNINE WAY

Angus Hotel & Almonds Bistro, 14 Scotland Road, Stanwix, CA3 9DG
☎ 01228 523546 www.angus-hotel.co.uk Map 85/400571
BB **D** ✗ £18, 6-9pm S3 D3 T4 F4 ⋙(Carlisle) Ⓥ Ⓑ Ⓓ ⛟🕭!🕭
◆◆◆◆ Free packed lunch for walk BRITAIN readers!

Craighead, 6 Hartington Place, CA1 1HL ☎ 01228 596767 (Mrs Pam Smith)
Map 85/406559 BB **B** ✗ nearby S1 D2 T1 F1 Closed Xmas ⋙(Carlisle)
Ⓑ Ⓓ ⊛ ⛟🕭!🕭 ◆◆◆

🚩◀ Knockupworth Hall, Burgh Road, CA2 7RF ☎ 01228 523531
(Patricia Dixon) www.knockupworthdi.co.uk Map 85/370566
BB **C** ✗ book first £10+, 7pm D2 T2 F1 Closed Dec-Feb ⋙(Carlisle)
Ⓥ Ⓑ Ⓓ ⊛ ⛟🕭🚗!

Abberley House, 33 Victoria Place, CA1 1HP ☎ 01228 521645
www.abberleyhouse.co.uk Map 85/406561
BB **C** ✗ nearby S3 D2 T2 F1 Closed Xmas ⋙(Carlisle)
Ⓑ Ⓓ ⊛🕭! ◆◆◆◆

🚩◀ Cambro House, 173 Warwick Rd, CA1 1LP ☎ 01228 543094
(David & Alice) davidcambro@aol.com Map 85/412559
BB **C** ✗ nearby D2 T1 Closed Xmas ⋙(Carlisle)
Ⓑ Ⓓ ⊛ ⛟🕭! ◆◆◆◆

🚩◀ Kenilworth Guest House, 34 Lazonby Terrace, London Road, CA1 2PZ
☎ 01228 526179 (Robert & Anne Glendinning) loopyloz54@hotmail.com
Map 85/414545 BB **C** ✗ nearby S1 D3 T1 F1 ⋙(Carlisle)
Ⓥ Ⓑ Ⓓ ⊛ ⛟🕭🚗 ◆◆◆

🚩◀ Rosemount Cottage, Burgh by Sands, CA5 6AN ☎ 01228 576440
(Paula Stevenson) www.rosemountcottage.co.uk Map 85/327592
BB **B** ✗ nearby D1 T2 F1 Ⓥ Ⓑ Ⓓ ⛟🕭🚗!🕭

● Cartmel (Grange-over-Sands)
Bank Court Cottage, The Square, LA11 6QB ☎ 015395 36593 (Mrs P C Lawson)
Map 96,97/378787 BB **C** ✗ nearby S1 D1 Closed Xmas ⋙(Grange)
Ⓓ ⊛ ⛟🕭🕭 ◆◆◆

● Coniston
LAKE DISTRICT
CUMBRIA WAY

☆ **Beech Tree House**
Yewdale Road, LA21 8DX ☎ 015394 41717
Map 96/302976
BB **C** ✗ nearby D6 T2 Closed Xmas
Ⓑ Ⓓ ⊛ ⛟🕭🚗 ◆◆◆◆

Charming 18th-century house with attractive gardens situated 150m from the village centre and all amenities. Ideally situated for a walking holiday or overnight stay on the Cumbria Way. Good drying facilities, ample parking. Ensuites available.

Lakeland House Guest House, Coffee & Eating Hse, Tilberthwaite Ave, LA21 8ED
☎ 015394 41303 www.lakelandhouse.com Map 96,97/304976
BB **C** S1 D3 T1 F5 Closed Xmas Ⓑ Ⓓ ⊛ ⛟🕭!🕭 ◆◆◆

Crown Hotel, LA21 8ED ☎ 015394 41243
www.crown-hotel-coniston.com Map 96, 97/304976
BB **D** ✗ £10, until 9pm D6 T4 F2 Closed Xmas
Ⓥ Ⓑ Ⓓ ⊛ ⛟🕭 ◆◆◆◆

NORTH WEST

☆ ☞ **Thwaite Cottage**
Waterhead, LA21 8AJ ☎ 015394 41367 (Marguerite & Graham Aldridge)
www.thwaitcot.freeserve.co.uk Map 96/311977
BB **C** ✗ nearby D2 T1 Closed Xmas
🅱 🅳 ⊗ 🐾🔥 ♦♦♦♦

A beautiful 17th C. cottage in a peaceful wooded garden, close to village and lake. Central heating, log fires, beamed ceilings. Bathrooms, private or en-suite. Off road parking. Non-smoking.

Waverley, Lake Road, LA21 8EW ☎ 015394 41127 (Jenny Graham)
Map 96,97/302974
BB **B** ✗ nearby S1 D1 T1 F1 Closed Xmas 🅱 🅳 ⊗ 🐾🔥🏠

☆ ☞ **Wilson Arms**
Torver, LA21 8BB ☎ 015394 41237 (Frances Mayvers)
Map 96,97/283941
BB **D** ✗ book first £, 6:30-9pm S1 D4 T1 F2 Closed Xmas
🆅 🅳 🐾🔥🏠🚗!🏠 ♦♦♦

Comfortable rooms with en-suite facilities, TV and tea/coffee making facilities. Good walking area, within easy reach of Coniston Water and the central lakes.

Orchard Cottage, 18 Yewdale Road, LA21 8DU ☎ 015394 41319 (Jean Johnson)
www.conistonholidays.co.uk Map 96,97/302976
BB **C** ✗ nearby D2 T1 Closed Xmas
🅱 🅳 ⊗ 🐾🔥🚗!Ⓜ ♦♦♦♦

Oaklands, Yewdale Rd, LA21 8DX ☎ 015394 41245 (Mr & Mrs J Myers)
www.oaklandsconiston.co.uk Map 96,97/302977
BB **C** ✗ nearby S1 D2 T1 🅱 🅳 ⊗ 🐾🔥🚗! ♦♦♦♦

☆ ☞ **Wheelgate Country Guest House**
Little Arrow, LA21 8AU ☎ 015394 41418 (Steve & Linda Abbott)
www.wheelgate.co.uk Map 96,97/290950
BB **D** ✗ nearby S2 D3 T1 Closed Xmas
🅱 🅳 ⊗🔥🚗 ♦♦♦♦♦ See SC also.

17th-century farmhouse with beamed ceilings, spacious en-suite bedrooms and cosy bar. Excellent breakfasts cater for all tastes. Ideally situated for access to central lakes, with superb local walks to suit all ages and abilities.

● Dent (Sedbergh)
YORKSHIRE DALES
DALES WAY
☞ Garda View Guest House, Main Street, LA10 5QL ☎ 015396 25209
(Rita Smith) rita@gardaview.co.uk Map 98/705870
BB **B** ✗ nearby S1 D2 T1 Closed Xmas 🅱 🅳 ⊗ 🐾🔥

Smithy Fold, Whernside, LA10 5RE ☎ 015396 25368 (Mrs G Cheetham)
www.smithyfold.co.uk Map 98/725859
BB **B** ✗ book first £13, 6:30-8pm D1 T1 F1 Closed Xmas ⋙(Dent)
🆅 🅳 🐾🔥🚗🏠 ♦♦♦

Stone Close, Main Street, LA10 5QL ☎ 015396 25231 (Janet Browning)
www.dentdale.com Map 98/705869
BB **C** ✗ book first £12.50, until 5:30pm S1 D1 T/F1 Closed Nov & Xmas
🆅 🅱 🅳 ⊗ 🐾🔥🏠Ⓜ ♦♦♦ Special diets catered for.

Stone Close Tea Room, Main Street, LA10 5QL ☎ 015396 25231
(Janet Browning) www.dentdale.com Map 98/705869
BB **C** D1 T2 🆅 🅱 🅳 ⊗ 🐾🔥🏠 ♦♦♦ Wheelchair access.

● Dubwath (Cockermouth)
LAKE DISTRICT
CUMBRIA WAY
☞ Ouse Bridge Hotel, Bassenthwaite Lake, CA13 9YD ☎ 017687 76322
www.ousebridge.com Map 89,90/197312
BB **D** ✗ £14, 7:15-8pm S2 D5 T1 F2 🆅 🅱 🅳 ⊗ 🐾🔥 ★★

● Dufton (Appleby)
PENNINE WAY & TEESDALE WAY
Ghyll View, CA16 6DB ☎ 017683 51855 (Mrs M Hullock) Map 91/691250
BB **B** ✗ nearby, 7pm S2 D1 T2 Closed Oct-Feb
🅱 🅳 🐾

Coney Garth, CA16 6DA ☎ 017683 52582 (Mrs J T Foster)
www.coneygarth.co.uk Map 91/685257
BB **B** ✗ book first £12, 7-7:30pm D1 T1 F1
🆅 🅱 🅳 ⊗ 🐾🔥🚗!🏠

● Eamont Bridge (Penrith)
River View, 6 Lowther Glen, CA10 2BP ☎ 01768 864405 (Mrs C O'Neil)
http://river-view.co.uk Map 90/524285
BB **B** ✗ nearby S2 D2 T2 ⋙(Penrith) 🅱 🅳 🐾🔥🏠

● Eskdale Green
LAKE DISTRICT

☆ **Forest How Guest House**
CA19 1TR ☎ 019467 23201
www.foresthow-eskdale-cumbria.co.uk Map 96/136999
BB **B** ✗ nearby S1 D3 T3 F1 Closed Xmas ⋙(Ravenglass & Eskdale)
🅱 🅳 ⊗ 🐾🔥🏠 ♦♦♦

Secluded, warm, comfortable guest house. Excellent home cooking. Delightful gardens with spectacular views. TVs, H&C, beverage trays. Some en-suite. Parking. Friendly and informal atmosphere. Brochure available.

● Gilsland (Brampton)
HADRIAN'S WALL & PENNINE WAY
☞ The Hill on the Wall, CA8 7DA ☎ 016977 47214 (Mrs Elaine Packer)
www.hadrians-wallbedandbreakfast.com Map 86/624668
BB **D** ✗ book first £15, 7-7:30pm D1 T2
🆅 🅱 🅳 ⊗ 🐾🔥 ♦♦♦♦♦Ⓢ

● Grange-over-Sands
☞ Corner Beech Guest House, 1 Methven Terr, Kents Bank Rd, LA11 7DP
☎ 015395 33088 (Ian Wright) www.cornerbeech.co.uk Map 96,97/402772
BB **D** ✗ book first £15, 6:30pm D3 T1 F1 Closed Dec-Jan
⋙(Grange-over-Sands) 🆅 🅱 🅳 ⊗ 🐾🔥🚗! ♦♦♦♦
Internet access available.

● Grasmere (Ambleside)
LAKE DISTRICT, COAST TO COAST WALK & CUMBRIA WAY

> ☆ **Dunmail House**
> Keswick Road, LA22 9RE ☎ 015394 35256 (Tony & Shirley Evans)
> www.dunmailhouse.com Map 90/339084
> BB **B** ✗ nearby S1 D3 T1 Closed Xmas
> B D ⊕ 🛏🛁 ♦♦♦♦
>
>
>
> A traditional stone house with a friendly family atmosphere. Beautiful views from all rooms and the spacious gardens. Convenient for lake and village. Non-smoking. Car park.
> enquiries@dunmailhouse.freeserve.co.uk

Silver Lea Guest House, Easedale Rd, LA22 9QE ☎ 015394 35657
(Dorothy Walker) www.silverlea.com Map 90/335079
BB **D** ✗ book first £13.50, 6:30pm D2 T2 Closed Feb-Dec
V B D ⊕ 🛏🛁 ♦♦♦♦⑤

Oak Lodge, Easedale Rd, LA22 9QJ ☎ 015394 35527 (Mrs Alison Dixon)
www.oaklodge-grasmere.co.uk Map 90/331081
BB **C** ✗ nearby D2 T1 Closed Xmas B D ⊕ 🛏🛁

> ☆ **Forest Side Hotel**
> Forest Side, LA22 9RN ☎ 015394 35250
> www.forestsidehotel.com Map 90/342080
> BB **C/D** ✗ £10.50, 6-9pm S10 D9 T9 F5 Closed Jan
> V B D ⊕ 🛏🛁🍴
>
>
>
> Family-run hotel just ten minutes' walk from the centre of Grasmere, set in 43 acres of wooded and landscaped gardens.
>
> Forest Side is an ideal base for exploring the Lake District or a stopover for the Coast to Coast Walk.
>
> Homecooked meals: traditional English breakfast. Packed lunches are available daily.
>
> Licensed bar and log fires. Non-smoking throughout. Tea/coffee making facilities and TV available in all rooms. Most rooms en-suite. Boot drying room.
>
> Self-catering apartments and large private car park also available.

● Grayrigg (Kendal)
DALES WAY

Punchbowl House, LA8 9BU ☎ 01539 824345 (Mrs D Johnson)
www.punchbowlhouse.co.uk Map 97/580972 BB **B/C** ✗ book first £16,
6:30pm D2 T1 Closed Mar-Dec V B D ⊕ 🛏🛁 ♦♦♦♦⑤

● Greystoke (Penrith)
Lattendales Centre for Wellbeing, Berrier Road, CA11 0UE ☎ 01768 483229
(Centre Manager) www.lattendales.org Map 90/436307
BB **B** ✗ book first £10, 7pm S6 D1 T6 Closed January
V B D ⊕ 🛏🛁

● Holton (Penrith)
LAKE DISTRICT

🚶 Beckfoot Country House, Guest Accommodation, CA10 2QB
☎ 01931 713241 (Mrs Lesley White) www.beckfoot.co.uk Map 90/500210
BB **D** ✗ nearby S1 D3 T2 F1 Closed Dec-Feb
V B D 🛏🛁🚗 ♦♦♦♦

● Hesket Newmarket (Caldbeck)
LAKE DISTRICT
CUMBRIA WAY

Newlands Grange, CA7 8HP ☎ 016974 78676 (Mrs Dorothy Studholme)
www.newlandsgrange.co.uk Map 90/350394
BB **B** ✗ book first £9.50, 6:30pm S1 D1 T1 F2 Closed Xmas
B D ⊕ 🛏🛁🚗! 🛏 See SC also.

● Kendal
LAKE DISTRICT
DALES WAY

🚶 Hillside Bed & Breakfast, 4 Beast Banks, LA9 4JW ☎ 01539 722836
(Mrs Joanne Buchanan) www.hillside-kendal.co.uk Map 97/513925
BB **C** ✗ nearby S3 D2 T1 Closed Xmas 🚍(Oxenholme)
B D ⊕ 🛏🛁 ♦♦♦

🚶 Sundial House, 51 Milnthorpe Road, LA9 5QG ☎ 01539 724468
(Sue & Andrew McLeod) info@sundialguesthousekendal.co.uk
Map 97/516916 BB **B/C** ✗ nearby S2 D2 T2 F/D/T1 Closed Xmas
🚍(Oxenholme) B D ⊕ 🛏🛁

> ☆ 🚶 **The Glen**
> Oxenholme, LA9 7RF ☎ 01539 726386 (Chris Green)
> www.glen-kendal.co.uk Map 97/534900
> BB **C** ✗ book first £18, 6-6:30pm S1 D3 T1 F2 Closed Xmas
> 🚍(Oxenholme) V B D ⊕ 🛏🛁🚗! 🛏 ♦♦♦♦
>
>
>
> We are situated in a quiet location on the outskirts of Kendal under 'The Helm', where there is a local walk & viewpoint of the Lakeland Mountains, but within short walk of country pub and restauarnt. Ideal for touring the Lakes & Yorkshire Dales.

● Kentmere (Kendal)
LAKE DISTRICT

Maggs Howe, LA8 9JP ☎ 01539 821689 (Mrs Christine Hevey)
www.smoothhound.co.uk/hotels/maggs Map 90/462041
BB **B** ✗ book first £12.50, 7pm S1 D1 T1 F1 Closed Xmas
V B D 🛏🛁🚗! 🛏

● Keswick
LAKE DISTRICT
CUMBRIA WAY

Melbreak House, 29 Church Street, CA12 4DX ☎ 017687 73398
(John, Jen & Carol Hardman) www.melbreakhouse.co.uk Map 89,90/269232
BB **B/C** ✗ nearby D7 T3 Closed Xmas
B D ⊕ 🛏🛁 ♦♦♦

NORTH WEST

☆ Seven Oaks Guest House

7 Acorn Street, CA12 4EA ☎ 017687 72088 (L Furniss & C Firth)
www.sevenoaks-keswick.co.uk Map 89,90/269232
BB **C** ✗ nearby D4 T2 F1 Closed Xmas
B D 🌐 🍴 👤 🚆 ! ◆◆◆

Enjoy a good night's sleep, a great breakfast,
and a glorious day out...

Relax at Seven Oaks

Centrally located for the town centre and Lake
Derwentwater and furnished with your comfort in mind.

☆ Tarn Hows

3-5 Eskin Street, CA12 4DH ☎ 017687 73217 (Mr & Mrs T Bulch)
www.tarnhows.co.uk Map 89, 90/268233
BB **C** ✗ book first £15 (groups only), 5-8pm S2 D5 T1 Closed Xmas
V B D 🌐 🍴 👤 🚆 ◆◆◆◆

Traditional Victorian residence pleasantly
situated in a quiet location, Tarn Hows is only
a few minutes walk from the town
centre, with easy access to the lake and
the surrounding fells. Private car park.
Non-smoking. Drying facilities.

☆ Hedgehog Hill

18 Blencathra Street, CA12 4HP ☎ 017687 74386 (Nel & Keith Nicholls)
www.hedgehoghill.co.uk Map 89,90/269233
BB **C** ✗ nearby S2 D3 T1 Closed Xmas
B D 🌐 🍴 👤 ◆◆◆◆

Wet clothes and boots are
welcome in our friendly
Victorian guesthouse near
town centre, fells and lake.
Freshly prepared breakfasts
with choice.
Packed lunches available.
Flasks filled for free.
All rooms with colour TV,
tea/coffee making facilities.
Most rooms en-suite.
Central heating.
Mountain views.
Motorcycle parking.
Non-smoking.
Credit cards accepted.
rambler@hedgehoghill.co.uk

☆ Glencoe Guest House

21 Helvellyn, CA12 4EN ☎ 017687 71016 (Teresa Segasby)
www.glencoeguesthouse.co.uk Map 89,90/269233
BB **C** ✗ nearby S1 D3 T2
B D 🌐 🍴 👤 ◆◆◆◆

Teresa & Karl await you with a warm friendly
welcome. Victorian home ensuring an
enjoyable stay in comfortable and relaxing
accommodation. Quiet. En-suites.
Excellent breakfasts. Keswick centre 5 mins.
Drying room. Free flask filling.
Weather reports, local knowledge and more.

☆ Cumbria House

1 Derwentwater Place, Ambleside Road, CA12 4DR ☎ 017687 73171
(Barry & Cathy Colam) www.cumbriahouse.co.uk Map 89,90/268232
BB **B** ✗ book first £15 (groups only), 6:45pm S3 D2 T3 F1 Closed Dec-Jan
V B D 🍴 👤 🚆 Ⓜ ◆◆◆◆ See Walking Holidays also.

We can't guarantee the
weather – but at least
we have an efficient
drying room and provide
a local weather forecast
twice a day.

Award-winning
breakfast using local
produce with plenty of
choice, home-made rolls,
marmalade and jams,
plus Fairtrade teas,
coffees and fruit juices.

Comfortable lounge with library of walking books.

At the UK's first Green Globe Benchmarked and 'climate-neutral' guesthouse,
be assured your stay will be as environmentally sustainable as possible.
We'll even give discounts to car-free guests.

Advice on walks freely given or Pace the Peaks with Cathy & Kim.

See Walking Holidays section and www.pacethepeaks.co.uk

☆ Greystones

Ambleside Road, CA12 4DP ☎ 017687 73108 (Robert & Janet Jones)
www.greystones.tv Map 89/268232
BB **C** ✗ nearby S1 D5 T2 Closed Xmas
B D 🌐 👤 ◆◆◆◆

Tranquil location with excellent fell views.
Short walk to the market square and Lake
Derwentwater. Eight delightful
en-suite rooms, each with TV and
refreshments tray. Aga cooked breakfasts.
Drying and storage facilities. Walks from
the front door. Non-smoking. Parking.

Clarence House, 14 Eskin St, CA12 4DQ ☎ 017687 73186 (Jenny & Pat Stokes)
www.clarencehousekeswick.co.uk Map 89,90/269232
BB **C** ✗ nearby D4 T1 F3 Closed Xmas B D 🌐 🍴 👤 🚗 ◆◆◆◆

☆ ➤ Hawcliffe House

30 Eskin Street, CA12 4DG ☎ 017687 73250 (Diane & Ian McConnell)
www.hawcliffehouse.co.uk Map 89,90/270232
BB **B** ✗ nearby D3 T2 Closed Xmas
B D 🌐 🍴 👤 ◆◆◆

Small, family run guest house.
Warm welcome assured.
Non-smoking.
Packed lunches available on request.
Short walk from town centre.

Call Diane for more information.

☆ Badgers Wood

30 Stanger Street, CA12 5JU ☎ 017687 72621 (Anne Paylor)
www.badgers-wood.co.uk Map 89,90/265235
BB **C** ⌖ nearby S2 D4 T1 Closed Xmas-Jan
Ⓑ Ⓓ ⊗ ♨ ◆◆◆◆

A friendly welcome awaits you at this delightful Victorian terraced house situated in a quiet cul-de-sac just a 2 minute walk from the heart of town, with its shops, restaurants and bus station.

All our comfortable, attractive rooms are en-suite, furnished to a high standard with colour TVs and tea/coffee making facilities and views of the fells.

Maps & guide books available. Owner's extensive fells knowledge gladly shared. Non-smoking.

☆ Hazeldene Hotel

The Heads, CA12 5ER ☎ 01768 772106
www.hazeldene-hotel.co.uk Map 89,90/264232
BB **D** ⌖ nearby D7 T1 F2 Closed Xmas-Jan
Ⓑ Ⓓ 🐕♨🏓 ◆◆◆◆

Hazeldene is a welcoming family-run hotel in a magnificent location, ideally placed for both town and country.

Well-appointed en-suite bedrooms, beautiful views & an excellent breakfast make Hazeldene Hotel the perfect haven for your visit to the Lake District National Park.

Games room with table tennis and pool table. Private parking is available for 8 cars.

Craglands Guest House, Penrith Road, CA12 4LJ ☎ 017687 74406
(Ella Ferguson) www.craglands-keswick.co.uk Map 89,90/279238
BB **C** ⌖ nearby S2 D3 T2 Ⓥ Ⓑ Ⓓ ⊗ 🐕♨ ☂! ◆◆◆◆

☆ High Hill Farm

High Hill, CA12 5NY ☎ 017687 74793 (Lillian and Keith Davies)
lillankei@btinternet.com Map 89/262238
BB **B** ⌖ nearby D2 T1 Closed Xmas
Ⓑ Ⓓ ⊗ 🐕♨Ⓜ

Former farmhouse, 5 mins level walk to town centre. B&B for non-smokers in 3 en-suite rooms with tea/coffee and beautiful views. Parking. Special breaks of 3 days plus – except bank holidays. Excellent centre for walking.

☆ ▥◀ Appletrees

The Heads, CA12 5ER ☎ 017687 80400 (John & Sue Armstrong)
www.appletreeskeswick.co.uk Map 89,90/264232
BB **C/D** ⌖ nearby S1 D5 T1 Closed Xmas
Ⓑ Ⓓ ⊗ 🐕♨

Victorian House overlooking Hope Park and lake. 2 mins walk to town centre, theatre and bus station. En-suite rooms. Colour TV (teletext). Tea/coffee making facilities. Excellent breakfasts. Drying room and secure cycle storage. Limited private parking. Non-smoking. Email: john@armstrong2001.fsnet.co.uk

☆ ▥◀ Littlefield

32 Eskin Street, CA12 4DG ☎ 017687 72949 (Maureen Hardy)
www.keswick98.fsnet.co.uk Map 89,90/270233
BB **B/C** ⌖ nearby S1 D3 T1 Closed Xmas
Ⓑ Ⓓ ⊗ 🐕♨

Small, friendly bed and breakfast.

Convenient for shops, lake and many lovely walks.

We pride ourselves on our warm, relaxed hospitality and attention to detail.

▥◀ Rivendell Guest House, 23 Helvellyn St, CA12 4EN
☎ 01768 773822 (Pat & Linda Dent & June Muse)
www.rivendellguesthouse.com Map 89,90/269233
BB **B** ⌖ nearby S2 D6 T4 F2
Ⓑ Ⓓ ⊗ 🐕♨!🏓Ⓜ

Cragside Guest House, 39 Blencathra St, CA12 4HX
☎ 01768 773344 (Wayne & Alison Binks)
www.smoothhound.co.uk/hotels/cragside Map 89,90/271234
BB **B** ⌖ nearby D2 T1 F1 Closed Xmas
Ⓑ Ⓓ ⊗ 🐕♨🏓 ◆◆◆ Veggie breakfasts.

▥◀ Lincoln Guest House, 23 Stanger Street, CA12 5JX ☎ 017687 72597
www.lincolnguesthouse.com Map 89,90/265236
BB **B/C** ⌖ nearby S2 D3 T1 F1
Ⓥ Ⓑ Ⓓ ⊗ 🐕♨

☆ ▥◀ Lakeside House

40 Lake Road, CA12 5DQ ☎ 017687 72868
www.lakesidehouse.co.uk Map 89,90/266232
BB **B** ⌖ book first £11, 6:30pm S6 D3 T8 F5
Ⓥ Ⓑ Ⓓ 🐕♨ See Groups also.

Large guesthouse in prime location: close to the lake, theatre and town, overlooking Hope Park and the fells beyond. Excellent drying facilities, large lounge, wholesome food. Friendly and informal, an ideal base for exploring the northern lakes.

Portland House, 19 Leonard Street, CA12 4EL ☎ 017687 74230 (Linda Ball)
www.portlandhouse.net Map 89,90/269233
BB **C** ⌖ nearby S1 D3 T1 F1
Ⓥ Ⓑ Ⓓ ⊗ 🐕♨ ☂! Wheelchair access.

NORTH WEST

● Kirkby Stephen
COAST TO COAST WALK

☆ **Redmayne House**
Silver Street, CA17 4RB ☎ 017683 71441 (Mrs C J Prime)
Map 91/774088
BB **B** ✗ nearby S1 D1 T1 F1 Closed Xmas ⋘(Kirkby Stephen)
Ⓓ ⊗ 🐾 👃 🏠

A spacious and attractive Georgian home set in a large garden.

Home-made bread and preserves, walkers' breakfasts, private sitting room, parking.

£20.00 - one price for all.

●▬◄ The Pennine Hotel, Market Sq, CA17 4QT ☎ 017683 71382
www.penninehotel.co.uk Map 91/775087
BB **B** ✗ £7-£8, until 9pm S2 D2 T2 F1 ⋘(Kirkby Stephen)
Ⓥ Ⓑ 🐾 👃 🏠

●▬◄ Lockholme, 48 South Road, CA17 4SN ☎ 017683 71321
(Mrs M E Graham) www.lockholme.co.uk Map 91/772079
BB **B** ✗ nearby S1 D1 T1 F1 Closed Xmas ⋘(Kirkby Stephen)
Ⓑ Ⓓ ⊗ 🐾 👃 ! Ⓜ

Fletcher House, Fletcher Hill, Market Street, CA17 4QQ ☎ 017683 71013
(Mr & Mrs S Bamford) www.fletcherhousecumbria.co.uk Map 91/774086
BB **C** ✗ nearby S1 D2 T2 ⋘(Kirkby Stephen)
Ⓑ Ⓓ ⊗ 🐾 👃 🚗 Veggie breakfasts.

The Manor House, Mellbecks, CA17 4AB ☎ 017683 72757 (Jean Leeson)
www.manorhouse.netfirms.com Map 91/777085
BB **C** ✗ nearby D2 F1 Closed Xmas ⋘(Kirkby Stephen)
Ⓑ Ⓓ ⊗ 🐾 👃 🚗 🏠

● Levens (Kendal)
LAKE DISTRICT

Birslack Grange Country Guest House, Hutton Lane, LA8 8PA
☎ 01539 560989 (Jean Carrington-Birch)
www.birslackgrange.co.uk Map 97/486866
BB **B** ✗ nearby S2 D2 T2 F1 Closed Jan
Ⓑ Ⓓ ⊗ 🐾 👃 🚗 ! 🏠 Ⓜ

● Long Marton (Appleby-in-Westmorland)
PENNINE WAY & TEESDALE WAY

Broom House, CA16 6JP ☎ 017683 61318 (Mrs Sandra Bland)
http://broomhouseappleby.co.uk Map 91/666238
BB **C** ✗ book first £ S1 D1 T1 F1 Closed Dec-Jan
Ⓥ Ⓑ Ⓓ ⊗ 🐾 👃 🚗 ◆◆◆◆

● Low Crosby (Carlisle)
HADRIAN'S WALL & CUMBRIA WAY

Madgwick, Green Lane, CA6 4QN ☎ 01228 573283 (M J Plane)
www.madgwickonwall.co.uk Map 85/445593
BB **B** ✗ nearby S1 T1 Closed Nov-Feb Ⓓ ⊗ 🐾 👃 !

● Matterdale (Penrith)
LAKE DISTRICT

●▬◄ Greenah, CA11 0SA ☎ 017684 83387 (Marjorie Emery)
www.greenah.co.uk Map 90/413249
BB **D** D1 T1 Ⓥ Ⓓ ⊗ 🐾 👃 🚗 !

● Motherby (Penrith)

☆ ●▬◄ **Motherby House**
CA11 0RJ ☎ 017684 83368 (Jacquie Freeborn)
www.motherbyhouse.co.uk Map 90/429285
BB **B** ✗ book first £14, 7pm F4 Closed Xmas
Ⓥ Ⓓ 🐾 👃 See SC also.

18th C. warm and friendly guest house with beamed lounge and log fires. Drying facilities. Packed lunches and flask filling. Excellent 3 course meal for healthy outdoor appetites. Near Ullswater Helve, Ilyn and Blencathra. Small groups & muddy boots welcome.

● Patterdale (Penrith)
LAKE DISTRICT
COAST TO COAST WALK

☆ **Wordsworth Cottage**
CA11 0NP ☎ 017684 82084 (Mrs Joan B Martin)
www.wordsworthcottage-ullswater.co.uk Map 90/340160
BB **C** ✗ nearby D2 T1 Closed Xmas
Ⓑ Ⓓ ⊗ 🐾 👃 !

A friendly welcome awaits you at this cosy Grade II-listed cottage. Built in 1670, it was once owned by Wordsworth himself. Ideal location for the Coast to Coast Walk, Helvellyn and high street ranges. View website for more details.

☆ **Old Water View**
CA11 0NW ☎ 017684 82175
www.oldwaterview.co.uk Map 90/398158
BB **C** ✗ nearby D4 T2 F2 Closed Xmas
Ⓑ Ⓓ ⊗ 🐾 👃

Elegant and welcoming, this bed & breakfast is beautifully situated on the banks of Goldrill Beck. Guests are welcome to enjoy the guest lounge and garden at any time during their stay. Telephone for a brochure or view the website. Credit cards accepted.

The White Lion Inn, CA11 0NW ☎ 017684 82214 Map 90/397157
BB **C** ✗ £7, until 9:30pm S2 D3 T3 Ⓥ Ⓑ Ⓓ 🐾 👃 🏠

●▬◄ Brotherswater Inn & Sykeside Camping Park, Brotherswater, CA11 0NZ
☎ 017684 82239 www.sykeside.co.uk Map 90/407130
BB **C** ✗ £10, 5:30-9:30pm D6 T8 Closed Xmas Ⓥ Ⓑ Ⓓ 🐾 👃 🏠 Ⓜ

●▬◄ Barco House, CA11 0NW ☎ 017684 82474 www.barcohouse.com
Map 90/397157 BB **D** ✗ nearby S3 D2 T2 Ⓥ Ⓑ Ⓓ ⊗ 🐾 👃

● Penrith
●▬◄ 27 Sandgate, CA11 7TJ ☎ 01768 865057 (Mrs V Bardgett)
Map 90/516302 BB **A** ✗ nearby D1 F1 Closed Xmas ⋘(Penrith)
Ⓑ Ⓓ ⊗ 🐾 👃 🚗 🏠

Acorn Guest House, Scotland Road, CA11 9HL ☎ 01768 868696
(Joyce or Anita) www.acorn-guesthouse.co.uk Map 90/510308
BB **C/D** ✗ nearby D4 T3 F1 ⋘(Penrith) Ⓥ Ⓑ Ⓓ ⊗ 🐾 👃

● Portinscale (Keswick)
LAKE DISTRICT
CUMBRIA WAY
▪◄ The Mount Guest House, CA12 5RD ☎ 017687 73970
(Lindsay & Ann Ferguson) www.mountferguson.co.uk Map 89/252236
BB C ✕ nearby S1 D1 T1 F1 Closed Xmas B D ⊗ ≜ ! ⌂

● Ravenglass
LAKE DISTRICT

☆ ▪◄ **Rose Garth**
Main Street, CA18 1SQ ☎ 01229 717275
www.rosegarth1.fsnet.co.uk Map 96/084964
BB B ✕ nearby S1 D3 T1 F1 Closed Xmas ⋙(Ravenglass)
B D ⌂ ≜ ⌂

Overlooking village green and estuary. All rooms en-suite, CH and tea making facilities. Near Eskdale and Wasdale. BR station in village. Walks: Cumbrian Coastal Way, Cumberland Way, Furness Way, Lakeland to Lindisfarne and Ravenglass to Scarborough routes.

▪◄ Muncaster Country Guest House, Muncaster, CA18 1RD ☎ 01229 717693
(Ron & Jan Stringer) www.muncastercountryguesthouse.com Map 96/099968
BB C ✕ book first £15, 7pm S2 D4 T1 F1 Closed Xmas ⋙(Ravenglass)
V B D ⊗ ≜ ⌂ ◆◆◆

● Rosthwaite (Borrowdale)
LAKE DISTRICT
COAST TO COAST WALK & CUMBRIA WAY

☆ ▪◄ **Scafell Hotel**
CA12 5XB ☎ 017 687 77208
www.scafell.co.uk Map 89/259149
BB C/D ✕ £21, 6:30-9pm S3 D7 T12 F2
V B D ⌂ ≜ ⌂ M ★★

A former coaching inn situated in the heart of the Borrowdale Valley, adjacent to the Allerdale Ramble, Cumbrian Way, Lakeland Way and Coast to Coast Walk footpaths.

24 en-suite rooms. Renowned for its fine food, bars and friendly service. A hotel through its superb location is frequented by walkers of all ages and abilities. Special breaks available.

Fax: 017687 77280
Email: info@scafell.co.uk

● Sedbergh
YORKSHIRE DALES
DALES WAY
Holmecroft, Station Road, LA10 5DW ☎ 015396 20754 (Mrs S Sharrocks)
www.holmecroftbandb.co.uk Map 97/650919
BB B ✕ nearby S1 D1 T1 D ⊗ ≜ !

▪◄ Wheelwright Cottage, 15 Back Lane, LA10 5AQ
☎ 015396 20251 (Miss M Thurlby)
antique.thurlby@amserve.net Map 97/659921
BB B ✕ nearby D1 T1 D ⊗ ≜ ! ⌂ ◆◆

☆ ▪◄ **St Mark's**
Cautley, LA10 5LZ ☎ 015396 20287 (Mrs Barbara Manwaring)
www.saintmarks.uk.com Map 98/690944
BB C ✕ book first £10.50, 7-7:30pm S1 T3 F1 Closed Xmas
V B D ⊗ ≜ ! ⌂ ◆◆◆

Treat yourself to the tranquil Howgill Fells (Cautley Spout 2 miles). Outstanding setting, Dales National Park. Former vicarage built in 1872, comfortable en-suite rooms (3 bath, 2 shower rooms), open fires, delicious aga-cooked breakfasts. Also workshops: embroidery, patchwork & quilting.

▪◄ Yew Tree Cottage, 35 Loftus Hill, LA10 5SQ ☎ 015396 21600
(Mrs Anne Jones) www.sedbergh.org.uk Map 97/658917
BB B ✕ nearby D1 T1 Closed Xmas
D ⊗ ≜ ! ⌂ ◆◆◆

Brantrigg, Winfield Rd, LA10 5AZ ☎ 015396 21455 (Linda Hopkins)
brantrigg@btinternet.com Map 97/658923
BB C ✕ nearby T1 Closed Xmas
B D ⊗ ≜ ⌂

● St Bees
COAST TO COAST WALK
Stonehouse Farm, Main Street, CA27 0DE ☎ 01946 822224 (Carole Smith)
www.stonehousefarm.net Map 89/971119
BB C ✕ nearby S1 D3 T2 F3 Closed Xmas ⋙(St Bees)
B D ⌂ ≜ ! ⌂ ◆◆◆

1 Tomlin House, Beach Road, CA27 0EN ☎ 01946 822284
(Mr & Mrs Whitehead) id.whitehead@which.net Map 89/963118
BB A/B ✕ nearby D1 T2 F1 Closed Xmas ⋙(St Bees)
B D ⌂ ≜ ⌂

Fairladies Barn Guest House, Main Street, CA27 0AD ☎ 01946 822718
(Susan & John Carr) www.fairladiesbarn.co.uk Map 89/970114
BB B ✕ nearby D5 T4 F2 ⋙(St Bees)
B D ⊗ ≜ ! ◆◆◆◆

● Staveley (Kendal)
LAKE DISTRICT
DALES WAY
Stock Bridge Farm, LA8 9LP
☎ 01539 821580 (Mrs Betty Fishwick) Map 97/475977
BB B ✕ nearby S1 D4 F1 Closed Nov-Feb ⋙(Staveley)
D ⊗ ≜ ! ⌂

▪◄ Ramblers Cottage, 1 School Lane, LA8 9NU ☎ 01539 822120
(Mrs Craven) www.ramblers-cottage.co.uk Map 97/469984
BB C ✕ nearby D1 T1 Closed Xmas ⋙(Staveley)
B D ⌂ ≜ ⌂ ! ⌂

NORTH WEST

● Threlkeld (Keswick)

LAKE DISTRICT

CUMBRIA WAY

☆ Scales Farm Country Guest House

CA12 4SY ☎ 01768 779660 (Alan & Angela Jameison)
www.scalesfarm.com Map 90/341268
BB **D** ✕ nearby D3 T2 FI Closed Xmas
B D ⊗ ☎ ♨ ⚘ ♨ ◆◆◆◆

Stunning views & a warm welcome await you at this 17th C. fells farmhouse sensitively modernised to provide accommodation of the highest standard. The farm is on the lower slopes of Blencathra, with a Lakeland inn next door.

● Troutbeck (Windermere)

LAKE DISTRICT

DALES WAY

☆ ☜◀ High Fold Guest House

LA23 1PG ☎ 015394 32200 (Les & Susan Bradley)
www.highfoldbedandbreakfast.co.uk Map 90/408027
BB **D** ✕ nearby D3 T2 FI
V B D ⊗ ☎ ♨ ! ◆◆◆◆

Former traditional Lakeland farm house, ideally placed for walking in the south Lakes and stopovers for the Westmorland Way, and other walks. Evening meals are available at two local pub-restaurants. All rooms en-suite with excellent views. AA & VisitBritain 4 diamonds.

● Ulpha (Broughton-in-Furness)

LAKE DISTRICT

Oakbank, Ulpha, Duddon Valley, LA20 6DZ
☎ 01229 716393 (Ray & Susan Batten)
susan@soakbank.freeserve.co.uk Map 96/201938
BB **C** ✕ book first £10, 7pm SI DI TI Closed Xmas
V D ☎ ♨ ⚘ ♨ ◆◆◆

● Ulverston

LAKE DISTRICT

CUMBRIA WAY

Rock House, 1 Alexander Road, LA12 0DE ☎ 01229 586879
(Ian and Linda Peters) www.rock-house.info Map 96,97/287779
BB **C** ✕ nearby SI F/D/T3 Closed Xmas ∿∿(Ulverston)
B D ⊗ ☎ ♨ ⚘ !

Dyker Bank, 2 Springfield Road, LA12 0DS
☎ 01229 582423 (M H Abbott) Map 96,97/284779
BB **B** ✕ nearby SI TI FI Closed Xmas ∿∿(Ulverston)
B D ⊗ ☎ ♨ ! ♨ Ⓜ

☜◀ St Mary's Mount, Belmont, LA12 7HD ☎ 01229 583372
(Marlon Bobbett) www.stmarysmount.co.uk Map 96,97/290788
BB **D** ✕ book first £17.50, 2:30-9pm SI D2 TI Closed Xmas ∿∿(Ulverston)
V B D ⊗ ☎ ♨ ⚘ !

● Watermillock (Ullswater)

LAKE DISTRICT

☆ ☜◀ Land Ends Country Lodge

CA11 0NB ☎ 017684 86438 (Barbara Murphy)
www.landends.co.uk Map 90/433245
BB **D** ✕ nearby S2 D4 T2 FI Closed Xmas-Jan
B D ☎ ♨ ♨ Ⓜ ◆◆◆ See SC also.

Peaceful setting in 25 acres with 2 lakes and lovely courtyard with flowers, pots and fishpond. Red squirrels, ducks, owls and other fabulous birdlife live in the grounds. Ullswater 1.3 miles. Rooms are light, clean and airy. Great breakfasts.

● Windermere

LAKE DISTRICT

DALES WAY

☆ ☜◀ Holly Lodge

6 College Road, LA23 1BX ☎ 015394 43873 (Anne & Barry Mott)
http://hollylodge20.co.uk Map 96,97/411985
BB **C** ✕ nearby SI D3 TI F4 Closed Xmas ∿∿(Windermere)
B D ⊗ ☎ ♨ ◆◆◆

Quietly situated in the village of Windermere, close to shops, restaurants, buses and trains.
Family run. Friendly atmosphere.
Good English breakfast.

Tel/Fax: 015394 43873, Mob: 07774 967805

e-mail: anneandbarry@hollylodge6.fsnet.co.uk

☆ Lynwood

Broad Street, LA23 2AB ☎ 015394 42550 (Mrs F Holcroft)
www.lynwood-guest-house.co.uk Map 96,97/413982
BB **B/C** ✕ nearby SI D4 TI F3 ∿∿(Windermere)
B D ⊗ ☎ ♨ ♨ ◆◆◆◆

Relax in our elegant Victorian house in the heart of Windermere. Each bedroom is individually furnished and smoke-free with en-suite shower and wc, colour TV, hairdryer & beverages. Convenient for bus and train stations and close to parking. We look forward to your stay with us.

☆ ☜◀ The Beaumont

Holly Road, LA23 2AF ☎ 015394 47075 (Denise Dixon)
www.lakesbeaumont.co.uk Map 96,97/413981
BB **D** ✕ nearby SI D7 TI FI ∿∿(Windermere)
V B D ⊗ ☎ ♨ ! ◆◆◆◆◆

The Beaumont is an elegant Victorian villa occupying an enviable position for all amenities in Windermere and an ideal base to explore the lakeland area. The Beaumont offers superb food, sincere hospitality and tranquility, yet only two minutes from the centre.

Brendan Chase, 1-3 College Road, LA23 1BU ☎ 015394 45638
(David Maloney) www.placetostaywindermere.co.uk Map 96,97/411985
BB **B** ✕ nearby S2 D2 T3 F5 ∿∿(Windermere) V B D ⊗ ☎

LANCASHIRE

● Burnley

PENNINE BRIDLEWAY

Rosehill House Hotel, Rosehill Ave, BB11 2PW ☎ 01282 453931
www.rosehillhousehotel.co.uk Map 103/834315
BB **D** ✕ £8+, 7-9:30pm S9 D21 T4 F4 �(Burnley)
Ⓥ Ⓑ Ⓓ 🐾🛁🚗❗🏇 ★★★

● Chipping (Clitheroe)

☆ ▪◄ **Rakefoot Farm**
Thornley Rd, Chaigley, BB7 3LY ☎ 01995 61332 (Mrs Pat Gifford)
www.rakefootfarm.co.uk Map 103/663416
BB **B/C/D** ✕ book first £15-£18, 5-7pm D2 T1 F2
Ⓥ Ⓑ Ⓓ 🐾🛁🚗❗🏇 ◆◆◆ See SC also.

17th C. farmhouse and traditional stone
barn on family farm. Original features,
woodburners, home cooked meals/
convenient restaurants, laundry, en-suite
and ground floor available. Longridge Fell/
Forest of Bowland/ AONB/ panoramic views.
Transport available. See Self-catering also.

● Clayton-le-Dale (Ribble Valley)

Rose Cottage Bed & Breakfast, Longsight Road, BB1 9EX ☎ 01254 813223
(Marje Adderley) www.smoothhound.co.uk/hotels/rosecott Map 103/667333
BB **C/D** ✕ nearby D2 T1 ⋅⋅⋅(Wilpshire/Ramsgreave)
Ⓥ Ⓑ Ⓓ ⊗ 🐾🛁❗🏇

● Clitheroe

☆ ▪◄ **Foxhill Barn**
Howgill Lane, Gisburn, BB7 4JL ☎ 01200 415906 (Janet & Peter Moorhouse)
www.foxhillbarn.co.uk Map 103/843467
BB **C** D1 T2 F1 Closed Xmas
Ⓓ ⊗ 🐾🛁🚗🏇 ◆◆◆◆

A newly converted barn with beautiful
panoramic views close to the
Lancashire/Yorkshire border. Many scenic
walks traversing the farm. Ribble Way and
Pendle nearby. Unwind afterwards with a
jacuzzi, or in our homely guest lounge with
wood burner and oak beams.

● Colne

☆ ▪◄ **Wickets**
148 Keighley Road, BB8 0PJ ☎ 01282 862002 (Mrs Etherington)
wickets@colne148.fsnet.co.uk Map 103/897402
BB **B/C** ✕ nearby D1 T1 Closed Xmas-Feb ⋅⋅⋅(Colne)
Ⓑ Ⓓ ⊗ 🐾🛁 ◆◆◆◆

Spacious Edwardian family home
providing quality accommodation in
attractive & comfortable en-suite
rooms. All the local amenities of the
town yet close to open countryside,
lovely walks & breathtaking views.
Pick up a bargain in the Mill shops.

● Eccleston (Chorley)

☆ ▪◄ **Parr Hall Farm**
Parr Lane, PR7 5SL ☎ 01257 451917 (Mike & Kate Motley)
parrhall@talk21.com Map 108/519174
BB **C** ✕ nearby S1 D9 T3 F2
Ⓑ Ⓓ ⊗ 🐾🛁🚗❗ ◆◆◆◆

Charming property with mature gardens
peacefully located in the countryside, a few
miles from the M6. Built in 1721, it has been
renovated, providing comfortable guest rooms
with en-suite facilities, TV & hospitality trays.
With many attractions nearby, it is a good
stopover from Scotland & the Lake District.

● Silverdale (Carnforth)

▪◄ Spring Bank House, 19 Stankelt Rd, LA5 0TA ☎ 01524 702693
(Mrs Nancy Bond) www.springbankhousesilverdale.co.uk Map 97/463749
BB **D** ✕ nearby S1 D1 T2 F1 ⋅⋅⋅(Silverdale) Ⓑ Ⓓ ⊗ 🐾🛁🚗 Ⓜ

● Wycoller (Colne)

▪◄ Parson Lee Farm, BB8 8SU ☎ 01282 864747 (Pat Hodgson)
www.parsonleefarm.co.uk Map 103/937385
BB **B** ✕ book first £9, 6:30-8pm D1 T1 F1 Closed Xmas
Ⓥ Ⓑ Ⓓ 🐾🛁🚗❗🏇 ◆◆◆

SELF-CATERING

CHESHIRE

● Audlem

Berry Cottage ☎ 01270 811573 (Jane Hardwick)
http://homepages.tesco.net/hardwork/index.html
£180-£350 Sleeps 4 + cot. 1 bungalow.
Canalside village. Rural, private. Donkeys, chickens. ⊗ 🏇 ★★★

● Macclesfield

Acorn Cottages ☎ 01260 223388 (Susan Bullock)
www.acorncottages-england.co.uk
£220-£320 Sleeps 2-9. 2 cottages. Oak beams, stone floors, undulating
scenery. ⊗ ★★★★

● Rainow

PEAK DISTRICT

☆ **Common Barn Farm**
☎ 01625 574878 (Mrs Rona Cooper)
www.cottages-with-a-view.co.uk
£250-£500 Sleeps 4-10. 2 cottages.
Fabulous views. Underfloor heating. Footpath from door. ⊗ ★★★★

Luxury barn conversion with power shower and
under-floor central heating. Situated in Peak
District NP with unrivalled views across the
Cheshire plain to the Welsh mountains. Located
close to Lamaload and Goyt Valley reservoirs,
midway between Macclesfield and Buxton.
Footpaths from door. Ideal base for walkers.

NORTH WEST

CUMBRIA

● Ambleside
LAKE DISTRICT

P F Quarmby ☎ 015394 32326 paulfquarmby@aol.com
£140-£240 Sleeps 4. 1 flat. Closed Nov-Feb
Opens onto garden. Private parking.   Ⓧ 🐾

The Haven ☎ 015394 32441 (Fiona Sparrow)
www.havengreen.fsbusiness.co.uk
£225-£345 Sleeps 4. 3 cottages. Close to shops and amenities. 🐾

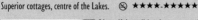

☆ **Grove Cottages**
☎ 015394 33074 (Peter & Zorika Thompson)
www.grovecottages.com
£250-£650 Sleeps 2-6. 4 cottages.
Superior cottages, centre of the Lakes. Ⓧ ★★★★-★★★★★

4 beautiful, traditional cottages set in our 200 acres of Stockghyll Valley. Magnificent views to Coniston Old Man and The Langdales but only 1½ miles from Ambleside shops and restaurants. Wonderful walks from your doorstep and a warm personal welcome.

☆ **Rydal Holiday Lettings**
☎ 015394 31043 (Neil Rowley)
www.steppingstonesambleside.com
£235-£415 Sleeps 2-4. 4 flats. Lovely apartments in idylic riverside setting.
Ⓧ 🐾 ★★★★ See B&B also.

Superbly situated apartments, furnished and equipped to high, clean standard with video and CD player. Large landscaped gardens with BBQ area and spectacular views. Ample private parking. Private water supply.

☆ **Riverside Lodge**
☎ 015394 34208 (Alan Rhone)
www.riversidelodge.co.uk
£285-£475 Sleeps 2. 2 cottages.
Idyllic riverside setting in Ambleside. Ⓧ 〰(Windermere) ★★★★

Riverside lodge is a property of immense charm and character with two attached 4-star holiday cottages.

Situated in an idyllic riverside setting just 500 yards from the centre of Ambleside in the heart of the English Lake District.

● Aspatria
Mark & Elaine Harris ☎ 01594 562974 www.rubiconsolutionsuk.co.uk
£155-£290 Sleeps 5. 1 cottage.
Ideal base for western Lakes/Solway coast.   Ⓧ 〰(Aspatria) 🐾

● Bassenthwaite
LAKE DISTRICT

Irton House Farm ☎ 017687 76380 (Mrs J Almond) www.irtonhousefarm.com
£295-£715 Sleeps 2-6. 5 apartments, 1 caravan.
Superb views. Table tennis, snooker/pool.   Ⓧ 🐾 ★★★★

Brook House Cottages ☎ 017687 76393 (Alison Trafford)
www.holidaycottageslakedistrict.co.uk
£100-£750 Sleeps 2-20. 3 cottages, 1 studio.
Village cottages & B&B by stream/farm. 🐾

● Bowness-on-Windermere
LAKE DISTRICT

Mr & Mrs E Jones ☎ 0151 228 5799 eejay@btinternet.com
£150-£280 Sleeps 2-3. 1 flat.
Lake views, central situation, well-equipped.   Ⓧ 〰(Windermere)

☆ **Mrs J Kay**
☎ 01925 755612
£205-£390 Sleeps 4. 1 flat. Closed Nov-March
Modern, central, lake view, private parking.
Ⓧ 〰(Windermere)

2 bedroom flat. Very attractively furnished. Central situation near shops, restaurants and places of interest. Lake view. Private parking. No dogs or children under 10. No smoking.

● Caldbeck
LAKE DISTRICT

Monkhouse Hill ☎ 016974 76254 (Jennifer or Andy Collard)
www.monkhousehill.co.uk
£330-£2,125 Sleeps 2-46. 9 cottages.
Award-winning. Rural setting. Evening meals. 🐾 ★★★★-★★★★★

Newlands Grange ☎ 016974 78676 (Mrs Dorothy Studholme)
studholme_newlands@hotmail.com
£100-£140 Sleeps 6. 1 caravan.
On working farm, lovely views.   Ⓧ See B&B also.

● Cockermouth
LAKE DISTRICT

Dr P S Davies ☎ 0141 9423704
www.kirkbraecottage.co.uk
£229-£511 Sleeps 2-6. 1 cottage.
Pubs & restaurants within walking distance.   Ⓧ ★★★★

Wood Farm Cottages ☎ 01900 829533 (Mrs A Cooley)
www.woodfarmcottages.com Grid ref: 119263
£270-£415 Sleeps 6. 2 cottages. Barn conversion, excellent walking. Ⓧ 🐾

● Coniston
LAKE DISTRICT

☆ **Coniston Country Cottages**
☎ 015394 41114 (Steve, Linda or Sharon)
www.conistoncottages.co.uk
£200-£750 Sleeps 2-7. 17 cottages. Quality cottages in superb surroundings.
Ⓧ 🐾 ★★★-★★★★★ See B&B also

Cosy Lakeland cottages in superb surroundings. Tastefully furnished and well-equipped. Easy access to central Lakes, with local walking to suit all ages and abilities.
Most cottages have free use of a nearby leisure club.

Elterwater

LAKE DISTRICT

☆ Langdale Cottages
☎ 0161 904 9445 (Robert & Pat Locke)
www.langdalecottages.co.uk
£230-£1,550 Sleeps 2-10. 1 house, 1 cottage. Leisure club. Unspoilt village. Luxury accommodation. ★★★-★★★★ RA member

Two luxury Lake District self-catering holiday cottages at the entrance to the Langdale valley, in the unspoilt village of Elterwater, Cumbria. These beautifully refurbished houses are set in well-landscaped gardens with fine views to the beck and fells.

Eskdale

LAKE DISTRICT

Mrs J Holland ☎ 01732 459168
£350-£650 Sleeps 8. 1 farmhouse.
17th century farmhouse, elevated position, stunning views.
RA member

Wha House ☎ 019467 23322 (Mrs Marie Crowe)
mariehodgkiss@aol.com
£180-£350 Sleeps 2. 1 cottage.
Ideal starting point for Scar/Harter Fell. See B&B also.

Irton Hall Country Cottages ☎ 0161 976 5440 (Steve Cottrell)
www.irtonhall.co.uk
£210-£440 Sleeps 5. 2 cottages.
Peacefully set in 19 acres of grounds. (Ravenglass)

Gamblesby

Church Villa ☎ 01768 881682 (Patricia Clowes)
www.gogamblesby.co.uk
£165-£425 Sleeps 2-6. 1 barn conversion, 3 cottages.
Tranquil, picturesque village. Views, gardens.
★★★-★★★★ See Helton also.

Grange-over-Sands

Lynn Branson ☎ 01253 813682
£180-£230 Sleeps 2. 1 cottage.
Adjoining amenities and long distance paths.
(Grange-Over-Sands)

Grasmere

LAKE DISTRICT

☆ Broadrayne Farm
☎ 015394 35055 (Mrs Jo Dennison Drake)
www.grasmere-accommodation.co.uk
£254-£580 Sleeps 2-5. 3 cottages. Dramatic views, quiet location, colour brochure. ★★★★ See Hostels & Groups also.

Broadrayne Farm is at the heart of the Lake District. Superb traditional cottages. Quiet location.Open fires, C/H & parking. Dogs welcome. Dramatic views. Classic Lakeland walks from front door. Brochure. Sauna and drying room on site. Resident owners.
Email: jo@grasmere-accommodation.co.uk

Greystoke

☆ Motherby House
☎ 017684 83368 (Mrs Jacquie Freeborn)
www.motherbyhouse.co.uk
£175-£296 Sleeps 4-6. 1 cottage. Closed Xmas
Converted coach house. See B&B also.

18th century warm and friendly guest house with beamed lounge and log fires. Drying facilities. Packed lunches and flask filling. Excellent 3 course meal for healthy outdoor appetites. Near Ullswater Helve, llyn and Blencathra. Small groups & muddy boots welcome.

Hawkshead

LAKE DISTRICT

Broomriggs ☎ 015394 36280 (Mrs Haddow) www.broomriggs.co.uk
£150-£340 Sleeps 3-4. 1 cottage.
Ideal for walking. Quiet, pleasant views. ★★★ See Sawrey also.

☆ High Dale Park Barn
Grizedale Forest ☎ 01229 860226 (Mr P Brown)
www.lakesweddingmusic.com/accomm
£195-£650 Sleeps 2-6. 17th century barn.
Quiet valley, superb position, many walks. ★★★

Idyllic setting in Grizedale Forest. Charming 17th century barn conversion. Two centrally heated units, sleeping six and two, or eight altogether. Totally non-smoking. Off road parking.

Fully fitted, well equipped kitchens. Popular catering service available.
Owner managed. Trout fishing nearby.
Secure undercover cycle storage. High Dale Park Barn is a recently converted 17th century barn that nestles in a small, peaceful valley within Grizedale Forest – Lakeland's largest forest area.
Woodland walks literally seconds away.
Email: peter@lakesweddingmusic.com

Helton

LAKE DISTRICT

Church Villa ☎ 01768 881682 (Mark Cowell) www.gogamblesby.co.uk
£185-£495 Sleeps 2-5. 2 cottages.
Beautiful views, log fire, garden. ★★★★ See Gamblesby also.

Keswick

LAKE DISTRICT

Hope Cottages ☎ 01900 85226 (Christine M England)
www.hope-farm-holiday-cottages.co.uk
£220-£420 Sleeps 3-4. 2 cottages. Closed Nov-Feb
Quiet and comfortable, lovely views/walks. ★★★

Mrs Smith ☎ 01992 463183
£90-£340 Sleeps 2-8. 2 flats.
Near bus station and Lake Derwentwater.

☆ Birkrigg
☎ 017687 78278 (Mrs Beaty)
£200-£340 Sleeps 1-4. 1 cottage.   Closed Jan
Pleasantly, peacefully situated, wonderful mountainous view.
🚫 ★★★

Enjoy the peace and quiet of a Lakeland valley, five miles from Keswick. Cosy oak beamed cottage converted from a stable nestled between the farm guesthouse and barn. Wonderful view of the Newlands range of mountains, Blencathra in the distance.

☆ Derwent House Holidays
☎ 01889 505678 (Mary & Oliver Bull)
www.dhholidays-lakes.com
£105-£375 Sleeps 2-6. 4 flats.
Central heating & parking. 🛏 ★★★

Traditional stone Lakeland building now four comfortable well-equipped self-catering holiday suites at Portinscale village on Derwentwater, 1 mile from Keswick. Central heating and linen included. Parking. Open all year. Short breaks. Prices £105 to £375. Some reductions for two people only.

☆ Brigham Farm
☎ 017687 79666 (N Green)
www.keswickholidays.co.uk
£140-£365 Sleeps 2-4. 6 apartments.   Lovely garden. Ample parking.
Owner maintained. 🚫 🛏 ★★★★ See The Studio (below) also.

Quietly situated 5 mins walk from town centre, former farmhouse converted to six spacious self-contained apartments. Handsomely furnished and well equipped, gas-fired CH, with garden and plenty of parking space. Carefully owner maintained.
Email: selfcatering@keswickholidays.co.uk

☆ The Studio
☎ 017687 79666 (N Green)
www.keswickholidays.co.uk
£140-£320 Sleeps 2-4. Apartments.   Tasteful barn conversion with stunning views. 🚫 ★★★★ See Brigham Farm (above) also.

Tasteful barn convesion in the lovely Vale of St Johns. Well equipped, handsomely furnished with beautiful views. Five miles from Keswick. Personally maintained.
selfcatering@keswickholidays.co.uk

☆ Croft House Holidays
☎ 017687 73693 (Mrs Jan Boniface)
www.crofthouselakes.co.uk
£230-£895 Sleeps 2-8. 5 cottages.   Stunning, panoramic views.
Peaceful rural settings. 🚫 ★★★★ RA member

Cottage and ground floor apartment in a Victorian country house and three other cottages – including a spacious barn conversion ideal for family reunions. All in Applethwaite village – just one mile from Keswick. Open all year, short breaks available.

● Kirkby-in-Furness
LAKE DISTRICT
The Annexe ☎ 01543 676552 (R C Clague-Smith) theannexeuk@aol.com
£175 Sleeps 2. 1 bungalow.   Duddon estuary, Furness fells,
Cumbrian Coastal Way. 🚫 🚶(Kirkby-In-Furness)

● Loweswater
LAKE DISTRICT
D Bell ☎ 01900 85227
£250-£280 Sleeps 2-6. 1 cottage.
Quiet country location, ideal for walking. 🛏

● Patterdale
LAKE DISTRICT

☆ Patterdale Hall Estate
☎ 017684 82308 (Sue Kay)
www.patterdalehallestate.com
£155-£484 Sleeps 2-6. 17 varying types..
Private 300 acre estate below Helvellyn. 🚫 🛏 ★★-★★★

Between Helvellyn and Ullswater, the private 300-acre Estate offers 17 self-catering properties in an idyllic setting with stunning views. Own foreshore, woodland and gardens. Perfect for leisurely holidays, many great walks and as a base for exploring the Lake District.

Lesley Hennedy ☎ 01539 622069 www.hartsop-fold.co.uk
£126-£434 Sleeps 5-6. 12 lodges.
Scandinavian lodges on small secluded site. 🚫 🛏 ★★★

● Penrith
Howscales ☎ 01768 898666 (Mrs E Webster) www.howscales.co.uk
£200-£475 Sleeps 2-4. 5 cottages.
Set in open, tranquil countryside. 🚫 🚶(Lazonby) 🛏 ★★★★

☆ Dukes Meadow
☎ 0121 705 4381 (Jane Hounsome)
www.dukesmeadow.co.uk
£150-£450 Sleeps 6. 1 pine lodge.
Quiet, peaceful location. 🚫

Three-bedroomed holiday lodge, recently refurbished to a high standard (including D/W). Good base for the north Lakes and Eden Valley, and within easy reach of the excellent facilities in Penrith (15 mins). Mon-Fri and weekend lets available.
Email: janeandben@hotmail.co.uk

☆ **Nether Cottages**
☎ 07901 825531 (Sandra)
www.nethercottages.co.uk
£295-£995 Sleeps 2-10. 1 cottage, 1 farmhouse.
Country walks from cottage or farmhouse.   ⊛ 👜 ★★★★-★

Nether Cottage (sleeps 4)
Sheriff Park Farmhouse (sleeps 10)

4 & 5-star accommodation.

Discount given if both properties
are booked together.

Cottage has two bedrooms, two bathrooms, dishwasher, washer, fridge/freezer,
spacious lounge, parking for two cars and own garden.

Farmhouse has five bedrooms, three bathrooms (two en-suite), two lounges,
large kitchen with Aga, dining room with garden views. Parking for five cars.
Large gardens with furniture, separate laundry room. Country walks from
farmhouse and cottage — a great place to relax with family and friends.

● Sawrey
LAKE DISTRICT
Broomriggs ☎ 015394 36280 (Mrs J Haddow) www.broomriggs.co.uk
£150-£500 Sleeps 2-6. Cottages & apartments.
Magnificent mountain/lake views, boats.
⊛ 👜 ★★★-★★★★★ See Hawkshead also.

● Silverdale
Dot McGahan ☎ 0114 2338619 dotmcgahan@aol.com
£180-£300 Sleeps 2-5. 1 cottage. Closed Feb
AONB/nature reserve location, lake views.   ⊛ 🚶(Silverdale) RA member.

● Ulverston
LAKE DISTRICT
St Mary's Mount ☎ 01229 583372 (Marion Bobbett)
www.stmarysmount.co.uk
£400-£500 Sleeps 4 + 2. 1 converted stable.
Lovely views. Peaceful location. Large garden.   ⊛ 🚶(Ulverston) 👜

● Wasdale
LAKE DISTRICT

☆ **The Screes Apartment**
☎ 07791 712768 (E O'Hara)
www.wasdalecottage.co.uk
£215-£355 Sleeps 4. 1 apartment.
Stunning views, 1/4 mile from lake.   ⊛

Delightful, comfortable 2 bedroom ground
floor apartment. Former barn, recently
converted to very high standard. Boasting
England's tallest mountain, the area is ideal
for high and low level walking all
year round.

● Watermillock
LAKE DISTRICT

☆ **Land Ends**
☎ 017684 86438 (Barbara Murphy)
www.landends.co.uk
£270-£550 Sleeps 2-5. 4 log cabins.
Peaceful 25 acre grounds, 2 ponds.   👜 ★★★ See B&B also.

For real countrylovers! Peaceful fellside
setting in 25 acres with 2 lakes. Red
squirrels, ducks, moorhens, owls and
fabulous birdlife on your doorstep. Lake
Ullswater only 1.3 miles. Dramatic
scenery and superb walks close by!
Warm and cosy interiors.

● Windermere
LAKE DISTRICT
Waters Edge Villa ☎ 015394 43415 (Mr & Mrs Judson)
www.lakewindermere.net
£230-£940 Sleeps 2-7. 3 apts in lakeland house.
Lake shore location with stunning views.   ⊛ ★★★★

Lake Lodge ☎ 07931 715753 (Mrs Nicola Walker)
www.lakelodge.co.uk
£240-£680 Sleeps 4. 1 pine lodge. Closed Nov-Feb
In a quiet area of 5-star park   ⊛ 🚶(Windermere)

LANCASHIRE

● Chipping
Outlane Head Cottage ☎ 01995 61160 (Mrs J Porter)
www.fellviewchipping.co.uk
£160-£210 Sleeps 2. 1 coach house.
Superb fell views, excellent walking. Woodburner.   ⊛ 👜 ★★★★

☆ **Rakefoot Farm**
☎ 01995 61332 (Mrs Pat Gifford)
www.rakefootfarm.co.uk
£95-£560 Sleeps 2-22. 4 cottages in barn conversion.   Woodburners,
meals, laundry, CH, panoramic views. 👜 ★★-★★★★ See B&B also.

Past winner of North West Tourist Board
Silver Award. Traditional stone barn
conversion. Family farm in the Forest of
Bowland. Most bedrooms en-suite, some
groundfloor. Original features with
comforts of modern living. Gardens,
games room, meals service.

● Clitheroe
Crimpton Cottages ☎ 01200 448278 (Mrs Elsie Miller)
www.crimptoncottages.co.uk
£100-£315 Sleeps 2-4. 3 cottages.
Cottages of character. Forest of Bowland.   👜 ★★★★

● Holcombe
Top o'th' Moor Cottage ☎ 07976 034196 (Michele Richardson)
www.topofthemoorcottage.com
£350 Sleeps 2. 1 cottage.
Snooker room, tennis court, panoramic views.   ⊛ ★★★★

NORTH WEST

GROUPS

CHESHIRE

SANDSTONE TRAIL

Haycroft Farm Camping & Caravan Site (SC) Spurstow, Tarporley
☎ 01829 260389 www.haycroftfarm.co.uk Map 117/554573
nearby [B] [D] See B&B also.

CUMBRIA

LAKE DISTRICT

Great Langdale Campsite (SC) Great Langdale, Ambleside, LA22 9JU
☎ 015394 37668 (The Warden)
www.ntlakescampsites.org.uk Grid ref: 287058
SC £4.50+pn Campsite field (book in advance). nearby [D]

High Wray Basecamp (SC) High Wray, Ambleside, LA22 0JE
☎ 015394 34633 (The Warden)
www.nationaltrust.org.uk/volunteering Grid ref: SD 373995
SC £64-£176 Min 8, max 22. 2 bunkhouse blocks. [D]

Kirkbeck House (SC) Lake Rd, Coniston, LA21 8EW ☎ 01539 730686 (Shona Potter) www.kirkbeckhouse.co.uk Map 96,97/301973
SC £1,200-£2,100 Min 10, max 20. Victorian gentleman's residence.
nearby [B] [D]

☆ **Lakeside House** (BB)
40 Lake Road, Keswick, CA12 5DQ
☎ 017687 72868
www.lakesidehouse.co.uk Map 89,90/266232
BB £22 Min 10, max 48. 1 guesthouse. [B] [D] See B&B also.

Large licensed guesthouse in prime location, close to town centre and lake. 22 bedrooms sleeping up to 48. Excellent drying facilities, spacious lounge, dinners available. There are many walks, of all levels, starting from the house. Group discounts given.

Brathay Exploration Group (SC) Brathay Hall, Ambleside LA22 0HP
☎ 015394 33942 www.brathayexploration.org.uk Map 90/366028
SC £238.76-£557.321 Max 32. 1 lodge. [D]

Low Wray Campsite (SC) Low Wray, Ambleside, LA22 9JA ☎ 015394 32810 (The Warden) www.ntlakescampsites.org.uk Grid ref: 372012
SC £4.50+pn Max 300. Campsite field (book in advance). Closed Nov-Feb
nearby [D]

☆**Tarn Outdoor Centre** (SC)
Tarn, Fell End, Ravenstonedale, CA17 4LN
☎ 015396 20832 (Alison Mells)
www.tarnoutdoor.co.uk
SC £1,260 Min 15, max 24 [D]

A unique and superb barn conversion in a traditional hill farm setting. Spectacular views over the Howgills and Uldale Valley. An idyllic base for walking. Unlimited routes from doorstep. Excellent modern facilities.

☆ **Smallwood House Hotel** (BB)
Compston Rd, Ambleside LA22 9DJ
☎ 015394 32330 (Christine & Anthony Harrison)
www.smallwoodhotel.co.uk
BB £33 Min 10, max 24. [B] [D] ◆◆◆◆ See B&B also.

We pride ourselves on a quality, friendly service in the traditional way.

Dinners and packed lunches . Drying facilities. Group discounts. Winter breaks. Leave your cars in our car park and walk from here.

Please telephone Anthony or Christine Harrison for a full brochure and tariff enq@smallwoodhotel.co.uk

COAST TO COAST WALK

Grasmere Independent Hostel (SC), Broadrayne Farm Grasmere LA22 9RU
☎015394 35055 (Mr Bev Dennison)
www.grasmerehostel.co.uk Grid ref: 336094
Bednight £14.50, SC £275-£350 Min 1, max 24.
nearby [B] [D] ★★★★ See Hostels & SC also.

HOSTELS, BUNKHOUSES & CAMPSITES

CUMBRIA

LAKE DISTRICT

COAST TO COAST WALK

☆ **Grasmere Independent Hostel** (IH)
Broadryne Farm Grasmere LA22 9RU ☎ 015394 35055 (Mr Bev Dennison)
www.grasmerehostel.co.uk Grid ref: 336094
Bednight 14.50 nearby
[B] [D] ★★★★ Hostel See Groups & SC also.

Quiet, clean and friendly. Ensuite bedrooms. Sleeps 24. Beds made up. Superb SC kitchens, dining, drying rooms, laundry, sauna, full C/H, parking. Fantastic walks from door. Individuals to whole hostel group hire welcome. Colour brochure. Hostel is behind farmhouse bev@grasmere-accommodation.co.uk

Catbells Camping Barn (CB) Newlands
☎ 017687 72645 (Mrs Ann Grave) Map 90/243208
Bednight £5.50 Min 1, max 12. [D]

YORKSHIRE DALES

Catholes Farm (B) Sedbergh ☎ 015396 20334 (Mrs Jean Handley)
Grid ref: SD653908
Bednight £7 Closed Dec-Feb [D]

Trans Pennine Trail

Take the Trail

If you're looking for a great way to get fit, de-stress and get closer to nature, try the Trans Pennine Trail. Whether you're a cyclist, walker or horse-rider, it's a trail for you. With around 350 miles of trail, covering Southport, Hornsea, the Peak District, Leeds and Chesterfield, you can easily explore many parts of Yorkshire. Much of the trail is flat so you can take it easy and enjoy the views; take the family or get away from it all, take your bike or just a picnic - it's up to you.

There are leaflets and maps available to tell you more, so get in touch and we'll be happy to help.

Phone us on: 01226 772 574.
www.transpenninetrail.org.uk

A Millennium Commission Lottery Project

Supported by YORKSHIRE FORWARD

NORTH WEST

Commanding superb views over Bassenthwaite Lake and Skiddaw, **Irton House Farm** is a working sheep farm of 246 acres. Our warm welcome invites you to share the peace and beauty of our surroundings. Good walking country - bring your camera to catch the stunning sunsets! We pride ourselves on our extremely high standard in our spacious and comfortable self-catering holiday homes for 2, 4 or 6 people. Ample parking. Games room, Go-karts and Trailer Rides. **For a warm and friendly welcome telephone Joan & Reg Almond on 017687-76380, Irton House Farm, Isel, Cockermouth, Cumbria CA13 9ST.**

Ribble Valley, Lancashire

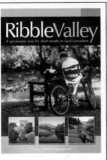

Plan your perfect country escape in the beautiful Ribble Valley, an Area of Outstanding Natural Beauty. For walking routes and a visitor's accommodation guide contact Clitheroe Tourist Information Centre
Tel. 01200 425566 or
E-mail: tourism@ribblevalley.gov.uk

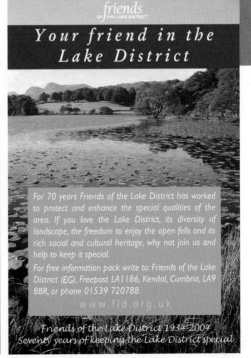

friends OF THE LAKE DISTRICT

Your friend in the Lake District

For 70 years Friends of the Lake District has worked to protect and enhance the special qualities of the area. If you love the Lake District, its diversity of landscape, the freedom to enjoy the open fells and its rich social and cultural heritage, why not join us and help to keep it special.

For free information pack write to: Friends of the Lake District (EG), Freepost LA1186, Kendal, Cumbria, LA9 8BR, or phone 01539 720788.

www.fld.org.uk

Friends of the Lake District 1934-2004
Seventy years of keeping the Lake District special

YORKSHIRE DALES FROM GUNNERSIDE VILLAGE, WEST YORKSHIRE

YORKSHIRE

BRITAINONVIEW.COM

ROBIN HOOD OF WAKEFIELD

Robin Hood of Sherwood, Prince of Robbers. Or so the legend goes. But was he really Robin Hood of Wakefield? Many argue that far from hailing from Nottingham, he was in fact a Yorkshireman who lived in Barnsdale forest that once covered the southern West Riding. The heroic outlaw has certainly left his name all over Yorkshire – Robin Hood's Bay, near Whitby, being the most well known.

But whether this is evidence enough, all agree Robin Hood's last resting place is Kirklees Priory in West Yorkshire. He went there to see the Prioress who was famed for her medicinal skills and she bled him to death in the gatehouse (her reasons remain a mystery). With his last breaths, Robin fired an arrow through the window and asked to be buried where it fell.

Six hundred years later, and 55 metres from the ruined Kirklees gatehouse, the gravestone lies overgrown and surrounded by twisted iron railings erected in Victorian times. The grave and twelfth-century nunnery now form part of the private Kirklees Estate that includes some fascinating fifteenth and eighteenth-century farm buildings. Calderdale Heritage Walks organises a guided tour of the grounds, Outlaws & Nuns, twice a year as part of a summer walks programme, which also includes tours of Ted Hughes' local childhood haunts, and visits the picturesque hilltop village of Heptonstall where the former Poet Laureate's wife, Sylvia Plath, is buried.

> Many argue that far from hailing from Nottingham, Robin Hood was in fact a Yorkshireman who lived in Barnsdale forest that once covered the southern West Riding.

The right to roam's introduction to Yorkshire in May and October last year had a huge impact on walkers in the Yorkshire Dales National Park, increasing open access from 4 to 62 per cent of the park – over 100,000 hectares. And new areas of the Wolds became accessible such as the previously off-limits Scoar Dale and Sylvan Dale, near Millington.

The Wakefield Way, a new 121km/75-mile circular route devised by West Riding Ramblers, was also inaugurated last year. Making use of canal towpaths, disused railway lines and four country parks around the city – Robin Hood of Wakefield would have approved.

Long Distance Paths

Cleveland Way CVL
Coast to Coast Walk.................C2C
Dales Way.................................DLS
Nidderdale Way.......................NID
Pennine Bridleway ....PNB
Pennine Way............................PNN
Teesdale Way...........................TSD
Trans Pennine Trail..................TPT
Yorkshire Wolds Way...............WDS

Public rights of way:
20,808km/2,922 miles

Mapped access land:

236 sq km/91 sq miles (Area 2, Lower North West) 1,344 sq km/519 sq miles (Area 4, Upper North West) 1,928 sq km/744 sq miles (Area 8, East)

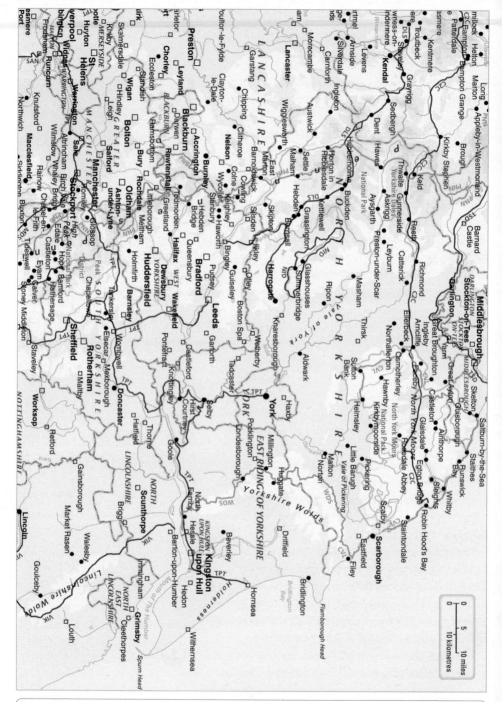

YORKSHIRE
LOCAL RAMBLERS GROUPS

EAST YORKSHIRE & DERWENT
AREA SECRETARY
Mr M Dixon, 8 Horseman Avenue,
Copmanthorpe, York, YO23 3UF
☎ 01904 706850

GROUP SECRETARIES
Beverley Mr J Roach, Hollins,
The Park, Swanland, HU14 3LU
☎ 01482 632117
Driffield Mr J R Jefferson, Delamere,
2 Spellowgate, Driffield, YO25 5BB
☎ 01377 252412
East Yorks Get Your Boots On
Mr Paul Rhodes, 23 Ash Street, York,
YO26 4UR ☎ 07749 840885
www.gybo.org.uk
Howden & Goole Marian Thomas,
46 Boothgate Drive, Howden, Goole,
DN14 7EW ☎ 01430 431766
Hull & Holderness Mrs Sue Ripley,
17 Clifford Avenue, Hull, HU8 0LU
☎ 01482 708026
www.hullramblers.org.uk
Pocklington Mr A F Ashbridge,
4 Burnaby Close, Molescroft, Beverley,
East Yorkshire, HU17 7ET
☎ 01482 861215
www.pocklingtonramblers.org.uk
Ryedale Mike McGrory, 2 Acres Close,
Helmsley, North Yorkshire, YO62 5DS
☎ 01439 770 940
Enquiries: 01482 882499 (Ray Fielden)
www.ryedaleramblers.org.uk
Scarborough & District Mr Dennis
Muir, 6 West Avenue, Scalby,
Scarborough, North Yorks, YO13 0QB
☎ 01723 377222
York Miss V Silberberg, 41 North
Parade, Bootham, York, YO30 7AB
☎ 01904 628134
www.communigate.co.uk/york/
yorkramblers2

NORTH YORKS & SOUTH DURHAM
AREA SECRETARY
Mr D G Lawrenson, Smithy Cottage,
Hunton, Bedale, North Yorkshire,
DL8 1QB ☎ 01677 450422
www.bigwig.net/nysd_ramblers

GROUP SECRETARIES
Barnard Castle Mr T Fenton, Garden
House, Westholme, Winston,
Darlington, Co Durham, DL2 3QL
☎ 01325 730895
www.barnardcastleramblers.org.uk
Cleveland Mr A Patterson, 141 Castle
Road, Redcar, TS10 2NF
☎ 01642 474864

Crook & Weardale Mrs K Berry,
11 Wood Square, Bishop Auckland, Co.
Durham, DL14 6QQ ☎ 01388 608979
http://members.aol.com/crookramblers
Darlington Mr Bryan Spark,
3 Thirlmere Grove, West Auckland,
Bishop Auckland, Co Durham,
DL14 9LW ☎ 01388 834213
www.bigwig.net/darlington.ramblers
Darlington Hills & Dales Jo Bird,
Middle Garth, Stainton, Barnard Castle,
DL12 8RD ☎ 01833 637756
Northallerton Mr M F Kent,
131 Valley Road, Northallerton, North
Yorkshire, DL6 1SN ☎ 01609 777618
http://web.onetel.net.uk/~murraykent
Richmondshire Mrs V Darwin,
4 Sycamore Avenue, Richmond, North
Yorks, DL10 4BN ☎ 01748 822 845

SOUTH YORKSHIRE & NE DERBYS
AREA SECRETARY
See www.syned-ramblers.org.uk or
contact our central office for details

GROUP SECRETARIES
Barnsley & Penistone Mrs C Wood,
25 Cloverlands Drive, Mapplewell,
Barnsley, S75 6EB ☎ 01226 384041
See Area website
Bolsover District Mrs J Lee,
193 Langwith Road, Bolsover,
Chesterfield, S44 6LU ☎ 07817 419250
See Area website
**Chesterfield & North East
Derbyshire** Mr Joe Kellett, 7 Brambling
Court, Chesterfield, S41 0ED
☎ 01246 229803 See Area website
Chesterfield 20s & 30s Gill Stone,
Garth Derwen, 195 Old Road,
Chesterfield, Derbyshire, S40 3QH
See Area website
Dearne Valley Mrs Pauline Gibbons,
6 Ruskin Avenue, Mexborough, South
Yorkshire, S64 0AU See Area website
Doncaster Mrs M Thompson,
31 Broom Hill Drive, Cantley 6,
Doncaster, South Yorkshire, DN4 6QZ
☎ 01302 371093 See Area website
Rotherham Metro District Mrs A
Balding, 2 Calcot Green, Swinton,
Mexbrough, South Yorks, S64 8SY
See Area website
Sheffield Mr Peter Wood,
17 Woodend Drive, Sheffield,
S Yorks, S6 5HB
☎ 0114 234 1217
www.sheffield.ramblers.care4free.net
Sheffield 20s & 30s Ms D Terry,
38 Linaker Road, Sheffield, S6 5DT
See Area website

WEST RIDING
AREA SECRETARY
Gwendoline Goddard, Spring Bank,
Hebden Bridge, West Yorks, HX7 7AA
☎ 01422 842558
www.ramblerswestriding.org.uk

GROUP SECRETARIES
Bradford Mr M J Pitt, Fairbank, Beck
Lane, Bingley, BD16 4DN
☎ 01274 563426
www.ramblerswestriding.org.uk
Calderdale Mrs D F Hall, 11 School
Close, Ripponden, Halifax, Yorks,
HX6 4HP ☎ 01422 823440
www.ramblerswestriding.org.uk
Castleford & Pontefract Mrs J A
Hartley, 2 Moorleigh Close, Kippax,
Leeds, LS25 7PB ☎ 0113 286 6737
www.ramblerswestriding.org.uk
Craven Ms D Lindsay, 15 Sycamore
Croft, Beeston, Leeds, LS11 6BB
☎ 0113 2776110
www.ramblerswestriding.org.uk
Dewsbury Michael Church,
58 Alexandra Crescent, Birkdale Road,
Dewsbury, West Yorkshire, WF13 4HL
☎ 01924 462811
www.ramblerswestriding.org.uk
Harrogate Mrs C Sandercock,
3 Burrell Close, Wetherby, LS22 6YA
☎ 01937 520174
www.willouby.demon.co.uk/
ramblersassociation/
harrogategroup.htm
Huddersfield Mr J M Lieberg,
11 Woodroyd Avenue, Honley,
Huddersfield, West Yorks, HD9 6LG
☎ 01484 662866
www.ramblerswestriding.org.uk
Keighley Mr Jeff Maud, 50 Cliffe Lane
South, Baildon, Bradford, West
Yorkshire, BD17 5LB ☎ 01274 597718
www.ramblerswestriding.org.uk
Leeds Ms J B Morton, 6 Lawns Green,
New Farnley, Leeds, West Yorkshire,
LS12 5RR ☎ 0113 279 0229
www.leedsramblers.org.uk
Leeds & Bradford 20s & 30s
Mr T R Williamson, 91 Valley Road,
Pudsey, LS28 9EU ☎ 0113 2570260
www.takeahike.org.uk
Lower Wharfedale The Revd David
Morling, Lorindell, 61 Layton Lane,
Rawdon, Leeds, LS19 6RA
☎ 0113 250 3488
www.ramblerswestriding.org.uk

YORKSHIRE

LOCAL RAMBLERS GROUPS continued

Ripon Mr A G Clothier,
49 Boroughbridge Road,
Knaresborough, N Yorkshire,
HG5 Ond ☎ 01423 865412
www.ramblerswestriding.org.uk

Wakefield Ms J Douglas, 19 Clifton
Avenue, Stanley, Wakefield, West
Yorkshire, WF3 4HB
☎ 01924 820732
www.ramblerswestriding.org.uk

Wetherby & District
Mrs Pauline Clarke, 7 Raby Walk,
Wetherby, W Yorks, LS22 6SA
☎ 01937 583378
www.ramblerswestriding.org.uk

LOCAL RAMBLERS PUBLICATIONS

PATHS & ROUTES

Airedale Way
by Douglas Cossar, ISBN 0 900613 95 5.
An 80km/50-mile riverside walk from
Leeds to Malham Tarn in the Dales, in 11
sections, 10 of them walkable as circular
walks, with additional walks in Airedale.
£4.50 + £1 p&p from 11 Woodroyd
Avenue, Honley, Holmfirth HD9 6LG.
Cheques to West Riding Area Ramblers'
Association.

Brontë Way
by Marje Wilson, ISBN 1 901185 05 6.
A 69km/43-mile walk from Oakwell Hall,
Birstall to Gawthorpe Hall, Padiham, via
a variety of places linked to the famous
literary family. In 11 sections walkable as
circular walks. £4.50 + £1 p&p as
Airedale Way above; cheques to West
Riding RA.

Chalkland Way
by Ray Wallis (Hull RA) 66km/40-mile
circular walk through the chalk hills of the
Yorkshire Wolds from Pocklington,
including chalk wolds, arable land and
woodland. A few steep hills but not too
strenuous. Colour leaflet (new edition
2003) free + A5 SAE to R Wallis, 75
Ancaster Avenue, Kingston upon Hull
HU5 4QR. Badge available from the
same source.

Dales Way Handbook
edited by West Riding RA. An annually
updated guide to accommodation and
transport along the path between Ilkley
and Windermere. £1.50 + £1 p&p as
Airedale Way above; cheques to West
Riding Area Ramblers' Association.

Danum Trail
A series of walks linking villages and
towns in Doncaster borough, readily
accessible by public transport and creating
a 80km/50-mile walk from Dome Leisure
Park Doncaster to the Glass Park, Kirk
Sandall, taking in the Earth Centre, short
sections of the Trans Pennine Trail,
historic villages and open countryside.
Colour foldout leaflet with map of the
route and notes on places of interest.
£1.30 from 31 Broom Hill Drive,
Doncaster DN4 6QZ. Cheques to
Ramblers' Association Doncaster Group.

Harrogate Dales Way Link
32km/20 miles from Valley Gardens,
Harrogate to Bolton Abbey, linking to the
Dales Way. A5 leaflet, 30p + SAE.
Sew-on badge available on completion,
£1.50 + SAE

Harrogate Ringway
(Harrogate Ramblers). 33.5km/21 miles
circular trail around this spa town, starting
from Pannal via Knaresborough, in easy
stages with public transport connections.
A5 leaflet, 30p + SAE. Sew-on badge
available on completion, £1.50 + SAE
Both from 20 Pannal Ash Grove, Harrogate
HG2 0HZ. Cheques to Harrogate
RA Group.

Kirklees Way
Circular walk around Huddersfield and
Dewsbury. £2.70 + £1 p&p as Airedale
Way above; cheques to West Riding Area
Ramblers' Association.

Knaresborough Round
32km/20 mile circular walk round this
ancient town, in two stages with bus
connections. A5 leaflet, 30p + SAE, as
Harrogate Dales Way above.

Minster Way
by Ray Wallis (Hull RA) An 83km/50-mile
signed walk established in 1980 between
the Minsters of Beverley and York,
crossing the Yorkshire Wolds and Vale of
York. A good variety of countryside, not
too strenuous but with some hills.
Guidebook with maps and colour photos,
dividing the route into 3 sections, £4 +
55p p&p from 75 Ancaster Avenue, Hull
HU5 4QR. Cheques payable to R Wallis.
Badge and accommodation list available
from same source.

Penistone Line Trail
Sheffield to Huddersfield by the Penistone
Line Partnership, supported by South
Yorkshire and North Derbyshire
Ramblers. 95km/60 miles divided into
several sections ranging from 2.5km/1.5
miles to 7.5km/4.75 miles, all between
stations on this attractive railway branch
through the south Pennines, linking
Lincoln and Huddersfield. Route
descriptions, background on the line,
overprinted OS maps. £4.95 + 55p (or
£2.95 + 55p p&p for RA or Partnership

members) from PLP, St Johns Community
Centre, Church Street, Penistone S36 9AR.
Cheques to Penistone Line Partnership.

Ripon Rowel Walk
by Les Taylor. 80km/50 mile circular
route from Ripon Cathedral via Masham,
with 12 circular walks of between 5km/3
miles and 24km/15 miles along the way.
£4.95 + 70p p&p from 49 Boroughbridge
Road, Knaresborough HG5 0ND. Cheques
to The Ripon Rowel. Order Rambles Around
Ripon (see below) at the same time and
get both books for £8 + 70p p&p.

Rotherham Ring Route
by Rotherham Metro Ramblers. An
80km/50-mile circular walk through the
gently rolling landscape around the
boundary of Rotherham borough
including many fine country parks. Pack of
10 leaflets in a plastic wallet plus bus
details and additional useful information
for beginners, £2 + £1 p&p from
Rotherham Visitor Centre, 40 Bridge Gate,
Rotherham S60 1PQ, tel 01709 835904.
Cheques to Rotherham TIC.

Sheffield Country Walk
3rd edition by Sheffield Ramblers and
Sheffield City Council. 87km/54.5 miles
through the countryside round Sheffield
via Eckington, Dronfield, Burbage,
Grenoside and Meadowhall, in ten
sections of around 8km/5 miles each,
linked by public transport, all with
separate colour route cards in an
attractive folder. £3.95 + 55p p&p from
Ramblers' Association Sheffield Group, 33
Durvale Court, Sheffield S17 3PT.
Cheques to Ramblers' Association
Sheffield Group.

Yorkshire Wolds Way
Accommodation Guide
(E Yorks & Derwent Area). 95p + SAE
from Mrs S M Smith, 65 Ormonde Avenue,
Kingston upon Hull HU6 7LT.

NEW **Wakefield Way**
by Douglas Cossar, ISBN 1 901184 74 9
(West Riding Ramblers). Describes a
120km/75-mile loop around the
boundary of Wakefield district in West
Yorkshire, from Anglers Country Park via
Gawthorpe, Catleford, Pontefract and

South Kirkby. Easily walked as 24 shorter walks (5.5km/3.5 miles to 13.5km/8.5 miles), both circular and linear, with public transport connections. £5.99 + p&p as Airedale Way above; cheques to West Riding Area Ramblers' Association.

SHORTER WALKS

Car-Free Countryside Walks accessible from York
by Patsy Pendegrass, ISBN 1 904446 04 03 (East Yorkshire and Derwent Ramblers). 15 walks from stations or bus stops over a wide area within easy reach of York, all 8km/5 miles to 19.5km/12 miles, some with shorter options. £4.99 + 50p p&p from Quacks Books, 7 Grape Lane, York YO1 7HU. Cheques to P M Pendegrass. All profits to Ramblers' Association.

NEW **Dearne Valley Walks**
(Dearne Valley Group) Seven leaflets: Broomhill, Bolton & Wath; Conisbrough to Sprotborough; Dearne Valley Ramble; Elsecar and Wentworth; River Don Walk; Swinton & Wath; Swinton & Rawmarsh. *Available free + SAE from Mrs Pauline Gibbons, 6 Ruskin Avenue, Mexborough, South Yorkshire, S64 0AU.*

East Riding Walks
(East Yorkshire and Derwent Ramblers). Four circular routes of around 14.5km/9 miles each with full description and photo, in a plastic case. £2 from 2

Spellowgate, Driffield YO25 7BB. Cheques to J Jefferson.

Rambles Around Ripon
by Ripon Ramblers 15 varied countryside walks 2km/1.5 miles to 20km/13 miles. £3.60 + 70p p&p from 49 Boroughbridge Road, Knaresborough HG5 0ND. Cheques to Rambles Around Ripon. Order Ripon Rowel Walk (see above) at the same time and get both books for £8 + 70p p&p.

All the following from 11 Woodroyd Avenue, Honley, Holmfirth HD9 6LG. Cheques to West Riding Area Ramblers' Association.
Country Walks in Mirfield, Emley, Thornhill and Denby Dale
(2002) by Douglas Cossar and John Lieberg, ISBN 1 901184 30 7. 17 circular walks of between 6km/3.75 miles and 12km/7.5 miles, with sketch maps, route descriptions, photos and public transport details. £4.75 + £1 p&p.

NEW **The Ramblers' Association Book of Kiddiwalks: Thirty short family rambles in and near West Yorkshire**
70th Jubilee Edition, by West Riding Ramblers, ISBN 0 900613 88 2. Easy walks 1.5km/1 mile to 6.5km/4 miles, devised principally with young families in mind, with lots of interest along the route, including some suitable for pushchairs. The book includes sketch maps, route descriptions, background notes and photos. All walks are accessible

by public transport, with details included. A welcome new edition for this popular guide covering every part of West Yorkshire as well as the southern Yorkshire Dales. £5.99 + £1 p&p.
Ramblers' Bradford Volume 1
by Douglas Cossar, ISBN 1 901184 22 6. 20 circular walks 3km/2 miles to 16km/10 miles, covering the whole of the district with an introduction to a variety of landscapes and a wealth of history, accessible by public transport. £4.95 + £1p&p.
Ramblers' Leeds Volume 1
East of Leeds by Douglas Cossar, ISBN 1 901184 23 4. 25 mostly circular walks, 5.5km/3.5 miles to 18.5km/11.5 miles, accessible by public transport. £4.95 + £1 p&p.
Ramblers' Leeds Volume 2
West of Leeds by Douglas Cossar, ISBN 1 901184 24 2. 24 mainly circular walks, 4km/2.5 miles to 14.5km/9 miles, offering a variety of landscapes and using the extensive footpath network in the area, accessible by public transport. £5.95 + £1 p&p.
Walks in and around Kirklees
12 varied, hand-illustrated walks in Huddersfield/Holmfirth area by Huddersfield Ramblers. £2.40 + £1 p&p.
More Walks in and around Kirklees
15 varied, hand-illustrated walks in Huddersfield/Holmfirth area by Huddersfield Ramblers. £2.40 + £1 p&p.

YORKSHIRE

BED & BREAKFAST

EAST YORKSHIRE & HUMBERSIDE

● Beverley
🚩 I Woodlands, HU17 8BT ☎ 01482 862752 (Sarah King)
www.number-one-bedandbreakfast-beverley.co.uk Map 106,107/029395
BB C ✕ book first £12, 7pm S1 D1 T2 Closed Xmas ⋘(Beverley)
Ⓥ Ⓑ Ⓓ ⊗ 🐾♨🚗! 🕭 ◆◆◆

🚩 5 Hurn View, Norfolk St, HU17 7DP ☎ 01482 880521
www.hurnview.co.uk Map 106,107/025400
BB D ✕ nearby S1 D1 T1 Closed Xmas ⋘(Beverley)
Ⓑ Ⓓ ⊗ 🐾♨🕭 ★★★

● Bridlington
☆ 🚩 **Rosebery House**
I Belle View, Tennyson Avenue, YO15 2ET ☎ 01262 670336 (Helen Gallagher)
helengallagher99@btinternet.com Map 101/186671
BB C ✕ nearby D3 T1 F3 Closed Xmas ⋘(Bridlington)
Ⓑ Ⓓ 🐾♨🕭 ◆◆◆◆ Veggie breakfasts.

A Grade II listed Georgian house with a long garden and sea view. Amenities close by. Ideal for walking and touring. Near Flamborough Head and Bempton Bird Reserve. High standard of comfort and friendliness. All rooms en-suite, CH, TV, tea/coffee facilities. Some parking. Vegetarians/vegans welcome, packed lunches available.

● Goole
TRANS PENNINE TRAIL
The Briarcroft Hotel, 49-51 Clifton Gardens, DN14 6AR ☎ 01405 763024
www.briarcrofthotel.co.uk Map 105,106,112/739241
BB C ✕ nearby S5 D5 T6 F1 Closed Xmas ⋘(Goole Town)
Ⓑ Ⓓ 🐾♨ ◆◆◆

● Huggate
The Wolds Inn, Driffield Road, YO42 1YH ☎ 01377 288217
(John & Jane Leaver) huggate@woldsinn.freeserve.co.uk Map 106/882550
BB C ✕ £9, 6:30-9pm S3 D2 T1 Closed Xmas
Ⓥ Ⓑ 🐾♨ ◆◆◆

● Londesborough (York)
YORKSHIRE WOLDS WAY
Towthorpe Grange, YO43 3LB ☎ 01430 873814 (Mrs P Rowlands)
towthorpegrange@hotmail.com Map 106/869437
BB A ✕ book first £10 D/S2 T/S1 Closed Xmas
Ⓥ Ⓓ ⊗ 🐾♨🚗 ◆◆

● Millington (York)
YORKSHIRE WOLDS WAY
🚩 Laburnum Cottage, YO42 1TX ☎ 01759 303055 (Mrs Maureen Dykes)
roger&maureen@labcott.fslife.co.uk Map 106/830517
BB C ✕ book first £9, 7pm T1 F1 Closed Dec-Feb
Ⓥ Ⓑ Ⓓ ⊗ 🐾♨🚗! 🕭 ◆◆◆

● North Ferriby
TRANS PENNINE TRAIL & YORKSHIRE WOLDS WAY
B&B at 103, 103 Ferriby High Road, HU14 3LA ☎ 01482 633637
(Margaret Simpson) www.bnb103.co.uk Map 106/999260
BB B ✕ nearby S1 D1 T1 F1 Closed Xmas ⋘(Ferriby)
Ⓑ Ⓓ ⊗ 🐾♨🕭 ◆◆◆

NORTH YORKSHIRE

● Ainthorpe (Whitby)
NORTH YORK MOORS
COAST TO COAST WALK
Rowantree Farm, Fryup Rd, YO21 2LE ☎ 01287 660396 (Mrs L Tindall)
krbsatindall@aol.com Map 94/704073
BB B ✕ book first £10 T1 F1 Closed Jan-Feb ⋘(Danby)
Ⓥ Ⓓ ⊗ 🐾♨ ◆◆◆

● Aldwark (York)
☆ 🚩 **Aldwark Manor**
YO61 1UF ☎ 01347 838146
www.marstonhotels.com Map 100/469631
BB D ✕ £35, 7-9:30pm D37 T12 F6
Ⓥ Ⓑ 🐾♨ ★★★★ Wheelchair access.

Incorporating an invigorating mix of old and new styles, Aldwark Manor is a great place to stay, convenient for York walks, the Nidderdale Way and the Castle Howard circular route.

Set in 100 acres of walkable parkland on the picturesque River Ure, the golf course and Reflections Leisure Club facilities are excellent, with indoor pool, spa and body treatments.

Aldwark Manor is a hotel with wonderful contrasts offering maximum comfort, and an award-winning restaurant offering fine dining, complemented by wonderful wines.

Please ask about our exclusive rates for walking parties.

● Askrigg (Leyburn)

YORKSHIRE DALES

Milton House, DL8 3HJ ☎ 01969 650217 (Mrs B Percival)
stay_miltonhouse@btinternet.com Map 98/948910
BB **B/C** ✗ nearby DI TI Closed Xmas 🅱 🅳 ⊛ 🐾 🛁 ♦♦♦♦

🢐🢐◀ Whitfield, Helm, DL8 3JF ☎ 01969 650565 (Mrs Kate Empsall)
www.askrigg-cottages.co.uk Map 98/934916
BB **C** DI TI Closed Xmas 🅱 🅳 ⊛ 🐾 🛁 🗲! 🏇 ♦♦♦♦

🢐🢐◀ Thornsgill House, Moor Rd, DL8 3HH ☎ 01969 650617
(Miss Wendy Turner) www.thornsgill.co.uk Map 98/949912
BB **C** ✗ nearby SI DI TI Closed Xmas
🅱 🅳 ⊛ 🐾 🛁 🚗 🗲 ♦♦♦♦

● Austwick (Settle)

YORKSHIRE DALES

PENNINE WAY

☆ 🢐◀ **Wood View Guest House**
The Green, LA2 8BB ☎ 015242 51190 (Sue & David Dewhirst)
www.woodviewbandb.com Map 98/766685
BB **D** ✗ nearby D4 TI FI
🆅 🅱 🅳 ⊛ 🐾 🛁 🚗 🏇 ♦♦♦♦

One of Austwick's oldest farmhouses (circa 1700), situated on the village green, with open fires and beamed ceilings.
Good walking & cycling in spectacular limestone scenery of the Yorkshire Dales National Park.

● Aysgarth (Leyburn)

YORKSHIRE DALES

☆ 🢐◀ **Stow House Hotel**
Aysgarth Falls, DL8 3SR ☎ 01969 663635
www.stowhouse.co.uk Map 98/014883
BB **D** ✗ book first £19.50, 7:30pm D5 T4 Closed Xmas
🆅 🅱 🅳 🐾 🛁 🗲! 🏇 ♦♦♦♦

Family run former Victorian Vicarage with magnificent views near Aysgarth Falls. Superb walks from the door. En-suite rooms, comfortable lounge and cosy bar. The house overlooks Wensleydale and Bishopdale and stands in 2 acres of garden with tennis and croquet lawns. Excellent food and hospitality.
Email: info@stowhouse.co.uk

● Buckden (Skipton)

YORKSHIRE DALES

DALES WAY & PENNINE WAY

🢐◀ Romany Cottage, BD23 5JA ☎ 01756 760365 (Tim & Gwen Berry)
www.thedalesway.co.uk/romanycottage Map 98/942772
BB **C** ✗ nearby SI DI T2 Closed Xmas 🅳 ⊛ 🐾 🛁 🚗 🏇

West Winds Yorkshire Tearooms, BD23 5JA ☎ 01756 760883
(Lynn Thornborrow) www.westwindsinyorkshire.co.uk Map 98/942772
BB **B** ✗ £8, Before 6pm SI DI TI Closed Jan-Feb 🆅 🅳 ⊛ 🐾 🛁 🗲!

Birks View, BD23 5JA ☎ 01756 760873 (Mrs A Huck) Map 98/943772
BB **B** ✗ nearby DI TI Closed Xmas 🅳 ⊛ 🐾 🛁

● Burnsall (Skipton)

YORKSHIRE DALES & DALES WAY

☆ **Burnsall Manor House Hotel**
BD23 6BW ☎ 01756 720231 (Mr J E Lodge)
www.manorhouseuk.co.uk Map 98/032614
BB **C** ✗ book first £10, 6:30-7:30pm D6 T3 Closed Xmas
🆅 🅱 🅳 🐾 🛁 🗲 🏇 ♦♦♦

A small private hotel on the bank of the River Wharfe, in the Yorkshire Dales National Park, with the Dalesway at the foot of the garden.
Mid-week 4 nights for 3 offer.
Email: joe@manorhouseuk.co.uk

● Castleton (Whitby)

NORTH YORK MOORS

🢐◀ Greystones, 30 High Street, YO21 2DA ☎ 01287 660744
(Mrs Della Wedgwood) thewedgwoods@aol.com Map 94/684079
BB **B** ✗ nearby D3 Closed Xmas ⋙(Castleton Moor)
🅱 🅳 ⊛ 🐾 🛁 🚗 🗲 ♦♦♦ Sauna available.

● Catterick Village (Richmond)

COAST TO COAST WALK

Rose Cottage Guest House, 26 High Street, DL10 7LJ
☎ 01748 811164 (Carol Archer) Map 99/249979
BB **C** ✗ book first £12, 6:30pm SI DI T2 Closed Xmas
🆅 🅱 🐾 🛁 🏇 Ⓜ ♦♦♦

● Cowling (Skipton)

PENNINE WAY

🢐◀ Woodland House, 2 Woodland Street, BD22 0BS ☎ 01535 637886
(Mrs Susan Black) www.woodland-house.co.uk Map 103/973432
BB **B** ✗ nearby DI TI 🅱 🅳 ⊛ 🐾 🛁 🚗 🗲 Ⓜ ♦♦♦♦

● East Marton (Skipton)

PENNINE WAY

Sawley House, BD23 3LP ☎ 01282 843207 (Joan Pilling)
jon@pilling16.fsnet.co.uk Map 103/909515
BB **B** ✗ nearby DI TI Closed Xmas ⋙(Gargrave) 🅳 🐾 🛁 🗲

● Egton Bridge

NORTH YORK MOORS & COAST TO COAST WALK

☆ 🢐◀ **Broom House**
Broom House Lane, YO21 1XD ☎ 01947 895279 (Mr & Mrs D White)
www.egton-bridge.co.uk Map 94/796054
BB **B** ✗ book first (groups only), 7pm SI D/T4 TI FI ⋙(Egton Bridge)
🆅 🅱 🅳 ⊛ 🐾 🛁 🚗 🗲! ♦♦♦♦Ⓢ See SC also.

An excellent place to stay. Comfortable en-suite rooms and an idyllic setting with views of the Esk valley. En-route Coast to Coast & Esk Valley Walks. Local pubs serving good meals within easy walking distance. In house evening meals for large parties.
Email: mw@broom-house.co.uk

YORKSHIRE

Ellerbeck (Northallerton)

CLEVELAND WAY

The Old Mill, The Old Mill House, DL6 2RY ☎ 01609 883466 (Mrs Gillian Shepherd) http://users.firenet.uk.com/ben.shepherd Map 99/433967 BB **C** ✕ nearby D2 T1 Closed Dec V D

Faceby (Middlesbrough)

NORTH YORK MOORS

CLEVELAND WAY & COAST TO COAST WALK

Four Wynds B&B, Whorl Hill, TS9 7BZ ☎ 01642 701315 (Sue Barnfather) Map 93/487033 BB **C** ✕ book first £9, 5-7pm D1 T1 F1 Closed Xmas V B D ◆◆◆

Filey

YORKSHIRE WOLDS WAY & CLEVELAND WAY

The Fairway, 11 Valley Road, Primrose Valley, YO14 9QX ☎ 01723 512174 (Mrs Ruth Milner) Map 101/118784 BB **C** ✕ nearby S1 D1 F1 Closed Xmas (Filey and Hunmanby) B D

Glaisdale (Whitby)

NORTH YORK MOORS

COAST TO COAST WALK

☆ **Red House Farm**

YO21 2PZ ☎ 01947 897242 (Tom or Sandra Spashett) www.redhousefarm.net Map 94/771049 BB **C** ✕ nearby S1 D2 T1 F1 Closed Xmas (Glaisdale) B D See SC also.

Listed Georgian farmhouse featured in Houses of the North Yorkshire Moors. Completely refurbished to the highest standards & retaining all original features. All bedrooms en-suite, with CH, TV & tea making facilities. Wonderful walking country. Coast to Coast Walk 400yds from house.

Glasshouses (Harrogate)

NIDDERDALE WAY

Arran House, 3 Glencoe Terrace, HG3 5DU ☎ 01423 712785 (Lynda Coates) suite4two@hotmail.com Map 99/175647 BB **C** ✕ nearby D1 T1 F1 Closed Xmas-Jan B D

Grassington (Skipton)

YORKSHIRE DALES

DALES WAY

Springroyd House, 8a Station Road, BD23 5NQ ☎ 01756 752473 (Mrs P Robertshaw) www.springroydhouse.co.uk Map 98/001639 BB **C** ✕ nearby D1 T/D2 Closed Xmas B D ◆◆◆

Lythe End, Wood Lane, BD23 5DF ☎ 01756 753196 (Andrew & Cynthia Colley) akandccolley@freeuk.com Map 98/000647 BB **C** ✕ nearby D1 F1 Closed Xmas B D

Scar Lodge, 13 Hardy Grange, BD23 5AJ ☎ 01756 753388 (Valerie Emmerson) www.scarlodge.com Map 98/003639 BB **C** ✕ nearby D2 Closed Xmas B D

Great Ayton

NORTH YORK MOORS

Crossways, 116 Newton Road, TS9 6DL ☎ 01642 724351 (Miss Sue Drennan) susieds@crossways26.fsnet.co.uk Map 93/563115 BB **B** ✕ nearby S2 D1 T1 (Great Ayton) B D ◆◆◆◆

Great Broughton

CLEVELAND WAY & COAST TO COAST WALK

Holme Farm, 12 The Holme, TS9 7HF ☎ 01642 712345 (Don Robinson) www.donathome.demon.co.uk Map 93/546062 BB **B** ✕ nearby D1 T2 D

Gunnerside (Richmond)

YORKSHIRE DALES

COAST TO COAST WALK & PENNINE WAY

Oxnop Hall, DL11 6JJ ☎ 01748 886253 (Mrs A I Porter) Map 98/931973 BB **D** ✕ nearby S1 D2 T2 Closed Nov-Feb V B D ◆◆◆◆

Harrogate

Amadeus Hotel, 117 Franklin Road, HG1 5EN ☎ 01423 505151 (Janet Frankland) www.acartha.com/amadeushotel Map 104/303560 BB **C** ✕ nearby S2 D2 T1 Closed Xmas (Harrogate) B D Ⓜ ◆◆◆◆

Hawes (Wensleydale)

YORKSHIRE DALES

PENNINE WAY

☆ **Dalesview**

East Marry, Gayle, DL8 3RZ ☎ 01969 667397 (Mrs S McGregor) Map 98/871893 BB **B** ✕ nearby D1 T1 Closed Dec-Feb B D

A modern comfortable bungalow situated in the picturesque village of Gayle, ½ mile from the small market town of Hawes. 100m from Pennine Way. Lovely views, quiet location, an ideal centre for touring, cycling and walking in the Yorkshire Dales.

☆ **Thorney Mire Barn**

Appersett, DL8 3LU ☎ 01969 666122 (Jane Hudson) www.thorneymirebarn.co.uk Map 98/853897 BB **D** ✕ £15, 7:30pm D2 T1 V B D ◆◆◆◆◆ Wheelchair access.

Luxurious 5 diamond accommodation in a 250-year-old stone barn 2 miles from Hawes. Generous rooms with quality furnishings. Double rooms have full en-suite bathrooms and the disabled-friendly ground floor twin/double has an en-suite shower room.

☆ **Thorney Mire House**

Appersett, DL8 3LU ☎ 01969 667159 (Mrs S Turner) www.thorneymire.yorks.net Map 98/852899 BB **B/C** ✕ nearby S1 D2 Closed Nov-Feb B D Ⓜ ◆◆◆◆

Recommended in the Which? Good Bed & Breakfast Guide. A warm welcome awaits you at our traditional Dales house, surrounded by woods, fells & meadows, a place to unwind. Excellent walking, ideal for bird watchers. Off road parking.

White Hart Inn, Main Street, DL8 3QL ☎ 01969 667259 (Diane Horner)
www.whiteharthawes.co.uk Map 98/875897
BB **C** ✕ £8.50, 7-8:30pm S1 D4 T2 Closed Xmas
Ⓥ Ⓓ 🐾♿🚗!🛁 ◆◆◆

● I lawnby (Helmsley)

☆ ✸◄ **The Hawnby Hotel**
Hilltop, YO62 5QS ☎ 01439 798202 (Dave & Kathryn Young)
www.hawnbyhotel.co.uk Map 100/542898
BB **D** ✕ book first £12, 7-9pm D6 T3 Closed Xmas
Ⓥ Ⓑ Ⓓ🐾♿🚗! ◆◆◆◆

Situated in an unspoilt village in the heart of the North Yorkshire Moors National Park. An ideal spot for a walking holiday. Group bookings available.

● Hebden (Skipton)

✸◄ Court Croft, Church Lane, BD23 5DX
☎ 01756 753406 (Mrs Philippa Kitching) Map 98/026630
BB **C** ✕ nearby T2
Ⓓ🐾♿🚗🛁 ◆◆◆ Tea garden.

● Helmsley

✸◄ Carlton Grange, YO62 5HH
☎ 01439 770259 (Mrs Ann Kirby) Map 100,94/615879
BB **A** ✕ book first £3 (light supper) D1 Closed Nov-Feb
Ⓥ Ⓓ🐾♿

● Hirst Courtney (Selby)

☆ ✸◄ **Royal Oak Inn**
Main St, YO8 8QT ☎ 01757 270633 (Steven Whitley)
www.royaloakinn-hotel.co.uk Map 105/611245
BB **C** ✕ £6, 6pm onwards S2 D2 T5 F1
Ⓥ Ⓑ🐾♿🚗!Ⓜ ◆◆◆

Traditional family run country pub on the Trans Pennine Trail. 7 miles from Selby with large medieval abbey. 30 minutes drive to the historic city of York. Large camping and caravanning field. Extensive menu with midweek sepcials.

● Horton-in-Ribblesdale (Settle)

The Golden Lion Hotel, BD24 0HB ☎ 01729 860206
(Michael & Tricia Johnson) www.goldenlionhotel.co.uk Map 98/807721
BB **D** ✕ £8, 7-9:30pm D2 T3 Closed Xmas ⋙(Horton-in-Ribblesdal)
Ⓥ Ⓑ🐾♿

● Hubberholme (Skipton)

☆ **Low Raisgill**
BD23 5JQ ☎ 01756 760351
Map 98/905786
BB **C** ✕ nearby D1 T1 Closed Xmas
Ⓥ Ⓑ Ⓓ⊛🐾♿🚗! ◆◆◆◆

Traditional Dales farmhouse built in 1608. Centrally situated in Langstrothdale in the National Park. Ideal base to tour or walk. Very quiet. Spacious en-suite rooms with lovely open views.

● Ingleby Arncliffe (Northallerton)

Longlands Farm, DL6 3JS ☎ 01609 882925
www.coast2coast.co.uk/longlandsfarm Map 93/437013
BB **B** ✕ nearby D1 T1 Ⓥ Ⓑ Ⓓ⊛🐾♿🚗

● Ingleton (Carnforth)

☆ **Ingleborough View Guest House**
Main Street, LA6 3HH ☎ 015242 41523 (Mrs Sue King)
www.ingleboroughview.com Map 98/695732
BB **C** ✕ nearby D3 T2 F1 Closed Xmas
Ⓑ Ⓓ⊛🐾♿🚗! ◆◆◆◆Ⓦ

Ingleborough View is located in a stunning position in the Yorkshire Dales. It is a cheerful, friendly and welcoming guesthouse with comfortable, well-equipped rooms. Great breakfasts with wide choice. Few minutes' walk to village shops, cafes and pubs.

☆ ✸◄ **The Dales Guest House**
Main Street, LA6 3HH ☎ 015242 41401 (Penny & Paul Weaire)
dalesgh@hotmail.com Map 98/692727
BB **B** ✕ book first £12, 6:30pm S1 D3 T1 Closed Xmas
Ⓥ Ⓑ Ⓓ🐾♿🛁 ◆◆◆

A friendly welcome, cosy en-suite rooms with lovely views and excellent home cooking will make your stay one to remember. The perfect base for exploring the Dales, Lakes and the Forest of Bowland. For details of bargain breaks and a brochure call Penny or Paul.

✸◄ Newbutts Farm, High Bentham, LA2 7AN ☎ 015242 41238
(Jean Newhouse) Map 98/696695
BB **B** ✕ book first £13.50, 6-7pm S2 D2 T2 F2
Ⓥ Ⓑ Ⓓ🐾♿🛁 ◆◆◆

The Station Inn, Ribblehead, LA6 3AS ☎ 015242 41274
www.thestationinn.net Map 98/779799
BB **C** ✕ £5, 6:30-8:30pm S1 D3 T1 F1 Closed Xmas ⋙(Ribblehead)
Ⓥ Ⓑ Ⓓ🐾♿🚗!🛁Ⓜ ◆◆◆ See Hostels also.

☆ ⌐ 🖛 **Riverside Lodge**
24 Main Street, LA6 3HJ ☎ 015242 41359 (Andrew Foley)
www.riversideingleton.co.uk Map 98/691727
BB **D** ✕ book first £15 D/T7 Closed Xmas
Ⓥ Ⓑ Ⓓ ⊗ 🐾 ♨ 🖬 ! ◆◆◆◆

Beautiful riverside location, rooms with views of Ingleborough or wooded riverbank. Nearby waterfalls walk, 2 ground floor rooms, all rooms en-suite, large lounge, open fire, T.V. Snooker table, sauna, licensed, conservatory dining room, private car park.

⌐ 🖛 Inglenook Guest House, 20 Main Street, LA6 3HJ ☎ 015242 41270 (Phil & Carolyn Smith) www.inglenookguesthouse.com Map 98/691727
BB **C** ✕ book first £14, 6:30pm D2 T2 F1
Ⓥ Ⓑ Ⓓ ⊗ 🐾 ♨ ◆◆◆◆

● Keld (Richmond)
YORKSHIRE DALES
PENNINE WAY & COAST TO COAST WALK

☆ **Butt House**
DL11 6LJ ☎ 01748 886374 (Ernest & Doreen Whitehead)
www.coasttocoastguides.co.uk/butthouse Map 91/893009
BB **C** ✕ book first £12, 7:30pm D2 T1 F1 Closed Oct-Feb
Ⓥ Ⓑ Ⓓ ⊗ 🐾 ♨ 🐾

Country house Bed and Breakfast on Coast to Coast Walk, Pennine Way, Herriot Way & Swale Way. Also available: the original Coast to Coast Accommodation Guide (2006 edition due out 5th January 2006). Price £3 to cover cost & postage.

● Kettlewell (Skipton)
YORKSHIRE DALES
DALES WAY

Lynburn, BD23 5RF ☎ 01756 760803 (Lorna Thornborrow)
lorna@lthornborrow.fsnet.co.uk Map 98/970720
BB **C** ✕ nearby D1 T1 Closed Xmas Ⓓ 🐾 ♨ ◆◆◆

● Kilburn (York)
NORTH YORK MOORS
CLEVELAND WAY

⌐ 🖛 Church Farm, YO61 4AH ☎ 01347 868318 (Mrs C Thompson)
churchfarmkilburn@yahoo.co.uk Map 100/516796
BB **B** ✕ book first £10, 6-8pm D1 F1 Closed Xmas
Ⓥ Ⓑ Ⓓ ⊗ 🐾 ♨ ♨ 🐾 ◆◆

● Kirkbymoorside (York)
NORTH YORK MOORS

Mount Pleasant, Rudland, Fadmoor, YO62 7JJ ☎ 01751 431579 (Mary Clarke)
www.mountpleasantbedandbreakfast.co.uk Map 100/657917
BB **B** ✕ book first £6.50, 6:30-8pm T1 F1 Closed Xmas
Ⓥ Ⓓ 🐾 ♨ 🐾 ◆◆◆

● Leyburn
The Haven, Market Place, DL8 5BJ ☎ 01969 623814 (Paula & David Burke)
www.havenguesthouse.co.uk Map 99/111904
BB **D** ✕ nearby D4 F2 Closed Xmas Ⓑ ⊗ 🐾 ♨ 🐾 ! ◆◆◆◆

● Malham (Skipton)
YORKSHIRE DALES
PENNINE WAY

☆ ⌐ 🖛 **River House Hotel**
BD23 4DA ☎ 01729 830315
www.riverhousehotel.co.uk Map 98/901628
BB **D** ✕ book first £15, 7-8pm S1 D6 T2 F1
Ⓥ Ⓑ Ⓓ ⊗ 🐾 ♨ ! ◆◆◆◆

A Victorian country house hotel, originally built in 1664, offering superb breakfasts & evening meals. Centrally located in this beautiful Dales village amidst stunning scenery, with the Pennine Way running just past the front door. A warm welcome awaits you on your arrival.

☆ ⌐ 🖛 **Beck Hall Guest House**
BD23 4DJ ☎ 01729 830332 (Simon Maufe)
www.beckhallmalham.com Map 98/898631
BB **C** ✕ £7.50, 6pm S1 D6 T3 F1 Closed Xmas
Ⓥ Ⓑ Ⓓ ⊗ 🐾 ♨ 🖬 ♨ ◆◆◆

A friendly family welcome to all at 18th C. Beck Hall. 3 nights price of 2 Nov-Feb midweek. Located on Pennine Way and Dalesway. Riverside location. Special diets catered for. Meals until 6pm or 2 pubs 100 yards away. Internet PC. Group discounts.

● Malton
YORKSHIRE WOLDS WAY
⌐ 🖛 Suddaby's Crown Hotel, 12 Wheelgate, YO17 7HP ☎ 01653 692038 (R N Suddaby) www.suddabys.co.uk Map 100/788718
BB **B** ✕ nearby D2 T3 F3 Closed Xmas ⋙(Malton) Ⓑ Ⓓ 🐾 ♨

● Masham (Ripon)
Bank Villa Guest House, HG4 4DB ☎ 01765 689605 www.bankvilla.com Map 99/224810 BB **D** ✕ book first £15, 7:30pm D3 T2 F1 Ⓥ Ⓑ Ⓓ ⊗ 🐾 ♨ 🐾 ! ◆◆◆◆

● Northallerton
COAST TO COAST WALK
⌐ 🖛 Alverton Guest House, 26 South Parade, DL7 8SG ☎ 01609 776207 (Mrs M Longley) www.alvertonguesthouse.com Map 99/367934
BB **B** ✕ nearby S3 D2 T1 F1 Closed Xmas ⋙(Northallerton)
Ⓑ Ⓓ ⊗ 🐾 ♨ 🐾 ◆◆◆

● Osmotherley (Northallerton)
NORTH YORK MOORS
CLEVELAND WAY & COAST TO COAST WALK
Stonehaven, Thimbleby, DL6 3PY ☎ 01609 883689 (Margaret Shepherd)
stonehaven1@tiscali.co.uk Map 99/449954
BB **B** ✕ book first £7.50, 6:30pm S1 D1 T1 Closed Xmas
Ⓥ Ⓑ Ⓓ 🐾 ♨ 🐾 Ⓜ ◆◆◆

● Pickering
NORTH YORK MOORS

103 Westgate, YO18 8BB ☎ 01751 472500 (Mrs R Metcalf) Map 100/793840
BB **B** ✕ nearby D2 T1 Closed Xmas ⋙(Nym)

Kirkham Garth, Whitby Road, YO18 7AT ☎ 01751 474931
(Mrs M Rayner) www.kirkhamgarth.co.uk Map 100/800840
BB **C** ✕ nearby SI DI TI FI Closed Xmas ⚍(Pickering)
🅱 🅳 ⊗ ♿ 🐾 ♦♦♦

Swan Cottage, Newton-upon-Rawcliffe, YO18 8QA ☎ 01751 472502
(Marjorie Heaton) Map 100,94/812907
BB **C** ✕ book first £12 DI TI Closed 1-12 ⚍(Newton-upon-Rawcliff)
Ⓥ 🅱 🅳 ⊗ 🐾 🐾 ♿ 🐾 ! 🐾 Ⓜ ♦♦♦♦

Vivers Mill, Mill Lane, YO18 8DJ ☎ 01751 473640
www.viversmill.com Map 100/796835
BB **C** ✕ nearby D5 T2 FI Closed Xmas
🅱 ⊗ ♿ 🐾 ♦♦♦♦

☆ **Bramwood Guest House**
19 Hallgarth, YO18 7AW ☎ 01751 474066 (Marilyn Bamforth)
www.bramwoodguesthouse.co.uk Map 100/800840
BB **C** ✕ book first £17.50, 6:30pm S2 D4 TI FI ⚍(Pickering)
Ⓥ 🅱 🅳 ⊗ 🐾 🐾 ♿ ! Ⓜ ♦♦♦♦Ⓢ See SC also.

Elegant Georgian Grade II listed building in quiet location close to town centre. All rooms are en-suite with TV & generous hospitality trays. Hearty breakfasts. Lounge with log fire & TV. Private parking. Charming walled garden. Steam railway nearby.

● **Preston-under-Scar (Leyburn)**
Hawthorn Cottage, DL8 4AQ ☎ 01969 624492 (Mrs Helen Francis)
www.hawthorn-wensleydale.com Map 99/071910
BB **C** ✕ book first £15, 7pm DI TI
Ⓥ 🅱 🅳 ⊗ 🐾 🐾 ♿ 🐾 ♦♦♦♦

● **Reeth (Richmond)**
YORKSHIRE DALES
COAST TO COAST WALK

Springfield House, Quaker Close , DL11 6UY ☎ 01748 884634
(Mrs Denise Guy) denise@guy426.fsnet.co.uk Map 98/039993
BB **B** ✕ nearby DI TI Closed Xmas
🅱 🅳 ⊗ 🐾 🐾 ♿ ♦♦♦♦ Free refreshments on arrival

The Buck Hotel, DL11 6SW ☎ 01748 884210
www.buckhotel.co.uk Map 98/038993
BB **D** ✕ £9, 6-9pm SI D6 T2 FI
Ⓥ 🅱 🅳 🐾 ♿ ! 🐾 ♦♦♦♦

Walpardoe, Anvil Square, DL11 6TE ☎ 01748 884626 (Ann Bain)
www.coast2coast.co.uk Map 98/038992
BB **A** ✕ nearby SI TI Closed Nov-Feb 🅳 🐾 ♿

Hillary House, 4 Hillary Terrace, DL11 6TG ☎ 01748 884171 (Clive Blodwell)
hillaryreeth@aol.com Map 98/039994
BB **A** ✕ nearby DI TI Closed Xmas
🅳 ⊗ 🐾 ♿

Elder Peak, Arkengarthdale Road, DL11 6QX ☎ 01748 884770
(Mrs M E Peacock) Map 98/036999
BB **B** ✕ nearby DI TI Closed Dec-Feb
🐾 ♿ 🐾 ♦♦♦

● **Richmond**
YORKSHIRE DALES
COAST TO COAST WALK

☆ **Willance House Guest House**
24 Frenchgate, DL10 7AG ☎ 01748 824467 (Thelma Jackson)
www.willancehouse.com Map 92/174012
BB **B** ✕ nearby SI DI TI FI Closed Xmas
🅱 🅳 ⊗ 🐾 🐾 ♿ 🐾 ♦♦♦♦

Willance House, once the home of Robert Willance the first alderman of Richmond, is the oldest in Richmond dating back to 1600. Set on a wide cobbled street just 2 mins walk from the market place. All rooms are en-suite with TV. Comfortable lounge for our guests. Discount for Ramblers bookings.

● **Ripon**
Bishopton Grove House, HG4 2QL ☎ 01765 600888 (Susi Wimpress)
wimpress@bronco.co.uk Map 99/301711
BB **B** ✕ nearby DI TI FI
🅱 🅳 🐾 ♿ 🐾 ♦♦♦

● **Robin Hood's Bay (Whitby)**
NORTH YORK MOORS
CLEVELAND WAY & COAST TO COAST WALK
South View, Sledgates, Fylingthorpe, YO22 4TZ
☎ 01947 880025 (Mrs Reynolds) Map 94/940048
BB **B** ✕ nearby D2 Closed Xmas 🅳 🐾 ♿

The Old School House, Fisherhead, YO22 4ST ☎ 01947 880723
www.old-school-house.co.uk Map 94/952049
BB **A** ✕ £6, 6-8pm D2 F8
Ⓥ 🅳 ⊗ 🐾 ♿ 🐾 ! See Groups also.

● **Rosedale Abbey (Pickering)**
NORTH YORK MOORS

☆ **Sevenford House**
Thorgill, YO18 8SE ☎ 01751 417283 (Mrs Linda Sugars)
www.sevenford.com Map 100,94/724949
BB **C** ✕ nearby DI TI FI Closed Xmas
🅱 🅳 ⊗ 🐾 🐾 ♿ 🐾 ! ♦♦♦Ⓢ

Originally a vicarage, built from the stones of Rosedale Abbey, Sevenford House stands in 4 acres of lovely gardens in the heart of the beautiful Yorkshire Moors National Park.

The tastefully furnished bedrooms offer wonderful views of valley and moorland and overlook Rosedale. There is a relaxing guests' lounge with open fire and shelves full of books. An excellent base for exploring the region with over 500 square miles of open moorland, with ruined abbeys, Roman roads and a steam railway. Non-smoking.
Email: sevenford@aol.com

YORKSHIRE

● Runswick Bay (Saltburn-by-the-Sea)
NORTH YORK MOORS
CLEVELAND WAY

☆ The Firs
26 Hinderwell Lane, TS13 5HR ☎ 01947 840433
www.the-firs.co.uk Map 94/791168
BB **D** ✕ book first £16.50, 6-9pm S1 D4 T2 F4 Closed Dec-Feb
Ⓥ Ⓑ Ⓓ 🐾🛏️🍵 ◆◆◆ See Groups also.

Situated at the top of the bank in the beautiful scenic coastal village of Runswick Bay. An ideal base for moors and coast, on the edge of the North Yorkshire Moors NP, Cleveland Way and Coast to Coast paths, 5 minutes from the beach.

● Saltburn-by-the-Sea (Middlesborough)
CLEVELAND WAY

🚲 The Rose Garden, 20 Hilda Place, TS12 1BP ☎ 01287 622947
(Rose Thacker) www.therosegarden.co.uk Map 94/661212
BB **C** ✕ nearby D/T2 T1 Closed Xmas-Jan ⚐(Saltburn)
Ⓑ Ⓓ⊗ 🐾🛏️ ◆◆◆◆

● Scarborough
CLEVELAND WAY

Brincliffe Edge Private Hotel, 105 Queens Parade, YO12 7HY ☎ 01723 364834
www.brincliffeedgehotel.co.uk Map 101/039895
BB **B** ✕ nearby S2 D5 F3 Closed Nov-Feb ⚐(Scarborough)
Ⓑ Ⓓ 🐾 ◆◆◆

🚲 Russell Hotel, 22 Ryndleside, YO12 6AD ☎ 01723 365453
www.russellhotel.net Map 101/033893
BB **C** ✕ book first £10, 5:45pm S1 D3 T2 F3 ⚐(Scarborough)
Ⓥ Ⓑ Ⓓ 🐾🛏️🚗!🐾 ◆◆◆◆

Brontes Guest House, 135 Columbus Ravine, YO12 7QZ ☎ 01723 362934
www.brontesguesthouse.co.uk Map 101/037892
BB **A** ✕ £5, 7pm S1 D2 T2 F2 Closed Xmas ⚐(Scarborough)
Ⓥ Ⓑ Ⓓ 🐾🛏️!

● Selby
TRANS PENNINE TRAIL

🚲 Hazeldene Guest House, 32-34 Brook Street, YO8 4AR ☎ 01757 704809
hazeldene@selbytourism.co.uk Map 105/610320
BB **D** ✕ book first £6, 6-7pm S4 D4 T5 F2 ⚐(Selby Town)
Ⓥ Ⓑ Ⓓ⊗ 🐾🛏️🍵

● Settle
YORKSHIRE DALES
PENNINE WAY

☆ Whitefriars Country Guest House
Church Street, BD24 9JD ☎ 01729 823753
www.whitefriars-settle.co.uk Map 98/819637
BB **B/C** ✕ nearby S1 D3 T3 F2 Closed Xmas ⚐(Settle)
Ⓑ Ⓓ⊗ 🐾🛏️! ◆◆◆◆

Delightful 17th C. family home, standing in secluded gardens in the heart of the market town of Settle. Ideal for walking, cycling & touring: Yorkshire Dales National Park, The Three Peaks and Settle-Carlisle Railway. Recommended by Which? Good B&B Guide.

Golden Lion Hotel, Duke Street, BD24 9DU ☎ 01729 822203
www.yorkshirenet.co.uk/stayat/goldenlion Map 98/819635
BB **D** ✕ book first £12, 6-10pm D10 T2 F2 ⚐(Settle)
Ⓥ Ⓑ Ⓓ 🐾🛏️🍵 ◆◆◆◆

● Skelton (Saltburn-by-the-Sea)
CLEVELAND WAY

🚲 Westerland's Guest House, 27 East Parade, TS12 2BJ
☎ 01287 650690 (B Bull) Map 94/655185
BB **B** ✕ book first £6, 6:30-7pm S2 D3 F1 Closed Xmas ⚐(Saltburn)
Ⓥ Ⓑ Ⓓ⊗ 🐾🛏️🚗!🐾 ◆◆◆◆

Wharton Arms, 133 High Street, TS12 2DY ☎ 01287 650618 (Pat Cummings)
p.cummings4@ntlworld.com Map 94/658189
BB **B** ✕ nearby S1 D1 T1 F2 Closed Xmas ⚐(Saltburn)
Ⓑ Ⓓ🐾🛏️🚗!🐾 ◆◆

● Skipton
YORKSHIRE DALES

☆ Low Skibeden House
Harrogate Rd, BD23 6AB ☎ 01756 793849 (Mrs Simpson)
www.yorkshirenet.co.uk/accgde/lowskibeden Map 104/012524
BB **C** ✕ nearby D2 T1 F2 Closed Xmas ⚐(Skipton)
Ⓑ Ⓓ⊗ 🐾🛏️ ◆◆◆◆

16th C. farmhouse. Quiet country location set in private grounds. Beautiful views, garden and parking. Offering home from home comforts and little luxuries in guests' lounge. Close to many areas of AONB. 2 mins by car to the market town of Skipton.

● Sleights (Whitby)
NORTH YORK MOORS
COAST TO COAST WALK

☆ Ryedale House
156 Coach Road, YO22 5EQ ☎ 01947 810534 (Pat Beale)
www.ryedalehouse.co.uk Map 94/866070 BB
B/C ✕ nearby S2 D2 Closed Nov-Mar ⚐(Sleights)
Ⓑ ⊗ 🐾🛏️ ◆◆◆◆

Welcoming home at foot of the moors in National Park 4 miles from Whitby. Magnificent scenery, superb walking, picturesque harbours, cliffs, beaches, scenic railways— it's all here!

Beautifully appointed rooms, private facilities, many extras. Guest lounge, extensive breakfast menu served with panoramic views, facing large landscaped gardens. Local inn and fish restaurant just a short walk. Minimum booking 2 nights. Regret no pets/children. B&B £24-28. Exclusive to non-smokers

● Staintondale (Scarborough)
NORTH YORK MOORS
CLEVELAND WAY

Plane Tree Cottage, YO13 0EY
☎ 01723 870796 (Mrs M A Edmondson)   Map 94,101/999983
BB **C** ✕ book first £14, 6:30pm D2 TI Closed Dec-Jan
Ⓥ Ⓑ ⊛ 🐾 ö 🛏 ◆◆◆

● Staithes (Saltburn-by-the-Sea)
NORTH YORK MOORS
CLEVELAND WAY

Brooklyn, Brown's Terrace, TS13 5BG ☎ 01947 841396 (Margaret Heald)
m.heald@tesco.net Map 94/782187
BB **B** ✕ nearby D2 TI Closed Xmas
Ⓓ 🐾 ö 🚗 ! 🛏 ◆◆◆

● Summerbridge (Harrogate)
NIDDERDALE WAY

◤▰ Dalriada, Cabin Lane, Dacre Banks, HG3 4EE
☎ 01423 780512 (Mrs J E Smith)   Map 99/196621
BB **B/C** ✕ nearby SI DI TI Closed Xmas
Ⓑ Ⓓ ⊛ 🐾 ö 🚗 ! 🛏 ◆◆◆

● Sutton Bank (Thirsk)
NORTH YORK MOORS
CLEVELAND WAY

High House Farm, YO7 2HJ
☎ 01845 597557 (Mrs K M Hope)   Map 100/521839
BB **B** ✕ book first £12, 6pm SI DI TI FI Closed Xmas
Ⓥ Ⓓ 🐾 ö 🚗 ! ◆◆◆

Cote Faw, YO7 2EZ ☎ 01845 597363 (Mrs J Jeffray)   Map 100/522829
BB **A** ✕ nearby SI DI TI Closed Xmas   Ⓓ 🐾 ◆◆

● Thwaite (Richmond)
NORTH YORK MOORS
PENNINE WAY

Kearton Country Hotel, DL11 6DR ☎ 01748 886277 (I & J Danton)
www.keartoncountryhotel.co.uk Map 98/892982
BB **C** ✕ book first £6, 6:30-8pm SI D3 T7 F2 Closed Jan
Ⓥ Ⓑ Ⓓ 🐾 ö ◆◆◆

● Whitby
NORTH YORK MOORS
CLEVELAND WAY & COAST TO COAST WALK

◤▰ Prospect Villa, 13 Prospect Hill, YO21 1QE ☎ 01947 603118 (J Gledhill)
janceeprospectvilla@hotmail.com Map 94/894105
BB **C** ✕ nearby S2 DI TI F2 Closed Xmas ∧∧∧(Whitby)
Ⓑ Ⓓ ⊛ 🐾 ö ◆◆◆

Storrbeck Guest House, 9 Crescent Avenue, YO21 3ED ☎ 01947 605468
www.storrbeck.fsnet.co.uk Map 94/894110
BB **B** ✕ nearby S5 D5 Closed Xmas ∧∧∧(Whitby)
Ⓑ Ⓓ ⊛ 🐾 ö ◆◆◆◆Ⓢ

Kimberley House Hotel, 7 Havelock Place, YO21 3ER ☎ 01947 604125
(Julie & Steve Walton) www.kimberleyhousehotel.co.uk Map 94/896112
BB **C** ✕ nearby SI D5 T2 F2 Closed Xmas-Jan ∧∧∧(Whitby)
Ⓥ Ⓑ Ⓓ ⊛ 🐾 ö ◆◆◆◆

Rosewood, 3 Ocean Rd, YO21 3HY ☎ 01947 820534 Map 94/890113
BB **B** ✕ nearby D2 ∧∧∧(Whitby)
Ⓥ Ⓑ Ⓓ ⊛ 🐾 ö ◆◆◆◆Ⓢ

◤▰ Saxonville Hotel, Ladysmith Ave , YO21 3HX
☎ 01947 602631 (Richard Newton)
www.saxonville.co.uk Map 94/891113
BB **D** ✕ £11, 7-8:30pm S4 D8 T9 F2 Closed Dec-Jan ∧∧∧(Whitby)
Ⓥ Ⓑ Ⓓ 🐾 ö ★★★ See Groups also.

Falcon Guesthouse, 79 Falcon Terrace, YO21 1EH ☎ 01947 603507
www.accommodation.uk.net/falconguesthouse.htm Map 94/897106
BB **B** ✕ nearby D/T/F2 ∧∧∧(Whitby) Ⓥ Ⓓ ⊛ ö

● Wigglesworth (Skipton)
YORKSHIRE DALES

◤▰ Cowper Cottage, BD23 4RP ☎ 01729 840598 (Marion Howard)
www.yorkshirenet.co.uk/stayat/cowper Map 103/810569
BB **C** ✕ nearby DI TI Closed Xmas
Ⓑ Ⓓ ⊛ 🐾 ö 🚗 ! ◆◆◆◆

● York
TRANS PENNINE TRAIL

Ambleside Guest House, 62 Bootham Crescent, Bootham, YO30 7AH
☎ 01904 637165 (Keith Hugill)
www.ambleside-gh.co.uk Map 105/598527
BB **D** ✕ nearby D4 TI FI Closed Jan ∧∧∧(York)
Ⓥ Ⓑ ⊛ ö ◆◆◆

☆ ◤▰ **Ascot House**
80 East Parade, YO31 7YH ☎ 01904 426826
www.ascothouseyork.com Map 105/616525
BB **D** ✕ nearby SI D8 T3 F3 Closed Xmas ∧∧∧(York)
Ⓥ Ⓑ 🐾 ö 🛏 ◆◆◆◆Ⓢ

A family run Victorian villa with four-poster and canopy beds. Situated midway between the Dales and Moors and fifteen minutes' walk from the historic York city centre. Delicious English, Continental and vegetarian breakfasts. Residential licence, sauna and private enclosed car park.

◤▰ Coxwold Tearooms, School House, YO61 4AD
☎ 01347 868077 (Mervyn Poulter)
www.coxwoldschoolhouse.co.uk Map 100/534771
BB **B** ✕ nearby D2 TI Closed Jan Ⓥ Ⓓ ⊛ 🐾 ö !

SOUTH YORKSHIRE

● Doncaster
◤▰ 10 Saxton Avenue , DN4 7AX ☎ 01302 535578 (Mrs A Gibbs)
johnrichard.gibbs@virgin.net Map 111/602020
BB **C** ✕ book first £10, 7:30pm S2 D2 T2 Closed Xmas ∧∧∧(Doncaster)
Ⓥ Ⓑ Ⓓ ⊛ 🐾 ö 🚗 ! Ⓜ

● Elsecar (Barnsley)
TRANS PENNINE TRAIL

Old Bank House, 85 Fitzwilliam St, S74 8EZ
☎ 01226 747960 (Ron Foster)
www.webco.co.uk/obh Map 110,111/384999
BB **B** ✕ nearby TI FI ∧∧∧(Elsecar) ö ! 🛏 ◆◆◆

YORKSHIRE

● Tankersley (Barnsley)
TRANS PENNINE TRAIL

☆ ▰◀ Tankersley Manor
S75 3DQ ☎ 01226 744700
www.marstonhotels.com Map 110,111/341993
BB **D** ✕ £29.50, 7-9:30pm S2 T22 F75
Ⓥ Ⓑ 🐾🛁 ★★★★ Wheelchair access.

Backing onto the accessible Trans Pennine Trail, Tankersley Manor sensitively incorporates a 17th-century building with a modern hotel with many original features retained.

Relax and enjoy a meal in the Manor Restaurant or the The Onward Arms, Tankersley Manor's own traditional pub, complete with beams and roaring fires.

The Reflections Leisure Club offers a heated indoor swimming pool, gym, steam, sauna and spa offering body treatments.

Take the time to explore the delights of South Yorkshire and its picturesque moorland scenery.

Please ask about our exclusive rates for walking parties.

WEST YORKSHIRE

● Greetland (Halifax)
Crawstone Knowl Farm, Rochdale Road, Upper Greetland, HX4 8PX
☎ 01422 370470 (Mrs Sylvia Shackleton) Map 104/081213
BB **B** ✕ nearby S1 D1 T1 F1 Closed Xmas ⋙(Sowerby Bridge)
Ⓑ Ⓓ ⊗ 🐾🛁🚗 ! 🏠 ◆◆◆

● Guiseley (Leeds)
DALES WAY

▰◀ Lyndhurst, Oxford Road, LS20 9AB ☎ 01943 879985
(Mrs Alison Button) www.guiseley.co.uk/lyndhurst Map 104/190421
BB **C** ✕ nearby D1 T1 ⋙(Guiseley) Ⓥ Ⓑ Ⓓ 🛁 Ⓜ ◆◆◆

● Haworth
PENNINE WAY

▰◀ Apothecary Guest House, 86 Main Street, BD22 8DP ☎ 01535 643642
(Mr N J Sisley) http://theapothecaryguesthouse.co.uk Map 104/030372
BB **B** ✕ nearby S1 D3 T2 F1 ⋙(Haworth) Ⓑ Ⓓ ⊗ 🐾🛁 ◆◆◆

Rosebud Cottage Guest House, 1 Belle Isle Rd, BD22 8QQ ☎ 01535 640321
(Miss Caroline Starkey) www.rosebudcottage.co.uk Map 104/034370
BB **D** ✕ book first £15, 5:30-7pm S1 D2 T1 F1 ⋙(Haworth)
Ⓥ Ⓑ Ⓓ ⊗ 🐾🛁🚗 ◆◆◆◆

▰◀ Aitches Guest House, 11 West Lane, BD22 8DU ☎ 01535 642501
(David Evans) www.aitches.co.uk Map 104/030372
BB **B** ✕ book first £15, 7pm S1 D3 T1 F1 ⋙(Haworth)
Ⓥ Ⓑ Ⓓ 🐾🛁🚗 ! 🏠 ◆◆◆◆

● Hebden Bridge
PENNINE WAY & PENNINE BRIDLEWAY

▰◀ Myrtle Grove, Old Lees Road, HX7 8HL ☎ 01422 846078
(Mrs M J Audsley) www.myrtlegrove.btinternet.co.uk Map 103/994278
BB **B** ✕ book first D1 F1 ⋙(Hebden Bridge)
Ⓥ Ⓑ Ⓓ ⊗ 🐾🛁🚗 ! 🏠 Ⓜ ◆◆◆◆
See SC also. Vegetarian/vegan food only.

▰◀ Mytholm House, Mytholm Bank, HX7 6DL
☎ 01422 847493 (Brenda & Jim Botten)
www.mytholmhouse.co.uk Map 103/983274
BB **C** ✕ book first £15, To suit. S1 D/T2 Closed Xmas ⋙(Hebden Bridge)
Ⓥ Ⓑ Ⓓ ⊗ 🐾🛁🚗 Ⓜ ◆◆◆◆Ⓢ

● Holmfirth (Huddersfield)
▰◀ Uppergate Farm, Hepworth, HD9 1TG
☎ 01484 681369 (Mrs Alison Booth)
www.uppergatefarm.co.uk Map 110/162068
BB **C** ✕ book first £10, 7-9pm T2 F1 Closed Xmas
Ⓥ Ⓑ Ⓓ ⊗ 🐾🛁🚗 ! ◆◆◆◆

● Marsden (Huddersfield)
PENNINE WAY

Pear Tree Cottage, 18 Grange Avenue, HD7 6AQ
☎ 01484 847518 (John & Heulwen Goodall)
http://mysite.wanadoo-members.co.uk/pear_tree_cottage Map 110/051120
BB **B** ✕ book first £ S1 D/T1 ⋙(Marsden)
Ⓥ Ⓓ ⊗ 🐾🛁 ! 🏠

● Meltham (Holmfirth)

☆ Durker Roods Hotel
Bishopsway, HD9 4JA ☎ 01484 851413
www.durkerroodshotel.co.uk Map 110/104105
BB **D** ✕ £10, 6-9:30pm S2 D18 T5 F5 Closed Xmas
Ⓥ Ⓑ Ⓓ 🐾🛁 ! 🏠 ★★★

An imposing manor house set in the foothills of the Peak District National Park. In the heart of 'Last of the Summer Wine' country, but within easy reach of the major motorway networks.

30 en-suite rooms. Welcoming bar with traditional bar meals. Elegant a la carte restaurant serving a mixture of British and Mediterranean cuisine. Guided walks can be arranged.

Stanbury (Keighley)
PENNINE WAY

☆ ◄ **Ponden House**
BD22 0HR ☎ 01535 644154 (Mrs Taylor)
www.pondenhouse.co.uk Map 103/992371
DD **D/D** ✗ book first £14.50, 7pm DI TI FI
Ⓥ Ⓑ Ⓓ 🐾🛏🏠Ⓜ ◆◆◆◆

Brontë Country.
Relax in a tranquil historic setting.
Enjoy panoramic views over reservoir and
moors, log fires, imaginative home cooking and
warm hospitality.
Call Brenda Taylor for a brochure.

Todmorden
PENNINE WAY

◄ Highstones Guest House, Rochdale Road, Walsden, OL14 6TY
☎ 01706 816534 (Heather Pegg) Map 103/939208
BB **B** ✗ book first £10, 7-7:30pm S1 D2 Closed Xmas ᴀᴀᴀ(Walsden)
Ⓥ Ⓑ Ⓓ ☺ 🐾🏠 ◆◆◆

Cross Farm, Mankinholes, OL14 6HB
☎ 01706 813481 (Lesley Parkinson) Map 103/960239
BB **B** ✗ nearby D/S2 T/S2 FI Closed Xmas ᴀᴀᴀ(Todmorden)
Ⓑ Ⓓ ☺ 🐾🛏🚶! ◆◆◆◆

SELF-CATERING

EAST YORKSHIRE

Huggate
English Village Cottage ☎ 07709 253618 (John Scrivens)
www.englishvillagecottage.co.uk
£416-£700 Sleeps 5. 1 property.
Quiet location. Wold's Way 5 minutes. ☺🏠

Wold Newton
Mrs Ann Gee ☎ 01262 470609
£225-£375 Sleeps 4-5. 1 cottage.
Comfortable warm 17th century cottage. Short breaks. 🏠 ★★★★

NORTH YORKSHIRE

Askrigg
YORKSHIRE DALES

Elm Hill Cottages ☎ 01969 624252 (Peter & Liz Haythornthwaite)
www.elmhillholidaycottages.co.uk
£185-£450 Sleeps 4-6. 2 cottages.
High quality, central heating, private parking. ☺ ★★★

Aysgarth Falls
YORKSHIRE DALES

☆ **Meadowcroft**
☎ 01792 280068 (M C Mason)
www.meadowcroftcottage.co.uk
£180-£336 Sleeps 5. 1 cottage.
Wensleydale, unspoiled village in National Park. ☺🏠 ★★★★

Wensleydale. Unspoilt village with pub
and shop. Modern comfortable
conversion of large traditional Dales
barn in heart of National Park. Network
of footpaths directly from cottage – a
walker's pardise. Lovely views. Secure
off-street parking and private paddock.

Ebberston
NORTH YORK MOORS

Cliff House Cottage Holidays ☎ 01723 859440 (Simon Morris)
www.cliffhouse-cottageholidays.co.uk
£225-£945 Sleeps 2-6. 6 cottages, 2 apts.
Indoor heated swimming pool. ★★★★

Egton Bridge
NORTH YORK MOORS

☆ **Broom House Cottages**
☎ 01947 895279 (M White)
www.egton-bridge.co.uk
£220-£595 Sleeps 2-4. 3 cottages. Riverside location, private garden.
Local inns. ᴀᴀᴀ(Egton Bridge) ☺ ★★★★ See B&B also.

Broom Cottage and Riverside Cottage, Egton
Bridge. North Yorkshire Moors National Park.
4-star cosy cottages well equipped to a high
standard. Quiet village setting with superb
views. For a virtual tour visit our website. For
further details and a brochure please phone or
Email: mw@broom-house.co.uk

Glaisdale
NORTH YORK MOORS

Red House Farm ☎ 01947 897242 (T J Spashett)
www.redhousefarm.net
£200-£567 Sleeps 2-4. 2 cottages, 1 studio flat.
Award winning, listed barn conversions. ᴀᴀᴀ(Glaisdale) 🏠 See B&B also.

Hawes
YORKSHIRE DALES

Mrs Metcalfe ☎ 01609 881302
info@adventuretoys.co.uk
£120-£300 Sleeps 4. 1 cottage. Cosy, open fire, fishing, short breaks. 🏠

Steve Birkin ☎ 01959 523071
sbirkin@tinyworld.co.uk
£130-£280 Sleeps 6. 1 cottage.
Idyllic. Walking biking. Secure storage. Telephone ☺🏠

Kirkbymoorside
NORTH YORK MOORS

Rose Cottage ☎ 01751 417588 (Mrs A M Wilson)
£150-£210 Sleeps 3. 1 cottage. Good walking country, in National Park. 🏠

YORKSHIRE

● Lealholm

NORTH YORK MOORS

Rachel Woolley ☎ 07889 199445
rachelsjewels@aol.com
£200-£300 Sleeps 4. 1 cottage.
Fully modernised, patio area. Stunning views. ∧∧(Lealholm) 🏠

● Leyburn

YORKSHIRE DALES

☆ **Throstlenest Cottages**
☎ 01969 623694 (Tricia Smith)
www.throstlenestcottages.co.uk
£200-£435 Sleeps 1-6. 6 cottages.   Closed Jan
Glorious view, rural, town half mile. ∧∧(Leyburn) ★★★ RA member

Six cosy, comfortable, well-equipped cottages converted from stone barns. All have a glorious panoramic view over Wensleydale and the high fells of Coverdale. Rural, yet town centre only half a mile. Sorry – no pets.

● Pateley Bridge

YORKSHIRE DALES

The Laundry ☎ 01423 711493 (Sarah Downs)
gms66@btopenworld.com
£125 Sleeps 2. 1 flat.   On Nidderdale Way. Walk to pub. ⊗ 🏠

● Pickering

NORTH YORK MOORS

☆ **Keld Head Farm Cottages**
☎ 01751 473974 (Penny & Julian Fearn)
www.keldheadcottages.com
£180-£998 Sleeps 2-8 + cot. 9 cottages.   Off peak discounts, couples, senior citizens. ⊗ ★★★★ See Groups also. Access category 3.

In open countryside on the edge of Pickering and the York Moors a picturesque group of stone cottages with beamed ceilings, stone fireplaces. Furnished with emphasis on comfort, some rooms with four-poster beds. Large gardens with garden house, play and barbecue area.

Let's Holiday ☎ 01751 475396 (John Wicks)
www.letsholiday.com
£270-£755 Sleeps 2-6. 1 cottage, 2 apts.
Indoor heated pool, jacuzzi and sauna ⊗ 🏠 ★★★★

Marilyn Bamforth ☎ 01751 473446 www.bramwoodguesthouse.co.uk
£195-£450 Sleeps 2-4. 2 cottages.
Tastefully converted stables, Grade II listed. ∧∧(Pickering)
⊗ ★★★★ RA member. See B&B also.

Wayside ☎ 07931 536209 (Mr & Mrs Honcharenko)
www.wayside-cottage.org.uk
£170-£380 Sleeps 4. 1 cottage.
Comfortable, well equipped, stone built cottage. ⊗ ★★★

☆ **Hungate Cottages**
☎ 07957 166950 (Giles Redman)
www.hungatecottages.co.uk
£400-£1,500 Sleeps 4-12. 11 cottages.
Free logs supplied. ∧∧(Pickering)

Luxury highly individual holiday cottages which have the unique appeal of being a short walk from the town centre, whilst retaining the tranquility and peacefulness of the countryside.
Easy access to the North Yorkshire Moors, York, Castle Howard, steam railway and the beautiful port towns of Whitby and Scarborough.
Please visit our website for further details.

Chestnut & Coronation Cottages ☎ 01653 698251 (David and Jane Beeley)
www.forgevalleycottages.co.uk
£195-£495 Sleeps 2-8. 2 cottages.
Please call for full colour brochure. ⊗ ∧∧(Matton) 🏠 ★★★★

● Richmond

YORKSHIRE DALES

Chetwynd Holiday Cottage ☎ 0131 449 7435 (Richard & Maureen Porter)
http://reeth-holiday-cottages.pwp.blueyonder.co.uk
£240 Sleeps 5. 1 cottage.
Three bedrooms (one ensuite), spacious, well-equipped. ⊗ 🏠

● Robin Hood's Bay

NORTH YORK MOORS

Lingers Hill Farm ☎ 01947 880608 (Mrs F Harland)
Grid Ref: NZ 94634 05241
£190-£340 Sleeps 2-4. 1 cottage. Cosy character cottage. 🏠 ★★★

Brudenell and Cranford Cottages ☎ 01947 840181 (Trevor & Tracey Robinson)
www.coast-country.info
£240-£380 Sleeps 2-4. 2 cottages.
Open fires, garden, cosy and characterful. ⊗ See Staithes also.

● Scarborough

NORTH YORK MOORS

☆ **Wrea Head View**
☎ 01484 659946 (Anne Carlton)
£240-£320 Sleeps 4.
1 bungalow. Closed Oct-Mar
Central heating and double glazing ⊗

Spacious 2 bed bungalows, rural aspect. Central for walking in National Park and coastal paths. Many local attractions. Large conservatory and garden with table and seating giving extensive views to castle and sea. Parking in drive for 2 cars. Brochure.

● Settle
YORKSHIRE DALES

Selside Farm ☎ 01729 860367 (Mrs S E Lambert)
www.cottageguide.co.uk/selsidefarm
£260-£425 Sleeps 2-6. I cottage, I barn conversion.
Centre Three Peaks. Selside, Horton-in-Ribblesdale. 🛁 ★★★★

● Skipton
YORKSHIRE DALES

Bankfoot Farm ☎ 07753 747912 (Peter Smith) www.bankfootsutton.co.uk
£391-£624 Sleeps 4-6. I cottage.
Well equipped farmhouse with amazing views. ⊛ 🛁 ★★★★

● Staithes
NORTH YORK MOORS

David Purdy ☎ 01751 431452
£230-£360 Sleeps 4. I cottage.
Coast, moors. On Cleveland Way. Harbourside 🛁 ★★

The Moorings ☎ 01947 840181 (Trevor & Tracey Robinson)
www.coast-country.info £375-£675 Sleeps 2-7. I cottage.
Stunning sea views, superb detached cottage. ⊛ See Robin Hood's Bay also.

● Whitby
NORTH YORK MOORS

Swallow Cottages ☎ 01947 603790 (Jill & Brian McNeil)
www.swallowcottages.co.uk
£140-£520 Sleeps 2-7. 4 cottages. Supervised by owners. ᴧᴧ(Whitby)
🛁 ★★★★

Grange Farm ☎ 01947 881080 (Denise Hooning) www.grangefarm.net
£725-£1,595 Sleeps 14. I farmhouse.
Excellent base to explore coast & moors. ⊛ ★★★★

☆ Aislaby Lodge Cottages
☎ 01947 811822 (Mrs S Riddolls)
www.aislabylodgecottages.co.uk
£200-£650 Sleeps 2-25 + 3 cots. 5 farmhouse cottages. Stunning views,
quiet location. Sleeps 25. ᴧᴧ(Ruswarp) 🛁 ★★★-★★★★

Traditional stone cottages with stunning views over Esk Valley. 4 miles from Whitby and coastal villages. Ideal Base for North Yorkshire Moors and coast. Excellent facilities, including laundry and drying room. Quiet location, ample parking.

The Crows Nest ☎ 01642 492144 (Mr E Tayler)
www.crowsnestwhitby.co.uk £145-£600 Sleeps 4-11. I house, 2 apartments.
Spacious five-bedroom house. Apartments. Panoramic views.
ᴧᴧ(Whitby) ⊛ 🛁 ★★★

WEST YORKSHIRE

● Hebden Bridge
Myrtle Grove ☎ 01422 846078 (Mr J A Holcroft)
www.myrtlegrove.btinternet.co.uk
£230-£410 Sleeps 4. I cottage. Secluded scenic historic stone weavers
cottage. ᴧᴧ(Hebden Bridge) ⊛ 🛁 ★★★ RA member. See B&B also.

Robin Hood Cottage ☎ 07977 459913 (Liz Woznicki)
www.robinhoodcottage.co.uk £150-£240 Sleeps 3. I cottage.
Cosy beams, real fire, weekends available. ⊛

GROUPS

NORTH YORKSHIRE
YORKSHIRE DALES

The Confluence Centre (SC/BB) Northcote, Kilnsey, Skipton, BD23 5PT
◻ 01756 753525 (Tim Illingworth) www.the.confluencecentre.co.uk
SC/BB £14+ Max 18. ✗ 🐾 D ⊛ ! ◓

NORTH YORK MOORS

The Firs (BB) 26 Hinderwell Lane, Runswick Bay, Whitby TS13 5HR
☎ 01947 840433 (Mandy Shackleton)
www.the-firs.co.uk Map 94/791168
BB £30 Min 2, max 24. Closed Nov-Feb
✗ 🐾 B D ◆◆◆◆ See B&B also

Keld Head Farm Cottages (SC) Pickering
☎ 01751 473974 (Penny & Julian Fearn) www.keldheadcottages.com
SC £180-£998 Min 2, max 44. 9 cottages
✗nearby 🐾 D B ★★★★ See SC also

The Old School House (SC/BB) Fisherhead, Robin Hood's Bay, YO22 4ST
☎ 01947 880723 www.old-school-house.co.uk Map 94/953049
BB £16, FB £22.50, SC £235pn Max 42. Field study centre.
✗ 🐾 D ⊛ ! ◓ See B&B also

Saxonville Hotel (BB) Ladysmith Ave, Whitby, YO21 3HX ☎ 01947 602631
www.saxonville.co.uk Map 94/892114
DBB £55.50 Min 20, max 42. Closed Dec-Jan, July-Aug ᴧᴧ(Whitby)
✗ 🐾 B D ⊛ ★★★⑤ See B&B also

CLEVELAND WAY & COAST TO COAST WALK

Whitby Backpackers At Harbour Grange (SC/IH/B)
Spital Bridge, Whitby YO22 4EF ☎ 01947 600817 (Birgitta)
www.whitbybackpackers.co.uk Map 94/901104
SC £200pn Max 24. ᴧᴧ(Whitby) ✗nearby 🐾 D ⊛ See Hostels also

HOSTELS, BUNKHOUSES & CAMPSITES

NORTH YORKSHIRE
YORKSHIRE DALES

Low Mill Outdoor Centre (BHB) Askrigg, Leyburn, DL8 3HZ ☎ 01969 650432
www.lowmill.com Grid ref: 907860 Bednight £8 ⊛

DALES WAY & PENNINE WAY

The Station Inn (B), Ribblehead, Ingleton ☎ 015242 41274
www.thestationinn.net Map 98/764792
Bednight £8.50 ᴧᴧ(Ribblehead) ✗ 🐾 D ◆◆◆ See B&B also

Skirfare Bridge Dales Barn (IH/BHB) Kilnsey ☎ 01756 761028 (Mrs J L
Foster) www.skirfaredalesbarn.co.uk Map 98/971689
Bednight £10 ✗nearby D ⊛

CLEVELAND WAY & COAST TO COAST WALK

Whitby Backpackers At Harbour Grange (IH) Spital Bridge, Whitby YO22 4EF
☎ 01947 600817 www.whitbybackpackers.co.uk Map 94/901104
Bednight £10 ✗nearby ᴧᴧ(Whitby) 🐾 ⊛ D See Groups also

SOUTH YORKSHIRE
TRANS PENNINE TRAIL

Greensprings Touring Park (C) Rockley Abbey Farm, Rockley Lane, Worsbrough,
Barnsley S75 3DS ☎ 01226 288298 (Mr R Hodgson) Map 110/330020
Camping £4.50 Closed Nov-Mar ✗nearby

YORKSHIRE

HEATHER COVERED MOORLAND ALONG THE CLEVELAND WAY

NORTH EAST

As if some of Britain's most beautiful coastline, dramatic uplands and spectacular moors were not already enough to tempt twitchy-footed ramblers to the region, the Forestry Commission dedicated all its land in the North East as open access land following the arrival of the right to roam last May. Walkers now have free rein to explore the famous forests at Hamsterley, Wark and Kielder – Europe's largest man-made woodland and home to red squirrels, deer and rare birds.

THE ALNWICK GARDEN

EUROPE'S LARGEST TREEHOUSE AT ALNWICK

Another record is held at nearby Alnwick, where the Alnwick Garden has finished building Europe's largest treehouse. Sitting 18 metres up in a copse of mature lime trees, the structure is more of a fantasy village than jerry-built child's den. But children will love exploring suspended walkways through the woodland canopy (also fully accessible by wheelchair) and the fantastic-sized adventure playground being developed below.

The treehouse is the latest in a massive re-development of Alnwick Castle's 12-acre walled garden, but the eleventh-century turreted castle still maintains the ancient tradition of Shrovetide Football.

> The Forestry Commission dedicated all its land in the North East as open access land following the arrival of the right to roam last May

Played between teams of up to 150 people, the ball was originally thrown from the castle's barbican and kicked through the town's streets into the pastures beyond, where a mass scramble ensued to take home the ball, which usually involved a swim across the River Aln. Since 1825, the ball has been taken to the field in a procession led by the Duke of Northumberland's piper. Similar events are held each Shrove Tuesday in Chester-le-Street and Sedgefield.

Elsewhere, the South Tyne Trail has now completed new waymarks and extensions that take the route 36.5km/23-miles from the Tyne's source near Garigill to Haltwhistle by Hadrian's Wall. And an extension to the Pennine Bridleway has been approved that will see it reach Byrness in Northumberland.

Long Distance Paths

Cleveland Way CVL

Hadrian's Wall Path ....HWP

Pennine Way..............................PNN

South Tyne Trail ....STY

St Cuthbert's Way ....STC

Teesdale Way..............................TSD

Public rights of way:

9,156km/5,686 miles

Mapped access land:

347 sq km/134 sq miles
(Area 4, Upper North West)
1,422 sq km/549 sq miles
(Area 5, North East)

New Year's Day   Sunday 1

Must visit the North York Moors this year !

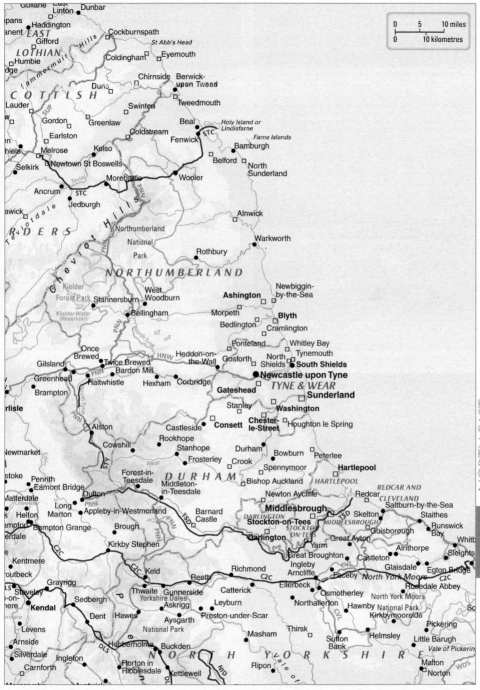

NORTH EAST
LOCAL RAMBLERS GROUPS

NORTHUMBRIA

AREA SECRETARY
Mrs J P Taylor, 2 The Poplars, Gosforth, Newcastle Upon Tyne, NE3 4AE
☎ 0191 285 3482)
http://northern.ra-area.org.uk

GROUP SECRETARIES
Alnwick Mr C Whitney, The Haven, Boulmer, Alnwick, Northumberland, NE66 3BW ☎ 01665 577420
See Area website
Berwick Mr John Bamford, 112 Main Street, Spittal, Berwick On Tweed, TD15 1RD ☎ 01289 302559
See Area website
Chester le Street Mr Brian Stout, 37 Kirkstone Drive, Carrville, Durham City, DH1 1AH ☎ 0191 3864089
See Area website
Derwentside Mrs S M Jeffreys, 7 Ferndene Court, Moor Road South, Newcastle Upon Tyne, Tyne & Wear, NE3 1NN ☎ 0191 285 8442
See Area website
Durham City Mr C Ludman, 5 Church Street, Durham, DH1 3DG
☎ 0191 386 6886 See Area website
Gateshead Mrs Hilary Clark, 15 Shibdon Park View, Blaydon, Tyne & Wear, NE21 5HA
☎ 0191 4143643
See Area website
Hexham Mrs R Blaylock, 10 Quatre Bras, Hexham, Northumberland, NE46 3JY ☎ 01434 604639
See Area website

Morpeth Miss M Siggens, 17 Kingswell, Carlisle Lea, Morpeth, Northumberland, NE61 2TY
☎ 01670 518031
See Area website
Northumbria Family Walking Mrs E Smith, 18 Bath Terrace, Newcastle Upon Tyne, NE3 1UH ☎ 0191 2132102
See Area website
Northumbria Short Circuits Mrs Mary Moore, 2 Kingsway Avenue, Gosforth, Newcastle Upon Tyne, NE3 2HS ☎ 0191 285 6890
See Area website
Northumbria Walking Group Ms G Atkinson, 39 Shearwater, Whitburn, Sunderland, SR6 7SF
See Area website
Ponteland Mr Colin Braithwaite, 105 Western Way, Ponteland, Newcastle Upon Tyne, NE20 9LY
☎ 01661 822929 See Area website
Sunderland Mrs P Jackson, 73 Houghton Road, Hetton-Le-Hole, Houghton Le Spring, DH5 9PQ
☎ 0191 526 0434
See Area website
Tyneside Mrs Pennie Porter, 4 Angerton Gardens, Fenham, Newcastle Upon Tyne, NE5 2JB See Area website

---

DID YOU KNOW?
You can search online for Ramblers Group walks. Visit
www.ramblers.org.uk/walksfinder

NORTH YORKS & SOUTH DURHAM

AREA SECRETARY
Mr D G Lawrenson, Smithy Cottage, Hunton, Bedale, North Yorkshire, DL8 1QB ☎ 01677 450422
www.bigwig.net/nysd_ramblers

GROUP SECRETARIES
Barnard Castle Mr T Fenton, Garden House, Westholme, Winston, Darlington, Co Durham, DL2 3QL
☎ 01325 730895
www.barnardcastleramblers.org.uk
Cleveland Mr A Patterson, 141 Castle Road, Redcar, TS10 2NF
☎ 01642 474864
Crook & Weardale Mrs K Berry, 11 Wood Square, Bishop Auckland, Co. Durham, DL14 6QQ ☎ 01388 608979
http://members.aol.com/crookramblers
Darlington Mr Bryan Spark, 3 Thirlmere Grove, West Auckland, Bishop Auckland, Co Durham, DL14 9LW ☎ 01388 834213
www.bigwig.net/darlington.ramblers
Darlington Hills & Dales Jo Bird, Middle Garth, Stainton, Barnard Castle, DL12 8RD
☎ 01833 637756
Northallerton Mr M F Kent, 131 Valley Road, Northallerton, North Yorkshire, DL6 1SN ☎ 01609 777618
http://web.onetel.net.uk/~murraykent
Richmondshire Mrs V Darwin, 4 Sycamore Avenue, Richmond, North Yorks, DL10 4BN ☎ 01748 822 845

NORTH EAST

LOCAL RAMBLERS PUBLICATIONS

Berwick Walks
by Arthur Wood, ISBN 0 9545331 0 0.
A beautifully hand-drawn and calligraphed pocket book with 24 town, coastal, countryside and riverside walks within a 19km/12-mile radius of Berwick upon Tweed, many of them shorter walks.
£4.95 + 50p p&p from Berwick Ramblers, 5 Quay Walls, Berwick upon Tweed TD15 1HB. Cheques to Ramblers' Association.

NEW **Walking the Tyne: Twenty-five walks from mouth to source**
by J B Jonas, ISBN 1 901184 70 6 (new

edition 2005, Northumbria Area). A route along all 133km/83 miles of this great river, divided into 25 linked, mainly circular walks of 8km/5 miles to 14.5km/9 miles, with suggestions for lunch stops, time estimates, public transport details, and notes on stiles, terrain and places of interest. Follows the North Tyne from Hexham to the source. £5.50.
NEW **Walking the North Tyne: Seventeen walks from Hexham to the source** by J B Jonas, ISBN 1 901184 82 X (Northumbria Area).
Complementing Walking the Tyne by the

same author, this volume follows the North Tyne branch of the river through remote northern countryside from Hexham to the source near Deadwater in the Kielder Forest area, including a walk alongside Kielder Water. Divided into sections, most of which are circular (3km/2 miles to 12km/7.5 miles. Total length of the walk is 76km/47.5 miles. Sketch maps, photos, route description and practical information. £5.
Both from 8 Beaufront Avenue, Hexham NE46 1JD. Cheques to J B Jonas, profits to Ramblers' Association.

BED & BREAKFAST

DURHAM

● Bowburn
Hillrise Guest House, 13 Durham Road West, DH6 5AU
☎ 0191 3770302 (George Webster)   www.hill-rise.com   Map 93/307376
BB **C** ✕ nearby S2 D2 T2 F1 Ⓥ Ⓑ Ⓓ ⊗ ☻ ◆◆◆◆

● Castleside (Consett)

☆ ▣◄ **Bee Cottage Farmhouse**
DH8 9HW   ☎ 01207 508224 (Melita & David Turner)
www.smoothhound.co.uk/hotels/beecottage.html Map 87/070453
BB **D** ✕ book first £18, 7pm D2 T2 F4 Closed Xmas
Ⓥ Ⓑ Ⓓ ⊗ ☻☺☻ ◆◆◆◆

On edge of Durham Dales with walking/cycling from our carpark. Ideal base for Durham, Beamish, Newcastle, Hadrian's Wall. Stunning views, relaxing. Licensed. Dinner available. Good, clean accommodation. All rooms en-suite, with TV and tea tray. Warm welcome guaranteed.

● Cowshill (Wearhead)
▣◄ Low Cornriggs Farmhouse, DL13 1AQ ☎ 01388 537600 (Janet Elliott)
www.alstonandkillhoperidingcentre.co.uk Map 86,87/845413
BB **C** ✕ book first £15, 6.30pm D2 T1 Closed Xmas
Ⓥ Ⓑ Ⓓ ⊗ ☻☺☻ ◆◆◆◆

● Durham
Hillrise Guest House, 13 Durham Road West, Bowburn, DH6 5AU
☎ 0191 377 0302 (George Webster)   www.hill-rise.com Map 93/306376
BB **D** ✕ nearby S1 D2 T2 F1 Closed Xmas Ⓑ Ⓓ ⊗ ☻ ◆◆◆◆

● Forest-in-Teesdale
PENNINE WAY & TEESDALE WAY
The Dale, DL12 0EL ☎ 01833 622303 (Mrs Jean Bonnett) Map 91/869298
BB **A** ✕ book first £10, 7pm D1 F1 Closed Dec-Feb
Ⓥ ⊗ ☻☺☻ Ⓜ

● Frosterley (Bishop Auckland)
▣◄ Newlands Hall, DL13 2SH ☎ 01388 529233 (Carol Oulton)
www.newlandshall.co.uk Map 92/043372
BB **C** F2 Closed Dec-Mar Ⓥ Ⓑ Ⓓ ⊗ ☻☺☻

● Middleton-in-Teesdale (Barnard Castle)
PENNINE WAY & TEESDALE WAY
Brunswick House, 55 Market Place, DL12 0QH ☎ 01833 640393
(Andrew & Sheila Milnes) www.brunswickhouse.net Map 91,92/946255
BB **C** ✕ book first £18, 7:30pm D3 T2 Closed Xmas
Ⓥ Ⓑ Ⓓ ⊗ ☻☺☻ ◆◆◆◆Ⓢ

Belvedere House, 54 Market Place, DL12 0QA ☎ 01833 640884 (Mrs J A Finn)
www.thecoachhouse.net Map 91,92/947254
BB **B** ✕ nearby D2 T1 Closed Xmas Ⓑ ⊗ ☻☺☻ ◆◆◆◆

▣◄ The Teesdale Hotel, Market Place, DL12 0QG ☎ 01833 640264
(Mr J Falconer) Map 91,92/947255
BB **D** ✕ £7.50, 7-9pm S4 D6 T3 F1 Ⓥ Ⓑ Ⓓ ☻☺☻

☆ **Wemmergill Hall Farm**
Lunedale, DL12 0PA ☎ 01833 640379 (Irene Stoddart)
www.wemmergill-farm.co.uk Map 91,92/901218
BB **B** ✕ book first £15, 6:30pm S/D1 T/F1 Closed Oct-Mar
Ⓥ Ⓑ Ⓓ ⊗ ☻☺☻ ◄ ◆◆◆◆

Adjacent to the B6276, Wemmergill Farm House provides a more than comfortable stop for the traveller: hiker, biker or driver (and passengers) can enjoy quality food and accommodation in traditional, peaceful surroundings. Panoramic views over Selset Reservoir from lounge/dining room.

▣◄ Lonton South Farm, DL12 0PL
☎ 01833 640 409 (Mrs Irene Watson) Map 91,92/954245
BB **B** ✕ nearby S1 D1 T1
Ⓓ ⊗ ☻☺☻ ◆◆◆

● Rookhope (Bishop Auckland)

☆ ▣◄ **The Rookhope Inn**
DL13 2BG ☎ 01388 517215 (Chris Jones)
www.rookhope.com Map 87/938428
BB **B** ✕ £6, 7pm T4 F1
Ⓥ Ⓑ Ⓓ ☻☺☻ ◄ ! Ⓜ See Groups also.

This is upper Weardale in the North Pennines, secluded 300 year old village inn offering en-suite accommodation, good food and cask ales. Groups of up to 12 welcome. Drying facilities, maps and excellent walking venues. BB: £25 / DBB: £33

● Stanhope
▣◄ Redlodge Guest House, 2 Market Place, DL13 2UN ☎ 01388 527851
www.redlodgegh.co.uk Map 92/996391
BB **B** S1 T2 Closed Xmas Ⓓ ⊗ ☻☺☻

NORTHUMBERLAND

● Bamburgh
The Sunningdale, 21/23 Lucker Rd, NE69 7BS ☎ 01668 214334
www.sunningdale-hotel.com Map 75/178347
BB **D** ✕ £14, 7pm S2 D8 T3 F5
Ⓥ Ⓑ Ⓓ ☻☺☻ ◄ ! ☻ ◆◆◆

● Bardon Mill (Hexham)
NORTHUMBERLAND NATIONAL PARK
PENNINE WAY & HADRIAN'S WALL
Twice Brewed Inn, Military Rd, NE47 7AN ☎ 01434 344534 (Brian Keen)
www.twicebrewedinn.co.uk Map 86,87/753669
BB **B** ✕ £6.50, 6-8:30pm S2 D4 T7 F1 Closed Xmas ▬▬(Bardon Mill)
Ⓥ Ⓑ ☻☺☻ ◆◆◆

▣◄ The Willows, Redburn, NE47 7EA ☎ 01434 344075
(Mrs Sandie Chesters) www.willows-hexham.co.uk Map 86,87/770645
BB **C** ✕ nearby S1 D1 T1 ▬▬(Bardon Mill)
Ⓥ Ⓓ ☻☺☻ ◄ ! ☻ ◆◆◆

● Beal (Berwick-upon-Tweed)
ST CUTHBERT'S WAY

☆ ✦⊲ **Brockmill Farmhouse**
TD15 2PB ☎ 01289 381283
www.lindisfarne.org.uk/brock-mill-farmhouse Map 75/060436
BB **C** ✗ nearby S1 D1 T1 F1 Closed Xmas
Ⓓ⊗🛏♿🚗 ◆◆◆◆

Brock Mill Farmhouse is peacefully situated 1½ miles from the A1 on the road to Holy Island. The St Cuthbert's Way is just 1½ miles away.

Ideally situated for touring and exploring north Northumberland and Borders. A warm welcome awaits in superbly furnished quality rooms with TV, tea making facilities, vanity units and 2 seater settees. Pick-ups available for ramblers. Evening meals nearby. Full English or vegetarian breakfasts.

● Bellingham (Hexham)
NORTHUMBERLAND NATIONAL PARK
PENNINE WAY

Lyndale Guest House, Riverside Walk, NE48 2AW ☎ 01434 220361
(Ken & Joy Gaskin) www.lyndaleguesthouse.co.uk Map 80/839833
BB **C** ✗ nearby S1 D2 T1 F1 Closed Xmas
Ⓑ Ⓓ🛏♿🚗! ◆◆◆ Veggie breakfasts.

● Berwick-upon-Tweed
✦⊲ Orkney Guest House, 37 Woolmarket, TD15 1DH ☎ 01289 331710
(Helen Rutherford) orkneyguesthouse@yahoo.co.uk Map 75/000528
BB **B** ✗ nearby D2 T2 F1 ⚑(Berwick-upon-Tweed)
Ⓑ Ⓓ🛏♿ ◆◆ Veggie breakfasts.

● Corbridge
HADRIAN'S WALL
✦⊲ The Hayes, Newcastle Rd, NE45 5LP ☎ 01434 632010
(Mrs M J Matthews) www.hayes-corbridge.co.uk Map 87/996643
BB **C** ✗ nearby S1 T1 F2 Closed Xmas ⚑(Corbridge)
Ⓑ Ⓓ⊗🛏♿🚗! ◆◆◆

☆ ✦⊲ **Dyvels Hotel**
Station Rd, NE45 5AY ☎ 01434 633633
dyvels.corbridge@virgin.net Map 87/989636
BB **B** ✗ £6, 5-8pm D1 T1 Closed Xmas ⚑(Corbridge)
Ⓥ Ⓑ Ⓓ🛏♿🚗

Cosy, friendly atmosphere. Fully stocked bar, offering a good selection of cask ales, lagers and fine wines. Separate restaurant, serving a full English breakfast and excellent home-cooked food. Beer garden. All rooms tastefully decorated and furnished and equipped with TV and beverage tray.

● Fenwick (Berwick-upon-Tweed)
ST CUTHBERT'S WAY

✦⊲ The Manor House, TD15 2PQ ☎ 01289 381016 (Christine Humphrey)
www.manorhousefenwick.co.uk Map 75/066401
BB **C** ✗ book first £15 D2 T1 F1 Closed Xmas Ⓥ Ⓑ Ⓓ⊗🛏♿🚗!

☆ ✦⊲ **Cherry Trees**
TD15 2PJ ☎ 01289 381437
Map 75/066401
BB **B** ✗ book first £12, 6-7:30pm D1 T1 F1 Closed Sep-Apr
Ⓥ Ⓑ Ⓓ🛏♿

Large detached house in large private grounds with ample parking. Ideally situated for St Cuthbert's Way, walking and touring. 6 miles to Holy Island. Spacious rooms, hospitality tray and countryside views.

● Greenhead (Brampton)
NORTHUMBERLAND NATIONAL PARK
HADRIAN'S WALL, PENNINE WAY & SOUTH TYNE TRAIL

10 Blenkinsopp Terrace, Bankfoot, CA8 7JN ☎ 016977 47429
(Robin & Jean Fuller) robingfuller@yahoo.co.uk Map 86/663645
BB **B** ✗ book first £8-£12, Xmas S1 D1 T/F1
Ⓥ Ⓑ Ⓓ⊗🛏♿🚗! Ⓜ

● Haltwhistle
NORTHUMBERLAND NATIONAL PARK
PENNINE WAY, HADRIAN'S WALL & SOUTH TYNE TRAIL

☆ ✦⊲ **Broomshaw Hill Farm**
Willia Road, NE49 9NP ☎ 01434 320866 (Mrs J Brown)
www.broomshaw.co.uk Map 86/707653
BB **C** ✗ nearby D2 T1 Closed Jan-Feb ⚑(Haltwhistle)
Ⓑ Ⓓ⊗🛏♿🚗! ◆◆◆◆◆Ⓖ

An 18th C. farmhouse enlarged and modernised to the highest standards. The house is quietly situated on the conjunction of footpath and bridleway leading to Hadrian's Wall. Easy access to major Roman sites, town and Hadrian's Wall. Warm welcome assured.

✦⊲ Hall Meadows, Main Street, NE49 0AZ ☎ 01434 321021
(Mrs Heather Humes) Map 86,87/708641
BB **B** ✗ nearby S1 D1 T1 Closed Xmas ⚑(Haltwhistle)
Ⓑ Ⓓ🛏♿🚗 ◆◆◆◆

✦⊲ Doors Cottage B&B, Shield Hill, NE49 9NW ☎ 01434 322556
(Lesley Lewis) www.doorscottage.co.uk Map 86,87/712649
BB **B** ✗ nearby D1 T1 Closed Xmas ⚑(Haltwhistle)
Ⓓ⊗🛏♿🚗! ◆◆◆

● Heddon-on-the-Wall
HADRIAN'S WALL

Ramblers' Repose, 8 Killiebrigs, NE15 0DD ☎ 01661 852419
(Mrs P.A. Millward) Map 88/130665
BB **C** ✗ nearby D1 T1 Closed Xmas ⊗♿ ◆◆◆ Veggie breakfasts.

● Hexham
HADRIAN'S WALL

Peth Head Cottage, Juniper, NE47 0LA ☎ 01434 673286 (Mrs Joan Liddle)
www.peth-head-cottage.co.uk Map 87/938587
BB **C** S1 D2 Closed Xmas Ⓑ Ⓓ⊗🛏♿🚗! ◆◆◆Ⓢ

NORTH EAST

● Once Brewed (Bardon Mill)
NORTHUMBERLAND NATIONAL PARK
PENNINE WAY, HADRIAN'S WALL & SOUTH TYNE TRAIL

☆ ▨◀ **Gibbs Hill Farm**
NE47 7AP ☎ 01434 344030 (Mrs Valerie Gibson)
www.gibbshillfarm.co.uk Map 86,87/750691
BB **B** ✕ nearby DI T4 Closed Xmas
Ⓥ Ⓑ Ⓓ ⊗ 🐾👤🚲! ◆◆◆◆ See Hostels also.

17th C. working farm on Hadrian's Wall.
Comfortable en-suite rooms, spectacular
views. Walking, birdwatching from hide on
Greenlee Lough Nature Reserve, stables,
trout fishing. Central for Roman sites,
Pennine Cycleways, Pennine Way and
Pennine Bridleway.

● Rothbury
NORTHUMBERLAND NATIONAL PARK
▨◀ **Well Strand, NE65 7UD**
☎ 01669 620794 (Helen & David Edes) Map 81/056016
BB **A** ✕ nearby SI DI TI Closed Xmas
Ⓓ ⊗ 🚲! 🛏 Veggie breakfasts.

● Stannersburn
NORTHUMBERLAND NATIONAL PARK

☆ ▨◀ **The Pheasant Inn**
NE48 IDD ☎ 01434 240382
www.thepheasantinn.com Map 80/721866
BB **D** ✕ £7.95-£15, 7-9pm D4 T/S3 FI Closed Xmas
Ⓥ Ⓑ 🐾👤🛏 ◆◆◆◆Ⓢ

380-year-old traditional family run country inn bursting with character and
charm, beamed ceiling, open fires.
Bar lunches and evening meals available daily.
Excellent area for walking and cycling in and around Kielder Water and Forest.

● Twice Brewed (Haltwhistle)
NORTHUMBERLAND NATIONAL PARK
HADRIAN'S WALL & PENNINE WAY
Saughy Rigg Farm, NE49 9PT ☎ 01434 344120 (Kath Dowle)
www.saughyrigg.co.uk Map 86,87/755675
BB **C** ✕ book first £14.50, 7-9pm SI D4 T4 F2 Closed Xmas
Ⓥ Ⓑ Ⓓ 🐾👤🚲! 🛏 ◆◆◆◆

● Warkworth (Morpeth)
Bide a While, 4 Beal Croft, NE65 0XL
☎ 01665 711753 (Mrs D Graham) Map 81/249053
BB **B** ✕ nearby DI TI FI Ⓑ Ⓓ👤🛏

● West Woodburn (Hexham)
PENNINE WAY
▨◀ Yellow House Farm, NE48 2SB ☎ 01434 270070 (Avril A Walton)
www.yellowhousebandb.co.uk Map 80/898870 BB **B** ✕ nearby DI TI FI
Closed Xmas Ⓑ Ⓓ ⊗ 🐾👤🚲! 🛏 ◆◆◆◆

● Wooler
ST CUTHBERT'S WAY

☆ ▨◀ **Winton House**
39 Glendale Road, NE71 6DL ☎ 01668 281362 (Terry & Veronica Gilbert)
www.wintonhousebandb.co.uk Map 75/991283
BB **C/D** ✕ nearby D2 TI Closed Dec-Feb
Ⓑ Ⓓ ⊗ 🐾👤🚲 ◆◆◆

Charming Edwardian house with
spacious, comfortable rooms.
Situated on a quiet road close to
village centre just 250m from St
Cuthbert's Way. Much praised
breakfasts, using local produce.
Walkers very welcome.

☆ ▨◀ **Tilldale House**
34/40 High Street, NE71 6BG ☎ 01668 281450 (Julia Devonport)
tilldalehouse@freezone.co.uk Map 75/990281
BB **C** ✕ nearby D3 T3
Ⓑ Ⓓ ⊗ 🐾👤🚲! 🛏 ◆◆◆◆ Special diets catered for.

Our stone built 17th C. home offers
spacious comfortable en-suite
bedrooms. An ideal base for
walking, cycling, fishing, golf or
riding. Located off the main road,
150 yards from St Cuthbert's Way.
Further details on request.

☆ ▨◀ **The Black Bull Hotel**
2 High Street, NE71 6BY ☎ 01668 281309
www.theblackbullhotel.co.uk Map 75/991280
BB **B** ✕ £10 D4 T5 F2
Ⓥ Ⓑ Ⓓ 🐾👤🛏 ◆◆◆◆

The Black Bull Hotel is a 17th-century inn
standing in the main street of Wooler, situated
in one of the most picturesque parts of north
Northumberland.

The en-suite bedrooms have TV, tea & coffee
making facilities, hair dryers and radio alarms.

TYNE & WEAR

● Newcastle upon Tyne
HADRIAN'S WALL
The Barn B&B, East Wallhouses, Military Rd, NE18 0LL ☎ 01434 672649
(Brenda Walton) www.smoothhound.co.uk/hotels/thebarn1.html
Map 87/047683 BB **C** ✕ nearby DI T2 Closed Dec Ⓑ ⊗ 🐾👤🛏

● South Shields
HADRIAN'S WALL
Seaways Guest House, 91 Ocean Road, NE33 2JL ☎ 0191 4271226
(Karon Dickinson) seawayshouse@aol.com Map 88/368674
BB **B** ✕ book first £8, 6:30-7pm S2 D3 T2 F2 Ⓥ Ⓑ Ⓓ👤

SELF-CATERING

DURHAM

● Barnard Castle

☆ **East Briscoe Farm Cottages**
☎ 01833 650087 (Emma Wilson)
www.eastbriscoe.co.uk
£120-£455 Sleeps 2-6. 6 cottages.
Beautiful countryside, superb area for walking. ★★★★

East Briscoe is a beautiful riverside estate which makes a superb base for walkers in scenic Teesdale. Offering well-equipped, comfortable cottages. Walkers welcome accreditation. Close to many new right to roam areas. Pets welcome in three cottages. Linen, towels and heating included.

Bramble Cottage ☎ 01833 638552 (Mrs C Young)
£280-£350 Sleeps 2-4. 1 cottage.
Detached cottage. Private location. Stunning views.

● Bowes

☆ **Mellwaters Barn**
☎ 01833 628181 (Mrs S Tavener)
www.mellwatersbarn.co.uk
£180-£500 Sleeps 2-4. 5 cottages.   Barn cottages, working farm, various walks.   ★★★★ Guide dogs accepted.

Mellwaters Barn is an old traditional stone-built dairy and granary that has been converted into 5 self-catering barn cottages for both disabled and able-bodied people. The cottages will sleep 2 to 4, up to a total of 12 people.
It is situated on a working farm just off the A66 down a farm lane and across a Grade II packhorse bridge in beautiful Teesdale near Barnard Castle. This is an Area of Outstanding Natural Beauty with many walks, and is situated in the first British European Geopark.
Mellwaters Barn dates back over 100 years and is situated in the centre of Steading with magnificent views down the valley to Bowes or up towards the moor.
The cottages have been designed to give maximum possible access as well as offering a homely and relaxing atmosphere. The beds are all adjustable for maximum comfort, the bathrooms have either a bath with shower above, or a level entry shower.
At the western edge of the farm is God's Bridge the best example of a natural bridge in the UK, and a Site of Special Scientific Interest (SSSI)

● Rookhope

Hole House ☎ 01388 517184 (Nick & Lorraine Thwaites)
nick@holehousefarm.wanadoo.co.uk
£320 Sleeps 4. 1 cottage.   Beamed ceiling and log fire. See Hostels also.

● Wolsingham
Mrs M Gardiner ☎ 01388 527538
£130-£233 Sleeps 4. 2 terraced cottages.
Cosy cottages, excellent scenic walking area. ★★★

Anne Molloy ☎ 01207 542545
£190-£310 Sleeps 4. 1 cottage.
Well equipped cosy retreat. Excellent walking.   RA member

NORTHUMBERLAND

● Embleton
Doxford Farm ☎ 01665 579348 (Sarah Shell) www.doxfordfarmcottages.com
£175-£550 Sleeps 2-7. 7 cottages.
Working farm on beautiful country estate. ★★★-★★★★

● Rothbury
NORTHUMBERLAND NATIONAL PARK
The Lodge & Gatehouse ☎ 01669 630210 (Jenny Sordy)
http://alnhamfarm.co.uk
£180-£460 Sleeps 4-6. 2 properties.
Tennis court, fishing. Excellent walking.   ★★★★

GROUPS

DURHAM

The Rookhope Inn (BB) Rookhope, Weardale DL13 2BG ☎ 01388 517215
(Chris Jones) www.rookhope.com Map 87/939428
BB £25, DBB £32 Min 1, max 14. Village inn. ✗ B D See B&B also.

HOSTELS, BUNKHOUSES & CAMPSITES

DURHAM

Hole House (B) Eastgate, Weardale ☎ 01388 517184 (Nick & Lorraine
Thwaites) nick@holehousefarm.wanadoo.co.uk Map 92/951398
BB £17.50 ✗ nearby B D   See B&B also.

NORTHUMBERLAND

NORTHUMBERLAND NATIONAL PARK
PENNINE WAY & HADRIAN'S WALL

☆ **Gibbs Hill Bunkhouse**
(B/IH) Once Brewed, Bardon Mill, Hexham NE47 7AP
☎ 01434 344030 (Mrs Valerie Gibson)
www.gibbshillfarm.co.uk Map 86,87/750691
Bednight £12 B D   See B&B also.

New bunkhouse sleeps up to 20 people. Ensuite showers, spacious cooking facilities, comfortable lounge. Ideal for families, weekly room rates, short breaks and special weekly rates for groups. Some evening meals available on-site. Pennine Bridleway – new stables on site.

NORTH EAST

207

VIEWS OVER FAN-Y-BIG AND PEN-Y-FAN, BRECON BEACONS

WALES

Twenty per cent extra free! That's the extent of new access that the Countryside and Rights of Way (CRoW) Act has added to walkers' maps in Wales. Since May last year, areas of open countryside that add up to more than all the existing national parks in Wales put together have been available to walkers under the Act.

ENJOYING ACCESS LAND NEAR PONTRHYDYGROES

New areas include the Cnewr Estate, near Sennybridge, containing Fforest Fawr's wild moorland and abandoned mountain tramways. The limestone plateau of Bwrdd Arthur near Llandonna and the watershed between Craig Ogwr and the Bwlch in the Rhondda valley can also be visited for the first time.

For those in need of a gentle introduction to walking, the Cerrig Camu/Stepping Stones project, funded by the Countryside Council for Wales, provides walks of between 3 to 5 miles that will keep you fit and will give you the chance to make new friends.

Troeon Tren/Rail Rambles enables people to enjoy walking without the need to use cars. Throughout the year there are around 90 walks, from the Aberystwyth Town Tour to a day's walking from Fairbourne to Machynlleth via Trawsfynydd, Craig-y-Llyn, Carnedd Llwyd, Cadair Idris and Minffordd – a challenging walk but worth the effort.

Llanwrtyd Wells, in Powys, may be the smallest town in Britain, but each year it organises several annual walks of varying demand and levity. Celebrating its silver jubilee this September, the Welsh International Four Day Walks has a choice of 10, 15 or 25-mile daily routes, as does the Lord Cranshaw Walk in February. Both take in the beautiful and rugged Cambrian Mountain surroundings. For those with a taste for the grain, the Saturnalia Walk offers free beer as you tour local Roman archaeology, and the Real Ale Ramble boasts 'beer checkpoints' as part of the Mid Wales Beer Festival in November.

You can find details of these and many other events on our website.

> For those with a taste for the grain, the Saturnalia Walk offers free beer as you tour local Roman archaeology, and the Real Ale Ramble boasts 'beer checkpoints'

Long Distance Paths

Cambrian Way	CAM
Clwydian Way	CLW
Glyndŵr's Way	GLN
Isle of Anglesey Coastal Path	ANC
Offa's Dyke Path	OFD
Pembrokeshire Coast Path	PSC
Severn Way	SVN
Usk Valley Walk	USK
Valeways Millennium Heritage Trail	VMH
Wye Valley Walk	WVL

Public rights of way:

33,211km/20,637 miles

Mapped access land:

 4,500 sq km/1,737 sq miles (Area 9, Wales)

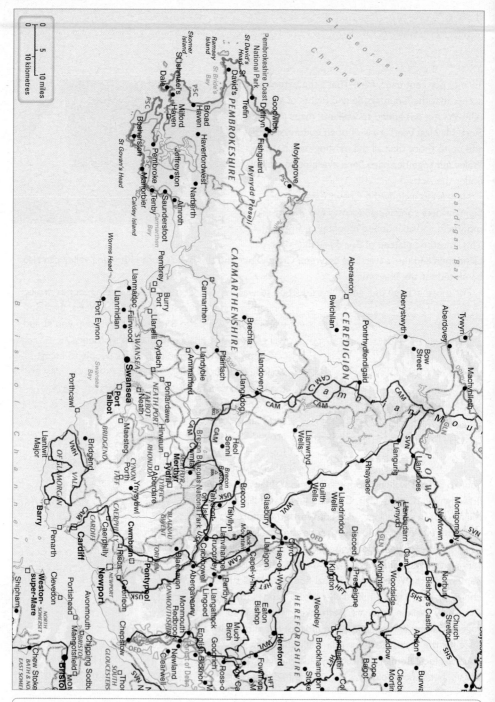

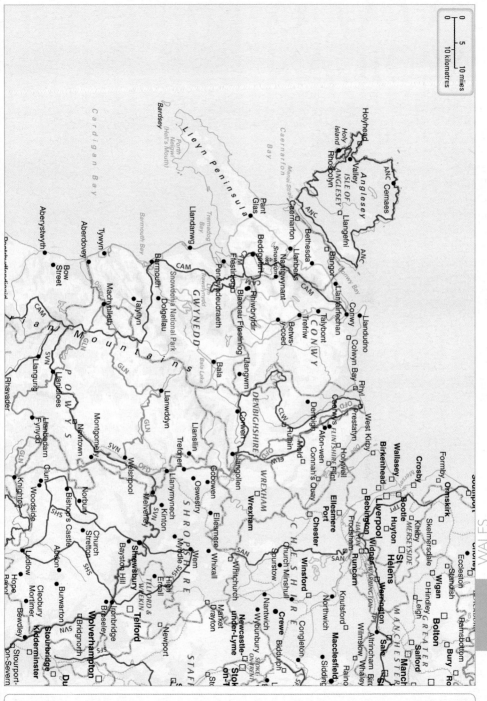

2006
CARDIGAN FESTIVAL OF WALKING
6 - 7 OCTOBER 2006

Cardigan and its surrounding area is truly a paradise for walkers. Whethe you are looking for a taste of the beautiful Cardigan Bay coastline, the history of Cardigan, the mysterious Te Valley, the magical Preseli Hills or th spectacular Ceredigon or Pembrokeshire Coastal Paths, Cardigan's Festival of Walking has it a

For further details contact the
Cardigan Festival of Walking on
01239 615554

WALES
LOCAL RAMBLERS GROUPS

CARMARTHENSHIRE
AREA SECRETARY
See www.ramblers.org.uk/info/localgroups or contact our central office for details.

GROUP SECRETARIES
Carmarthen & District Mr David Bush, 31 Eldergrove, Llangunnor, Carmarthenshire, Dyfed, SA31 2LQ
☎ 01267 230994
http://mysite.freeserve.com/beauchamp
Dinefwr Mr David Foot, Ty Isaf, Taliaris, Llandeilo, SA19 7DE
☎ 01550 777623
http://mysite.freeserve.com/beauchamp/index.html
Llanelli See www.ramblers.org.uk/info/localgroups or contact our central office for details.

CEREDIGION
AREA SECRETARY
Sue Johnson, 16 Clos Ceitho, Llanbadarn Fawr, Aberystwyth, SY23 3TZ ☎ 01970 612649

GROUP SECRETARIES
Aberystwyth Shirley Kinghorn, 16 Bryn Glas, Llanbadarn, Aberystwyth, Dyfed, SY23 3QR ☎ 01970 624965
http://users.aber.ac.uk/dib/AberRamblers
Cardigan & District See http://mysite.wanadoomembers.co.uk/beauchamp/index.html or contact our central office for details
Ceredigion See www.ramblers.org.uk/info/localgroups or contact our central office for details.
Lampeter Mr D G Hughes & Ms J McDowall, Ddol Brenin, Ffarmers, Llanwrda, SA19 8PZ ☎ 01558 650339
www.lampeterwalkers.org.uk

GLAMORGAN
AREA SECRETARY
Mr J E Thomas, 7 Parc Afon, Porth, Mid Glamorgan, CF40 1JF
☎ 01443 681082

GROUP SECRETARIES
Bridgend & District Mr John Sanders, 3 Bryn Rhedyn, Pencoed Bridgend, CF35 6TL ☎ 01656 861835
http://freespace.virgin.net/alex.marshall/ramblers.htm
Cardiff Ms Diane Davies, 9 Cyncoed Rise, Cyncoed, Cardiff, CF23 6SF
☎ 029 2075 2464
www.btinternet.com/~cardiff.ramblers
Cynon Valley Mr Allan Harrison, 8 Stuart Street, Aberdare, Mid Glamorgan, CF44 7LY
☎ 01685 881824
http://freespace.virgin.net/alex.marshall/cynon.htm
Maesteg Mr S S Luke, 33 Maiden Street, Maesteg, CF34 9HP
☎ 01656 733729
Merthyr Valley Mr A J Richards, 8 St Davids Close, Penpedairheol, Hengoed, Mid Glamorgan, CF82 8BL
☎ 01443 833719
Neath Port Talbot Mr David Davies, 2 Cwrt Coed Parc, Maesteg, CF34 9DG
☎ 01656 733021
Penarth & District Mrs L Davies, 3 Barrians Way, Barry, Vale Of Glamorgan, CF62 8JG
☎ 01446 407595
http://freespace.virgin.net/alex.marshall/penarth.htm
Taff Ely Mr J T Roszkowski, 18 Parc Y Coed, Creigiau, Nr Cardiff, CF15 9LX
☎ 02920 891455
http://www.apyule.demon.co.uk/taffely.htm
Tawe Trekkers Mr O D Morgan, 100 Bryn Road, Brynmill, Swansea, SA2 0AT ☎ 07766 652837
Tiger Bay Ramblers Ms C Ley, 42 Ty Wern Avenue, Cardiff, CF14 6AW
☎ 029 20628892
www.tigerbayramblers.org.uk
Vale of Glamorgan Mr I D Fraser, 44 Millfield Drive, Cowbridge, Vale Of Glamorgan, CF71 7BR
☎ 01446 774706
http://freespace.virgin.net/alex.marshall/Vale.htm
West Glamorgan Zetta Flew, 8 Meadow Croft, Southgate, Swansea, SA3 2DF ☎ 01792 232060
http://homepage.ntlworld.com/alex.thomas

GREATER GWENT
AREA SECRETARY
Mr Mike Williams, 7 Cwm Sor Close, New Inn, Pontypool, NP4 0NN
☎ 01495 753040 www.ra-gga.co.uk

GROUP SECRETARIES
Gelligaer Mrs D Price, 26 Tyn Y Coed, Ystrad Mynach, Caerphilly, CF82 7DD
☎ 01443 813220
www.gelligaer-ramblers.co.uk
Islwyn Ms M Thomas & Ms A Thomas, 15 Carlton Terrace, Cross Keys, Newport, NP11 7BU ☎ 01495 273057
www.islwyn-ramblers.itgo.com
Lower Wye Mr R D Davies, 5 Crown Meadow, Coal Way, Coleford, Glos, GL16 7HF ☎ 01594 837157
www.lowerwyeramblers.co.uk
North Gwent Mr A Nicholas, 31 Windsor Road, Brynmawr, Blaenau Gwent, NP23 4HE ☎ 01495 311088
www.northgwentramblers.co.uk
Pontypool Mrs Barbara Whitticase, Glantawell, Llanfihangel Talyllyn, Brecon, Powys, LD3 7TH ☎ 01874 658386
www.pontypool-ramblers.co.uk
South Gwent Mr K Phillips, 39 Penylan Close, Bassaleg, Newport, Gwent, NP10 8NW ☎ 01633 894172
http://south-gwent-ramblers.co.uk

NORTH WALES
AREA SECRETARY
Mr Ron Williams, 11 Fron Las, Holywell, Clwyd, CH8 7HX ☎ 01352 715723

GROUP SECRETARIES
Bangor-Bethesda Mr N Fernley, Fedw Crymlyn Aber, Llanfairfechan, Gwynedd, LL33 0LU ☎ 01248 354724
Berwyn Mrs Sue Kay, Erw Fain, Llantysilio, Llangollen, Clwyd, LL20 8BU
☎ 01978 861793
Caernarfon/Dwyfor Ms E Watkin, Ty N Lon, Bethel, Caernarfon, Gwynedd, LL55 1UW ☎ 01248 671243
Clwydian Mr E Ankers, 14 Bron Yr Eglwys, Mynydd Isa, Mold, Clwyd, CH7 6YQ ☎ 01352 754659
Conwy Valley Mr F R Parry, 2 Derwen Avenue, Rhos On Sea, Colwyn Bay, LL28 4SP ☎ 01492 547967
Deeside Mr Jim Irvine, 30 St Davids Drive, Connahs Quay, Flintshire, CH5 4SR ☎ 01244 818577
www.deesideramblers.org.uk
Eryri 20.30 Delyth Roberts, Tre Wen, Groeslon, Waunfawr, Caernarfon, LL55 4EZ ☎ 01286 650295
www.walk20.30.btinternet.co.uk

WEST GLAMORGAN

WALES

LOCAL RAMBLERS GROUPS continued

Meirionydd Ms V Goslin, 4 Highgate,
Penrhyndeudraeth, Gwynedd, LL48 6RG
☎ 01766 770770
Vale of Clwyd Mr M R Wilkinson,
49 Victoria Road West, Prestatyn,
Denbighshire, LL19 7AA
☎ 01745 888137
www.voc-ramblers.org.uk
Walkers on Wales Dr F Lloyd-Williams,
Plas Wern, Waen, St Asaph, LL17 0DY
☎ 07702 955344
www.walkersonwales.fsnet.co.uk
Wrexham Mr Paul Davies, 5 Glyndwr
Road, Wrexham, LL12 8DG
☎ 01978 362253
Ynys Mon
See www.ramblers.org.uk/info/localgroups
or contact our central office for details

PEMBROKESHIRE
AREA SECRETARY
See www.ramblers.org.uk/info/localgroups
or contact our central office for details.

GROUP SECRETARIES
Pembrokeshire Ms C M Morris,
24 St Lawrence Close, Hakin, Milford
Haven, Dyfed, SA73 3NE
☎ 01646 697 543
www.pembrokeshireramblers.org.uk

DID YOU KNOW?
Ramblers Group walks are now online at
www.ramblers.org.uk/walksfinder

POWYS
AREA SECRETARY
Mr K M Jones, I Heyope Road,
Knucklas, LD7 1PT ☎ 01547 520 266
www.powysramblers.org.uk

GROUP SECRETARIES
4 Wells Miss M Emery,
Pantgwyn, Hundred House,
Builth Wells, Powys, LD2 3TE
Enquiries: ☎ 01982 570366 (J Beagley)
www.fourwells.powysramblers.org.uk
East Radnor Mr K M Jones, I Heyope
Road, Knucklas, LD7 1PT
☎ 01547 520 266
Welshpool Mrs Lynda Dabinett,
Pentre Isaf, Llangyniew, Welshpool,
Powys, SY21 0JT ☎ 01938 810069

LOCAL RAMBLERS PUBLICATIONS

The Pioneer Ramblers 1850-1940
by David Hollett, ISBN 1 901184 54 4.
The history of walking is full of vivid
incidents and striking characters, many of
them captured in this new book. Thus
George Allen, who walked a thousand
miles to advance vegetarianism, shares a
cover with Lawrence Chubb, the severely
conservative first secretary of the Open
Spaces Society, and the young communists
who trespassed on Kinder Scout in 1932
jostle with Victorian mountaineers and
natural history enthusiasts. The pictures
are a delight. *North Wales Ramblers, £8.95
+ £1 p&p from 69 Wethersfield Road,
Prenton CH43 9YF. Cheques to North Wales
Area RA.*

CEREDIGION
**Cardigan Centre for Walkers –
Aberteifi Canolfan Cerddwyr**
by Cardigan and District Ramblers.
Collection of 11 graded walks of between
5km/3 miles and 16km/10 miles in and
around Cardigan, with connecting bus
service information, on attractive cards in a
pack. Bilingual Welsh/English.
*£5.50 + 50p p&p from G Torr, Parc-y-Pratt,
Cardigan SA43 3DR. Cheques to Cardigan
and District Ramblers.*

Lampeter Walks – Llwybrau Llanbed
by Lampeter Ramblers, ISBN 1 901184
58 7. Newly revised edition of this book
of 16 walks 2.5km/1.5 miles to 13km/8
miles, with route maps, background notes
on geographical and historical context and
accommodation listings, with colour
illustrations and line drawings by Robert
Blayney. Bilingual Welsh/English.
*£4.95 + £1 p&p from Lampeter Bookshop,
21 Bridge Street, Lampeter SA48 7AA.
Cheques to Lampeter Ramblers.*

DENBIGHSHIRE
Clwydian Way
by David Hollett, ISBN 1 901184 36 6.
Circular route around Denbighshire,
looping through some of the best, but
relatively unknown, walking country in the
region, including details of 12 short circular
walks. *£5.95 + £1.55 p&p from PO Box
139, Llanfairpwllgwyngyll LL61 6WR.
Cheques to The Ramblers' Association North
Wales Area.*

GLAMORGAN
Capital Walks and The Capital Walk
Cardiff Ramblers have produced two
books of countryside walks around Cardiff,
with a total of 30 short circular walks
between about 5km/3 miles and
18km/11.5 miles. These link up into a
circular Capital Walk around the city of
61km/38 miles starting from Swanbridge.
*Both books are out of print, but walk
descriptions are available to download from
the website at
www.btinternet.com/~cardiff.ramblers*

Valeways Millennium Heritage Trail
by B Palmer and G Woodnam (Vale of
Glamorgan). Fascinating 99km/62-mile
circular walk with various spurs linking up
many places of historical, geographic and
geological interest, developed by a
partnership of the RA, Vale of Glamorgan
Council and other organisations. Pack with
attractive descriptive booklet and 16 route
cards with map and route details in easy
sections. *£6.99 + £1.50 p&p from
Valeways, Unit 7 BCEC, Skomer Road, Barry
CF62 9DA. Cheques to Valeways.*

Walking Around Gower
4th edition by Albert White, ISBN 0
951878 01 8 (West Glamorgan Ramblers).

10 circular walks of between 8km/5 miles
and 21km/13 miles around the Gower
peninsula, going out along the coast and
returning inland, including extensive notes
on scenery, wildlife and history.

**Walking Around Northern Gower
and the Swansea Valley**
by Peter Beck and Peter J Thomas, based
on an original work by Albert White, ISBN
0 951878 11 5. 10 circular walks that can
be split into 25 shorter circuits, giving
options of between 8km/5 miles and
21km/13 miles in the former mining area
north of Swansea and the Gower
peninsula. Includes overprinted OS maps
and extensive background notes.
*Both £7.50 each post free from Peter Beck,
24 Hazelmere Road, Sketty, Swansea SA2
0SN. Cheques to The Ramblers' Association.*

MONMOUTHSHIRE
Lower Wye Rambles
2nd edition, edited by Allan Thomas and
Gill Nettleship. 16 walks in the Lower
Wye Valley, part of the Wye Valley Area of
Outstanding Natural Beauty, between
Chepstow and Monmouth, 4-14km/2.5-9
miles, some linking together to make
longer walks and including parts of the
Wye Valley Walk, with clear colour maps.
*£3.75 from 1 Mounton Close, Chepstow
NP16 5EG. Cheques to Lower Wye
Group RA.*

Walks you will enjoy
Pack of 18 walks in east Radnorshire and
northwest Herefordshire on laminated
pocket-sized cards. *£4.50 (£3.75 to RA
members) from East Radnor Publications, 1
Heyope Road, Knucklas LD7 1PT. Cheques
to East Radnor Publications.*

WALES

BED & BREAKFAST

ANGLESEY

● Cemaes
ISLE OF ANGLESEY COASTAL PATH

◄═ Tredolphin Guest House, Cemaes Bay, LL67 0ET
☎ 01407 710388 (Frances & Bill O'Donnell) Map 114/370935
BB **C** ✕ nearby S2 D2 T1 F2 Closed Xmas
B D ⊗ 🐾👖 ★★★ Guide dogs welcome.

● Rhoscolyn (Holyhead)
ISLE OF ANGLESEY COASTAL PATH

Glan Towyn, LL65 2NJ ☎ 01407 860380 (Carol Gough)
www.glantowyn-rhoscolyn.co.uk Map 114/272752
BB **B** ✕ nearby S1 D2 T1 Closed Dec-Jan
B ⊗ 🐾👖🚗! ★★★

● Valley (Holyhead)
ISLE OF ANGLESEY COASTAL PATH

Ty Mawr, LL65 3HH ☎ 01407 740235 (Mrs Anne Lloyd)
www.angleseybedandbreakfast.co.uk Map 114/296784
BB **C** ✕ nearby S1 D2 T1 Closed Xmas-Jan ᴡᴡ(Valley)
D ⊗ 👖🚗📚 ★★★

CARMARTHENSHIRE

● Brechfa (Carmarthen)

☆ ◄═ **Glasfryn Guest House and Restaurant**
SA32 7QY ☎ 01267 202306
www.glasfrynbrechfa.co.uk Map 146/526303
BB **C** ✕ £10-£15, 7-9pm D2 T1
V B D 🐾👖!📚 ★★★

Situated at the edge of the Brechfa Forest. Six miles from the A40. Ideal centre for walking, cycling and touring South, West and Mid Wales. 15 minutes from National Botanic Gardens and Aberglesni gardens (Garden Lost in Time). Licensed restaurant. Excellent home-cooked food.
All rooms en-suite. Brochures available.

● Llandovery
BRECON BEACONS & CAMBRIAN WAY

☆ **LLanerchindda Farm**
Cynghordy, SA20 0NB ☎ 01550 750274 (Lynn & Martin Hadley)
www.cambrianway.com Map 160/808429
BB **C** ✕ £12, 7pm S3 D7 T6 F4 ᴡᴡ(Cynghordy)
V B D 🐾👖🚗!📚Ⓜ ★★ See Groups also.

Our Bed & Breakfast at a remote sheep farm 7 miles north-east of LLandovery is a very popular base for walking clubs and groups.
With 42 beds in 20 mainly en-suite rooms, plus excellent facilities including drying room and map room with 20 well documented walks, we are understandably very popular.

Our special offer: Sun-Fri (5 nights) DBB – £166.50 (minimum 12), transport and packed lunches extra – single supplement in certain circumstances.

Email: martin@cambrianway.com.

☆ **Dan-y-Parc Farm Guest House**
Cynghordy, SA20 0LD ☎ 01550 720401 (Mrs Diane Brown)
www.danyparcholidays.co.uk Map 146,160/795378
BB **B** ✕ book first £15, 7pm S1 D1 T1 F1 Closed Xmas ᴡᴡ(Llandovery)
V B D 🐾👖🚗!📚 ★★★

Beautifully situated 17th C. farmhouse bordering the Brecon Beacons and Cambrian mountains. Comfortable en-suite rooms with tea/coffee making facilities, hearty homecooked English or vegetarian breakfasts & homemade evening meals. Woodland walk and waymarked routes nearby. Pets very welcome.

● Llandybie

☆ **The Glynhir Estate**
Glynhir Mansion, Glynhir Road, SA18 2TD ☎ 01269 850438 (Justine Jenkins)
www.theglynhirestate.com Map 159/639152
BB **D** ✕ book first £17, 7pm S1 D3 T1 F2 Closed Xmas ᴡᴡ(Llandybie)
V B D ⊗ 🐾🚗!

200-acre estate nestling in the foothills of the Black Mountain.
Explore its secret valleys and rivers - wonderful walking country with spectacular scenery and plenty of wildlife. Perfect for groups, excellent home-cooked food and a large private car park.

● Llangadog
BRECON BEACONS

🥾⊂ Cynyll Farm, SA19 9BB ☎ 01550 777316 (Mrs Jackie Dare)
cynyllfarm@clara.co.uk Map 146,160/718301
BB **B** ✕ book first £13-£14, approx 7pm D1 F1 Closed Xmas ⋘(Llanwrda)
Ⓥ Ⓑ Ⓓ ⊛ 🐾🛏 ﹗ ★★★

CEREDIGION

● Aberystwyth
🥾⊂ Marine Hotel, Promenade, Marine Terrace, SY23 2BX
☎ 0800 0190020 (Freephone) Map 135/583821
BB **C** ✕ £8-£18.95, 6:30-8:30pm S6 D24 T6 F12 ⋘(Aberystwyth)
Ⓥ Ⓑ Ⓓ🐾🛏🚲 Ⓜ Wheelchair access.

● Bow Street (Aberystwyth)
🥾⊂ Garreg Lwyd, Penygarn, SY24 5BE
☎ 01970 828830 (Mrs A Edwards) Map 135/625852
BB **B** ✕ nearby S1 D1 T1 F1 ⋘(Aberystwyth) Ⓓ 🐾🛏🚲 ★★

● Bwlchllan (Lampeter)

☆🥾⊂ Rhyd-y-Groes (Pescatarian B&B)
SA48 8QN ☎ 01570 470188 (Melvyn & Eve Twitchett)
www.milford.co.uk/wales Map 146/565597
BB **C** ✕ book first £14, 6-9pm S1 D1 T1
Ⓥ Ⓑ Ⓓ⊛🐾🛏🚗﹗🚲 ★★★

Tranquil setting in 4½ acres of unspoiled Welsh countryside, with stream and woodland walk. Ideal base for red kite country. Enjoy a slice of Welsh butter cake on arrival. Comfortable, well-equipped rooms with uninterrupted views. Home-cooking using fresh duck eggs.

● Pontrhydfendigaid (Ystrad Meurig)
CAMBRIAN WAY

☆🥾⊂ Black Lion Hotel
Mill St, SY25 6BE ☎ 01974 831624 (Giles Polglase)
www.blacklionhotel.co.uk Map 135,147/731666
BB **D** ✕ £7:50, 5-9pm D2 T2 F1 ★★★
Ⓥ Ⓑ Ⓓ🐾🛏🚗﹗🚲 Ⓜ ★★★

The Black Lion Inn is set in a fold of the Cambrian Mountains close to Strata Florida Abbey and Cors Caron Nature Reserve. Log fire, beamed ceilings and traditional music. Homemade food & real ale. Guided/self-guided walks arranged.

CONWY

● Betws-y-Coed
SNOWDONIA/ERYRI

🥾⊂ Glan Llugwy, LL24 0BN ☎ 01690 710592 (Graham & Jean Brayne)
jean@glanllugwy.fsnet.co.uk Map 115/784565
BB **B** ✕ nearby S1 D2 T1 F1 Closed Xmas ⋘(Betws-y-Coed)
Ⓓ⊛🐾🛏﹗ ★★

☆ Fairy Glen Hotel
Beaver Bridge, LL24 0SH ☎ 01690 710269 (Mr & Mrs B Youe)
www.fairyglenhotel.co.uk Map 115/799547
BB **C/D** ✕ book first £15, 7pm S1 D5 T1 F1 Closed Nov-Feb
⋘(Betws-y-Coed) Ⓥ Ⓑ Ⓓ🐾🛏 ★★

Built in the 17th C, commended for its food and hospitality in the 21st C. The hotel where you can enjoy your walking, relaxation and food. Residents licensed bar. Private car park. fairyglen@youe.fsworld.co.uk

☆ The Ferns Non-Smokers Guest House
LL24 0AN ☎ 01690 710587 (Deborah & Ian Baxter)
www.ferns-guesthouse.co.uk Map 115/795562
BB **B/C** ✕ nearby D6 T1 F2 ⋘(Betws-y-Coed)
Ⓑ Ⓓ⊛🐾🛏 ★★★

The Ferns Non-Smokers Guest House is conveniently situated in the village of Betws. All rooms en-suite with TV, beverage trays, clocks and hairdryers. Ian & Deborah will make every effort to ensure that your stay is a comfortable one. Which? Recommended.

☆🥾⊂ The Old Courthouse
Henllys, Old Church Rd, LL24 0AL ☎ 01690 710534 (Mark & Gillian Bidwell)
www.guesthouse-snowdonia.co.uk Map 115/795568
BB **C/D** ✕ nearby D7 T1 F1 Closed Jan ⋘(Betws-y-Coed)
Ⓑ Ⓓ🐾🛏﹗Ⓜ ★★★

Comfortable non-smoking guesthouse in the village, ideal centre for Snowdon, Siabod, Tryfan. Many lake and forest walks from the door. Train/bus 5mins' walk. All en-suite. Heating. Car park. Drying facilities. Riverside garden. Vegetarians welcome.

☆🥾⊂ Afon View Non Smokers Guest House
Holyhead Road, LL24 0AN ☎ 01690 710726 (Keith Roobottom)
www.afon-view.co.uk Map 115/795562
BB **C** ✕ nearby S1 D4 T1 F1 Closed Xmas ⋘(Betws-y-Coed)
Ⓑ Ⓓ⊛🐾🛏﹗ ◆◆◆◆

A warm welcome awaits you from your host Keith. Mountain bike hire is available nearby – secure overnight storage. You can choose from four-poster, twin, doubles and single room, all with en-suite shower. Guests who appreciate a relaxed, comfortable environment are well cared for here.

Park Hill Hotel, Lanrwst Rd, LL24 0HD ☎ 01690 710540
(Jaap & Ghislaine Buis) www.park-hill-hotel.co.uk Map 116/801565
BB **D** ✕ book first £17, 7pm D5 T4 ⋘(Betws-y-Coed)
Ⓥ Ⓑ Ⓓ🐾🛏﹗★★★

Bryn Bella Guest House, Lon Muriau, Llanwrst Rd, LL24 0HD
☎ 01690 710627 (Mark Edwards) www.bryn-bella.co.uk Map 116/800565
BB **C** ✕ nearby D5 Closed Xmas ⋘(Betws-y-Coed)
Ⓑ Ⓓ⊛🐾🛏 Ⓜ ★★★★

WALES

● Conwy
CAMBRIAN WAY

☆ Glan Heulog Guest House
Llanrwst Road, LL32 8LT ☎ 01492 593845 (Stan & Vivien Watson-Jones)
www.walesbandb.co.uk Map 115/779772
BB C ✗ nearby D4 T2 F1 Closed Xmas ⋙(Conwy)
Ⓥ Ⓑ Ⓓ ⊗ 🛉🛏💺🔥!💺 ★★★

Beautiful Victorian house coveniently situated in the World Heritage town of Conwy. Non-Smoking en- suite rooms, centrally heated with TV, beverage trays, clock radio and hairdryers. Lounge and conservatory to relax in. Car parking.

● Llandudno
CAMBRIAN WAY

▪🍽◀ Lakelands Guest House, 36 Lloyd Street, LL30 2YG
☎ 01492 874260 (Glen Jones)
www.lakelands-guesthouse.co.uk Map 115/779821
BB C ✗ nearby D5 T1 F1 ⋙(Llandudno) Ⓥ Ⓑ Ⓓ 🛉🛏💺

No. 9 Guest House, 9 Chapel Street, LL30 2SY
☎ 01492 877251 (Amanda Miller)
numbernine@34gg.freeserve.co.uk Map 115/780823
BB B ✗ book first £10, 6pm S2 D3 T2 F2 ⋙(Llandudno)
Ⓥ Ⓑ Ⓓ ⊗ 🛉🛏💺 ★★ Wheelchair access.

▪🍽◀ Vine House, 23 Church Walks, LL30 2HG
☎ 01492 876493 (Amanda Jacob) www.vinehouse.org.uk Map 115/778827
BB B ✗ nearby D2 F2 ⋙(Llandudno)
Ⓥ Ⓑ Ⓓ ⊗ 🛉🛏💺🔥!💺 ◆◆◆

● Llanfairfechan
SNOWDONIA/ERYRI
CAMBRIAN WAY

☆ ▪🍽◀ Rhiwiau Isaf
LL33 0EH ☎ 01248 681143 (Ruth Carrington)
www.rhiwiau.co.uk Map 115/678732
BB C ✗ book first £10, 6:15pm S2 D2 T2 F2 Closed Xmas
⋙(Llanfairfechan) Ⓥ Ⓑ Ⓓ ⊗ 🛉🛏💺🔥! ★★

Set in secluded valley only 5 minutes from A55. Views across the Menai Straits to Anglesey. Walk through our 16 acres of woods onto the Snowdonia National Park, Carneddau and North Wales Path. Extremely comfortable en-suite rooms (all non-smoking). Own car park.

● Talybont
The Lodge Hotel, LL32 8YX ☎ 01492 660766
www.thelodgehotelconwy.co.uk Map 115/768694
BB D ✗ £20, 7pm D5 T5 F3 ⋙(Tal-y-Cafn) Ⓥ Ⓑ Ⓓ 🛉🛏💺🔥💺
Wheelchair access.

● Trefriw
SNOWDONIA/ERYRI

☆ ▪🍽◀ Crafnant Guest House
LL27 0JH ☎ 01492 640809 (Mike & Jan Bertenshaw)
www.trefriw.co.uk Map 115/780631
BB C ✗ nearby D3 T1 F1 Closed Xmas-Jan ⋙(Llanrwst)
Ⓑ Ⓓ ⊗ 🛉🛏💺! ★★★

Whether you've discovered the mountain lakes which nestle above our village, conquered Snowdon or just strolled in the stunning Conwy Valley then rest assured of the comfort and warm welcome of Crafnant House. All bedrooms have cast-iron beds with fresh white linen.

GWYNEDD

● Aberdovey
SNOWDONIA/ERYRI

▪🍽◀ Awel Y Mor, 4 Bodfor Terrace, LL35 0EA ☎ 01654 767058
(Mrs Jennifer Johnson) www.awelymor-aberdovey.co.uk Map 135/612959
BB C ✗ nearby S1 D3 T2 F1 ⋙(Aberdovey)
Ⓑ Ⓓ ⊗ 🛉🛏💺🔥💺 ★★★

● Bala
SNOWDONIA/ERYRI

☆ ▪🍽◀ Abercelyn Country House
Llanycil, LL23 7YF ☎ 01678 521109 (Mrs Lindsay Hind)
www.abercelyn.co.uk Map 125/914349
BB D ✗ book first £18, 7:30pm D1 T1 F1 Closed Xmas
Ⓥ Ⓑ Ⓓ ⊗ 🛉🛏💺🔥!Ⓜ ★★★★

Walker-friendly accommodation in a former Grade II listed rectory in own grounds. Home cooking using local produce. Visitors can be met by car. Drying room. Walking guides and maps. Guided walking. Self-catering available.

☆ Fronderw Country House
Stryd y Fron , LL23 7YD ☎ 01678 520301 (Paul Short)
www.fronderwhouse.co.uk Map 125/915361
BB D ✗ £25 S1 D4 T1 F1 Closed Xmas-Jan
Ⓥ Ⓑ Ⓓ ⊗ 🛉🛏💺 ★★★★

Enjoying spectacular lake & mountain views, our early 17th C. Dower House is an ideal base for touring and walking holidays. Fully refurbished. Off street parking. Imaginative cuisine and outstanding wine list. Close to many local walks and attractions.

● Barmouth
SNOWDONIA/ERYRI
CAMBRIAN WAY

▪🍽◀ The Gables, Mynach Rd, LL42 1RL
☎ 01341 280553 (Mrs D Lewis) Map 124/609166
BB B ✗ nearby S1 D2 F1 Closed Dec-Feb ⋙(Barmouth)
Ⓑ Ⓓ ⊗ 🛉🛏💺🔥!💺 ★★★

☀ Bryn Melyn Hotel, Panorama Road, LL42 IDQ
☎ 01341 280556 (Mrs Lisa Hunt) www.brynmelyn.co.uk Map 124/619157
BB **D** ✗ £21.95, 6-8pm D5 T2 F2 ⚌(Barmouth)
Ⓥ Ⓑ Ⓓ ⚌🚲👤⛅!🏠Ⓦ

● Beddgelert (Caernarfon)
SNOWDONIA/ERYRI
CAMBRIAN WAY

Plas Colwyn Guest House, LL55 4UY ☎ 01766 890458 (Lynda Osmond)
www.plascolwyn.co.uk Map 115/589482
BB **C** ✗ nearby SI D2 TI F2 Closed Xmas Ⓑ Ⓓ ⊗ ⚌👤🚲!🏠 ★★

Gwesty Plas Tan-Y-Graig, LL55 4LT ☎ 01766 890310 (John & Rae Duffield)
www.plastanygraig.co.uk Map 115/587483
BB **C** ✗ nearby D2 T2 FI Closed Xmas Ⓑ Ⓓ ⊗ ⚌👤⛅ ★★★

● Bethesda (Bangor)
SNOWDONIA/ERYRI
CAMBRIAN WAY

☆ ☀ **Snowdon Lodge, Nant Ffrancon**
LL57 3LX ☎ 01248 600500
www.snowdonlodge.com Map 115/634642
BB **C** ✗ nearby S5 D5 TI2 F5
Ⓥ Ⓑ Ⓓ ⊗ ⚌👤Ⓜ See Yr-Ocar in SC also.

Snowdon Lodge used to be a motel and has been transformed into a beautiful retreat centre for self-catering and bed & breakfast accommodation, along with residential group facilities.

This venue is renowned for its peaceful, tranquil surroundings. A perfect holiday location providing opportunities to walk in the Snowdonia National Park.

Facilities include Internet access, lounge and a shop for gifts, snacks and non-alcoholic beverages.

● Blaenau Ffestiniog
SNOWDONIA/ERYRI
CAMBRIAN WAY

☆ ☀ **Bryn Elltyd Guest House**
Tanygrisiau, LL41 3TW ☎ 01766 831356 (Ann & Bob Cole)
www.accommodation-snowdonia.com Map 124/681448
BB **B** ✗ book first £12, 7.30pm SI D2 T2 FI ⚌(Blaenau Ffestiniog)
Ⓥ Ⓑ Ⓓ ⊗ ⚌👤⛅!🏠Ⓜ ★★★ Guided walks.

One of the leading environmentally-friendly guest houses in Wales, located in a secluded mountain setting in the centre of Snowdonia National Park, ideal for all outdoor activities. Sauna, drying room, evening meals & packed lunches. Discount for ramblers and groups.

Dolawel Guest House, Rhiwbrydfir, LL41 3HS
☎ 01766 830511 (Alister Haveron) www.dolawel.co.uk Map 115/697463
BB **C** ✗ nearby DI TI F2 ⚌(Blaenau Ffestiniog)
Ⓥ Ⓑ Ⓓ ⚌👤⛅ ★★★Ⓖ

☆ **Cae Du**
Manod, LL41 4BB ☎ 01766 830847 (Chris Carswell & Sue Ashe)
www.caedu.co.uk Map 124/709438
BB **B** ✗ book first £14, 7pm D2 TI Closed Xmas ⚌(Blaenau Ffestiniog)
Ⓥ Ⓑ Ⓓ ⊗ ⚌👤🚲! ★★★

Picturesque 16th C. former farmhouse in magnificent mountain setting. Stunning panoramic views, comfortable en-suite rooms, log fires, 2 lounges, satellite TV, private parking. Beautiful mature gardens and ponds. Centrally located for exploring Snowdonia with varied walks direct from Cae Du, guide if required. Great views, great walks, great home cooking, all make for ramblers to unwind with Chris & Sue. "It's our home – make it yours".

● Dolgellau
SNOWDONIA/ERYRI
CAMBRIAN WAY

☆ **Dwy Olwyn**
Coed-y-Fronallt, LL40 2YG ☎ 01341 422822 (Mrs N Jones)
www.dwyolwyn.co.uk Map 124/734183
BB **A/B** ✗ book first £12, 7pm DI TI F2 Closed Dec
Ⓥ Ⓓ ⊗ ⚌👤 ★★★

"View of Cader Idris from Dwy Olwyn". A warm welcome awaits you in this comfortable guesthouse, set in an acre of landscaped gardens. Peaceful position only 10 mins walk into town. Ideal for touring Snowdonia NP, sandy beaches, gauge railways, RSPB sanctuary, picturesque walks including famous Precipice Walk above Mawddach estuary. Spacious bedrooms with colour TV, clock radio, hairdryer. Good home cooking. Lounge with selection of maps, guide books and leaflets. Cleanliness and personal attention assured. Car parking available.

☆ ☀ **Ivy House**
Finsbury Square, LL40 IRF ☎ 01341 422535 (J S & M Bamford)
www.ukworld.net/ivyhouse Map 124/727177
BB **B** ✗ book first £15, 6:30-7:30pm D3 T2 FI Closed Xmas
Ⓥ Ⓑ Ⓓ ⚌👤🚲!🏠 ◆◆◆

At the centre of an idyllic walking area, a country town guesthouse, offering home made food: big breakfasts, evening meals and packed lunches. Fully centrally heated, licensed, all bedrooms have TV, hairdryers & tea/coffee making facilities, most en-suite. Email: marg.bamford@btconnect.com

WALES

Tanyfron, Arran Road, LL40 2AA ☎ 01341 422638 (Elfed & Sue Rowlands)
www.tanyfron.co.uk Map 124/735176
BB B/C ✗ nearby D1 T1 F1 Closed Jan ▣ ▣ ⊗ ☖ ★★★★

◄▨ The Clifton, Smithfield Square, LL40 1ES ☎ 01341 422554
(Geoff & Teresa Challenor) www.clifton-house-hotel.co.uk Map 124/728177
BB D ✗ £12, 6:30 onwards S1 D3 T3 Closed Dec
▣ ▣ ▣ ⊗ 🐾☖🚗! ◆◆◆◆

◄▨ Penycoed Hall, LL40 2YP ☎ 01341 423403 (Madge & Nigel Hawkins)
www.snowdoniaguesthouse.co.uk Map 124/724183
BB D ✗ nearby D2 T2 F2 ▣ ▣ ▣ ⊗ 🐾☖🚗!🏠

● Llanberis (Caernarfon)
SNOWDONIA/ERYRI
Mount Pleasant Hotel, High Street, LL55 4HA ☎ 01286 870395
www.waterton.org.uk/mph Map 114,115/577602
BB B/C ✗ £14, 6-9pm S2 D2 T1 F2 ▣ ▣ ▣ 🐾☖🚗!🏠

◄▨ Snowdon Cottage, 7 Pentre Castell, LL55 4UB
☎ 01286 872015 (Carol Anne Gerrard) Map 115/585596
BB B ✗ nearby S1 D1 T1 ▣ ▣ ⊗ 🐾☖🚗🏠Ⓜ

● Llandanwg (Harlech)
SNOWDONIA/ERYRI
Glanygors Guest House, LL46 2SD ☎ 01341 241410 (Gweneth Evans)
Map 124/570285 BB B ✗ nearby D1 T1 F1 ⋘(Llandanwg)
▣ ▣ ⊗ 🐾☖🚗!🏠 ★★★

● Nantgwynant (Caernarfon)
SNOWDONIA/ERYRI
Pen-y-Gwryd Hotel, Pen-y-Gwryd, LL55 4NT ☎ 01286 870211 & 870768
www.pyg.co.uk Map 115/660558 BB D ✗ book first £22, 7:30pm
S1 D8 T6 F1 Closed Xmas ▣ ▣ ▣🐾🏠 ★★ Closed weekdays Jan-Feb.

● Pant Glas (Garndolbenmaen)
SNOWDONIA/ERYRI

☆ ◄▨ Hen Ysgol (Old School)
Bwlch Derwin, LL51 9EQ ☎ 01286 660701 (Terry & Sue Gibbins)
www.oldschool-henyysgol.co.uk Map 123,115/456474
BB C ✗ book first £13-£16, 7pm D1 T1 F1 Closed Xmas
▣ ▣ ▣ ⊗ 🐾☖🚗!🏠 ★★★

A beautiful, historical 'Welsh Not' country school provides a unique base for walking the re-opened network of paths linking Snowdonia with Lleyn Peninsular & Bardsey Island. Delicious home cooked evening meals and choice of breakfast menu. Terry & Sue offer a warm welcome.

● Penrhyndeudraeth (Porthmadog)
SNOWDONIA/ERYRI

☆ Talgarth
LL48 6DR ☎ 01766 770353 (Hilary & Paul Davies)
hilary@talgarthbb.freeserve.co.uk Map 124/615398
BB B ✗ book first £12, 7pm S2 D1 Closed Xmas
⋘(Penrhyndeudraeth) ▣ ▣ ⊗ 🐾

Ideally situated in the walkers' paradise that is Snowdonia. Glorious views, friendly welcome. Warm & comfortable B&B with superb range of cooked food. Optional evening meal and packed lunches. Open all year round. Member of WTB Welcome Host scheme.

● Talyllyn (Tywyn)
SNOWDONIA/ERYRI
CAMBRIAN WAY

◄▨ Dolffanog Fawr Country House, LL36 9AJ ☎ 01654 761247
(Lorraine Hinkins) www.dolffanogfawr.co.uk Map 124/729104
BB D ✗ book first £17.50, 7pm D2 T2 Closed Nov-Feb
▣ ▣ ▣ ⊗ 🐾☖🚗 ★★★★

● Tywyn
SNOWDONIA/ERYRI
CAMBRIAN WAY
Hendy Farm, LL36 9RU ☎ 01654 710457 (Anne Lloyd-Jones)
www.hendyfarmholidays.co.uk Map 135/594013
BB D ✗ nearby D2 T1 Closed Nov-Mar ⋘(Tywyn)
▣ ▣ ⊗ ☖🚗!🏠 ★★★

MONMOUTHSHIRE

● Abergavenny
BRECON BEACONS
CAMBRIAN WAY & USK VALLEY WALK
◄▨ The Guest House, 2 Oxford Street, NP7 5RP ☎ 01873 854823
(Jenny Taylor) theguesthouseabergavenny@hotmail.com Map 161/303147
BB C S1 D2 T3 F1 ⋘(Abergavenny) ▣ ⊗ 🐾☖🚗!🏠 ★

◄▨ Park Guest House, 36 Hereford Road, NP7 5RA ☎ 01873 853715
(Neil & Julia Herring) www.abergavenny.net Map 161/303146
BB C ✗ nearby S1 D4 T1 F1 Closed Xmas ⋘(Abergavenny)
▣ ▣ 🐾☖ ★★

● Chepstow
OFFA'S DYKE
◄▨ Upper Sedbury House, Sedbury Lane, Sedbury, NP16 7HN
☎ 01291 627173 (Christine Potts) www.smoothound.co.uk/hotels/uppersed.html
Map 172/547943 BB B ✗ nearby D3 T2 F1 Closed Xmas ⋘(Chepstow)
▣ ▣ ⊗ 🐾☖ ★★

Southam, Welsh Street, Chepstow, NP16 5LU (Maureen & Richard Langston)
maureenlangston@hotmail.com Map 172,162/527943
BB C ✗ nearby D2 T1 F1 Closed Xmas ▣ ▣ ⊗ 🐾☖! See SC also.

● Llanfihangel Crucorney (Abergavenny)
BRECON BEACONS
OFFA'S DYKE
Penyclawdd Farm, NP7 7LB ☎ 01873 890591 (Ann Davies)
www.penyclawdd.co.uk Map 161/312200
BB C ✗ nearby S/D/F1 D2 T2 F1 Closed Xmas ⋘(Abergavenny)
▣ ▣ ⊗ 🐾☖🚗🏠 ★★★

● Llangattock-Lingoed (Abergavenny)
BRECON BEACONS
OFFA'S DYKE
The Old Rectory, NP7 8RR ☎ 01873 821326 (Karen Ball)
www.rectoryonoffasdyke.co.uk Map 161/362201
BB C ✗ book first £12.50, 6:30-7pm S1 D2 T1
▣ ▣ ▣ ⊗ 🐾☖🚗! ★★★

● Monmouth
OFFA'S DYKE & WYE VALLEY WALK
◄▨ Penylan Farm, The Hendre, NP25 5NL ☎ 01600 716435
(Cathy & Dave Bowen) www.penylanfarm.co.uk Map 161/445162
BB C ✗ book first £12, 7:30pm D1 T1 F1 Closed Xmas
▣ ▣ ▣ ⊗ 🐾☖🚗! ★★★

☆ 🍴 Church Farm Guest House
Mitchel Troy, NP25 4HZ ☎ 01600 712176 (Rosey & Derek Ringer)
www.churchfarmmitcheltroy.co.uk Map 162/492103
BB **C** ✕ book first £15, 7-7:30pm S2 D3 T2 F3 Closed Xmas
🆅 🅱 🅳 ⊗ 🍳♿🛏! 🛁 Ⓜ ◆◆◆ See SC also.

Set in large garden with stream, a 16th C. former farmhouse with oak beams and inglenook fireplaces. Excellent base for Wye Valley, Forest of Dean and Black Mountains. Central heating. Mainly en-suite bedrooms. Groups welcome (discounts available). Also self-catering unit.

🍴 Casita Alta, 15 Toynbee Close, Osbaston, NP25 3NU ☎ 01600 713023
www.monmouthbedandbreakfast.co.uk Map 162/502143
BB **C** ✕ nearby S/DI D/TI Closed Xmas
🆅 🅱 🅳 🍳♿🛏! ★★

Ramblers Rest, 7 Levitsfield Close, NP25 5BZ ☎ 01600 715611
(Mrs M C Atkins) secretswd@hotmail.com Map 162/496133
BB **C** ✕ book first £7.50, To suit SI DI TI
🆅 🅱 🅳 ⊗ 🍳♿🛏 Ⓜ

● Pandy (Abergavenny)
BRECON BEACONS
OFFA'S DYKE
The Lancaster Arms, Old Hereford Road, NP7 8DW ☎ 01873 890699
(Mrs Sandra Lyon) www.lancaster-arms.supanet.com Map 161/334221
BB **C** ✕ £7, 7pm onwards T2 Closed Xmas
🆅 🅱 🍳♿🛏! 🛁 ★★ Free camping.

Brynhonddu Country House B&B, Bwlch Trewyn Estate, NP7 7PD
☎ 01873 890535 (Mrs Carol White)
www.brynhonddu.co.uk Map 161/326224
BB **C** ✕ nearby SI D2 TI FI Closed Xmas 🅱 🅳 🍳♿🛏 🛁 ★★

● Redbrook (Monmouth)
OFFA'S DYKE & WYE VALLEY WALK
Tresco, NP25 4LY ☎ 01600 712325 (Mrs M Evans) Map 162/536101
BB **B** ✕ nearby S2 DI TI FI Closed Xmas 🅳 ⊗ 🍳♿! 🛁 Ⓜ

NORTH EAST WALES

● Bodfari (Mold)
OFFA'S DYKE & CLWYDIAN WAY
🍴 Moel-y-Park, Mountain View, The Bungalow, Afon-Wen, CH7 5UB
☎ 01352 720338 (Mrs H L Priestley) hlpriestley@aol.com Map 116/127716
BB **B** ✕ nearby D2 TI Closed Xmas
🅱 ⊗ 🍳♿🛏 🛁

● Caerwys (Mold)
OFFA'S DYKE
🍴 Plas Penucha, CH7 5BH ☎ 01352 720210 (Mrs N Price)
www.plaspenucha.co.uk Map 116/108733
BB **C** ✕ book first £15, 7pm S4 D2 T2 Closed Xmas
🆅 🅱 🅳 ⊗ 🍳♿🛏! 🛁 ★★★

● Corwen

☆ 🍴 Bron-y-Graig
LL21 0DR ☎ 01490 413007
www.north-wales-hotel.co.uk Map 125/082433
BB **D** ✕ book first £18, 6:30-9pm S/D/T8 F2
🆅 🅱 🅳 🍳♿🛏 🛁 ◆◆◆◆◆Ⓦ

Bron-y-Graig is a superbly located AA 5-diamond guest house set in the Upper Dee Valley between Llangollen and Bala – ideal for Offa's Dyke, Clwydian Way, the Berwyns and the Dee Valley – on the edge of Snowdonia National Park.

Its 10 en-suite luxury bedrooms can be configured as single, double, twin or triple rooms. Prices are £29.50pppn for bed and breakfast, single rooms are £39.50pppn.

Chose from our excellent a la carte menu and take dinner, bed and breakfast at £39.50pppn (see www.north-wales-hotel.co.uk for full details and conditions).

Member of Walkers Welcome Scheme with minibus available.

● Denbigh
Cayo Guest House, 74 Vale Street, LL16 3BW ☎ 01745 812686
stay@cayo.co.uk Map 116/055663
BB **B** ✕ nearby SI D2 T3 Closed Xmas 🅱 ⊗ 🍳♿🛏 🛁 ◆◆◆

● Llangollen
OFFA'S DYKE

☆ 🍴 New Ross
Dinbren Rd, LL20 8TF ☎ 01978 861334 (Mrs E A Roberts)
www.newrosstlan.co.uk Map 117/217418
BB **C** ✕ nearby D2 TI Closed Xmas
🅱 🅳 ⊗ 🍳♿🛏! ★★★★

Set in a spectacular location by Offa's Dyke Path and overlooking Llangollen marina. The warm welcome and excellent breakfast inspired one visitor to comment: "wonderful, friendly, relaxing B&B. Immaculate and with views to die for."

Squirrels, Abbey Rd, LL20 8SP ☎ 01978 869041 (Mrs Lilian Speake)
www.squirrels-b-and-b.co.uk Map 117/211423
BB **C** ✕ nearby D3 T2
🅱 🅳 ⊗ 🍳♿🛏 🛁 ★★★

WALES

☆ Oakmere

Regent Street, LL20 8HS ☎ 01978 861126 (Lyndsey Knibbs)
www.oakmere.llangollen.co.uk Map 117/218418
BB **C** ✗ nearby D4 T2
Ⓥ Ⓑ Ⓓ ⊗ 🛏🍴👤🛁🚗! ◆◆◆◆

Large country house set in its own grounds, five minutes' walk from Llangollen's town center. Easy access to Offa's Dyke and the Dee Valley Way. Rooms either en-suite or with private facilities providing a relaxing atmosphere of spacious comfort. Private parking and non-smoking.

● Llangwm (Corwen)

Bryn Awel B&B, LL21 0RB ☎ 01490 420610 (Jenni Miller)
www.brynawelbnb.com Map 125/963439
BB **B** SI DI TI Closed Xmas
Ⓓ ⊗ 🛏🛁🚗! ★★ Walking routes, notes and maps available.

PEMBROKESHIRE

● Amroth (Narberth)
PEMBROKESHIRE COAST PATH & NATIONAL PARK

Ashdale Guest House, SA67 8NA ☎ 01834 813853 (Roy & Edith Williamson)
Map 158/160071 BB **B** ✗ book first £9.50, 6pm SI D4 T3 F0
Closed Nov-Feb 🚶(Kilgetty) Ⓓ 🛁🚗!

● Bosherston (Pembroke)
PEMBROKESHIRE COAST PATH & NATIONAL PARK

St Govan's Country Inn, SA71 5DN ☎ 01646 661643
trefalen@trefalen.force9.co.uk Map 158/966947
BB **C** ✗ £8, 7-9pm SI D2 T2 FI Ⓥ Ⓑ 🛏🚗! ★★★

● Broad Haven (Haverfordwest)
PEMBROKESHIRE COAST PATH & NATIONAL PARK

🛏🍴 Albany Guesthouse, 27 Millmoor Way, SA62 3JJ ☎ 01437 781051
(Mrs Morgan) www.albanyguesthouse.co.uk Map 157/861138
BB **C** ✗ nearby SI DI TI Closed Oct-Feb Ⓑ Ⓓ ⊗ 🛏🛁! ★★★

● Dale (Haverfordwest)
PEMBROKESHIRE COAST PATH & NATIONAL PARK

Allenbrook, SA62 3RN ☎ 01646 636254 (Elizabeth Webber)
www.ukworld.net/allenbrook Map 157/811059
BB **D** ✗ nearby SI DI TI FI Closed Xmas
Ⓑ Ⓓ ⊗ 🛏🛁🚗! ★★★★

🛏🍴 Point Farm, SA62 3RD ☎ 01646 636541
www.pointfarm.info Map 157/815053
BB **C** ✗ nearby D2 FI Closed Dec-Feb Ⓓ ⊗ 🛏🛁🚗! Ⓜ ★★★

● Dyffryn (Goodwick)
PEMBROKESHIRE COAST PATH & NATIONAL PARK

Ivybridge, Drim Mill, SA64 0JT ☎ 01348 875366
www.ivybridge.cwc.net Map 157/943371
BB **C** ✗ book first £17.95, 6:30-7:30pm SI D3 T3 F4 Closed Xmas
🚶(Fishguard) Ⓥ Ⓑ Ⓓ 🛏🛁🚗! 🍴 ★★★

● Fishguard
PEMBROKESHIRE COAST PATH & NATIONAL PARK

Cartref Hotel, 15-19 High Street, SA65 9AW ☎ 01348 872430
(Mrs Kristiina Bjorkqvist) www.cartrefhotel.co.uk Map 157/956369
BB **D** ✗ £16, 6:30-8:30pm S4 D2 T2 F2 🚶(Fishguard Harbour)
Ⓥ Ⓑ Ⓓ 🛏🛁🚗! 🍴 ★★

● Goodwick (Fishguard)
PEMBROKESHIRE COAST PATH & NATIONAL PARK

🛏🍴 6 New Hill Villas, SA64 0DS ☎ 01348 874076 (Anne Strawbridge)
garyann@glowinternet.net Map 157/947385
BB **B** ✗ nearby DI FI Closed Xmas 🚶(Fishguard)
Ⓑ Ⓓ ⊗ 🛏🛁🚗! 🍴

● Haverfordwest

☆ 🛏🍴 Cuckoo Mill Farm

Pelcomb Bridge, SA62 6EA ☎ 01437 762139 (Margaret Davies)
cmflimited@aol.com Map 157,158/933172
BB **B** ✗ book first £13-£15, 6-8:30pm SI D2 TI FI 🚶(Haverfordwest)
Ⓥ Ⓑ Ⓓ ⊗ 🛏🛁🚗 ★★★

Mixed farm in central Pembrokeshire. Country walking. Six miles to coastal path. Meal times to suit guests. Excellent home cooking. Cosy farmhouse. Warm, well-appointed rooms. En-suite facilities. Gold Welcome Host.

College Guest House, 93 Hill St, St Thomas Green, SA61 1QL ☎ 01437 763710
(Colin Larby) www.collegeguesthouse.com Map 157,158/951152
BB **D** ✗ nearby SI D2 T2 F3 🚶(Haverfordwest)
Ⓑ Ⓓ 🛏🛁🚗! 🍴 ★★★

● Jeffreyston (Kilgetty)
PEMBROKESHIRE COAST PATH

Jeffreyston Grange, SA68 0RE ☎ 01646 650159 (Tony Hesslegrave)
tony@hesslegrave.fsnet.co.uk Map 158/089065
BB **B** ✗ book first £10, 6:30pm D3 T2 FI Closed Jan-Feb
Ⓥ Ⓑ Ⓓ ⊗ 🛏🛁🚗! Wheelchair access.

● Manorbier (Tenby)
PEMBROKESHIRE COAST PATH & NATIONAL PARK

Honeyhill, Warlows Meadow, SA70 7SX ☎ 01834 871906 (Susan Robinson)
honeyhillbandb@aol.com Map 158/064983
BB **B** ✗ nearby SI D2 TI FI 🚶(Manorbier)
Ⓑ Ⓓ ⊗ 🛏🛁! ★★★

● Moylegrove (Cardigan)
PEMBROKESHIRE COAST PATH & NATIONAL PARK

🛏🍴 Swn-y-Nant B&B, SA43 3BW ☎ 01239 881244
www.moylegrove.co.uk Map 145/117446
BB **C** ✗ book first £15 D2 TI Closed Jan
Ⓥ Ⓑ Ⓓ ⊗ 🛏🛁🚗! ★★★

● Narberth

☆ Highland Grange Farm Guest House

Roberston Wathen, SA67 8EP ☎ 01834 860952 (Naomi Jones)
www.highlandgrange.co.uk Map 158/077154
BB **B/C** ✗ book first £12-£15, 6:30pm S2 D2 T2
Ⓥ Ⓑ Ⓓ ⊗ 🛏🛁🚗 ◆◆◆ⓒ

Spacious, quality groundfloor B&B. Central, A40 hilltop village location bordering National Park. Forest, castles, river, walking, country inn restaurant nearby. Excellent birdwatching, access to SSSI. Large guest lounge, books, boardgames etc, teas. Delicious choice of breakfast.

● Pembroke
PEMBROKESHIRE COAST PATH & NATIONAL PARK

◄═▪ High Noon Guest House, Lower Lamphey Road, SA71 4AB
☎ 01646 683736 (The Barnikel Family) www.highnoon.co.uk
Map 157,158/990011 BB **B** ✕ nearby S3 D3 T1 F2 Closed Xmas
▰(Pembroke) Ⓑ Ⓓ ⊗ 🐾♨ 🚗! ♨ ★★

● Saundersfoot
PEMBROKESHIRE COAST PATH & NATIONAL PARK

Jubilee Guest House, SA69 9HH
☎ 01834 813442 (Diane Cotton) Map 158/135046
BB **B** ✕ book first £10, 6:30pm S1 D4 T1 F1 ▰(Saundersfoot)
Ⓥ Ⓑ Ⓓ 🐾♨ ♨ ★★ Facilities available for disabled guests.

● St Davids
PEMBROKESHIRE COAST PATH & NATIONAL PARK

☆ Ramsey House
Lower Moor, SA62 6RP ☎ 01437 720321 (Ceri & Elaine Morgan)
www.ramseyhouse.co.uk Map 157/747250
BB **D** ✕ nearby D3 T3 Closed Nov-Feb
Ⓑ Ⓓ ⊗ 🐾♨ 🚗! ◆◆◆◆

Quality 4-diamond accommodation catering exclusively for adults. Quiet location situated just half mile from centre of St Davids, coast path and cathedral. Ideal for walking, bird watching, watersports and beaches. Congenial relaxed hospitality and licensed bar complete your enjoyment.

☆ Lochmeyler Farm Guest House
Llandeloy, Pen-y-Cwm, Solva, SA62 6LL ☎ 01348 837724 (Mrs M M Jones)
www.lochmeyler.co.uk Map 157/855275
BB **C** ✕ book first £15, 7pm S2 D5 T4 F4 Closed Xmas
Ⓥ Ⓑ Ⓓ 🐾♨ ♨ ★★★★★

15 en-suite non-smoking luxury bedrooms, TV & refreshment facilities. Centre St Davids peninsula. Ideal for exploring Pembrokeshire Coast Path & countryside. B&B £25-35 pppn. Optional evening dinner £15 pp. Closed Christmas and New Year. 10% discount on advance bookings for inclusive evening dinner, B&B for 7 nights or more. Email: stay@lochmeyler.co.uk

● St Ishmael's (Haverfordwest)
PEMBROKESHIRE COAST PATH & NATIONAL PARK

◄═▪ Skerryback Farmhouse, Sandy Haven, SA62 3DN ☎ 01646 636598
(Mrs M Williams) www.pfh.co.uk/skerryback Map 157/852074
BB **C** ✕ nearby D1 T1 F1 Closed Xmas
Ⓑ Ⓓ ⊗ 🐾♨ 🚗! ★★★

● Tenby
PEMBROKESHIRE COAST PATH

Sea Breezes B&B, 18 The Norton, SA70 8AA ☎ 01834 842753
www.seabreezesonline.co.uk Map 158/132007
BB **B** ✕ nearby S/D1 D/T2 ▰(Tenby) Ⓥ Ⓑ ♨ ♨ ★★

◄═▪ Glenholme, Picton Terrace, SA70 7DR ☎ 01834 843909
(Sandra Milward) www.glenholmetenby.co.uk Map 158/134002
BB **C** ✕ nearby S1 D4 T1 F2 ▰(Tenby)
Ⓥ Ⓑ Ⓓ ⊗ 🐾♨ ♨ ★★★

● Trefin (St Davids)
PEMBROKESHIRE COAST PATH & NATIONAL PARK

Bryngarw, Abercastle Rd, SA62 5AR ☎ 01348 831211
(Anthony & Judith Johnson) www.bryngarwguesthouse.co.uk
Map 157/842325 BB **D** ✕ book first £20, 7pm D4 T2 Closed Nov-Dec
Ⓥ Ⓑ Ⓓ ⊗ 🐾♨ ★★★

◄═▪ Hampton House, 2 Ffordd-y-Felin, SA62 5AX ☎ 01348 837701
(Vivienne & Chris Prior) viv.kay@virgin.net Map 157/840324
BB **B** ✕ nearby S1 D1 T1 Closed Xmas
Ⓑ Ⓓ ⊗ 🐾♨ 🚗! ♨ ★★★ Veggie breakfasts.

POWYS

● Brecon
BRECON BEACONS
USK VALLEY WALK

☆ Lodge Farm
Talgarth, LD3 0DP ☎ 01874 711244 (Mrs M Meredith)
marionlodgefarm@fwi.co.uk Map 161/173344
BB **D** ✕ book first £16, 7pm D1 T1 F1 Closed Xmas
Ⓥ Ⓑ Ⓓ ⊗ ♨ ♨ ★★★

Welcome to our 17th century farm house situated in the Brecon Beacons National Park, well placed for walking the Black Mountains and Brecon Beacons. En-suite bedrooms, tea-making facilities. Good, freshly prepared food including vegetarian. Non-smoking. FHB members.

The Beacons, 16 Bridge Street, LD3 8AH ☎ 01874 623339
(Melanie & Stephen Dale) www.s-h-systems.co.uk/hotels/beac.html
Map 160/042285 BB **B/C** ✕ book first £7.95-£20, 6:30-9pm D8 T2 F4
Ⓥ Ⓑ ⊗ 🐾♨ 🚗! ★★★★

The Grange , The Watton, LD3 7ED ☎ 01874 624038 (Meryl, Ian & John)
www.thegrange-brecon.co.uk Map 160/048283
BB **B** ✕ nearby D4 F4 Closed Xmas
Ⓑ Ⓓ ⊗ 🐾♨ ★★★ Guide dogs accepted.

☆ ◄═▪ The Old Mill
Felinfach, LD3 0UB ☎ 01874 625385
Map 161/091332
BB **B** ✕ nearby D1 T2 Closed Nov-Jan
Ⓑ Ⓓ 🐾♨ ★★★Ⓦ

A 16th C. converted corn mill, peacefully situated in its own grounds. Inglenook fireplace, exposed beams, TV lounge, beverage trays. Ideally situated for walks & touring the Brecon Beacons NP & Black Mountains or just relaxing. Local inn within walking distance. A friendly welcome awaits you.

WALES

☆ ⬛ The Castle of Brecon Hotel
Castle Square, LD3 9DB ☎ 01874 674611
www.breconcastle.co.uk Map 160/043288
BB D ✕ 6-9pm S1 D20 T/D16 F6
Ⓥ Ⓑ Ⓓ 🛏🛁♿🚗! 🎵Ⓜ ★★

Historic venue in the National Park set above the River Usk, with south-facing gardens and superb views of your walks on the Brecon Beacons.

Walker-friendly hotel with expert advice on hand to help plan your walks for individuals or groups alike.

The Borderers Guesthouse, 47 The Watton, LD3 7EG ☎ 01874 623559
www.borderers.com Map 160/046283
BB D ✕ nearby D3 T3 F3 Closed Xmas
Ⓑ Ⓓ⊛🛏🛁♿ ◆◆◆

☆ ⬛ Plas-y-Ffynnon
Battle, LD3 9RN ☎ 01874 611199 (Gill Badham)
www.breconbeaconsbandb.co.uk Map 160/009310
BB B ✕ nearby D3 T2
Ⓑ Ⓓ⊛🛏🛁🚗!🎵Ⓜ ★★★

Plas-y-Ffynnon is a 5-minute drive from Brecon. A great place to stay for a walking break in the Brecon Beacons National Park. Stunning views into the hills, lovely garden full of wildlife, tremendous breakfasts and a warm welcome from Gill & Colin Badham.

☆ ⬛ The Coach House
12-13 Orchard Street, LD3 8AN ☎ 07005 978099 (Marc & Tony)
www.coachhousebrecon.co.uk Map 160/040284
BB C ✕ book first £17, 6-8pm S2 D4 T2 F2
Ⓥ Ⓑ Ⓓ⊛🛏🛁🚗! ★★★★Ⓦ

Superior comfort (refurbished) in central location. All rooms en-suite, television and tea/coffee making facilities. A non-smoking house, private parking, beautiful garden, close to restaurants & pubs. Indulge in 4-star luxury. "My tastes are simple. I am always satisfied with the best" — Oscar Wilde

⬛ Canal Bank, Ty Gardd, LD3 7HG
☎ 01874 623464 (Peter & Barbara Jackson)
www.accommodation-breconbeacons.co.uk Map 160/047281
BB D ✕ nearby D2 T1 Closed Xmas Ⓑ Ⓓ⊛🛏🛁🚗!🎵

⬛ The Beacon, 4 The Watton, LD3 7ED
☎ 01874 625862 (Joanna & Dafydd Jones)
www.beaconguesthouse.co.uk Map 160/048283
BB B ✕ £7, 6-8pm T1 Ⓥ Ⓑ Ⓓ⊛🛏🛁🚗!

● Builth Wells
WYE VALLEY WALK

⬛ Little Smithfield, Cwmbach, LD2 3RS
☎ 01982 552973 (Mrs Philippa Wright)
andrew.wright91@virgin.net Map 147/024548
BB C ✕ book first £15, 7:30pm S2 D2 F1 Closed Xmas
Ⓥ Ⓑ Ⓓ⊛🛏🛁🚗!🎵 ★★★

☆ Dol-Llyn-Wydd Farmhouse
LD2 3RZ ☎ 01982 553660 (Biddy Williams)
Map 147/042488
BB B ✕ book first £12.50, 7:30-8:30pm S2 D1 T2 Closed Xmas
🚌(Builth Road) Ⓥ Ⓑ Ⓓ⊛🛏🛁🚗! ★★

17th C. farmhouse beneath the Eppynt Hills. Superb area for walking, touring, bird watching. Elan Valley, Black Mountains, Hay-on-Wye. 1 mile from Builth Wells, B4520 Upper Chapel, 1st left down lane – 200 yds, on left. Bike lockup garage. Wye Valley Walk.

● Capel-y-Ffin (Abergavenny)
BRECON BEACONS
CAMBRIAN WAY & OFFA'S DYKE

The Grange, NP7 7NP ☎ 01873 890215/157 (Griffiths Family)
www.grangeguesthouse.co.uk Map 161/251315
BB B ✕ book first £14, 7-7:45pm S1 D1 T1 F2 Closed Dec-Feb
Ⓥ Ⓑ Ⓓ🛏🛁🚗!🎵 ★

● Crickhowell
BRECON BEACONS
CAMBRIAN WAY

⬛ Dragon Hotel, High Street, NP8 1BE ☎ 01873 810362
(Andrew & Sian Powell) www.dragonhotel.co.uk Map 161/217183
BB D ✕ £6-£15, 6:30-9:30pm S2 D6 T6 F1 Closed Xmas
Ⓥ Ⓑ Ⓓ🛏🛁 ★★

⬛ Ty Croeso Hotel, The Dardy, NP8 1PU ☎ 01873 810573 (Linda Jarrett)
www.ty-croeso.co.uk Map 161/206183
BB D ✕ £18, 7-9pm S2 D4 T2 Closed Jan
Ⓥ Ⓑ Ⓓ⊛🛏🛁🚗!Ⓜ

● Discoed (Presteigne)
OFFA'S DYKE

☆ Gumma Farm
LD8 2NP ☎ 01547 560243 (Mrs Anne Owens)
www.ukworld.net/gummafarm Map 137, 148/288651
BB B ✕ book first £15, 6-8pm S1 D1 T1 Closed Xmas
Ⓥ Ⓑ Ⓓ⊛🛏🛁♿!🎵Ⓜ ★★★★

350-acre working farm accommodation at its best. 3 front rooms overlooking meadows & woodland. Peaceful. Guest lounge. Full breakfast. Antique furnishings. En-suite/private facilities. TV. Tea/coffee. All for £25. A perfect haven. Evening meal ordered in advance. Brochures available.

● Glasbury (Hay-on-Wye)
WYE VALLEY WALK

Aberllynfi B&B, HR3 5NT ☎ 01497 847107 (Catherine Sturgeon)
www.hay-on-wye.co.uk/aberllynfi Map 161/179390
BB B ✕ nearby S1 T2 Closed Xmas Ⓓ⊛🛏🛁🚗!

● Hay-on-Wye
BRECON BEACONS
OFFA'S DYKE & HEREFORDSHIRE TRAIL

Fernleigh, Hardwick Road, Cusop, HR3 5QX ☎ 01497 820459
(Winnifred Hughes) Map 161,148/235422
BB A ✕ nearby D2 T1 Closed Nov-Feb Ⓥ Ⓑ Ⓓ⊛🛏🛁Ⓜ

La Fosse Guest House, Oxford Road, HR3 5AJ ☎ 01497 820613
(Bob and Annabel Crook) www.hay-on-wye/lafosse.co.uk Map 161/232423
BB **B** ✕ nearby D4 T1 Closed Xmas 🅱 🅳 ⊗ 🐾🍴🌿 ★★

🏠◀ Old Black Lion Inn, 26 Lion Street, HR3 5AD ☎ 01497 820841
www.oldblacklion.co.uk Map 161,148/231423
BB **D** ✕ £9 1 , 6.30-9:30pm S2 D5 T2 F1 Closed Xmas
🆅 🅱 🅳 🐾🛁🍴 ★★★

Oxford Cottage, Oxford Road, HR3 5AJ ☎ 01497 820008 (Ed Moore)
www.oxfordcottage.co.uk Map 161,148/232423
BB **B** D2 T1 🅳 ⊗ 🌿 Kitchen for guests.

🏠◀ Baskerville Hall Hotel, Clyro Court, Clyro, HR3 5LE ☎ 01497 820033
www.baskervillehall.co.uk Map 161/208428
BB **D** ✕ £8, 7-9pm S7 D10 T12 F5 Closed Xmas
🆅 🅱 🅳 🐾🛁🌿 See Groups also.

● Heol Senni (Brecon)
BRECON BEACONS

🏠◀ Maeswalter Farm, LD3 8SU ☎ 01874 636629 (Mrs M J Mayo)
bb@maeswalter.co.uk Map 160/931236
BB **D** ✕ book first £12, 6:30-7pm D3 T1 F1
🆅 🅱 🅳 ⊗ 🐾🛁🚗🍴 ◆◆◆

● Knighton
GLYNDWR'S WAY & OFFA'S DYKE

The Fleece House, Market Street, LD7 1BB ☎ 01547 520168
(Mrs Dana Simmons) www.fleecehouse.co.uk Map 148,137/284723
BB **C/D** ✕ nearby T3 🚶(Knighton)
🅱 🅳 ⊗ 🛁🍴 ★★★ Local information available.

🏠◀ The Plough, 40 Market Street, LD7 1EY ☎ 01547 528041
sarahscotford@aol.com Map 148,137/284723
BB **C** ✕ £3 (bar snacks), 7-9pm S4 D1 T3 Closed Xmas 🚶(Knighton)
🆅 🅱 🐾🛁🍴

☆ **The George & Dragon**
4 Broad Street, LD7 1BL ☎ 01547 528532 (Justin & Helen Rees)
www.thegeorgeknighton.freeserve.co.uk Map 148,137/286723
BB **D** ✕ £7, 7-9pm D2 T3 🚶(Knighton)
🆅 🅱 🅳 🐾🛁🍴

16th-century coaching inn located in the heart of Wales offering a warm and friendly welcome from the new owners.

Historic Knighton is an ideal base for walking Offa's Dyke Path and is also the gateway to Glyndwr's Way.

Quality accommodation, home cooking and a range of real ales and wines ensure a memorable stay. Five en-suite rooms with a separate boot/drying room. Leaflet and further information available on request.

● Llanbadarn Fynydd (Llandrindod Wells)
GLYNDWR'S WAY

Hillside Lodge Guest House, LD1 6TU ☎ 01597 840364
(Mr W T & Mrs B Ainsworth) Map 136/085764
BB **B** ✕ nearby T1 F2 Closed Xmas 🅱 🅳 ⊗ 🐾🛁🚗🍴🌿 ★★★

● Llandrindod Wells

☆ **Holly Farm**
Howey, LD1 5PP ☎ 01597 822402 (Mrs Ruth Jones)
www.ukworld.net/hollyfarm Map 147/049589
BB **C** ✕ book first £12, 7pm D2 T2 F1 Closed Xmas
🚶(Llandrindod Wells) 🆅 🅱 🅳 ⊗ 🐾🛁🌿 ◆◆◆

Tastefully restored Tudor farmhouse on working farm in peaceful location. En-suite bedrooms with breathtaking views over fields and woods. CTV and beverage trays. Two lounges, log fires, delicious cuisine using farm produce. Excellent area for walking, birdwatching or relaxing. Near red kite feeding station. Weekly reductions. Packed lunches. Safe parking.
Call Mrs Ruth Jones for a brochure.

● Llangurig (Llanidloes)
WYE VALLEY WALK

🏠◀ The Old Vicarage, SY18 6RN ☎ 01686 440280 (Margaret Hartey)
www.theoldvicaragellangurig.co.uk Map 147/912799
BB **B/C** ✕ book first £15, 7pm D3 T2 F1 Closed Xmas
🆅 🅱 🅳 🐾🛁Ⓜ ◆◆◆◆

🏠◀ Plas Bwlch Farm, SY18 6RT ☎ 01686 440659 (Mrs Pauline Wheeler)
petebarguse@aol.com Map 135,136/882807
BB **B** ✕ nearby D1 T1 🆅 🅱 🅳 ⊗ 🐾🛁🚗 ★★★Ⓦ

● Llanidloes
GLYNDWR'S WAY

Lloyds Hotel & Restaurant, Cambrian Place, SY18 6BX ☎ 01686 412284
(Tom Lines & Roy Hayter) www.lloydshotel.co.uk Map 136/955844
BB **D** ✕ book first £28.50, 8pm S2 D3 T2 Closed Xmas-Feb
🆅 🅱 🅳 ⊗ 🐾🛁 ★★★

● Llanigon (Hay-on-Wye)
BRECON BEACONS, OFFA'S DYKE & WYE VALLEY WALK

The Old Post Office, HR3 5QA ☎ 01497 820008 (Linda Webb)
www.oldpost-office.co.uk Map 161/213401
BB **C/D** D1 T1 F1 Closed Xmas 🅱 🅳 ⊗ 🐾🛁🌿

● Llanwddyn (Oswestry)
GLYNDWR'S WAY

☆ 🏠◀ **The Oaks**
Lake Vyrnwy, SY10 0LZ ☎ 01691 870250 (Michael & Daphne Duggleby)
www.vyrnwyaccommodation.co.uk Map 125/017190
BB **D** ✕ nearby D1 T2 Closed Xmas
🆅 🅱 🅳 ⊗ 🐾🛁🚗🍴🌿 ★★★

Located by Lake Vyrnwy on Glyndwr's Way. A warm and friendly welcome into a comfortable family home. Brilliant breakfasts. Excellent for walkers.
Email: mdugg99@aol.com

WALES

☆ ▉◄ Gorffwysfa
4 Glyn Dir, Lake Vyrnwy, SY10 0NB ☎ 01691 870217
www.vyrnwy-accommodation.co.uk Map 125/019190
BB **C** ✕ £12.50, 7pm D2 T1 F1
Ⓥ Ⓑ Ⓓ ⊛ 🐾🛏🚗! 🍴 Jacuzzi for walkers.

Listed, restored Victorian cottage overlooking Lake Vyrnwy and the dam. Situated in the nature reserve. Close to Snowdon. Bird-watching, cycling, walking and watersports are available locally. A very warm welcome with glowing log-fires and sumptuous food awaits you.

● Llanwrtyd Wells
▉◄ Neuadd Arms Hotel, The Square, LD5 4RB ☎ 01591 610236
(Lindsay Ketteringham) www.neuaddarmshotel.co.uk Map 147/879467
BB **C** ✕ £13.50, 6:30-8:30pm S6 D7 T8 ᨘᨘ(Llanwrtyd Wells)
Ⓥ Ⓑ Ⓓ 🐾🛏! 🍴Ⓜ ★

☆ ▉◄ Belle Vue Hotel
LD5 4RE ☎ 01591 610237 (Eileen & Bernie Dodd)
www.bellevuewales.co.uk Map 147/879467
BB **B** ✕ £4-£14, 6:30-9:30pm S4 D3 T8 F2 Closed Xmas
ᨘᨘ(Llanwrtyd Wells) Ⓥ Ⓑ Ⓓ 🐾🛏 🚗 🍴 See Groups also.

Situated midway between Builth Wells and Llandovery on the A483 trunk road. Built in 1843 the Belle View Hotel is the oldest hotel in Llanwrtyd Wells. Combining village pub and local meeting place, which gives this small, comfortable, family-run hotel the charm and character of the friendly inhabitants of this town.

● Llanymynech
OFFA'S DYKE
▉◄ Orchard Holidays, Unity House, Llandrinio, SY22 6SG
☎ 01691 831976 (Mrs Maxine Roberts)
www.orchard-holidays.com Map 126/290160
BB **B** ✕ nearby S3 D2 T2 F1 Closed Nov-Feb
Ⓑ Ⓓ ⊛ 🐾🛏🚗! ★★★

● Machynlleth
GLYNDWR'S WAY
▉◄ Maenllwyd, Newtown Road, SY20 8EY ☎ 01654 702928 (Mrs M Vince)
www.cyber-space.co.uk/maenllwyd.htm Map 135/752008
BB **C** ✕ nearby D4 T3 F1 Closed Xmas ᨘᨘ(Machynlleth)
Ⓑ Ⓓ 🐾🛏🚗! 🍴 ◆◆◆◆

▉◄ Dyfiguest, 20 Ffordd Mynydd, Griffiths, SY20 8DD ☎ 01654 702562
(Carol Handcock) www.dyfiguest.co.uk Map 135/747012
BB **C** ✕ nearby S1 D1 ᨘᨘ(Machynlleth)
Ⓥ Ⓑ Ⓓ ⊛ 🐾🛏🚗! ★★★★Ⓖ Ⓦ

☆ ▉◄ Talbontdrain Guest House
Uwchygarreg, SY20 8RR ☎ 01654 702192
www.talbontdrain.co.uk Map 135/777959
BB **C** ✕ book first £15, 7:30pm S2 D1 T1
Ⓥ Ⓑ Ⓓ ⊛ 🐾🛏🚗! 🍴

Remote and comfortable farm guesthouse – Glyndwr's Way runs through the yard. Home made food with generous helpings. Newly renovated for 2006. Much more information on the website.

● Montgomery
OFFA'S DYKE
Dragon Hotel, SY15 6PA ☎ 01686 668359 (Mark & Sue Michaels)
www.dragonhotel.com Map 137/222964
BB **D** ✕ £7-£20, 7-9pm S2 D9 T5 F4
Ⓥ Ⓑ Ⓓ 🐾🛏🚗! 🍴 ★★★

☆ ▉◄ Hendomen Farmhouse
Hendomen, SY15 6HB ☎ 01686 668004 (Jo & Bruce Lawson)
www.offasdykepath.com Map 137/218981
BB **C** ✕ nearby S1 D1 T1
Ⓑ Ⓓ ⊛ 🐾🛏🚗! 🍴 ★★

Stay in Montgomery and walk the Dyke. Transport of walkers between Knighton and Llangollen and Glyndwr's Way. Discounts for 3 nights. Owners are walkers. Flexible breakfast times. 5 pubs (1 with pool) nearby. Fabulous views. Email: bruce.lawson@btinternet.com

● Presteigne
OFFA'S DYKE
Carmel Court, King's Turning Road, LD8 2LD ☎ 01544 267986
(Marenee & Terry Monaghan) www.carmelcourt.co.uk Map 148,137/320639
BB **B** ✕ nearby S1 D5 T3 F2 Closed Xmas Ⓑ Ⓓ 🐾🛏🚗! 🍴 ★★

▉◄ Lower Dolley Farm, Dolley Green, LD8 2EE ☎ 01547 560430
(Claire & Neil Reid-Warrilow) reidwarrilow@aol.com Map 148,137/284654
BB **B** ✕ book first £8, 7:30pm D3 Ⓥ Ⓑ Ⓓ ⊛ 🐾🛏🚗! 🍴

● Rhayader
WYE VALLEY WALK
Brynteg, East Street, LD6 5EA ☎ 01597 810052 (Mrs B Lawrence)
brynteg@hotmail.com Map 147,136/972681
BB **B** ✕ nearby S1 D2 T1 Closed Xmas
Ⓑ Ⓓ ⊛ 🐾🛏🚗! Ⓜ ★★★ Local footpath information.

The Horseshoe, Church Street, LD6 5AT ☎ 01597 810982 (Mrs P Bishop)
www.rhayader.co.uk/horseshoe Map 147,136/969680
BB **B** ✕ book first £12, 7pm S2 D2 T1 Closed Xmas
Ⓥ Ⓑ Ⓓ ⊛ 🐾🛏🚗! 🍴 ★★★

● Talybont-on-Usk (Brecon)
BRECON BEACONS
▉◄ Gethinog, LD3 7YN ☎ 01874 676258 (Christina & Roy Gale)
www.gethinog.co.uk Map 161/108233
BB **C** ✕ book first £15, 7pm D1 T1 Closed Xmas
Ⓥ Ⓑ 🐾🛏!

● Talyllyn (Brecon)

BRECON BEACONS
USK VALLEY WALK

▪☜◀ Dolycoed, LD3 7SY
☎ 01874 658666 (Mrs Mary Cole) Map 161/107271
BB **B** SI DI TI Ⓑ Ⓓ ⊛ 👃 ♨ 🛏

● Welshpool

GLYNDWR'S WAY & OFFA'S DYKE

Tynllwyn Farm, SY21 9BW ☎ 01938 553175 (Jane & Caroline Emberton)
www.tynllwynfarm.co.uk Map 126/215086
BB **D** ✕ book first £14, 6:30pm DI T4 Closed Xmas ᠁(Welshpool)
Ⓥ Ⓑ Ⓓ ⊛ 🐾 👃 🛏 ! 🛁 ★★★

Severn Farm, SY21 7BB ☎ 01938 555999 (T & J Jones)
www.severnfarm.co.uk Map 126/231070
BB **B** ✕ nearby S2 DI TI F2 Closed Xmas ᠁(Welshpool)
Ⓓ ⊛ 🐾 👃 🛏 ! 🛁

The Royal Oak Hotel, The Cross, SY21 7DG ☎ 01938 552217 (Neil Benbow)
www.royaloakhotel.info Map 126/225075
BB **D** ✕ £15-£20, 6:30-9:30pm S8 D8 T7 F2 ᠁(Welshpool)
Ⓥ Ⓑ Ⓓ 🐾 👃 ! 🛁 Ⓜ ★★★Ⓦ

▪☜◀ Ty-Isaf, Llanerfyl, SY21 0JB ☎ 01938 820143 (Sheenagh Carter)
sheen.carter@virgin.net Map 125/024082
BB **C** ✕ book first £10, 6:30-9pm DI FI
Ⓥ Ⓑ Ⓓ ⊛ 🐾 👃 🛏 ! 🛁 ★★★

SOUTH WALES

● Blaenavon

BRECON BEACONS
CAMBRIAN WAY

☆▪☜◀ **Red Rooster B&B**
23 Broad Street, NP4 9NE ☎ 01495 791840 (Gail Johnson)
www.blaenavonrooster.supanet.com Map 161/248095
BB **B** ✕ £5, 6-8pm D2 TI
Ⓥ Ⓑ Ⓓ 🐾 👃 🛏 ! 🛁 Wheelchair access & bath hoist.

Attractive building at the heart of Blaenavon Booktown.

Blaenavon is a World Heritage Site by virture of the ironworks, Big Pit National Mining Museum and the historic landscape of its industrial past. Blaenavon is partly within the Brecon Beacons National Park.

Email: blaenavonrooster@supanet.com

● Bridgend

VALEWAYS MILLENNIUM HERITAGE TRAIL

▪☜◀ Alexandra Guest House, 44 Coity Road, CF31 1LR ☎ 01656 650761
(Mrs Jean O'Neill) Map 170/906802
BB **B** ✕ nearby S4 DI TI F2 Closed Xmas ᠁(Bridgend) Ⓑ 🐾 👃

● Cwmtaf (Merthyr Tydfil)

BRECON BEACONS

▪☜◀ Llwyn Onn Guest House, CF48 2HT ☎ 01685 384384 (Mrs M Evans)
www.llwynonn.co.uk Map 160/012115
BB **D** D6 T4 FI Closed Xmas Ⓑ Ⓓ 🐾 👃 🛏 ★★★

● Fairwood (Swansea)

☆▪☜◀ **Seren Retreat**
Bryncoch Farm, SA2 7LB ☎ 01792 371421 (Rex & Alaea Beynon)
www.serenretreat.com Map 159/556921
BB **C/D** D2 F4
Ⓥ Ⓑ Ⓓ ⊛ 🐾 👃 🛏 ! ▲ ▲★★

Idyllic 23-acre farm with ancient oak forest, river and wildflower meadows. Ideal base to explore the natural beauty of the Gower peninsula. Walkers can follow the river from our farm down the Ilston valley to Three Cliffs Bay. Most rooms are en-suite.

● Ffairfach (Llandeilo)

▪☜◀ 9 Towy Terrace, SA19 6ST ☎ 01558 822742 (Annie Allen)
aj@anniedavisallen.co.uk Map 159/628216 BB **B** ✕ book first £9, 7-8pm
D2 Closed Nov-Feb ᠁(Ffairfach/Llandeilo) Ⓥ Ⓓ ⊛ 🐾 👃 !

● Llanmadoc (Gower)

▪☜◀ Tallizmand, SA3 1HA ☎ 01792 386373 (Mrs A Main)
http://tallizmand.co.uk Map 159/444933 BB **C** ✕ book first £17, 6pm
SI DI TI Closed Xmas Ⓥ Ⓑ Ⓓ ⊛ 🐾 👃 🛏 ★★★Ⓦ

▪☜◀ Forge Cottage, SA3 1DB ☎ 01792 386302 (Mike Downie)
www.forgecottagegower.co.uk Map 159/446932
BB **C** ✕ nearby DI TI FI Closed Xmas-Jan Ⓥ Ⓑ ⊛ 🐾 👃 🛏 ★★★

● Llanrhidian (Gower)

☆▪☜◀ **North Gower Hotel**
SA3 1EE ☎ 01792 390042
www.northgowerhotel.co.uk Map 159/501919
BB **B** ✕ £5, 6-9pm D/S10 TI F7 Closed 1-12
Ⓥ Ⓑ Ⓓ 🐾 👃 🛏 ! 🛁 ★★

Privately owned, professionally run 2-star AA hotel.

Our central Gower location overlooking the Loughar Estuary is an ideal base for exploring the beautiful Gower peninsula.

All our rooms are en-suite with modern facilities. We can provide our guests a full laundry service and a clothes drying service. Our hotel prides itself on its catering standards, from light snacks up to a four course dinner, and also provides a packed lunch on request.

We also have discounts for group bookings and mid-week breaks.

For more information visit our website.

● Port Eynon (Gower)

☆ 🖃 **Culver House Hotel**
SA3 1NN ☎ 01792 390755 (Mark & Susan Cottell)
www.culverhousehotel.co.uk Map 159/468853
BB **D** ✗ nearby S3 D4 T3 F1 Closed Nov-Jan
Ⓑ Ⓓ ⊗ ☺ 🏠 ★★

A family-run hotel with a warm friendly atmosphere, superb food and quality service. Most rooms have beautiful seaviews with en-suite facilities. Ideally situated for rambling the Gower peninsula. Groups welcome. Discounts available.

● Swansea

🖃 The Coast House, 708 Mumbles Road, SA3 4EH ☎ 01792 368702
(Jan & Len Clarke) www.thecoasthouse.co.uk Map 159/622877
BB **C** ✗ nearby S1 D3 F2 Closed Nov-Dec Ⓥ Ⓑ ☺ 🏠 ★★★

● Ynysybwl
BRECON BEACONS

☆ **Tyn-y-Wern**
CF37 3LY ☎ 01443 790551 (Mrs Hermione Bruton)
www.tyn-y-wern.co.uk Map 170/065945
BB **C** D2 T1 Closed Xmas
Ⓑ Ⓓ ⊗ 🚲 ☺ 🐴 🏠 ★★★ See SC also.

A Victorian mine manager's residence lovingly restored to its former glory. Offers a tranquil country retreat just 30 minutes from Cardiff. Spectacular walking. Phone for brochure.

SELF-CATERING

ANGLESEY

● Brynsiencyn
Cerrig Y Barcud Holidays ☎ 01248 430056 (Julia Harfitt)
www.cerrigybarcud.co.uk
£160-£535 Sleeps 2-4. 4 cottages.
Tranquil location superb views. Adults only. ⊗ ★★★★★

● Hermon

☆ **Gwenallt Cottage**
☎ 0114 263 1507 (C Waterhouse)
http://gwenalltcottage.mysite.wanadoo-members.co.uk
£199-£399 Sleeps 3. 1 cottage.
Close to fabulous beaches and walks. ⊗ 🏠

Pretty mill cottage, beams, log-burning fire, mod cons, private garden, furniture and BBQ. Located near four fabulous beaches and forest, Maltraeth cob, Newborough, Aberffraw, Cable Bay, Rhosneigr. Sleeps 2/3. Peaceful location, outstanding natural beauty, history and wildlife.
Mob: 07875 648446

● Llanerchymedd

☆ **Bryntglwys Farmhouse & Tyddyn Truan Cottage**
☎ 01248 490078 (Jeni Farrell)
www.bryneglwyscottages.co.uk
£230-£672 Sleeps 6-10. 1 cottage, 1 farmhouse.
Beautiful houses, peaceful heart of Anglesey. 🏠 ★★★★

A warm welcome. Perfect location for enjoying coastal and historic walks. Anglesey's Coast to Coast walk on the doorstep! Impressive stone farmhouse (sleeps 10) and pretty cottage (sleeps 6). Both offer a high standard of comfort and facilities.

CEREDIGION

● Aberporth
Frances & Peter Miller ☎ 01239 810595 milldrove@aol.com
£180-£350 Sleeps 4. 2 cottages.
Rural setting. Walks & beach minutes away. ⊗ 🏠

☆ **Penffynnon Properties**
☎ 01239 810387 (Jann Tucker)
www.aberporth.com
£250-£1,000 Sleeps 4-8. 6 varying types.
Close to Pembrokeshire Coast Path. 🏠 ★★★★★

Dolphin Cottage.
Eight miles from Pembrokeshire Coast Path, and 250m from Aberporth's Blue Flag beaches, our houses are in their own grounds reached by a private road and have good sea views. Aberporth has a range of shops and two pubs.

● Aberystwyth
Mr & Mrs James ☎ 01974 202877
www.selfcatering-aberystwyth.co.uk
£175-£395 Sleeps 2-8. 2 houses, 1 flat.
Great base for mountain and coastal walks. 🚂(Aberystwyth) 🏠 ★★★★

● Cardigan
Sally Sparkes ☎ 01239 68293
lglanafon.bach@virgin.net £150-£320 Sleeps 2. 1 cottage.
Village location, linen, CH, log fire. ⊗ 🏠 ★★★★

● Llwyndafydd
Tyhen Farm Cottages ☎ 01545 560346 (Roni Kelly)
www.tyhenswimminglessons.co.uk
£221-£688 Sleeps 2-6. 7 cottages. Closed Nov-Jan
Private indoor heated pool & facilities. ⊗ 🏠

● Machynlleth
Magda Corser ☎ 01654 781335
www.kitevalleycottage.co.uk
£190-£415 Sleeps 2-5. 1 cottage, 1 flat.
Secluded hillfarm setting. Superb walkers base. 🚂(Dovey Junction)
⊗ 🏠 ★★★★

● New Quay

☆ Romantic Garden Cottage
☎ 01545 560846 (Mr N Makepeace)
www.romantic-garden-cottage.co.uk
£250-£415 Sleeps 2. 1 property. Peaceful location. Good walking.
Gardens; dolphins. ⊗ ★★★★★ KA member

Well-appointed, comfortable, high-quality accommodation with central heating. Set in beautiful gardens, surrounded by birds: red kite; peregrine; chough etc. Just a stroll down the bridlepath to the unspoilt National Trust coastline and marine reserve.

CONWY

● Betws-y-Coed
SNOWDONIA/ERYRI

Penmachno Cottages ☎ 01690 760167 (Molly Gorman)
http://penmachno-cottages.co.uk
£75-£300 Sleeps 6. 1 static caravan.
Stunning views, forest. Secluded. Welcome groceries. ⊗

GWYNEDD

● Bala
SNOWDONIA/ERYRI

☆ J H Gervis
☎ 01992 892331
www.backofbeyond.co.uk/RF
£240 Sleeps 2-8. 1 cottage.
Isolated with mountain views, wood stove.

An 18th century stone cottage, Grade II listed. Isolated, situated high on a hillside above Bala Lake. 3 bedrooms, 3 sitting rooms. Wood burning stove. Well equipped kitchen. Kids' room. Snowdon 1 hour by car, the sea 45 mins. Walks from the doorstep.
email: jandmgervis@btinternet.com

● Bangor

☆ Yr-Ocar
☎ 0870 534 2342 (Hoseasons (ref W7250))
www.yr-ocar.co.uk
£500-£1,000 Sleeps 13. 1 house. Perfect for family or small groups.
⊗ 🐾 ★★★★ See Snowdon Lodge in B&B also.

Yr-Ocar accommodates up to 13 people and is nestled in tranquil woodlands in the heart of Snowdonia, surrounded by dramatic mountain scenery. Yr-Ocar's main house has five bedrooms and two annex rooms. Recently refurbished to an extremely high standard.

● Barmouth
SNOWDONIA/ERYRI

Val & Tom Bethell ☎ 01341 247033 bethellvt@btopenworld.com
£125-£225 Sleeps 2. 1 cottage. Closed Jan
Delightfully rural. Sea/mountain views. Peaceful ⋘(Dyffryn Ardudwy) ⊗ 🐾

● Beddgelert
SNOWDONIA/ERYRI

☆ Brackenbury
☎ 01751 430624 (David Jackson)
davjackson@supanet.com
£277-£405 Sleeps 4. 1 cottage.
Central heating, open fire, riverside location. ⊗ 🐾

Grade II listed cottage overlooking the village green and the adjacent river Glaslyn.
Features conservatory, en-suite bathroom to front bedroom, central heating, open fire, enclosed back garden and parking for two cars. Shops, pubs and church nearby. Prices include electricity and central heating costs.

Glaslyn Leisure Ltd ☎ 01766 890880 (Mrs Joan Firth)
www.snowdonia-cottages.net
£275-£750 Sleeps 1-6. 5 cottages. Excellent accommodation, village location. Families/groups. ⊗ ★★★★★

● Bethesda
SNOWDONIA/ERYRI

Ogwen Valley Holidays ☎ 01248 600122 (Mrs Jill Jones)
www.ogwensnowdonia.co.uk
£160-£550 Sleeps 2-6. 1 flat, 1 cottage.
Convenient, carefree holiday location. Mountain views. 🐾 ★★★★

● Bryncrug
SNOWDONIA/ERYRI

☆ Dolgoch Holiday Homes
☎ 01564 205299 (Mrs L Fraley)
www.dolgochfalls.com
£210-£525 Sleeps 4-8. 4 houses.
Mountain views, walks, waterfall, steam railway. 🐾 ★★★-★★★★

Four recently refurbished holiday homes. Built on remains of watermill. Beautiful countryside, views. Woodland, mountain walks. Near Dolgoch Falls, Talyllyn Steam Railway, Cadair Idris, lake and coast. Fishing, birdwatching, cycling, golf, horseriding, watersports, beaches nearby. Well equipped including washing machines and dryers.

● Dolgellau
SNOWDONIA/ERYRI

Mrs O Williams ☎ 01341 430277
£150-£180 Sleeps 6. 1 caravan. Closed Nov-Feb
Working farm. Estuary views, countryside walks. ⊗ 🐾

Bwthyn Gwyn ☎ 0117 927 7452 (Paul Craig)
www.cottageguide.co.uk/bwthyngwyn
£210-£475 Sleeps 4. 1 cottage.
17 C. stone beamed cottage. ⋘(Llwyngwril) ⊗ 🐾

WALES

☆ **Brynygwin Isaf**
☎ 01341 423481 (Mr Gauntlett)
www.holidaysinwales.fsnet.co.uk
£136-£719 Sleeps 2-24. 2 cottages, 2 parts country house.
Walk guidesheets provided. Large bird-rich garden. 🐾

Two self-contained sections of family country house built 1806 with large, comfortably furnished rooms, superb views, extensive garden and character cottages. 1 mile from Dolgellau. Over 30 walk guidesheets provided. Log fires. Open all year. Children and pets welcome. Email: holidays_wales@onetel.com

● Garndolbenmaen
SNOWDONIA/ERYRI

Grant Busby ☎ 07769 862350
grant@fbusby.fsnet.co.uk
£199-£250 Sleeps 5. 1 cottage.
Quiet rural location, peaceful garden. 🚫 🐾

● Llanberis
SNOWDONIA/ERYRI

Wilson's Holidays ☎ 01286 870261 (Lesley Wilson)
www.wilsons-holidays.co.uk
£395-£1,075 Sleeps 16. 1 house.
Spacious, well equipped. Off road parking. 🐾 ★★★★

● Porthmadog
SNOWDONIA/ERYRI

Rhos Country Cottages ☎ 01758 720047 (Anwen Jones)
www.rhos-cottages.co.uk
£200-£1,000 Sleeps 2-8. 4 varying types.
Good walks from your door. 🐾 ★★★★★

MONMOUTHSHIRE

● Abergavenny
BRECON BEACONS

Eunice Wafford ☎ 01873 890726
www.blackmountains.net
£195-£360 Sleeps 4-6. 1 farmhouse annexe.
Stunning views. Ideal for birdwatching. 🚫 🐾 ★★★★

● Chepstow

☆ **Caroline Banks**
☎ 020 8882 7855
bankscaroline@aol.com
£195-£295 Sleeps 5. 1 cottage.
Courtyard garden, all modern conveniencies. 〰(Chepstow)

An excellent base for the Wye Valley and Offa's Dyke walks. Refurbished old cottage, all modern facilities. Pretty, secluded garden. Close to historic Chepstow town centre. 3 interconnecting bedrooms – comfortable place to relax at the end of the day.

● Hendre

Penylan Farm ☎ 01600 716435 (Cathy Bowen)
www.penylanfarm.co.uk
£175-£450 Sleeps 6. 1 cottage.
New character barn conversion. Modern luxuries. See B&B also.

● Monmouth

Church Farm ☎ 01600 712176 (Rosey & Derek Ringer)
www.churchfarmmitcheltroy.co.uk
£150-£450 Sleeps 2-8. 1 barn conversion.
Wing of 16th century farmhouse. 🚫 🐾 RA member. See B&B also.

● Trellech

Mrs S D M Poulter ☎ 01600 86068 1alanpoulter@beeb.net
£150-£550 Sleeps 1-6. 1 cottage.
Characterful C17 stone property. Historic village. 🐾 ★★★★★Ⓖ

NORTH EAST WALES

● Llangollen

☆ **Tan Y Ddol**
☎ 01206 855244 (Mrs Judith Watts)
tanyddol@msn.com
£240-£450 Sleeps 2-5. 1 house.
Maps and guides available. 🚫 ★★★★

Tan Y Ddol is a modern house ideally placed for walking the beautiful Dee valley and surrounding hills.
A wide variety of easy and challenging walks are available straight from the door, including the Llangollen Canal and Offa's Dyke Path.

PEMBROKESHIRE

● Moylegrove
PEMBROKESHIRE COAST NATIONAL PARK

☆ **Ty Newydd Cottage**
☎ 01239 881280 (Mrs Dawn Cotton)
jaybillimoria@jaybillimoria.demon.co.uk
£285-£398 Sleeps 2-5. 3 cottages.
Coast Path within 10 mins walk. 🐾

The three Ty Newydd properties are in Moylegrove on the north Pembrokeshire coast.
Ceibwr Bay and the coastal path are three quarters of a mile down the lane.
There are many coastal and inland footpaths and beaches in the area.

● Roch
PEMBROKESHIRE COAST NATIONAL PARK

Maureen & Richard Langston ☎ 01437 710492
www.cuffernmanorcottages.co.uk
£224-£819 Sleeps 2-10. 4 cottages.
Coastal Path nearby. Short breaks available. 🚫 🐾 See B&B also.

● Saundersfoot
PEMBROKESHIRE COAST NATIONAL PARK

☆ **Admirals Mews**
☎ 01834 870000
www.admiralsmews.co.uk
£272-£3,300 Sleeps 2-14. 6 cottages. Heated pool. Breathtaking views.
Coast path, beach. ⚲(Saundersfoot) ★★★★★ See Tenby also.

Winner of the *Sunday Times* 'Best of the Best' award.

Located on the cliff-top overlooking Saundersfoot Bay.

Stunning accommodation with large balconies for outside dining, luxury kitchens and bathrooms with jacuzzi baths.

Heated indoor pool with jet-stream swimming.

Ideally positioned in the beautiful Pembrokeshire Coast National Park with glorious walks from your front door!

Saundersfoot harbour and village are just a short stroll away with wonderful restaurants, pubs and miles of golden sands.

● St Davids
PEMBROKESHIRE COAST NATIONAL PARK

St Nons Bay Cottages ☎ 01437 720616 (Thelma M Hardman)
www.stnbc.co.uk
£175-£2195 Sleeps 2-16. 4 cottages.
Beautiful location, near Coast Path.
⊗ 🐾 ★★★★★ See Groups also.

☆ **Park House**
☎ 02920 752402 (Shelagh Thompson)
www.stdavids.co.uk/selfcatering/park_house
£350-£650 Sleeps 2-6. 1 house.
Central location. Beautiful walks in national park. ⊗

Cosy character cottage in town centre, hidden on a private lane. Excellent base for coastal walks in the beautiful National Park, straight from the house. Imaginatively renovated and furnished, central heating and log fire.
No smokers or dogs.
Email: parkhousestdavids@btinternet.com

● St Dogmaels
Trenewydd Farm Cottages ☎ 01239 612370 (Cheryl Hyde)
www.cottages-wales.com
£190-£865 Sleeps 4-9. 5 cottages.
Coastal Path, River Valleys, Bluestone country. 🐾 ★★★★★

REMEMBER TO USE YOUR DISCOUNT VOUCHERS!
Turn to p7 and save money on any establishment where you see ⌫ next to their entry.

● Tenby
PEMBROKESHIRE COAST NATIONAL PARK

☆ **Celtic Haven Ltd**
☎ 01834 870000
www.celtichaven.com
£272-£2,445 Sleeps 2-12. 26 cottages. Private beach access. Coast path, golf, pool. ⚲(Manorbier) 🐾 ★★★★★ See Saundersfoot also.

An award winning village set in the Pembrokeshire Coast National Park. 26 5-star luxury cottages nestling above a private beach and set in acres of parkland.

An amazing spa with over 80 therapies and treatments awaits to pamper you, whilst the headland golf course and the coast path walks are ideal for the more energetic!

Celtic Haven really is a unique escape with its own superb terrace restaurant, heated pool and fitness suite.

POWYS

● Brecon
BRECON BEACONS

Wern-Y-Marchog ☎ 01874 665329 (Ann Phillips) www.wernymarchog.co.uk
£125-£425 Sleeps 1-6. 1 bungalow, 2 apts.
Centre of national park. Superb walkers' base. 🐾 ★★★★

● Hay-on-Wye
S Meredith ☎ 01544 370278
£150-£600 Sleeps 2-6. 1 cottage.
Detached cottage, stunning scenery. Two bathrooms. ⊗

● Lake Vyrnwy
SNOWDONIA/ERYRI

☆ **Eunant**
☎ 01691 870321 (Bronwen Davies)
eunant@terrafirmatravel.com
£237-£385 Sleeps 1-7. Gites.
Gorgeous lakeside scenery, edge of Snowdonia. 🐾

Lovely self-catering accommodation; large farmhouse, woodburning stove, spacious conservatory. Fabulous walking, cycling and fishing in this area of outstanding natural beauty, on the edge of the beautiful Berwyn hills, not far from Snowdonia. Castles, beaches and more...

● Llanidloes
The Old Weather Station ☎ 01939 220421 (Jan Rouse)
prouse@young-st-chambers.com
£750-£1,200 Sleeps 20-22. 1 lodge/house.
Perfect large group venue. 🐾 ★★★

WALES

● Machynlleth

SNOWDONIA/ERYRI

Lynn & John Williams ☎ 01654 702952
www.lynn.john.williams.care4free.net
£170-£220 Sleeps 4-5. 1 cottage.
Local walks, wildlife, rivers, varied landscape. ᗰ(Machynlleth) ⊗ 🏠 ★★★

● Welshpool

☆ **Orchard Holidays**
☎ 01691 831976 (Mrs Maxine Roberts)
www.orchard-holidays.com
£180-£285 Sleeps 2-16. 5 cottages & apts.   Closed Nov-Feb
Fishing , parking, fine views.   ⊗ ★★★ See B&B also.

Birdsong is your alarm call. Choose to walk
Offa's Dyke, Severn Way or Glyndwr's Way.
Visit Powys Castle or relax in the tranquil
gardens. Ideal touring base for Chester, mid-
Wales coast, Snowdonia and Shropshire.
B&B also available.
Email: info@orchard-holidays.com

SOUTH WALES

● Gower
Mrs E Stone ☎ 01792 391175
pittonxfarmhouse@hotmail.co.uk
£300-£700 Sleeps 6. 1 farmhouse.
Varied scenery. Central heating. Separate shower.   ⊗ 🏠 RA member

● Pontypridd

BRECON BEACONS

☆ **Tyn-y-Wern Country House**
☎ 01443 790551 (Mrs Hermione Bruton)
www.tyn-y-wern.co.uk
£200-£335 Sleeps 2-4. 2 lodges.   Beautiful location, Welsh valleys,
spectacular walking.   ⊗ 🏠 ★★★★ See B&B also.

Stylish conversion of old building offering
modern facilities in tranquil country retreat
just 30 minutes from Cardiff.
Spectacular walking. Phone for further
inormation.
OS Map 170 - 065945
Email: tynywern2002@yahoo.co.uk

DID YOU KNOW?
The Ramblers website features accommodation
along 100 Long Distance Paths
and is linked to our Group Walks Finder.
Visit www.ramblers.org.uk

● Port Eynon

☆ **Gower Holiday Village**
☎ 01792 390431 (Cathy Harris)
www.gowerholidayvillagewales.co.uk
£135-£545 Sleeps 4-8. 23 bungalows.   Closed Jan-Feb
⊗ 🏠 ★★★-★★★★

Gower Holiday Village, located in an area of outstanding natural beauty, is
ideally situated for walking the beaches and hills of the Gower Peninsula.
We have 23 letting 2 and 3 bedroom bungalows to sleep 4, 6 and 8 people.
Our free heated indoor pool also has a spa bath and sauna.
Our conference centre has its own catering facilities for groups plus laundry and
drying rooms. Bed linen and electricity is supplied free of charge.
Our Village Shop boasts an in-house bakery, off licence, post office and
hairdressers. Pets are welcome at £25 per week.
Non-smoking bungalows also available.

Email: enquiries@gowerholidayvillagewales.co.uk

GROUPS

CARMARTHENSHIRE

BRECON BEACONS & CAMBRIAN WAY

☆ **Llanerchindda Farm** (BB/SC)
Cynghordy, Llandovery SA20 0NB ☎ 01550 750274
www.cambrianway.com Map 160/808429
BB £28, SC £240 Min 12 max 42. 3 cottages. ✕ 🐾 Ⓑ Ⓓ
ᗰ(Cynghordy) ⬥ 🚗 ★★★ See B&B also.

Large farmhouse set high in the Cambrian mountain foothills with stunning
views over the Brecon Beacons.
Popular with groups. Excellent facilities. Drying room, map room, licensed.
20 rooms (15 ensuite) sleeps up to 42. Famous home made food.
20 walks programmes including the Cambrian Way.
Email:nick@cambrianway.com

GWYNEDD

SNOWDONIA/ERYRI

☆ **Panteinion Hall** (BB)
Ffordd, Panteinion, Friog, Fairbourne ☎ 01341 250519 (Paul & Helen)
www.panteinionhall.co.uk Grid Ref: 624124
BB £28.50, DBB £42.50 Min 8, max 30. Country guesthouse.
⋙(Fairbourne) ✗ 🐾 B D !

A large
9-bedroomed
country guest
house situated in
the lovely
Panteinion valley,
which offers:

Exclusive use for groups of eight of more, within walking distance to Cader Idris,
and Fairbourne beach.
Extensive walks and activities close by, and a beautiful outlook.
Ideal for walking, golfing, photography and fishing.
Outward-bound activities arranged with notice.
Large log fire in the winter.
Four course candlelit evening meals
Bar includes 240 malt whiskys

MONMOUTHSHIRE

BRECON BEACONS

☆ **The Old Pandy Inn** (BB)
Hereford Rd, Pandy, Abergavenny, NP7 8DR
☎ 01873 890208 (Alan Bridgewater) www.theoldpandyinn.co.uk
Map 161/335226 BB £14.75 + Max 28.
✗ 🐾 B D ⊗ ! 🚗

Come walking in the Black Mountains and stay at the Old Pandy Inn.

Situated at the foot of the Black Mountains in Pandy, (OS 335226) Offa's Dyke
path 400yds away. The market town of Abergavenny is nearby.
The Black Mountain Lodge is the ideal place to stay and recharge after a
long day's walk.

We can accommodate large groups of up to 20 in three rooms and also have an
ensuite room that sleeps 8 within the Inn. Our Inn offers cask ales and full range
of day and evening meals. Mid week specials available.
Email: Pandyinn@beeb.net

PEMBROKESHIRE

PEMBROKESHIRE COAST NATIONAL PARK

High View (SC) St Davids ☎ 01437 720616 (Thelma Hardman)
www.stnbc.co.uk 4 cottages Map 175/740731
SC £395-£2,195 Min 2, max 16. ✗ nearby B ⊓ ⊗ ! 🚗 See SC also.

Millenium Youth Hostel (SC) Lawrenny, SA68 0PN
☎ 01646 651270 www.lawrenny-village.co.uk
SC £175pn (sole use) Min 10, max 23.
✗ nearby 🐾 D ⊗ ★★★★ hostel

☆ **Pen Rhiw Centre for Groups** (SC/BB)
St Davids, Haverfordwest, SA62 6PG ☎ 01437 721821
www.penrhiw.co.uk
BB £46, SC £2,500 1 hostel.
✗ 🐾 B D ⊗ ! 🚗 ★★ hostel

In the stunning setting of the St Davids
Peninsula we are in the heart of an area
steeped in natural beauty and
ancient history.
Pen Rhiw is a fine, early Victorian
rectory. Secluded grounds, wildflower
meadow, beautiful coastal walks.

POWYS

☆ **Belle Vue Hotel** (BB)
Llanwrtyd Wells ☎ 01591 610237 (Eileen & Bernie Dodd)
www.bellevuewales.co.uk Map 147/879467
BB £19.50 Min 10, max 24. ✗ 🐾 B D ⋙(Llanwrtyd Wells)
! 🚗 See B&B also

Situated midway between Builth Wells and Llandovery on the A483 trunk road.
Built in 1843 the Belle Vue Hotel is the oldest Hotel in Llanwrtyd Wells.
Combining village pub and local meeting place and so giving this small,
comfortable, family run hotel the charm and character representative of the
friendly inhabitants of this town.

BRECON BEACONS

Baskerville Hall Hotel (BB) Clyro Court, Clyro, Hay-on-Wye, HR3 5LE
☎ 01497 820033 www.baskervillehall.co.uk
Map 161/208428
BB £16 1 hotel and 1 bunkhouse. Min 1, max 60.
✗ 🐾 B D See B&B also.

WALES

Capel-y-Ffin YHA (BB/SC) Castle Farm, Capel-y-Ffin, Ilanthay, NP7 7NP
☎ 01873 890650 www.yha.org.uk
Map 161/250328
BB £10.80-£13.80, SC £7-£10 Min 5, max 40.
✕ 🐾 Ⓓ ⊛ ! ★★ See Hostels also.

☆ **Ty'r Morwydd House** (BB)
Pen-y-Pound, Abergavenny NP7 5UD ☎01873 855959
Map 161/298146
BB £20 Min 12, max 75. ⋙(Abergavenny)
✕ 🐾 Ⓓ ⊛ ★★★

Come walking in the glorious Brecon Beacons and Black Mountains.

Stay in Abergavenny, an historic market town in the Welsh Marshes.

3 star hostel. 72 beds in twin and single rooms.
Full/half board accommodation. Bed & Breakfast. Packed lunches.
Good wholesome food. Self-catering barbecue. Self-catering available Christmas, New Year and August.

Fax: 01873 855443
Email: enq@tyrmorwydd.co.uk

SOUTH WALES

BRECON BEACONS

The Rhongyr Isaf Centre (SC) Pen-y-Cae, Upper Swansea Valley, SA9 1GB
☎ 01639 730518 enquiries@absoluteadventure Map 160/849146
Bednight £12 Min 10, max 42. ✕ nearby
🐾 Ⓓ ⊛ ! 🚗 See Hostels also.

HOSTELS, BUNKHOUSES & CAMPSITES

CARMARTHENSHIRE

Old Stables Bunkhouse (B) Rhiw-yr-Hwch, Llandovery
☎ 01550 720856 (Pauline Nutt)
www.outdoorlifeventures.co.uk Grid Ref: 728357
Bednight £13 ⋙(Llandovery) ✕ 🐾 Ⓓ ⊛ ★★★

CEREDIGION

☆ **Maes-y-Môr** (IH)
25 Bath St, Aberytwyth
☎ 01970 639270 (Mererid Jones) www.maesymor.co.uk
Bednight £17
⋙(Aberystwyth) ✕ nearby Ⓓ

All eight bedrooms are decorated and furnished to a very high standard with colour TV tea/coffee making facilities. Kitchen and launderette facilities.
Lock-up shed.
80 metres from the beach on the Ceredigion Coast Path.

GWYNEDD

SNOWDONIA/ERYRI

Llwyn Celyn Bach (C) Llanberis ☎ 07796 420179 (Fiona Davies)
daviesllanberis@aol.com Grid Ref: SH573595
Camping £3 🐾 nearby Ⓓ

MONMOUTHSHIRE

OFFA'S DYKE

The Rickyard (B) Wonaston, Monmouth ☎ 01600 740128
www.rickyardbunkhouse.co.uk Map 162/457124
Bednight £12, Camping £8 per tent
✕ nearby 🐾 Ⓑ Ⓓ Ⓜ ⊛ 🚗 ! 🏍

PEMBROKESHIRE

PEMBROKESHIRE COAST NATIONAL PARK

Tycanol Farm (C/CB/B/IH/BHB/OC) Newport ☎ 01239 820264
www.caravancampingsites.co.uk/pembrokeshire/tycanolfarm.htm
Map 157, 145/0433 Bednight £10 ✕ nearby Ⓑ Ⓓ

POWYS

BRECON BEACONS

Canal Barn Bunkhouse (B) Ty Camlas, Canal Bank, Brecon, LD3 7HH
☎ 01874 625361 (Ralph Day) www.canal-barn.co.uk Map 160/052280
Bednight £12.50 ✕ nearby Ⓓ ⊛ ★★★★

Capel-y-Ffin (YHA) Castle Farm, Capel-y-Ffin, Ilanthay, NP7 7NP
☎ 01873 890650 www.yha.org.uk Map 161/250328
BB £13.80, SC £10 Closed Dec-Jan ✕ 🐾 Ⓓ ⊛ ★★ See Groups also.

SOUTH WALES

BRECON BEACONS

The Rhongyr Isaf Centre (B) Pen-y-Cae, Upper Swansea Valley, SA9 1GB
☎ 01639 730518 enquiries@absoluteadventure
Map 60/849146
Bednight £12 Min 10, max 42.
✕ nearby 🐾 Ⓓ ⊛ ! 🚗 See Hostels also.

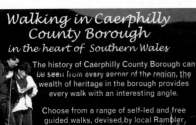

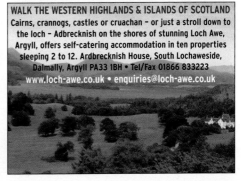

VIEW FROM SCHIEHALLION BACK DOWN THE SUMMIT PATH TO LOCH TUMMEL

SCOTLAND

Recent legislation means Scotland now enjoys some of the most enlightened access arrangements in Europe, allowing walkers the freedom to explore over 64,750 sq km/25,000 square miles of wild mountain, forest, glen and rugged coastline.

This alone would surely prompt Voltaire to repeat his eighteenth-century declaration "We look to Scotland for all our ideas of civilisation", but the Frenchman would be equally impressed by the perfectly balanced structure that is the Falkirk Wheel.

CATERAN TRAIL, SPITTAL OF GLENSHEE

This spectacular feat of engineering can be reached as an easy day trip from Edinburgh or Glasgow. The Wheel is the world's only rotating boat lift, and effectively links two canals by lifting boats up 35 metres using the Archimedean principle of water displacement and requiring just one and a half kilowatts of additional power — about the same amount of energy used to power a hairdryer. Walkers can explore the network of paths around the wheel, taking in the Forth & Clyde and Union canals as well as the Antonine Wall.

> Wherever you roam in Scotland this year you're guaranteed unparalleled access to some of the wildest and most spectacular landscapes in Britain.

The West Highland Way has recently celebrated its silver jubilee and to mark the anniversary 1,000 local children walked the entire length of the 153km/95-mile route, assisted by mountain rescue teams, local Ramblers volunteers and rangers. The 341km/212-mile Southern Upland Way celebrated its 21st birthday with numerous events along the route which runs through Dumfries & Galloway, South Lanarkshire and the Scottish Borders.

The Cateran Trail, Scotland's newest waymarked long distance path, follows historic drove roads once used by marauding Caterans (cattle thieves) who thrived in Highland Perthshire during the Middle Ages. The first guided completion of the circuit took place during the Blairgowrie and East Perthshire Walking Festival in October last year.

Plans to develop the Speyside Way with the addition of six new sections linking Aviemore to Newtonmore are well under way. The proposed extension will add 33km/20.5 miles to the 135kn/84-mile route, which meanders alongside the river Spey through Scotland's 'whisky country' and Cairngorms National Park.

Wherever you roam in Scotland this year you're guaranteed unparalleled access to some of the wildest and most spectacular landscapes in Britain.

Long Distance Paths

Cateran Trail	CAT
Cowal Way	COW
Fife Coastal Path	FFC
Great Glen Way	GGN
Pennine Way	PNN
Rob Roy Way	RRY
Southern Upland Way	SUP
Speyside Way	SPS
St Cuthbert's Way	STC
West Highland Way	WHL

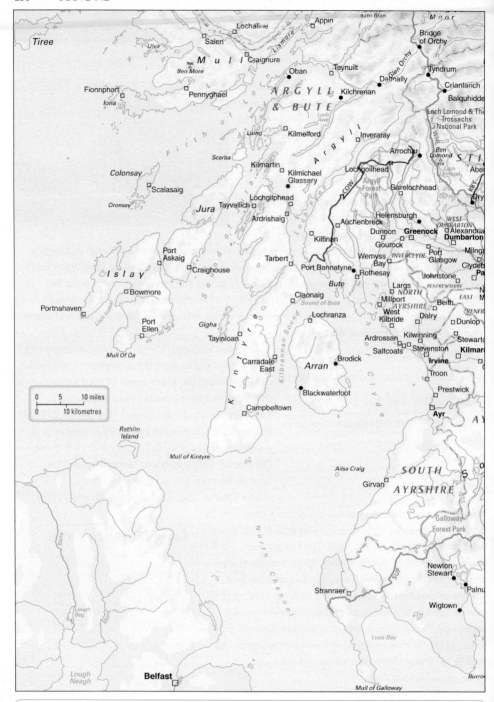

Tiree

Lochaline   Appin   nam Bian   M o o r

Salen   Bridge
of Orchy

Ulva

Craignure   Glen Orchy

M u l l

Ben More   Taynuilt   Tyndrum
966

Oban   Dalmally   Crianlarich

Fionnphort   A R G Y L L   Kilchrenan   Balquhidde
Pennyghael   & B U T E   Loch Lomond & The
Iona   Loch   Trossachs
Awe   National Park

Luing   Kilmelford   Inveraray   WH L

A r g y l l

Scarba   Arrochar   Ben   S T I
Lomond   Abe
Colonsay   Kilmartin   Lochgoilhead   974   Loch
Kilmichael   Lomond
Scalasaig   Glassary   Argyll   Garelochhead   Dry
Oronsay   Forest
Lochgilphead   Park   Helensburgh   RR Y
Jura   Tayvallich   WEST
Ardrishaig   Auchenbreck   DUNBARTON
Dunoon   Greenock   Alexandria
Kilfinan   Dumbarton
Port   Gourock
Askaig   Tarbert   Wemyss   INVERCLYDE   Port   Milnga
I s l a y   Craighouse   Bay   Glasgow   Clyde
Port Bannatyne   Rothesay   Johnstone   Pa
Bowmore   Bute   Largs   RENFREWSHIRE
Claonaig   NORTH   EAST   M
Portnahaven   Sound of Bute   Millport   AYRSHIRE   RENFR
Lochranza   West   Beith
Port   Gigha   Kilbride   Dalry   Dunlop
Ellen   Tayinloan   Ardrossan   Kilwinning   Stewart
Mull Of Oa   Saltcoats   Stevenston   Kilmar
Carradale   Brodick   Irvine
East   Arran   Troon
Blackwaterfoot   Prestwick

C l y d e

0   5   10 miles   Campbeltown   Ayr
0   10 kilometres

Rathlin   A Y
Island
Mull of Kintyre   Ailsa Craig   SOUTH   S
Girvan   AYRSHIRE

Galloway
Forest Park

Bann

Newton
Stewart   Palnu
Stranraer   Wigtown

Lough
Beg   Luce Bay

Lough   Belfast   Mull of Galloway   Burro
Neagh

K i n t y r e

K i l b r a n n a n   S o u n d

S o u n d   o f   J u r a

F i r t h   o f   L o r n

L i s m o r e

N o r t h   C h a n n e l

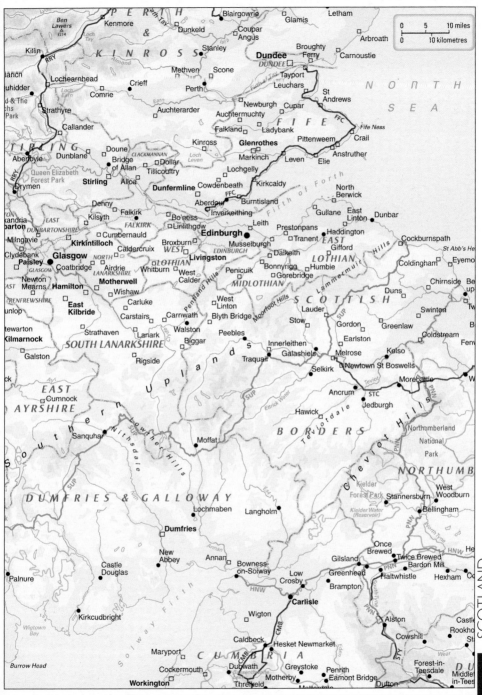

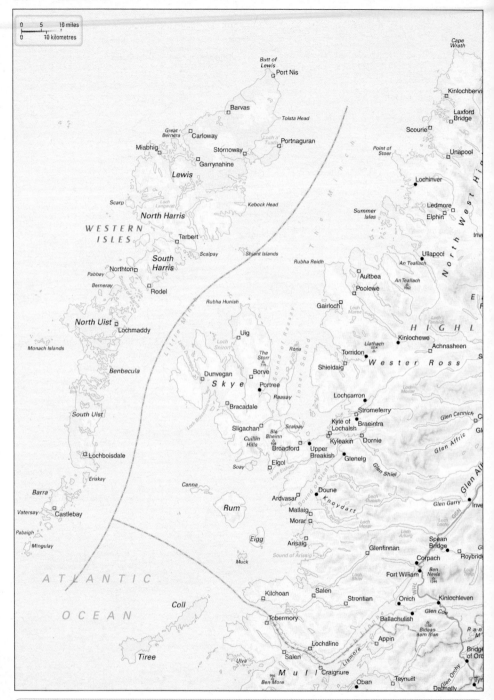

0   5   10 miles
0   10 kilometres

Cape Wrath

Butt of Lewis
Port Nis

Kinlochbervi

Barvas
Tolsta Head
Laxford Bridge

Scourie

Great Bernera
Carloway
Loch a Tuath
Portnaguran

Point of Stoer
Unapool

Miabhig
Stornoway

Lochinver

Garrynahine

Lewis

Ledmore

Scarp
Loch Langavat
Kebock Head
Summer Isles
Elphin

North Harris

Inve

WESTERN ISLES
Tarbert

Ullapool

An Teallach

North West Hi

Scalpay
Shiant Islands
Rubha Reidh

South Harris

Northton
Aultbea
An Teallach

Pabbay

An Teallach 1062

Berneray
Rodel
Poolewe

Rubha Hunish
Gairloch
Loch Maree

Loch Fannich

North Uist
Loch Snizort

Uig
HIGHL
Kinlochewe

Lochmaddy

Liathach 1054

Achnasheen

Monach Islands
Loch Dunvegan

Rona
Torridon

Loch Fada

Shieldaig
Wester Ross
S

Benbecula

The Storr 719
Borve

Loch Fada
Dunvegan
Skye
Portree

Loch Morlir

South Uist

Bracadale
Raasay

Lochcarron

Loch Boisdale
Loch Breakish

Stromeferry

Glen Cannich

Sligachan
Scalpay
Kyle of Lochalsh
Braeintra

Lochboisdale

Cuillin Hills
Bla Bheinn 928
Broadford
Kyleakin
Dornie

Gl

Eriskay

Upper Breakish
Glenelg

Glen Affric

Barra
Canna
Soay
Elgol

Loch Eishort

Glen Shiel

Glen Alb

Vatersay
Castlebay
Ardvasar
Doune

Loch Hou

Rum
Mallaig

Knoydart
Loch Quoich
Glen Garry

Inve

Pabaigh
Morar

Loch Morar

Loch Arkaig
Loch Lochy

Mingulay
Eigg
Arisaig

Spean Bridge
Gl

Glenfinnan
Muck
Sound of Arisaig

Corpach
Roybrid

Fort William
Ben Nevis 1344

Loch

ATLANTIC

Kilchoan
Salen
Strontian
Onich
Kinlochleven

OCEAN
Coll

Tobermory
Ballachulish
Glen Coe

Ra n
M

Bidean nam Bian 1150

Lochaline
Appin
Bridge of Orc

Tiree
Salen
Glen Orchy

Ulva
Mull
Craignure

Ben More 966
Oban
Taynuilt
Tyn

Dalmally

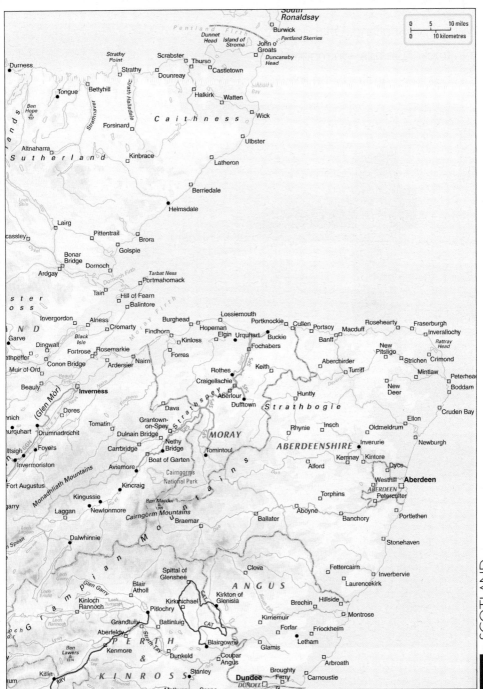

Walking in Scotland. On roads.
On tracks. On hills. On mountains.
On beaches. And now, on line.

www.visitscotland.com/walking

Near Kinlochewe, North West Highlands

Live it. Visit *Scotland*.
visitscotland.com 0845 22 55 121
The No.1 booking and information service for Scotland

You can now explore Scotland's dramatic landscape without even putting your boots on. Our new website is a one-stop-shop to finding information on all kinds of walking in Scotland. You can browse over 750 walking routes, search our extensive 'Walkers Welcome' accommodation database, even find route summaries for all 284 Scottish Munros. Start your visit to the most accessible, diverse and unspoilt walking experiences in the UK at **visitscotland.com/walking**

VW422

SCOTLAND
LOCAL RAMBLERS GROUPS

CENTRAL, FIFE AND TAYSIDE
AREA SECRETARY
Mr David Galloway, 5 Doocot Road, St Andrews, Fife, Scotland, KY16 8QP
☎ 01334 475102

GROUP SECRETARIES
Blairgowrie & District Miss A M McRuvie, 5 Grampian Crescent, Kirriemuir, Angus, DD8 4TW
☎ 01575 572415

Brechin Ms Ursula Shone, 4 Park Road, Brechin, Angus, DD9 7AF
☎ 01356 626087

Broughty Ferry Miss M Cameron, 19 Gillies Place, Broughty Ferry, Dundee, DD5 3LE
☎ 01382 776250

Dalgety Bay & District Mr D Thomson, Sand Dollar House, High Street, Aberdour, Burntisland, KY3 0SW ☎ 01383 860324
www.dalgetybayramblers.org.uk

Dundee & District Mrs A C Cowie, 32 Ballindean Terrace, Dundee, Tayside, DD4 8PA ☎ 01382 507682

Forfar & District Mrs Jenny Mcdade, 21 Duncan Avenue, Arbroath, DD11 2DA ☎ 01241 870695

Glenrothes Mr Doug Jolly, 16 Orchard Drive, Glenrothes, Fife, Scotland, KY7 5RG ☎ 01592 757039

Kinross & Ochil Karen Bernard, Flat 9, 3 Stirling Road, Milnathort, Kinross, KY13 9XS
☎ 01577 861421

Kirkcaldy Mr W H Gibson, Flat 5, 2 Darney Terrace, Kinghorn, Fife, KY3 9RF
☎ 01592 891 319

Perth & District Miss E J Bryce, 2 Hawarden Terrace, Jeanfield, Perth, PH1 1PA ☎ 01738 632645

St Andrews Ms P J Ritchie, 63 St Michaels Drive, Cupar, Fife, KY15 5BP
☎ 01334 653667

Stirling, Falkirk & District Ms J A Cameron, 17 Buchany, Doune, FK16 6HD
☎ 01786 841178

Tayside Trekkers Mrs M Nicol, 7 Coastguard Cottages, Fife Ness, Crail, Anstruther, KY10 3XN
☎ 01333 450611
www.taysidetrekkers.co.uk

West Fife Mrs M E Wrightson, 24 Orwell Place, Dunfermline, KY12 7XP
☎ 01383 729 994

GRAMPIAN
AREA SECRETARY
Anne Macdonald, 64 Grant Road, Banchory, Aberdeenshire, AB31 5UU
☎ 01330 823 255

GROUP SECRETARIES
Aberdeen Miss A M Mitchell, 32 Gordon Road, Mannofield, Aberdeen, AB15 7RL ☎ 01224 322580
www.aberdeenramblers.org.uk

Inverurie Ms M T Corley, 60 Gray Street, Aberdeen, AB10 6JE
☎ 01224 318 672

Moray Mrs E M Robertson, Abbey Bank, Station Road, Urquhart, By Elgin, Moray, IV30 8LQ ☎ 01343 842489

Stonehaven Mr I Forbes, 11 Burnside Gardens, Stonehaven, AB39 2FA
☎ 01569 766553

HIGHLAND & ISLANDS
AREA SECRETARY
Mr Brian Spence, 19 Redwood Avenue, Milton Of Leys, Inverness, IV2 6HA
☎ 01463 772602
www.highlandramblers.org.uk

GROUP SECRETARIES
Badenoch & Strathspey Miss C Jack, 13 Muirton Place, Boat Of Garten, PH24 3JA ☎ 01479 831275
www.highlandramblers.org.uk/badenoc handstrathspey

Inverness Mrs Moira Livingstone, 'Nooralain', 21 Green Drive, Inverness, IV2 4EX ☎ 01463 231985
www.highlandramblers.org.uk/inverness

Lochaber & Lorn Mr K Van Rein, Glenduror House, Duror, Appin, PA38 4BS ☎ 01631 740395
www.highlandramblers.org.uk/ lochaberandlorn

LOTHIAN & BORDERS
AREA SECRETARY
Arthur Homan-Elsy, 55 Deanburn Road, Linlithgow, West Lothian, EH49 6EY
☎ 01506 842897
www.lothian-borders-ramblers.org.uk
All Groups listed on website.

GROUP SECRETARIES
Balerno Mr R J Bayley, 65 Silverknowles Drive, Edinburgh, EH4 5HX

Coldstream Mrs M A Taylor, East Cottage, Lees Farm, Kelso Road, Coldstream, TD12 4LJ
☎ 01890 883137

East Berwickshire Mrs E Windram, 20 Hinkar Way, Eyemouth, Berwickshire, TD14 5EQ
☎ 018907 51048

Edinburgh Miss D Giles, 81b Lothian Street, Bonnyrigg, Midlothian, EH19 3AF

Edinburgh Young Walkers Ms H K Brown, 20 Claremont Park, Edinburgh, EH6 7PJ

Linlithgow Mr J B & Mrs J G Davidson, 16 Friars Way, Linlithgow, EH49 6AX
☎ 01506 842504

Livingston Mrs V McGowan, 4 Larbert Avenue, Deans, Livingston, EH54 8QJ
☎ 01506 438706

Midlothian Walkers & Hillwalkers Miss L J McKie, 48 The Square, Newtongrange, Dalkeith, Midlothian, EH22 4PX

Musselburgh Mr G C Edmond, 54 Northfield Gardens, Prestonpans, East Lothian, EH32 9LG ☎ 01875 810729

North Berwick Mrs I R McAdam, 23 Gilbert Avenue, North Berwick, East Lothian, EH39 4ED ☎ 01620 893657

Tweeddale Mrs F Hunt, 8 Craigerne Drive, Peebles, EH45 9HN
☎ 07763 169896

STRATHCLYDE, DUMFRIES & GALLOWAY
AREA SECRETARY
Mrs E Lawie, Burnside Cottage, 64 Main Street, Glenboig, Lanarkshire, ML5 2RD
☎ 01236 872959

GROUP SECRETARIES
Bearsden & Milngavie Ms E Gallacher, 4 Kirkville Place, Blairardie, Glasgow, G15 6JE (membership enquiries Andrew Summers
☎ 0141 942 6505) www.bearsden-and-milngavie-ramblers.co.uk

Biggar Mrs I L Macdonald, Tigh Na Cloich, 2 Glasgow Road, Lanark, ML11 9UE ☎ 01555 661748

Clyde Valley Mr Harry Read, 6 Maybole Gardens, Hamilton, Lanarkshire, ML3 9EU ☎ 01698 828207
www.cvramblers.supanet.com

Cumbernauld & Kilsyth Mrs H Shearer, 7 Avonhead Avenue, Cumbernauld, Glasgow, G67 4RB
☎ 01236 780136)

Cunninghame Mrs C Jeffers, 12 Thornhouse Avenue, Irvine, Ayrshire, Scotland, KA12 0LT
www.cunninghameramblers.org.uk

SCOTLAND

Trust us to keep you out there.

Polly Murray, Adventurer; Tiso sponsored athlete.

Tiso have been supplying outdoor clothing and equipment to climbers, walkers, explorers and adventurers for over 40 years and are Scotland's leading outdoor specialist. Come and benefit from our experience.

Ayr, Aberdeen, Belfast, Blackford, Dundee, Edinburgh, Glasgow, Inverness, Leith, London, Newcastle, Ratho, Stirling.

www.tiso.com

TRUST US TO KEEP YOU OUT THERE

LOCAL RAMBLERS GROUPS continued

Dumfries & Galloway Jean Snary,
7 Birchwood Place, Lockerbie Road,
Dumfries, DG1 3EB
☎ 01387 267450

Eastwood Mrs A P Fulton,
132 Greenwood Road, Clarkston,
Glasgow, G76 7LQ
www.eastwood-ramblers.org.uk

Glasgow Denise Connell,
14a Carment Drive, Shawlands,
Glasgow, G41 3PP
☎ 0141 632 0832

**Glasgow Region Under 40 First
Footers (GRUFF)**
Mr C M Duncan, Flat 1/1, 12 Forbes
Place, Paisley, PA1 1UT
☎ 0141 842 1823
www.geocities.com/
GRUFF_RAMBLERS

**Helensburgh & West
Dunbartonshire** Una Campbell,
5 Dalmore House, Dalmore Crescent,
Helensburgh, G84 8JP ☎ 01436 673726
http://website.lineone.net/~g_fiann

Inverclyde Mrs Hilary Graham, Clune
House, Clune Brae, Clunebraehead,
Port Glasgow, PA14 5SW
☎ 01475 705569
www.inverclyderamblers.org.uk

Kilmarnock & Loudoun Ms M Bush,
14 Goatfoot Road, Galston, Ayrshire,
KA4 8BJ ☎ 01563 821331
www.freewebs.com/kilmarnockandloud
ounramblers

Mid Argyll & Kintyre Mrs Brenda
Nicholson, 14 Wilson Road,
Lochgilphead, Argyll, PA31 8TR
☎ 01546 603026

Monklands Ms C McMahon,
4 Blackmoor Place, New Stevenston,
Motherwell, ML1 4JX ☎ 01698 833983
www.monklandsramblers.org.uk

Paisley Ms M Docherty, 22 Douglas
Road, Renfrew, PA4 8BB
☎ 0141 561 4416

SLOW – S Lanark Older Walkers
Ms M A Rankin, 18 Cherrytree
Crescent, Larkhall, Lanarkshire,
ML9 2AP
☎ 01698 885995

South Ayrshire Mrs K Graham,
113 Logan Drive, Troon, KA10 6QE
☎ 01292 311704

Strathkelvin Miss M Lang,
69 Redbrae Road, Kirkintilloch,
Glasgow, G66 2DE
☎ 0141 776 4161

LOCAL RAMBLERS PUBLICATIONS

**DUNBARTONSHIRE AND
LANARKSHIRE**
Easy Walks Around Milngavie
by Bearsden and Milngavie Ramblers and
East Dunbartonshire Council. Free leaflet
available from Milngavie Library.
☎ 0141 956 2776.

Walk Strathkelvin
by John Logan (Strathkelvin Ramblers)
with introduction by Cameron McNeish,
historical essays by Don Martin and
nature notes by Ian McCallum, ISBN 1
901184 44 7. Handsome book of over

70 walks, mainly short and easy walks
taking half an hour to two hours, plus
longer walks in the Campsies, canalside
and disused railway line trails, illustrated
with over 40 maps. *£7.99 from
Strathkelvin Ramblers, 25 Anne Crescent,
Lenzie, Kirkintilloch G66 5HB, cheques to
Strathkelvin Ramblers.*

FIFE
**NEW Cupar Walks: Explore Fife's
Farming Heritage**
by St Andrews Ramblers. Free colour
leaflet offering a large variety of walks

around this historic market town and out
into the surrounding countryside. 14
different routes, ranging from 3km/2
miles to 14km/9 miles, and from surfaced
paths in parks to rough country and
woodland tracks.

Maps, detailed route descriptions, photos.
Produced in association with ScotWays
and funded by Scottish Natural Heritage
and Sport Scotland. *Send 22x11cm SAE to 63 St Michaels
Drive, Cupar KY15 5BP, or contact St
Andrews Tourist Information Centre.*

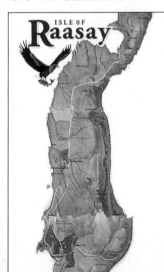
SCOTLAND

BED & BREAKFAST

ARGYLL & BUTE

● Arrochar
LOCH LOMOND & THE TROSSACHS
Lochside Guest House, Main Street, G83 7AA ☎ 01301 702467 (Maria & Iain Gourlay) www.stayatlochlomond.com/lochside Map 56/299045
BB **C** ✗ nearby S1 D3 T1 F1 Closed Xmas ᗊᗊ(Arrochar)
Ⓑ Ⓓ ⊛ ♿ ★★★

● Bridge of Orchy (Argyll)
WEST HIGHLAND WAY
⌇⌁ Inveroran Hotel, PA36 4AQ ☎ 01838 400220
www.inveroran.com Map 50/274414 BB **D** ✗ £8-£15 S1 D3 T3 F1
Closed Xmas Ⓥ Ⓑ Ⓓ ⭗♿⛬ 🐾 ★★

● Dalmally
LOCH LOMOND & THE TROSSACHS
Craig Villa Guest House, PA33 1AX ☎ 01838 200255 (A W Cressey)
www.craigvilla.co.uk Map 50/168273
BB **B** ✗ nearby D2 T2 F2 Closed Xmas ᗊᗊ(Dalmally)
Ⓑ Ⓓ ⊛ ⭗♿🚗 ! ★★★

Craigroyston, Monument Rd, PA33 1AA ☎ 01838 200234
(Mrs Sandra Boardman) www.craigroyston.com Map 50/158271
BB **B** ✗ nearby S1 D1 T1 Closed Xmas ᗊᗊ(Dalmally)
Ⓑ Ⓓ ⊛ ⭗♿🚗⛬ ★★★Ⓦ

● Helensburgh
LOCH LOMOND & THE TROSSACHS
Balmillig, 64B Colquhoun Street, G84 9JP ☎ 01436 674922
(Anne & John Urquhart) www.balmillig.co.uk Map 56/297830
BB **C/D** ✗ nearby D1 T1 F1 Closed Xmas ᗊᗊ(Helensburgh Central)
Ⓑ Ⓓ ⭗♿🚗 ★★★★

● Kilchrenan (Taynuilt)
⌇⌁ Roineabhal, PA35 1HD ☎ 01866 833207 (Maria Soep)
www.roineabhal.com Map 50/033239 BB **D** ✗ book first £30, 7pm
D2 T1 Ⓥ Ⓑ Ⓓ ⊛ ⭗♿🚗! ⛬ ★★★★

● Kilmichael Glassary (Lochgilphead)
The Horseshoe Inn, PA31 8QA ☎ 01546 606369
www.horseshoeinn.biz Map 55/852930 BB **C** ✗ £9, 6-9pm D2 T2 F1
Closed Xmas Ⓥ Ⓑ ⭗♿🚗⛬

● Oban
Kathmore, Soroba Road, PA34 4JF ☎ 01631 562104 (Mrs M Wardhaugh)
www.kathmore.co.uk Map 49/860292
BB **B** ✗ nearby D4 T3 F2 Closed Xmas ᗊᗊ(Oban)
Ⓑ Ⓓ ⊛ ⭗♿ ★★★

CENTRAL BELT

● Aberdour (Fife)
FIFE COASTAL PATH
⌇⌁ Aberdour Hotel, 38 High Street, KY3 0SW ☎ 01383 860325
www.aberdourhotel.co.uk Map 65,66/189852 BB **D** ✗ £15, 6-9pm
D6 T6 F4 ᗊᗊ(Aberdour) Ⓥ Ⓑ Ⓓ ⭗♿🚗! Ⓜ ★★★

● Crieff
⌇⌁ James Cottage, 77 Burrell Street, PH7 4DG ☎ 01764 655814
(Michael Lynch) www.jamescottage.co.uk Map 52,58/860213
BB **C** ✗ book first £10, 7-8pm D2 T1 F1
Ⓥ Ⓑ Ⓓ ⊛ ⭗♿🚗! ⛬ ★★★★

● Dunbar
Springfield Guest House, Belhaven Road, EH42 1NH ☎ 01368 862502
(Joy Smeed) Map 67/669787
BB **B** ✗ book first £12, 6pm S1 D2 T1 F1 Closed Dec ᗊᗊ(Dunbar)
Ⓥ Ⓓ ⊛ ⭗♿ ★★

● Edinburgh
Barrosa Guest House, 21 Pilrig Street, EH6 5AN ☎ 0131 554 3700
(Miss Y Pretty) Map 66/264753 BB **C/D** ✗ nearby D3 T3 F2
Closed Xmas ᗊᗊ(Waverley) Ⓑ ⊛ ♿⛬ ★★

Borodale, 7 Argyle Place, (off Melville Drive), EH9 1JU ☎ 0131 667 5578
(Mrs C A Darlington) catherine@darlington496.freeserve.co.uk
Map 66/256724 BB **C** ✗ nearby S1 D1 T1 F1 Closed Xmas
ᗊᗊ(Waverley) Ⓑ Ⓓ ★★★

Aarajura, EH10 4PQ ☎ 0131 2296565 (Ross & Lorna) www.aarajura.co.uk
Map 66/241723 BB **D** ✗ nearby S1 D3 T2 F4 ᗊᗊ(Haymarket)
Ⓥ Ⓑ Ⓓ ⊛ ⭗♿⛬

⌇⌁ Kirklea Guest House, 11 Harrison Road, EH11 1EG ☎ 0131 3371129
www.kirklea-guest-house.co.uk Map 66/234722
BB **C** ✗ nearby S2 D2 T1 F1 ᗊᗊ(Haymarket)
Ⓥ Ⓑ Ⓓ ⊛ ♿⛬ ★★★

● Glasgow
⌇⌁ Adelaide's, 209 Bath Street , G2 4HZ ☎ 0141 248 4970
www.adelaides.co.uk Map 64/584657
BB **C** ✗ nearby S2 D2 T2 F2 Closed Xmas ᗊᗊ(Glasgow Central)
Ⓑ Ⓓ ⊛ ⭗♿ ★★

● Haddington
⌇⌁ Eaglescairnie Mains, Gifford , EH41 4HN ☎ 01620 810491
(Barbara Williams) www.eaglescairnie.com Map 66/516689
BB **C/D** S2 D1 T1 Closed Xmas Ⓑ Ⓓ ⊛ ⭗♿🚗⛬ ★★★★

DUMFRIES & GALLOWAY

● Castle Douglas
⌇⌁ Buittle Bridge, East Logan, DG7 3AA ☎ 01556 660324
(Mrs Susan Matthews) sue-jeff@supanet.com Map 84/809640
BB **C** ✗ £12, 7-8:30pm D1 T1 Closed Xmas Ⓥ Ⓓ ⭗♿⛬

● Kirkcudbright
Number 3 B&B, 3 High Street, DG6 4JZ ☎ 01557 330881 (Miriam Baker)
www.number3-bandb.co.uk Map 83,84/681509
BB **C** ✗ nearby D1 T2 Closed Xmas
Ⓑ Ⓓ ⊛ ⭗♿⛬ ★★★★

● Langholm
⌇⌁ Carnlea, 16 Hillside Crescent, DG13 0EE ☎ 013873 80284
(Meg Braithwaite) http://myweb.tiscali.co.uk/meg.braithwaite/index.html
Map 79/370839 BB **B/C** ✗ nearby D1 T1 Closed Xmas
Ⓑ Ⓓ ⊛ ⭗♿🚗⛬ ★★★

● Lochmaben (Lockerbie)
Ardbeg Cottage, 19 Castle Street, DG11 1NY ☎ 01387 811855 (Bill Neilson)
bill@neilson.net   Map 78/081826
BB **B**   ✕ book first £10, 6:30pm   D/TI TI   Closed Xmas
Ⓥ Ⓑ Ⓓ ⊗ 🍵♨🚗 ★★★

● Moffat
SOUTHERN UPLAND WAY
🏴‍☠ Seamore House, Academy Road, DG10 9HW ☎ 01683 220404
(Heather & Allan Parkinson)   www.seamorehouse.co.uk Map 78/083055
BB **B**   ✕ nearby, Xmas   D2 TI F2   Ⓑ Ⓓ 🍵♨🚗!♨ ★★★

🏴‍☠ Morag, 19 Old Carlisle Road, DG10 9QJ ☎ 01683 220690 (Mrs L Taylor)
morag_moffat44@btopenworld.com   Map 78/093046
BB **B/C**   ✕ nearby   SI D2 TI   Closed Xmas   Ⓑ Ⓓ 🍵♨🚗 ★★★

North Nethermiln, Old Carlisle Road, DG10 9QJ ☎ 01683 220325
(Heather Quigley)   Map 78/093046
BB **A**   ✕ £8, 6-9pm   S/TI D2 FI   Closed Xmas   Ⓥ Ⓓ ⊗ 🍵♨🚗!

☆ **Bridge House**
Well Road, DG10 9JT ☎ 01683 220558 (Danyella & Russell Pearce)
www.bridgehousemoffat.co.uk Map 78/091057
BB **C**   ✕ £20   D4 T2 FI
Ⓥ Ⓑ Ⓓ ⊗ 🍵♨🚗🏍 ★★★

A fine Victorian property, Bridge House lies in attractive gardens in a quiet residential area on the fringe of the town.
Family-run, the atmosphere is friendly and relaxed.
The chef/proprietor provides excellent dinners for both residents and non-residents.

● New Abbey
🏴‍☠ Abbey Arms Hotel, 1 The Square, DG2 8BX ☎ 01387 850489
enquiries@Abbeyarms.netlineuk.net Map 83/963662
BB **C**   ✕ £7.50, until 8pm   SI D2 T5 F2   Closed Xmas
Ⓥ Ⓑ Ⓓ 🍵♨🏍 ★★

● Newton Stewart
Kilwarlin, 4 Corvisel Road, DG8 6LN ☎ 01671 403047 (Mrs Hazel Dickson)
hazel@kilwarlin.plus.com Map 83/409650
BB **B**   ✕ nearby   SI DI FI   Closed Nov-Feb
Ⓓ 🍵♨🚗 ★★★Ⓦ

Benera, Corsbie Rd, DG8 6JD ☎ 01671 403443 (Mrs E.M.Prise)
ethel_prise@hotmail.com Map 83/405655
BB **B**   ✕ nearby   DI TI   Closed Nov-Mar
Ⓑ Ⓓ ⊗ 🍵♨🚗! ★★★

☆ **Sherwood**
4 Stronord, Palnure, DG8 7BD ☎ 01671 401174 (Mrs G Pullen)
Map 83/450643
BB **B**   ✕ book first £6, 7pm   DI TI   Closed Xmas
Ⓥ Ⓑ Ⓓ 🍵♨🚗!

Galloway Forest trails direct from the door. Cairnsmore of Fleet opposite. Red squirrels are daily visitors along with numerous bird life. Come and enjoy Scotland's secret corner. Non-smoking, en-suite rooms.

🏴‍☠ Bargaly Estate, Bargaly House, Palnure, DG8 7BH ☎ 01671 401048
(Gene & Peter Jones)   www.bargaly.net Map 83/464664
BB **C**   ✕ book first £10-£15, 6:30-9pm   D2 TI
Ⓥ Ⓑ Ⓓ ⊗ 🍵♨🚗!♨ See SC also.

☆ 🏴‍☠ **Eskdale**
Princes Avenue, DG0 6ES ☎ 01671 404195 (Mrs Marie Sergeant)
peter-sergeant@ntlworld.com Map 83/409652
BB **B**   ✕ nearby   SI DI TI
Ⓥ Ⓑ Ⓓ ⊗ 🍵♨

Comfortable house offering spacious bedrooms and a friendly welcoming atmosphere.
Within 5 minutes' walk of Newton Stewart's varied amenities and easy access to all that Galloway has to offer the outdoor enthusiast. Forest, hill and coastal walks all nearby.

● Sanquhar
SOUTHERN UPLAND WAY
Newark Farm, DG4 6HN ☎ 01659 50263 (Frances Barbour)
www.newarkfarm.com Map 71,78/789091
BB **A**   ✕ book first, to suit   DI F2   🚌(Sanquhar)
Ⓥ Ⓑ Ⓓ 🍵♨🚗🏍 ★★★Ⓦ   Access Category 2

● Wigtown (Newton Stewart)

☆ 🏴‍☠ **Hillcrest House**
Maidland Place, Station Rd, DG8 9EU ☎ 01988 402018 (Deborah Firth)
www.hillcrest-wigtown.co.uk Map 83/433550
BB **C/D**   ✕ book first £15, 7pm   D2 T2 FI
Ⓥ Ⓑ Ⓓ 🍵♨🚗!♨ ★★★

Beautiful Victorian villa providing bright, spacious accommodation in Wigtown—Scotland's National Book Town. Perfect base for exploring the mountains, forests and coastline of this unspoilt and largely undiscovered part of SW Scotland.

HIGHLAND

● Aviemore
CAIRNGORMS & SPEYSIDE WAY
🏴‍☠ Ravenscraig Guest House, Grampian Road, PH22 1RP ☎ 01479 810278
(Jonathan Gatenby)   www.aviemoreonline.com Map 35,36/895131
BB **C/D**   ✕ nearby   S2 D3 T3 F4   Closed Xmas   🚌(Aviemore)
Ⓑ Ⓓ 🍵♨🚗 ★★★

🏴‍☠ Cairngorm Guest House, Grampian Road, PH22 1RP ☎ 01479 810630
(Gail and Peter Conn)   www.cairngormguesthouse.com Map 35,36/895131
BB **B**   ✕ nearby   D5 T3 F2   Closed Xmas   🚌(Aviemore)
Ⓑ Ⓓ ⊗ 🍵♨ ★★★

● Ballachulish (Argyll)
Park View, 18 Park Road, PH49 4JS ☎ 01855 811560 (Mrs Diana Macaskill)
www.glencoe-parkview.co.uk Map 41/080582
BB **B**   ✕ nearby   SI D2 TI   Closed Xmas
Ⓓ 🍵♨ ★★★Ⓦ Veggie breakfasts.

● Braeintra (Plockton)

☆ **Soluis Mu Thuath**
IV53 8UP ☎ 01599 577219 (Margaret Arscott)
www.highlandsaccommodation.co.uk Map 24/864324
BB **C** ✕ book first £12.50, 7:30pm D1 T3 F1 ↝(Strome Ferry) Ⓥ Ⓑ
Ⓓ ⊘ 🐾♿☕❗🛁 ★★ Facilities available for disabled guests.

Ideally situated for Torridon, Kintail, Skye or Glen Carron for the energetic, and the picture postcard village of Plockton for the less energetic, Soluis Mu Thuath is a family run guest house where a warm welcome awaits all walkers.

● Corpach (Fort William)
WEST HIGHLAND WAY & GREAT GLEN WAY

🚌🍴 Mansfield Guest House, PH33 7LT ☎ 01397 772262
(Toby & Bev Richardson) www.fortwilliamaccommodation.com Map 41/101768
BB **C** ✕ book first, 7pm S1 D2 T2 F2 ↝(Corpach)
Ⓥ Ⓑ Ⓓ ⊘ 🐾☕❗ ★★★

🚌🍴 Ramsay House, 7 Pobs Drive, PH33 7JP ☎ 01397 772419
www.corpach.free-online.co.uk Map 41/094770
BB **B** ✕ nearby D2 T1 Closed Dec ↝(Corpach)
Ⓥ Ⓑ Ⓓ ⊘ 🐾☕❗

● Dalwhinnie
CAIRNGORMS

☆ 🚌🍴 **The Inn at Loch Ericht**
PH19 1AG ☎ 01528 522257 www.priory-hotel.com Map 42/636842
BB **C** ✕ £11.50, until 9:30pm S2 D10 T13 F2
Closed Xmas ↝(Dalwhinnie)
Ⓥ Ⓑ Ⓓ 🐾☕♿🚗🍴 ★

Sited off the main north-south road from Perth to Inverness, The Inn at Loch Ericht offers a special welcome to ramblers.

Dalwhinnie village is at the gateway to the Cairngorm National Park and an excellent place to unwind.

Econony backpacker's accommodation and mountain bike hire also available.

Call us at the number above, or Fax: 01528 522270
Visit our website (above) or Email: reservations@priory-hotel.com

● Doune (Knoydart)

☆ **Doune Stone Lodges**
PH41 4PL ☎ 01687 462667 (Martin Davies)
www.doune-knoydart.co.uk Map 33/705035
BB **D** F3 Closed Oct-Mar
Ⓥ Ⓑ Ⓓ ⊘ 🐾♿🛁🚗❗ See Groups also.

Remote and unique holiday setting on the western tip of Knoydart with views to the magnificent Skye Cuillin.
Spectacular low and high level walking.

There is no road access – we collect you from Mallaig in our own boat.
Full board available.

Enjoy every comfort: delicious home cooking, a warm welcome and total relaxation. Mountains, sea, boat trips, wildlife – a truly great escape.

● Drumnadrochit (Inverness)
GREAT GLEN WAY

☆ 🚌🍴 **Loch Ness Clansman Hotel**
Loch Ness-side, IV3 8LA ☎ 01456 450326 (Mr Ian Miller)
www.lochnessview.com Map 26/572349
BB **D** ✕ £6-£12, 6:30-9pm S2 D12 T6 F4 Closed Xmas
Ⓥ Ⓑ Ⓓ 🐾☕🚗 ★★★

The only Loch Ness-side hotel. Stunning views from the observation lounge bar and restaurant.
Free pick up for B&B from Drumnadrochit (4 minutes) or Abriachan/Lochlaite (5 minutes).

🚌🍴 Bridgend House, Village Green, IV63 6TX ☎ 01456 450865
(Rosalyn Luffman) www.scotlandsbestbandbs.co.uk/bridgend.htm
Map 26,35/508299 BB **C** ✕ nearby S1 D1 T1 Closed Dec-Feb
Ⓥ Ⓑ Ⓓ ⊘ 🐾☕❗ ★★★★Ⓦ

● Durness (Lairg)
Glengolly House, Durine, IV27 4PN ☎ 01971 511255 (Martin Mackay)
www.glengolly.com Map 9/401678
BB **C** ✕ nearby D1 T1 F1 Closed Xmas
Ⓑ Ⓓ ⊘ 🐾♿🚗 Veggie breakfasts.

● Fort Augustus
GREAT GLEN WAY

☆ 🍴 **St Joseph's Bed & Breakfast**
Fort William Road, PH32 4DW ☎ 01320 366771 (Ann Taylor)
stjosephsftaug@tiscali.co.uk Map 34/375088
BB **C** ✕ nearby D2
Ⓥ Ⓑ Ⓓ ⊛ 🐾🛏🚗❗🧺

St Joseph's is a former hospital run by the Benedictine nuns from around 1871.
Fort Augustus has a lot to offer. Enjoy peace & tranquility or be energetic. Walk along the Great Glen Way with stunning views over Loch Ness.

● Fort William
WEST HIGHLAND WAY & GREAT GLEN WAY

Craig Nevis Guest House, Belford Road, PH33 6BU ☎ 01397 702023
www.craignevis.co.uk Map 41/108741 BB **B** ✕ nearby S2 D3 T3 F1
Closed Xmas 🚌(Fort William) Ⓑ Ⓓ ⊛ 🛏❗

Glenlochy Guest House, Nevis Bridge, PH33 6LP ☎ 01397 702909
(Hugh MacPherson) www.glenlochy.co.uk Map 41/114742 BB **D** ✕ nearby
S1 D7 T3 F2 Closed Xmas 🚌(Fort William) Ⓑ Ⓓ ⊛ 🐾🛏 ★★★

☆ 🍴 **Distillery House**
Nevis Bridge, PH33 6LR ☎ 01397 700103 (Stuart and Mandy McLean)
www.stayinfortwilliam.co.uk Map 41/113744
BB **D** ✕ nearby S2 D3 T2 F1 Closed Xmas 🚌(Fort William)
Ⓑ Ⓓ ⊛ 🐾🛏🚗❗🧺 ★★★★ See SC also

Set in the grounds of the old Glenlochy Distillery against the backdrop of Ben Nevis. Lovely home cooked breakfast and well equipped en-suite bedrooms. Recommended in the *Daily Mail* article 'Great Glen Way'.
Enjoy a complimentary whiskey upon arrival. Email: disthouse@aol.com

🍴 Alltonside Guest House, Achintore Road, PH33 6RW ☎ 01397 703542
(Elizabeth Ann Allton) www.alltonside.co.uk Map 41/085718
BB **B** ✕ book first £ D3 T2 F1 🚌(Fort William)
Ⓥ Ⓑ Ⓓ ⊛ 🛏🧺 ★★★

🍴 11 Castle Drive, Lochyside, PH33 7NR ☎ 01397 702659 (Mrs M Grant)
www.moygrant.co.uk Map 41/118758 BB **B** ✕ book first £12 D1 T1
Closed Xmas 🚌(Fort William) Ⓥ Ⓓ 🐾🛏🚗❗🧺 ★★★

🍴 Ashburn House, Achintore Rd, PH33 6RQ ☎ 01397 706000
(Christine MacDonald) www.highland5star.co.uk Map 41/095732
BB **D** ✕ nearby S3 D4 Closed Xmas 🚌(Fort William) Ⓑ Ⓓ ⊛ 🐾🛏

● Foyers (Inverness)
🍴 Riverside B&B, 11 Riverside, IV2 6YH ☎ 01456 486737
riverside112005@yahoo.co.uk Map 26/493209
BB **B** ✕ £6, 7pm S1 D2 Ⓥ Ⓑ Ⓓ 🐾🛏

● Garve
🍴 Birch Cottage, 6/7 Station Road, IV23 2PS
☎ 01997 414237 Map 20/395611
BB **C** ✕ £8.50-£15, 7-8pm D2 T1 🚌(Garve) Ⓥ Ⓑ Ⓓ ⊛ 🐾🛏🚗

● Glenelg (Kyle)
Marabhaig, 7 Coullindune, IV40 8JU ☎ 01599 522327
(Mrs Margaret Cameron) Map 33/808189
BB **B** ✕ book first £12, 6-8:30pm D3 T1 Closed Xmas-Jan
Ⓥ Ⓑ Ⓓ ⊛ 🐾🛏🚗❗ ★★★

● Glenurquhart (Inverness)
🍴 Shenval B&B, IV63 6TW ☎ 01456 476363 (Pierre Lebrun)
www.glenaffric.info/shenvalpage.htm Map 26/407297
BB **A** ✕ book first £14, 7:30pm D2 T1 Closed Jan
Ⓥ Ⓓ ⊛ 🐾🛏🚗❗ Organic food.

● Helmsdale (Sutherland)
Broomhill House, Navidale Road, KW8 6JS ☎ 01431 821259 (Mrs S Blance)
www.blancebroomhill.com Map 17/037160
BB **B** ✕ book first £14, 6:30pm D1 T1 Closed Xmas 🚌(Helmsdale)
Ⓥ Ⓑ Ⓓ 🐾🛏🚗❗🧺 ◆◆◆

● Invergarry
GREAT GLEN WAY
🍴 Craigard Guest House, PH35 4HG ☎ 01809 501258
(Robert & Barbara Withers) www.craigard.saltire.org Map 34/292010
BB **B/C** ✕ nearby S1 D4 T2 Ⓥ Ⓑ Ⓓ ⊛ 🐾🛏🚗❗

● Invermoriston (Inverness)
GREAT GLEN WAY
🍴 Riverbank Lodge, IV63 7YA ☎ 01320 351287 (Mrs M C Hill)
www.visitscotland.com Map 34/418169
BB **B** ✕ nearby D2 T1 Closed Nov-Feb
Ⓥ Ⓑ Ⓓ ⊛ 🐾🛏🚗❗🧺 ★★★★

🍴 Briarbank, Alltsigh, IV63 7YD ☎ 01320 351246 (Wendy Potter)
briarbank@hotmail.com Map 34/457191
BB **B** ✕ book first £9, 6:30pm D2 T2 F1 Ⓥ Ⓑ Ⓓ ⊛ 🐾🛏🚗❗

● Kincraig (Kingussie)
CAIRNGORMS
Insh House, PH21 INU ☎ 01540 651377 (Nick & Patsy Thompson)
www.kincraig.com/inshhouse Map 35/836038
BB **B** ✕ nearby S2 D1 T1 F1 Closed Nov-Dec
Ⓑ Ⓓ ⊛ 🐾🛏🚗❗🧺 ★★★

● Kingussie
CAIRNGORMS

☆ **Ardselma**
The Crescent, PH21 1JZ ☎ 07786 696384 (Valerie Johnston)
valerie.ardselma@aol.com Map 35/757009
BB **B** ✕ nearby S1 D1 T3 F2 Closed Xmas 🚌(Kingussie)
Ⓑ Ⓓ 🐾🛏🚗❗🧺

Situated within the Cairngorms National Park, Ardselma is quiet and peaceful, set in its private grounds of three acres with ample parking and safe bicycle storage. Large bedrooms, log fire sitting room, 5 mins from train station and less from bus stop.

● Kinlochewe (Achnasheen)
Hill Haven, IV22 2PA ☎ 01445 760204 (David & Lilah Ford)
www.kinlochewe.info Map 19/029620
BB **D** ✕ nearby D2 T1 Ⓥ Ⓑ Ⓓ ⊛ 🐾🛏🚗❗ ★★★

SCOTLAND

● Kinlochleven
WEST HIGHLAND WAY
🚶🍽 Hermon, 5 Rob Roy Rd, PH50 4RA ☎ 01855 831383 (Miss MacAngus)
hughenamacangus@tiscali.co.uk Map 41/189622
BB **B** ✗ nearby DI T2 Closed Dec-Jan
🅱 🅳 🛁🐾🚗 ! 🧺 Ⓜ

Edencoille Guest House, Garbhien Rd, PH50 4SE ☎ 01855 831358
(Elsie Robertson) www.kinlochlevenbed&breakfast.co.uk Map 41/181617
BB **B/C** ✗ £15, 6:30-9pm D2 T2 F2
Ⓥ 🅱 🅳 🛁🐾🚗 ! ★★★

☆ **An Tigh na Cheo Guest House**
Garbhein Road, PH50 4SE ☎ 01855 831434 (Nicola Lyden)
www.tigh-na-cheo.co.uk Map 41/182617
BB **C** ✗ nearby S2 D6 T6 FI
Ⓥ 🅱 🅳 ⊗ 🛁🐾 ! Facilities available for disabled guests.

The ideal accommodation on the
penultimate stop of the famous West
Highland Way.
With views of Am Bodach Mountain and
River Leven, we offer walkers practical yet
luxurious accommodation including en-suite
baths, open fires and drying room facilities.

● Lochcarron (Strathcarron)
Aultsigh, Croft Road, IV54 8YA ☎ 01520 722558 (Ms M Innes)
moyra.innes@btinternet.com Map 25/905400
BB **B** ✗ nearby DI TI FI Closed Xmas
🅳 ⊗ 🐾🚗 🧺

● Lochinver (Sutherland)
🚶🍽 Ardglas Guest House, IV27 4LJ ☎ 01571 844257
(Arthur & Meryl Quigley) www.ardglas.co.uk Map 15/093231
BB **A** SI D4 TI F2 Closed Xmas
Ⓥ 🅳 ⊗ 🐾🚗 Ⓜ ★★★

Ardmore House, 80 Torbreck, IV27 4JB ☎ 01571 844310
(Mrs Sandra Macleod) Map 15/069247
BB **B** DI TI Closed Nov-Feb
🅳 ⊗ 🛁 ★★★★

● Nethy Bridge (Inverness)
CAIRNGORMS
SPEYSIDE WAY
🚶🍽 Mondhuie, PH25 3DF ☎ 01479 821062 (David Mordaunt)
www.mondhuie.com Map 36/991207
BB **A** ✗ book first £10, 7:30pm DI TI Closed Nov-Dec 🚍(Broomhill)
Ⓥ 🅳 ⊗ 🐾🛁🚗 ! 🧺 See SC also.

Tigh na Fraoch Guest House, PH25 3DA ☎ 01479 821400 (Jeniffer Carrott)
www.carrott-photographic.com Map 36/000206
BB **C** ✗ £10, 7:30pm D3 T2
Ⓥ 🅱 🅳 ⊗ 🐾🛁🚗 ! 🧺

● Newtonmore (Kingussie)
CAIRNGORMS
🚶🍽 The Pines, Station Rd, PH20 IAR ☎ 01540 673271 (Colin Walker)
www.pinesnewtonmore.co.uk Map 35/713986
BB **C** ✗ nearby SI D3 T2 Closed Xmas 🚍(Newtonmore)
🅱 🅳 ⊗ 🐾🛁 ! 🧺

☆ 🚶🍽 **Craigerne House Hotel**
Golf Course Rd, PH20 IAT ☎ 01540 673281 (David & Jane Adamson)
www.craigernehotel.com Map 35/716991
BB **C** ✗ £20.50, 7-9pm SI D3 T6 FI Closed Xmas 🚍(Newtonmore)
Ⓥ 🅱 🅳 ⊗ 🐾🛁🚗 🧺

A detached Victorian villa with mature
gardens commanding magnificent views of
the Monadhliath and Cairngorm Mountains
and the Spey Valley. Only 100 yards from
the centre of Newtonmore, 'the walking
centre of Scotland'. Most rooms en-suite
with tea/coffee making facilities.

● Onich (Fort William)
Tom-Na-Creige, PH33 6RY ☎ 01855 821405 (Mr & Mrs Flynn)
www.tom-na-creige.co.uk Map 41/036613
BB **B** ✗ nearby D2 TI Ⓥ 🅱 🅳 ⊗ 🐾🛁🚗 🧺

● Spean Bridge
GREAT GLEN WAY
🚶🍽 Marlaw, 3 Lodge Gardens, PH34 4EN ☎ 01397 712603
(Ros & Roy Griffiths) www.marlawbandb.co.uk Map 41,34/220816
BB **C** ✗ nearby D2 TI Closed Xmas 🚍(Spean Bridge)
🅱 🅳 🐾🛁 ! 🧺

🚶🍽 Achnabobane Farmhouse, PH34 4EX ☎ 01397 712919 (Neil & Elizabeth
Ockenden) www.achnabobanefarmhouse.dial.pipex.com Map 41,34/195810
BB **D** ✗ £14, 7pm SI DI TI FI 🚍(Spean Bridge)
Ⓥ 🅱 🅳 ⊗ 🐾🛁🚗 ! 🧺 ★★★Ⓦ

● Tongue (Sutherland)
🚶🍽 Rhian Guest House, Rhian Cottage, IV27 4XJ ☎ 01847 611257
(Mrs J M Anderson) www.rhiancottage.co.uk Map 10/588555
BB **D** ✗ nearby D2 T2 FI Ⓥ 🅱 🅳 ⊗ 🐾🛁🚗 ! 🧺 ★★★

● Torridon
Ben Bhraggie, Diabaig, IV22 2HE ☎ 01445 790268 (Mrs I Ross)
Map 24,19/802605 BB **A** ✗ book first £10.50, 7:30pm SI DI TI
Closed Nov-Feb Ⓥ 🅱 ⊗ 🐾 !

Benview, Inveralligin, IV22 2HB ☎ 01445 791333 (Mrs Mary Mackay)
Map 24/845577 BB **A** D2 TI Closed Dec 🅳 ⊗

● Ullapool
🚶🍽 The Ceilidh Place Clubhouse, West Argyle Street, IV26 2TY
☎ 01854 612103 www.theceilidhplace.com Map 19/126939
BB **B** ✗ £20, 6:30-9pm S4 T3 F4 Ⓥ 🅳 🐾🧺 Ⓜ

● Urquhart (Moray)
SPEYSIDE WAY
🚶🍽 The Old Church of Urquhart, Parrandier, Meft Rd, IV30 8NH
☎ 01343 843063 (Andreas Peter) www.oldkirk.co.uk Map 28/284632
BB **B** ✗ book first £11, 7pm DI TI FI Ⓥ 🅱 🅳 🐾🚗 ! 🧺 ★★★★

ISLE OF ARRAN

● Blackwaterfoot (Brodick)
Lochside , KA27 8EY ☎ 01770 860276 (Marjorie Bannatyne)
george.bannatyne@virgin.net Map 68,69/903268 BB **B** ✗ book first £9,
6:30pm SI D2 TI FI Closed Xmas Ⓥ 🅱 🅳 🐾🛁 🧺 See SC also.

● Brodick

☆ **Rosaburn Lodge**
KA27 8DP ☎ 01770 302383
www.smoothhound.co.uk/hotels/rosaburn.html Map 69/009367
BB **C** ✕ nearby D3 T2 Closed Xmas
Ⓑ Ⓓ ☺ 🐾⛄🏊🚗 ! ★★★

Beautifully located on the banks of River Rosa, nearest guest house to the Arran Hills. Comfortable bedrooms and bathrooms. Excellent breakfasts. Private parking.

ISLE OF BUTE

● Port Bannatyne
Russian Tavern at Port Royal Hotel, 37 Marine Rd, PA20 0LW ☎ 01700 505073
(Olga Crawford) www.russiantavern.co.uk Map 63/071672
BB **C** ✕ £18, 7-10pm S1 D1 T2 F1 Closed Dec-Mar
Ⓥ Ⓑ Ⓓ ☺ 🐾👤🏊 CAMRA Scottish Pub of the Year 2005.

ISLE OF SKYE

● Portree
Cuaig, 7 Kitson Crescent, IV51 9DP
☎ 01478 612273 (Catherine MacLeod) Map 23/483483
BB **B** S1 D1 Closed Nov-Apr ☺ ★★★

● Upper Breakish
Tir Alainn, 8 Upper Breakish, IV42 8PY ☎ 01471 822366 (Pam & Ron Davison)
www.visitskye.com Map 32/680231
BB **B** ✕ book first £15, 7-7:30pm S1 D1 F1 Closed Nov-Dec
Ⓥ Ⓑ Ⓓ ☺ 🐾👤🏊🚗 !🌿 ★★★★ Guided walking available.

NORTH EAST SCOTLAND

● Buckie

☆ 🍴 **Rosemount B&B**
62 East Church Street, AB56 1ER ☎ 01542 833434 (Mrs Alison Temple)
rosemountbb@btinternet.com Map 28/428657
BB **C** ✕ book first £4.50+, 6-8pm D1 T2 Closed Xmas
Ⓥ Ⓑ Ⓓ ☺ 🐾👤! ★★★★

Family-run Victorian house with splendid views over the Moray Firth. Based at the beginning of the Speyside Way. Ideal for coastal, castle or forest walks. Residents' lounge with sea views. En-suite facilities. No smoking. Off-road parking available.

● Dufftown (Keith)
SPEYSIDE WAY
🍴 Errolbank, 134 Fife Street, AB55 4AQ ☎ 01340 820229 (Mrs J Smart)
jeandsmart@errolbank.freeserve.co.uk Map 28/327397
BB **A** ✕ nearby S1 D1 F3 Ⓑ Ⓓ 🐾👤🚗 !🌿

● Inverurie
🍴 Glenburnie Guest House, Blackhall Road, AB51 4JE
☎ 01467 623044 (Iain Ogilvie) Map 38/770216
BB **B** ✕ nearby D1 T5 Closed Dec 🚗(Inverurie)
Ⓥ Ⓓ 🏊🚗

● Kirkton Of Glenisla (Blairgowrie)
CAIRNGORMS
CATERAN TRAIL
🍴 Kirkside House B&B, PH11 8PH ☎ 01575 582313
kirksidehouse@btinternet.com Map 44/212604
BB **C** ✕ nearby D2 T1
Ⓥ Ⓑ Ⓓ ☺ 🐾👤🏊🚗 !🌿

● Letham (Angus)
🍴 Whinney-Knowe, 8 Dundee Street, DD8 2PQ ☎ 01307 818288
(Ellen Mann) www.whinneyknowe.co.uk Map 54/525485
BB **B** ✕ book first £10, 6-8pm S1 D2 T1
Ⓥ Ⓑ Ⓓ 🐾👤🌿 ★★★

● Rothes (Elgin)
SPEYSIDE WAY
🍴 Eastbank Hotel, 15-17 High Street, AB38 7AU ☎ 01340 831564
(Mrs Maureen Humphreys) www.eastbankhotel.activehotels.com
Map 28/277491 BB **B** ✕ £7-£15, until 8:30pm S3 D3 T4 F2
Ⓥ Ⓑ Ⓓ 🐾👤🏊🚗 !🌿 ◆◆◆ Group discounts also.

● Tomintoul (Ballindalloch)
CAIRNGORMS
SPEYSIDE WAY
🍴 Morinsh, 26 Cults Drive, AB37 9HW ☎ 01807 580452
(Mrs Jean Birchall) www.tomintoul-glenlivet.org.uk Map 36/166189
BB **A** ✕ nearby S1 D1 T1 Closed Xmas
Ⓓ ☺ 🐾👤🚗 !🌿

ORKNEY ISLANDS

● Sanday
Ladybank, KW17 2BL ☎ 01857 600339 (Denise Thomson)
Ladybank@btinternet.com Map 5/681399
BB **B** ✕ book first £12, 6-7pm S1 D2 T1
Ⓥ Ⓑ Ⓓ ☺ 🐾👤🚗 ! Ⓦ

PERTH & KINROSS

● Blairgowrie
CATERAN TRAIL
🍴 Shocarjen House, Balmoral Rd , PH10 7AF ☎ 01250 870525
(Mrs Shonaidh Beattie) shocarjen@btinternet.com Map 53/180456
BB **B** ✕ book first £8, 7pm D1 T1 Closed Xmas
Ⓥ Ⓑ Ⓓ ☺ 🐾👤🏊🚗 !🌿 ★★★★

SCOTLAND

● Killin
LOCH LOMOND & THE TROSSACHS & ROB ROY WAY

☆ ▰◄ **Dall Lodge Country House**
Main Street, FK21 8TN ☎ 01567 820217
www.dalllodgehotel.co.uk Map 51/572335
BB **C** ✗ nearby S2 D4 T2 Fl Closed Nov-Feb
Ⓥ Ⓑ Ⓓ 🐾🍴♨!🛏 ★★★

Country house on the outskirts of the picturesque village, overlooking the River Lochay, with own moorings and spectacular views of the mountains. Perfect base for relaxing, outdoor pursuits or touring. All rooms are en-suite. Visit our website for full information.

● Perth
Beeches, 2 Comelybank, PH2 7HU ☎ 01738 624486 (Pat & Brian Smith)
www.beeches-guest-house.co.uk Map 53, 58/124245
BB **B** ✗ nearby S2 D1 Tl Closed Xmas ⋙(Perth) Ⓑ Ⓓ ⊗ 🐾🍴 ★★★

▰◄ Lorne Villa, 65 Dunkeld Road, PH1 5RP ☎ 01738 628043
(Harry MacFadyen) www.lornevilla.co.uk Map 58,53/111243
BB **B** ✗ book first £10, 6pm S3 D2 T2 Fl ⋙(Perth)
Ⓥ Ⓑ Ⓓ ⊗ 🐾🍴🚗!🛏

● Pitlochry
▰◄ The Atholl Centre, Atholl Rd, PH16 5BX ☎ 01796 473044
http://athollcentre.users.btopenworld.com Map 52,53/941580
BB **B** ✗ nearby S1 D1 T4 F2 Closed Xmas ⋙(Pitlochry)
Ⓑ Ⓓ ⊗ 🐾 See Groups also. Guide dogs welcome.

● Stanley (Perth)
Glensanda House, Six Acres, Station Road, PH1 4NS ☎ 01738 827016
www.a1touristguide.com/glensandahouse/ Map 53/108334
BB **B** ✗ nearby S1 D1 Tl Closed Xmas Ⓑ ⊗ 🐾🛏 ★★★

SCOTTISH BORDERS

● Ancrum (Jedburgh)
ST CUTHBERT'S WAY

☆ **Cheviot View**
The Green, TD8 6XA ☎ 01835 830563 (Julie & Michael O'Sullivan)
www.cheviotview.co.uk Map 74/626243
BB **C** ✗ nearby D1 T2 Closed Xmas
Ⓑ Ⓓ ⊗ 🐾🍴🚗🛏 ★★★

Enjoy friendly welcome and creature comforts of a traditional Scottish village. Super views and walks including St Cuthbert's Way. Good suppers nightly across the green. Stay 2 nights with car lifts for convenience. Tasty packed lunches and expert language tuition available.

● Galashiels (Selkirk)
SOUTHERN UPLAND WAY & ST CUTHBERT'S WAY
Ettrickvale, 33 Abbotsford Road, TD1 3HW ☎ 01896 755224 (Mrs S Field)
www.ettrickvalebandb.co.uk Map 73/499352
BB **B** ✗ book first £7, 6-8pm D1 T2 Closed Xmas
Ⓥ Ⓑ Ⓓ 🐾🛏 ★★★

☆ ▰◄ **Over Langshaw Farm**
TD1 2PE ☎ 01896 860244 (Mrs Sheila Bergius)
www.organicholidays.com Map 73/514390
BB **C** ✗ book first £15, approx 7:30pm D1 Fl
Ⓥ Ⓑ Ⓓ ⊗ 🐾🍴🚗!🛏 ★★★

A relaxed and friendly hillside farm. B&B in the farmhouse or SC in The Henhoose with excellent facilities and lots of character. The farm is run organically, the food delicious. Close to the Southern Upland Way, the area is unspoilt and ideal for walkers. No midges!

● Jedburgh
ST CUTHBERT'S WAY
▰◄ Riverview, Newmill Farm, TD8 6TH ☎ 01835 862145
(Elizabeth Kinghorn) http://mysite.freeserve.com/riverviewbandb
Map 74/659227 BB **B** D2 Tl Closed Nov-Mar Ⓑ Ⓓ ⊗ 🐾🛏 🚗★★★

☆ **Ferniehirst Mill Lodge**
TD8 6PQ ☎ 01835 863279
(Alan & Christine Swanston) www.ferniehirstmill.co.uk Map 80/654171
BB **B** ✗ book first £15, 7:30pm S2 D2 T4
Ⓥ Ⓑ Ⓓ ⊗ 🐾🛏 ★

Just 2½ miles south of Jedburgh, this chalet-style guesthouse is set in its own grounds of 25 acres beside Jed Water. Homecooking including vegetarian. Dogs welcome. A country-lover's paradise. Email: ferniehirstmill@aol.com

● Kelso
Border Hotel, Woodmarket, TD5 7AX
☎ 01573 224791 (E Galbraith) Map 74/728340
BB **B** ✗ nearby S3 D2 Tl F3 Closed Xmas 🐾🛏

● Morebattle (Kelso)
ST CUTHBERT'S WAY
▰◄ Linton Farm, TD5 8AE ☎ 01573 440362 (Mrs Mary Ralston)
ralston@ecosse.net Map 74/773264
BB **B** ✗ book first £10 S1 D1 Tl Closed Nov-Feb Ⓥ Ⓑ Ⓓ ⊗ 🐾🛏🚗!

● Peebles
Whitestone House, Innerleithen Road, EH45 8BD
☎ 01721 720337 (Mrs M Muir)
www.aboutscotland.com/peebles/whitestone.html Map 73/251408
BB **B** ✗ nearby S1 D1 T2 Fl Closed Xmas Ⓓ ⊗ 🛏 Ⓜ ★★★

● Selkirk
▰◄ Ivy Bank, Hillside Terrace, TD7 4LT ☎ 01750 21270
(Mrs Janet MacKenzie) lannet@aol.com Map 73/473286
BB **B** ✗ nearby S1 D1 Tl Closed Xmas-Jan Ⓑ Ⓓ 🐾🛏🚗!🛏 ★★

● Traquair (Innerleithen)
SOUTHERN UPLAND WAY
The School House, EH44 6PL ☎ 01896 830425 (Mrs J A Caird)
www.old-schoolhouse.ndo.co.uk Map 73/331344
BB **B** ✗ book first £12, 6:30pm D1 Tl Fl Closed Xmas
Ⓥ Ⓓ 🐾🍴🚗!🛏 ★★

● Walston (Carnwath)

🛏🍴 Walston Mansion Farmhouse, ML11 8NF ☎ 01899 810334
(Margaret Kirby)   kirby-walstonmansion@talk21.com   Map 72/057454
BB **A** ✕ £10, 7pm D1 T1 F2 Ⓥ Ⓑ Ⓓ 🛋🛁🐾 ★★★

SHETLAND ISLANDS

● Walls

☆ 🛏🍴 **Burrastow House**
ZE2 9PD ☎ 01595 809307
www.users.zetnet.co.uk/burrastow-house   Map 3/223493
BB **D** ✕ £35, 7:30-9pm D3 T1 F1 Closed Nov-Mar
Ⓥ Ⓑ Ⓓ ⊗ 🛋🛁🍴🐾   Wheelchair access.

18th-century 'Haa' house overlooking Vaila Sound on Shetland's most westerly
point. All food is home cooked and a great deal home produced.

STIRLING

● Aberfoyle
LOCH LOMOND & THE TROSSACHS
ROB ROY WAY

🛏🍴 Inchrie Castle, The Covenanters Inn, FK8 3XD ☎ 01877 382347
www.stonefieldhotels.com Map 57/517007
BB **D** ✕ £19.50, 7-9pm S6 D19 T17 F3 Closed Xmas
Ⓥ Ⓑ Ⓓ🛋🛁🍴 ★★★

Corrie Glen B&B, Manse Rd, FK8 3XF ☎ 01877 382427
(Pauline & Steven Alexander) www.corrieglen.com Map 57/519003
BB **C** D2 T1 Closed Dec-Feb
Ⓑ Ⓓ ⊗ 🛋🛁 ★★★

● Balquhidder
LOCH LOMOND & THE TROSSACHS
ROB ROY WAY

🛏🍴 Kings House Hotel, FK19 8NY ☎ 01877 384646
www.kingshouse-scotland.co.uk Map 51,57/543209
BB **D** ✕ £13-£15, until 8:30pm D5 T2 Closed Xmas
Ⓥ Ⓑ Ⓓ🛋🛁🚗! ★★

● Bridge of Allan (Stirling)
🛏🍴 5a Bed & Breakfast, 5a Kenilworth Road, FK9 4DU ☎ 01786 833930
(Liz Wrathmell) lwrathmell@hotmail.com Map 57/795975
BB **B** ✕ book first £10 D1 T1 ⚶(Bridge of Allan)
Ⓥ Ⓑ Ⓓ ⊗ 🛋🛁🚗!

● Crianlarich
LOCH LOMOND & THE TROSSACHS
WEST HIGHLAND WAY

🛏🍴 Inverardran House, FK20 8QS ☎ 01838 300240 (John & Janice Christie)
www.inverardran.demon.co.uk Map 364/239725
BB **B** ✕ book first £7.50, until 9:30pm D3 T2 ⚶(Crianlarich)
Ⓥ Ⓑ Ⓓ ⊗ 🛋🛁🚗!🐾

☆ 🛏🍴 **Suie Lodge Hotel**
Glen Dochart, FK20 8QT ☎ 01567 820417
www.suielodge.co.uk Map 51/488278
BB **C/D** ✕ £9, until 8:30pm S2 D4 T3 F1 Closed Xmas
Ⓥ Ⓑ Ⓓ🛋🛁🚗 ★★

Delightful former shooting lodge in scenic
Glen Dochart surrounded by many Munros
and overlooking the river Dochart on the
A85. Comfortable accommodation, TVs,
clock radios in all rooms & CH. Relaxing bar
with open fire. Restaurant offering a wide
range of locally produced Scottish fare.

● Drymen (Glasgow)
LOCH LOMOND & THE TROSSACHS, WEST HIGHLAND WAY & ROB ROY WAY

Ceardach, Gartness Road, G63 0BH
☎ 01360 660596 (Mrs Betty Robb) Map 57/477884
BB **B** ✕ nearby D1 T1 F1 Closed Xmas Ⓓ ⊗ 🛋🛁🍴🐾 ★★

Hillview B&B, The Square, G63 0BL ☎ 01360 661000 (Mrs Irene Mullen)
drymen-taxis@btconnect.com Map 57/473885
BB **B** ✕ nearby S1 D1 T1 F1 Closed Xmas
Ⓓ ⊗ 🛋🛁🍴🐾

Green Shadows, Buchanan Castle Estate, G63 0HX ☎ 01360 660289
(Gail Lisa Goodwin) www.visitdrymen.co.uk Map 57/460887
BB **C** ✕ nearby S1 D1 T1 F1 Closed Dec-Jan
Ⓑ Ⓓ ⊗ 🛋🛁🚗! ★★★

● Falkirk
🛏🍴 Ashbank Guest House, 105 Main St, Redding, FK2 9UQ
☎ 01324 716649 (Mrs Betty Ward) www.bandbfalkirk.com Map 65/922787
BB **C** ✕ nearby D1 T1 F1 Closed Xmas ⚶(Polmont)
Ⓑ Ⓓ ⊗ 🛋🛁🚗! ★★★

● Tyndrum
LOCH LOMOND & THE TROSSACHS & WEST HIGHLAND WAY
🛏🍴 Glengarry House, FK20 8RY ☎ 01838 400224 (Paul & Jen Lilly)
www.glengarryhouse.com Map 50/335298
BB **C** ✕ nearby D1 T1 F1 Closed Xmas ⚶(Tyndrum Upper)
Ⓑ Ⓓ ⊗ 🛋🛁🚗! ★★★ See SC also.

SELF-CATERING

ARGYLL & BUTE

● Acharacle

☆ **Dalilea Bungalow**
☎ 01207 504828 (Mrs C M Gregson)
www.dalileabungalow.co.uk
£195-£465 Sleeps 6. 1 bungalow, 2 caravans. 🐾
An unforgettable experience in captivating scenery. 🐾

Situated high in the western Highlands in
Ardnamurchan, set amidst spectacular scenery
in an idyllic rural location, one bungalow and
two caravans in 2-acre grounds. Modernised
bungalow sleeps 6, Sky/DVD etc.
Fantastic walks and beautiful beaches.
2 caravans sleep 4/6.

SCOTLAND

● Dunoon

LOCH LOMOND & THE TROSSACHS

Lyall Cliff ☎ 01369 702041 (Mr P Norris) www.lyallcliff.co.uk
£200-£600 Sleeps 4-8. 2 houses.
Beautifully situated spacious accommodation on promenade. ⊗ ★★★

● Inveraray

The Anchorage ☎ 07751 105345 (Margaret Muir) www.scottisholidays.co.uk
£230-£350 Sleeps 6 +cot. 1 bungalow.
Loch facing bungalow, cosy open fire. ⊗ 🌿 ★★★

● Kilmelford

Mrs G H Dalton ☎ 01866 844212 www.assc.co.uk/maolachy
£220-£330 Sleeps 1-2 +cot. 1 cottage.
Great walking among hills and forests. ★★★Ⓦ

● Oban

☆ **The Melfort Club**
☎ 01852 200257 (Carolyn Stoddart)
www.melfortvillage.co.uk
£330-£1,050 Sleeps 4-10. 32 cottages.
Fantastic walking area, local walks booklet. 🌿 ★★★★

A small holiday village nestled in the hills and oak woods at the head of Loch Melfort, amid some of the most beautiful scenery on the west coast of Scotland. A really relaxing holiday is guaranteed by the combination of beautifully furnished cottages, excellent leisure facilities and a friendly rural atmosphere.

● Taynuilt

Mrs Butcher ☎ 01592 266601
£275-£425 Sleeps 6. 1 cabin.
Lochside. No fishing permit required. 🌿

CENTRAL BELT

● Biggar

Carmichael Cottages ☎ 01899 308336 (Richard Carmichael)
www.carmichael.co.uk/cottages
£190-£595 Sleeps 2-6. 14 cottages & houses.
Great walking country. Lovely cosy cottages.
⊗ 🌿 ★★-★★★★

Anglers Holiday Cottages ☎ 01899 308697 (John or Gwen)
www.anglersholidaycottages.co.uk
£225-£350 Sleeps 4. 1 cottage.
Location southern uplands. Fly fishing, walks. ★★★

● Maybole

☆ **Balbeg Holiday Lodges**
☎ 01655 770665 (Mrs L Sinclair)
www.balbeg.co.uk
£175-£1,800 Sleeps 4-16. 1 lodge, 2 cottages, 1 house.
Quality self-catering accommodation. ⊗ 🌿 ★★★-★★★★

Quality self-catering accommodation in 300 acre country estate. Excellent base for Galloway Hills (10 mins), within easy reach of Arran, Ben Lomond. Local walks from the front door.
The estate has two playparks, a nature pond, playing field and acres of woodland walks.

Email: info@balbeg.co.uk

DUMFRIES & GALLOWAY

● Castle Douglas

☆ **Rose Haugh Laurieston**
☎ 01224 595561 (Miss A C Paterson)
a.c.paterson@abdn.ac.uk
£270-390 Sleeps 6. 1 house.
Galloway Hills & Southern Upland Way.

Well-appointed, comfortable, high-quality accommodation with central heating. Set in beautiful gardens, surrounded by birds: red kite; peregrine; chough etc. Just a stroll down the bridlepath to the unspoilt National Trust coastline and marine reserve.

● Kirkcudbright

☆ **High Kirkland Holiday Cottages**
☎ 01557 330684 (Mrs Dunlop)
www.highkirkland.co.uk
£200-£750 Sleeps 4-10. 3 cottages. Utility room. Excellent drying facilities, tumbledrier. ⚊(Kirkcudbright) 🌿 ★★★-★★★★

Situated on Cannee Farm 1 mile from Kircudbright, 3 cottages accommodate 4-10 persons. Excellent base for coastal and hill walking. This is a beautiful town, known as 'the artists' town', with an interesting harbour, a fishing fleet, golf course, wildlife park and birdwatching.

● Moffat

☆ **Fran Considine**
☎ 01784 740892
www.holidayelegance.co.uk
£250-£425 Sleeps 2-6. 1 apartment.
Luxury refurbished Victorian villa. Splendid views. ⊗ ★★★★

Spacious, elegant, two-bedroomed luxury apartment in prestigious former Victorian villa. Newly refurbished, furnished and equipped to a high standard. Splendid views. Wonderful walks. Overlooks Moffat town and the Moffat hills. Private parking. Mobile tel: 07977 428223
Email: fran_considine@yahoo.com

● Newton Stewart

Bargaly House ☎ 01671 401048 (Gene & Peter Jones)   www.bargaly.net
£250–£650 Sleeps 2-6. 3 cottages.
Cottages in grounds of historic estate.   ⊗ 🛏 See B&B also.

● Thornhill

☆ **Templand Cottages**
☎ 01848 330775 (Andrew & Ruth Snee)
www.templandcottages.co.uk
£260–£540 Sleeps 2-6. 6 cottages.
Beautiful unspoilt location, ideal for walking.   ⊗ 🛏

Six luxury well-equipped cottages with heated pool/sauna, games room and cycle hire. Located in valley near the river Nith (famous for salmon) and Southern Upland Way. Attractive village of Thornhill with shops, restaurants and pubs only half a mile away.

HIGHLAND

● Aviemore
CAIRNGORMS

☆ **High Range Chalets**
☎ 01479 810636 (Mrs J Hyatt)
www.highrange.co.uk
£200–£500 Sleeps 2-6. 8 chalets.   Peaceful complex with stunning
mountain views. ⋙(Aviemore) 🛏 ★★★★ See Hostels also.

1-3 bedroom chalets sleeping 2-6, providing all that is necessary for your comfort. Situated in its own birch woodland park with magnificent views of the Spey valley and Cairngorm mountains. Five hundred yards from Aviemore centre. Ristorante, pizzeria and bar on site.

● Fort Augustus
Miss J Ellice ☎ 01809 501287 www.ipw.com/aberchalder
£200–£1,400 Sleeps 2-12. 3 varying types.
Deer stalking and fishing.   ⊗ 🛏

● Fort William
Distillery Cottages ☎ 01397 700103 (S Mclean) www.distillerycottages.co.uk
£240–£490 Sleeps 2-4. 3 apartments.   West Highland Way and Ben Nevis.
⋙(Fort William) ⊗ 🛏 ★★★ See B&B also.

● Invergarry
Ardochy House Cottages ☎ 01809 511292 (Mr C Sangster)
www.ardochy.ukgateway.net
£225–£445 Sleeps 4-6. 3 cottages. Variety of walks and Munros nearby. ⊗ 🛏

● Kingussie
CAIRNGORMS
Tim Barraclough ☎ 0115 9254002 claigan@aol.com
£300–£800 Sleeps 2-8. I cottage.
Newly refurbished, en-suites, drying/storage.
⋙(Kingussie) ⊗ 🛏

☆ **Landseer and Carrick Houses**
☎ 01926 640560 (Mary E Wheildon)
www.carrickhousekingussie.co.uk
£195–£600 Sleeps 5-6 + cot. 2 houses.
For Scotlands mountain peaks & rushing rivers. ⋙(Kingussie) 🛏 ★★★

Lanseer House and Carrick House.

Two traditional granite houses at the foot of both the Cairngorms and Monadhliath Mountains.

Each offer three most comfortable bedrooms and well-equipped homely public rooms. These popular accommodations offer a splendid base from which to walk the Cairngorm National Park -- explore the many outdoor activities, spot the wildlife and encompass the district.
Quiet village location, easy parking with local amenities.

Email: m_e_wheildon@hotmails.com

● Mallaig
Anne Skea ☎ 01687 462261 a.skea@tesco.net
£250–£475 Sleeps 6. I cottage. ⋙(Morar) ⊗

● Nethy Bridge
CAIRNGORMS
Mondhuie ☎ 01479 821062 (David Mordaunt) www.mondhuie.com
£95–£285 Sleeps 3-6. 2 chalets.   Closed Nov
Speyside Way. Owner is a mountaineer. ⋙(Broomhill) 🛏 See B&B also.

Stables Cottage ☎ 01309 672505 (Mr & Mrs Patrick)
www.speysidecottages.co.uk
£125–£720 Sleeps 2-9. I hayloft, I smithy (both converted).
On Speyside Way. Explore Abernethy walks.   ⊗ 🛏 ★★★

● Portree
Corrie Cottages ☎ 01478 640324 (Dorothy Morrison)
www.corriecottages.co.uk
£110–£275 Sleeps 1-4. 2 cottages. Set in a rural crofting community. 🛏 ★★

● Strontian
Ness Cottage ☎ 01967 402028 (Mrs Collins) www.nesscottage.com
£200–£375 Sleeps 5. I cottage.
Traditional cottage. Woodburner, views, good walking. 🛏

● Thurso
Dunnet Head Outdoor Activities ☎ 01847 851774 (Brian Sparks)
www.dunnethead.co.uk
£150–£450 Sleeps 2-4. I cottage, I caravan.   Closed Nov-Jan
En-suite rooms.   ⊗ ★★★

● Ullapool
Corran Self-catering ☎ 01854 612501 (Barbara D Peffers)
www.corranullapool.co.uk
£350–£600 Sleeps 6. I house.
Traditional village house, mountains, sea views   ⊗

SCOTLAND

☆ **Custom House**
☎ 01854 612107 (Mrs P Campbell)
www.ullapool.co.uk/customhouse
£180–£300   Sleeps 2-4.   1 cottage.   Closed Nov-March
Quiet conservation area, near shops/harbour.

One self-catering cottage sleeping 2-4 people.
This cottage is part of a modernised listed sandstone property in a quiet conservation close to shops, restaurants, the harbour, sea and hills.

ISLE OF ARRAN

● Blackwaterfoot
Lochside   ☎ 01770 860276 (Mrs M Bannatyne)
george.bannatyne@virgin.net   £220–£380   Sleeps 2-6.   2 cottages.
Centrally heated, near beach/village. Aga.   See B&B also.

NORTH EAST SCOTLAND

● Kintore
Kingsfield House   ☎ 01467 632366 (Mrs J Lumsden)
www.holidayhomesaberdeen.com   £275–£475   Sleeps 4 + cot.   1 cottage.
Closed Dec-Feb   Tranquil position overlooking fields.   ★★★★

● Tomintoul
CAIRNGORMS

☆ **Ballinlish**
☎ 01425 277644 (R M Clifford)
ballinlish@postmaster.co.uk
£400–£900   Sleeps 10.   1 house.
★★★★   RA member

Well appointed modernised former hunting lodge, large garden, stunning views, fantastic walks, close to Speyside Way. Four double rooms each with ensuite plus two single rooms.
All linen and towels included.

PERTH & KINROSS

● Aberfeldy
Garth House   ☎ 01887 830515 (Lady Eveline Bright)   www.garthhouse.co.uk
£215–£650   Sleeps 5-10.   2 apartments.
Well situated for hill walking.

FOUND SOMEWHERE GOOD
THAT'S NOT IN THIS GUIDE?
Fill in the Recommendation Form on p311
and send it to the editor at our central
office or email:
yearbook@london.ramblers.org.uk

● Crieff

☆ **Gamekeepers Cottages & Norwegian Lodges**
☎ 01764 652586 (Stephen Brown)
www.monzievaird.com
£350–£1000   Sleeps 2-8.   23 lodges, 1 cottage.
Fishing, designated designed landscape   ★★★★Ⓦ

Gamekeeper's Cottage & Norwegian Lodges in a designated designed landscape.

Beautiful, mature and extensive grounds. Private and well spread out.

Elevated positions with magnificent views.

"Holidays like they used to be" — space — wildlife — bring your dog — build dens and dams — net tadpoles — paddle — walk— tennis –fishing.
Large local path network on our doorstep. Many other local activities.

● Glenshee
CAIRNGORMS

☆ **Finegand Cottages**
☎ 01250 885234 (Mrs Shona Haddon)
www.finegandestate.com
£158–£399   Sleeps 2-7.   4 cottages.
Individually sited, well equipped, magnificent views.   ★★

4 individual traditional highland cottages in this beautiful glen with its winding river. South edge of Cairgorm National Park: 17 Munros nearby; historic walks such as the Cateran Trail and Lairig Guru. Small trout loch and wonderful bird life.
Email: finegand@tesco.net

SCOTTISH BORDERS

● Cockburnspath

☆ **Kittiwake Cottage**
☎ 01324 613098 (Susan Crooks)
www.kittiwake-cottage.com
£350–£550   Sleeps 7-8.   1 house.
Stunning panoramic sea views. Log fire.

New three-bedroom cottage in cliff-top conservation village at the end of the Southern Upland Way. Excellent base for coastal walks, Borders and Edinburgh. Sheltered sandy beach and picturesque harbour five minutes walk.
Log fire and secluded patio garden.

STIRLING

● Balmaha
LOCH LOMOND & THE TROSSACHS

Montrose House ☎ 01224 743586 (Rona Livingstone)
www.geocities.com/loch_lomond_uk £300-£1,000 Sleeps 8 + cot. 1 flat.
West Highland Way, Loch Lomond. Hill views. 🏠 RA member

● Killin
LOCH LOMOND & THE TROSSACHS

☆ Wester Lix Cottages
☎ 01567 820990 (Mrs Gill Hunt)
www.westerlix.co.uk
£350-£995 Sleeps 4-8. 6 cottages.
Jonna's refurbished for summer, steading easter 🏠 ★★★

Six cottages in a peaceful retreat located in a secluded forest clearing, but at the same time within easy reach of nearby villages, local amenities and outdoor activities. Features of the location include our own private lochan fed from the burn that runs through the site.

● Tyndrum
LOCH LOMOND & THE TROSSACHS

Glengarry House ☎ 01838 400224 (Paul & Jen Lilly)
www.glengarryhouse.com
£220-£320 Sleeps 4-6. 1 chalet. West Highland Way, plenty of Munros.
🚌(Tyndrum Upper/Lower) ⊗ 🏠 ★★ See B&B also.

GROUPS

CENTRAL BELT

The Burgh Lodge (SC) Back Wynd, Falkland, Cupar, Fife, KY15 7BX
☎ 01337 857710 www.burghlodge.co.uk
Bednight £12 ✕ nearby ⊗ D 🍳 ★★★★
See Hostels also.

HIGHLAND

☆ Doune Bay Lodge (SC/BB)
Doune, Knoydart ☎ 01687 462565 (Liz Tibbetts)
www.doune-knoydart.co.uk Map 33/705035
FB £50, SC £750 Min 6, max 14. 1 lodge.
✕ 🍳 D ! 🚌 See B&B also.

Remote and unique holiday setting on the western tip of Knoydart with views to the magnificent Skye Cuillin. Enjoy every comfort: delicious home cooking, a warm welcome and total relaxation. Mountains, sea, boat trips, wildlife – a truly great escape.

ISLE OF ARRAN

☆ Kilmory Lodge (SC)
Kilmory, KA27 8PQ ☎ 01770 870345 (Ann Rhead)
www.kilmoryhall.com Grid ref: NS 960215
SC £230pn Min 15, max 23. 1 bunkhouse.
✕ nearby ⊗ B D ! 🚌 ★★★

Modern, comfortable bunkhouse on the beautiful Island of Arran, one hour from Scottish mainland. Bordering a Specially Protected Area (SPA) Arran's Coastal Way, beaches, forestry, hill and mountain walks are all within 5 to 30 minutes of this budget accommodation.

ISLE OF EIGG

☆ Glebe Barn Field Centre & Independent Hostel (BB/SC)
PH42 4RL ☎ 01687 482417
www.glebebarn.co.uk Map 39/483853
BB £19 Bednight £9 Min 14, max 24.
✕ (groups only) ⊗ 🍳 D ! 🚌 See Hostels also.

Comfortable self-catering accommodation for large groups, families or individuals in attractive 19th-century barn. (Full catering optional.) Enjoy magnificent views, richly varied walks, abundant wildlife and fascinating archaeology, history and geology.

PERTH & KINROSS

The Atholl Centre (BB/SC) Atholl Rd, Pitlochry PH16 5BX ☎ 01796 473044
(Jean Marzetti) http://athollcentre.users.btopenworld.com
BB £20, SC £1,540 Min 2, max 34. 🚌(Pitlochry)
✕ ⊗ 🍳 B D See B&B also.

STIRLING

☆ Inverardran Cottage (SC)
Crianlarich, FK20 8QS ☎ 01259 760734 (Christina Murray)
www.ochils.com Map 50/392250
SC £819 Min 1, max 18. 1 cottage. 🚌(Crianlarich)
✕ nearby ⊗ D

Situated on the A85 at Crianlarich, the cottage is ideally positioned for Glencoe, Fort William and the southern Highlands. Fully equipped for self-catering. Restaurants and bars within easy walking distance. Bus and rail link to Glasgow, Stirling, Oban and Fort William.

SCOTLAND

HOSTELS, BUNKHOUSES & CAMPSITES

CENTRAL BELT

The Burgh Lodge (IH) Back Wynd, Falkland, Cupar, Fife, KY15 7BX
☎ 01337 857710 www.burghlodge.co.uk
Bednight £12 ✕ nearby 🄳 🐾 ⊗ ★★★★ See Groups also.

HIGHLAND

Bunroy Park Camping Site (C) Roy Bridge, Inverness ☎ 01397 712332
www.bunroycamping.co.uk Map 41/274806
Camping up to £4.50pppn Closed Nov-Feb ⚌(Roy Bridge) 🐾nearby ★★★★

CAIRNGORMS NATIONAL PARK

High Range Caravan and Camping Park (C) Grampian Rd, Aviemore, PH22 1PT
☎ 01479 810636 (Mrs J Hyatt) www.highrange.co.uk
£14-£15 per pitch ⚌(Aviemore) ✕ 🐾 🄳 See SC also.

Shemas Backpackers Lodge (IH) Mallaig, Inverness ☎ 01687 462764
Bednight £13 ✕ nearby ⚌(Mallaig) 🄳 ⊗

Sail Mhor Croft Hostel (IH) Dundonnell, IV23 2QT ☎ 01854 633224
www.sailmhor.co.uk Map 19/064983
Bednight £10 ⊗ 🄳 On Teallach Ridge route.

☆ The Wild Goose Backpackers' Hostel (IH)
Lochiel Crescent, Banavie, Fort William ☎ 01397 772531
www.great-glen-hostel.co.uk
Bednight £13.50
✕ nearby 🄳 ⊗

Located on the Great Glen Way and cycle route within the village of Banavie, just three miles from Fort William, is Scotland's newest backpackers' hostel, serving the accommodation needs of walkers, cyclists, individuals on activity holidays, families and groups.

Enjoy a relaxing break to the Scottish Highlands. Be inspired with fantastic views of Ben Nevis. Take an evening walk along the banks of the Caledonian Canal and Neptune's Staircase. Or enjoy a glass of wine or beer on the patio.

Above all, share your experiences with like-minded travellers.

Quality hostel accommodation sleeping 40. We are open all year from January 2006. Give us a call or visit our website for more information.

ISLE OF EIGG

Glebe Barn Field Centre & Independent Hostel (IH/OC) PH42 4RL
☎ 01687 482417 www.glebebarn.co.uk Map 39/483853
Bednight £10-£12 Closed for individual bookings Oct-Apr
🄳 ⊗ See Groups also.

NORTH EAST SCOTLAND

☆Rattray Head Hostel (IH)
Rattray, Peterhead ☎ 01346532236 (Rob Keeble & Val Porter)
www.rattrayhead.net/hostel Map 30/103577
Bednight £11
🐾 🄳 ⊗

Open Easter 2006.
Isolated non-smoking lighthouse shore station on 11 miles of beach and dunes, in one of the driest and sunniest midge-free areas of Scotland. Our green hostel has an environmental policy, is dog and wheelchair friendly, and offers 2 rooms of 5 beds including 2 doubles.
Bookswap and video libraries. Laundry room. Photo ID is essential to ensure guest security. Price includes drinks and a welcome food pack.

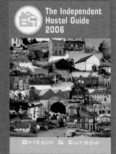

WALKING HOLIDAYS

BRITAIN

The companies listed here have chosen to advertise with us and their inclusion should not imply any recommendation by the Ramblers' Association

Bob Close Coach Assisted Walking Holidays, 40 Spring Hill, Kingswood, Bristol, BS15 1XT. Tel 01179 672459 Fax 01179 671986 Web www.bobswalkingholidays.co.uk Coach assisted walking holidays. Long distance walks 7-8 days. No leader. Choose your distance. Youth Hostel accommodation. Small friendly groups. Coach carries your luggage. Covers: UK

Byways Breaks, 25 Mayville Road, Liverpool L18 OHG Tel 0151 722 8050 Web www.byways-breaks.co.uk Self-led walking & cycling holidays. Flexible routes, comfortable accommodation, luggage transported. Covers: Shropshire, Welsh borders, Offa's Dyke, Cheshire

Wycheway Country Walks, 39 Sandpiper Crescent, Malvern, Worcestershire WR14 1UY, Tel 01886 833828, E: wb@wychewaycountrywalks.co.uk Web www.wychewaycountrywalks.co.uk Guided & self-guided walking holidays and short breaks. Itineraries to suit your requirements. Choose from over 30 trails and holidays throughout England and Wales

Instep Linear Walking Holidays, 35 Cokeham Road, Lancing, West Sussex, BN15 OAE Tel 01903 766475 Fax 01903 766475 Email walking@instephols.co.uk Web www.instephols.co.uk Coast to Coast Merchandise, Tee & Sweatshirts, Badges, Videos, Maps, Guide Books. Covers: Cumbria, The Dales, North Yorkshire

OVERSEAS

ENGLAND

Hambledon Hotel Guided and unescorted walks, tailor-made to suit you. 11, Queen's Road, Shanklin, Isle of Wight PO37 6AW. ☎ 01983 862403 (Bill Grindley) www.step-by-step.co.uk
See advert on page 48

Archaeology Holidays – Lindum Heritage, 7 Ridgeway, Nettleham, Lincolnshire, LN2 2TL Tel 01522 851388 Email info@lindumheritage.co.uk Web www.lindumheritage.co.uk Archaeology and history short breaks, historic setting. Excavation. Free brochure. Covers: Archaeology, history, UK holidays, short breaks

Curlew Guided Walking, 26 De Vitre Cottages, Ashton Road, Lancaster LA1 5AN Tel 01524 35601 Email info@curlewguidedwalking.co.uk Web www.curlewguidedwalking.co.uk Walking holidays and short breaks, comfortable accommodation and transport included. Covers: Lake District, Yorkshire Dales, Hadrian's Wall and other areas of Northern England

Footprints of Sussex, Pear Tree Cottage, Jarvis Lane, Steyning, West Sussex BN44 3GL Tel 01903 813381 Fax 01903 816533 Web www.footprintsofsussex.co.uk 7/9 night holidays on the South Downs Way, including baggage transfers Covers: South Downs

Lodge in the Forest - Lovely Alpine lodge in the forest (Matlock/Chatsworth/Peak District) with luxury pool for guided walking, self-guided or just to relax. Competitive rates. www.lodgeintheforest.co.uk 020 8741 8277

Orchard Trails, 5 Orchard Way, Horsmonden, Tonbridge, Kent TN12 8JX Tel 01892 722680 Fax 01892 722680 Email Grabham@btinternet.com Web www.kent-esites.co.uk/orchardtrails Unescorted walking/cycling holidays. Kent and East Sussex. Luggage transported. Covers: Kent, East Sussex

Pace the Peaks - with Cathy and Kim, Cumbria House, 1 Derwentwater Place, Ambleside Road, Keswick CA12 4DR 017687 73171 E: cathy@pacethepeaks.co.uk Web: www.pacethepeaks.co.uk. Local Knowledge – they key to wonderful walking. Join Cathy for guided fell walks or practical navigation. Individuals or groups welcome.

Cornwall's Roseland Peninsula is a walker's paradise. An unspoilt area of outstanding natural beauty. Country cottages to splendid waterside residences available. 4 The Quay, St Mawes, Cornwall TR2 5DG. www.portscathoholidays.co.uk 01326 270 900

Celtic Trails, PO Box 11, Chepstow, Monmouthshire, NP16 6ZD. Tel 01600 860846 Fax 01600 860843 Email info@bestbritishwalks.com Quality walking holidays, luggage transfer, short breaks. High standard service and organisation. Covers: Cotswold Way, Hadrians Wall Path, Dales Way, Norfolk Coast Path, South West Coast Path, Exmoor and Dartmoor, Offa's Dyke Path, Wye Valley Walk

WALES, SCOTLAND AND IRELAND

People call this an
exercise bike.

It doesn't move.

Funny bike.

Blacks
THE OUTDOOR EXPERTS

www.blacks.co.uk

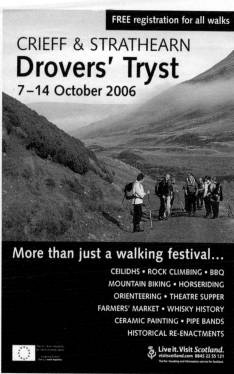

WALKER'S TOOLKIT

CONTENTS

MAPS FOR WALKERS

Ordnance Survey maps

The best and most comprehensive walkers' maps of Britain are the 1:25 000 scale Ordnance Survey (OS) Explorer series in orange covers. They include a range of geographical features and landmarks at a high level of detail, including field boundaries, heights shown as contours and 'spot heights', railway stations and tram stops. They also show rights of way (except in Scotland), permissive paths, many long-distance paths, off-road cycle paths, open access land in England and Wales, locations of shorter circular walks and nature trails, information centres and visitor attractions.

Another OS series, 1:50 000 Landranger maps in pink and silver covers, include footpaths and selected tourist attractions, but show less detail; OS are now marketing them as maps for planning days out rather than navigating on the ground.

Bookshops, information centres, larger newsagents and even some garages stock their local OS sheets. Maps can also be bought from specialist retailers, over the internet or direct from the OS, who can also supply a free Mapping Index showing all the sheet numbers.

Ordnance Survey ☎ 0845 605 0504
www.ordnancesurvey.co.uk

Or buy OS maps online from **Aqua3** through the Ramblers website and earn a **10% discount** with free postage. The Ramblers receive a 10% donation for every map sold this way.

Ordnance Survey Ireland see p304.

Other paper maps

While no other publisher covers all of Britain at detailed scales, a number of other specialist publishers do offer maps of use to walkers. The most important is Harvey who produce very clear specialist walkers' maps of certain popular upland areas and long-distance paths at 1:25 000 and 1:40 000 scales. The maps also usually include useful information and addresses, and most are printed on weatherproof paper.

Harvey Maps ☎ 01786 841202 (credit card hotline) www.harveymaps.co.uk

In urban areas street atlases can be more useful than OS maps: the Philips series is probably the best for walkers since off-road paths, parks and open spaces and even some signed routes are clearly shown.

Philips ☎ 020 7644 6940 (general enquiries), 01903 828503 (mail order), www.philips-maps.co.uk.

Electronic maps

Electronic mapping systems for home PCs enable you to print OS maps at a variety of scales, to plan and annotate routes and link up to a GPS or pocket PC to take out on your walk – but make sure your hardware is compatible with the system you want to buy. The main suppliers are:

Anquet Maps ☎ 0845 270 9020, www.anquet.co.uk
Hillwalker (ISYS) ☎ 0845 166 5701, www.hillwalker.org.uk
memory-map ☎ 0870 740 9040, www.memory-map.co.uk
TrackLogs ☎ 01298 872537, www.tracklogs.co.uk

Mapping websites allowing you to view extracts from Landranger and street maps by grid reference, postcode or place name include www.streetmap.co.uk, www.multimap.com and the OS site.

Learning about maps

Map Reading Made Easy, free from the OS or downloadable from their website, is an excellent brief introduction. See the Maps section on our website which lists course providers and suggestions for further reading (also available as a printed factsheet – FS2, see p308).

Two particularly useful books are available from us. *Navigation and Leadership: a manual for walkers* (£4 + p&p) is the Ramblers' official 'bible' on the use of map and compass and leading group walks. Julian Tippett's *Navigation for Walkers* (£8.99 + p&p) is a great beginners' guide which includes OS map extracts.

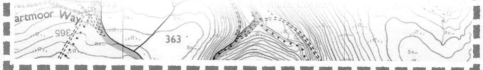

PUBLIC TRANSPORT

Help avoid pollution and congestion by combining walking and public transport. You can plan more flexible routes such as linear walks, and forget worries like parking, car crime and whether or not you should have a pint along the way.

Use National Rail for information about services and fares; their website also has an online journey planner. For long distance coaches, use National Express and Scottish City Link. Traveline has information on local bus, metro/underground, tram/light rail and ferries. When planning a walk it's handy to have a map of your route to hand. In London contact Transport for London or try Transport Direct, an online multi-modal journey planner for the whole of the UK.

There is an increasing number of services for countryside visitors, especially in popular areas during the summer; they often run on Sundays and bank holidays and offer economical ticket deals for those planning linear walks. See the information section of our website, and www.countrygoer.org.

Travel information for people with disabilities is available from Tripscope.

We encourage our Areas and Groups to organise walks by public transport wherever possible, and our annual Welcome to Walking Week, coinciding with In Town Without My Car Day (European car-free day) in September includes a wide range of car-free walks. Ramblers walk leaders in need of advice on organising walks by public transport should contact the countryside team at our central office, who can put you in touch with our network of regional transport contacts.

CIE see p304
Countrygoer ☎ 01943 607868
www.countrygoer.org
National Express ☎ 020 7529 2000
www.nationalexpressgroup.com
National Rail ☎ 0845 748 4950
www.nationalrail.co.uk
Scottish Citylink ☎ 0141 332 9644, ☎ 0870 550 5050 (enquiries and bookings)
www.citylink.co.uk
Translink see p304
Transport Direct
www.transportdirect.info
Transport for London ☎ 020 7222 1234
www.tfl.gov.uk
Traveline ☎ 0870 608 2608, textphone 0870 241 2216
www.traveline.org.uk
Tripscope ☎ 0845 758 5641,
www.tripscope.org.uk

NATIONAL PARKS

Association of National Park Authorities
☎ 029 2049 9966
www.anpa.gov.uk

Council for National Parks
☎ 020 7924 4077
Wales office:
☎ 029 2045 0433
www.cnp.org.uk
Works to protect and enhance the national parks of England and Wales, and areas that merit national park status, and promote understanding and quiet enjoyment of them for the benefit of all.

Scottish Council for National Parks
☎ 01505 682447
www.scnp.org.uk
Works to protect and enhance national parks in Scotland and to promote the case for new national parks.

Brecon Beacons
☎ 01874 624437
Brecon Beacons Visitor Centre (Mountain Centre)
☎ 01874 623366
Brecon Beacons Park Society –

Cymdeithas Parc Bannau Brycheiniog
☎ 01639 730179
www.breconbeaconsparksociety.org
Organise a programme of free led walks in the Park.

The Broads
☎ 01603 610734
www.broads-authority.gov.uk

Cairngorms
☎ 01479 873535
www.cairngorms.co.uk

Dartmoor
☎ 01626 832093
High Moorland Visitor Centre
☎ 01822 890414
www.dartmoor-npa.gov.uk

Dartmoor Preservation Association
☎ 01822 890646
www.dartmoorpreservation.com
Aims to protect, preserve and enhance the natural beauty, cultural heritage and scientific interest of Dartmoor, and to preserve public access and commoners' rights.

Exmoor
☎ 01398 323665

Dulverton Visitor Centre
☎ 01398 323841
www.exmoor-nationalpark.gov.uk

Lake District
☎ 01539 724555
www.lake-district.gov.uk
Visitor information and walk suggestions
Brockhole Visitor Centre
☎ 015394 46601
Friends of the Lake District
☎ 01539 720788
www.fld.org.uk
Cares for the countryside and wildlife of the Lake District.

Loch Lomond & The Trossachs
☎ 01389 722600
National Park Gateway Centre
☎ 0845 345 4978
www.lochlomond-trossachs.org

New Forest
☎ 023 8028 6821
www.newforestnpa.gov.uk
Lymington Visitor Information Centre
☎ 01590 689000
www.thenewforest.co.uk
The New Forest's designation as a

national park came into effect in March 2005. It is expected the park will open officially in 2006.

North York Moors
☎ 01439 770657
Moors Information Centre
☎ 01439 772737
Park Information Centre
☎ 01845 597426
www.moors.uk.net

Northumberland
☎ 01434 605555
Once Brewed Visitor Centre
☎ 01434 344396
www.northumberland-national-park.org.uk

Peak District
☎ 01629 816200
www.peakdistrict.org
Visitor information
www.visitpeakdistrict.com

Pembrokeshire Coast – Arfordir Penfro
☎ 0845 345 7275

www.pembrokeshirecoast.org.uk
Visitor Centre
☎ 01437 720392
stdavids.pembrokeshirecoast.org.uk

Snowdonia – Eryri
☎ 01766 770274
www.eryri-npa.co.uk
Information Centre
☎ 01690 710426
www.snowdonia-npa.gov.uk

Cymdeithas Eryri – Snowdonia Society
☎ 01690 720287
www.snowdonia-society.org.uk
Works to protect Snowdonia National Park.

South Downs
Sussex Downs Conservation Board
☎ 01243 558700
East Hampshire AONB Office
☎ 023 9259 1362
www.vic.org.uk
These two adjoining AONBs work to protect, conserve and enhance

the natural beauty of the South Downs. A public consultation has been carried out on government proposals to designate this area as a national park.

Society of Sussex Downsmen
☎ 01273 771906
www.sussexdownsmen.org.uk
Aims to preserve and protect the South Downs.

South Downs Campaign
☎ 01273 563358
www.southdownscampaign.org.uk
Grouping of organisations including the Ramblers campaigning for the adoption of the South Downs as a national park.

Yorkshire Dales
☎ 0870 166 6333
www.yorkshiredales.org.uk
Visitor centre
☎ 01969 667450
www.destinationdales.org

AONBs & FOREST PARKS

Association for AONBs – Cymdeithas dros AoHNE
☎ 01451 862007
www.aonb.org.uk

Arnside/Silverdale
☎ 01524 761034
www.arnsidesilverdaleaonb.org.uk

Blackdown Hills
☎ 01823 680681
www.blackdown-hills.net

Cannock Chase
☎ 01889 882613
Visitor Centre ☎ 01543 876741
www.cannockchasedc.gov.uk/canno
ckchase/countryside.htm
Forest Centre
☎ 01889 586593
www.forestry.gov.uk/website/recrea
tion.nsf/LUWebDocsByKey/
Museum of Cannock Chase
☎ 01543 877666

Chichester Harbour
☎ 01243 512301
www.conservancy.co.uk

Cornwall
☎ 01872 322350
www.cornwall-aonb.gov.uk

Chilterns
www.chilternsaonb.org

Chiltern Society
☎ 01494 771250
www.chilternsociety.org.uk

Clwydian Range
☎ 01352 810614
www.denbighshire.gov.uk
(under Countryside Services)

Cotswolds
☎ 01451 862000
www.cotswoldsaonb.com

Cranborne Chase & West Wiltshire Downs
☎ 01725 516925
www.dorsetcc.gov.uk/
cranbornechase

Dedham Vale & Stour Valley
☎ 01473 583176
www.dedhamvalestourvalley.org

Dorset
☎ 01305 224279
www.dorsetaonb.org.uk

East Devon
☎ 01395 517557
www.eastdevonaonb.org.uk

East Hampshire
See South Downs under National Parks

Forest of Bowland
☎ 01772 534140
www.forestofbowland.com

Gower
☎ 01792 635741
www.goweraonb.org

High Weald
☎ 01580 879500
www.highweald.org

Howardian Hills
☎ 01653 627164

Isle of Anglesey – Ynys Môn
☎ 01248 752429
www.anglesey.gov.uk

AONBs & FOREST PARKS

Isle of Wight
☎ 01983 823855
www.wightaonb.org.uk

Isles of Scilly
☎ 01720 423486
www.ios-aonb.info

Kent Downs
☎ 01622 221522
www.kentdowns.org.uk

Kielder
☎ 01434 220643
www.kielder.org

Lincolnshire Wolds
☎ 01507 609740
www.lincswolds.org.uk

Llyn
☎ 01758 704083
www.gwynedd.gov.uk

Malvern Hills
☎ 01684 560616
www.malvernhillsaonb.org.uk

Mendip Hills
☎ 01761 462338
www.mendiphillsaonb.org.uk

Nidderdale
☎ 01423 712950
www.nidderdaleaonb.org.uk

Norfolk Coast
☎ 01328 850530
www.norfolkcoastaonb.org.uk

North Devon
☎ 01237 423655
www.northdevon-aonb.org.uk
Includes Braunton Burrows
Biosphere Reserve.

North Pennines
☎ 01388 528801
www.northpennines.org.uk

North Wessex Downs
☎ 01488 685440
www.northwessexdowns.org.uk

Northumberland Coast
☎ 01670 534088
www.northumberland.gov.uk

Quantock Hills
☎ 01278 732845
www.quantockhills.com

Shropshire Hills
☎ 01588 674080
www.shropshirehillsaonb.co.uk

Solway Coast
☎ 016973 33055
www.solwaycoastaonb.org.uk

South Devon
☎ 01803 861384
www.southdevonaonb.org.uk

South Hampshire
☎ 023 8028 5356
www.hants.gov.uk/coast

Suffolk Coast and Heaths
☎ 01394 384948
www.suffolkcoastandheaths.org

Surrey Hills
☎ 01372 220653
www.surreyhills.org

Sussex Downs
See South Downs under
National Parks

Tamar Valley
☎ 01579 351681
www.tamarvalley.org.uk

Wye Valley
☎ 01600 713977
www.wyevalleyaonb.co.uk

SARAH BOVE

COMMUNITY FORESTS

National Community Forest Partnership
☎ 01684 311880
www.communityforest.org.uk
Umbrella organisation for England's 12 community forests partnerships, regenerating large areas on the urban fringe for forestry, conservation and recreation.

Forest of Avon
☎ 0117 953 2141
www.forestofavon.org.uk

Central Scotland Forest
☎ 01501 822015
www.csct.co.uk

Forest of Marston Vale
☎ 01234 767037
www.marstonvale.org
Let's Go website promoting walks and sites in the Forest and in the rest of Bedfordshire:
www.letsgo.org.uk

Forest of Mercia
☎ 01543 370737
www.forestofmercia.co.uk

Great Western
☎ 01793 466324
www.forestweb.org.uk

The Greenwood
☎ 01623 758231
www.greenwoodforest.org.uk

Mersey Forest
☎ 01925 816217
www.merseyforest.org.uk

National Forest
☎ 01283 551211
www.nationalforest.org

Red Rose Forest
☎ 0161 872 1660
www.redroseforest.co.uk

South Yorkshire Forest
☎ 0114 257 1199
www.syforest.co.uk
Greensites website:
www.greensites.co.uk
South Yorkshire interactive environmental website with walking information.

Tees Forest
☎ 01642 300716
www.teesforest.org.uk

Thames
☎ 01708 641880
www.thameschase.org.uk

Watling Chase
☎ 01992 555256
http://enquire.hertscc.gov.uk/cms/wccf/default.htm

THE COUNTRYSIDE CODE (ENGLAND AND WALES)

RESPECT – PROTECT – ENJOY

If you follow the Countryside Code wherever you go, you'll get the best enjoyment possible and you'll help to protect the countryside now and for future generations.

Be safe – plan ahead and follow any signs

Even when going out locally, it's best to get the latest information about where and when you can go; for example, your rights to go onto some areas of open land may be restricted while work is carried out, for safety reasons, or during breeding season. Follow advice and local signs, and be prepared for the unexpected.

Leave gates and property as you find them

Please respect the working life of the countryside, as our actions can affect people's livelihoods, our heritage, and the safety and welfare of animals and ourselves.

Protect plants and animals, and take your litter home

We have a responsibility to protect our countryside now and for future generations, so make sure you don't harm animals, birds, plants or trees.

Keep dogs under close control

The countryside is a great place to exercise dogs, but it's every owner's duty to make sure their dog is not a danger or nuisance to farm animals, wildlife or other people.

Consider other people

Showing consideration and respect for other people makes the countryside a pleasant environment for everyone – at home, at work and at leisure.

For further advice, including advice for land managers, contact: Countryside Agency or Countryside Council for Wales (see opposite).

SCOTTISH OUTDOORS ACCESS CODE

Everyone has the right to be on most land and water for recreation, education and for going from place to place providing they act responsibly. These access rights and responsibilities are explained in the Scottish Outdoor Access Code.

The key things are:

When you're in the outdoors

● take personal responsibility for your own actions and act safely
● respect people's privacy and peace of mind help land managers and others to work safely and effectively

● care for your environment and take your litter home
● keep your dog under proper control
● take extra care if you're organising an event or running a business

If you're managing the outdoors

● respect access rights
● act reasonably when asking people to avoid land management operations
● work with your local authority and other bodies to help integrate access and land management
● respect rights of way and customary access

For more detailed advice contact Scottish Natural Heritage, Outdoor Access Scotland (see p275).

NATIONAL GOVERNMENT ORGANISATIONS

CABE
(Commission for Architecture and the Built Environment)
☎ 020 7960 2400
www.cabe.org.uk
CABE Space
(Parks and public open spaces)
www.cabespace.org.uk
Non-departmental public body championing the creation of great buildings and public spaces.

Citizens Advice Bureaux National Association
☎ 020 7833 2181

www.nacab.org.uk
Online advice:
www.adviceguide.org.uk
Free advice on civil rights and legal matters: phone or visit website for addresses of local offices.

Citizens Advice Scotland (CAS)
☎ 0131 667 0156
www.cas.org.uk
Free advice on civil rights and legal matters: phone or visit website for addresses of local offices, or use online advice guide

Countryside Agency
☎ 01242 521381
www.countryside.gov.uk
During 2006, the function of English Nature and the Countryside Agency will be taken over by a new body, Natural England.
Countryside access helpline:
☎ 0845 100 3298
www.countrysideaccess.gov.uk

CADW - Welsh Historic Monuments
☎ 029 2050 0200
www.cadw.wales.gov.uk
Guardian of the built heritage in Wales.

Countryside Council for Wales - Cyngor Cefn Gwylad Cymru
☎ 0845 130 6229
www.ccw.gov.uk
Wildlife conservation authority and advisor on sustaining natural beauty, wildlife and the opportunity for outdoor enjoyment in Wales and its inshore waters, including overseeing national trails.
Countryside Code website:
www.codcefngwlad.org.uk

Directgov
www.direct.gov.uk
Principal internet portal for government departments and services.

DCMS
(Department for Culture, Media and Sport)
☎ 020 7211 6200
www.culture.gov.uk

Defence Estates
(manages MoD lands)
☎ 0121 311 2140
www.defence-estates.mod.uk
Information on access to MoD lands and contact telephone numbers for details of firing times.

NATIONAL GOVERNMENT ORGANISATIONS

DEFRA
(Department for Environment, Food & Rural Affairs)
☎ 0845 933 5577
www.defra.gov.uk
Conservation Walks register:
countrywalks.defra.gov.uk
Lists walks in England on countryside managed under environmental schemes providing public access.

Department for Transport (DfT)
☎ 020 7944 8300
www.dft.gov.uk
In Town Without My Car (Car-free day):
www.itwmc.gov.uk
Highway Code online
(rules and advice for all road users):
www.highwaycode.gov.uk

English Heritage
☎ 0870 333 1181
www.english-heritage.org.uk
Responsible for protecting many of England's historic buildings, landscapes and archaeological sites, including many properties open to the public.

English Nature
☎ 01733 455000
www.english-nature.org.uk
Champions the conservation of wildlife and natural features. During 2006 the function of English Nature & Countryside Agency will be taken over by a new body, Natural England.

Environment Agency
☎ 0870 850 6506
www.environment-agency.gov.uk
Responsible for protecting and enhancing the environment, including maintaining flood defences and rivers.

Forestry Commission
☎ 0845 367 3787
www.forestry.gov.uk
Protects and expands Britain's forests and woodlands and increases their value to society and the environment, both by managing its own woodlands and making grants to other landowners.

Highway Authorities
see Local Authorities (p276)

Historic Scotland
☎ 0131 668 8600
www.historic-scotland.gov.uk
Agency of the Scottish Executive that safeguards Scotland's built heritage.

MAGIC
(Multi-Agency Geographic Information for the Countryside)
www.magic.gov.uk
Project to create a single website for rural and countryside information about England on the web, including mapping boundaries of protected areas. Partnership of the Countryside Agency, DEFRA, English Heritage, English Nature, the Environment Agency, Forestry Commission, ODPM.

Met Office
☎ 0870 900 0100
www.metoffice.com
Official weather service with very informative website.

Ministry of Defence
see Defence Estates

National Assembly for Wales – Cynulliad Cenedlaethol Cymru
☎ 029 2082 5111
www.wales.gov.uk

NHS
(National Health Service)
☎ 020 7210 4850
www.nhs.uk

Office of the Deputy Prime Minister
☎ 020 7944 4400
www.odpm.gov.uk
Deals with planning, regional and local government.

Ordnance Survey
see Maps (p266)

Scottish Avalanche Information Service
www.sais.gov.uk
Forecasts for five key climbing areas in Scotland during the winter season.

Scottish Environmental Protection Agency
(SEPA)
☎ 01786 457700
www.sepa.org.uk
Aims to provide an efficient and integrated environmental protection system that will both improve the environment and contribute to sustainable development.

Scottish Executive
☎ 0131 556 8400
www.scotland.gov.uk

Scottish Natural Heritage
☎ 0131 447 4784
www.snh.org.uk
Responsible for the care, improvement and responsible enjoyment of Scotland's natural heritage.

Outdoor Access Scotland:
☎ 01738 444177
www.outdooraccess-scotland.com
Details about Statutory Access Rights and the Scottish Access Code.

Sports Council for Wales – Cyngor Chwaraeon Cymru
and Welsh Institute for Sport, Sophia Gardens, Cardiff CF11 9SW,
☎ 029 2030 0500
www.sports-council-wales.co.uk

Sport England
(English Sports Council)
☎ 0845 850 8508
www.sportengland.org

SportScotland
(Scottish Sports Council)
☎ 0131 317 7200
www.sportscotland.org.uk

Outdoor Training Centre:
☎ 01479 861256
www.glenmorelodge.org.uk

LOCAL AUTHORITIES

In this section we list councils in Britain with primary responsibility for footpaths and access to whom problems should be reported. Many of them also promote walking locally and can provide information about walking routes, parks and countryside areas.

You can send your report either to our central office, or you can report the problem directly to the local authority, but please send us a copy too.

If you wish, use the Path/Access Problem Report Form on p285. You can request further forms from

Ramblers' Association offices and you can also report problems our website. Otherwise, don't forget to report what the problem is, where it is and when you noticed it.

Alphabetical order.
Councils covering only a part of an historic county are listed under the council area's name, not the county's name: for example, West Dunbartonshire is listed under 'W'.

ENGLAND

Barking and Dagenham
(Outer London Borough) Civic
Centre, Dagenham RM10 7BN
☎ 020 8592 4500
www.barking-dagenham.gov.uk

Barnet
(Outer London Borough) Hendon
Town Hall, The Burroughs, London
NW4 4BG
☎ 020 8359 2000
www.barnet.gov.uk

Barnsley
(Metropolitan Borough) Town Hall,
Barnsley S70 2TA
☎ 01226 770770
www.barnsley.gov.uk

**Bath & North East
Somerset**
(Unitary Authority) Trimbridge
House, Trim Street, Bath BA1 2DP
☎ 01225 477500
www.bathnes.gov.uk

Bedfordshire
(County Council) County Hall,
Cauldwell Street, Bedford
MK42 9AP
☎ 01234 363222
www.bedfordshire.gov.uk

Bexley
(Outer London Borough) Civic
Offices, Broadway, Bexleyheath
DA6 7LB
☎ 020 8303 7777
www.bexley.gov.uk

Birmingham
(Metropolitan Borough) The
Council House, Victoria Square,

Birmingham B1 1BB
☎ 0121 303 9944
www.birmingham.gov.uk

Blackburn with Darwen
(Unitary Authority) Town Hall,
Blackburn BB1 2LX
☎ 01254 585585
www.blackburn.gov.uk

Blackpool
(Unitary Authority) Municipal
Buildings, PO Box 77, Town Hall,
Blackpool FY1 1AD
☎ 01253 477477
www.blackpool.gov.uk

Bolton
(Metropolitan Borough) The
Wellsprings, Bolton BL1 1US
☎ 01204 333333
www.bolton.gov.uk

Bournemouth
(Unitary Authority) Town Hall,
Bourne Avenue, Bournemouth
BH2 6DY
☎ 01202 451451
www.bournemouth.gov.uk

Bracknell Forest
(Unitary Authority) Market Street,
Bracknell RG12 1LR
☎ 01344 424642
www.bracknell-forest.gov.uk

Bradford City
(Metropolitan Borough) City Hall,
Channing Way, Bradford BD1 1HY
☎ 01274 435681
www.bradford.gov.uk

Brent
(Outer London Borough) Town
Hall, Forty Lane, Wembley

HA9 9EZ
☎ 020 8937 1234
www.brent.gov.uk

Brighton & Hove
(Unitary Authority) Town Hall,
Bartholomew Sq, Brighton
BN1 1JA
☎ 01273 290000
www.brighton-hove.gov.uk

Bristol City
(Unitary Authority) The Council
House, College Green, Bristol
BS1 5TR ☎ 0117 922 2000
www.bristol-city.gov.uk

Bromley
(Outer London Borough) Civic
Centre, Stockwell Close, Bromley
BR1 3UH ☎ 020 8464 3333
www.bromley.gov.uk

Buckinghamshire
(County Council) County Hall,
Aylesbury HP20 1UA
☎ 01296 395000
www.buckscc.gov.uk

Bury
(Metropolitan Borough) 21 Broad
Street, Bury BL9 0AW
☎ 0161 253 5000
www.bury.gov.uk

Calderdale
(Metropolitan Borough) Northgate
House, Halifax HX1 1UN
☎ 01422 357257
www.calderdale.gov.uk

Cambridgeshire
(County Council) Shire Hall,
Cambridge CB3 0AP
☎ 01223 717111

www.cambridgeshire.gov.uk
See also Peterborough

Camden
(Inner London Borough) Camden
Town Hall, Judd Street, London
WC1H 9JE ☎ 020 7278 4444
www.camden.gov.uk

Cheshire
(County Council) Goldsmith
House, Hamilton Place, Chester
CH1 1SE ☎ 01244 602424
www.cheshire.gov.uk
Countryside and Walking
Information:
www.cheshire.gov.uk/countryside

City of London
*See Corporation of London, see also
London*

Cornwall
(County Council) County Hall,
Truro TR1 3AY ☎ 01872 322000
www.cornwall.gov.uk

Corporation of London
Guildhall, London EC2P 2EJ
☎ 020 7606 3030
www.cityoflondon.gov.uk

Coventry
(Metropolitan Borough) Council
House, Earl Street, Coventry
CV1 5RR ☎ 024 7683 3333
www.coventry.gov.uk

Croydon
(Outer London Borough) Taberner
House, Park Lane, Croydon
CR9 3JS ☎ 020 8686 4433
www.croydon.gov.uk

Cumbria
(County Council) The Courts,
Carlisle CA3 8NA
☎ 01228 606060
www.cumbria.gov.uk

Darlington
(Unitary Authority) Town Hall,
Darlington DL1 5QT
☎ 01325 380651
www.darlington.gov.uk

Derby
(Unitary Authority) The Council
House, Corporation Street, Derby
DE1 2FS ☎ 01332 293111
www.derby.gov.uk

Derbyshire
(County Council) County Offices,
Matlock DE4 3AG ☎ 01629 580000
www.derbyshire.gov.uk

Devon
(County Council) Lucombe House,
Topsham Road, Exeter EX2 4QW
☎ 01392 382000
www.devon.gov.uk

Doncaster
(Metropolitan Borough) 2 Priory
Place, Doncaster DN1 1BN
☎ 01302 734444
www.doncaster.gov.uk

Dorset
(County Council) County Hall,
Dorchester DT1 1XJ
☎ 01305 251000
www.dorsetforyou.com/index.jsp

Dudley
(Metropolitan Borough) Council
House, Priory Road, Dudley
DY1 1HF ☎ 01384 818181
www.dudley.gov.uk

Durham
(County Council) County Hall,
Durham DH1 5UB
☎ 0191 383 3000
www.durham.gov.uk

Ealing
(Outer London Borough) 14-16
Uxbridge Road, London W5 2HL
☎ 020 8825 5000
www.ealing.gov.uk

East Riding of Yorkshire
(Unitary Authority) County Hall,
Beverley HU17 9BA
☎ 01482 393939
www.eastriding.gov.uk

East Sussex
(County Council) County Hall, St
Anne's Crescent, Lewes BN7 1UE
☎ 01273 481000
www.eastsussexcc.gov.uk

Enfield
(Outer London Borough) Civic
Centre, Silver Street, Enfield
EN1 3XA ☎ 020 8379 1000
www.enfield.gov.uk

Essex
(County Council) County Hall,

Chelmsford CM1 1LX
Switchboard: 08457 430 430
www.essexcc.gov.uk

Gateshead
(Metropolitan Borough) Civic
Centre, Regent St, Gateshead,
NE8 1HH ☎ 0191 433 3000
www.gateshead.gov.uk

Gloucestershire
(County Council) Shire Hall,
Gloucester GL1 2TH
☎ 01452 425000
www.gloucestershire.gov.uk

Greenwich
(Inner London Borough) Woolwich
Town Hall, Wellington Street,
London SE18 6PW
☎ 020 8854 8888
www.greenwich.gov.uk

Hackney
(Inner London Borough) Town Hall,
Mare Street, London E8 1EA
☎ 020 8356 3000
www.hackney.gov.uk

Halton
(Unitary Authority) Municipal
Building, Kingsway, Widnes
WA8 7QF
☎ 0151 424 2061
www.halton.gov.uk

Hammersmith and Fulham
(Inner London Borough) Town Hall,
King Street, London W6 9JU
☎ 020 8748 3020
www.lbhf.gov.uk

Hampshire
(County Council) Mottisfont Court,
High Street, Winchester SO23 8ZF
☎ 0800 028 0888 Free helpline for
calls made within Hampshire
01962 870500 – calls from within
the UK
www.hants.gov.uk

Haringey
(Outer London Borough) Civic
Centre, High Road, London
N22 4LE ☎ 020 8489 0000
www.haringey.gov.uk

Harrow
(Outer London Borough) Civic
Centre, Station Road, Harrow

HA1 2XГ ☎ 020 8863 5611
www.harrow.gov.uk

Hartlepool
(Unitary Authority) Civic Centre,
Hartlepool TS24 8AY
☎ 01429 266522
www.hartlepool.gov.uk

Havering
(Outer London Borough) Town
Hall, Main Road, Romford
RM1 3BB
☎ 01708 434343
www.havering.gov.uk

Herefordshire
(Unitary Authority) 35 Hafod Road,
Hereford HR1 1SH
☎ 01432 260000
www.herefordshire.gov.uk

Hertfordshire
(County Council) County Hall,
Hertford SG13 8DQ
☎ 01438 737555
www.hertscc.gov.uk

Hillingdon
(Outer London Borough) Civic
Centre, Uxbridge UB8 1UW
☎ 01895 250111
www.hillingdon.gov.uk

Hounslow
(Outer London Borough)
Civic Centre, Lampton Road,
Hounslow TW3 4DN
☎ 020 8583 2000
www.hounslow.gov.uk

Hull
see *Kingston upon Hull*

Isle of Wight
(Unitary Authority) County Hall,
Newport PO30 1UD
☎ 01983 821000
www.iow.gov.uk

Isles of Scilly
Town Hall, St Mary's TR21 0LW
☎ 01720 422537
www.scilly.gov.uk

Islington
(Inner London Borough) 222
Upper Street, London N1 1XR
☎ 020 7527 2000
www.islington.gov.uk

Kensington and Chelsea
(Inner London Borough)
Town Hall, Hornton Street,
London W8 7NX
☎ 020 7361 3000
www.rbkc.gov.uk

Kent
(County Council) County Hall,
Maidstone ME14 1XQ
☎ 0845 824 7247
http://www.kent.gov.uk/
www.kent.gov.uk/countrysideaccess

Kingston upon Hull
(Unitary Authority) Guildhall, Hull
HU1 2AA ☎ 01482 300300
www.hullcc.gov.uk

Kingston upon Thames
(Outer London Borough) Guildhall,
Kingston upon Thames KT1 1EU
☎ 020 8547 5757
www.kingston.gov.uk

Kirklees
(Metropolitan Borough) Market
Street, Huddersfield HD1 1WG
☎ 01484 221000
www.kirkleesmc.gov.uk

Knowsley
(Metropolitan Borough) Muncipal
Buildings, Archway Road, Huyton
L36 9UX ☎ 0151 489 6000
www.knowsley.gov.uk

Lambeth
(Inner London Borough) Town
Hall, Brixton Hill, London
SW2 1RW ☎ 020 7926 1000
www.lambeth.gov.uk

Lancashire
(County Council) County Hall,
Fishergate, Preston PR1 8XJ
☎ 0845 053 0000
www.lancashire.gov.uk

Leeds
(Metropolitan Borough) Civic Hall,
Calverley Street, Leeds LS1 1UR
☎ 0113 234 8080
www.leeds.gov.uk

Leicester
(Unitary Authority) New Walk
Centre, Welford Place, Leicester
LE1 6ZG ☎ 0116 254 9922
www.leicester.gov.uk

Leicestershire
(County Council) County Hall,
Glenfield, Leicester LE3 8RJ
☎ 0116 232 3232
www.leics.gov.uk

Lewisham
(Inner London Borough) Town
Hall, London SE6 4RU
☎ 020 8314 6000
www.lewisham.gov.uk

Lincolnshire
(County Council) County Offices,
Newland, Lincoln LN1 1YL
☎ 01522 552222
www.lincolnshire.gov.uk

Liverpool
(Metropolitan Borough) Municipal
Buildings, Dale Street, Liverpool
L69 2DH ☎ 0151 233 3000
www.liverpool.gov.uk

London
Greater London Authority and
Mayor of London (strategic only):
City Hall, The Queen's Walk,
London SE1 2AA
☎ 020 7983 4100
www.london.gov.uk
Transport for London: see p267

Luton
(Unitary Authority) Town Hall,
Luton LU1 2BQ
☎ 01582 546000
www.luton.gov.uk

Manchester
(Metropolitan Borough) Town Hall,
Albert Sq, Manchester M60 2LA
☎ 0161 234 5000
www.manchester.gov.uk

Medway
(Unitary Authority) Civic Centre,
Strood, Rochester ME2 4AU
☎ 01634 306000
www.medway.gov.uk

Merton
(Outer London Borough) Civic
Centre, London Road, Morden
SM4 5DX ☎ 020 8274 4901
www.merton.gov.uk

Middlesbrough
(Unitary Authority) Middlesbrough
Council PO Box 99A

Town Hall, Middlesbrough
TS1 2QQ ☎ 01642 245432
www.Middlesbrough.gov.uk

Milton Keynes
(Unitary Authority) PO Box 113,
Civic Offices, 1 Saxon Gate East,
Central Milton Keynes, MK9 3HN
☎ 01908 252406
www.mkweb.co.uk/countryside

Newcastle
(Metropolitan Borough) Civic
Centre, Barras Bridge, Newcastle
upon Tyne NE99 1RD
☎ 0191 232 8520
www.newcastle.gov.uk

Newham
(Outer London Borough) Town
Hall, London E6 2RP
☎ 020 8430 2000
www.newham.gov.uk

Norfolk
(County Council) County Hall,
Martineau Lane, Norwich
NR1 2DH ☎ 0844 800 8020
www.norfolk.gov.uk

North East Lincolnshire
(Unitary Authority) Municipal
Offices, Town Hall Square, Grimsby
DN31 1HU ☎ 01472 313131
www.nelincs.gov.uk

North Lincolnshire
(Unitary Authority) Pittwood
House, Ashby Road, Scunthorpe
DN16 1AB ☎ 01724 296296
www.northlincs.gov.uk

North Somerset
(Unitary Authority) Town Hall,
Weston-super-Mare BS23 1UJ
☎ 01934 888888
www.n-somerset.gov.uk

North Tyneside
(Metropolitan Borough) Strategic
Services, Pametrada Building, Davy
Bank, Wallsend, Tyne & Wear,
NE28 6WJ ☎ 0191 200 5000
www.northtyneside.gov.uk

North Yorkshire
(County Council) County Hall,
Northallerton DL7 8AH
☎ 01609 780780
www.northyorks.gov.uk

Northamptonshire
(County Council) County Hall,
Northampton NN1 1DN
☎ 01604 236236
www.northamptonshire.gov.uk

Northumberland
(County Council) County Hall,
Morpeth NE61 2EF
☎ 01670 533000
www.northumberland.gov.uk

Nottingham
(Unitary Authority) The Guildhall,
South Sherwood Street,
Nottingham NG1 4BT
☎ 0115 915 5555
www.nottinghamcity.gov.uk

Nottinghamshire
(County Council) Trent Bridge
House, West Bridgford,
Nottingham NG2 6BJ
☎ 0115 982 3823
www.nottinghamshire.gov.uk

Oldham
(Metropolitan Borough) Civic
Centre, West Street, Oldham
OL1 1UG ☎ 0161 911 3000
www.oldham.gov.uk

Oxfordshire
(County Council) County Hall,
New Road, Oxford OX1 1ND
☎ 01865 792422
www.oxfordshire.gov.uk

Peterborough
(Unitary Authority) Town Hall,
Bridge Street, Peterborough
PE1 1PJ ☎ 01733 747474
www.peterborough.gov.uk

Plymouth
(Unitary Authority) Civic Centre,
Plymouth PL1 2AA
☎ 01752 668000
www.plymouth.gov.uk

Poole
(Unitary Authority) Civic Centre,
Poole BH15 2RU ☎ 01202 633633
www.poole.gov.uk

Portsmouth
(Unitary Authority) Civic Offices,
Guildhall Square, Portsmouth
PO1 2BG ☎ 023 9283 4092
www.portsmouth.gov.uk

Reading
(Unitary Authority) Civic Centre,
Reading RG1 7TD ☎ 0118 939 0900
www.reading.gov.uk

Redbridge
(Outer London Borough) PO BOX
No.2, Town Hall, 128-142 High
Road, Ilford, IG1 1DD
☎ 020 8854 5000
www.redbridge.gov.uk

Redcar and Cleveland
(Unitary Authority) Langbaurgh
Town Hall, Fabian Road, South
Bank, Middlesbrough TS6 9AR
☎ 08456 126 126
www.redcar-cleveland.gov.uk

Richmond upon Thames
(Outer London Borough) Civic
Centre, 44 York Street,
Twickenham TW1 3BZ
☎ 020 8891 1411
www.richmond.gov.uk

Rochdale
(Metropolitan Borough) PO Box
39, Municipal Offices, Smith Street,
Rochdale OL16 1LQ
☎ 01706 647474
www.rochdale.gov.uk

Rotherham
(Metropolitan Borough) The Crofts,
Moorgate Street, Rotherham,
S60 2TH ☎ 01709 382121
www.rotherham.gov.uk

Rutland
(Unitary Authority) Catmose,
Oakham LE15 6HP
☎ 01572 722577
www.rutnet.gov.uk

Salford
(Metropolitan Borough) Civic
Centre, Chorley Road, Swinton,
Salford M27 5DA
☎ 0161 794 4711
www.salford.gov.uk

Sandwell
(Metropolitan Borough) PO Box
2374, Oldbury B69 3DE
☎ 0121 569 2200
www.sandwell.gov.uk

Sefton
(Metropolitan Borough) Sefton

Plus, Bootle One Stop Shop, 324-342 Stanley Road, Bootle, L20 6ET
☎ 0845 140 0845
www.sefton.gov.uk

Sheffield
(Metropolitan Borough) Town Hall, Sheffield S1 2HH ☎ 0114 272 6444
www.sheffield.gov.uk

Shropshire
(County Council) Shirehall, Abbey Foregate, Shrewsbury SY2 6ND
☎ 0845 678 9000
www.shropshire-cc.gov.uk
See also Telford

Slough
(Unitary Authority) Town Hall, Bath Road, Slough SL1 3UQ
☎ 01753 552288
www.slough.gov.uk

Solihull
(Metropolitan Borough) PO Box 18, Council House, Solihull, West Midlands B91 3QS
☎ 0121 704 6000
www.solihull.gov.uk

Somerset
(County Council) County Hall, Taunton TA1 4DY
☎ 0845 345 9166
www.somerset.gov.uk

South Gloucestershire
(Unitary Authority) The Council Offices, Castle Street, Thornbury BS35 1HF ☎ 01454 868686
www.southglos.gov.uk

South Tyneside
(Metropolitan Borough), Town Hall & Civic Offices, Westoe Road, South Shields NE33 2RL
☎ 0191 427 1717
www.southtyneside.info

Southampton
(Unitary Authority) Civic Centre, Southampton SO14 7LY
☎ 023 8022 3855
www.southampton.gov.uk

Southend on Sea
(Unitary Authority), Ground Floor, Civic Centre, Victoria Avenue, Southend-on-Sea, SS2 6ER
☎ 01702 215000
www.southend.gov.uk

Southwark
(Inner London Borough) Town Hall, Peckham Road, London SE5 8UB ☎ 020 7525 5000
www.southwark.gov.uk

St Helens
(Metropolitan Borough) Town Hall, Victoria Square, St Helens WA10 1HP ☎ 01744 456789
www.sthelens.gov.uk

Staffordshire
(County Council) St Chad's Place, Stafford, ST16 2LR
☎ 01785 223121
www.staffordshire.gov.uk
See also Stoke-on-Trent

Stockport
(Metropolitan Borough) Town Hall, Edward Street, Stockport SK1 3XE
☎ 0161 480 4949
www.stockport.gov.uk

Stockton-on-Tees
(Unitary Authority) Municipal Buildings, PO Box 11, Church Road, Stockton-on-Tees TS18 1LD
☎ 01642 393939
www.stockton.gov.uk

Stoke-on-Trent
(Unitary Authority) Civic Centre, Glebe Street, Stoke-on-Trent ST4 1RN ☎ 01782 234234
www.stoke.gov.uk

Suffolk
(County Council) Endeavour House, Russell Road, Ipswich, IP1 2BX ☎ 01473 583000
www.suffolkcc.gov.uk

Sunderland
(Metropolitan Borough) PO Box 100, Civic Centre, Burdon Road, Sunderland, SR2 7DN
☎ 0191 520 5555
www.sunderland.gov.uk

Surrey
(County Council) Contact Centre, Floor 3, Conquest House, Wood Street, Kingston upon Thames, KT1 1AB ☎ 0845 600 9009
www.surreycc.gov.uk

Sutton
(Outer London Borough) Civic Offices, St Nicholas Way, Sutton

SM1 1EA ☎ 020 8770 5000
www.sutton.gov.uk

Swindon
(Unitary Authority) Civic Offices, Euclid Street, Swindon SN1 2JH
☎ 01793 463000
www.swindon.gov.uk

Tameside
(Metropolitan Borough) Council Offices, Wellington Road, Ashton-under-Lyne, Tameside OL6 6DL
☎ 0161 342 8355
www.tameside.gov.uk

Telford & Wrekin
(Unitary Authority) Civic Offices, Telford TF3 4LD ☎ 01952 202100
www.telford.gov.uk

Thurrock
(Unitary Authority) Civic Offices, New Road, Grays RN17 6SL
☎ 01375 652652
www.thurrock.gov.uk

Torbay
(Unitary Authority) Civic Offices, Castle Circus, Torquay TQ1 3DR
☎ 01803 201201
www.torbay.gov.uk

Tower Hamlets
(Inner London Borough) Town Hall, Mulberry Place, 5 Clove Crescent, London E14 2BG
☎ 020 7364 5000
www.towerhamlets.gov.uk

Trafford
(Metropolitan Borough) Town Hall, Talbot, Stretford M32 0YX
☎ 0161 912 2000
www.trafford.gov.uk

Wakefield
(Metropolitan Borough) Town Hall, Bond Street, Wakefield WF1 2QL
☎ 01924 306090
www.wakefield.gov.uk

Walsall
(Metropolitan Borough) Civic Centre, Walsall WS1 1TP
☎ 01922 650000
www.walsall.gov.uk

Waltham Forest
(Outer London Borough) Town Hall, Forest Road, London E17 4JF

☎ 020 8496 3000
www.lbwf.gov.uk

Wandsworth
(Inner London Borough) Town Hall, Wandsworth High Street, London SW18 2PU
☎ 020 8871 6000
www.wandsworth.gov.uk

Warrington
(Unitary Authority) Town Hall, Warrington WA1 1UH
☎ 01925 444400
www.warrington.gov.uk

Warwickshire
(County Council) Shire Hall, Warwick CV34 4RA
☎ 0845 090 7000
www.warwickshire.gov.uk

West Berkshire
(Unitary Authority) Council Offices, Faraday Road, Newbury RG14 2AF
☎ 01635 42400
www.westberks.gov.uk

West Sussex
(County Council) County Hall West Street, Chichester, PO19 1RQ
☎ 01243 777100
www.westsussex.gov.uk

Westminster
(Inner London Borough) P.O. Box 240, Westminster City Hall, 64 Victoria Street, London SW1E 6QP
☎ 020 7641 6000
www.westminster.gov.uk

Wigan
(Metropolitan Borough) Town Hall, Library Street, Wigan WN1 1YN
☎ 01942 244991
www.wiganmbc.gov.uk

Wiltshire
(County Council) County Hall, Bythesea Road, Trowbridge BA14 8JN ☎ 01225 713000
www.wiltshire.gov.uk
See also Swindon

Windsor and Maidenhead Royal Borough
(Unitary Authority) Town Hall, St Ives Road, Maidenhead SL6 1RF
☎ 01628 798888
www.rbwm.gov.uk

Wirral
(Metropolitan Borough) Town Hall, Brighton Street, Wallasey CH44 8ED ☎ 0151 606 2000
www.wirral.gov.uk

Wokingham
(Unitary Authority) Civic Offices, Shute End, Wokingham RG40 1GY
☎ 0118 974 6000
www.wokingham.gov.uk

Wolverhampton
(Metropolitan Borough) Civic Centre, St Peters Square, Wolverhampton WV1 1SH
☎ 01902 556556
www.wolverhampton.gov.uk

Worcestershire
(County Council) County Hall, Spetchley Road, Worcester WR5 2NP ☎ 01905 763763
www.worcestershire.gov.uk

York City
(Unitary Authority) Guildhall, 9 St Leonard's Place, York YO1 1QN
☎ 01904 613161
www.york.gov.uk

WALES

Blaenau Gwent
Municipal Offices, Civic Centre, Ebbw Vale NP23 6XB
☎ 01495 350555
www.blaenau-gwent.gov.uk

Bridgend – Pen y Bont
Civic Offices, Angel Street, Bridgend CF31 1LX
☎ 01656 643643
www.bridgend.gov.uk

Caerphilly – Caerffilli
Council Offfices, Nelson Road, Tredomen, Ystrad Mynach CF82 7WF ☎ 01443 815588
www.caerphilly.gov.uk

Cardiff – Caerdydd
County Hall, Atlantic Wharf, Cardiff
CF10 4UW ☎ 029 2087 2000
www.cardiff.gov.uk

Carmarthenshire – Caerfyrddin
County Hall, Carmarthen SA21 1JP
☎ 01267 234567
www.carmarthenshire.gov.uk

Ceredigion
Penmorfa, Aberaeron SA46 0PA
☎ 01545 570881
www.ceredigion.gov.uk

Conwy
Bodlondeb, Conwy LL32 8DU
☎ 01492 574000
www.conwy.gov.uk

Denbighshire – Sir Ddinbych
Council Offices, Wynnstay Road,
Ruthin LL15 1YN
☎ 01824 706000
www.denbighshire.gov.uk

Flintshire – Sir y Fflint
County Hall, Mold CH7 6NB
☎ 01352 752121
www.flintshire.gov.uk

Gwynedd
Swyddfa'r Cyngor, Caernarfon
LL55 1SH ☎ 01286 672255
www.gwynedd.gov.uk

Isle of Anglesey – Ynys Môn
Swyddfa'r Sir, Llangefni LL77 7TW
☎ 01248 750057
Highways department:
☎ 01248 752300
www.anglesey.gov.uk

Merthyr Tydfil
Civic Centre, Castle Street,
Merthyr Tydfil CF47 8AN
☎ 01685 725000
www.merthyr.gov.uk

Monmouthshire – Sir Fynwy
County Hall, Cwmbran
NP44 2XH ☎ 01633 644644
www.monmouthshire.gov.uk

Neath Port Talbot – Castell-nedd
Civic Centre, Neath SA13 1PJ
☎ 01639 763333
www.neath-porttalbot.gov.uk

Newport – Casnewydd
Civic Centre, Newport
NP20 4UR ☎ 01633 656656
www.newport.gov.uk

Pembrokeshire – Sir Benfro
County Hall, Haverfordwest
SA61 1TP
☎ 01437 764551
www.pembrokeshire.gov.uk

Powys
County Hall, Llandrindod Wells
LD1 5LG ☎ 01597 826000
www.powys.gov.uk

Rhondda Cynon Taff
The Pavillions, Cambrian Park,
Clydach Vale CF40 2XX
☎ 01443 484400
www.rhondda-cynon-taff.gov.uk

Swansea – Abertawe
County Hall, Oystermouth Road,
Swansea SA1 3SN
☎ 01792 636000
www.swansea.gov.uk

Torfaen
Civic Centre, Pontypool NP4 6YB
☎ 01495 762200
www.torfaen.gov.uk

Vale of Glamorgan – Bro Morgannwg
Dock Offices, Barry Docks, Barry
CF63 4RT ☎ 01446 700111
www.valeofglamorgan.gov.uk

Wrexham – Wrecsam
Wrexham LL11 1WF
☎ 01978 292000
www.wrexham.gov.uk

Ynys Môn
See Isle of Anglesey

SCOTLAND

Aberdeen
Town House, Broad Street,
Aberdeen AB9 1AQ
☎ 01224 522000
www.aberdeencity.gov.uk

Aberdeenshire
Woodhill House, Westburn Road,
Aberdeen AB16 5GB
☎ 0845 606 7000
www.aberdeenshire.gov.uk

Angus
The Cross, Forfar DD8 1BX
☎ 0845 277 7778
www.angus.gov.uk

Argyll and Bute
Kilmory Castle, Lochgilphead, Argyll
PA31 8RT ☎ 01546 602127
www.argyll-bute.gov.uk

Clackmannanshire
Council Offices, Greenfield, Alloa
FK10 2AD ☎ 01259 452000
www.clacks.gov.uk

Dumfries & Galloway
Council Offices, English Street,
Dumfries DG1 2DD
☎ 01387 260000
www.dumgal.gov.uk

Dundee
Council Offices, 21 City Square,
Dundee DD1 3BY
☎ 01382 434000
www.dundeecity.gov.uk

East Ayrshire
Council Offices, London Road
Centre, London Road, Kilmarnock
KA3 7DG ☎ 0845 724 0000
www.east-ayrshire.gov.uk

East Dunbartonshire
Council Offices, Tom Johnston
House, Civic Way, Kirkintilloch
G66 4TJ ☎ 0141 578 8000
www.eastdunbarton.gov.uk

East Lothian
Council Buildings, Haddington
EH41 3HA ☎ 01620 827827
www.eastlothian.gov.uk

East Renfrewshire
Council Offices, Eastwood Park,
Rouken Glen Road, Giffnock
G46 6UG ☎ 0141 577 3001
www.eastrenfrewshire.gov.uk

Edinburgh
City Chambers, High Street,
Edinburgh EH1 1YJ
☎ 0131 200 2000
www.edinburgh.gov.uk

Eilean Siar – Western Isles
Sandwick Road, Stornoway
HS1 2BW ☎ 01851 703773
www.w-isles.gov.uk

Falkirk
Municipal Buildings, Falkirk FK1 5RS
☎ 01324 506070
www.falkirk.gov.uk

Fife
Fife House, North Street,
Glenrothes KY7 5LT
☎ 01592 414141
www.fife.gov.uk

Glasgow
City Chambers, George Square,
Glasgow G2 1DU
☎ 0141 287 2000
www.glasgow.gov.uk

Highland
Glenurquhart Road, Inverness
IV3 5NX ☎ 01463 702000
www.highland.gov.uk

Inverclyde
Municipal Buildings, Clyde Square,
Greenock PA15 1LX
☎ 01475 717171
www.inverclyde.gov.uk

Midlothian
Midlothian House, 40 Buccleuch
Street, Dalkeith EH22 1DJ
☎ 0131 270 7500
www.midlothian.gov.uk

Moray
Council Offices, High Street, Elgin
IV30 1BX

☎ 01343 543451
www.moray.gov.uk

North Ayrshire
Cunninghame House,
Friar's Croft, Irvine KA12 8EE
☎ 01294 324100
www.north-ayrshire.gov.uk

North Lanarkshire
Civic Centre, Motherwell
ML1 1TW ☎ 01698 403200
www.northlan.gov.uk

Orkney Islands
Council Offices, School Place,
Kirkwall, Orkney KW15 1NY
☎ 01856 873535
www.orkney.gov.uk

Perth & Kinross
Council Offices, 2 High Street,
Perth PH1 5PH ☎ 01738 475000
Public transport unit
☎ 0845 3011130
www.pkc.gov.uk

Renfrewshire
Municipal Buildings, Cotton Street,
Paisley PA1 1BU ☎ 0141 842 5000
www.renfrewshire.gov.uk

Scottish Borders
Council Headquarters, Newtown
St Boswells, Melrose TD6 0SA
☎ 01835 824000
www.scotborders.gov.uk

Shetland Islands
Town Hall, Lerwick ZE1 0HB
☎ 01595 693535
www.shetland.gov.uk

South Ayrshire
Council Offices, Wellington Square,
Ayr KA7 1DR
☎ 00845 601 2020
www.south-ayrshire.gov.uk

South Lanarkshire
Council Offices, Almada Street,
Hamilton ML3 0AA
☎ 01698 454444
www.southlanarkshire.gov.uk

Stirling
Council Offices, Viewforth,
Stirling FK8 2ET
☎ 0845 277 7000
www.stirling.gov.uk

West Dunbartonshire
Council Offices, Garshake Road,
Dunbarton G82 3PU
☎ 01389 737000
www.west-dunbarton.gov.uk

West Lothian
West Lothian House, Almondvale
North, Livingstone EH54 6QG
☎ 01506 777000
www.westlothian.gov.uk

Western Isles
See Eilean Siar

North Devon & Exmoor Walking and Cycling Festival

Great scenery, Great Walks, Great Accommodation, ALL YEAR GREAT OUTDOOR HOLIDAYS

- Self-Guided walking and Cycling Holidays • Guided Group Holidays • Easy to follow route directions • Friendly accommodation arranged • Luggage transfer included

Annual Walking & Cycling Festival 26th April to 2nd May 2006

Celebrating the Beauty and Variety of the North Devon Countryside.

- Great choice of Guided Walks and Rides • Outings suitable for all abilities • Experienced and friendly guides
- Group sizes restricted for guaranteed enjoyment
- FREE Entertainment during the festival

Tel: **01271 88 31 31**
www.westcountrywalks.co.uk
www.walkcyclenorthdevon.co.uk

sponsored by

TARKA
Springs

MULLACOTT PARK

Project Part financed by the European Union

PATH/ACCESS PROBLEM REPORT FORM

Please complete this form to report a footpath or access problem and return it to the address below.

WHERE WAS THE PROBLEM? Please give as much information as you can.

Path report ☐   **Access report** ☐

District_____   Nearest Town/Village_____

Parish/Community_____

From (place) _____   _____

Grid ref._____

To (place)_____   At Grid ref._____

Grid ref._____

Path N° if known_____   **(and if applicable)**
Grid ref._____

Date problem encountered_____

County/unitary authority_____

WHAT WAS THE PROBLEM? Be precise and quote a grid reference for any specific point. Draw a sketch map if you think it will help. If anyone spoke to you, please give details, including their name and address if known.

WHAT TO DO NEXT Give us your details

Name_____

Address_____

_____

Email_____

Telephone_____**Tick box for more Report Forms** ☐

Send this form to
Your local Ramblers representative or the Ramblers' Association,
2nd Floor, 87-90 Albert Embankment, London SE1 7TW.
Telephone 020 7339 8500 • Fax 020 7339 8501

VICTORINOX

You're miles away from anywhere.
Your rucksack strap breaks.
The nearest shop is a **long** way away...

Mountaineers, adventurers, sailors, even astronauts, have all thanked Victorinox for coming to the rescue in life's little (and big) emergencies...

If you're **serious** about the outdoors, you'll never leave home without the most useful and famous multi-tool ever invented - a Victorinox Swiss Army knife.

The scissors, corkscrew and screwdriver have all saved the day so many times. But have **you** got any better ideas?

...No matter how wacky your suggestion, we want to know what gadgets you'd like to see on a Swiss Army knife.

The best five entries we receive will each win a Victorinox Voyager (pictured below right) worth £40.

✚ VICTORINOX

Cut out the form and post it to the address below, or e-mail marketing@burton-mccall.co.uk

---

My suggestion for a different tool on a Victorinox swiss army knife would be...

....

....

Name: ....

Address: ....

....

City: ....

Postcode: ....

Telephone: ....

E-mail: ....

Send your entries to:
Victorinox Swiss Army knife Competition, Burton McCall Ltd, 163 Parker Drive, Leicester, LE4 0JP.

ENVIRONMENT AND COUNTRYSIDE

BEN
(Black Environment Network)
☎ 01286 870715
www.ben-network.org.uk
Promotes equality of opportunity
with respect to ethnic communities
in the preservation, protection and
development of the environment.

BTCV
(British Trust for Conservation
Volunteers) ☎ 01302 572244
www.btcv.org
The UK's largest practical
conservation charity helping
volunteers take hands-on action to
improve the rural and urban
environment including improving
access to the outdoors.

**Campaign to Protect Rural
England (CPRE)**
☎ 020 7981 2800
www.cpre.org.uk
Promotes the beauty,
tranquillity and diversity of rural
England by encouraging the
sustainable use of land and other
natural resources in town and
country.
*See also CPRW/YDCW,
ruralScotland*

CPRW/YDCW
(Campaign for the Protection of
Rural Wales – Ymgyrch Diogelu
Cymru Wledig)
☎ 01938 552525
www.cprw.org.uk

Aims to help the conservation
and enhancement of the
landscape, environment and
amenities of the countryside,
towns and villages of rural
Wales. See also CPRE, rural
Scotland

ENCAMS
(Envrionmental Campaigns)
☎ 01942 612639
www.encams.org.uk
Environmental charity
aiming to achieve litter
free and sustainable
environments by working
with community groups,
local authorities, businesses
and other partners.

Environmental Transport Association (ETA)
☎ 0800 212810
www.eta.co.uk
Campaigns for a sound and sustainable transport system and provides an environmental alternative to the other motoring organisations.

Everyone Campaign
see Scottish Environment LINK

Friends of the Earth
☎ 020 7490 1555
www.foe.co.uk
Scotland: ☎ 0131 554 9977
www.foe-scotland.org.uk
The world's largest federation of environmental campaigning groups.

Greenpeace UK
☎ 020 7865 8100
www.greenpeace.org.uk
Researches and campaigns on the environment using non-violent direct action.

Groundwork UK
☎ 0121 236 8565
www.groundwork.org.uk
Federation of trusts working in poor areas to help build sustainable communities through joint environmental action.

IWA
(Inland Waterways Association)
☎ 01923 711114
www.waterways.org.uk
Campaigns for the conservation, use, maintenance, restoration and development of inland waterways in England and Wales.
See also Scottish Inland Waterways Association.

John Muir Trust
☎ 0131 554 0114
www.jmt.org
Conserves and protects wild places by acquisition; currently owns seven areas in the Scottish Highlands and Islands totalling 20,000ha/50,000 acres.

Keep Britain Tidy
see ENCAMS

National Trust
☎ 0870 458 4000
Wales: ☎ 01492 860123
www.nationaltrust.org.uk
Protects, through ownership, countryside, coastline and historic buildings in England, Wales and Northern Ireland.

National Trust for Scotland
☎ 0131 243 9300
www.nts.org.uk
Protects, through ownership, countryside, coastline and historic buildings.

Open Spaces Society
☎ 01491 573535
www.oss.org.uk
Works to protect common land and footpaths in England and Wales.

RSPB
(Royal Society for the Protection of Birds)
☎ 01767 680551
Scotland: ☎ 0131 311 6500
Wales: ☎ 029 2035 3000
www.rspb.org.uk
Works for a healthy environment rich in birds and wildlife, including managing over 150 nature reserves.

ruralScotland
(Association for the Protection of Rural Scotland)
☎ 0131 225 7012
www.aprs.org.uk
Scotland's rural champion.
See also Campaign for the Protection of Rural Wales, CPRE

Scottish Environment LINK
☎ 01738 630804
www.scotlink.org
Everyone campaign:
www.everyonecan.org
Voluntary organisations working together to care for and improve Scotland's heritage for people and nature. Also manages the LEARN project. See Wildlife and Countryside Link also

Scottish Inland Waterways Association
www.siwa.org.uk
Coordinates the conservation and use of the waterway network.
See also IWA

Scottish Wildlife Trust
☎ 0131 312 7765
www.swt.org.uk
Protects all forms of wildlife and the environment, with over 120 reserves. Part of The Wildlife Trusts network.

Transport 2000
☎ 020 7613 0743
www.transport2000.org.uk
National campaign for environmental and sustainable transport.

Wildlife and Countryside Link
☎ 020 7820 8600
www.wcl.org.uk
Liaison service for all the major non-governmental organisations in the UK concerned with the protection of wildlife and the countryside.
See also Scottish Environment LINK

Wildlife Helpline National Service
☎ 01522 544245
www.wildlifehelpline.org.uk
Information on the identification of British wildlife and wild flowers and contacts for wildlife organisastions.

Wildlife Trusts
☎ 0870 036 7711
www.wildlifetrusts.org
Partnership of 46 local groups throughout Britain and junior group Wildlife Watch protecting wildlife in town and countryside, and maintaining 2,400 nature reserves.

Woodland Trust
☎ 01476 581135
Scotland: ☎ 01764 662554
Wales: ☎ 01686 412508
www.woodland-trust.org.uk
Protects Britain's native woodland heritage by conserving and managing over 1,000 sites, all with public access, and creating new woodlands.

WWF-UK
☎ 01483 426444
www.wwf-uk.org
Aims to conserve and protect endangered species and address global threats to nature.

WALKING AND OUTDOOR ACTIVITIES

Backpackers Club
www.backpackersclub.co.uk
Promotes and encourages
backpacking for the benefit of
its members.

BMC (British Mountaineering Council)
☎ 0870 010 4878
www.thebmc.co.uk
Protects the freedoms and
promotes the interests of
climbers, hillwalkers and
mountaineers.

British Horse Society
☎ 0870 120 2244
www.bhs.org.uk
Works to improve the
welfare of horses through
education, training and
promoting the interests of
horse-riders and owners,
including defending
bridleways.

British Orienteering Federation (BOF)
☎ 01629 734042
www.britishorienteering.org.uk

British Upland Footpath Trust (BUFT)
☎ 0870 010 4878
Aims to improve the quality of
footpath works and deal with
erosion problems on upland paths.

British Walking Federation (BWF)
www.bwf-ivv.org.uk
British affiliate of the International
Volkssport Federation, organising
non-competitive walking events.

British Waterways
☎ 01923 201120
www.britishwaterways.co.uk
Leisure information on waterways
including walking:
www.waterscape.com

Byways and Bridleways Trust
www.bbtrust.org.uk
Aims to protect Britain's ancient
minor highways, publishes *Byway
and Bridleway* magazine.

Camping and Caravanning Club
☎ 024 7669 4995
www.campingandcaravanningclub.co.uk
Runs 90 members' sites throughout
the UK, offers technical advice and
membership benefits.

Confraternity of St James
☎ 020 7928 9988
www.csj.org.uk
Promotes modern use of the old
European pilgrimage routes of Saint
James/Santiago de Compostela.

Countrygoer
☎ 01943 607868
www.countrygoer.org
Promotes the use of public
transport for countryside visits and
publicises information about
services through the website.

CTC (Cyclists' Touring Club)
☎ 0870 873 0060
www.ctc.org.uk
Campaigning for cyclists' rights,
lobbying government and other

agencies to promote, invest in
and facilitate cycling, also
organises club activities.

Defence Estates for walks on MOD lands
see *National Government*

Disabled Ramblers
www.disabledramblers.co.uk
Aims to improve countryside
access for disabled people
and organises regular rambles
and visits.

Duke of Edinburgh's Award
☎ 01753 727400,
Publications:
☎ 0131 553 5280
www.theaward.org
Operates a challenging and
rewarding personal
development programme for
people aged 14-25.

Fieldfare Trust
☎ 01334 657708
www.fieldfare.org.uk
Works with people with
disabilities and countryside
managers to improve access to the
countryside for everyone.

Gay Outdoor Club (GOC)
☎ 01673 861962
http://goc.uk.net/
Organises walking and other
outdoor activities for lesbian, gay,
bisexual and transgender people
across the UK.

Go Outdoors (Outdoor Industries Association)
☎ 020 8842 1111
www.go-outdoors.org.uk
Trade body for manufacturers and
retailers of outdoor clothing and
equipment in Britain and Ireland.

Green Space (Urban Parks Forum)
☎ 0118 946 9060
www.green-space.org.uk
Helps those committed to the
planning, design, management
and use of public parks and open
spaces.

Hillphones
www.hillphones.info
Recorded information on deer-stalking between August and October in selected areas to assist those planning walks and climbs. Provided in conjunction with the Mountaineering Council of Scotland.

Institute of Public Rights of Way Officers (IPROW)
☎ 0700 078 2318
www.iprow.co.uk
Professional body for local authority rights of way officers in England and Wales; also run a variety of training courses.

Living Streets
☎ 020 7820 1010
www.livingstreets.org.uk
Defends the rights of pedestrians and campaigns for living streets.
See also Walk to School, Walking Bus

Long Distance Walkers Association
www.ldwa.org.uk
Works to further the interests of those who enjoy long-distance walking, including documenting the long-distance path network in its *Handbook* and *Strider* magazine.

Mountain Bothies Association (MBA)
www.mountainbothies.org.uk
Maintains around 100 simple, unlocked shelters in remote country.

Mountaineering Council of Scotland (MCS)
☎ 01738 638227
www.mountaineering-scotland.org.uk
Representative body for climbers, walkers and others who enjoy the Scottish mountains.

Boots Across Scotland
www.bootsacrossscotland.org.uk
Provides support for injured hillwalkers and climbers, and promotes mountain safety.

Paths for All Partnership
☎ 01259 218888
www.pathsforall.org.uk
Paths to Health:
www.pathstohealth.org.uk

Partnership of 17 Scottish organisations working to create path networks for walkers of all abilities to walk, cycle and ride for recreation, health and sustainable transport. Also coordinates local Paths to Health walking for health schemes in Scotland.

Railway Ramblers
www.railwayramblers.org.uk
Discovers and explores old railway lines and promotes their use as footpaths and cycleways.

Red Rope
☎ 01274 493995 (Titch Kavanagh)
www.redrope.org.uk
The socialist walking and climbing club.

Scottish Avalanche Information Service
see SportScotland (p275)

ScotWays
☎ 0131 558 1222
www.scotways.com
Works for the preservation, defence, restoration and acquisition of public rights of land in Scotland, including publc rights of way.

Sensory Trust
☎ 01726 222900
www.sensorytrust.org.uk
Works to make green space accessible to as many people as possible.

Sustrans
☎ 0845 113 0065
www.sustrans.org.uk
Works on practical projects to encourage people to walk and cycle more; champions the National Cycle Network, some of which includes off-road mixed use routes also suitable for walkers.

SHYA (Scottish Youth Hostels)
☎ 0870 155 3255
www.syha.org.uk
Providers of budget accommodation and countryside activities. See also YHA

Wainwright Society
www.wainwright.org.uk
Set up in commemoration of renowned hillwalker and author A Wainwright.

Walk to School (National Walking to School Initiative)
www.walktoschool.org.uk
Encourages walking to school and promotes National Walk to School Week (late September). Partnership of TravelWise, Living Streets and Dorset County Council. International Walk to School Day: www.iwalktoschool.org

Walking Bus
☎ 0870 420 3236
www.walkingbus.org
Information about walking buses (schemes in which groups of children walk to school according to a set route and timetable).

Walking-Routes
www.walking-routes.co.uk
Extensive links to sites with online route descriptions.

Walking the Way to Health Initiative – Cerdded Llwybr Iechyd
Joint initiative of the Countryside Agency. CCW and British Heart Foundation using walking to improve the health of people in England who currently get little exercise.
England: contact the WHI team at the Countryside Agency
☎ 01242 533258
www.whi.org.uk
Wales: contact the WW2H team at the Countryside Council for Wales:
☎ 0845 130 6229
www.ww2h.org.uk
Scotland: *see Paths for All Partnership (Paths to Health)*

YHA England & Wales
☎ 0870 870 8808
Walking holidays and accommodation booking:
☎ 0870 241 2314
Edale Activity Centre:
☎ 01433 670302
www.yha.org.uk
Providers of budget accommodation and countryside activities. *See also SYHA*

FIRST AID AND HEALTH

British Red Cross
☎ 020 7235 5454
www.redcross.org.uk
Cares for people in crisis by
supporting the statutory rescue,
health and welfare services, and
providing first aid training.

**Mountain Rescue
Committee of Scotland**
☎ 01360 770431
www.mrc-scotland.org.uk
Representative and coordinating
body for mountain rescue in
Scotland.

Mountain Rescue Council
www.mountain.rescue.org.uk
Secretary: ☎ 01457 869506
Official coordinating body for
mountain rescue in England and
Wales.

NH3 Direct
(medical advice and information):
☎ 0845 4647
www.nhsdirect.nhs.uk
See also NHS p275

RADAR
(Royal Association for Disability and
Rehabilitation)
☎ 020 7250 3222,
minicom ☎ 020 7250 4119
www.radar.org.uk
Run by and for disabled people to
campaign and advise on disability
issues.

**RNLI (Royal National
Lifeboat Institution)**
☎ 0800 543210
www.lifeboats.org.uk
Aims to save lives at sea by
operating lifeboats and search and
rescue facilities in Britain and Ireland.

**St Andrew's Ambulance
Association**
☎ 0141 332 4031
www.firstaid.org.uk
Scotland's premier provider of first
aid training and services.

St John Ambulance
☎ 0870 010 4950
www.sja.org.uk
Leading first aid, transport and care
charity in in England, Northern
Ireland, Channel Islands and Isle
of Man.

St John Ambulance Wales
☎ 029 2062 9308
www.stjohnwales.co.uk
Teaches first aid and life-saving skills
in Wales.

TOURISM

Tourist Information
For your local tourist or visitor
information centre, see your
phonebook. The local centre can
give you numbers of centres in
other areas, or you can find a full
list at www.visitbritain.com

VisitBritain
☎ 020 8846 9000 (not an
information line: for Tourist
Information please visit the Visit
Britain website and look up your
nearest centre)
www.visitbritain.com

VisitScotland
Visitor information and
accommodation:
☎ 0845 225 5121
or 01506 832121
www.visitscotland.com
Walking in Scotland website:
http://walking.visitscotland.com

**Wales Tourist Board –
Bwrdd Croeso Cymru**
Information and booking line:
☎ 0870 121 1251,
minicom ☎ 0870 121 1255
www.visitwales.com

292

LOCAL MILLETS STORES

ABERDEEN	167/168 Union Street AB11 6BB	01224 596230
ABERGAVENNY	Unit 3 Cibi Walk NP7 5AJ	01873 858944
ABERYSTWYTH	3 Great Darkgate Street SY23 1DE	01970 612119
ALDERSHOT	1/2 Wellington Centre GU11 1DB	01252 345979
ALTRINCHAM	101 George Street WA14 1RN	0161 9269794
AMBLESIDE	Unit 12 Market Cross Shopping Ctre LA22 9BT	01539 433956
ANDOVER	29 High Street SP10 1LJ	01264 324877
ANTRIM	43/45 Castle Centre BT41 4DN	02894 468714
ASHFORD	Unit 24 Park Mall TN24 8RY	01233 634192
AYLESBURY	13 Market Square HP20 2PZ	01296 397599
AYR	58 High Street KA7 1PA	01292 610516
BAKEWELL	Unit 3 Rutland Square DE45 1BZ	01629 815143
BALLYMENA	Unit 33 Fairhill BT43 6UG	02825 646098
BANBURY	9 High Street OX16 5DZ	01295 263189
BANGOR	261 High Street LL5 7IPB	01248 361263
BARNSTAPLE	91 High Street EX31 1HR	01271 342937
BASILDON	21A Town Square SS1 4IBA	01268 272771
BASINGSTOKE	11/12 Potters Walk RG21 7GQ	01256 364649
BATH	25/28 High Street BA1 5AJ	01225 471500
BEDFORD	3 West Arcade, Church Street MK40 1LQ	01234 357375
BELFAST	1 Cornmarket BT1 4DA	02890 242264
BEVERLEY	16 Butcher Row HU17 0AE	01482 868132
BEXLEYHEATH	119 The Broadway DA6 7HF	0208 3035089
BICESTER	26/27 Crown Walk OX26 6HY	01869 324854
BIGGLESWADE	2 Market Square SG18 8AP	01767 312089
BIRKENHEAD	32/34 Borough Pavement CH41 2XX	0151 6661350
BIRMINGHAM	35 Union Street B2 4SR	0121 6431496
BIRMINGHAM	62 New Street B2 4 DU	0121 6430885
BISHOP AUCKLAND	63/65 Newgate Street DL14 7EW	01388 602555
BISHOP STORTFORD	26 South Street CM23 3AT	01279 651452
BLACKPOOL	22 Church Street FY1 1EW	01253 628430
BLANCHARDSTOWN	Unit 149 Blanchardstown Ctr DUBLIN 15	00353 18222160
BODMIN	27/31 Fore Street PL31 2HT	01208 79003
BOGNOR REGIS	38 London Road PO21 1PZ	01243 837340
BOLTON	53/55 Victoria Square BH1 1RY	01204 366563
BOSCOMBE	13 Sovereign Centre BH1 4SX	01202 300720
BOSTON	16 Market Street PE21 6EH	01205 361753
BOURNEMOUTH	39 Old Christchurch Road BH1 1DS	01202 295911
BRACKNELL	46 High Street RG12 1LL	01344 485524
BRADFORD	43A Darley Street BD1 3HN	01274 725343
BRAINTREE	86/88 High Street CM7 1JP	01376 554742
BRECON	16 High Street LD3 7AL	01874 624634
BRENTWOOD	7 Chapel High CM14 4RY	01277 223669
BRIDGEND	Brackla Street Centre CF31 1EB	01656 657945
BRIDGWATER	5 Fore Street TA6 3NQ	01278 422243
BRIGHTON	153 Western Road BN1 2DA	01273 329435
BRISTOL	9/10 Transom House BS1 6A	0117 926 4892
BRISTOL	10 Broadmead BS1 3HH	0117 9221167
BROMLEY	65 High Street BR1 1JY	0208 460 0418
BURGESS HILL	Unit 77 Church Walk, The Martlet RH15 9BQ	01444 258448
BURNLEY	64/66 St James Square BB11 1NH	01282 831803
BURTON ON TRENT	12 St Modwens Walk DE14 1HL	01283 562488
BURY ST EDMUNDS	2 Buttermarket IP33 1DB	01284 755521
BUXTON	53/55 Spring Gardens SK17 6BJ	01298 25660
CAMBERLEY	33 High Street GU15 3RB	01276 65680
CAMBRIDGE	18/19 Sidney Street CB2 3HG	01223 307406
CANTERBURY	47 Burgate CT1 4BH	01227 479698
CARDIFF	109/111 Queen Street CF1 4BH	02920 340341
CARDIFF	10 Duke Street CF10 1AY	02920 390887
CARLISLE	59 English Street CA3 8JU	01228 529206
CARMARTHEN	1 Red Street SA31 1QL	01267 235906
CHELMSFORD	34 High Chelmer CM1 1XR	01245 269989
CHELTENHAM	117 High Street GL50 1DW	01242 520692
CHELTENHAM	240 High Street GL50 3HF	01242 262592
CHESHAM	35 High Street HP5 1BW	01494 791920
CHESTER	15/17 Northgate CH1 1HA	01244 329331
CHICHESTER	4 South Street PO19 1EH	01243 786627
CHIPPENHAM	17/18 High Street SN15 3ER	01249 652533
CHISWICK	167 Chiswick High Road W4 2DR	0208 9945807
CIRENCESTER	34 Cricklade Street GL7 1JH	01285 651250
COLCHESTER	17/18 High Street CO1 1DB	01206 574615
COLCHESTER	16 Short Wyre Street CO1 1LN	01206 577040
COVENTRY	19 Smithford Way CV1 1FY	02476 837048
COVENTRY	41 Smithford Way CV1 1FY	02476 224841
CRAWLEY	16 Haslett Avenue RH10 1HS	01293 541005
CREWE	7 Queensway CW1 2HH	01270 255446
CROYDON	52 High Street CR0 1YB	0208 688 6066
CROYDON	40/44 St George's Walk CR0 1YJ	0208 6881730
CWMBRAN	14 Monmouth Walk NP44 1PE	01633 871279
DARLINGTON	5/7 East Row DL1 5PZ	01325 485806
DERBY	1 East Street DE1 2AU	01332 342368
DEVIZES	29 The Brittox SN1 0IAJ	01380 730281
DONCASTER	54 High Street DN1 1BE	01302 739659
DORCHESTER	16 Cornhill DT1 1BQ	01305 251637
DORKING	5 South Street RH4 2DY	01306 887227
DUDLEY	205/206 High Street DY1 1PB	01384 252974
DUMFRIES	28 Munches Street DG1 1ET	01387 739954
DUNDEE	23 Cowgate DD1 2MS	01382 223744
DUNSTABLE	14 Nicholas Way LU6 1TD	01582 663460
EASTBOURNE	146/148 Terminus Road BN21 3AN	01323 728340
EAST GRINSTEAD	23 London Road RH19 1AL	01342 300977
EDINBURGH	12 Frederick Street EH2 2HB	0131 220 1551
EDINBURGH	Unit 6 Princess Mall EH1 1BQ	0131 558777
ELGIN	Unit 13 St Giles Centre IV30 1EA	01343 556550
ELTHAM	122 Eltham High Road SE9 1BJ	0208 8502822
ELY	26 Market Place CB7 4NT	01353 664023
ENFIELD	21 Palace Gardens EN2 6SN	0208 363 1682
ENNISKILLEN	Unit 24 Erneside Centre BT74 6JQ	02866 328580
EPSOM	17 High Street KT19 8DD	01372 721557
EVESHAM	33 Bridge Street WR11 4SQ	01386 446759
EXETER	207 High Street EX4 3EB	01392 255811
EXMOUTH	42 Chapel Street EX8 1HW	01395 267144
FALMOUTH	11 Market Strand TR11 3DB	01326 313348
FAREHAM	80/82 Osborne Mall PO16 0PW	01329 283088
FARNBOROUGH	Unit 5/7 The Mead GU14 7RT	01252 371663
FARNHAM	2/3 West Street GU9 7DN	01252 711338
FLEET	158 Fleet Road GU13 8BE	01252 620636
FELIXSTOWE	52 Hamilton Road IP11 7AJ	01394 672203
GALWAY	Unit 37 Headford Road	00353 91569433
GATESHEAD	31 The Galleria NE11 9YP	0191 460 3153
GLASGOW	71 Union Street G1 3TA	0141 221 1678
GLASGOW	Unit 2B Sauchiehall Street G2 2ER	0141 332 5617
GLENROTHES	56 Unicorn Way, Kingdom Centre KY7 5NU	01592 753217
GLOUCESTER	4 Southgate Street GL1 2DH	01452 412803
GRAVESEND	Unit 4 Anglesea Centre DA11 0AU	01474 362889
GREAT YARMOUTH	20/21 Market Place NR30 1LY	01493 857040
GREENOCK	45 Hamilton Way PA15 1RQ	01475 726425
GRIMSBY	22 Baxtergate, Freshney Place DN31 1QL	01472 362449
GUERNSEY	9 The Pollet GY1 1WQ	01481 725888
GUILDFORD	21 Friary Street GU1 4GH	01483 573476
HALIFAX	11 Crown Street HX1 1TT	01422 342644
HAMILTON	17 Duke Street ML3 7DT	01698 284691
HANLEY	10/12 Upper Market Square ST1 1NS	01782 214560
HARLOW	5 Eastgate CM20 1HP	01279 438165
HARROGATE	15/15A Beulah Street HG1 1QH	01423 526677
HARROW	324A Station Road HA1 2DX	0208 4273809
HASTINGS	12/13 York Building, Wellington Pl TN34 1NN	01424 203589
HAVERFORDWEST	25 Bridge Street SA61 2AZ	01437 767300
HAVERHILL	17 High Street CB9 8AD	01440 713682
HAYWARDS HEATH	98 South Street RH16 4LJ	01444 457214
HEMEL HEMPSTEAD	221 The Marlowes HP1 1WR	01442 265218
HEREFORD	12/14 Eign Gate HR4 0AB	01432 264196
HERTFORD	18 Fore Street SG14 1BZ	01992 584427
HIGH WYCOMBE	4/5 Church Street HP11 2DE	01494 522100
HITCHIN	26 Market Place SG5 1DT	01462 432567
HORSHAM	18 West Street RH12 1TV	01403 262851
HOUNSLOW	156 High Street TW3 1LR	0208 5 704309
HULL	24/26 King Edward Street HU1 3SS	01482 210389
HUNTINGDON	Unit 5 St Germain Walk PE29 3FG	01480 413554
ILFORD	154 High Road IG1 1LL	0208 478 7341
INVERNESS	24 High Street IV1 1JQ	01463 714387
IPSWICH	14/16 Carr Street IP4 1EJ	01473 211797
ISLE OF MAN	13 The Strand Shopping Centre IM1 2ER	01624 615668
JERSEY	29/31 King Street JE2 4WS	01534 725449

LOCAL MILLETS STORES

KENDAL	26/28 Highgate LA9 4SX	01539 736866
KESWICK	85/87 Main Street, Cumbria CA12 5DT	01768 775524
KETTERING	3/5 Newland Street NN16 8JH	01536 481261
KIDDERMINSTER	21 The Bull Ring DY10 2AZ	01562 740127
KINGSTON	3/5 Thames Street KT1 1PH	0208 546 5042
LANCASTER	7 Cheapside LA1 1LY	01524 841043
LEAMINGTON SPA	23/31 The Parade CV32 4BC	01926 889012
LEEDS	24 St Johns Centre, 110 Albion Street LS2 8LQ	0113 2457273
LEEDS	117/118 Kirkgate LS1 6BY	0113 242 9892
LEEDS — WHITEROSE	Unit 28 Whiterose Centre LS11 8LU	0113 276 1149
LEEK	34 Derby Street ST13 5AB	01538 383731
LEICESTER	121/123 Granby Street LE1 6FD	0116 254 2402
LEIGH	33 Spinning Gate Ctre, Ellesmere St WN7 4PG	01942 671944
LEIGHTON BUZZARD	47 High Street LU7 1DN	01525 371623
LETCHWORTH	5 Commerce Way, Garden Sq Centre SG6 3DN	01462 679583
LEWISHAM	205 Lewisham High Street SE13 6LY	0208 852 1909
LICHFIELD	19 Tamworth Street WS13 6JP	01543 262003
LINCOLN	321/322 High Street LN5 7DW	01522 567317
LIVERPOOL	15 Ranelagh Street L1 1JW	0151 709 7017
LIVINGSTONE	Unit 68, Almomdvale Centre EH54 6HR	01506 437 728
LLANDUDNO	80 Moystn Street LL30 2RP	01492 872511
LLANELLI	42 Stepney Street SA15 3YA	01554 751657
LONDON HARROW	324A Station RoadHA1 2DX	0208 4273809
LONDON KENSINGTON	176 Kensington High Street W8 7RG	0207 9377141
LOUGHBOROUGH	4 Market Street LE11 3EP	01509 236413
LOUTH	78 East Gate LN11 9PG	01507 602711
LOWESTOFT	71 London Road North NR32 1LS	01502 572239
LUTON	Unit 125 Arndale Centre LU1 2TN	01582 724514
LYMINGTON	52 High Street SO41 9AG	01590 675144
MACCLESFIELD	45 Mill Street SK11 6NE	01625 427477
MAIDSTONE	Unit 34A Fremlin Walk ME14 1QT	01622 764137
MANCHESTER	Unit 49 Arndale Centre M4 2HU	0161 832 7547
MANCHESTER	133 Deansgate M3 3WR	01618 351016
MANSFIELD	48 Westgate NG18 1RR	01623 629446
MERRY HILL	11 Merry Hill, Brierley Hill DY5 !QX	01384 261671
MIDDLESBROUGH	40 Linthorpe Road TS1 1RD	01642 240863
MILTON KEYNES	21/23 Crown Walk MK9 3AH	01908 672322
MONMOUTH	21 Monnow Street NP25 3EF	01600 719187
NEATH	12 Queen Street SA11 1DL	01639 637216
NEWARK	25 Middlegate NG24 1AL	01636 640842
NEWBURY	68/69 Northbrook Street RG13 1AE	01635 40070
NEWCASTLE U LYME	53 High Street ST5 1PN	01782 612968
NEWCASTLE U TYNE	121/120 Grainger Street NE1 5AE	0191 232 1100
NEWPORT (GWENT)	3 Llanarth Street, Gwent NP20 1HS	01633 246 309
NEWPORT (Isle of Wight)	21 St James Square PO30 1UX	01983 525995
NEWRY	Unit 30, Buttercrane Quay BT35 8HJ	02830 263565
NEWTON ABBOT	17 Queen Street TQ12 2AQ	01626 353405
NEWTOWNABBEY	Unit 70/71, Abbey Centre BT37 9AQ	02890 865520
NORTHAMPTON	24 Market Square NN1 2DX	01604 621898
NORWICH	9/11 St Stephens Street NR1 3QN	01603 622708
NORWICH	Boston House, 5 Orford Hill NR1 3QB	01603 625645
NOTTINGHAM	12 Exchange Walk NG1 2NX	0115 9417456
NUNEATON	14/15 Abbey Gate Centre CV11 4HL	02476 385625
OBAN	71 George Street PA34 5NN	01631 571122
ORPINGTON	178 High Street BR6 0JW	01689 826794
OXFORD	42/43 Queen Street OX1 1ET	0865 790676
OXFORD	17 Turl Street OX1 3DH	01865 247110
PAIGNTON	37/39 Victoria Street TQ4 5DD	01803 529578
PAISLEY	29 The High Street PA1 2AF	0141 8471013
PENZANCE	105 Market Jew Street TR18 2LE	01736 363204
PERTH	182/186 High Street PH1 5PA	01738 622248
PETERBOROUGH	47 Bridge Street PE1 1HA	01733 341371
PETERBOROUGH	97 Bridge Street PE1 1HG	01733 561000
PETERSFIELD	8 Rams Walk GU32 3JA	01730 260317
PLYMOUTH	39/40 New George Street PL1 1RW	01752 665521
PONTYPRIDD	80 Taff Street CF37 4SD	01443 400086
POOLE	9 Kingland Crescent BH15 1TA	01202 661307
PORTSMOUTH	213/215 Commercial Road PO1 4BJ	02392 851653
PRESTON	28 Market Place PR1 2AR	01772 884433
PRESTON	23 Miller Arcade PR1 2QA	0177 2250242
PUTNEY	98 High Street SW15 1RB	0208 788 2300
RAMSGATE	8 Queen Street CT11 9DR	01843 594220
READING	4/5 St Mary's Butts RG1 2LN	0118 959 5228
REDCAR	15/17 High Street TS10 3BZ	01642 483924
REDDITCH	12 Kingfisher Walk D97 4CY	01527 69229
REDHILL	29 High Street RH1 1RD	01737 765177
RHYL	60/62 High Street LL18 1ET	01745 353178
RICHMOND	36/37 The Quadrant TW9 1BP	0208 940 2805
RINGWOOD	7 The Furlong Centre BH24 1AT	01425 480047
ROMFORD	42/44 South Street RM1 1RB	01708 743751
ROTHERHAM	18 Howard Street S60 1QU	01709 382502
RUGBY	Uuit 28 Clock Towers Shopping Centre CV21 3JT	
SAFFRON WALDEN	37/39 King Street CB10 1EU	01799 529343
SALISBURY	38/39 Old George Mall SP1 2AF	01722 341 583
SCARBOROUGH	6/7 Westborough YO11 1UH	01723 367869
SCUNTHORPE	116 High Street DN15 6HB	01724 849890
SHEFFIELD	71 The Moor S1 4PF	0114 2722194
SHREWSBURY	6/7 Mardol Head SY1 1HD	01743 353686
SITTINGBOURNE	119 High Street ME10 4AQ	01795 472544
SKIPTON	30 Sheep Street BD23 1HX	01756 793754
SLOUGH	186/188 High Street SL1 1JS	01753 520981
SOLIHULL	50 Drury Lane B91 3BG	0121? 113817
SOUTHAMPTON	104 East Street SO14 3HH	02380 228797
SOUTHEND	4/19 York Road SS1 2BH	01702 463316
SOUTHPORT	4/8 Tulketh Street, Merseyside PR8 1AQ	01704 534017
SOUTHSEA	5 Palmurston Road PO5 3QQ	02392 732461
St. ALBANS	19/21 French Row AL3 5DZ	01727 856328
St. HELENS	2/4 Cotham Street WA10 1SQ	01744 739941
STAFFORD	13 Gaolgate Street ST16 2BQ	01785 251912
STAINES	111A High Street TW18 4PQ	01784 469820
STAMFORD	63 High Street PE9 2LA	01780 481346
STIRLING	20/22 Murray Place FK8 1DQ	01786 451141
STOCKPORT	29/31 Princes Street SK1 1SU	0161 477 4160
STRATFORD UPON AVON	Unit 21A Town Square Centre CV37 6JN	01789 414857
STROUD	34 Kendrick Street GL5 1AQ	01453 764646
SUDBURY	14 North Street CO10 1RB	01787 375883
SUTTON	86 High Street SM1 1JG	0208 643 4251
SUTTON COLDFIELD	56 The Parade B72 1DS	01213 554931
SWANSEA	234 High Street SA1 1NZ	01792 655637
SWINDON	Sub Unit 4 The Parade SN1 1BA	01793 514941
TALLAGHT	Unit 315 The Square DUBLIN 24	003531 4621119
TAUNTON	20 East Street TA1 3LP	01823 332782
TELFORD	207 Dean Street TF34BT	01952 201002
TONBRIDGE	70 High Street TN9 1SD	01732 355247
TORQUAY	49 Union Street TQ1 1ET	01803 297588
TROWBRIDGE	40 The Shires BA14 8AT	01225 762871
TRURO	11 Pydar Street TR1 2AX	01872 240973
TUNBRIDGE WELLS	37 Camden Road TN1 2PS	01892 519891
UCKFIELD	136 High Street TN22 1QN	01825 766176
WAKEFIELD	28 Westgate WF1 1YJ	01924 371120
WALSALL	9 The Bridge, West Midlands WS1 1LR	01922 624462
WARRINGTON	28 Golden Square Shopping Centre WA1 1QE	01925 417050
WATFORD	Unit A8 The Harlequin Centre WD1 2TB	01923 212427
WELWYN GARDEN CITY	41 Wigmores North AL8 6PG	01707 330260
WEST THURROCK	Unit 338 Lakeside RM20 2ZH	01708 864366
WESTON-S-MARE	98 High Street BS23 1HS	01934 621930
WEYMOUTH	74 St Mary Street DT14 8PJ	01305 786002
WHITEHAVEN	19/20 King Street CA28 7LA	01946 694655
WHITEROSE (LEEDS)	Unit 28 White Rose Centre LS11 8LU	0113 2761149
WIGAN	24/26 Market Street WN1 1HX	01942 245330
WIMBLEDON	34 The Broadway SW19 0BB	0208 946 6644
WINCHESTER	149 High Street SO23 9AY	01962 841970
WINDSOR	42 Peascod Street SL4 1DE	01753 620405
WITNEY	Unit 18A, Woolgate OX28 6AP	01993 778775
WOKING	31 Commercial Road GU21 1XR	01483 721551
WOKINGHAM	37 Peach Street RG4 0IXJ	01189 798097
WOLVERHAMPTON	2 Wulfrun Centre WV1 3HF	01902 423797
WORCESTER	7/8 The Shambles WR1 2RF	01905 25672
WORTHING	95 Montague Street BN11 3BN	01903 236066
WREXHAM	24 Queen Street LL11 1AL	01978 261267
YATE	5 West Walk BS37 4AX	01454 312823
YEOVIL	22 Middle Street BA20 1LY	01935 423156
YORK	4/6 Market Street YO1 8ST	01904 620618
YORK	Unit 3, Queens House, Micklegate YO1 6JH	01904 653567

JUST WHAT YOU'D EXPECT
FROM A STORE
DEVOTED TO PRACTICAL
OUTDOOR STUFF.

AN AD THAT DOUBLES
AS LOO PAPER.

The UK's largest walking festival

Isle of Wight
walking festival

6 to 21 May 2006

ISLE OF WIGHT 2006 WALKING FESTIVAL

hf holidays — Quality Walking Specialists Since 1913

ISLE of WIGHT COUNCIL

millets — The Outdoor Store

RED FUNNEL
THE ORIGINAL ISLE OF WIGHT FERRIES
Travel Partner

www.isleofwightwalkingfestival.co.uk

High Barn Oils
Linseed Oil

Edge of Wales Walk, 1 Dolfor, Aberdaron, Gwynydd, LL53 8BP Tel 01758 760652, Fax 01758 760582 Email enquiries@edgeofwales.co.uk Web www.edgeofwales.co.uk. Walking holidays on the Llŷn Peninsula – Accommodation, transport, luggage transfer. Covers: The Llŷn Peninsula in North Wales.

Omega 3 + 6 + 9 in one natural plant oil to simulate the body and calm the mind

Superior Culinary Linseed Oil and Linseed 'Pure Oil Dinner' Pods for health, vitality and well-being. NEW! 100% vegetarian Vege Pods

Grown and pressed in the English countryside to capture Nature's goodness

Order direct from the farm at

01403 730326
www.highbarnoils.co.uk

PODS: £11.75 (plus p&p)
Oil: £13 (plus p&p)

A taste of Sussex MEMBER

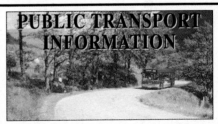

PUBLIC TRANSPORT INFORMATION

The Highland Council publishes a full colour map showing all public transport routes in the Highlands & Islands.

A series of local travel guides are published in association with the map giving detailed timetable information
The publications are available free of charge from:

PUBLIC TRANSPORT SECTION,
TEC SERVICES, GLENURQUHART ROAD,
INVERNESS, IV3 5NX
Tel: 01463 702458 Fax: 01463 702606
Email:
public.transport@highland.gov.uk

Walk all over Britain...

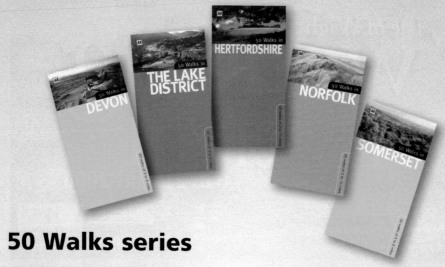

50 Walks series

- **37 counties covered across Great Britain**

1001 Walks in Britain

- **Removable walks can be kept in the plastic wallet for on-the-move reference**

With the AA's best–selling range of walking guides

Britain's largest travel publisher

PUBLISHERS

Aurum Press
☎ 020 7637 3225
www.aurumpress.co.uk

Cicerone Press
☎ 015395 62069
www.cicerone.co.uk

Countryside Books
☎ 01635 43816
www.countrysidebooks.co.uk

Frances Lincoln
☎ 020 7284 4009
www.franceslincoln.com

Harvey Maps
☎ 01786 841202
www.harveymaps.co.uk

Jarrold
☎ 01264 409206
www.totalwalking.com

Kittiwake
☎ 01650 511314
www.kittiwake-books.com

memory-map
☎ 0870 740 9010
www.memory-map.co.uk

Rucksack Readers
☎ 01786 824 696
www.rucsacs.com

Sigma Leisure
☎ 01625 531035
www.sigmapress.co.uk

LUGGAGE CARRIERS & HOSTEL BOOKING

Aberchalder
☎ 01809 501411

AMS
☎ 01324 823144
www.ams-scotland.com

Bag Tag
☎ 01983 861559
www.bagtagiow.co.uk

Bike and Hike
☎ 01877 339788
www.bikeandhike.co.uk

Brigantes
☎ 01729 830463
www.pikedaw.freeserve.co.uk/walks

CarryLite
☎ 01434 634448
www.carrylite.com

Coast to Coast Holidays
☎ 01642 489173
www.coasttocoast-holidays.co.uk

Coast to Coast Packhorse
☎ 01768 371777
http://cumbria.com/packhorse

Compass (Carry a Bag)
☎ 01242 250642
www.compass-holidays.com

Great Glen Baggage Transfer
☎ 01320 351322
www.invermoriston.freeserve.co.uk
/BaggageTransfer

Great Glen Travel
☎ 01809 501222
www.greatglentravel.com

IBHS
www.hostel-scotland.co.uk

Loch Ness Travel
☎ 01456 450550
www.lochnesstravel.com

Pembrokeshire Discovery
☎ 01437 710720
www.pembrokeshirediscovery.co.uk

Sherpa Van Project
☎ 0871 520 0124
www.sherpavan.com

southernuplandway.com
☎ 0870 835 8558
www.southernuplandway.com

Tony's Taxis
☎ 01437 720931
www.tonystaxis.co.uk

Travel-Lite
☎ 0141 956 7890
www.travel-lite-uk.com

Trossachs Transfers
☎ 01360 660466
www.trossachs-transfers.co.uk

Way Forward
☎ 01750 42271
www.thewayforward.org

YHA
☎ 0870 770 8868
www.yha.org.uk

FAQ RIGHT TO ROAM

Where does the new legislation apply?

The Countryside and Rights of Way (CRoW) Act provides a legal right of access to 1.3million hectares of open, uncultivated countryside in England and Wales, which is defined in the legislation as mountain, moor, heath and down, as well as registered common land. See p304 for access arrangements in Scotland.

ORDNANCE SURVEY MAPPING
© CROWN COPYRIGHT

How can I find out where I can walk?

Ordnance Survey is in the process of reissuing all of its Explorer maps to show access land, which is indicated by a light yellow area surrounded by a narrow pale orange border. Orange 'i' symbols pinpoint access information points.

In addition, in England the Countryside Agency provides an open access website where walkers can find details of access land throughout the country; while in Wales the Countryside Council for Wales hosts a similar resource. See p273.

What am I allowed to do on access land?

The new law provides a right of access for walkers only, and does not confer any additional rights for cyclists or horse-riders (though where additional rights are currently allowed or tolerated, they are likely to continue). Dogs are permitted on some areas of open country, but must be kept on a lead on access land between 1 March and 31 July and at any time in the vicinity of livestock. Furthermore, dogs may be banned temporarily or permanently from some areas of land. Access at night is permitted but may be subject to local restrictions. Walkers are responsible for their own safety at all times.

How is access managed locally?

Access is managed by local authorities or, in national parks, by the national park authority. They have the power to enact and enforce by-laws that will apply to open access land in their jurisdiction, subject to consultation with the relevant local access forum and countryside body. They also have powers to set up the necessary infrastructure to make the new access land easily available to walkers including the power to appoint wardens, erect and maintain notices and improve means of access.

What is a local access forum?

Local access forums, made up of landowners, users and others with an interest in the land, have been established to advise access authorities on the local application of the new law. This may mean commenting on access management or the need for signage or the necessity or otherwise of a proposed long-term local access restriction.

Are landowners able to close their land for any reason?

The Act allows landowners to close their land for up to 28 days a year (including some Saturdays and Sundays) for any reason. The Countryside Agency and the Countryside Council for Wales should be informed of these closures and can make the information publicly available. Landowners may apply for further closures or restrictions, on a temporary or permanent basis, for public safety, land management or fire risk. There may also be restrictions to protect wildlife or areas of historic interest or on the grounds of national security.

What should I do if I see a misleading notice?

If the notice is about a local restriction then call the Countryside Access helpline or the Countryside Council for Wales (see p273) and they will advise you. For any other notices please contact your local authority (see p274) using the report form on page p285, and then inform the Ramblers' Association.

What if there is no way onto the access land?

Access authorities must provide ways of getting to access land, ideally in consultation with the landowner but by order if necessary. If you find there is no way of getting to the access land then please contact your local authority (see p276) using the report form on page p285, and then inform the Ramblers' Association, but remember that not all access points will be available immediately. For more information see www.ramblers.org.uk/freedom

FAQ RIGHTS OF WAY

Here we answer some of the most frequently asked questions about Rights of Way in England and Wales. A fuller version of this text is available as a factsheet (Basics of Footpath Law – FS7, see p308) and on our website.

What is a right of way?
A right of way is a path that anyone has the legal right to use on foot, and sometimes using other modes of transport.

➤ **Public footpaths** are open only to walkers, and may be waymarked with yellow arrows

➤ **Public bridleways** are open to walkers, horse-riders and pedal cyclists, and may be waymarked with blue arrows

➤ **Byways Open to All Traffic** (BOATs) are open to all classes of traffic including motor vehicles, though they may not be maintained to the same standard as ordinary roads, and may be waymarked with red arrows

Legally, a public right of way is part of the Queen's highway and subject to the same protection in law as all other highways, including trunk roads.

What are my rights on a public right of way?
Your legal right is to 'pass and repass along the way'. You may stop to rest or admire the view, or to eat or drink, providing you stay on the path and do not cause an obstruction. You can also take with you a 'natural accompaniment', which includes a pram, pushchair or wheelchair (though you may find the surface of the path is not always suitable), or a dog. However, you should ensure that dogs are under close control. Note that there is no requirement for stiles to be suitable for use by dogs.

How do I know whether a path is a public right of way or not?
The safest evidence is the official 'definitive map' of public rights of way. These maps are available for public inspection at the offices of local surveying authorities (see Local Authorities p276). In addition, public rights of way information derived from them is shown by the Ordnance Survey on its Explorer and Landranger maps.

Some rights of way are not yet shown on definitive maps. These can quite properly be used, and application may be made to surveying authorities for them to be added to the map. The Inner London boroughs are not required to produce definitive maps, though this does not mean there are no rights of way in Inner London.

How does a path become public?
In legal theory most paths become rights of way because the owner 'dedicates' them to public use. In fact very few paths have been formally dedicated, but the law assumes that if the public uses a path without interference for some period of time – set by statute at 20 years – then the owner had intended to dedicate it as a right of way.

A public path that has been unused for any amount of time does not cease to be public (except possibly in Scotland). The legal maxim is 'once a highway, always a highway'.

Paths can also be created by agreement between local authorities and owners or by compulsory order, subject, in the case of objection, to confirmation by the Secretary of State for the Environment, Food and Rural Affairs, or the National Assembly for Wales.

Can a landowner put up new gates and stiles where none exist presently?
No. Not without seeking and getting permission from the highway authority and then complying with any conditions to that permission. Maintaining stiles and gates is primarily the owner's responsibility, but the local authority must contribute 25% of the cost if asked and may contribute more if it wishes. If stiles and gates are not kept in proper repair the authority can, after 14 days' notice, do the job itself and send the bill to the owner.

How wide should a path be?
The path should be whatever width was dedicated for public use. This width may have arisen through

usage, or by formal agreement, or by order, for example if the path has been diverted. The width may be recorded in a statement accompanying the definitive map but in many cases the proper width will be a matter of past practice on that particular path.

Is it illegal to plough up or disturb the surface of a path so as to make it inconvenient to use?

Yes, except where the path is a footpath or bridleway that runs across a field (as opposed to alongside a field edge). In this case the landowner can plough or otherwise disturb the path surface provided it is not reasonably convenient to avoid doing so. The path must be restored within 24 hours of the disturbance, or within two weeks if this is the first such disturbance for a particular crop. The restored path must be reasonably convenient to use, have a minimum width of 1m for a footpath or 2m for a bridleway, or the legal width (see above) if known, and its line must be clearly apparent on the ground.

What about crops growing on or over a path?

The landowner has a duty to prevent a crop (other than grass) from making the path difficult to find or follow. The minimum widths given above apply here also, but if the path is a field-edge path they are increased to 1.5m for a footpath, 3m for a bridleway. You have every right to walk through crops growing on or over a path, but stick as close as you can to its correct line. Report the problem to the local authority (see p276): it has power to prosecute the landowner or cut the crop and send the owner the bill.

Can a farmer keep a bull in a field crossed by a public path?

Only a bull of up to ten months in age. Bulls over ten months of a recognised dairy breed (Ayrshire, British Friesian, British Holstein, Dairy Shorthorn, Guernsey, Jersey and Kerry) are banned from fields crossed by public paths under all circumstances. All other bulls over ten months are banned unless accompanied by cows or heifers. If any bulls act in a way that endangers the public, an offence may be committed under health and safety legislation.

What is an obstruction on a path?

Anything that interferes with your right to use it, for example a barbed wire fence across the path or a

heap of manure dumped on it. Dense undergrowth is not normally treated as an obstruction but is dealt with under path maintenance. Local authorities have a duty 'to prevent as far as possible the stopping up or obstruction' of paths.

Can I remove an obstruction to get by?

Yes, provided that you are a bona fide traveller on the path and have not gone out for the specific purpose of moving the obstruction, and that you remove only as much as is necessary to get through. If you can easily go round the obstruction without causing any damage, then you should do so.

Are horses allowed on public paths?

Horse riders have a right to use bridleways and byways. They have no right to use footpaths, and if they do they are committing a trespass against the owner of the land, unless the use is by permission. If use of a footpath by riders becomes a nuisance the local authority can ban them with a traffic regulation order or byelaw. This makes such use a criminal offence rather than an act of trespass.

Are pedal cyclists allowed on public paths?

Pedal cyclists have a right to use bridleways and byways, but on bridleways they must give way to walkers and riders. Like horse riders, they have no right to use footpaths and if they do so they are committing a trespass against the owner of the land, unless use is by permission. As with horse-riding (see above), use of any right of way by cyclists can be controlled by traffic regulation orders and byelaws imposed by local authorities. Infringement of byelaws or orders is a criminal offence. Under the Highways Act 1835, it is an offence to ride a bicycle on the pavement at the side of a road, and under the Fixed Penalty Offences Order 1999 a person who rides on a pavement can be fined on the spot by a police officer.

Is it illegal to drive cars or motorcycles on public paths?

Anyone who drives a motor vehicle on a footpath or bridleway without permission is committing an offence. This does not apply if the driver stays within 15 yards of the road, only goes on the path to park and does not obstruct the right of passage. The owner of the land, however, can still order vehicles off even within 15 yards from the road. Races or speed trials on paths are forbidden. Permission for other types of trials on paths may be sought from the local authority, if the landowner consents.

SARAH BOVE

What is trespass?

A person who strays from a right of way, or uses it other than for "passing and repassing" commits trespass against the landowner.

In most cases, trespass is a civil rather than a criminal matter. A landowner may use "reasonable force" to compel a trespasser to leave, but not more than is reasonably necessary. Unless injury to the property can be proven, a landowner could probably only recover nominal damages by suing for trespass. But of course you might have to meet the landowner's legal costs. Thus a notice saying 'Trespassers will be Prosecuted', aimed for instance at keeping you off a private drive, is usually meaningless. Criminal prosecution could arise only if you trespass and damage property. However, under public order law, trespassing with an intention to reside may be a criminal offence under some circumstances. It is also a criminal offence to trespass on railway land and sometimes on military training land.

 # OUTDOOR ACCESS IN SCOTLAND

What is the Land Reform (Scotland) Act?

The Land Reform (Scotland) Act 2003 establishes a statutory right of responsible access and is accompanied by the Scottish Outdoor Access Code (p272). For a full explanation visit http://www.ramblers.org.uk/scotland

How will the Act affect my access to the Scottish countryside?

There has long been a general presumption of access to all land unless there is a very good reason for the public to be excluded. The access legislation confirms this presumption, and walkers in Scotland now have a statutory right of access to all land, except for areas such as railway lands, quarries, harbours, airfields and defence land where other laws apply.

Walkers should act responsibly when exercising their right of access, and follow the Scottish Outdoor Access Code (see p272).

Are there rights of way in Scotland?

Yes, but they are less extensive than in England and Wales because there is a tradition of access to most land. Rights of way do exist, but there is no legal obligation on local authorities to record them, so they don't appear on Ordnance Survey maps, though paths and tracks are shown on these maps as geographical features and you have a right to walk on most of these. ScotWays (see p290) keeps a catalogue of rights of way, signs many of them and maps and describes the major rural routes in its publication *Scottish Hill Tracks*. It is expected that 'core paths' will largely supersede the existing arrangements for rights of way.

What is a Core Path?

Local authorities have new duties and powers to develop Core Path Networks by adopting and improving existing paths and creating new ones. Councils have until February 2008 to produce plans for these networks. Core paths will eventually appear on OS Explorer maps. Scottish Natural Heritage and local authorities have developed The Scottish Paths Record database as a tool to help develop path networks.

OUTSIDE BRITAIN

EUROPE

European Ramblers Association

(ERA) c/o Klub âesk˜ch TuristÛ, Archeologická 2256, CZ-155 00 Praha 5 – Luřiny
☎ +420 2 5162 7356
www.era-ewv-ferp.org
Federation of 26 national organisations including the Ramblers' Association working for walking and climbing, protecting the countryside and creating international long distance paths (E-Paths). The website is a good source of information on walking in Europe and member organisations' contact details.

Hostelling International

(International Youth Hostels Federation) 2nd Floor Gate House, Fretherne Road, Welwyn Garden City, AL8 6RD, UK
☎ 01707 324170
www.iyhf.org (has links to national sites)

CHANNEL ISLANDS

Alderney Tourist Information
☎ 01481 822333
www.visitaldemey.com

Guernsey Tourist Board
☎ 01481 723552
www.visitguernsey.com

Herm Tourist Information
☎ 01481 722377
www.herm-island.com

Jersey Tourist Information
☎ 01534 500700
www.jersey.com

Sark Tourist Information
☎ 01481 832345
www.sark.info

NORTHERN IRELAND

Countryside Access and Activities Network for Northern Ireland
☎ 028 9030 3930
www.countrysiderecreation.com
Responsibilities include the province's network of 14 Waymarked Ways.

Northern Ireland Tourist Board
☎ 029 9024 6609 (information)
www.discovernorthernireland.com
London: information available from Bord Fáilte (see Republic of Ireland)

Ordnance Survey of Northern Ireland
☎ 028 9025 5755
www.osni.gov.uk

Translink
☎ 028 9089 9400
Enquiry line: ☎ 028 9066 6630
www.translink.co.uk
Operates integrated public transport services including Northern Ireland Railways, Citybus and Ulsterbus.

Ulster Federation of Rambling Clubs
☎ 028 9066 6358
www.ufrc-online.co.uk

REPUBLIC OF IRELAND

Fáilte Ireland (Tourism Ireland)
☎ +353 (0)1 602 4000
www.ireland.ie

Walking website:
www.walking.travel.ie

CIE
(Córas Iompair Éireann)
☎ +353 (0)1 703 2358

Rail enquiries: ☎ +353 (0)1 836 6222
Bus enquiries: ☎ +353 (0)1 836 6111 www.cie.ie
Operates integrated public transport services including Iarnród Éireann (Irish Rail), Bus Éireann and Dublin Bus

Mountaineering Council of Ireland
☎ +353 (0)1 625 1115
www.mountaineering.ie

National Waymarked Ways Advisory Committee
Irish Sports Council:
☎ +353 (0)1 860 8800
www.walkireland.ie

Ordnance Survey Ireland - Suirbhéireacht Ordanáis Éireann
☎ +353 (0)1 802 5300
www.osi.ie

ISLE OF MAN

Manx Footpaths Conservation Group
manxfootpaths.iomonline.co.im

VisitIsleofMan – Cur jee shilley er Ellan Vannin
☎ +44 (0)1624 686801
www.visitisleofman.com

THE RAMBLERS BOOKSHOP

WALKING IN BRITAIN

walk BRITAIN 2006
Packed with useful information and details of 2,500
places to stay   **£5.99 (free to members)**
Long Distance Walkers' Handbook: 7th edition
Comprehensive directory of trails in UK   **£12.99**
Long Distance Path Chart Colour map of UK
network   **£9.95**
Land's End to John O'Groats Walk Route suggestions
and advice by Andrew McCloy   **£11.99**
Ramblers' Regional Guides
Directories of places to walk
London (all of Greater London)   **£1.50**
West Midlands
(Hereford, Worcs, Shrops, Staffs, Warks)   **£1.50**
Yorkshire (including Dales and Moors)   **£1.50**
An older series of free guides is available covering
other areas: please enquire for details.
Collins Rambler's Guides
30 walks in each colour volume
Ben Nevis and Glen Coe by Chris Townsend   **£9.99**
Connemara by Paddy Dillon   **£9.99**
Dartmoor by Richard Sale   **£9.99**
Isle of Skye by Chris Townsend   **£9.99**
Yorkshire Dales by David Leather   **£9.99**
*Walking in Britain (FS1) Outline of access arrangements,
transport, accom, parks etc*   **FREE**
Walk South East England Colour booklet   **FREE**

PATHS AND ROUTES

Angles Way
Norfolk Broads-Suffolk Brecks: route guide with
accommodation by RA Norfolk/Suffolk   **£2.70**
Birmingham Greenway
Sutton Park to Bournville by Fred Willits   **£4.95**
Calderdale Way Around Calderdale, W Yorks **£4.95**
Cambrian Way S–N Wales by Tony Drake   **£5.50**
Capital RING Inner London Circular Official guide to
whole route by Colin Saunders   **£12.99**
Walking the Ceredigion Coast   **FREE**
Chiltern Way from Hemel Hempstead   **£9.99**
Cleveland Way
Around North York Moors and coast
National Trail Guide by Ian Sampson   **£12.99**
Accommodation and information guide   **FREE**
Clwydian Way Circular from Prestatyn   **£6.95**
Coast to Coast Walk St Bees to Robin Hood's Bay
Harvey strip map and guide west: St Bees to Keld **£9.95**

Harvey strip map and guide east to R Hood's Bay **£9.95**
Cotswold Way Chipping Campden to Bath
Guide by Mark Richards   **£4.95**
Harvey strip map and guide   **£9.95**
Handbook: Accommodation list and practical info **£2.95**
Cumbria Way Ulverston to Carlisle
Official Ramblers Guide by John Trevelyan   **£2.99**
Harvey strip map and guide   **£9.95**
Dales Way Leeds, Bradford or Ilkley to Bowness
Harvey strip map and guide   **£9.95**
Handbook and accommodation list   **£1.50**
Ebor Way Helmsley to Ilkley route card pack **£4.99**
Essex Way Epping to Harwich   **£5.00**
Fife Coastal Path
Long Distance Guide by Hamish Brown   **£12.99**
Glyndwr's Way Knighton to Welshpool   **£12.99**
For accommodation guide see Offa's Dyke Path
Great Glen Way Fort William to Inverness
Long distance route guide by Jacquetta Megarry **£10.99**
Harvey strip map and guide   **£9.95**
Accommodation and services guide   **FREE**
Greater Ridgeway See under Ridgeway
Green Chain Walk Thames Barrier, Thamesmead,
Erith to Chislehurst, Crystal Palace   **£3.50**
Gritstone Trail Disley to Kidsgrove   **FREE**
Hadrian's Wall Path Wallsend to Bowness
National Trail guide by Anthony Burton   **£12.99**
Essential guide to walking the trail   **£3.95**
Harvey strip map and guide   **£9.95**
Accommodation guide   **FREE**
Heart of England Way *Stafford to Bourton on the
Water: Guide by John Roberts*   **£7.50**
Accommodation list   **FREE**
Icknield Way See under Ridgeway
Isle of Anglesey Coastal Path route card pack **£1.50**
Isle of Wight Coastal Path and inland trails **£3.00**
Jubilee Trail (Dorset)
Forde Abbey to Bokerley Dyke   **£4.50**
Jubilee Walkway Central London map/guide   **FREE**
London Loop near-circular walk around Outer London
Official guide to whole route by David Sharp **£12.99**
Macmillan Way Boston to Abbotsbury   **£9.00**

PLEASE NOTE
Postage and packing is charged even on
free items. Please see order form on
p309 for details.

Macmillan Way West Castle Cary to Barnstaple **£6.25**

Monarch's Way Worcester to Shoreham

1 The Midlands: Worcester to Stratford **£5.95**

2 The Cotswolds, Mendips & Sea, to Charmouth **£6.95**

3 The South Coast, The Downs and Escape **£6.95**

Nene Way Badby to Wansford, leaflet pack **£3.00**

New River Path Islington–Hertford **FREE**

Nidderdale Way circ around Nidderdale, N Yorks

Route card pack and accommodation list **£2.95**

Harvey strip map and guide **£6.95**

North Downs Way Farnham to Dover

National Trail guide **£12.99**

Harvey strip map and guide west, to the Medway **£9.95**

Harvey strip map and guide east, to Dover **£9.95**

Offa's Dyke Path Chepstow to Prestatyn

National Trail Guide south, to Knighton **£12.99**

National Trail Guide north, to Prestatyn **£12.99**

Offa's Dyke/Glyndwr's Way accommodation list **£4.00**

Walking the Peddars Way & Norfolk Coast Path

with Weavers Way Guidebook with accom **£2.70**

Pembrokeshire Coast Path Amroth to Cardigan

National Trail Guide by Brian John **£12.99**

Accommodation list **£2.50**

Pennine Bridleway Derbyshire to the South Pennines

National Trail Guide **£12.99**

Harvey strip map and guide **£9.95**

Accommodation and information guide **FREE**

Pennine Way Edale to Kirk Yetholm

National Trail Guide south to Bowes **£12.99**

National Trail Guide north to Kirk Yetholm **£12.99**

Accommodation and transport pack **FREE**

Pilgrim's Trail Winchester to Portsmouth **£2.99**

Ridgeway/Greater Ridgeway (see also Peddars Way)

Ridgeway National Trail Avebury to Ivinghoe **£12.99**

Harvey strip map and guide **£9.95**

National Trail Companion:

accom, practical information **£3.95**

Wessex Ridgeway Marlborough to Shaftesbury **£4.50**

Icknield Way Ivinghoe to Knettishall Heath **£4.50**

Icknield Way accommodation list **£1.00**

Rob Roy Way Drymen to Pitlochry **£10.99**

Robin Hood Walks Nottingham to Edwinstowe **£4.95**

Saints' Way Padstow to Fowey **£3.99**

Sandlings Walk Ipswich to Southwold **£4.75**

Sandstone Trail Frodsham to Whitchurch **FREE**

Shropshire Way circular from Wem **£6.99**

Solent Way outline leaflet **FREE**

Pub Walks along the Solent Way including full linear

route Christchurch to Emsworth **£7.95**

South Downs Way Eastbourne to Winchester

Along the South Downs Way in both directions **£6.00**

Harvey strip map and guide **£9.95**

South West Coast Path Guide Concise route

directions, accommodation, practical information **£7.00**

Southern Upland Way Portpatrick to Cockburnspath

Long distance route guide by Anthony Burton **£12.99**

Accommodation leaflet **FREE**

Speyside Way Buckie to Craigelachie, Tomintoul,

Aviemore

Accommodation and information **FREE**

St Cuthbert's Way Lindisfarne to Melrose **£9.99**

St Swithun's Way Winchester to Farnham **£3.99**

Staffordshire Way Mow Cop to Kinver Edge

Official guide **£5.00**

Accommodation list (with Way for Millennium) **FREE**

Stour and Orwell Walk Felixstowe to Manningtree,

linking with Suffolk Coast and Heaths Path **£4.00**

Suffolk Coast and Heaths Path

Felixstowe to Lowestoft **£4.00**

Test Way Inkpen Beacon to Totton **FREE**

Thames Path Thames Barrier to Source

Official National Trail Guide by David Sharp **£12.99**

Thames Path Companion: accom, practical info **£4.75**

Three Castles Path Windsor to Winchester

Route guide by East Berkshire Ramblers **£2.95**

Accommodation guide **FREE**

Trans Pennine Trail (E8)

Map/guide West Irish Sea – Yorkshire **£4.95**

Map/guide Central Derbyshire & Yorkshire **£4.95**

Map/guide East Yorkshire – North Sea **£4.95**

Accommodation and visitor guide **£4.95**

Two Moors Way Dartmoor to Exmoor

Route guide by Two Moors Way Association **£4.95**

Accommodation list **50p**

Vanguard Way Croydon to Newhaven: Route guide

by Vanguards Rambling Club **£2.95**

Viking Way Barton upon Humber to Oakham **£3.95**

Way for the Millennium (Staffs) Newport to Burton

upon Trent **£3.50**

For accommodation guide see Staffordshire Way

Wealdway Gravesend to Eastbourne **£5.00**

Weavers Way *See under Peddars Way*

Wessex Ridgeway *See under Ridgeway*

West Highland Way Glasgow to Fort William

Long distance route guide **£14.99**

Accommodation, practical information **FREE**

Wye Valley Walk Chepstow to Plynlimon, including

accommodation guide **£9.00**

Yorkshire Wolds Way Filey to Hull

National Trail Guide by Roger Ratcliffe **£12.99**

Accommodation and information guide **FREE**

WALKING FOR EVERYONE

Walking for Health by Dr W Bird & V Reynolds.
Comprehensive full-colour guide   **£14.99**
Take 30 Practical booklet on walking for health   **FREE**
Take 30 Poster10-week healthy walking plan   **FREE**
Walking for health factsheet (FS18)   **FREE**
Walking for everyone (FS11) Includes advice on
finding easier walks, walking with children and access
to the outdoors for people with disabilities   **FREE**
The Walker's Companion A miscellany of walking
facts, tit-bits and information   **£9.99**
Walking: getting started (FS16)   **FREE**
Walking: a useful guide Booklet answering common
questions about walking, with useful addresses and
contacts   **FREE**
Walking facts and figures (FS12)   **FREE**
Preparing Walks Guidebooks   **£2.50**
Discovering new routes A report of the Volunteers'
Conference 2000 on outreach work   **FREE**

TECHNICAL & LEADERSHIP ADVICE

Navigation and Leadership Practical official Ramblers'
guide for planning and navigating group walks   **£4.00**
Navigation for Walkers by Julian Tippett,
with colour illustrations & OS map extracts, ideal for
beginners   **£8.99**
Maps and navigation (FS2)   **FREE**
Clothing, equipment and safety (FS3)   **FREE**
Leading group walks (FS6)   **FREE**
Leading group walks in remote areas or demanding
conditions (GWSP1)   **FREE**
Walk leader's checklist on laminated card   **FREE**
Let's Get Going Advice on leading group walks for
people with disabilities and other special needs   **FREE**
Guidelines for Events: Long Distance Walkers
Association manual on organising challenge walks**£1.70**

FOOTPATHS, ACCESS, COUNTRYSIDE

Rights of Way: A guide to law and practice
('Blue Book') 3rd edn full guide to law in England &
Wales   **£20**
Footpath Worker Authoritative Journal on footpath
law and related matters, including regular updates to
'Blue Book' *(free to RA Groups/Areas)*   **4 issues £12**
Animals and Rights of Way (CAN4) Walking with
your dog, dangerous animals on paths etc   **FREE**
Basics of Footpath Law (FS7) Introduction in question
and answer form   **FREE**
Defending public paths What the Ramblers'

Association does to defend public paths and how you
can help   **FREE**
The Economic and Social Value of Walking in
England A report for the Ramblers   **FREE**
Footpath erosion (FS14) How serious is the problem,
and what can walkers do about it?   **FREE**
Freedom to Roam A celebratory supplement   **FREE**
Freedom to Roam Guides
edited by Andrew Bibby
Forest of Bowland   **£7.99**
Peak District East & South   **£7.99**
Peak District West & North   **£7.99**
Pennine Divide   **£7.99**
See p14 for Readers' discount and second series
Freedom to Roam in England and Wales (FS8)
The Countryside & Rights of Way Act explained **FREE**
Golf Courses (CAN2): their impact on paths   **FREE**
Managing conflict over access to open country
A case study of the Peak National Park   **FREE**
Meeting the challenges of the new millennium
A proposal for a wider New Forest
National Park   **FREE**
Paths for people for parish and community councils.
Also in bilingual Welsh/English version.   **FREE**
Reporting path problems Includes a report form and
general guidance. Also available in Welsh.   **FREE**
Rights of Way and development (CAN3) Planning
permission and proposed path changes   **FREE**
Roads used as Public Paths and Byways Open To All
Traffic (CAN1) A detailed guide   **FREE**
You're Either Quick or Dead Locations where
walkers need safe, convenient road crossings   **FREE**

Ramblers' Cloth badge (free with orders over £20)**£1**

ABOUT THE RAMBLERS

About the Ramblers' Association (FS4)   **FREE**
Annual report 2004/5 published April 2006   **FREE**
Legacies How to remember the RA in your will **FREE**
Waymarking the future A strategic framework for the
growth and development of the RA 2002-2007 **FREE**
Tom Stephenson: A 1970s tribute   **60p**

MAPS: We do not sell walkers' maps, but we do
maintain a map library which members can use for a
small fee. Please contact us for details on ☎ 020 7339
8500.
WALKING INFORMATION ONLINE An expanding
range of the material listed on this page, and more, is
available to download from www.ramblers.org.uk/info

THE RAMBLERS BOOKSHOP ORDER FORM

Item	Quantity	Price

Continue on a plain piece of paper if necessary

POSTAGE CHARGES

Please add these as follows:

● **UK Addresses**

Orders up to £4, add £1

Orders over £4 add £1.70 for first item, then £1.50 per item

Orders including Rights of Way (the 'Blue Book'): Minimum p&p charge £5

● **Other European addresses**

Orders up to £4, add £1.50

Orders over £4 add £2.20 for first item, then £1.70 per item

Orders including Rights of Way (the 'Blue Book'): Minimum shipping charge £6.50

● **All other addresses**

Orders up to £4, add £2.20

Orders over £4 add £4 for first item, then £1.70 per item

Orders including Rights of Way (the 'Blue Book'): Minimum shipping charge £12

FREE PUBLICATIONS

● Up to 2 free publications can be ordered without any additional charge when ordered with paid-for items only

● You can order up to two free publications sent on their own to a UK address on payment of a 50p p&p charge.

● Otherwise postage charges per 5 items are: UK addresses £1.50, European addresses £2.50, all other addresses £3.50.

PAYING BY CHEQUE & POSTAL ORDER

We can accept cheques or postal orders in UK pounds, made payable to the Ramblers' Association. We cannot accept cheques in any other currency, including Euro. Please don't send cash in the post.

PAYING BY CREDIT OR DEBIT CARD

We accept Visa, Mastercard, Switch and Delta cards only.

Telephone orders Please call us on ☎ 020 7339 8500 (international ☎ +44 20 7339 8500) on Mondays to Fridays 10:00–17:00 hrs. You can also take out a membership subscription by telephone.

Internet shopping You can order books and merchandise, make donations and join the Ramblers by credit or debit card at our website, **www.ramblers.org.uk**. You can also view a range of our free literature online at the site.

Total cost of items

Total postage (shipping) charges

Donation to Ramblers' Association

Grand total

Name

Address

Postcode   Country

Send this form and your payment to:
Ramblers' Association (Sales), 2nd Floor Camelford House, 89 Albert Embankment, London SE1 7TW, UK Please allow 14 days for delivery to UK, 28 days to rest of the world.

RECOMMENDATION/FEEDBACK FORM

FOUND SOME GOOD DIGS THAT AREN'T IN THE GUIDE?   ☐

or

HAVE A COMPLAINT ABOUT ACCOMMODATION IN THIS EDITION?   ☐

Your name and address _____

_____

Name and full postal address of the establishment _____

_____

Email (if known) _____

Comments

WHAT DO YOU THINK OF walk BRITAIN 2006?

ANY SUGGESTIONS TO IMPROVE FUTURE EDITIONS?

THANK YOU. PLEASE RETURN THIS FORM TO THE PUBLICATIONS TEAM:

RAMBLERS' ASSOCIATION, 2ND FLOOR CAMELFORD HOUSE
87-90 ALBERT EMBANKMENT, LONDON SE1 7TW

opticron
www.opticron.co.uk

DBA Oasis Binoculars

Simply among the best lightweight roof prism waterproof binoculars money can buy, the DBA Oasis are designed specifically for todays' birdwatcher and wildlife enthusiast.

Available in full size 8x42 & 10x42 and compact 8x21 & 10x25, with prices starting from just £249, DBA Oasis binoculars can be tested at specialist retailers nationwide.

For more information and your nearest stockist telephone us on

01582 726522

DBA Oasis 8x42   DBA Oasis 10x42   DBA Oasis 8x21   DBA Oasis 10x25

DBA Oasis Monoculars

Derived directly from DBA Oasis binoculars and delivering an unbeatable combination of resolution, colour reproduction and viewing comfort. Price £249.

Models also available as 20x42 & 25x42 pocket telescope kits. Price £349.
(Components also sold separately.)

DBA Oasis 8x42
DBA Oasis 10x42

For more information on the complete range of Opticron equipment and a copy of our current Catalogue call 01582 726522 or visit our on-line Catalogue at www.opticron.co.uk

PO Box 370, Unit 21, Titan Court, Laporte Way, Luton, Beds, LU4 8YR, UK Fax: 01582 723559 E-mail: sales@opticron.co.uk

ACCOMMODATION INDEX

INDEX